Effective Learning and Teaching of Writing
A Handbook of Writing in Education
Second Edition

STUDIES IN WRITING

VOLUME 14

Series Editor:

Gert Rijlaarsdam, *University of Amsterdam, The Netherlands*

Editorial Board:

Linda Allal, *University of Geneva, Switzerland*
Eric Espéret, *University of Poitiers, France*
David Galbraith, *Staffordshire University, UK*
Joachim Grabowski, *University of Heidelberg, Germany*
Ronald Kellogg, *St. Louis University, USA*
Lucia Mason, *University of Padova, Italy*
Marta Milian, *Universitat Autonoma Barcelona, Spain*
Sarah Ransdell, *Florida Atlantic University, USA*
Liliana Tolchinsky, *University of Barcelona, Spain*
Mark Torrance, *Staffordshire University, UK*
Annie Piolat, *University of Aix-en-Provence, France*
Païvi Tynjala, *University of Jyväskylä, Finland*
Carel van Wijk, *Tilburg University, The Netherlands*

Springer publishes the international book series *Studies in Writing*, founded by Amsterdam University Press and continued by Kluwer Academic Publishers. The intended readers are all those interested in the foundations of writing and learning and teaching processes in written composition. The series aims at multiple perspectives of writing, education and texts. Therefore authors and readers come from various fields of research, from curriculum development and from teacher training. Fields of research covered are cognitive, socio-cognitive and developmental psychology, psycholinguistics, text linguistics, curriculum development, instructional science. The series aim to cover theoretical issues, supported by empirical research, quantitative as well as qualitative, representing a wide range of nationalities. The series provides a forum for research from established researchers and welcomes contributions from young researchers. All studies published in the Series are peer-reviewed.

Effective Learning and Teaching of Writing
A Handbook of Writing in Education
Second Edition

edited by

Gert Rijlaarsdam
University of Amsterdam, The Netherlands
Utrecht University, The Netherlands

Huub van den Bergh
Utrecht University, The Netherlands

Michel Couzijn
University of Amsterdam, The Netherlands

KLUWER ACADEMIC PUBLISHERS

Library of Congress Cataloging-in-Publication Data

A C.I.P. Catalogue record for this book is available
from the Library of Congress.

ISBN 1-4020-2724-9 (hard); ISBN 1-4020-2725-7 (soft);   e-ISBN 0-4020-2739-7
Printed on acid-free paper.

© 2005 Kluwer Academic Publishers
All rights reserved. This work may not be translated or copied in whole or in part without the written permission of the publisher (Springer Science+Business Media, Inc., 233 Spring Street, New York, NY 10013, USA), except for brief excerpts in connection with reviews or scholarly analysis. Use in connection with any form of information storage and retrieval, electronic adaptation, computer software, or by similar or dissimilar methodology now know or hereafter developed is forbidden.
The use in this publication of trade names, trademarks, service marks and similar terms, even if the are not identified as such, is not to be taken as an expression of opinion as to whether or not they are subject to proprietary rights.

Printed in the United States of America.

9 8 7 6 5 4 3 2 1

springeronline.com

TABLE OF CONTENTS

EFFECTIVE LEARNING AND TEACHING OF WRITING: STUDENT INVOLVEMENT IN THE TEACHING OF WRITING   1
Gert Rijlaarsdam & Huub van den Bergh

PART ONE: STUDIES IN LEARNING TO WRITE

EMERGENT WRITING IN KINDERGARTEN AND THE EMERGENCE OF THE ALPHABETIC PRINCIPLE   17
Madelon Saada-Robert, Kristine Balslev, & Katja Mazurczak

LOOKING AT READING AND WRITING THROUGH LANGUAGE   31
Maria da Graça L. C. Pinto

REWRITING TO INTRODUCE PUNCTUATION IN THE SECOND GRADE: A DIDACTIC APPROACH   47
Sofía Vernon, Mónica Alvarado, & Paula Zermeño

CONTEXTUAL FACTORS ENHANCING COGNITIVE AND METACOGNITIVE ACTIVITY DURING THE PROCESS OF COLLABORATIVE WRITING   59
Marta Milian Gubern

METACOGNITIVE REGULATIONS, PEER INTERACTIONS AND REVISION OF NARRATIVES BY SIXTH GRADERS   77
Yviane Rouiller

THE DIRECTIVITY OF TEACHER STRATEGIES IN COLLABORATIVE WRITING TASKS   91
Christina Díez, Juan José Anula, Fernando Lara, & Pilar Pardo

MAKING DIGITAL ANNOTATIONS USING THE WORLD WIDE WEB   105
Henrry Rodríguez & Sandra Brunsberg

POPULAR CULTURE: 121
A RESOURCE FOR WRITING IN SECONDARY ENGLISH
CLASSROOMS
Douglas McClenaghan & Brenton Doecke

THE GARDEN OF THOUGHT – ABOUT WRITING POEMS IN UPPER 131
SECONDARY SCHOOL
Per-Olof Erixon

USING A STRUCTURED WRITING WORKSHOP TO HELP GOOD 141
READERS WHO ARE POOR WRITERS
Ronald L. Honeycutt & Ruie Jane Pritchard

DEAF WAYS OF WRITING NARRATIVES: 151
A BILINGUAL APPROACH
Maria Koutsoubou

STYLISTIC IMITATION AS A TOOL IN WRITING PEDAGOGY 169
Uwe Geist

IMPROVING ARGUMENTATIVE WRITING BY FOSTERING 181
ARGUMENTATIVE SPEECH
Sergio Crasnich & Lucia Lumbelli

MONITORING LOCAL COHERENCE THROUGH BRIDGING 197
INTEGRATION
Lucia Lumbelli & Gisella Paoletti

LEARNING TO WRITE INSTRUCTIVE TEXTS BY READER 209
OBSERVATION AND WRITTEN FEEDBACK
Michel Couzijn & Gert Rijlaarsdam

LEARNING TO READ AND WRITE ARGUMENTATIVE TEXT BY 241
OBSERVATION OF PEER LEARNERS
Michel Couzijn & Gert Rijlaarsdam

THE UPTAKE OF PEER-BASED INTERVENTION IN THE WRITING 259
CLASSROOM
Eva Lindgren

PART TWO: STUDIES IN HOW TO TEACH WRITING

TEACHING WRITING: USING RESEARCH TO INFORM PRACTICE 275
Roger Beard

IMPACT OF REGULAR PHILOSOPHICAL DISCUSSION ON 291
ARGUMENTATIVE SKILLS:
REFLECTION ABOUT EDUCATION IN PRIMARY SCHOOLS
Emmanuèle Auriac-Peyronnet & Marie-France Daniel

ACTION RESEARCH. 305
A STUDY ON USING AN INTEGRATIVE-NARRATIVE METHOD TO
TEACH L2 WRITING IN A HONG KONG PRIMARY SCHOOL
Anita Y. K. Poon

TEACHING HOW TO WRITE ARGUMENTATIVE TEXTS AT PRIMARY 323
SCHOOL
Milagros Gárate & Angeles Melero

TEACHING WRITING – TEACHING ORAL PRESENTATION 339
Susanne Munch

WRITING TO LEARN: 349
CONSTRUCTING THE CONCEPT OF GENRE IN A WRITING
WORKSHOP
Milly Epstein-Jannai

WRITING "IN YOUR OWN WORDS": 367
CHILDREN'S USE OF INFORMATION SOURCES IN RESEARCH
PROJECTS
Rob Oliver

METACOGNITION TO LEARN HOW TO WRITE TEXTS AT SCHOOL 381
AND TO DEVELOP MOTIVATION TO DO IT
Anne-Marie Doly

FOSTERING NOVICES' ABILITY TO WRITE INFORMATIVE TEXTS 393
Lieve Vanmaele & Joost Lowyck

ADAPTING TO THE CLASSROOM SETTING: 417
NEW RESEARCH ON TEACHERS MOVING BETWEEN TRADITIONAL
AND COMPUTER CLASSROOMS
Kate Kiefer & Mike Palmquist

ASSESSMENT OF ARGUMENTATIVE WRITING 427
Ron Oostdam

DIGITAL INFORMATION LITERACY: 443
TEACHING STUDENTS TO USE THE INTERNET IN SOURCE-BASED
WRITING
Caroline M. Stern

"DOWN THE PLUGHOLE": 455
THE PITFALLS OF TESTING THE WRITING OF L2 PUPILS
Geri Smyth

PART 3: STUDIES IN WRITING TO LEARN

COMPOSING A SUMMARY — 469
Monica Alvarado & Ana Laura de la Garza

ENHANCING THINKING DISPOSITIONS THROUGH INFORMAL WRITING: EXPERIENCES IN SCIENCE CLASSES — 481
Tamar Levin & Tili Wagner

FOSTERING REFLECTIVE WRITING BY STRUCTURING WRITING-TO-LEARN TASKS — 499
Gissi Sarig

REFLECTIVE WRITING & REFLECTIVE THINKING: THE IMPLICATIONS OF INTRODUCING REFLECTIVE PRACTICE INTO A PROFESSIONAL DOCTORATE PROGRAMME IN PHARMACY — 519
Peter Sayers

WRITING TO LEARN: CONDUCTING A PROCESS LOG — 533
Rachel Segev-Miller

LEARNING BY WRITING HYPERTEXT: A RESEARCH BASED DESIGN OF UNIVERSITY COURSES IN WRITING HYPERTEXT — 547
Elmar Stahl & Rainer Bromme

THE EFFECT OF STUDENT PRIOR EXPERIENCE, ATTITUDES, AND APPROACHES ON PERFORMANCE IN AN UNDERGRADUATE SCIENCE WRITING PROGRAM — 561
Charlotte E. Taylor & Helen Drury

CHILDREN'S WRITING STRATEGIES: PROFILES OF WRITERS — 574
Anat Shapira & Rachel Hertz-Lazarowitz

WRITING-TO-LEARN AND GRAPH-DRAWING AS AIDS OF THE INTEGRATION OF TEXT AND GRAPHS — 587
Gisella Paoletti

REFERENCES   599

AUTHOR INDEX   645

SUBJECT INDEX   655

LIST OF CONTRIBUTORS   667

EFFECTIVE LEARNING AND TEACHING OF WRITING

Student involvement in the teaching of writing

GERT RIJLAARSDAM*/** & HUUB VAN DEN BERGH**

*University of Amsterdam, & **Utrecht University, the Netherlands

1. CONTINUITY AND CHANGE

This book is a state of the art with a caleidoscopic character. Although by no means we claim to publish a representative sample of chapters, it is *a* state of the art, in all its variety. It focuses on the learning and teaching of writing, and is a sequel to the book we published in 1996, with Amsterdam University Press (Rijlaarsdam, Van den Bergh & Couzijn, 1996a). In 2002, no copies were left, and no successor had been published with the same amount of variety as in 1996. Therefore we took the opportunity to publish a new volume, inviting all kinds of researchers, varying form linguists to educationalists to psychologists to contribute. That is one thing we agree upon as volume editors: research on teaching is a multidisciplinary enterprise, so many aspects have to be covered when we try to understand what writing is and how we can improve the learning of writing. We also agreed upon asking some of the 1996 authors to reprint an updated chapter, to stress the continuity of research: these chapters are certainly not out of date. There is a tendency in research to think that only the newest and most modern things count: literature older than ten years is seen as hopelessly old. Less is true. Many studies in the present volume are outspokenly modern, but definitively rooted in older work.

Great changes are taking place in the educational landscape. The diversity of the school population, in terms of multilingualism, or in terms of heterogeneity, new

Rijlaarsdam, G. & Van den Bergh, H. (2004). Effective learning and teaching of writing: Student involvement in the teaching of writing.
Rijlaarsdam, G. (Series Ed.) & Rijlaarsdam, G., Van den Bergh, H., & Couzijn, M. (Vol. Eds.) (2004). Studies in Writing. Vol. 14, Effective Learning and Teaching in Writing, 2nd Edition, 1 - 16.

communication technologies, new ways of expression, globalisation, etc. When we compare the 1996 volume we edited in this series with the present volume, all kinds of differences can be traced, and we will deal with some in this introduction. Some of these differences are due to the changing world in which we teach and learn. Other differences stem from changing perspectives and themes in writing research (constructivism, situated learning etc.). We tend to think that these differences indicate progress in research. And progress is needed. What Anita Poon in her chapter describes as the typical composition lesson in Hong Kong is something we all recognize as the dominant classroom, despite all our endeavors to improve practice (Poon, this volume: 307):

> Typically writing is taught based on a prescribed textbook in primary schools. Most teachers simply stick to the textbook and adopt a very traditional method. A typical composition lesson goes as follows: the teacher teaches the class a sample of writing in the unit, which usually consists of several sentences describing a person or an object. Then, with the help of some guiding questions, the teacher asks the class to do parallel writing, which means to write a similar text by changing simply the names, pronouns, numbers or some details of the original text. Finally, the students copy the answers to the guiding questions in their exercise books, and submit their 'composition'.

Although we are moving in primary education from 'text as a bundle of sentences', from sentence oriented composition to text oriented and even to reader oriented composition, many of the features of this lesson description stay intact: textbook (or national curriculum) driven, aimed at deductive learning (applying new learning content in a piece of writing), presentational in teaching methodology, narrowing down the concept of writing into testing new knowledge. Yes I know: there are other lessons, and teachers develop wonderful teaching strategies and teaching scenario's, and some of these teachers show their insights and work in this volume, but in general writing lessons are uninspired and not stimulating. As Roger Beard analyzes from research on the implementation of the Literacy strategy, referring to a report with the revealing title *The Teaching of Writing in Primary School: Could do Better* (Beard, this volume: 283):

> an over-reliance on duplicated worksheets;
>
> an over-reliance on a stimulus to inspire pupils to write without the necessary teaching in the form of modelling or other forms of scaffolding. (...)
>
> in many schools, [there is a lack of] (...) an appropriate balance between reading and writing. In 300 literacy hours observed (...) there was no shared writing in three-quarter of the lessons;
>
> while pupils were being given opportunities to write in subjects other than English, the skills learned in literacy lessons were being insufficiently transferred to work in other subjects. More could be done to use these lessons to teach the genre features of writing which are commonly used in other subjects.

And, he adds (Beard, this volume: 284):

> The use of duplicated worksheets may reflect a teaching approach in which pupils are allocated practice or small-scale tasks in writing, perhaps focused on a particular linguistic structure or other component of writing. The finding that such approaches are sometimes over-relied upon has been a recurrent one in English primary school inspection findings. As long ago as 1978, a survey of a nationally representative sample

of primary [in this case 7-11] schools reported that books of English exercises were used in nearly all classes of 9 and 11 year olds (DES, 1978). The authors of the survey added that the use of such exercises do not necessarily help pupils to write fluently and with purpose [the exercises typically being short tasks, involving little 'authorship'].

The dominant patterns of Hong Kong and England are apparent and the resemblances are striking: sentence oriented, textbook/worksheet driven, lack of authorship. The experience of the excited student Rob Oliver presents will be a very rare phenomenon in these lessons:

'If you think about it. Wow! I made a book, nobody ever wrote it. I didn't copy it. I did it by myself, with some help, books and things. You have that feeling...I really did it.....This was the first one, not really the first one, but the first one with those words.'
(Oliver, this volume: 377)

The research presented in this volume may contribute to better practice and research. In this introduction, we deal with three topics: new insights in learning to write (section 2), in writing to learn (section 3), and research in writing (section 4). We choose to introduce all chapters via these three topics, instead of listing them; in section 4 we deal with some future developments in writing research.

2. ABOUT LEARNING TO WRITE

The most frequent cliché about writing is that writing is a complex task. It certainly is. Writing is fun (authorship: 'Mama, I can write!'), meaning making is fun (contributing to the world), but learning to write requires cognitive and affective investments. For the sake of analysis, in our work we make the distinction between writing and learning to write.

There is much instruction in language arts classes, but how much learning is there? Although the teacher's core task is to create opportunities for learning, often little comes of it in practice. What we see in classrooms, is practising, doing exercises. Students spend a lot of time on reading and writing tasks. They carry out tasks, sometimes get some feedback when they have finished, and then go back to other tasks. That students learn anything at all may be considered something of a miracle.

At least two basic assumptions that underlie the literacy curriculum in practice should be questioned. First, there is the adage 'practice makes perfect': when students have to learn to *write,* then they have to *write* a paper; when students have to learn to *read*, then they have to *read*. Second, there is the principle of maximum task similarity: when students have to learn to write a *paper*, then they have to write a *paper*. Both principles seem so evident that they are not often questioned. Together they form the obviously shortest route to success: why should you do something other than practising the final task when you want to acquire the skill to execute the final task fluently? Yet, we would like to question these two principles.

Practise makes perfect. This assumption might be valid in instances where automaticity or fluency is the aim of learning, that is, after basic skills and strategies are acquired, practising helps to integrate the components into one fluent execution of the task. But before that stage of learning, a lot has to be learnt from other types of learning activities. When making curriculum decisions, we should keep in mind that writing (an essay, a letter, a summary) and learning-to-write (an essay, a letter, a summary) are two different cognitive activities. The act of writing is complex and effortful. When students compose a written text, most of them are completely involved in writing, in completing the writing task, in writing a text that fulfils the aim of the task. Given the complexity of composing, the involvement in all kinds of sub-processes as generating content, structuring information, translating information into language, checking and revising the results against rhetorical aims, language rules, spelling rules etc., it is clear that learners cannot learn much during practising: they are simply not in a situation where they can learn. That's not to say no one does: good students may take the opportunity to practise as an opportunity to learn. They are active learners: they see writing assignments not as just writing tasks but also as learning-to-write tasks. They have enough effort for dual tasking: to write and to learn from that writing at the same time. In doing so, they develop metacognitive and meta-communicative skills; skills that are necessary to develop to become a proficient language user. Good learners develop these skills under their own steam. What societies want us to do nowadays, is to help *all* students in developing these skills. That is why practising, as the major learning activity in literacy curricula, is not enough.

Therefore, many studies in this book describe and study the effects of alternative 'didactic sequences' or lesson scenario's, which are similar in that they pay less attention to the writing activity itself, but more to other learning activities that could enhance the quality of the learning outcome. Many instances of research in this volume provide good and tested examples of writing lessons in which writing itself plays a less dominant role than in practice. We will present and discuss these studies shortly in section 2.1.1 of this introduction.

Similarity of tasks. Writing essays has to be learnt by writing essays. The problem with this principle is that it neglects the human capacity of transfer, the capacity to adjust what was learnt in one specific situation to another, somewhat different situation. In most traditions, there is a certain awareness that text types relate to each other in a sort of cumulative way: narratives then expositions then argumentation, or description goes before analysis. In the Netherlands, textbooks have only recently started to relate reading and writing (and speaking and listening) exercises to each other around a certain rhetorical theme or speech act (complaining, persuasion, argumentation). And we think we may go further: why don't throw the doors wide open, raising the question from which modality we can learn the most for another modality? Traditionally, reading is said to influence writing: analyze a text on certain features about argumentation, and then apply these features in a writing assignment. Nevertheless, why do we not consider the opposite? Does producing a text with certain features facilitate the recognition of these features, say an argumentation structure? Is writing a hypertext-formatted text beneficial for writing (and reading) 'linear' texts? (See Braaksma, Rijlaarsdam & Van den Bergh, 2001 for an experiment.) What we plead for is to distinguish the mode of the final, target task (for instance, writing) from the mode of the learning tasks that support the final target task and to connect the communicative modes, discourse functions and speech acts where possible and efficient. Studies in this book that pay attention to connections between modes, functions and speech acts are introduced in section 2.2.

2.1 Alternative Learning Activities in Learning to Write Studies

Doing a writing task is not equivalent to a learning-to-write task. Learning processes require at least some awareness raising, at some point in the process. This moment can be built into the task itself, the task environment, the focus of instruction, the feed back phase etc. At a certain point in the learning-to-write process a learner must experience a difficulty, a threshold to overcome. This might produce some discomfort, as Milly Epstein formulates in her chapter (Epstein, this volume: 367):

> They also require study and a willingness to examine the cultural-linguistic surroundings in which we find ourselves, an activity that is liable to produce a certain *discomfort*. This is however a fertile discomfort, as it is a means of stimulating learning about written texts and the frameworks that affords their construction. Simultaneously, it seems to me that this is a type of investment that promises a unique yield for each and every reader and writer – both teachers and learners.

Peter Sayers (this volume, 523-535) noticed something similar. PhD-students in his study create 'interim styles', styles that indicate that they are in the transition phase from writing academic texts to reflective writing: it is hard for them, difficult, although they can write, and while learning, they develop 'interim styles', mostly generated by affective reasons. Learning to write reflective journals is more than learning to write. It requires personal development, and is therefore hard and difficult, causing affective resistance in first instance.

2.1.1 Exchanging Positions in the Learning-To-Write Process

Both studies deal with adult writers and affective discomfort. But creating *cognitive discomfort* as a motor for learning is suggested in some educational interventions in this book. When Sofía Vernon, Mónica Alvarado, & Paula Zermeño introduce punctuation for young children, they realize that learning to punctuate accurately assumes knowledge of the writing system and awareness of the units, which is lacking at that early moment. Then they decide to raise this awareness via interpretation problems:

> This leads to a dilemma in educational practices. How can we teach children who cannot write conventionally to punctuate texts if the awareness of the units that are delimited by punctuation is a result of the knowledge of the writing system? It seems to us that the solution is to allow children to face problems of interpretation in their own texts as well as to provide them with suitable writing models in terms of analysing conventionally written texts (Vernon, Alvarado & Zermeño, this volume: 49).

Writers are placed in the reader's role. Not to improve their reading skills, but to *experience text problems*. One of the difficulties of writing is to incorporate a reader in the writing process, to anticipate on readers processes, to guide readers' processes and to check the resulting text on reader's understanding. The writer must learn to

distantiate from her text, to distantiate from her writer's role. Several studies try to realize this educational goal.
1) Writers write a text and then *experience* the effect of their text on readers. This alternation of reader-writer roles is part of some interventions in this book. In one of the Couzijn & Rijlaarsdam chapters, writers learn how the text they wrote is experienced by real peer readers; this simple intervention generates a strong learning and transfer effect (Couzijn & Rijlaarsdam, this volume: 209 - 240).
2) Writers write a text and then describe and analyze their writing processes, by *reconstructing* their writing process, supported by electronic tools ('playing back the text production process') with supportive questions from a peer (Lindgren, this volume: 259 - 274).
3) Writers write and/or revise collaboratively. In doing so, they become aware of choices by discussing alternatives, constantly *changing positions* from writing to reading to writing (see chapters by Marta Milian (59 - 76) and Yviane Rouiller (77-89). Specifying the contect of the writing task ('writing for younger students') can support this process (see Milian, this volume)

What all these learning activities have in common is that they place the writer in the role of the reader in order to enhance reader awareness. An effective writing curriculum requires that students play different roles. First, they must be in a position to experience communication, to experience the effects of written and spoken communication. That is, they have to participate in communication. As writers/speakers, they must experience how their texts affect readers and listeners; as readers/listeners, they must experience texts and formulate their responses (see Figure 1).

Role: Participant   Role: Participant

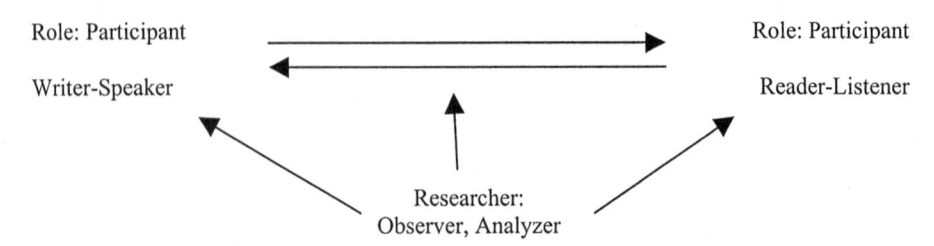

Writer-Speaker   Reader-Listener

Researcher:
Observer, Analyzer

Figure 1. Student-as- learner participation model in the L1-curriculum.

This role differentiation seems similar to what Britton (1972) introduced, when he distinguished the participant from the observer role in language users:

> As participants, we use language to interact with people and things and make the wheels of the world [...] go around. As participants, we use language to inform, instruct, persuade, plan, argue, and explain. Free from the demands of the worlds, as spectators we use language to create make-believe play; do day dream; to relate and to listen to experiences, gossip and tales; to read or write fiction, drama, and poetry (Britton, 1972: 8).

Yet our perspective to distinguish between participant and observer is different from Britton's, because it focusses on the student-as-learner of language use, and not the student-as-language user.

The observer role is the focus one of the studies by Couzijn & Rijlaarsdam (this volume: 241-258). Couzijn & Rijlaarsdam show that 15-year old learners can learn to write argumentative texts effectively by observing other learners/writers, instead of writing themselves. These participants are released from the complex activity of writing and therefore are (presumably) more attentive to learning from and about writing. The fact that these participants are placed in the role of learner instead of writer could have made them more receptive to learning. They were not loaded with the double task of writing a piece and learning from the writing at the same time.

In other studies presented in this volume, observation is part of complex multifaceted interventions, which makes it difficult although not impossible to single out the effect of observation. In the intervention Sergio Crasnich and Lucia Lumbelli (this volume: 181 - 196) describe and test, one of the components is an observation of the comprehension processes of an experienced reader when reading argumentative texts. In this intervention, the act of writing is limited, nevertheless much learning is generated. In another study, Lumbelli and Paoletti (this volume: 197 - 208) provided learners with audio-tapes, containing experts' spontaneous comprehension processes of target texts which

> '...contained all the flaws and redundancies of oral language; the expert reader's uncertainty had been fully verbalised, so that uncertainty about the possible different interpretations of the same passage could be traced back to uncertainty about which processes would most adequately integrate the explicit information, as read and decoded.' (Lumbelli & Paoletti, this volume: 206)

A similar procedure was implemented in Milagros Gárate & Angeles Melero's study when teaching 11-years-olds using counter argumentation in argumentative writing, inspired by Vygotsky:

> '...using the modelling technique carried out by an expert, thereby making, from a Vygotskian perspective, the passage from the interpsychological to the intrapsychological easier.' (Gárate & Melero, this volume: 329)

Uwe Geist (this volume: 169 - 179) focuses on classic imitation as a learning activity, building on the natural habits of learning, moving from the unconscious to semi consciousness, which again is a matter of awareness raising:

> The unreflected, casual and random use of imitation we practise all the time is uncontrolled, e.g., it often becomes an imitation of the 'ends', and not of the 'means', as Dewey formulates it, and imitation thus loses its element of analysis, of 'close observation and judicious selection' which makes it 'an intelligent act' (Dewey, 1916: 42). The potential in imitation I want to activate is precisely this semi-conscious analytical component of observation and selection. In its semi-consciousness, it provides access to funds of techniques which are commonly shared, but which are too subtle, too varied, too contextually determined to be formulated in common rules or instructions. (Geist, this volume: 171)

If we refer to Figure 1, Geist focuses in this teaching sequence on the learner-as-researcher role, when 'students are asked to describe in detail how the different writers have used the language to bring forth these particular impressions' (Geist, this volume: 174). Contrary to the other observation studies students do not observe writing processes or comprehension processes, but try to reconstruct the relation between text features and reading experiences. This is a variant of inductive learning, construing 'scales of texts', an effective way to teach composition (Hillocks, 1986).

Experiencing communication and communicative effects supports the development of intentional cognition (Galbraith & Rijlaarsdam, 1999: 94), a necessary element of the ability to direct writing towards communicative goals. Students can be helped to incorporate goals within the writing process by 'procedural facilitation', they can be offered external prompts which encourage them to consider different possible goals and courses of action at different points within the process (Galbraith & Rijlaarsdam, 1999: 96). Another way to facilitate learners is to help them to decompose the task, to solve the conflict between idea generation and text production (see section 2.1.2). But effective writing depends not just on how goal-directed writing is, but also on the writer's ability to co-ordinate all the different processes involved. Therefore learners need to have access to these processes, to 'models', to become aware of these processes and the management of these processes.

2.1.2 Scaffolding Content Generation

A remarkable number of studies concentrates on content generation, in some respect. The assumption here is that writing is difficult because it requires different cognitive activities at the same time (content generation and organization, text organization and production, revision), which are strongly interactive. If the writing curriculum can make writing easier by decomposing the whole process into meaningful elements, than writing a text becomes easier and requires less cognitive effort. Focussing on content as a scaffold in this process implies that these researchers conceive writing as a meaning creating process, rather than an instrumental process to convey meaning.

We see this focus among others in the chapters by Emmanuèle Auriac-Peyronnet & Marie-France Daniel (this volume: 291-304), Anita Poon (305-323), Milagros Gárate & Angeles Melero (325-340), and Sergio Crasnich & Lucia Lumbelli (181-196). Auriac & Daniel train groups successfully in primary education by philosophical discussions in generating content for argumentative texts, including reader oriented counter arguments. Poon tries to get away from the traditional frozen contents, trying to enrich the creativity both in terms of content and language, focussing on teacher-led classroom discussions. Gárate & Melero implemented a successful multi-method intervention, aimed at argumentative text writing, using counter arguments, as in Auriac & Daniel's study. Among other elements group writing and scaffolding were included. Their choice to improve argumentative skills is embedded in social aims (Gárate & Melero, this volume: 326):

> It is our firm belief that learning to present arguments is difficult but that it helps to build up complex linguistic and cognitive abilities and leads to pupils' having more tolerant attitudes, thereby giving citizens a more enlightened moral code.

One of the elements of their complex intervention is the use of scaffolding, focussed on conceptualisation, precisely as stated above for compensating the complexity of the writing process (Gárate & Melero, this volume: 328):

> To compensate for this complexity, we gave the pupils an important piece of help: a series of cards which, as a whole, represent the external argumentative scheme, and which are directed more towards conceptualisation processes rather than those of textualisation.

2.1.3 Raising Interest in Writing

Until now, the actions to improve the writing curriculum focused on the pedagogical techniques to make didactic sequences more effective. Another focus is to raise students' interest in writing, assuming that increased interest leads to more involvement in learning. Although in most studies in this book the content of writing is well chosen, it is chosen as a means to improve the writing, not as a goal. In two studies, on the contrary, the choice of content is the primary educational goal. As Uwe Geist states in his chapter: 'The worst that can happen is that learning to write becomes emptied of content' (Geist, this volume: 171).

In McClenaghan & Doecke' study (this book: 121-130), the authors expand the notion of written text, using out of school cultural practices as a resource for writing in secondary school:

> Popular cultural texts – digital media texts, chat groups, the internet – play a particularly significant role in adolescents' communicational webs. Such concepts are important, not simply because they highlight new forms of communication, but because they sensitise us to the ways in which literacy practices are bound up with the network of relationships in which people find themselves. Individuals do not simply 'read' or 'write' or 'speak' or 'listen' (i.e., the traditional way in which we conceptualise the components of the English curriculum); these acts are social practices, embedded in specific sets of social relationships, which are mediated in technologically complex ways (...).(McClenaghan & Doecke, this volume: 124)

McClenaghan & Doecke report some interesting classroom experiences when trying to expand the notion of text and to relate school teaching to out of school communication. At the same time, Erixon reports on a study in which he tried to understand student's perceptions about the dualism students have to deal with when writing in private at home is introduced into the public space of the school (Erixon: 131-140). From his study, it becomes clear that students experience a clear difference between private home writing and school writing, even if the genre is poetry. Erixon concludes:

> We have, however, to accept that genuine communication between students may be less easy to establish. As a result of projects like *The Garden of Thought* ritual activities are expressed alongside elements of communication. That is certainly a step in the right direction. (Erixon, this volume: 140)

A more traditional move to enhance interest in writing, is developing (research) projects in class, where writing supports the development of the project, and writing is the ultimate educational aim. Susanne Munch (341-349) in secondary and Rob

Oliver (369-382) in primary education report on these kinds of writing environments.

2.2 Connecting Communicative Modes

Many chapters deal with at least two modes of communication. Some authors see reading as facilitating progress in writing:

> My assumption is that consciousness of the reading process develops through the sharpening of generic principles and by paying attention to the restrictions that genre dictates to readers and writers alike (Epstein, this volume: 354).

In most studies where writing and reading are connected, reading and writing activities are interwoven in the intervention or the lesson studied, (for instance the chapters by Madelon Saada-Robert, Kristine Balslev, & Katja Mazurczak, Maria da Graça Pinto, Sergio Crasnich & Lucia Lumbelli, Lucia Lumbelli & Gisela Paoletti, Milagros Gárate & Angeles Melero, Couzijn & Rijlaarsdam). In these instances, reading is the facilitating mode for writing.

Writing has the lead in a very few cases. When Vernon, Alvarado, & Zermeño (this volume: 47-58) plan to teach very young children interpunction, they realize that "It is writing that defines the unit "word". (p. 48). It is interesting to see how they teach funny lessons about a theme in the 'lower skills' domain (interpunction). In Couzijn & Rijlaarsdam, the claim is tested that under particular circumstances, there is more transfer from writing to reading than from reading to writing. Indeed, when students learn about writing argumentative texts by observing writers, they learn more than when they write, and the transfer to reading tasks is significant.

Oral skills and writing are connected in studies focussing on scaffolding content generation (see section 2.1.2) and collaborative work where oral speech facilitates writing and awareness raising (for instance Milian: 59-76; Rouiller: 77-89).

The relation between the communicative modes is a means-end relation in most instances: oral activities contribute to content generation or awareness raising; reading facilitates the acquistion of genre knowledge, reader awareness, awareness of coherence etc. In one study, the relation is not additional but substitutional: by writing you learn to read (Couzijn & Rijlaarsdam, this volume: 241-258). The underlying assumption in their study is that in the case of argumentative texts, the skills to analyse an argumentative text argumentatively (argumentative structure) and rhetorically mirror the skills to generate, structure and formulate an argumentative text. This assumption is a leading principle in Susanne Munch's chapter (this volume: 341-349). She reports of a curriculum where writing and oral skills are both target skills. She ties these skills into one frame of reference when evaluating writing and oral presentations (this volume: 348).

We underline this trend. Teaching communicative skills has much to do with teaching genre awareness: relations between effect and text features, within a certain context. When the theoretical framework to assess the quality of communication can exceed the communicative modes to a certain degree, there is a lot to be gained. Combined with our model of alternating student roles in the language curriculum, a shared framework supports the development of the communicative competence. That implies more emphasis on pragma-linguistic and textual aspects of language use, instead of syntax and grammar. It also implies more emphasis on the dynamics of language use and communication, on how meaning is (re-)constructed, on the process of meaning creation in the writer, the reader, in the communication partners, and between the communication partners.

Aiming at the development of communicative competence means an emphasis on developing the *strategic competence*, which embodies communicative strategies, built on declarative and procedural knowledge about what works in which circumstances. Strategic knowledge can be acquired in two different ways: direct teaching and consciousness-raising (Cohen, 1991; Oostdam & Rijlaarsdam, 1995). Consciousness-raising implies that the participant can step aside during an act of communication and notice, for instance, what happens during the conversation, or estimate whether the discussion will result in the desired effect, or anticipate whether the reader will agree, when he is writing a letter of complaint. The *Strategic competence* plays a role in language processing or communication tasks: in planning a specific problem solving strategy, interpreting language in a communicative context and in planning, executing and monitoring language processing.

In short, three distinguishable paradigm shifts shape the modern language arts currriculum in upper primary and in secondary education:
1) Pragmalinguistic shift: What makes communication effective under what circumstances? Adding language use to the language system, extending the focus from the sentence level to the textual level, the rhetoric level and the sociolinguistic level. Adding conditional knowledge (what works when?) to declarative and procedural knowledge.
2) Strategic knowledge in communication: How do cognitive (reading and writing processes) and communicative processes work? Adding to the curriculum: intrapersonal and interpersonal communication processes, to communication results.
3) Strategic knowledge in learning-to-write: How to learn from particular events for future use (abstraction, generalization, transfer) in order to develop skills for life long learning. This shift implies that the curriculum includes the process of learning from language use to improve communication, which includes learning to state learning goals, to plan tasks, to monitor task execution, and transfer learning results.

This curriculum requires that students can play different roles as we presented in section 2.1.1. to experience and analyze communicative effects. Combining written and oral communicative situations can enhance the learning result.

3. WRITING TO LEARN

The ongoing discussion in the USA about writing across the curriculum (WAC), the dissemination efforts of the WAC-movement, and growing the interest in writing in higher education (Björk, Bräuer, Rienecker, & Stray Jörgensen, 2003), did increase the interest in writing as a learning activity. The problem of the writing-to-learn paradigm is the same as the learning-to-write paradigm: nothing is learnt by just writing, as the theme likes to suggest. Writing can be used as a learning activity in certain conditions, tailored to the learning task and the expected learning outcomes. Gisela Paoletti shows in her chapter that in some instances, writing is not the best choice (this volume: 593-603). She provides a sound theoretical explanation in her discussion for why graphics are more effective in this case than writing.

One subtheme in this volume is Writing from Sources, or synthesis writing. Monica Alvarado & Ana Laura de la Garza (this volume: 473 - 483) report a study with 9-years-olds on summarizing a text. Focus in this classroom based study is to learn to delete in order to find the main idea, instead of starting with the most difficult task in summarizing, namely the identification of the main idea. In Rob Oliver's study primary school students learn to use several sources in one research report.

Tamar Levin and Tilly Wagner report about a long intervention (three semesters) in four eight grade science classes. Their focus is the effect of informal writing tasks on thinking dispositions. Some examples of these tasks in a learning unit on Heat and Temperature are presented on page 492 of this volume:

> Story: Tell the story of a group of water particles that were heated up from a temperature of 20°C below zero to 150°C above zero.
>
> Diary: An additional sun has appeared in the sky of our planet. The sun radiates continuous heat on the earth. Write a diary of your own or the diary of someone else describing the effect on our world.
>
> Debate: Two children, Dan and David, have an argument:
> Dan: In my computer game, the hero shoots a tank using a small rifle and the tank evaporates.
> David: That's impossible. The tank is made of iron. Iron is a metal and no heat exists that can cause the tank to evaporate. Continue the argument.

This list shows that the authors try to stimulate imagination, and that writing is the means to stimulate imagination. Imagination should contribute to thinking dispositions like 'Looking at issues from a number of persectives' and 'Appreciation of metacognition'. Writing is a means to develop imagination, which is a means to developt thinking dispositions. This causal chain seems to work well: the experimental ('writing') group outperformed the control group significantly in thinking dispositions.

There are also chapters on writing as a learning tool. Gissi Sarig (this volume: 503-521) provides a theoretical framework, tried out in practice and illustrated with children's work. Her Reflective Cycle can be applied in various learning contexts where reflective thinking is called for. At the heart of learning is a text. The teacher may stimulate nine different dialogic responses to this text. In a section on misuses and pitfall, it becomes clear that working with this cycle needs intelligent investment from teachers and learners. Peter Sayers invests in his chapter in moving students in a doctorate programme of Pharmacy toward reflective writing and thinking, despite their training in academic writing. He shows that his students also invest, albeit in developing interim styles as a consequence of the affective resistance. Rachel Segev-Miller (this volume: 537-551) shows that investment in reflective writing in a course on writing with sources results in a rich reservoir of self-reported cognitive and meta-cognitive strategies, which enriched the writing-from-sources course.

Elmar Stahl and Rainer Bromme (this volume: 553-565) introduce a new approach in this theme. They designed a course for university students to learn from writing hypertexts, describe the course design and embed their choices in learning theories.

Charlotte Taylor & Helen Drury (this volume: 567-579) report about students characteristics in their faculty (attitude, prior experiences with writing etc.), related to writing quality, to sort out basic student profiles. These profiles form the staring point of course design:

> 'Armed with this information we can thus make changes to the writing curriculum to account for our different student profiles emphasizing the development of a positive attitude to writing through building confidence.'(this volume: 575).

A similar but different study is reported by Anat Shapira & Rachel Hertz-Lazarowitz (this volume: 580-592). Similar because of the aim: collecting data about learner features that may contribute to the effectiveness of the course. Different because of the applied methodology (study of writing processes) and the domain: Shapira and Hertz-Lazarowitz contribute to the domain of learning-to-write and not to the domain of writing-to-learn. But because of the similarity of the aim of study, we placed Taylor & Drury and Shapira & Hertz-Lazarowitz next to eachother.

4. THE STUDY OF WRITING

Comparing this volume in the *Studies in Writing* series with the 1996 volume (Rijlaarsdam, Van den Bergh & Couzijn, 1996), it is tempting to infer some trends in the study of writing, and to predict some of the contents of the next volume in the next decade. In short, we list some features that stroke us.

Writing environments: from writing to text design. Not only the act of writing changes now that the environment changes, but also the way we see writing. In a few chapters new tools that support writing or the learning of writing are presented (see the reviewers tool in Hennry Rodriguez' chapter (this volume: 105-120) and the writing process play back tool Eva Lindgren implemented in her study (this volume: 259-274). In the chapters by Rob Oliver (this volume: 369-382) and Caroline Stern (this volume: 447-457) we experience how the availability and use of internet affect writing. At the same time, we perceive glimpses of changing conceptions of writing, related to the changes in the writing environment. Rob Oliver is most outspoken in this volume about this change. Children in his study are no longer seen as witers, but as text producers, and sign-makers. His carefully analysis of children copying and pasting text from the internet in 'research reports' results in six strategies of text importation. Seeing writing as a form of text importation is really a new perspective on writing.

Having access to digital texts when 'making texts' makes it easier and more inviting to add other signs than text: the concept of text will broaden (including pictures, see for instance Oliver and the texts Anita Poon presents) to powerpoint presentations (Doecke & McClenaghan). Designing hypertext will not be far away (see the chapter by Elmar Stahl & Rainer Bromme on hypertext design as an mode of instruction, this volume: 553-565). Are we moving from studies of writing to studies in document design?

Iterative design studies. Inspired by the way new technology is constructed and tested, in educational research a new methodology of research has been developed (see for methodologies Reigeluth, 1999; Van den Akker, Branch, Gustafson, Nieveen, & Plomp, 1999). This approach is new for writing studies and therefore scarcely represented in this volume (Vanmaele & Lowyck: 395-417; Doly: 383-394). The most important feature of design studies is that they focus on designing lesson scenario's or didactic sequences, and test and design them iteratively. These studies do not focus on varying one variable in teaching – for instance observational learning – to test the effect of this variable by confronting this sequence with another one without observational learning. They focus on the study of feasibility and intrinsic effect. Step by step these designs are tested in various situations (varying from comments from teachers on to classroom testing).

The advantages of design studies are manifold. Two of the most striking one's are the involvement of teachers (real classroom situations) and the research methodology. Design studies try to solve an educational problem. In this respect, design studies have much in common with what some authors have called action research in this volume (Poon: 305-323; Levin & Wagner: 485-501; Doecke & McClenaghan: 121-130). That implies that design studies are closer to classroom practice, closer to teachers, closer to implementation. At the other hand, design studies are more rigoured in research design and methods, and offer the opportunity to collect *qualitative and quantitative* data to measure the effect of the design.

To quote Marta Milian (this volume: 60):

> Research on writing instruction faces the challenge of elaborating a theory of teaching and learning writing in school contexts. The consideration of writing instruction as a scenario where intellectual, together with personal and social development is being built constitutes a firm ground to be explored. Observation and analysis of classroom literacy events as privileged settings for the development of thinking and learning strategies concerning writing competence becomes one of the main research paths to gather evidence of some of the factors contributing to a successful and effective writing instruction model.

Differentiation and heterogeneity in classrooms. The major approach in this volume seem to assume that one and the same type of intervention supports learning to write and writing to learn effectively. Only a very few studies recognize that differences in students could affect the rate and quality of learning. Geri Smyth (this volume: 459-471) shows that the testing system in Scotland deprives bilingual children; she extends this finding to teaching. Maria Koutsoubou (this volume: 151- 167) present findings of the bilingual effect in deaf students; she also studies the interactions between the balance of bilingualism and conditions of writing. Ron Honeywell and Ruie Jane Pritchard (this volume: 141-150) present a study on the specific strategies of students who are good readers but poor writers, and present an effective course to improve the writing of these students.

We think that the study of differences is underrepresented in this volume and that in the future more research will deal with multilingualism, multiculturalism and learning styles. In the European Union, learning at least one foreign language is compulsory in all member states. The already increasing temporary migration of adults during study, internationalisation of communication at the work place, will require adults to deal with at least two languages and cultures with a certain level of profiency. Writing in two languages will be the default situation for many students in the future. We expect more studies on bilingual and bicultural writing in the next decade.

At the same time, the need for differentiation in regular education and for special education is growing. As writing researchers, we must be able to develop and test different paths to Rome.

The same holds for the writing-to-learn paradigm. Most researchers in this field seem to assume that writing-to-learn is effective for all. An exception in this volume is the study by Charlotte Taylor and Helen Drury (this volume: 567-579). They study the writing strategies of students in order to adapt the teaching strategy to the students' preferred learning style preferences. Gisela Paoletti shows in her study (this volume: 593-603) that writing is not the most effective learning activity in all circumstances. We feel that the proposed effect of writing for learning is too easily generalized over learning tasks and learner types. A theory that explains in which circumstances (learner type, learning task) writing is an effective learning activity is welcomed.

Teacher studies. We welcome in this volume teachers as authors or co-authors (McClenaghan, Munch, Geist, de la Garza, Zermeño). In other studies in this volume researchers work closely with teachers, in natural circumstances (Saada, Poon, Oliver, Doly, Levin & Wagner). Presenting and analysing their years of experience, teachers provide writing education and research with valuable best practices as mixes of all kind of theoretical insights, within the natural boundaries of classroom practice. Teachers are the gatekeepers of educational progress. Research or educational policy only contribute in a very limited and indirect way. Therefore we hope that in the next decade, more studies will focus on teachers, as Kate Kiefer and Michael Palmquist do in this volume (419-429). They update their 1996 study (Kiefer & Palmquist, 1996) allowing us to share in their developments. In first instance they were interested in how the computer in the classroom affected writing lessons. But now they found that it's not the dichotomy between traditional and computer classrooms that makes a difference in the quality of teaching (Kiefer & Palmquist: 427). It is the effective and ineffective use of classroom writing time that is the key component (Kiefer & Palmquist: 426). Kiefer & Palmquist highlight the complexity of interactions that affect student and teacher performance in *any instructional context*. Studies in the domain of writing that focus on the way teachers plan to implement effective patterns of interaction (teacher-student; student-student) can rely on studies by Christina Díez' team (Díez, Anula, Lara, & Pardo: 91-103).

Measuring writing. In this selection of chapters, minimal attention is paid to measuring writing. The only study focusses fully on measurement is Ron Oostdam's chapter on measuring argumentation (this volume: 431-446). Some other chapters provide us with details about how writing is measured (among others Koutsoubou: 151-167; Vanmaele & Lowyck: 395-417; Couzijn & Rijlaarsdam: 209-240). Where possible and available, we included information about how writing was measured in chapters, mostly in appendices. Reporting educational studies on writing should include a concise description of the independent and the dependent variable: the two communicating vessels of research. The increasing bilingualism in Europe and other parts of the world will help us to understand the fine distinctions in genres and speech acts in the different languages. This may result in clearer understanding of the particular features of tasks, texts, and genres when we design and test writing lessons.

EDITORS' NOTE

The publication of this peer-reviewed volume is due to the efforts of many. We thank authors for the accurate way they responded to our questions; reviewers for their thorough, deep and helpful critique and advices; native English speaking authors in this volume for helping non-native English authors with linguistic advices. Although the size of the volume submerged us from time to time, we were happy to notice that authors felt that making this volume was a joint enterprise.

EMERGENT WRITING IN KINDERGARTEN AND THE EMERGENCE OF THE ALPHABETIC PRINCIPLE

MADELON SAADA-ROBERT, KRISTINE BALSLEV & KATJA MAZURCZAK

University of Geneva, Switzerland

Abstract. This chapter focuses on effective learning and teaching to write in kindergarten, considering L1. The research is part of a larger program that aims at exploring the relationship between learning to write and learning to read in the classroom, from kindergarten to grade two, where spelling becomes autonomous (children from 4 to 8 years old; see Rieben & Saada-Robert, 1997; Saada-Robert & Balslev, 2001). The actual results focus on the impact of emergent writing practices on the awareness of the alphabetic principle in a comprehensive way. They point out the benefit of teaching writing simultaneously with reading, from the very beginning of school culture acquisition.

Keywords: Emergent writing, developmental models, situated research in kindergarten

1. INTRODUCTION

Fostering learning and teaching to write and spell since the very beginning of school or even in kindergarten is a controversial, challenging and complex question that concerns researchers as well as politicians, practitioners and parents. Besides historical and cultural reasons that can explain the practices of teaching to read *before* teaching to write or spell, what are the scientific reasons actually given by psycholinguistics and didactics? What do we know about the processes of acquisition involved in reading and in writing/spelling? Does reading lead to writing, or the reverse, or are they both acquired in parallel? In short, is there a strictly defined "beginning" of literacy and an order of acquisition between reading and writing/spelling? During the last 20 years, a large number of studies in cognitive psycholinguistics has focused on very specific components such as phonological awareness, whereas others have recently contributed to question the complex relations

Saada-Robert, M., Balslev, K., & Mazurczak, K. (2004). Emergent writing in kindergarten and the emergence of the alphabetic principle.
In Rijlaarsdam, G. (Series Ed.) & Rijlaarsdam, G., Van den Bergh, H., & Couzijn, M. (Vol. Eds.), Studies in writing. Vol. 14, Effective learning and teaching of writing, 2nd Edition, Part 1, Studies in learning to write, 17 - 30 .

between learning to read and to spell (see Perfetti, Rieben & Fayol, 1997, for models and empirical results).

When taking such results into account, a new question arises, as a challenge for *situated research*: can results from experimental studies (occurring in a laboratory) "simply" be transferred to the educational field and more precisely to the everyday practices of reading and writing in the classroom? Is there a type of research, a methodological paradigm that could afford the challenge of aiming both at scientific knowledge and proposing reflexive tools for practitioners in their professional life? We propose here to consider that cognitive psycholinguistic studies (see below) are relevant for their results on two main points: on the components and processes involved in reading and writing/spelling, and on the developmental steps of the acquisition for each component. These studies lead to a clear identification of the components of literacy that will be transposed in didactic settings; they also lead to a more precise knowledge of learning strategies, and allow a better anticipation for the next step to be acquired by the learner. We also propose to consider that these studies are to be newly questioned from a *situated point of view* (Balslev & Saada-Robert, 2002; Saada-Robert & Balslev, in press), because they avoid the cultural and historical conditions in which knowledge occurs and is socially taught and learned.

For these reasons, emergent writing/spelling[1] is presently studied in a situated way, i.e., through effective processes of learning and teaching in the classroom[2]. Focusing on the field of emergent literacy in school or kindergarten, our team's research program relies on the intersection of three scientific areas: *socioconstructivism* (Piaget - Vygotsky), cognitive and genetic *psycholinguistics* and *didactic* theoretical models.

2. THEORETICAL FRAMEWORK

Whereas socioconstructivism is used as an epistemological frame underlying the processes of situated teaching/learning, psycholinguistics studies provide us with models of acquisition and concepts dealing with the processes occurring in the classroom. On the other hand, the analysis of our results is essentially didactic-oriented, in the sense that the processes of teaching and learning are analyzed conjunctly regarding literacy, even if the results presented here only concern the children's progression.

Four developmental models dealing with the acquisition of reading/writing and their relationships[3] are pointed here (Ehri, 1997; Frith; 1985; Rieben & Saada-

---

[1] *We shall use from now on the general concept of emergent writing, but it also concerns emergent spelling since the communicative situation of writing a short "text" is spontaneously converted by young children in the task of spelling words.*

[2] *This research occurred in the "Maison des Petits", a public school of Geneva linked to the university. We are grateful to the students and the teachers, M. Auvergne and J. Girard for their contribution.*

[3] *Although not being developmental models, other works are particularly convincing concerning the links between reading and writing and more particularly in regard of the processes in*

Robert, 1997; Seymour, 1997) for their common features as well as the contradictions they raise. In the first place, Frith's *linear stage model* (1985) suggests a first logographic stage that relies on reading, a second alphabetic stage related mainly to spelling, and a final orthographic stage requiring reading. Secondly, Ehri's *interactive stage model* (1997) presents a parallel evolution of spelling and reading. Both follow the same path, from a prealphabetic stage, through an alphabetic one (partial and full), and finally to an orthographic stage. Third, Seymour (1997) states that both logographic and alphabetic strategies develop in parallel, through reading and spelling, forming the dual foundation of later orthographic and morphographic strategies (*parallel foundation's model*). Finally, Rieben & Saada-Robert's model (1997) describes the acquisition of literacy in the classroom as a change in the dominance of either logographic, alphabetic and orthographic strategies that appear at the same time, in reading as well as in spelling (*interactive dominance-like phases*). This last model contrasts with a successive and discrete stages model (Frith); it shows that reading and spelling develop in parallel (like Ehri's and Seymour's models), and that several strategies can appear at the same time (like Seymour's model), the progression being marked by the dominance of first logographic strategies, then alphabetic, finally orthographic strategies (like Frith's and Ehri's models). Being analyzed with children aged 5 to 8, these models do not focus on the early roots of this acquisition, neither on the effects of emergent writing.

Concerning emergent writing as a possible root for the acquisition of the alphabetic principle, the effects of invented spelling on reading acquisition are stressed as strong hypothesis by several researchers (Ehri, 1997; Ferreiro, 1988; Frith, 1985; Jaffré, 1997). The psychogenesis of writing/spelling is analyzed by Ferreiro (1988) based on children's productions. Writing is considered as a conceptual construct that develops very early in successive stages through various cognitive conflicts occurring during the problem solving of writing tasks. Children discover the alphabetic system following five developmental stages: 1) understanding the difference between drawing and writing; 2) building up the principle of variety and quantity of letters in the word; 3) using letters in one-to-one correspondence with the syllable; 4) gradually making alphabetic hypotheses by understanding that letters or chains of letters are words; finally 5) phonologising and spelling. However, this model does not explain the influence of invented writing on the acquisition of the alphabetic principle, whereas other models do, such as in Jaffré (1997), Frith (1985) and Ehri (1997). For Jaffré (1995), invented writing leads to the discovery and the ontogenetic reconstruction of the alphabetic principle. According to his studies, the evolution begins with an early morphologic and logographic phase in writing. Children's writing then evolves toward the alphabetic principle, followed by a second logographic phase where words are considered as segmented units. Finally the orthographic phase appears while the main regularities and the most frequent irregularities are taken into account. In short, invented writing evolves from a morphographic and logographic form to alphabetic spelling. These results are comforted by Ehri's studies (1997). She points out that invented spelling, as an early practice of writing,

---

set (Caramazza & Hillis, 1991, adapted by Zesiger & de Partz, 1995; Ehri, 1997; Gombert, Bryant & Warrick, 1997; Perfetti, 1997).

reflects children's knowledge on the *orthographic system* and determines the speed with which they progress in learning to read. According to her, teaching to spell through settings of *invented spelling of words* would have a better influence on word reading than traditional teaching of spelling. Moreover, phonological *awareness* (long considered as a prerequisite to the acquisition of reading/spelling) appears more likely to evolve in relation with the knowledge of letters and the development of reading/spelling skills. Nevertheless, phonological awareness and phonemic segmentation remain major components of the acquisition of the alphabetic system. Finally, the impact of writing/spelling on the alphabetic principle is a key point of Frith's model (1985). As presented above, this model shows that early logography develops through reading, while *the alphabetic principle is acquired through spelling*. Later on, orthographic regularities and the specificities of the written system require reading. The question we focus on here aims at effective teaching and learning practices. At the beginning of school or kindergarten, should learning to read be a foundation for learning to write, as it is most likely to be practiced? Or should reading and writing both be considered at the same time? Or even could learning to write be fostered before learning to read? Such questions cannot be directly answered. Another question should first be answered prior to the latter: do emergent writing practices in kindergarten lead to the awareness of the alphabetic principle? More specifically, the research questions we focus on here are the following: 1) How do emergent writing strategies evolve? 2) Are emergent writing[4] strategies occurring in the classroom linked to the awareness of the alphabetic system? 3) What are the relationships between the sublexical skills occurring in didactic settings (writing strategies) and the ones taking place in psycholinguistic tasks (letter naming, letter writing and phonological awareness)?

3. METHODOLOGICAL FRAMEWORK

The methodological paradigm of *situated research* is used here. It deals both with scientific knowledge and the achievement of practical concerns about the efficiency of teaching/learning processes (Saada-Robert & Balslev, in press).

Subjects are 18 four-year-old children (the mean age is 4;3 in September) in one classroom with their teacher. They are observed four times during one school year (September, November, February, June) on two different cues. First, linguistic skills are individually tested on letter identification[5], letter spelling[6] and phonological

---

[4] *We deal here with emergent writing rather than with invented spelling. Occurring in the classroom, the setting aims at a "written production" within a textual dimension that differs from the known spelling tasks. Moreover, children's writing emerges in the social context of kindergarten that differs from the individual conditions of invented spelling experimentations.*
[5] *The child is shown each letter of the alphabet (in the developmental acquisition frequency order) and is asked if he can tell the name of the letter or its sound.*
[6] *The child is asked to write as many letters as possible, even those that he cannot name. He is asked to write them as he thinks they should be written.*

awareness[7]. These tasks are chosen among others, considering their explicative value concerning the alphabetic acquisition. Second, didactic sequences in emergent reading (with a picture book) and writing are video recorded at the four times. Emergent writing that occurs in collective interactive setting shall be stressed as a condition for the alphabetic principle awareness. Children are asked to 'write as they know' what the picture they have just drawn tells. The didactic sequence is conceived in several phases. First children make a drawing about one of the book's episodes chosen from the emergent reading story. They are then asked to 'write what the drawing says'; and are encouraged to 'write as they already know, even if they still don't write as the bigger children or the teacher do'; later on, the drawing and writing productions are discussed with the teacher or the researcher; the record of the discussion is then transcribed and used for the emergent writing production's analysis. Finally, the children, collecting all their drawings and writings, discuss their progress with the teacher and their parents. Following the transcription of complete on-line observations (using video records), the data analysis consists in a comprehensive description of emergent writing strategies occurring in didactic settings. Their relationship to the awareness of the alphabetic principle is then analyzed through children's scores at the psycholinguistic tasks.

4. RESULTS

Regarding acquisition of the alphabetic system, our results focus on the transition between the logographic and the alphabetic phases of literacy acquisition. In order to investigate this transition, results are presented in three parts: 1) description of the emergent writing strategies encountered with four year-old children; 2) strategies' evolution during the school year; and finally 3) results on the alphabetic system acquisition: letter naming, letter spelling and phonemic awareness.

4.1 Emergent Writing Strategies

In order to analyze the children's productions, writing strategies are defined according to two criteria: their content (adapted from previous studies, i.e., Ehri, 1990; Ferreiro, 1988; Saada-Robert & Hoefflin, 2000; Saada-Robert & Favrel, 2001) and their developmental complexity (Frith, 1985; Ehri, 1997; Seymour, 1997, Rieben & Saada-Robert, 1997). They are listed below (table 1) in a developmental order, going from the more basic strategies (for example scribbles or waves) to the more complex ones (use of letters in phonographic correspondence).

At four years old in kindergarten, children mainly produce logographic and (partial) alphabetic strategies, confirming previous studies. The logographic strategies are twofold (see fig.1). First, they involve the use of signs or marks characterized by 1) the intention to produce meaning and 2) the awareness of the writings' representational nature and of its difference with drawings. Children make discontinuous and

---

[7] *Phonological segmentation at the beginning of words: from animal pictures, the child starts by naming the animals, then is asked to say the sound he hears at the very beginning of the word. The words are all bisyllabic and the first vowels are of CV, VC, or CCV type.*

quick scribbles or waves (pictorial imitation of the writer's gesture, IMP in fig.1) and produce some isolated units resembling letters or numbers, pseudo-letters and some awkwardly drawn letters (semiographic marks, GRA in fig.1). Second, the logographic strategies in writing involve the use of known letters (logographically memorized without the corresponding name or sound, LOG in fig.1) written in lines, and the more evolved strategy of writing different words with different letters and a number of letters that changes according to the length of the word to be written[8] (VNP in fig.1). Alphabetic strategies are first used while children become aware of the necessity to write only the letters that are in phonetic correspondence with the word to be written. After the first awareness that written words are composed of *discontinuous signs* representing concepts that are also spoken words, the logographic strategies lead to a more abstract awareness, i.e., written words are made of *letters that have to differ* according to the quality of the different spoken words. The alphabetic strategy deals with a third type of constraint, still more complex and requiring. The written words are strictly composed of the *precise letters that fit the exact phonological components* of the spoken words. This requirement is first applied to the first sound heard in the word, or to the rime (for example, *city* could be written *S I*), later to the syllable (*city* could be written *S T*, see the SYL strategy in fig.2), last to the phoneme (*S I T I*, see the ALP strategy in fig.2). Finally, for the population of this study, lexical strategies take into account the segmentation of the words, the blank spaces that mark the external limits of the word unit (LEX in fig.2). Later in the acquisition process, the orthographic strategies add a new constraint to the learner: the constraint dealing with the whole word unit, written altogether as a visual and a spelled unit, involving the specificities of each written system.

Table 1. Emergent Writing Strategies

Logographic strategies	Use of signs/marks	IMP:	pictural imitation
		GRA:	semiographic strategies
	Use of letters without phonographic correspondence	LOG:	production of letters from the logographic memory, in line
		VNP:	principle of variety and number of letters without sound analysis
Alphabetic strategies	Use of phonographic correspondence	SYL:	syllabic strategies
		ALP:	alphabetic strategies
		LEX:	lexical strategies

Figures 1 and 2 illustrate the writing strategies. Figure 1 shows the variety of strategies composing the logographic phase preceding the alphabetic awareness. The use of semiotic marks, of non-conventional discontinuous signs, of pseudo-letters, and the use of very few known letters (known as pictures before being known by name

---

[8] *As shown by Ferreiro (1988), the length of the word can be its effective graphic length (train being shorter than locomotive) or, at that developmental level, the representational length of the concept (train being obviously much longer than the sole locomotive).*

or sound) spelled in different ways according to the spoken words, characterize the logographic phase in a positive constructivist manner preceding the alphabetic one.

The pictural imitation (IMP) strategies contain semiopictural strategies (scribbles) and graphic imitations of the writer's gesture (waves).

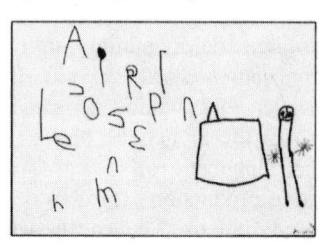

The semiographic strategy (GRA) is composed of discontinuous graphic signs, pseudo-letters, a few known letters (from the first name or familiar words) and numbers, dispatched all over the paper sheet.

This production shows a LOG strategy: the letters are produced in line without phonetic correspondence but they match with the writing project: the child "reads" his production, recalling his project, but the pointing of the letters does not fit the length of the line.

The child understands that print necessarily contains different letters for different words and a minimum number of letters, depending on the spoken words. Nevertheless the writing project is most often not recalled, the child being focused on the variation and number of the letters he writes (VNP strategy).

Figure 1. Examples of logographic writing strategies.

This example shows the awareness of the alphabetic principle. The child wrote
"Léo rentre à la maison avec son papa" (Leo goes back home with his dad).
The syllabic strategy (SYL) is used for "la maison" = L M S, and "son" = S, in an attempt of phonographic correspondence marked with consonants. The alphabetic strategy (ALP) drives the writing of the other words ("ront" for "rentre", "AVC" for "avec").
Finally, "Leo", "papa" and "Theodore" (the child's name) are conventionally written with the lexical strategy (LEX) that involves the constraint of the word segmentation in addition to the alphabetic strategy.

Figure 2. Examples of alphabetic writing strategies in one text.

This definition of the logographic phase is consistent with Frith (1985) and Seymour (1997), whereas others (Ehri, 1997; Sprenger-Charolles & Casalis, 1996; Sprenger-Charolles, Siegel & Béchennec, 1997) consider this phase as pre-alphabetic or even non-linguistic, by stating that the reading/writing process only starts *with the use of letters matched with sounds*. In a developmental and constructivist point of view however, this position appears as reductionist. The results presented here also point out that the alphabetic phase includes several evolving strategies that can be syllabic, alphabetic or lexical. A constructivist approach of the children's emergent writing productions leads to consider the acquisition process as both discontinuous and continuous. The gap between the logographic and the alphabetic strategies is well marked by the use of phonographic strategies. On the other hand, the continuity from the first to the second appears in the links children make between spoken and written words, well before the phonographic correspondence. The first link deals with the early use of discontinuous signs for writing (opposed to drawing) in order to communicate and produce meaning as in speech. Second, the progressive use of letters, and then the necessity of change in the variety and number of letters according to the spoken words, are previous strategies leading to the more constraining and later link of phonography between spoken and written words that characterizes the alphabetic phase.

4.2 Evolution of Strategies during the School Year

Regarding acquisition of the alphabetic system and within the evolution of emergent writing strategies, our results focus on two important transitions. The first one is the transition between the use of signs (GRA strategies) and the use of letters (LOG and VNP strategies). The second one concerns the awareness that letters must be used in phonographic correspondence, i.e., the transition between the LOG and VNP strategies (logographic phase) to the SYL strategies (alphabetic phase).

Table 2 presents the frequencies and percentages of emergent writing strategies for the group of 18 children at the four times during the year. Each production is written according to one or more strategies. At the beginning of the year (T1), only 16 children were present and they wrote in a single homogeneous way.

Four points can be stressed from these results. At first, the quantity of total writing strategies increases[9] from T1 to T4 (16, 27, 33, 43). At T1, each production is homogenously composed and the strategies are exclusively IMP, GRA (dominant with 56.3%) and LOG. From T2 on, the increasing number of strategies indicates that *different strategies appear in one single production*, even more so at T4 (end of the year) than at T3 or T2.

Secondly, concerning the type of strategies that evolve, it is mostly the more complex strategies that increase, whereas the basic strategies tend to stabilize or decrease. Logographic strategies, essentially GRA, dominant at T1 and still at T2, decrease from 56.3% to only 7% at T4. LOG and VNP strategies become dominant

---

[9] *The changes pointed out in this research cannot be statistically tested because of the low number of strategies and subjects.*

at T3 (30.3% and 24.2%) and remain approximately at the same percentage at T4 (23.3% for both of them). Alphabetic strategies, mainly SYL and ALP increase. There are none at T1 and they become very close to dominance at T4 (respectively 11.6 and 18.6). When added together, SYL and ALP strategies are dominant with 30.2% of all the strategies observed at T4. Lexical strategies that concern the word segmentation in addition to the alphabetic principle also increase from none at T1 to 9.3% of all the strategies used at T4.

Table 2. Emergent Writing Strategies from T1 to T4 (N = Frequencies, % = Percentages)

	T1 n = 16	T2 n = 27	T3 n = 33	T4 n = 43
IMP: Semiopictural and graphic imitation	18.8	7.4	6.1	7.0
GRA: Semiographic units	56.3	44.4	12.1	7.0
LOG: Logographic use of letters	25	18.5	30.3	23.3
VNP: Principle of variety and number of letters	-	18.5	24.2	23.3
SYL: Syllabic correspondance	-	-	6.1	11.6
ALP: Alphabetic correspondence	-	3.7	12.1	18.6
LEX: Lexical segmentation	-	7.4	9.1	9.3

Regarding the dominant strategies, they evolve from semiographic ones (GRA) at T1 and T2, to the logographic use of letters (LOG and VNP) at T3 and T4, with a strong presence of alphabetic strategies at T4 (SYL and ALP totaling 30.2% of the strategies).

The last point concerns persistent strategies that do not decisively decrease with time, such as the basic imitative pictural strategy (IMP: discontinuous scribbles and waves). Table 2 shows that all strategies are present at T3 and T4, even the more basic ones. The choice of strategies enlarges with time and children finally use basic strategies as well as evolved ones, depending on the constraint of the task and the didactic context. In contrast with Ferreiro (1988) who explains progression of writing in terms of discrete stages, our results show that acquisition in situated writing appears as a change in a dominance of strategies, which confirms the results of a previous research (Rieben & Saada-Robert, 1997) and not in replacement of a less evolved strategy by a more complex one. In short, these results show that four year-old children in kindergarten evolve during one year in their writing from a logographic phase to the alphabetic one. They also point out the difficulty to isolate these two phases insofar as learning/teaching occurs in ecological contexts and is analyzed within a developmental constructivist approach. The evolution occurs through changes in the dominance of strategies and not in the replacement of simple ones by complex ones. The two main evolutions occur at T3 with the passage from GRA to LOG and VNP, i.e., the passage from the use of semiographic marks to the use of letters, and at T4 with the passage from letters without phonographic correspondence to use of phonographic correspondence, either applied to the syllable or to the phoneme. Moreover, regarding the evolution within children, only two of them use the same strategies as dominant ones between T1 and T4, whereas the sixteen other children progress from one dominance to the next ones. The results also show, in a descriptive way, that emergent writing settings in kindergarten are good conditions for the acquisition of the alphabetic system's awareness.

4.3 Results Concerning the Alphabetic System

The question dealing with the links between emergent writing strategies and the *alphabetic* system leads to compare results that are drawn from the psycholinguistic tasks (individual conditions) and from the didactic settings (class conditions). These two conditions offer different data concerning the acquisition of the alphabetic system. They allow considering the evolution from discontinuous graphic signs and pseudo-letters, to letters used in a logographic way, finally to letters used in phonographic correspondence. The following points are described: 1) evolution from T1 to T4 of the amount of *letters spelled in individual task* and the evolution of the number of *discontinuous graphic signs written in didactic settings* (figure 3) that are not yet letters; 2) progression of the amount of *named* and *spelled letters in individual task* and the amount of *written letters in didactic settings* (figure 4); 3) evolution of *phonemic awareness* (individual task) and the number of *phonographic correspondences in didactic settings* (figure 5).

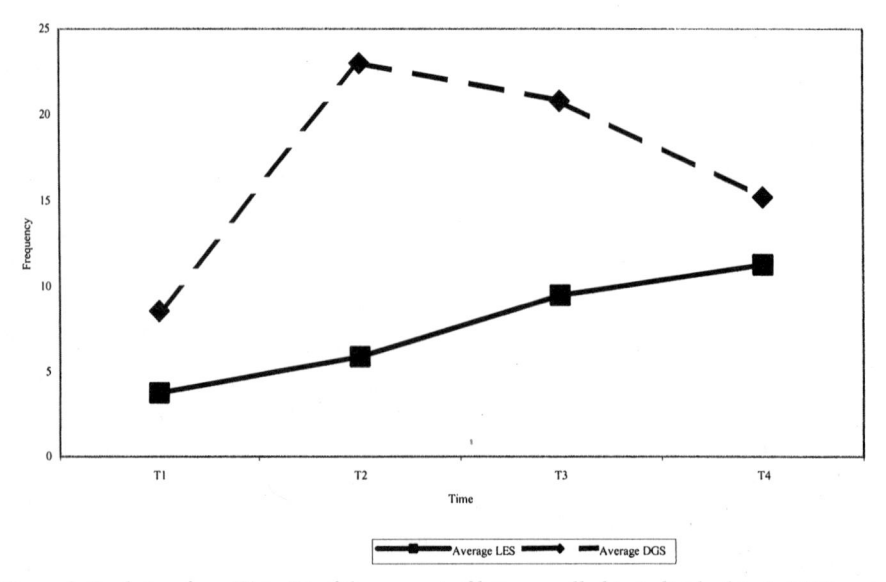

Figure 3. Evolution from T1 to T4 of the amount of letters spelled in individual task (LES) and the number of discontinuous graphic signs written in didactic settings (DGS).

Figure 3 shows a difference in the evolution of the two results. The amount of discontinuous graphic signs (DGS curve) produced in the four didactic settings rapidly increases between T1 and T2, then decreases. Children where asked to "write as they know, as they can, the story of the drawing" they previously made. At T4 this amount is not far from the amount of letters written by the same children when asked to "write as you know all the letters you know" (LES curve). Whereas the amount of known letters that are written progresses in a linear way (LES), the amount of any discontinuous sign for producing meaning (DGS) increases considerably from T1 to T2 then decreases. At T2 and T3, children produce an important amount of graphic signs when they are asked to "write the story". They are fully involved in the class setting, while they spell very few known letters in the task condition. But their written production decreases at T4, as if they became aware of *the necessity to use letters* in order to write. We can here hypothesize that the class condition offers children a way to enter the writer's social role, to become aware of the first properties of written language (made of discontinuous graphic signs) and of the necessity to use conventional signs that are letters in order to represent spoken messages. Furthermore they are going to learn the name, the sound and the pictural form of the letters from the teacher and other partners of the classroom. How does letter knowledge evolve during one school year at four years old? Letter knowledge involves letter naming, spelling and writing (figure 4).

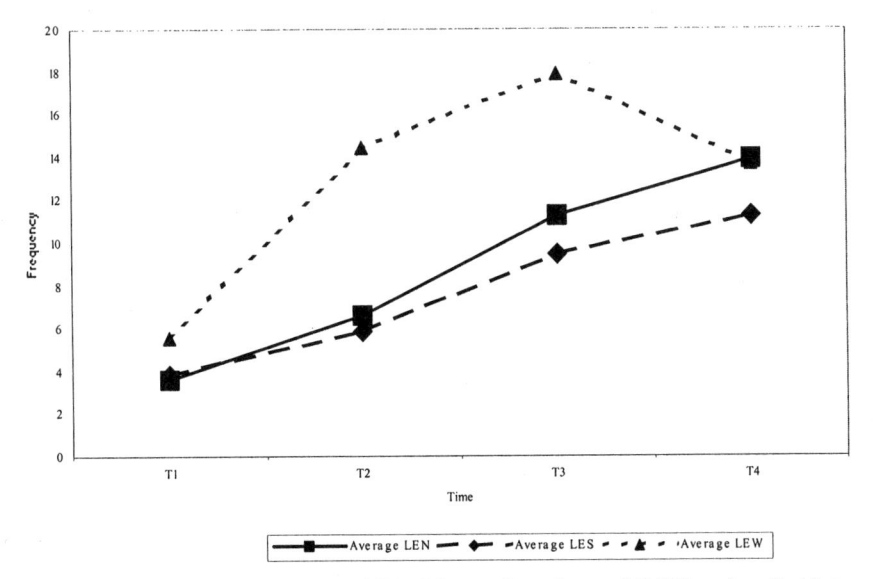

Figure 4. Progression between T1 and T4 of the number of named (LEN) and spelled letters (LES) in individual tasks and the number of written letters produced in didactic settings (LEW).

Figure 4 shows that from the beginning of the school year (T1) and increasingly at T2 and T3, children in didactic settings write letters (LEW curve) in addition to the discontinuous signs mentioned in figure 3, even if they cannot name them (LEN curve) or spell them (LES curve). These two last curves are slightly different, the named letters being more frequent than the spelled ones. Again, writing in didactic settings seems to be more productive at the beginning of the year, but strongly decreases with time. At T4, the amount of written letters in the didactic condition becomes equal to the amount of named letters in the task condition, as if children start to realize that they cannot write just any letter for all the different spoken words they intend to write. Thus, the role of known letters on the written production is marked, but in reverse, at the beginning of the acquisition process, the hypothesis can be made of the role of writing any letters, a lot of letters, as a drive to assert the limits of this strategy and the necessity to learn their name and spelling. We can also notice from the qualitative individual productions that during the class settings, the children write or know different letters than during the individual task situation. The amount of named, spelled and written letters appears to become much the same at T4, but there are individual differences between these three skills for most children, which indicates that there is no stability in their letter knowledge. Considering their age, these results are not surprising, the alphabetic system being still in construction. The third figure deals with the other main component of the alphabetic system: phonographic correspondence.

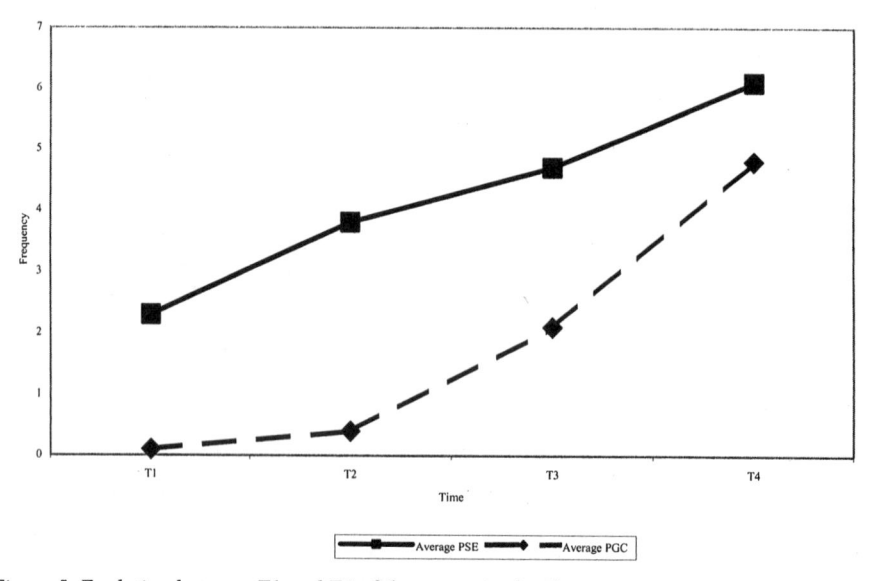

Figure 5. Evolution between T1 and T4 of the scores in the phonemic segmentation task (PSE, maximum score = 12) and the number of phonographic correspondences used in didactic settings (PGC).

In Figure 5, the results concerning the phonological segmentation (PSE curve) and the phoneme/grapheme correspondence (PGC curve) are shown. They both evolve between T1 and T4. Nevertheless, the scores in the phonological segmentation task are higher than the amount of letters spelled in phonographic correspondence at T1, T2 and T3. Only at T4 do the results become very close. As expected the task of segmenting the first sound heard in a word is easier than searching for the proper letter corresponding to each of the segmented sounds that compose a word. Phonologic segmentation appears to be part of the alphabetic system acquisition, with letter knowledge and phonographic correspondence.

In addition and concerning the relations between strategies occurring in didactic settings and skills appearing in the psycholinguistic individual tasks, some hypotheses can be formulated. At T1, few letters are named, spelled or written. This could explain why children mainly use logographic strategies; for example, children who use the IMP strategy name and spell four letters at most. At T2 and T3, the knowledge of letters, their naming, spelling or writing, (LEN, LES and LEW) increases and a parallel could be drawn with the evolution of the strategies. More the children become aware that letters are necessary to write, more they produce with the LOG and VNP strategies. At T4, children realize that any letter cannot be written for any word and any sound in the word: they use more and more alphabetic strategies along with the phonographic processes.

5. FINAL QUESTIONS ON TEACHING

Consistent with Frith's model (1985), our results show that through emergent writing, children become aware of the alphabetic principle. Furthermore, the evolution in emergent writing appears in the form of changes in the dominance of strategies (Rieben & Saada-Robert, 1997). They describe the children's progression concerning letter naming, spelling, phonological awareness, letter use in emergent writing as well as their writing strategies. In didactic settings, children progressively realize that letters must be used for writing (transition between T2-T3) and that they cannot write any letters for any words (transition between T3-T4). Emergent writing settings practiced in school before formal and direct instruction on the principle, or at the same time, appear to be a good way towards the acquisition of the alphabetic system.

In short, the results obtained in school settings suggest an alternative way to the acquisition of the alphabetic system through mere phonological and letter knowledge training. Regarding teaching, this conclusion leads to a hypothesis concerning the links between emergent reading and emergent writing, since emergent writing seems to play an important role in the acquisition of the alphabetic principle. Therefore emergent writing activities in early education should help the process of learning to read. One question concerning teaching to write arises from our results. As shown above, most children write letters in didactic settings without being able to name them, this first logographic knowledge leading to the necessity of learning the letters' name and sound. But on the other hand, some children spell letters when they are explicitly and individually asked to; at the same time, they still "write" waves, scribbles or pseudo-letters in the didactic settings of emergent writing. It means then that some formal knowledge is not used in didactic settings. So the question is: how can teachers optimize the activation of this knowledge? What properties of the didactic settings are able to foster this activation? Among these properties, what are the *on-line regulations* from teachers that are likely to induce this activation? These are the questions our research team is now going to focus on, through microgenetic-situated studies.

LOOKING AT READING AND WRITING THROUGH LANGUAGE

MARIA DA GRAÇA L. C. PINTO

University of Porto, Portugal

Abstract. Although writing has its own set of characteristics and its psycholinguistic processing follows different patterns, it cannot be seen in isolation from oral language or reading. Indeed, it can be said that oral and written language *nourish* each other, and this interaction should be borne in mind when they are practised. A first step towards dealing with writing in a meaningful way is proposed here through a language method (Girolami-Boulinier, 1984) and three reading techniques (indirect, semi-direct and silent direct) (Girolami-Boulinier, 1993; Girolami-Boulinier & Cohen-Rak, 1985). The language method trains learners to immediately identify the semantic groups of sentences they hear and produce, as well as the nature and function of the head words – "mots-centres" according to Girolami-Boulinier (Girolami-Boulinier, 1987: 38) – of sentence elements. The logical organisation that the proposed language method implies should also be taken into account. The reading techniques improve speaking and prevent writing errors which have to do with language misunderstandings and misuses, with misperceptions at the level of speaking and listening, and with lack of attention. This approach will benefit orthography in its broadest sense, from mere decoding to language mastery, punctuation and style. Furthermore, it prepares learners to exercise and cultivate the different writing practices required by today's society.

Keywords: Oral and written language *continuum,* language method, language awareness, language structuration, sentence construction, lexical nature and function identification, immediate grasping of the meaning of verbal productions, noun/pronoun expansions, vocabulary enlargement, indirect, semi-direct and silent direct reading, literacy.

1. INTRODUCTION

In modern societies, it is almost unthinkable not to be able to read or write – to be illiterate. Due to social, economic and cultural factors, however, our very notion of

---

Pinto, M. da Graça L. C. (2004). Looking at reading and writing through language.
In Rijlaarsdam, G. (Series Ed.) & Rijlaarsdam, G., Van den Bergh, H., & Couzijn, M. (Vol. Eds.), Studies in writing. Vol. 14, Effective learning and teaching of writing, 2nd Edition, Part 1, Studies in learning to write, 31 - 46.

literacy has undergone a change of meaning. No longer merely the ability to read and write, literacy "is viewed as an advancing set of knowledge, skills, and strategies, which individuals build on throughout life." (OECD, 2000: 18). A literate person is one who "cultivates and exercises the social practices which use writing" (Soares, 1998: 47).

It is unimaginable in our graphocentric societies that oral language could develop without the influence of written language. For practical reasons, the qualifications "oral" and "written" are used in this text to distinguish modalities of use of language as a code (Marcuschi, 2001: 25 and 26) though oral and written language should not be seen as a dichotomy, as two opposite poles (p. 34), but as a gradual differentiation (p. 43) based upon a conception of language and text which has to be seen as a set of social practices (p. 15). Thus, before children start school and become active users of written language, their language development should be encouraged through the use of literacy events, by which they are surrounded. Although school is generally seen as the literacy agency *par excellence* (see Kleiman, 1998: 176; Rojo, 2001: 65), the role of the family as an effective literacy agency cannot be underestimated, as numerous literacy events take place in the family context[1].

When oral and written language are viewed in this way they cannot be seen as antagonic skills, as two activities implying a dramatic change from the contextual dependence of oral language to the autonomy usually associated with written language, but as a *continuum* which consists of different ways of putting into practice natural language according to different demands. In other words, it should not be forgotten that, in terms of language development in a graphocentric society, the child already possesses a certain level of language knowledge, a vision of the language and a written representation of the spoken language before starting primary school and in early schooling (cf. Marcuschi, 1998: 105).

It is no wonder then that, according to Bentolila, the better a child masters the oral code the more success s/he will have in reading and writing tasks (Bentolila, 1994: 2). And the same author considers that access to the written code will be facilitated if the child has managed to acquire a certain distance from the oral, and consequently if s/he has already acquired the ability to grasp the different oral language components and to understand how and why the oral language functions.

With regard to the language *continuum*, Kavanagh says (Kavanagh, 1991: vii): "A few years ago [...] [s]poken language and written language were considered two separate and distinctly different skills or parallel processes in different modalities.

---

[1] *The OECD Programme for International Student Assessment (PISA) 2000 also leads us to confirm the role of the family as an important literacy agency, i. e., as a provider of (literacy) events, based upon indicators such as "discussing political or social issues; discussing books, films or television programmes; listening to music together; discussing how well the student was doing in school; eating the main meal with the student; and spending time just talking." (OECD, 2001: 147). Therefore, educational success may be linked "to positive synergies between the home and school environments" and "communication between parents and children can be of educational benefit" (OECD, 2001: 147). The Swiss document on the same programme also highlights the influence of the language spoken at home on the results obtained with the test. Once again we are faced with the family as a crucial literacy agency (see IRDP, n. d., section: "Résultats en lecture: faisceau de variables influentes").*

[...] But, authors [...] of the six chapters of this book, and the editor, believe that there is a *language continuum*; the skills of reading and writing (*literacy*) are built upon [...] the oral language acquired in *infancy* and the first years of life."[2].

The aim of this chapter, as the title suggests, is to show, on the one hand, the influence of successful mastering of oral language – based upon a language method (cf. Girolami-Boulinier, 1984, 1987, 1989, 1993) which helps learners to immediately grasp and identify the different units of speech when the subject is speaking and listening – on the acquisition of writing. On the other hand, it is also to show the influence of reading – at first by means of the indirect reading technique (cf. Girolami-Boulinier, 1993; Girolami-Boulinier & Cohen-Rak, 1985) – on the improvement of oral language development and on the preparation for entrance into the written world in an active way. The silent direct reading technique preceded by the indirect and the semi-direct reading techniques (cf. Girolami-Boulinier, 1993; Girolami-Boulinier & Cohen-Rak, 1985) as well as the aforementioned language method will help those who are beginning to read and write to become proficient in both skills and aware of the mechanisms inherent to them.

The sequence indirect, semi-direct, and silent direct reading refers to a process which becomes less and less mediated not only by another reader but also by oral language/reading aloud. This process begins with the oral reproduction of what is previously read aloud by another person who serves as a mediator because the child cannot yet read alone, and ends with silent reading, the kind of reading which, according to Cagliari, should prevail in school (Cagliari, 2001: 59, note 24). Silent reading is supposed to be performed by anyone who can already read and is not expected to be mediated by reading aloud. It is also qualified as direct (see Girolami-Boulinier & Cohen-Rak, 1985: 11) because, as the child can already read alone, s/he does not need the mediation of another person as happened with indirect reading when the child could not yet read alone. Very often, for the teacher to check progress, the child who is practising the silent direct reading is asked to reproduce orally, without looking at the text, what s/he has just read silently before reproducing what has been read in written form, without the presence of the model. In fact, silent direct reading is mainly meant to practise writing and consolidate spelling. It can be expected that the practice of silent reading will lead not only to correct written reproduction of the model, but also, when required, to fluent reading aloud, without hesitations, respecting idea units – reading and comprehension are to be taken as a whole –, paying attention to pauses and correctly reproducing the "speech song" ("la chanson du discours"), according to Girolami-Boulinier (Girolami-Boulinier, 2000: 83). In this context, practising of silent direct reading is preferred to the immediate practising of reading aloud because through silent direct reading the child is given the access to the written material for as long as necessary in order to master correct pronunciation and spelling before reproducing the text. During the time the child is reading silently s/he should feel a connection between what s/he is

---

[2] *It is, however, interesting to observe, following the ideas of De Lemos (De Lemos, 1998: 20), how the acceptance of the idea of writing as a knowledge to be taught and learned instead of seeing in it a direct relationship (a continuum) between oral and written language emphasises the idea of a gap between both modalities, i.e., a discontinuity.*

reading silently with what s/he already possesses in his/her inner language so that when the reproduction takes place the child appears to be translating directly from his/her inner language what s/he has read. In other words, reading aloud should sound like speaking. From this perspective, language has to be seen in a broader sense and not confined either to a phonic or a graphic manifestation.

Due to their distinct cognitive and linguistic implications, indirect reading and silent direct reading serve different purposes: the former aims mainly to improve different aspects of (oral) language, even in children who can already read alone, and the latter aims to improve both orthography and writing when the child has already learned how to read and write. In the first case, attention is especially paid to the oral stimulus and, in the second, to the visual one. Moreover, silent reading helps the reader to feel that written material may be accessed without the mediation of sound but certainly relying on inner language. When the reader has become proficient, reading aloud represents another way of giving form to what has already been read silently: both readings should be so close that they should appear to be simultaneous; in other words, the reader finds in the act of reading aloud a phonic manifestation of inner language (cf. Girolami-Boulinier 1988: 24).

Furthermore, the purpose of the language method proposed here is to train children from an early age to be sensitive both to the way language is organized and to the different writing practices they will need to exercise as members of their societies. In fact, the earlier learners are prepared for literacy requirements, the better they will perform in terms of oral and written expression and comprehension in any knowledge domain. The implications of this method on their logical reasoning should also be taken into account.

2. THE CONTRIBUTION OF ORAL LANGUAGE TO THE MASTERING OF WRITTEN LANGUAGE

From a developmental point of view, children first perceive the speech chain as a sound *continuum,* which they learn to decompose in order to identify its components. In other words, for language to develop, it has to be seen as an object to be constructed based upon deconstructions, which lead to new constructions, i.e., it is an object which is also exposed to (a special type of) "manipulation". This kind of "manipulation", which is supposed to lead to classification, relies on a sound input and is mediated by the sensory memory, which is characterized by its shortness. Oral language, unlike the objects the child is used to manipulating, can be neither touched nor seen by the child. It is an object which obliges the child to use auditory perception in order to operate the necessary classification. Moreover, due to its symbolization *role*, language may also be deemed to help in the construction/knowing of other objects, besides being an object of knowledge (cf. Sinclair-deZwart, 1972: 364). But, the relationship between the subject and the object/language should be seen in a state of permanent renewal because language as an object is never stable, due to its use in different contexts (cf. De Lemos, 1998: 21).

If, in the realm of L1 the term *learning* is sometimes used alongside the term *acquisition*, the reason may be that it is important to create the necessary conditions for the child to become aware as early as possible of the existence of the units (at first the discrete units) which compose the above-mentioned sound *continuum*, or speech chain. Undoubtedly, if from an early age the child is exposed to different oral language events, such as the reading of stories and books, the recounting of stories and daily experiences, the reproduction of songs and rhymes, this will lead to an easier and closer relationship with language in general and to the instilling of a certain awareness at different language levels (phonetic/phonological, morphological, lexical and syntactic).

To lead the child to the discovery that each act of his/her life has a verbal translation and that the objects, animals and persons s/he knows also possess a verbal existence seems to be one of the first steps in language awareness development. For example, we may make the gestures of jumping, walking, eating, clapping hands, and ask the child to tell us what we are doing. On the other hand, we may say "laugh", "run", "drink", etc., and ask the child to mimic the actions translated by the words (cf. Girolami-Boulinier, 1993: 12-13). Other exercises may be done to name and identify objects or pictures representing different items (cf. Girolami-Boulinier, 1993: 12). In languages such as Portuguese, where the articles usually precede the nouns and the verbs are conjugated, the children are instructed to give the nouns without any article (cf. Girolami-Boulinier, 1993: 12) and the verb in the base form (cf. Girolami-Boulinier, 1993: 13). The aim of this kind of exercise is to allow children to become acquainted with the discrete units of their language and, what is more, to feel that the language forms they are used to saying may look different (have different endings or be expanded in different ways) according to the contexts in which they appear. This very simple language exercise already leads the child to gain a certain distance from his/her language – instilling the beginnings of language awareness –, to feel that language also obeys certain rules and to see it as an object which is not passive. In fact, it may even offer resistance to the speaker forcing him/her to make the necessary adaptations.

Subsequently, due to the importance of the child mastering the notion of three ("quantité «3»" – see Girolami, 2001: 9) before beginning to learn to read and write (Girolami-Boulinier, 1993: 29), it is advisable to familiarize the child with three-element sentences, normally consisting of a subject, a verb and an object (the classical SVO structure). The child is then expected to construct a similar sentence when s/he is faced with three words: two nouns with no pre-determiner and a verb in the base form, and to say the nouns (without pre-determiners) and the verb in the base form when a three-element sentence is proposed (cf. Girolami-Boulinier, 1993: 20-22).

If one proposes, for example,

"beber"   "sumo"   "rapaz"

(drink)   (juice)   (boy)

the child is expected to say "O rapaz bebe sumo" ("The boy drinks juice") based upon his/her language experience, and his/her pragmatic knowledge. On the other hand, if one proposes:

"O pai lê o jornal"

(The father reads the newspaper)

the child is expected to identify "pai" ("father"), "ler" ("read") and "jornal" ("newspaper").

By means of this kind of language exercise, the child becomes familiar with the verb/act as well as with the head words (nouns, pronouns or verbs) – "mots-centres" according to Girolami-Boulinier (Girolami-Boulinier, 1987: 38) – of the elements of the structures: s/he is not only asked to place them in the correct positions with the necessary additions (articles, endings, etc.), but also to identify them when they appear in a sentence with the necessary agreement.

The number of elements may vary according to the child's language development and school level. In other words, the act/action represented by the verb of the structure may be completed by means of different objects and complements (direct and indirect objects and adverbial complements) according to the meaning to be conveyed.

With regard to the complements of verbs/actions, it is important that the child learns both to identify the nature (nouns, pronouns or verbs) of the head words of the elements of the sentence and their function (subject, object, complement) so that the sentence makes sense to him/her immediately. (See Girolami-Boulinier's functions table ("tableau des fonctions"): Girolami-Boulinier, 1989: 45 and 47; 2000: 74-75.).

If one considers the sentence:

"As flores crescem no jardim"

(The flowers grow in the garden),

the child is expected to identify the act, i.e., the verb in the base form "crescer" ("grow"), and look for the complement which completes its sense "no jardim" "in the garden"). After this, the subject of the sentence – "as flores" ("the flowers") – should be easily identified (see Girolami-Boulinier, 1987: 34). The child begins to interiorize the different roles assigned to the elements (subject, direct or indirect objects, and adverbial complements) which complete the sense of the verb/act and may even be able to show them in any graphic representation, without needing to know the metalinguistic labels of the different functions.

The most important aim of this language exercise is to train the child to grasp the nature and function of the elements of the sentences as s/he listens to them or reads them (Girolami-Boulinier, 1987) before learning the grammar labels normally attributed to them. This language method helps to create the necessary distance between the order of occurrence of the elements of the sentence and their function. It is perhaps worthwhile remembering that in some languages the subject does not occur systematically in the first position of the sentence. Nevertheless, the child is not supposed to identify the first element of the sentence as the subject. If s/he does so, we have to conclude that s/he has not yet grasped how to turn around the verb/act leading to an immediate understanding of the sentence.

Another way to contribute to the awareness of the existence of linguistic units as discrete entities is the expansion of the head words ("mots-centres") of the noun phrases and prepositional phrases which may figure as elements of the sentences (see Girolami-Boulinier, 1993: 72 and ff.).

A noun, for example, may be expanded by means of (pre)determiners, adjectives, post-modification ("compléments du nom") including relatives ("relatives") (Girolami-Boulinier, 1984: 22; 1993: 78; 2000: 81-82). For example, the noun "jardim" (garden) may be expanded in different ways:

1. Pre-determiner + noun	"<u>um</u> jardim"	(<u>a</u> garden)
2. Pre-determiner + <u>adjective</u> + noun	"um <u>belo</u> jardim"	(a <u>beautiful</u> garden)
3. Pre-determiner + adjective + noun + <u>post-modification ("complément du nom")</u>	"um belo jardim <u>para passear</u>"	(a beautiful garden <u>to go for a walk</u>)
4. Pre-determiner + adjective + noun + post-modification ("complément du nom") + <u>relative</u>	"um belo jardim para passear <u>que fica ao lado de minha casa</u>"	(a beautiful garden to go for a walk, <u>which is next to my house</u>)

This way of expanding the noun – restricting its meaning but contributing at the same time to the enlargement of the child's vocabulary – is useful in the classroom because pupils will undoubtedly benefit from the different suggestions made. For example, in the case of pre-determiners different suggestions may be made ("o" ("the"), "um" ("a/one"), "este" ("this"), "aquele" ("that"), etc.). Leading the child to notice that different words may be used before the noun according to certain language principles and aims is an important step towards looking at language as a game or puzzle consisting of different pieces, some of which may be moved around or exchanged. The same can be said about the other types of noun (and pronoun) expansions (by means of adjectives and post-modification including relatives). This type of language exercise encourages the awareness of different parts of speech, which is not only important in terms of oral language development but also in terms of written language.

When the child is taught to identify the nouns in noun phrases and to recognize that they may exist in isolation, s/he is prepared, for example, not to judge nouns and determiners as whole blocks, as only one word. This may be illustrated by the answers of Portuguese children attending pre-school and the first year of primary school. They were asked how many words there were in the sentence "O menino come um bolo" ("The child eats a cake"). Portuguese children attending the first year of primary school where asked the same question about the sentence "Olha um passarinho" ("Look at the bird"). Indeed, in the first sentence, they counted "<u>o menino</u>" and "<u>um bolo</u>", as one word each and thus said that the sentence contained three words ("O menino" / "come" / "um bolo"). The same happened with the second sentence. They said that it contained two words ("Olha" / "um passarinho") showing again that "<u>um passarinho</u>" was taken as only one word. That is to say, they did not yet consider the pre-determiner a word. If they had been used to identifying the head words of the noun phrases and their expansions, they would certainly not have done so. Moreover, when Portuguese children from pre-school to the fourth year of primary school were asked if "o" (the Portuguese masculine singular definite article corresponding to the English "the") was a word, it was observed that some of them did not consider it a word because it only had one letter. Some of them did not recognize that "o" could be either a word when corresponding to the article or a letter, and referred to it only as a letter (Pinto, unpublished).

It is therefore advisable to train the child to identify isolated nouns inserted in the noun phrases where they already appear expanded by means of pre-determiners, adjectives or post-modification including relatives. This is the kind of exercise that reinforces the importance of seeing language as being composed of discrete units which may look different depending on the context and which may be replaced by other units, as long as their nature and function are not violated.

When the child begins to reason in language as has been suggested above, it may happen that, due to the complexity of the language or to his/her restricted vocabulary, some linguistic units will not be identified correctly although s/he already reveals a certain level of morphological awareness. To illustrate this statement, it may be mentioned the case of a child who understood the Portuguese word "nação" (nation) – the meaning of which she did not yet know – as a Portuguese noun-phrase "na São" containing two words she already knows: "na", the contraction of the Portuguese preposition "em" and the Portuguese feminine singular definite article "a", and "São" the nickname of her maid. This is a constructive error we may expect from children familiar with language manipulation: it already reveals a certain morphological awareness and the search for meaning in the speech chain. In fact, speech should always make sense to the child; language – except in certain specific cases – must always make sense when heard or read, as well as when spoken or written. If the child does not understand what s/he is listening to or reading, it is necessary to discover the reason and find out if the child is used to working out the semantic groups and subgroups within the sentence and within the different paragraphs that constitute the text or the speech. If one takes for granted that language is a means to be understood and that language has to be based upon meaning, then the identification of the semantic groups within the sentence and their main elements is crucial. When the child is able to identify the semantic groups of the sentence and their head words ("mots-centres"), s/he is also expected to be able to grasp the main idea conveyed by the sentence. Little by little, depending on his/her language and textual experience, s/he will discover the reason why nouns and verbs are respectively expanded and completed in a certain way.

To grasp the nature and the function of the words is important because there exist forms which are apparently similar but whose nature and function have nothing in common. Indeed, the existence of dependent (see, for example, verb, noun and adjective endings) and independent linguistic units (the different parts of speech) has to be taken into account, as well as certain word components which may present similar forms. When, in the above mentioned example concerning the misunderstanding of the word "nação" ("nation"), the child misunderstood the first syllable "na" of the Portuguese word "nação" ("nation"), which is neither a dependent nor an independent form, with the word "na" (the contraction of the Portuguese preposition "em" with the feminine singular definite article "a") which possesses linguistic independence and which appears in many noun-groups such as "na escola" ("at school"), it is evident that the nature and function of the word "nação" was not identified. In other words, the child made a lexical identification error. In this case what is important is the fact that the child is already beginning to feel that certain pieces of this linguistic puzzle may occur in different contexts. The same morphological reasoning occurred when a child attending the first year of primary school, when faced with the word "umbigo" ("navel"), suggested it was possible to say "um bigo, dois bigos". That is to say, she also mixed the Portuguese cardinal numeral "um" ("one"), which coincides with the Portuguese masculine indefinite article "um" ("a"), with the first syllable of the word "<u>um</u>bigo". She then detached the other syllables of "um<u>bigo</u>" as if they constituted a word *"bigo" and exchanged the numeral "um" ("one") for the numeral "dois" ("two"). This kind of language manipulation already indicates a degree of language awareness and certain sensitivity towards the different possibilities of expanding nouns.

The correct identification of the head words in the noun phrases (for example the identification of "jardim" ("garden") in the noun phrase "um belo jardim" ("a beautiful garden"), as well as the correct identification of the elements of the sentence (for example "as flores" ("the flowers")/ "crescem"("grow")/ "no jardim" ("in the garden") in the sentence "as flores crescem no jardim" ("the flowers grow in the garden"), and the identification of the act/verb "crescer" ("grow") and of the components which complete its meaning ("as flores" and "no jardim") play a very important role in language development because they imply the understanding of the semantic groups of the sentence and consequently an accurate grasp of the meaning conveyed. It is also important that the child should identify the main verb of the sentence and should refer to it in the base form. Moreover, the child also has to become sensitive to the verb endings, which are dependent on the number and person of the subject of the sentence. This is another step towards the development of morphological awareness and of the idea that an action may be represented in different verb forms according to agreement conditions. In Portuguese, the utterance conditions the person of the verb depending on the number (singular or plural) and person (in the case of the pronouns) of the subject of the sentence. If the agreement concerns the noun, then gender also has to be taken into account.

The language method described so far, aims to make the learner immediately grasp the meaning of what s/he is listening to or reading and to understand that it is necessary to know previously what to say when one wishes to say or write something. Although speaking and writing present different features due to their distinct planning strategies (local planning vs. pre-planning) and production timings (see Urbano, 1999; Crystal, 2001), the speaker, and not only the writer, is also expected to use language in such a way as to translate his/her thoughts in a meaningful way.

This method also helps to develop an awareness of language organisation, of the way the different language "pieces" of various sizes and levels (morphological, lexical, syntactic) fit together, as well as of the nature (determiners, nouns, adjectives, adverbs, verbs, etc.) and function (subject, direct and indirect object, complement) of the words in order to get meaning from language.

As has been outlined before, it is important to identify the nature and the function of the words, as there are forms which are apparently similar but whose nature and function have nothing in common. Furthermore, the immediate grasp of the function and nature of certain words which sound alike but which are different as far as function, nature and written form are concerned (for example: "à" and "há") or which have written forms which differ only in accentuation ("e"/"é"; "esta"/"está") – as a matter of fact, attention is not always paid to accentuation by our school children – also helps children to look at written language from another perspective. This way of looking at aspects which characterize language in general emphasizes the *continuum* between oral and written language.

In general, language is supposed to convey meaning and it is up to the teachers to show the learner that behind the external language organization which corresponds to "how to say" and "when to say" there is, a "what to say". Practising oral and written language in this way, leading the learner to judge the correspondence between thinking and language, also constitutes the basis of maturity in terms of thinking and reasoning, which is required by any domain of study. If the learner is familiar with different possibilities of translating certain mental representations and aware that certain ways of communicating them are more suitable than others, s/he is doubtless prepared to face any kind of topic because s/he has developed the feeling that the role language plays in learning and in communicating is essential.

3. READING AT THE SERVICE OF ORAL AND WRITTEN MASTERING

Although reading and writing are distinct skills in psycholinguistic processing terms, they are activities which *nourish* each other. Reading *nourishes* writing, and writing, in so far as it leads to greater distancing between the object/language and the subject/writer-speaker, allows reading (especially aloud) to be seen as a "materialization" of inner language – "matérialisation du langage intérieur" (Girolami-Boulinier, 1988: 24). But writing is also improved by language methods, which help to show how language works. A suitable approach to language from an early age may then contribute to the enrichment of oral and written language as manifestations of language in general. Reading also improves oral language and may lead the child to become familiar with various aspects of language, from its sonority to its style, including the different language levels (phonetic/phonological, morphological, lexical and syntactic) and punctuation.

Due to their educational implications and potential, indirect, semi-direct and silent direct reading techniques have been selected for consideration in this chapter (Girolami-Boulinier, 1993; Girolami-Bouliner & Cohen-Rak, 1985). The indirect reading technique is the most suitable for use in the early stages, to awaken in the child the idea of language as a living process and to develop certain cognitive activities, such as attention and memory, which are absolutely essential. Besides, it trains the child to look at the speech *continuum* as being made up of discrete units, therefore in a constructive way and helps him/her to develop a certain level of linguistic awareness before attempting reading or writing. Consequently, when s/he begins to write s/he will not be surprised that lexical items which compose the speech *continuum* possess spatial independence, translated by the separation of words by blanks according to their nature and function.

It must be remembered that orthography relies on conventions and that orthography may closely follow the grammatical organization of the language. It is then possible to conclude that if the child is acquainted with language (de)composition from an early age, s/he will accept the rules of this language (game) much more easily.

3.1 The Indirect Reading Technique

The indirect reading technique (see Girolami-Boulinier & Cohen-Rak, 1985: 11, note 1) consists of the oral reproduction by the learner of a group of words always corresponding to an idea unit (a semantic group) that is read aloud beforehand by someone who masters reading and who is familiar with this reading technique: a parent, a teacher or an older friend/pupil. It is an exercise which may be practiced both by two people (parent and child, for example) and in a classroom with different children. When this reading exercise is practiced in the classroom it obliges the children to be particularly attentive because no one knows who is going to be asked to reproduce the semantic group requested. Due to the cognitive effort it requires, it can obviously only be used for short periods. The indirect reading technique is also useful because it may make the child think s/he is already reading, when s/he has no yet learned to read, although s/he is only repeating what someone else has read.

The length of the semantic groups to be reproduced orally varies according to the age of the learner. The learner's memory span conditions the length of the semantic groups, which may range from a noun-phrase, which may be a single noun or a noun preceded by a determiner, to a whole sentence, depending on the learner's ability to retain information. In the case of a sentence such as:

"A tartaruga do meu vizinho come bocadinhos de miolo de pão à mão"

(My neighbour's tortoise eats bits of bread from your hand)

oral reproduction of either the whole sentence or different semantic groups according to the learner's age and retention ability may be proposed. When the whole sentence proposal is not suitable, it is advisable to propose, according to the child's retention ability, for example,

Two semantic groups:	"A tartaruga do meu vizinho//"
	"come bocadinhos de miolo de pão à mão";
Three semantic groups:	"A tartaruga do meu vizinho//
	come bocadinhos de miolo de pão //
	à mão";
Four semantic groups:	"A tartaruga do meu vizinho//
	come/ /
	bocadinhos de miolo de pão//
	à mão";
Six semantic groups:	A tartaruga//
	do meu vizinho/ /
	come/ /
	bocadinhos/ /
	de miolo de pão/ /
	à mão.

This procedure is to be respected throughout the text to be read to the child. The main purpose of this exercise is to learn to *listen*, to *retain* and to *reproduce* the semantic groups proposed orally, following the model and therefore keeping as close as possible to it. As a result, children not only to develop different aspects of oral language performance but also familiarize as future writers/readers with the correct reading of the written material they may be faced with later.

Depending on the population and aims – because indirect reading may also be practiced with children who can already read –, it may be used to improve articulation, to correct pronunciation, to enable children to acquire new words and consequently to enlarge their vocabulary. It may also improve attention, memory, speed of articulation (with its implications in terms of working memory), as well as encourage children to pay attention to the oral stimulus in order to reproduce it correctly. What is more, it calls the learner's attention to the sonority of the language – the speech song ("la chanson du discours"), according to Girolami-Boulinier (Girolami-Boulinier, 2000: 83). This reading technique helps children to be sensitive to and respect the logical organization of language, very often in relation to punctuation, which learners will have to use when writing. It will also help children to become familiar with narrative style – in the case of the reading of stories – or with other styles if they are exposed to other types of texts, and with unfamiliar morphological and syntactic aspects of language, which will lead to a gradual discovery of language as a system full of potential. When this reading technique is used properly and the texts used well chosen, it also encourages the learner to love his/her language, to experiment with it and make it as lively as possible in the different contexts of use. Language should obviously make sense to the emitter and to the receiver. If, in some cases, indirect reading is practiced using material which at first sight does not make any sense to the learner (even though it respects the semantic groups), it is because the aim of the exercise in this particular case is to improve articulation and call the listener's attention to the stimulus, without requiring at the same time attention to the meaning of the stimulus. In this special case, the oral stimulus, and not the meaning, is the target of the task. In fact, the child may even enjoy pronouncing unfamiliar words. Besides this pleasurable aspect, this kind of task may also constitute a challenge; it may feed the child's curiosity about new words and therefore about new meanings, contributing to better mastery of his/her language. All children like novelties, new challenges, and they should not be prevented from enjoying the opportunity to be confronted with them. Moreover, language and speech are objects in permanent construction, deconstruction and reconstruction and learners cannot but benefit from the resistance they may offer.

Indirect reading is also an advantage when it comes to writing (and speaking). Effectively, a child's linguistic experience, also resulting from this reading technique, cannot be ignored when s/he enters the written world as an active agent. Since indirect reading is based on semantic groups, it leads the child not to identify reading with spelling or mere decoding. Looking at reading in this way means that to read is not only to spell. Reading should go beyond spelling because it must include the understanding of what is being decoded. That is to say, indirect reading reproduces the natural way of speaking. Its aim is to produce fluent readers and proficient writers, who can be expected to produce texts based upon a mental lexicon made up of meaningful lexical items, which are not subject to undesirable interferences which are nothing but the result of language and speech misuse and misunderstanding.

3.2 The Semi-direct Reading Technique

Between the indirect and the direct silent reading technique there is another technique, the semi-direct reading technique (Girolami-Boulinier, 1993: 35-37), which is used by children who are beginning to write. It consists of giving the children the chance to correctly reproduce – not only orally but also in written form (without the presence of the model) – the word(s) they have retained from the semantic groups given to them orally and in written form. In this way, the child begins to become aware of the (ortho)graphic image of the words so that s/he may reproduce them correctly and without interference from his/her mispronunciations or the inadequate auditory images they may possess in their mental lexicon.[3]

3.3 The Silent Direct Reading Technique

The direct silent reading technique (Girolami-Boulinier & Cohen-Rak, 1985: 11, note 2) is at first undertaken silently by the learners (always respecting the organisation of language in semantic groups). As soon as they feel they can reproduce the first semantic group orally and in written form without looking at the text, they may be asked to do so. They then go on through the text, following the same procedure. In order to supervise the operation, the teacher may ask the pupils to indicate with their finger the amount of material they are able to retain and reproduce. Reproducing by semantic groups avoids the identification of reading with spelling and follows the principle that the act of reading has to take into account comprehension. Moreover, pupils are required to learn to *see*, to *retain* and to *reproduce/write* the semantic groups compatible with their memory span because the reproduction takes place in the absence of the model. It is always advisable to ask the pupil to first reproduce orally the semantic group s/he is supposed to write because the teacher sometimes needs to check the way the child reads in order to correct production if necessary. Neither incorrect pronunciation nor incorrect spelling should be kept in the child's mental lexicon. This kind of reading technique is designed to improve spelling and punctuation at an early stage as well as to familiarize the learner with agreement rules (thereby avoiding errors of gender and number), with accentuation, with new vocabulary, and with written style. Although punctuation may not seem very important, its proper use shows us if the child articulates his/her ideas successfully and attributes different degrees of importance to them. The correct use of full stops, commas and semi-colons is proof of perfect mastery of the organization of written material. Portuguese children attending the second, third and fourth year of primary school have been found not to use commas or not to know how to use them in their texts and some children from the second year use no punctuation or only a full stop

---

[3] *See Levelt (Levelt, 1989: 6): "[...] mental lexicon–the store of information about the words in one's language."*

at the end of their texts (Pinto, 1999: 509-510). Through the silent reading technique the child is confronted with this aspect of writing, which s/he cannot help using in his/her writing as a means of showing that language has rules of organization according to what we wish to communicate.

4. EXAMPLES OF WRITING PROBLEMS AND SUGGESTIONS FOR PREVENTION

Bearing in mind that orthography has also to do with the way language is structured, and that it is much more than a "cosmetic" aspect at the level of a phoneme-grapheme conversion, the use of the above-demonstrated language method and reading techniques would prove beneficial in preventing orthographical/writing errors (see Girolami-Boulinier, 1984: 127 and ff.; Pinto, 1994: 205 and ff.; 1998: 158 and ff.)[4].

Lexical identification/separation errors – "fautes d'identification [...] d'individualisation" according to Girolami-Boulinier (Girolami-Boulinier, 1984: 133) –, such as:

aquilo	→	"a quilo"
abrigar	→	"a brigar"
Ia	→	"e a"
havia	→	" a via"
a certa	→	"acerta"
outra vez	→	"ou traves"
está	→	"esta"
e	→	"é"
à	→	"a"
ao	→	"ou"

are intimately connected with the way language is composed of discrete units possessing a particular nature and function and may be prevented using the above-demonstrated language method (see Girolami-Boulinier, 1984, 1987, 1993; Pinto 1994, 1998, 2001). There are also morphological errors which have to do with the verb endings and which may also benefit from the practice of the demonstrated language method.

Phonetic/perceptual errors, such as:

pregar	→	"pergar"
fez	→	"vez"
repente	→	"repende"
deixou	→	"deijou"
tábua	→	"tádoa"

are closely linked to auditory misperceptions, which could be prevented by the indirect reading technique (Girolami-Boulinier, 1993: 32-33).

Gender and number errors, such as:

---

[4] *All the Portuguese examples mentioned in this section are from Pinto (see, for example, Pinto 1994, 1997, 1998).*

outra	→	"outro"
uma	→	"um"
a	→	"o"
Seguintes	→	"seguinte"

are the result of not making the agreements required by the head words of the noun phrases and their expansions. They require attention training through the indirect and the silent direct reading techniques.

And finally, usage errors such as:

admirado	→	"ademirado"
cheio	→	"xeio"
tomar	→	"tumar"
mesa	→	"meza"
homem	→	"omem"
força	→	"forsa"
enorme	→	"inorme"

which may be solved by means of the silent direct reading technique, a technique which, as has been demonstrated, leads the learner to correctly associate the auditory and graphic images of the words (see Girolami-Boulinier, 1984: 129-130; Girolami-Boulinier & Pinto, 1996: 35-38; Pinto, 1994: 203; 1997; 1998: 161; 1999: 506).

5. CONCLUSION

Looking at language this way, it is unthinkable to consider oral and written language (and consequently talking/listening and writing/reading) without taking comprehension into account. Although speech differs from writing in several ways (Crystal, 2001: 26-28), it is important to consider the general structure of language and its contexts of use. Moreover, it is also advisable to see oral and written language as different ways of using language because written language can include different degrees of textual genres, on a *continuum* from "oral" texts to academic essays, just as oral language covers a *continuum* from spontaneous oral style to the prepared lecture (Marcuschi, 2001: 38). According to Jakobson, bearing in mind the way language is structured, it is possible to say that "Speaking [as well as writing] implies the selection of certain linguistic items and their combination in linguistic units of a higher degree of complexity." (Jakobson, 1963: 45-46). Therefore if, from an early age, children are acquainted with the way language is composed by means of suitable methods and techniques, they will quickly become aware of the potentialities of the language. Furthermore, when children feel that language is an object which may be constructed, deconstructed and reconstructed endlessly because it is made of (dependent and independent) units/forms which can be combined – obviously according to certain rules –, they may conclude that language relies on an economy of resources at the service of language creativity.

With regard to writing, it is a skill which obliges the learners to be even more aware of the potential of language because it can exist on its own, and because it may contribute to logical organization. Indeed, the writer can verify what is written in order to improve it and make it as close as possible to the idea s/he wishes to convey. It is then up to the teachers and parents to prepare the child to deal with language (oral and written) with the dignity it deserves avoiding any kind of undesirable future misuse and misunderstanding. In order for children to reach the desired proficiency in writing without problems a good knowledge of oral language is advocated before they begin writing and during the first years of their writing experience, as well as familiarity with adequate reading techniques. On the other hand, because of this writing experience better speaking and reading performances and higher levels of thinking organization can be expected.

In conclusion, this way of dealing with oral and written language obliges the learner to be aware of the creative implications of the way language is constructed/structured from an early age. It therefore affords the possibility of preparing citizens to exercise and cultivate social writing practices they may need and to explore the full potential of language.

AUTHOR'S NOTE

All the quotations and titles from non-English sources were translated into English by the author and are of her entire responsibility.

ACKNOWLEDGMENTS

Special thanks go to my colleague João Veloso for his useful comments and for formatting this text. I am also grateful to my colleague Catherine Evangelista who helped me with the English.

REWRITING TO INTRODUCE PUNCTUATION IN THE SECOND GRADE: A DIDACTIC APPROACH

SOFÍA A. VERNON*, MÓNICA ALVARADO*, & PAULA ZERMEÑO**

*Universidad Autónoma de Querétaro, México & **Escuela Maxei, Querétaro, México

Abstract. This chapter presents a didactic sequence aimed at introducing punctuation in the second grade. The teacher worked with 21 boys and girls (7 and 8 years of age). Based on Olson and Kamawar (2002) and Ferreiro and Pontecorvo (1996), we assumed that the use of punctuation would be enhanced through the writing of texts that required the students to delimit boundaries between quoted speech and narrative text. Jokes were chosen as target texts. The didactic sequence included the production of three drafts that were revised with the teacher and other students in collaborative tasks, as well as exercises specially designed to facilitate the distinction between direct and indirect speech and the inclusion of hyphens for quoted speech, capital letters and other punctuation marks. The first drafts show an almost total lack of punctuation. In second drafts, children can differentiate direct speech through the use of punctuation and through lexicalization. Final drafts include a more conventional use of hyphens, and the use of other punctuation devices to delimit clauses and sentences. The findings are related to the theoretical framework and suggestions for educators are given.

Keywords: Writing development, punctuation, didactic sequence, quoted speech.

1. INTRODUCTION

Punctuation has been a neglected area of study for modern linguistics (Catach, 1980). Probably because of this, there have been few studies about the use children make of punctuation marks at different moments of their lives (Simone, 1996). What teachers observe everyday (at least in Mexico), as a result, is an almost complete lack of punctuation marks during the elementary school years, while high school and university faculty often complain about their students' lack of abilities in the use of punctuation.

Vernon, S. A., Alavaroda, M., & Zermeño, P. (2004). Rewriting to introduce punctuation in the second grade: A didactic approach.
In Rijlaarsdam, G. (Series Ed.) & Rijlaarsdam, G., Van den Bergh, H., & Couzijn, M. (Vol. Eds.), Studies in writing. Vol. 14, Effective learning and teaching of writing, 2nd Edition, Part 1, Studies in learning to write, 47 - 58.

Pedagogical traditions in Mexico (as in many other countries) are hard to define, mainly because there are no studies about how punctuation is taught and evaluated. Although it is compulsory for all schools to teach punctuation, there is a lack of precision about what and how it should be taught. Teachers are provided with a national program with a list of punctuation marks and other associated graphic forms (such as capital letters) at the beginning of each school term. No additional information is given about their function in the texts.

Thus, the teaching of punctuation is left to teachers' intuition. What we have observed in classrooms and textbooks is that teachers usually present the information through manual-like definitions about the use of punctuation marks, followed by exercises in which children have to place the missing mark (the one that has just been defined) in a list of unrelated written sentences. Only one of the numerous graphic signs is exercised at a time. Numerous discrepancies between the children occur when solving the tasks, but these are generally not discussed openly in class. It is also common to find teachers trying to explain the use of punctuation by referring to the way a text should be read aloud. Often, teachers explain that when students find a full stop, they should stop, take a deep breath and count to three (or five), but should stop for a shorter period of time when they find a period, and a shorter period of time still when they get to a comma. These explanations are rounded out by explanations that have to do with the "completeness" of ideas: A complete idea should end in a period, but commas should separate incomplete ideas.

These observations reflect the fact that, during most of the twentieth century, writing was considered as a transcription of speech, or at least defined by reference to spoken language. Punctuation, in particular, has been considered as a device used to transcribe pause and other prosodic phenomena. Nunberg (1990) has argued that, even if punctuation originally had this function, "the fit between punctuation and intonation was at best only approximate, and the two systems came to diverge increasingly over the course of development of print traditions" (p. 12).

One of the most important functions of the punctuation system is to reveal structure (Simone, 1996). Both for the reader and the writer, it is an important aid in grasping the organization and the function of a text. One might assume that the organization of a text relies heavily upon the units of spoken language (words, sentences, clauses, and, in the case of written accents, syllables and phonemes). If so, the awareness of these units is crucial to learners. Many authors, however, have shown that there are no obvious parallelisms between the awareness of oral and of written units of language. For example, it is a well known fact that phonemes are not a "natural" unit of analysis in the spoken language, and that awareness only begins when children learn to read and write or are being subjected to a training program (Adams, 1990). Every literate speaker of Spanish or French knows that placing written accents in a word is by no means an easy task. Awareness of words is not obvious either. Ferreiro (1999) states, "It is writing that defines the unit "word". There is not an awareness of the word, at the oral level, that is then applied to writing, but the other way around: from the written word to the oral word." Béguelin (2002) has recently pointed out that the sentence is a unit only in writing, because it is delimited by punctuation (beginning capital letter and final period), even if, in writing, that which is delimited by capital letters and periods, is variable. Furthermore, he states that the notion of the sentence is inadequate to describe orality, and that, except when reading aloud, there is no correspondence between prosodic features and punctuation.

This leads to a dilemma in educational practices. How can we teach children who cannot write conventionally to punctuate texts if the awareness of the units that are delimited by punctuation is a result of the knowledge of the writing system? It seems to us that the solution is to allow children to face problems of interpretation in their own texts as well as to provide them with suitable writing models in terms of analyzing conventionally written texts.

The purpose of this chapter is to present a didactic sequence, which was aimed at introducing the use of punctuation in written compositions in the second grade. That is, to help children become aware of the punctuation marks used when a differentiation between direct and reported speech is central to the text.

2. THEORETICAL FRAMEWORK

Olson and Kamawar (2002) have argued that, as children learn to read, they become aware that written signs represent language. An important strategy which allows children to use language in order to refer to language, and thus to become aware of meta-representational properties of writing, is to establish the differences between direct and quoted speech. Punctuation marks that allow children to make this distinction seemed a good start for our purposes.

Ferreiro and Zuccermaglio's (1996) empirical study suggests that Olson and Kamawar's (2002) theoretical assumptions are correct, in that one of the first uses of punctuation in children's development is marking quoted speech. The authors analyze second and third graders' written productions in Spanish and Italian of the traditional story of *Little Red Riding Hood*. The productions were not part of any school project. The researchers analyzed only those texts that included some form of quoted speech (77 from second grade and 82 from third grade in the Spanish sample). Twelve percent of the texts did not include any punctuation marks. Another 27% included only an initial capital letter and a final full stop that indicated the boundaries of the text. The rest of the texts showed "a concentration of punctuation marks inserted in pieces of quoted speech." (p. 181). Children used a wider variety of punctuation marks within quoted speech as well. Even when children did not make use of conventional punctuation, their use of punctuation marks was coherent. For example, commas were used to separate elements in lists, they used exclamation marks for interjections and onomatopoeias, and they used full stops and commas to show the boundaries of narrative and quoted speech. The authors mention that, in the Spanish sample, many of the signs used in a conventional way were those that appear in pairs in Spanish written texts (question and exclamation marks, and, to a lesser extent, hyphens).

Children used some creative ways to show the taking of turns between the wolf and Little Red Riding Hood or the grandmother. Some children found a lexical solution through the use of declarative verbs that marked the beginning and end of each turn of speech; others used a combination of declarative verbs and the use of punctuation marks, such as colons or quotation marks. Others, in turn, had a contrastive solution. They preferred the use of punctuation marks to show the beginning and end of the intervention of one of the speakers, followed by a lack of punctuation marks in the reply.

2.1 Jokes and the Justification of their Use to Improve Punctuation

In order to introduce punctuation in a group of beginner writers, we had to find a suitable task that would encourage children to write. We thought that the writing task should take into account all of the following considerations:

1) We doubted that near-conventional punctuation would appear after the first writing attempt, but would rather appear after children faced problems related to interpretation. Thus, allowing others to read the written production, and checking on the effect the text produced upon the reader would be extremely important. Collaborative re-writing at some stage of the didactic sequence was considered a must. The importance of role-change of writers-readers and the effects of reader feedback have been documented by Lumbelli and by Couzijn, in this volume.

2) Texts should be short for two reasons. First, because we believe it is important for children to read normalized, published texts that can serve as models for their own writing. Second, because children would have to read their own (and other children's) texts several times in order to produce several drafts. Additionally, since texts would be revised several times over a long period of time (a month at least), intentioned texts had to be memorable.

3) Since direct and indirect speech were the main foci of analysis, the wording itself was of utter importance. Texts should also include a narrator and direct speakers, so that the distinction between quoted and unquoted speech became a central part of the writing activity.

4) The finished texts should be conventional enough to allow other readers to understand and enjoy. We considered that texts had to be aimed at a particular audience and should be published and distributed.

We considered that the writing of jokes took all these considerations into account. In our experience, the telling of jokes becomes a favorite pastime for most seven and eight-year olds.

2.2 The Linguistic Specificity of Jokes

The writing of jokes serves other educational purposes as well. For one thing, the inclusion of direct speech creates the need to distinguish what the speaker said and what the speaker meant or intended. The context created by the joke is equally important. Words and expressions in jokes often have a double meaning. Also, jokes often play with words that are meant by the speaker in one way, but can be understood by the listener in another way, due to the context in which it was said. In oral language, gesture, intonation and stress provide the clues for understanding. However, in writing, the clues must be found in the text itself, and punctuation makes a central contribution. Dealing with language in which linguistic clues are the only way to get the meaning is very important in children's semantic development (Olson, 1994). At about the age of our students (seven or eight years of age), children start making the distinction between what was said and what was intended; between what the speaker said and what he "should have said" (Torrance and Olson, 1985). This distinction builds upon the developing awareness of intentional mental states and the understanding of communicative intention ("what a speaker or writer thinks a listener or reader thinks", as Olson, 1994: 128, puts it.). This understanding of communicative intention develops throughout the school years.

2.3 The Difference between Spanish and English Punctuation

Although there seems to be only one system of punctuation which is used in alphabetic languages (Nunberg, 1990), some conventions seem to be established locally. This is the case in which direct speech is signaled in Spanish as opposed to English. In the latter, direct speech is introduced by placing quotation marks at the beginning and end of the quotation. In Spanish, however, direct speech is usually introduced by placing hyphens at the beginning and end of quotations (although end marks are not always obligatory.) In order to make clear the differences that can occur in Spanish and other alphabetic languages, such as English, we will transcribe a excerpt of Roald Dahl's *James and the Giant Peach* (English edition, 1961: 16; Spanish edition, 1996: 24) in both languages:

"What's the matter with you?" Aunt Sponge demanded.
"It's *growing*!" Aunt Spiker cried. "It's getting bigger and bigger!"
"What is?"
"The peach, of course!"
"You're joking!"
"Well, look for yourself!"
"But my dear Spiker, that's perfectly ridiculous. That's impossible. That's – that's – that's – Now, wait *just* a minute – No – No – that can't be right – No – Yes – Great Scott! The thing really *is* growing!"

In the Spanish translation, the dialogue looks like this:

— ¿Qué es lo que te pasa? – inquirió la tía Sponge.
—¡Está *creciendo*! — exclamó la tía Spiker. ¡Se está haciendo más y más grande!
— ¿Pero qué?
— ¡Qué va a ser! ¡El melocotón!
— ¡Estás de broma!
— ¡Compruébalo tú misma!
— Pero querida Spiker, eso es totalmente ridículo. Eso es imposible. Eso es ... eso es ... eso es ... No, espera un momento... No... No... No puede ser cierto... No... Sí... ¡Santo Cielo! ¡Esa cosa *está* creciendo de verdad!

Several differences can be observed in the use of punctuation besides the use of double hyphens (one at the beginning and one at the end of the quotation) to introduce direct speech (note that hyphens do not appear at the end when the quoted speech is followed by another quoted speech). Question and exclamation marks, unlike most other European languages, appear in Spanish both at the beginning and end of sentences. Hyphens that appear in the English version are translated into Spanish as leaders (…).

In most cases, not only hyphens or quotation marks delimit a quotation. Periods and exclamation or interrogation marks do so as well.

2.4 Main Hypothesis

The main objective of the intervention was to help students distinguish direct speech through the use of hyphens. However, we hypothesized that other punctuation marks would become necessary for the children in the process of organizing a text so that it could be understood. Another hypothesis was that establishing contrasts a) between quotations and reported speech, b) between one speaker and another speaker when taking turns and c) between the beginning and ending of each of the above would lead them to introduce punctuation marks. In other words, 1) do these contrasts appear in students' productions? 2) Is there an evolution between first draft, second draft and final version?

3. SUBJECTS AND PROCEDURE

Twenty-one second graders (11 boys, 10 girls; mean age 7 years, 8 months) participated in this study. They all attended the same classroom in an elementary school in Queretaro, Mexico. All of the children were middle-class, Spanish native speakers.

The didactic sequence took approximately 20 hours, distributed over two months (in the middle part of the school year), with 30-50 minute sessions. The teacher attended four preliminary sessions, in order to ensure her full understanding of the didactic sequence, and attended another weekly session to discuss children's progress and modes of intervention. The teacher was in charge of all of the sessions. The sequence involved the following steps:

3.1 Production of First Drafts

1) First, the teacher encouraged children to tell jokes to the whole class.
2) Each child wrote his/her favourite joke (first draft).

3.2 Production of Second Drafts

3) Children read jokes from several magazines. Teacher centred their attention on how they could differentiate when different speakers intervened (use of hyphens), and the presence of capital letters and full stops. All of these jokes included a narrator and two speakers.
4) Exercises were given in their notebooks where children had to:
- Correct small texts (between 6 and 10 lines of text) by placing punctuation marks (mainly periods and capital letters). These texts were all written in lowercase letters, and there was a total absence of punctuation. Two more similar ex-

ercises were given in which upper- and lower-case letters were mixed (in beginning, middle and end positions).
- Decide whether to use upper- or lower-case letters in blank spaces in a short story. These included the first letter in the text, the first letter after a full stop, and the first letter in proper names and common nouns. In these two exercises, children compared their corrections and discussed the reasons underlying their decisions.
- Identify speakers and narrator in printed short jokes and stories. Children were asked to read the text individually. After that, children were asked to distinguish what was "said" by the teller of the story (the narrator) and what was actually said by each one of the characters. Children were ask to identify any marks that showed when a character spoke.
- Identify upper-case letters, exclamation and question marks and comment about what they thought their function in the text was.

5) The whole group made corrections on one of the students' first drafts, as the teacher wrote what they indicated on the text, using an overhead projector. Use of beginning capital letter, final full stop, and differentiation of speakers and turns of speech were emphasized.

6) In groups of 3, children made comments about their first drafts. Later on, each author wrote a second draft.

3.3 Production of Third Drafts

7) The teacher told a joke and then wrote it on the board, as the children indicated what she should write. Children indicated the use of punctuation marks. The teacher pointed out interpretation problems (for example, how to differentiate between speakers and the difficulties in identifying whether a character was speaking or another character was reporting what a character had said.)

8) Children did more exercises of the same kind in their notebooks (see production of second draft), and some new exercises were included. Mainly:
- Placing the appropriate punctuation marks in texts (mainly hyphens, periods, interrogation and exclamation marks) in small texts. Children worked individually, and after that they discussed their work in pairs.
- Writing stories, taking special care in introducing upper-case letters, full stops, and hyphens to introduce direct speech. Their texts were revised in small groups, with the teacher pointing out problematic passages in texts.

9) Each child wrote a third draft, re-read this draft and corrected it for the final version.

10) Jokes were published in the school's newspaper, which is distributed to all students, teachers and parents.

4. RESULTS

In this analysis, we will discuss the ways in which the children differentiated direct and indirect speech; how they indicated speaker's turns; and how they contrasted the beginning and end of quotations. Additional mention will be made concerning the use of full stops at the end of the text, capital letters to start the text and periods (including full-stops) in children's jokes. Some examples will be given. As it is impossible to include a large number of examples, we will rely heavily upon the texts produced by a few of the children.

4.1 First Drafts

First drafts show an almost total lack of punctuation. Only one of the children started the text with a capital letter, and one of them mixed upper- and lower-case letters in most of the words, in both beginning, middle and end positions. Ten of the children included a final full stop to show the boundary of the written text. None of them used any other punctuation marks.

With one exception, children distinguished quoted speech through the use of verbs like "say" or "shout" (lexicalization). It is interesting to note that 18 of the children either used two verbs to introduce direct speech (for example "shout", followed by "say") or made use of the same verb both at the beginning and end of the quote. Mariana (age 7;4), for instance, wrote the following (versions will be transcribed exactly as they appear in the child's text, followed by the closest possible translation into English within brackets, using a normalized spelling):

> (...) y cuando bolbio a ber la leche le grito a su mama y le dijo mama mama el pan se esta tomando mi leche

> and when he saw the milk again he shouted to his mother and he said mother mother the bread is drinking my milk

The only child (Alam, age 7;8) that did not use lexicalization to signal quoted speech (and continued this way in all his versions) used juxtaposition. He had probably understood that the use of "say" in a repetitive way makes jokes less effective. In the first version, quoted speech was not differentiated, and could only be distinguished by the reader through contextual clues:

> Era una vez franquinstain y Dracula y iban en un carro y franc iba manejando iva a 140 franc y iba una viejita en enmedio de la ca rretera caminando y Dracula franc la viejita la viejita franc la viejita y lo agarra de los hombros franc la viejita franc la viejita y la atropello uf franc pence que te la ibas a echar.

> There was once frankenstein and Dracula and they were in a car and frank was driving he was going at 140 frank and an old lady was walking in the middle of the road and Dracula frank the old lady the old lady and grabs frank from the shoulders frank the old lady frank the old lady and runs over her oof frank I thought you were going to get her

4.2 Second Drafts

In second drafts, all of the children seemed to deliberately establish the limits of direct speech. Although 20 children started using hyphens to do so (mostly at the beginning, but not at the end of quotes), 19 of them used lexicalization as well. All of the children were able to delimit turns of speech,

Establishing contrasts between direct and indirect speech seemed to be more difficult. Thus, 50% of the children who used hyphens at the beginning and end of direct speech, made use of them whenever they used verbs such as "say" or "shout", in reported speech as well. This is an example from a boy (7; 9):

> (...) y los pilotos dijeron – Tiren maletasno podemos sostener tanto peso y tiraron maletas y y ano que donada y – los pilotosdijeron lo mismo y tiraron el piso y el mexicano dijo – yo me tiro por mi pays ielruso – dijo lo mismo (...)

> (...) and the pilots said – Throw away your bags we can't handle the weight and they threw away the bags and there was nothing left and – the pilots said the same and they threw away the floor and the Mexican said – I throw myself for my country and the Russian – said the same (...)

Only one of the children (age 7;5) started using exclamation marks in his second draft to establish boundaries between the beginning and end of quotes. He did not use a hyphen, even though he used this punctuation mark consistently in all other cases of direct speech. It is possible that, in this case, the child felt that boundaries were sufficiently clear through the use of opening and end signs (¡!).

Mariana, whose first draft we have seen previously, is the only child who did not use hyphens in her second draft. Instead, she used periods to establish the presence of a quotation as well as to delimit sentences and clauses:

> Había una vez en la casa de Pepito. Su mamá le dijo a Pepito que se fuera a desayunar. Y agarró su pan y lo puso en su leche. Y cuando volvió a ver su leche le grito a su mamá. Y le dijo. Mamá mamá el pan se esta tomando mi leche.

> Once upon a time in Pepito's house. His mother told Pepito to go and have breakfast. And he took his bread and put it in his milk. And when he looked at his milk again he shouted to his mother. And he said. Mother mother the bread is drinking my milk.

In her text, periods seem to be insufficient to delimit sentences and clauses. Probably that is the reason for an additional "and" to be added.

Whereas periods had not been used in first drafts to divide one clause or sentence from the other, 57% of the children started using them in their second drafts. All of them included a capital letter after each period.

4.3 Final Drafts

In their final drafts, all of the children used hyphens to signal direct speech. Only 2 of them did so when introducing reported speech through the use of verbs such as "say". Except for Alam, all of the children used verbs to introduce direct speech, together with hyphens. However, three children continued with the use of two verbs to establish the boundaries of direct speech.

Eighty percent of the children began to make use of exclamation and/or interrogation signs in a conventional way, at the same time as using hyphens for quotes. All of the children made some use of periods to delimit sentences or clauses and placed a capital letter after each period. Only two of the children, who had not used periods in their previous drafts, delimited these units both by a period and the use of "and". Only one child (age 8;0) used quotation marks to indicate the name of a hotel:

> One day 1 man recommended to 1 chinese man the hotel "John the great". The chinese man went to the hotel and asked the owner – Can I spend the night in 1 of your rooms –. The owner said – I only have the bloody-hand room. The Chinese man answers – Not me! I am afraid! (…)

Only two of the children used commas. In this case, commas had exactly the same uses as periods. Both appear in the final text in alternation.

Table 1 indicates the frequency of texts that include punctuation in each of the drafts:

Table 1. Frequency of Texts with Punctuation Marks (N = 21)

Punctuation	1	2	3
Capital letter beginning text	1	18	21
Capital letters after periods within text	0	12	21
Ending full stop	10	15	21
Periods (within text)	0	12	21
Exclamation or question marks	0	1	18
Hyphens for direct speech	0	20	21
Hyphens for reported speech	0	10	2
Quotation marks	0	0	1
Comma	0	0	2

No. of draft

5. DISCUSSION

The didactic sequence we have presented above was an effective way to introduce punctuation. Even if most texts did not achieve a conventional use, they all incorporated signs that organize the text.

Our results confirm of Ferreiro and Pontecorvo's (1996) findings. In their samples, most punctuation marks appeared in pieces of quoted speech. Although the children of this study did not incorporate punctuation in their first drafts, hyphens were used by 20 out of the 21 written productions by the second draft. That is, insertions of speech seem to be salient, probably because children can establish contrasts between narrative discourse and quoted speech, on the one hand, and because verbs such as "say" or "shout" often introduce characters' verbal responses. Precisely because of this use of verbs, the contrast between direct and reported speech appears to be more difficult to establish. Our results suggest that difficulty in contrasting direct and indirect speech is only temporary: While 10 children introduced hyphens in reported speech in the second draft, only 2 did so in the third, and final, draft. Once children have begun to delimit quoted speech, the alternation between speakers' turns is not problematic, at least when writing texts where the desired effect depends upon this alternation. Once the children have been able to delimit quoted speech, exclamation and question marks appear as an alternative means to set boundaries (in the final drafts), adding information about the speaker's intentions.

From an adult point of view, children often use excessive repetition in their writing. Lexical reiteration may be playing an important role in delimiting quoted speech. In the first drafts, this was the only means children used to set boundaries. The number of reiterated verbs diminished in the second draft and almost disappeared by the third draft.

The capability to signal direct speech seems to set the conditions for children to start establishing boundaries between clauses and sentences. As children diminish their use of lexical reiteration and start making use of more conventional hyphens, they also start using periods within the text.

Finally, the use of short, memorable texts such as jokes, in which direct speech occurs naturally, proved to be a good strategy for introducing punctuation. Other types of texts (stories, for example) could prove difficult to start reflections about the use of punctuation because of their length. We assume that a didactic sequence like the one we have presented here would be ideally followed up through the production of short, well known stories with fixed dialogues between characters.

This experience shows that teachers should take the following into account:

1) The difference between direct and indirect speech, between common and proper nouns (upper- and lower case-letters), between statements, questions and exclamations, and the limits within sentences or clauses are by no means "natural" distinctions for children.
2) Punctuation marks are best understood when presented in combination, so that children can establish similarities and differences between them.
3) The teaching of punctuation should involve writing complete, meaningful and organized texts. Having a potential, real reader in mind facilitates the task. Having an addressee makes the children attempt to achieve conventional writing.
4) Target texts should require the use of the language function that the adult wants them to become aware of.
5) Narrative texts that include direct speech seem to be the best choice. Our results show that quoted speech are probably the easiest fragments to delimit in a text
6) Encouraging social interaction and discussion between children in the writing process, allows them to identify and solve problems more effectively.
7) A higher degree of awareness is reached about punctuation when children are asked to revise and correct their texts several times. In between these different

attempts, children should do different activities, unrelated to their project, but that allow them to reflect about the use of punctuation in other types of texts and sentences.

CONTEXTUAL FACTORS ENHANCING COGNITIVE AND METACOGNITIVE ACTIVITY DURING THE PROCESS OF COLLABORATIVE WRITING

MARTA MILIAN GUBERN

Universitat Autònoma de Barcelona, Spain

Abstract. Writing instruction faces the challenge of elaborating a theory of writing in school contexts through the observation and analysis of how cognitive benefits of written language are reached. Different perspectives on the concept "context", considered in studies on written composition, are integrated in a model of context interaction that becomes the theoretical basis to the research. The relationship among four contexts within the collaborative composition process of an explanatory text are explored: the context of the writer, gathering the experience and knowledge on written language and written language use formerly acquired by the writer; the context of reception or social context of written language use; the context of the task, where the composition process develops; and the context of teaching and learning writing. Eleven-year-olds try to explain to eight-year-old readers the laws of light reflection through a kaleidoscope. Data analysis is carried out in a multiple case study in natural settings applied to verbal interactions among the participants in five collaborative writing groups. The parameters observed refer to: a) characteristics of the composition process, aiming to find out any general procedures in the processes followed by different groups; b) explicit references to readers, aiming to establish the influence of the context of reception; c) explicit utterances including references to the second person pronoun, to follow the presence of the different contexts involved in the process, d) reformulations of the text being written, known as "attempted text", aiming to observe the writers' consideration of the different contexts participating in the composition process. The results show the relevance of the context of reception in the writers' representation of the task and of the text, and acknowledge the presence of multiple contexts dynamically interacting in the context of the task. The study concludes that group work enhances knowledge building on discursive situations, on language, and on writing composition strategies, and argues for the importance of designing instructional sequences that allow the negotiation of explicit learning goals and the monitoring and control of one's own learning and writing process.

Keywords: writing process, context interaction, knowledge building, task representation, collaborative writing, collaborative learning.

Milian, M. (2004). Contextual factors enhancing cognitive and metacognitiev activity during the process of collaborative writing.
In Rijlaarsdam, G. (Series Ed.) & Rijlaarsdam, G., Van den Bergh, H., & Couzijn, M. (Vol. Eds.), Studies in writing. Vol. 14, Effective learning and teaching of writing, 2nd Edition, Part 1, Studies in learning to write, 59 - 76.

1. INTRODUCTION

The consideration of written language acquisition as a factor which contributes to the intellectual and social development of individuals has stressed the so-called cognitive advantages of written language (Vygotsky, 1978). Written language activities modify and extend both the knowledge and strategies of students about written language and language itself, increase the control that the writers have on their own knowledge and favor its translation into new writing situations.

Research on writing instruction faces the challenge of elaborating a theory of teaching and learning writing in school contexts. The consideration of writing instruction as a scenario where intellectual, together with personal and social development is being built constitutes a firm ground to be explored. Observation and analysis of classroom literacy events as privileged settings for the development of thinking and learning strategies concerning writing competence becomes one of the main research paths to gather evidence of some of the factors contributing to a successful and effective writing instruction model.

A theory about writing at school must consider the object of knowledge – written composition – and the scenarios where it is taught and learned: the context of the classroom, the context of the pupil and the context of the teacher.

1.1 The Concept of Context in Written Composition Studies

In the first studies on the process of written composition in the field of cognitive psychology, the context usually appeared as restricted to the mental context of the writer, and the social context meant simply the "rhetorical context" from a general perspective, without any variation (Hayes and Flower, 1980). The contribution of the socioconstructivist perspective establishes the removal of the almost unique attention paid to the mental context of the writer in favor of the external, social context in which the writer is placed. Some articles stress the diversified character of both the rhetorical context and the writer's context (Bizzell, 1982; Brandt, 1986, 1992) and contribute to an integrative vision of cognitive and social perspectives. The process of composition is understood as a dialogue between writer and reader: they both share a common social knowledge, although at different levels, and create a context from the dynamic knowledge showed in their intersubjectivity (Brandt, 1986; Bronckart, 1997; Flower, 1994; The New London Group, 1996).

Nystrand (1989, 1990), Flower (1994) and Witte (1992), following Bakhtin, suggest a contextual space in which the negotiation between the sociocultural context of the writer and the context of social use of written language takes place. It is a dynamic space, determined by the potential dialogue between the context of the writer and the context of reception or context of the written use, socioculturally marked. This space constitutes a new context that is being created during the process of elaboration of the text; it becomes modified according to the dynamics of the process and the factors contributing to it. Flower mentions the "construction of negotiated meaning", Nystrand names it "reciprocity between writer and reader", and he also defines the text as "the space for semantic potential" between writer and reader. Witte talks about double identity of the writer: the identity "situated" in the production space and the identity "projected" towards the context of written language use, both identities constantly interacting during the process.

Starting from the consideration of written language as a phenomenon originated in social interaction, Rubin (1988) suggests the following elements as parts of the concept:

1) The social representations of contexts of written language use, which conform a ground of "type contexts". This vision is related to Malinowski's idea of cultural context (1923), taken up by the London School (Halliday, 1978). The concept of "discourse genres", as well as the concepts of "type of text" and "type of discourse", constitute the basic concepts referring to the uses of language related to contextual parameters which determine its main features (Freedman, 1994, 1996).

2) The dynamic construction of context during the elaboration of the text, or negotiation between writer and reader. The writer establishes a certain context together with the reader, through the clues that the writer offers in the text, defined by the social parameters of communication.

3) The cooperation in the construction of the discourse, a growing phenomenon in our society, considered as a factor easing the task and mediating in the construction of knowledge.

4) The "social valence" attributed to the text, which establishes the attitudes related to the use of written language and to the written language as "a different language". This social valence determines a virtual context of the text, shaped by the written language representations that non-expert writers have, or representations of written language held by those who do not know how to write, or by those who pretend to write in a certain context – academic field, second language areas, etc. According to this, the representations of the written world offered by the school are framing the representations that the pupils build about written language and its uses (Heath, 1983; Cook-Gumperz, 1986).

1.2 A Model of Context Interaction

The construction of a model of context interaction tries to gather the different perspectives of "context" that contribute to written production with the intention of giving account of the interrelationship established among them. In this model (Fig. 1) four contexts are distinguished: (a) the context of the writer, (b) the context of reception, (c) the context of production of the text or context of the task, and (d) the context of learning written language and its uses.

```
┌──────────────┐  ┌──────────┐  ┌──────────────┐
│   of the     │◄─┤          ├─►│      of      │
│              │─►│          │◄─│  RECEPTION   │
│ learning context │ learning context │ learning │
│              │  │          │  │              │
│  Knowledge   │  │          │  │  Addressee   │
└──────▲───────┘  └────▼▼▼▼▼─┘  └──────▲───────┘
       │           ┌──────────┐        │
       │           │communicate│        │
       └───────────┤ interact ├────────┘
                   │knowledge │
                   │transforming│
                   └──────────┘
```

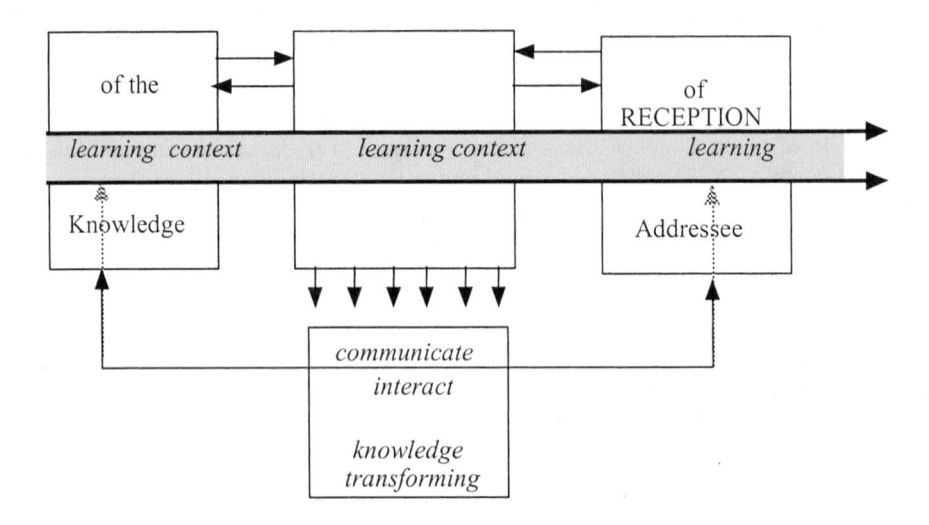

Figure 1. Model of contexts interaction in the process of written composition.

The context of production is located in the central area. This area is settled in a certain space and time, and at the same time it represents a virtual and dynamic space in which the communication between writer and reader is being built. Both the reception context and the context of the writer join in this area. Some connections are established between the conditions and specific requests for a specific situation and what the writer already knows – knowledge of varied nature: about the situations of written language uses, about the elements that shape it (addressee, intention, topic, social area, etc.), about the procedures for elaborating a written discourse. All this knowledge has been previously elaborated in other previous writing situations, and it is reactivated and updated for every new use. Thus the level of knowledge about the written situations will depend on the writer's experience, and it will also be influenced by the "social valence" attributed to the text in her personal context and by her own representation of the task and of the context of reception, modified themselves by the "social valence" attributed to the text in these contexts (Heath, 1983; Rubin, 1988).

The context of production represents the space for negotiation between the writer's intention and the addressee's expectations. It is a space of virtual communication between them. At the same time it is a space for knowledge transformation: acquired and updated knowledge is being modified according to the challenge brought for by the task. Learning is promoted in this active negotiation environment, provided that certain conditions be accomplished in two different areas: the context of reception, acting as a challenge but also as a guide for the writer, and the context of production as a space for mediating to fulfill the aims of the task.

Research on the differences between expert and non-expert writers and also research in the classrooms on the conditions that help to manage the complexity of the composition process (Bereiter and Scardamalia, 1987; Florio and Clark, 1982; Flower, 1979; Sperling, 1996, among others) points out to the convenience of suggesting writing tasks for real situations, as well as the need of promoting mediation tools during the process (Freedman, 1987; Freedman, Flower, Hull and Hayes, 1995; Gere and Stevens, 1985; Graves, 1983). The aim of these mediation tools is either to facilitate the task through the presence of an intermediate addressee -the interaction with an adult or other pupils during the process of writing: "writing conference" or "peer conference"-, or the suggestion of collaborative writing tasks. Another objective of the mediation is to contribute to the writer's awareness of the knowledge being used and the procedures for managing it, implied in the activity of writing.

In this central context the following activities, shown through the interaction among participants, are carried out:

1) Communicating: negotiation between writer and addressee. Carried out starting from the writer's double identity.
2) Interacting: connections among the participants in the task. Interaction acts as a mediation tool for the representation of the task and the text, and for the carrying out and control of the implied operations.
3) Knowledge transforming: relationship between acquired knowledge, being operational zed and adapted to the situation, and the knowledge built during the process.

There is still another broader context acting as the background of the process of composition of each text: the school context. It is in this area where learning and teaching takes place; this context, institutional and social, comes across the other contexts and influences all of them. The interaction between the two levels, writing and learning to write, implies the organization of the context of production, in such a way that it allows the mediation for the construction of knowledge that it offers the conditions required to change the intersubjective negotiation for the internalization of the knowledge.

2. RESEARCH DESIGN

2.1 Research Aims

The present chapter focuses on the analysis of the context functions in the activities carried out at school, concretely in a writing activity elaborating an explanatory text about the laws of light beams transmission. The questions to be answered are the following:

1) What is the influence of the real context of reception of the text in a composition task carried out at school?
2) How does the negotiation among the context of reception, the context of the classroom and of the school and the individual context of the writers take place?
3) At what stage may the context of the task be a context of learning? Is there a possibility for understanding the situation of collaborative writing as a mediating element in the construction of knowledge?

4) Which is the balance between context of the task and context of learning, between "doing" and "learning how to do"?

2.2 Parameters of the Observation Context

The pupils of the sixth form of primary education (aged 11-12) in a public school organize an exhibition of kaleidoscopes – previously made by themselves as a practical activity in the subject of observation sciences – addressed to the second form pupils in the same school. As addenda to the exhibition, the pupils edit a short explanatory brochure. One of the texts included in this brochure must give an answer to a question about how kaleidoscopes work, a question referring to the phenomenon of light reflection. It is knowledge already available to the writers. But now this knowledge will have to be adjusted to the level of knowledge of the addressees to make them understand the apparent paradox of the multiplication of images from a reduced number of objects when crushing with the surface of the mirrors through the phenomenon of reflection.

This experience is carried out in two classrooms of Primary, 6th form, ages about 10 and 11, 26 and 24 pupils, divided in groups of 3 or 4 participants. The elaboration of the text, one per group, takes two sessions, one hour and a half each. In every group a student Teacher acted as an observer. The trainee must obtain additional information about the sessions. However, the relationship between the pupils and the student Teacher turns the latter, in the eyes of the pupils, into a mediator for the explanation of the task: the pupils feel empowered to ask him/her for help along the sessions. Consequently, the student stimulates and may, eventually, help managing the group.

Following the literature on the situation of explanation from the point of view of text linguistics (Adam, 1992; Coltier, 1986; Combettes and Tomassone, 1988), from the point of view of natural logics (Borel, 1981; Grize, 1981) and also from the point of view of the research on explanatory discourse at school and on the pupils' difficulties to cope with explaining (Brassart, 1990; Coltier and Gentilhomme, 1989; Garcia-Debanc and Roger, 1986; Halté, 1989; Sutton, 1995; Vérin, 1995), the parameters of the writing situation observed are the following:
- A situation of explanation of the kaleidoscope: Why do we always see a different image when turning it to the left or to the right?
- Expert/non-expert relationship between writers and addressees: 6th form pupils (aged 11-12) / 2nd form pupils (aged 7-8)
- A neutral relationship with regard to the object under explanation: a topic belonging to the science subject.
- Absence of a predefined textual superstructure: importance of the pragmatical situation of explanation.

The challenges suggested to the writers (pupils) are mainly as follows:
- To assume and maintain their condition of experts by checking the distance between their knowledge and the addressees' knowledge on the topic, as well as their condition of pupils of a higher form

- To adapt their knowledge on the general phenomenon of light transmission to the object kaleidoscope, and also to adjust it to the knowledge of the addressees.
- To adapt the knowledge and experience in writing and scientific explanatory discourse to the suggested situation and to the context of teaching and learning.

2.3 Data Collection

The data presented here belong to the observation of the process of composition in five of the groups of work, randomly selected from the two classes:
1) An overall representation of the level of addressees' knowledge on the topic, gathered during a previous session in which the younger students answered a questionnaire.[1]
2) Transcription of the tape recording with the interactions among participants in each of the five groups during the two work sessions.
3) Drafts and texts elaborated in groups during these two sessions.
4) Final version of the texts.

The analysis of these five groups is based chiefly in the oral interactions inside each group during the process. The remaining abovementioned materials act basically as a support for the interpretation of the data or the global vision of the task.

3. ANALYSIS AND RESULTS

Protocols of verbal interactions among the participants in five collaborative groups along two class sessions constitute the data of analysis, together with the successive versions of the text being elaborated, in order to find out how the interactions referred to above contribute to learning. The parameters observed refer to: a) characteristics of the collaborative composition process, aiming to find any general features in the processes followed by the different groups to establish a possible relationship between working in group and learning; b) explicit references to readers, aiming to establish the influence of the social context of reception; c) explicit utterances including references to the second person pronoun, to follow the presence of the different contexts involved in the process; d) reformulations of the text being written, known as "attempted text", aiming to observe the incidence of the different contexts participating in the composition process in the writers' activity.[2]

---

[1] *The questionnaire was presented to the younger students in a previous session. They should answer the following questions: 1) What do you see when looking through the kaleidoscope eye-hole?; 2) What happens when you turn the kaleidoscope to the right or to the left?; 3) Why do we see so many images?; 4) What is inside the tube?*

[2] *The research questions are broadly referred to in these parameters. Characteristics of the collaborative process (parameter a) and reformulations of the text being written (parameter d) are clearly addressing questions 3 and 4, that is to say, will give evidence of how the context of the task and the context of learning interact, by showing how much time – in turns – they devote to elaborate knowledge and how they contribute to build learning through planification, and also through revision; and how variations in the text being written can be related to learning and especially to what learning issues. Parameters b and c – references to*

3.1 The Composition Process

The procedure followed for the analysis in this part presents the following steps: (a) establishing episodes or phases in the development of the process[3]; (b) establishing categories for the units of analysis in order to be able to generalize; (c) establishing comparisons between the processes followed by the various groups.

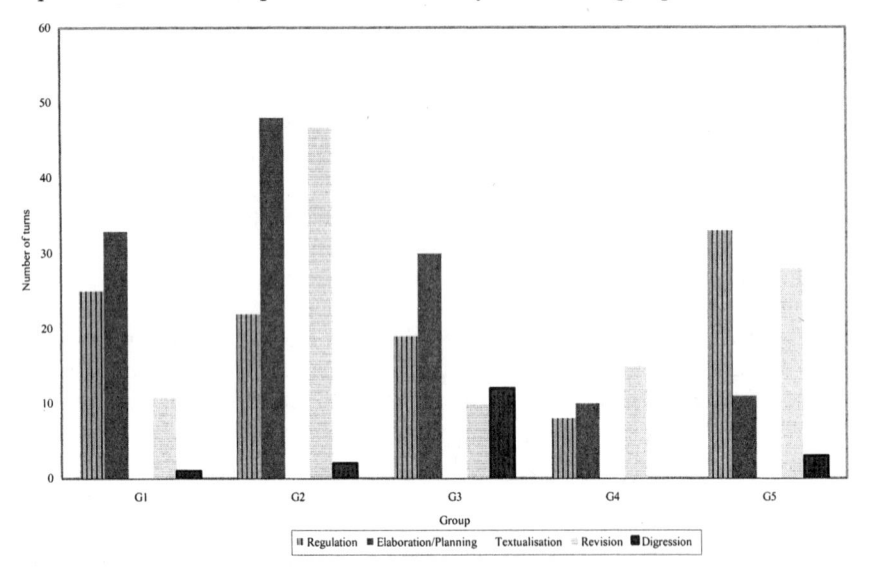

Figure 2. Distribution of episodes by categories according to the number of turns in five groups.

The categories taken into consideration are: Regulation of the process, Elaboration and Planning, Textualisation, Revision and Digression. The chronological vision of the distribution of episodes by categories in each group reveals the different dynamics followed in each group, as it is shown in Figure 3. This fact shows the diversity of the processes and the diversity of factors causing these processes, as well as the differences in the representation of the task and the way of managing it).

---

readers and uses of the second person as indicators of the different addressees contributing to the task – try to answer questions 1 and 2, referring to the context of reception and to the context of the task as the mirror of all the contexts interacting within.

[3] *Delimitation of episodes in the verbal protocols giving account of a shared activity is always controversial. Episodes in these protocols are established following a descriptive procedure, and categories are established following this description. The categories broadly correspond to the operations carried out by students during the writing process. Two external raters have checked the segmentation in episodes. The agreement among these raters and the researcher goes from 82% to 95% in all groups. Divergence among raters corresponds mainly to boundaries between episodes – one or two speech turn is the maximum difference stated-, they fully agree in the established categories.*

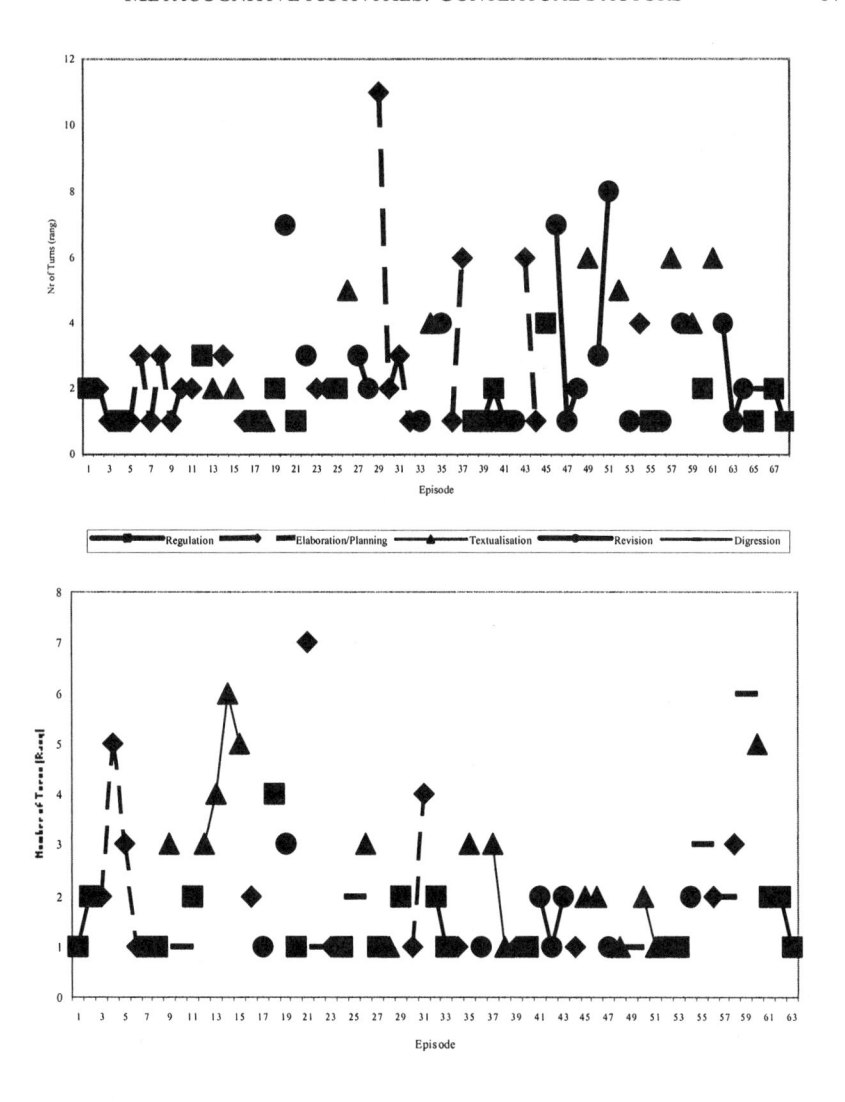

METACOGNITIVE ACTIVITIES: CONTEXTUAL FACTORS 67

Figure 3. Distribution of activities in subsequent episodes along the process for two different groups (Group 2 at the top, Group 3 below). At the Y-axis the number of turns in rang[4].

In spite of all the differences, however, we should also mention the coincidences, as shown in the graphic of the distribution in percentages of the episodes by categories and by groups (figure 4). As it is shown in figure 4, all groups follow the same operations, though at different moments along the two sessions and allocating a differ-

---

[4] *Rang indicates the number of turns: From 0 to 10 turns, rang 1; from 10 to 20, rang 2 ; from 20 to 30, rang 3. For example, rang 11 indicates 100 to 110 turns.*

ent amount of time – in number of turns – to each of them. Differences among groups refer mainly to the revision operation, though an imbalance between planning/elaboration and revision episodes is a relevant datum (see, for example, groups 1 and 3, where they spend more turns in elaborating and less turns in revising, whereas in groups 5, 4 and 2, there is a more regular quantitative distribution between the planning/elaboration and revision operations). This can be justified following closely the dynamics of work in every group, but it is not going to be presented in this chapter.

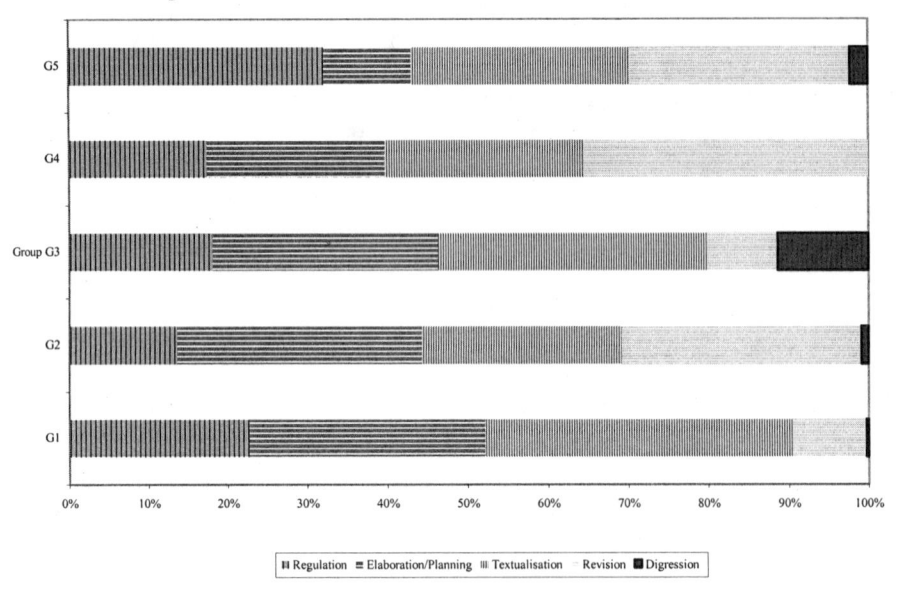

Figure 4. Distribution of episodes according to categories of activities and groups (Groups 1-5) in percentages.

3.2 References to the Addressees

To give account of the writers' representation of the addressees we may observe the amount of references to these addressees during the process, and also the kind of references they use. The qualitative analysis of the reference linguistic forms conveys information related to the challenges offered to the writers by the context of reception. Along the writing process, all groups refer to the addressees in some way or other. They become part of the task. In all groups the student writers refer to addressees by using a pronoun or a general noun clause: *they, them; the younger students, second-form kids.* What is more relevant in their references belongs to the semantic field, expressed mainly by the verb. The verbs refer mainly to the level of knowledge of the addressees – *to know, to understand, to realize, to have clear*-, or to the condition of experts assumed by the writers – *to explain, to say, to make them think.*

Example: In group 3, they are discussing about the use of the word *multiply*. They are not sure the addressees will be able to understand this word in a different context out of the specific field of the arithmetical operation.
    778 E- "multiply"? "reproduce" may be better.
    779 P- "reproducing" is what a mirror does.
    780 X- Yes, but this is still more difficult to understand to them!
    .../...
    864 P- *multiply*!
    865 E- which reproduces
    866 X- Let them look the word up in the dictionary!
    867 E- A first-form kid does not know how to use a dictionary!
    868 X- But he must learn to use it!
They end up by looking in the dictionary themselves to find a solution. They find it: *repeat several times*

Concerning the amount of references to the readers along the process, the analysis of occurrences by groups and by sessions, according to the total number of speech-turns, gives a greater concentration of references in the first session, mainly uttered by the observer, who is probably trying to help with the representation of the task.

3.3 Uses of the Second Person

The communicative relations established among the various speakers, either real or projected in the context of production, may be followed from the use of the second person in the dialogs. The analysis of these second person forms takes into account both morphological categories and the categories of speaker, enunciator and addressee[5] (Kerbrat-Orecchioni, 1980, 1990; Maingueneau, 1993). Table 1 shows the categories and the people they refer to.

"Speaker" refers to the individual who is physically uttering the words, either the pupils or the observer. "Enunciator" refers to the one who takes in charge the words being uttered. In this situation, utterances may be attributed to a single pupil, to the group as a voice, to the observer, or to the teacher of the class, who in some way or other, is present in the task as the "giver of instructions". "Addressee" refers to the interlocutor every speaker is directing their words. Among the uses included in the group "addressee", it is important to underline the category impersonal or general, which appears frequently in all the working groups. This general addressee is in accordance with the role of "destinator" (Maingueneau, 1990). It works as a potential addressee, which often is wrongly identified with the enunciator or utterer, or with the role of "coenunciator" (Culioli, 1990), that is to say, an addressee presented both as an utterer and receiver of a discourse valid for both positions. "You", an example

---

[5] *These categories follow Kerbrat-Orecchioni's framework on the interactive situation between participants presented in her study on Les interactions verbales (Verbal interaction) (1990-94), as well as the proposals presented by Maingueneau referring to the analysis of conversations in literary texts*

of the circular nature of communication, appears when elaborating the thematical contents, where the propositional content of the statement becomes a generic statement.

Table 1: Categories of Discourse Participants Represented by the Use of the 2nd Person

Linguistic forms	Speaker	Enunciator[6]	Addressee
V (verb) P (pronoun) Ps (possessive) I (interpellation)	pupil(s): A observer: O	single pupil: 6_1 pupil-group: 6_3 observer: O Teacher: M	single pupil: 6_1 pupil-group: 6_3 observer: O pupils of 2nd: 2 impersonal/general: G

Example Group 3[7]:

598 Obs.	It would happen the same with hard paper instead of mirrors; they would form a different image, because you move them
599 E.	Cause you move them, //and they change//
600 Obs.	//and they change their position//
601 E	...their position... and... that's it!
602 X	And that's it. But in this case the images wouldn't be so beautiful! Because you would always see the same!
603 E	No, you wouldn't always see the same!
604 X	I mean, you would always see...

The comparison inside the groups is shown in figure 5.

---

[6] The term "enunciator" may seem a bit strange to English readers. It refers to the author of the utterance, the one who takes in charge what is being said. The Latin stem where it derives from is shared in the Roman languages: French: énonciation, Spanish: enunciación. In English it corresponds to "utterer" which may be a confusing word, putting together the meanings of "speaker" and "utterer" in the sense of "the one who takes in charge what is being said".

[7] In English it is a bit difficult to show the use of "you" as referring to an impersonal or general addressee. In the example, every participant uses "you"; there is no change to the first person even though each one apparently is referring to his/her personal experiences. They are using the pronoun "you" in a general sense: "you" is anybody in a similar situation, so it relates to a hypothetical situation where anybody could be placed: what happens to the individual may be considered as general, beyond the concrete circumstances of the interlocutors.

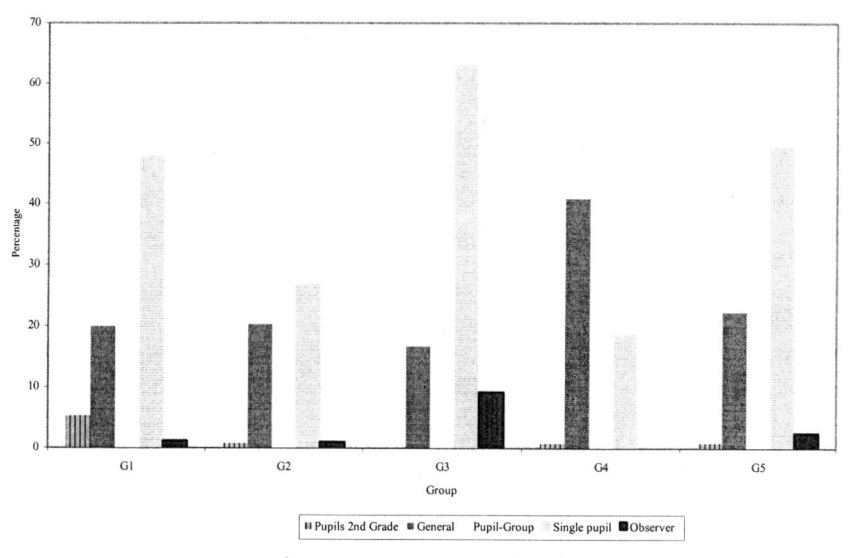

Figure 5. Distribution of 2nd person forms according to the category of addressee in percentages.

Some observations:
- Low percentage of uses addressing the real addressees: pupils of 2nd form.
- Low percentage of uses addressing the observer. The differences show the role that the different groups give him/her, from a close familiarity or participation (G3) to the minimal direct interpellations (G4).
- Occurrences concerning the interpellations addressed to the participants, considered both individually (6_1) or as a group (6_3) are extremely varied among groups.
- The percentage of occurrences addressed to a general addressee, concerning the elaboration of the topic, almost reaches the 20 % of all the references, in all the groups, except in G4 (40%). Relating these data to the category of speaker and enunciator, what comes to light is that the pupils acting as a group, in the role of enunciators, mostly use the second person referred to a general addressee, that it to say, the pupils themselves assume the authorship and, consequently, they assume the elaboration of the content.

3.4 Reformulations

The concept of reformulation has been used diversely related to the linguistic use. From the different notions implied by the word "reformulation" in the field of language sciences, we may underline: (a) the notion of interactive completion, related to the notion of verbal acts of textual composition (Kotschi, 1986); and (b) the notion of metalinguistic activity (Bouchard, 1988, 1993; Camps, 1994a; Camps et al.,

1997; Darras and Delcambre, 1989; David and Jaffré, 1997; Fabre, 1987; Scardamalia et al., 1982).

The first of these notions refers to the construction of the discourse as a dynamical and shared process, not an individual one. Some verbal acts take place in this process, meant to evaluate or to reformulate the already produced discourse, in order to solve possible difficulties or communicative problems, in the sense of paying attention to the produced statement and offer an alternative version to the first formulation. The "interactive achievement" represents an act in which the interlocutors collaborate negotiating a suitable formulation[8].

The notion of metalinguistic activity is understood as a backwards operation to the statements produced by the utterer or by other participants (Camps et al., 1997; Camps and Milian, 2000). It implies an activity of thinking about the language, in which the knowledge on the language and its use, shown in the changes introduced by the reformulated statement, play an important role[9].

The concept of reformulation is related to the notion of attempted text (Camps, 1994a; Camps and Milian, 2000). It refers to the successive reformulations of the text being written, which become the traces of the factors having an influence on the process. These changes may offer information on the representations that the writers have about the text, about the elements that conform it, about its explanatory power, about who will read it besides the addressee, about the adjustment required by the written language norms, etc.

The presentation of reformulations as a grid allows the observation of the changes in the attempted text and the exact elements that are being modified, as well as who suggests them and in what order does the suggestion or modification take place. The dynamics of the group within the task process becomes evident from the localization of the speaker and the turn, and at the same time helps determining the length of the negotiation of a certain piece of text, and of the level of intervention of the participants. Table 2 shows an episode of reformulation.

Two general comments can be done when analyzing the reformulations: the negotiation of the contract for the conversation and communication – among participants and among writers/utterers and addressees; and the reflection about language and its suitability to the situation of communication. There are no differences among groups: in all the groups there appear reformulations that show the capacity for judgment and reflection on the language; in all the groups there are given examples of reformulation that show the adequacy to the communicative situation.

---

[8] *This concept is known as "interactional achievement" (Goodwin, 1979, Schegloff, 1982; "complétude interactive", Roulet, 1987; "accomplissement interactif", Gülich, 1986, 1993.*
[9] *De Gaulmyn (1994) and Bouchard (1996) use the terms "conversational writing" and "writing conversation" to refer to the situations of collaborative writing, where participants speak to write and where the distance between text production and text reception allows considering the text as an object to experiment and apply the writer's knowledge and intentions.*

Table 2. Episode of Reformulation[10]

240 P	And	In the other end			
243 E		In the other end			
244 X		In the other end			
252 X		In the other end			
253 E	And	in the other end			
		In the other end			
254 P		In the other end we place			
256 P		is placed			
260 X		placed			
261 E		placed			
		placed	One		
262 X			One		
263 E			Paper		
264 X			paper or plastic		
265 E				translucid	
			one paper or plastic	translucid[11]	
266 X				translucid	
267 P			one paper or plastic	translucid	
268 E				translucid	
270 P					which can have different colours
271 E					which can have
272 X					different colours
Text		In the other end is placed	one paper or plastic	translucid	which can have different colours[12]

The following remarks refer to the possibilities offered by the analysis of the reformulations in order to get information on the process of collaborative composition:

- The active participation of the members in the group in the task shows a shared attention to the operations being carried out. The pupils participate effectively as "person-plus" (Perkins, 1995), that is to say, the suggestions of the attempted

---

[10] See appendix A for the full transcription of this episode.

[11] The position of the adjective shows the different word order in a Roman language versus English. I kept the disposition of Catalan, for it reflects more clearly the sense of the interventions.

[12] The final sentence in this episode is: "In the other end a paper or translucid film is placed, which can have different colors." The reformulations in this episode give evidence of the hesitations, proposals and counterproposals in relation to the utterers' position concerning the kaleidoscope (they are doubting between explaining how to build a kaleidoscope or explaining how it is built).

text gather all the members of the group together and allow them either to discover possible solutions to the problems that are risen along the process or to detect problems previously not perceived from an individual perspective.

- The narrow span of the changes, generally without a written basis, allows us mentioning the restrictions of the working memory and of the attention, but it also reveals a shared representation of the composition process, gathering new fragments of the text linearly towards the left and also without having a global idea of what they are producing, as in the knowledge telling model of composition process. It appears to happen following these premises, but sometimes the reformulations do not add text to the left but reorganize, and even project or anticipate new text as Bouchard (1996) suggests according to a pragmatic and semantic representation of the task, not strictly in syntactic terms.

On the other hand, the analysis of the verbal protocols points out to the presence of implication and negotiation among group members in order to make the text fit to the situation and the addressees. The dedication to the elaboration and reelaboration of the topic contents is also stressed. This brings us closer to the "knowledge transforming" model, although we must accept that the representation of the text as a product which guides the pupils becomes incomplete and, sometimes, even nonexistent. The lack of a global vision of the text causes the lack of explicit criteria for its elaboration, and the writers follow their own experience as science textbooks readers – precision in the words, detail – and they also follow their experience in the school writing tasks – attention to the written language norms.

4. SOME CONCLUSIONS

In the framework of the writing activities analyzed, the following conclusions are to be mentioned, in relation to the aforementioned questions and the hypothesis underlying the model of context interaction:

4.1 Influence of the Context of Reception in the Context of School Writing

All along the task we analyzed how the context of reception and its representation on the part of the students helped guiding them in the representation of the task. The relationship between the personal context of the pupils and the context of reception meant a constant challenge to play the role of experts, leading them to reinterpret their knowledge on the topic. References to the addressee, reformulations in the text along the process to make it adjust the reception demands, as well as the amount of time devoted to elaboration and revision give evidence of the importance of this context to guide the writing task.

4.2 Negotiation among Different Contexts in the Context of Production

The aim of suggesting collaborative composition tasks pretends to stimulate the cooperation among equals to build knowledge and to negotiate the procedures to be followed, as well as to help building bridges between utterer and addressee through the mediation of the participants. The role of mediator has been played by the pupils themselves through their constant split between expert writers and readers of the text, as if they were pupils of 2nd form in the act of reading, as is it shown by the analysis of references to the addressees and of the uses of 2nd person forms. However, the observation of the context of production through the comparison of the episodes followed by the groups has brought evidence of the differences among the composition process followed by them and among the factors that determine their dynamics. Any group has succeeded in establishing a shared representation both of the task and of the text; the vagueness of the main features of explanatory texts has perhaps contributed to it, together with the lack of experience of addressing a kind of readers who demanded the role of experts on the part of the writers. We should also mention the lack of guidance to the task on the part of the teacher.

4.3 The School Context as a Learning Context

We observed how the communicative situation and the situation of working in groups has an influence on the students' awareness of the writing situations, of the language adequacy to certain intentions and conditions and of the procedures that lead to the task achievement. The knowledge being used is, on the one hand, already existing knowledge on the part of the writers, who is adapted and updated according to the discursive situation. On the other hand, more knowledge is being elaborated along the process with the contribution of all members of the group, driven by the need to solve emerging difficulties. Thus, the process of learning along the process becomes evident. Working in groups also promotes the attention to certain control on the process operations and control on the text. Again, even though they reach a high degree of involvement in the task, and show their capacity to face different problems and solve them collaboratively, the lack of the teacher guidance in this task may have contributed to certain indefinition of the role of students.

4.4 "Doing" Versus "Learning To Do"

Even though the pupils show an intense activity related to knowledge construction, they also show their role of learners from the lack of orientation and knowledge in certain issues. The classroom context and the writing activities suitable for promoting the transfer from the shared regulation into an intra-psychological regulation requires the presence of a certain self-awareness, of a control on the activity – of the existence of learning objectives and the monitoring of these objectives through the formative evaluation tools. In this sense, there is a need of a didactic intervention as suggested in the model of didactic sequence (Camps, 1994a). The task being analyzed lacks the teacher guidance, as it is shown in the process followed by the students and in the task outcome. This consideration contributes to stress the benefits of the model of didactic sequence as a teaching and learning tool.

APPENDIX A: COMPLETE PASSAGE FOR TABLE 2
REFORMULATIONS ARE IN ITALICS.

240 P (makes a proposal)- And in the other end...
241 X- *No, first a full stop.*
242 P- Full stop.
243 E- *No,* In the other end... no. ahhhm...
244 X- *Yes. In the other end...*
245 E- Nooo. 'Cause first we need to empty it. First of all we have to put the things inside. If we cover it from both ends, how are we going to put them inside?
246 X- But this is an explanation of an already built kaleidoscope!
(......)
247 X- *This is an explanation of a kaleidoscope, not of how it is being built!*
248 P (laughs)
249 Obs.- You're right!
250 X- It doesn't matter the way we begin to explain! Well, if we begin saying why it is... and that inside there are tiny objects...
251 E (makes noises)
252 X (dictates)- In the other end...
253 E- And in the other end... *No* In the other end... *The "and" doesn't fit here.*
254 P (rereads and makes a proposal) In the other end...we place...
255 E- No.
256 P (repeats)- ...is placed...
257 E (writes)- placed. This is a draft, isn't it?
258 Obs.- Yes, it is.
259 E- Ahh!
260 X- ...placed...
261 E- ...placed... placed....one...
262 X-...one...
263 E- ...paper...
264 X- – paper or plastic...
265 E- ...translucid...
266 X- ... translucid.
267 P- *...a paper or plastic translucid*
268 E (finishes writing)- translucid.
269 X- *Comma, comma, put a comma.*
270 P- which can have different colors
271 E (writes)- ...which can have...
272 X (dictates)- ...different colors.

METACOGNITIVE REGULATIONS, PEER INTERACTIONS AND REVISION OF NARRATIVES BY SIXTH-GRADERS

YVIANE ROUILLER

University of Lausanne, Switzerland

Abstract. This chapter concerns a study aimed at determining the effects of peer interactions on the regulation processes involved in narrative writing. The research is carried out in three sixth-grade classrooms (age 11-12 years) which have followed an instructional sequence designed to optimize processes of metacognitive regulation during narrative text production. The effects of two experimental conditions – (1) individual production, (2) dyadic production involving collaborative planning and revision of a joint text composed of individually drafted episodes – are compared with respect to the revisions introduced between the initial draft and the final text. Transfer effects from dyadic text production to subsequent individual text production are also analyzed. Relevant findings show that although more revisions are carried out during dyadic collaboration, this effect shows no transfer; on the other hand, the different types of revision observed under each condition do show significant transfer to individual production.

Keywords: revision, planning, metacognition, peer interaction, narratives, transfer, dyads.

1. INTRODUCTION

The study presented here focuses on the regulation of writing. It adopts a metacognitive approach (Allal & Saada-Robert, 1992) in which relationships are sought between two levels of regulation: the regulating effects of instruction (resulting from teacher interventions, peer interactions, instructional activities proposed to the learner) and the student's processes of self-regulation. The general aim of the study is to understand more clearly how the writer integrates instructional guidance within his own action system, and how such guidance can be better oriented to enhance student regulation of reading and writing (Salomon, Globerson & Guterman, 1989).

According to Flavell's initial definition (1976: 232), metacognition is

---

Rouiller, Y. (2004). *Metacognitive regulations, peer interactions and revision of narratives by six[th] graders.*
In Rijlaarsdam, G. (Series Ed.) & Rijlaarsdam, G., Van den Bergh, H., & Couzijn, M. (Vol. Eds.), *Studies in writing. Vol. 14, Effective learning and teaching of writing, 2nd Edition, Part 1, Studies in learning to write,* 77 - 89.

> "knowledge concerning one's own cognitive processes and products or anything related to them .... Metacognition refers, among other things, to the active monitoring and consequent regulation and orchestration of these processes in relation to the cognitive objects or data on which they bear, usually in the service of some concrete goal or objective"

Concerning the relevance of this concept for writing instruction, several questions must be raised: what conditions are required in order to optimize metacognitive regulation of writing in a classroom context? In other words, which types of instructional situations favor metacognitive processes that are likely to regulate writing?

The present study examines peer interaction as a means of fostering metacognitive regulation processes. If we consider that metacognitive processes regulate cognitive processes at varying levels of consciousness, then peer interactions could be particularly effective as a means of stimulating active self-regulation. They offer occasions for verbalization that bring processes situated at the threshold of awareness to an explicit, conscious level, thereby progressively enabling the learner to use these processes as tools. A dialogue implies repeated verbalizations that the subject would not otherwise make on his own, and can thus induce metacognitive processes leading to automization of new forms of self-regulation. Previous research has shown effects of peer interactions on production processes in the course of a collaborative writing condition, but most studies have not verified whether this condition can assure transfer effects to a subsequent individual writing task.

In our study, several aspects of the effects of peer interaction on the regulation of writing are studied through experimentation comparing individual and dyadic conditions of text production, but this chapter focuses on results concerning revision. The general hypothesis of the study is defined as follows. In a situation of narrative text production, a dyadic condition (implying cooperative interactions between students writing a joint text) will induce qualitative and quantitative differences in the regulation of the writing processes, as compared to an individual condition (in which each student writes a text without peer interaction). These differences will be observed not only during the initial situation involving texts produced under dyadic and individual conditions, but will also transfer to a second situation of text production, about 10 days later, in which all subjects write a text individually.

Studies such as those conducted by Gilly (1988) have shown that when two children work together this does not necessarily imply an authentically interactive work sequence. It is necessary for learners to cooperate actively, confront their answers and argue about their positions in order for their reciprocal reactions to have a mutually beneficial impact. This consideration lies at the basis of our study and leads us to design an instructional situation so as to promote cooperative exchanges between the members of a dyad who have to produce a jointly composed text.

2. CONCEPTUAL FRAMEWORK

The conceptual framework has been constructed on the basis of two related areas of research. The first relationship concerns the articulations between processes of writing, such as planning, monitoring, reviewing, translating, as defined by Hayes & Flower (1980) and general aspects of metacognitive functioning (self- regulation and metacognitive knowledge). The second relationship concerns the effects on writing processes of the interactions of the student writer with his environment: that is, with his peers, with instructional material, with the teacher. Here we will briefly review the major references that have helped us to understand each relationship.

2.1 Metacognition and Writing

Although metacognition needs to be considered as a system including regulation processes, metacognitive knowledge, and the dynamic relationships between the two, the study presented in this chapter focuses on regulation processes without further inquiry into the construction of metacognitive knowledge.

Several authors classify different types of regulation processes (Brown & Palinscar, 1982; Kluwe, 1987; Allal & Saada-Robert, 1992). From a functional viewpoint, Brown & Palinscar (1982) consider that regulations – which are implicit and automatized – can become conscious when difficulties or new situations are encountered. In this perspective, it can be hypothesized that social interaction can increase the probability of active confrontations and thus raise the subject's awareness of his mode of functioning. The model adopted here (Allal & Saada-Robert, 1992) distinguishes three operations of regulation (planning, monitoring, adjustment) which run continually in a non-linear manner, and can be activated at different levels of complexity: on-line task execution, as well as management of relations between task, situation and context.

In research on writing, and especially in models derived from theories of problem-solving, metacognitive processes are often present, even though they are not necessarily designated as such. For example, in the well-known model of Hayes & Flower (1980: 11), three operations – "planning, monitoring, reviewing" – interact directly with the text 'produced so far' in order to guide the central operation of "translating". Espéret (1984: 180) distinguishes two levels of organization of the processes involved in writing: the overall monitoring of the writing activity (activated by the writer's representations) and the operations linked to text generation. He assumes that there is a functional dependence of the second level on the first, but postulates reciprocal influences between the two levels. In the interactive model proposed by Allal (1993: 5), the operations of metacognitive regulation, which intervene in both a top-down and bottom-up manner, constitute "an 'interface' which assures the coordinated functioning of two other components of the subject's cognitive activity: his representational network of task-relevant concepts and of contextual factors, and the production processes mobilized to accomplish the task".

Although metacognitive regulations are necessarily present in all aspects of writing, they are reflected in a particularly salient way in the activities of planning and revision. Studies of planning shed light on the representations and processes of anticipation which guide writing (Burtis, Bereiter, Scardamalia & Tetroe, 1983; Fayol & Schneuwly, 1987; Higgins, 1992).

Studies of revision examine reflective and decision-making processes leading to transformations of a text that is being produced or has already been produced. Several models have been developed to account for these processes and can provide elements for interpreting children's revision processes. Bereiter and Scardamalia (1987), for example, define three basic operations articulated in a cyclical model (compare, diagnose, operate), while Hayes, Flower, Schriver, Stratman, & Carey (1987) study links between judgment activity, the writer's intention, his knowledge base and other external elements.

One important point to note is that planning and revision can be facilitated by the writer's degree of mastery of various components of the writing task. Since the quantity and kind of monitoring during writing vary according the type of text being produced (Rijlaarsdam, Van den Bergh & Breetvelt, 1993), the writer's knowledge of text superstructure is likely to affect his revision activity.

With respect to the type of text considered in our study (i.e., narration), existing studies suggest that the superstructure is mastered, at least orally, by 11-year-olds (Espéret, 1984; Fayol, 1983). For Gordon & Braun (1985: 63), knowledge of the narrative superstructure facilitates planning: it is a "composing framework which provides children with metacognitive control over comprehension (and writing)", improving children's access to prior knowledge. Roussey (1990) shows that the writer's mastery of the notion of superstructure considerably improves his performance on text revision tasks. Research by Espéret (1989) shows that knowledge of the narrative framework facilitates performance on all structural levels of text production. In the sequential model he has developed, fundamental questions are raised regarding the role of the narrative framework (Espéret, 1984: 193), e.g., "est-il une représentation relativement statique activée par un processus métacognitif ..., ou constitue-t-il lui-même une structure opérative ...?"

2.2 Peer Interaction and Writing

According to Menez (1984: 171), the social structure of exchanges determines social relations and meanings which, in turn, elicit cognitive regulations. In the more restricted field of school learning, research has dealt with three dimensions of interactions which provoke regulations (Allal, 1988): interactions between teacher and student (e.g., Crahay, 1981), interactions between student and instructional material (e.g., Salomon, Perkins & Globerson, 1989) and interactions between students (e.g., Allal, 1985). Concerning peer interactions in classroom settings, Cazden (1986) differentiates three situations: spontaneous help, peer tutoring and collaborative situations. For Stodolsky (1984), it is important to distinguish two forms of collaboration: "complete cooperation" involving a common goal and a joint task, and a more limited form of "cooperation" in which there is a division of labor to attain a common goal. In addition, peer interactions have been studied with respect to their effects on different aspects of learning: products, results or performances (Skon, Johnson & Johnson, 1981), operations or cognitive processes (Doise, Mugny & Perret-Clermont, 1975), regulation of one's own and others' activity (Allal, 1985).

In the field of written text production, Bereiter and Scardamalia (1987) point out that writing usually suffers from a lack of the interaction which stimulates oral production in conversation. Since, from their point of view, regulations result from discrepancies between the text being produced and the intended text, greater dissonance can be expected when two persons focus on the same text, providing that their interaction involves appropriate forms of confrontation (without excessive dependence of one student on the other). According to Daiute (1989; in Roussey & Gombert, 1992) interactions can replace the internal dialogue on which expert control of production is based.

A literature review by DiPardo & Freedman (1988) reveals interesting findings concerning the effect of collaboration on text production. Nystrand (1986), for example, states that children working in a group approach the revision of their text at a reconceptualization level, whereas children working alone remain at a "correction of mistakes" level. Other studies are concerned with the conditions of efficient interaction. Freedman (1987) notes that subjects collaborate much better when they work on a joint task, whereas Bruffee (1985) and Elbow (1981) show the importance of the process leading to consensus.

Concerning revision, Cohen & Scardamalia (1983; in Olson, 1990: 24) state that "children (who do not often revise) do not suffer from a lack of competence but rather a lack of understanding of processes relevant to revision". In a comparative study of four writing conditions (presence/absence of peer interaction and of revision lessons), Olson concludes that peer interaction has a stronger influence on type and amount of revision than does a revision lesson. Peer conferencing seems to be effective for poor as well as good writers, but poor writers tend to remain dependent on other students' questions, whereas good writers can adopt a critical perspective when revising texts on their own (Russel, 1985).

3. METHOD

3.1 Subjects

The subjects are students from three sixth-grade classes (age 11-12 years) from public schools in Geneva. The population attending these schools is representative of the canton as a whole as far as the children's nationality and the socio-economic distribution of their families are concerned. The teachers of these classes have adopted the instructional approach to text production suggested by Bronckart and collaborators (Bronckart et al., 1985; Pasquier & Dolz, 1990). All the children in each class participated in the writing sequences, but those whose mother tongue was not French and who had not attended school in Geneva for at least three years were not included in the sample of 15 students per class selected for the experimentation.

In each class, children were divided into five strata on the basis of their first-term grades in French. This criterion, which provides a global measure of the child's language performance in school, was considered preferable to a writing pretest. Within each stratum, two children were assigned to the dyadic condition and a third child to the individual condition. The assignments were made in agreement with the teacher, taking into account affinities between children so as to favor constructive interactions within each dyad. The sample was thus composed of 5 dyads (10 subjects) and 5 matched individual subjects in each of the three classes.

3.2 Experimental Design

The experimentation took place in a classroom setting. Although measures were taken to match the children assigned to the two experimental conditions, the complexity of the variables affecting classroom learning does not guarantee that the two groups are fully equivalent. Nor can we be sure that optimal interactive functioning was present in all dyads. In other words, an overall instructional "treatment" was designed in the context described, and then the ways were sought to analyze relations between variables intervening in the treatment.

The experimentation consisted in two narrative text production sequences. In each sequence, text production was based on ten pictures corresponding to the episodes of the classical narrative superstructure. The use of pictures was intended to restrain the range of content so that the children could concentrate on text composition (in the sense of "mise en texte", Fayol & Schneuwly, 1987). Both sequences involve texts written for real audiences (i.e., production of storybooks for second-grade classes in the same school).

Each sequence was organized in four successive phases. The sequence began with discussions – in small groups and with the entire class – discussions aimed at defining the conditions of text production (aim, audience, type of text, etc.) and at activating relevant knowledge and skills. In the second phase, the children wrote a story outline and then produced a complete first draft. In the third phase, the children revised their drafts (which had been typed with their errors by the experimenter so as to encourage revision). In the last phase, the storybooks were communicated to the second-grade classes.

For the first text production sequence, three different series of pictures were distributed systematically across subjects in order to avoid the effect of a particular story. Under the dyadic condition, two students were involved in collaborative planning and revision of a joint text which was composed of individually drafted parts (one student drafted the first half, the other student the second half). This procedure was chosen to increase the necessity for verbalization between children and to make revision more dynamic due to the necessary coordination of the partial texts produced by each child. Under the individual condition, each subject carried out all phases of the instructional sequence on his own, with – at most – some brief, incidental interactions with nearby classmates.

In the second production sequence, all subjects produced a narrative text individually on the basis of one set of pictures (unknown to all). This sequence constitutes a posttest which allows us to determine whether there is evidence of transfer of the competencies developed under the dyadic condition to subsequent individual production. In addition, an interview was conducted with each subject in order to obtain indications of his metacognitive awareness of writing processes.

3.3 Method of Analysis

The analysis presented here will focus on the transformations carried out between the drafts and the final versions of the texts. The transformations were analyzed by a method developed on the basis of studies carried out by our research group (Allal, 1993; Allal, Michel-Rouiller & Saada-Robert, in press).

More than 1700 transformations were identified in the 75 texts produced by the students. The method of analysis provides a precise means of identifying the transformation units, each of which is then classified along four dimensions simultaneously: level of language affected by the transformation, type of transformation, function of the transformation, optional vs. conventional transformation. The subcategories of each dimension are listed in Figure 2.

	Level of language affected by the transformation	Codes
Word		M
Group		P
Proposition		G
Sentence		H
Text		T
	Type of transformation	
Addition		A
Deletion		S
Substitution		R
Rearrangement (particularly transfer of location)		D
	Function of transformation	
Semantic/lexical concerns		S
Textualisation[1]		T
	connection/segmentation	
	cohesion	
	modalisation	M
Spelling[2]		
	phonogramic	P
	morphogramic	M
	other aspects such as logogramic, ideogramic	O
	Optional vs. conventional transformation	
Optional (not required by the conventional standards of written language)		O
Conventional revision (respects the conventions of written language)		C
Conventional error located (but not accurately corrected)		R
Introduction of an error		E

Figure 2. Dimensions of classification.

Transformation units are defined as observable differences between the draft and the final text. Figure 3 shows the five transformations from the record of subject 2341. The non-transformed elements appear in parentheses, the transformation outside the parentheses; for example, the first transformation involves addition of the word

---

[1] *Sub categories adopted from Schneuwly (1988).*
[2] *Sub categories adapted from Betrix-Köhler (1991), on the basis of work by Catach (1980).*

"jour" between the words "un" and "son". This transformation concerns the text written for the second picture (col. P). It is coded as a transformation affecting the group (col 1.), carried out by addition (col. 2), having a cohesive function (col. 3), and it is a conventional correction.

S	Tr	P	Text of transformation	1	2	3	4	Remark
2341	1	2	(un) jour (son chat et lui)	G	A	H	C	
2341	2	2	son (chat) -> le (chat)	M	R	H	O	augmente la redondance
2341	3	3	(des biscuit)s	M	A	G	C	
2341	4	3	(mangèrent des biscuits) et (Le facteur laissa)	T	A	X	E	déjà "et" entre les 2 propos. précédentes
2341	5	6	(clefs). (Tout...)	H	A	O	C	segmentation déjà effectuée

Legenda: Columns
S   subject code
Tr   number of the transformation
P   number of the picture
1   level of language affected by the transformation
2   type of transformation
3   function of the transformation
4   optional vs. conventional transformation

Figure 3. Illustration of coding.

The data were coded by the author on the basis of a detailed eight-page protocol. A separate blind coding was carried out on a sample of 150 transformations by an external rater. An acceptable degree of inter-rater agreement was attained: 87.3% for unit identification and respectively 90.8%, 96.2%, 84.7, 94.7% for classifications along the four dimensions.

The effect of experimental conditions on the products (text 1 and text 2) was analyzed by F tests (on number of transformations, and number of words) and by chi^2 tests on the dimensions of transformations. Results of the F and the chi tests were considered as significant at $p < .05$.

4. RESULTS

The tables showing the effects of the experimental conditions on student revisions all have the same structure: in the first column are the data for the first production sequence (initial text – P1), during which the students produced under either individual or dyadic conditions; in the second column are the results for the second text (posttest – P2) written individually by all subjects who had previously composed a text under individual or dyadic conditions.

4.1 Number of Transformations

If we consider the number of transformations carried out by the children during the first sequence (Table 1), we see that the texts revised in collaboration contain significantly more transformations than those revised individually (F (1, 28) = 4.8266, p = .0365). In the second production sequence, students from both conditions carry out a comparable number of transformations, and the difference between conditions is no longer significant (F (1, 43) = .0949, p = .7596)

Table 1. Number of Transformations by Experimental Condition and by Product

	Initial text (P1)		Individual posttest (P2)	
	Individual	Dyad	Individual	Dyad
Mean	19.5	34	19.5	20.8
Standard deviation	19.9	16	15.6	11.6
Range	0 - 71	17 - 69	0 - 51	5 - 56

The mean number of words written under each condition is remarkably similar for each text (see Table 2): no significant differences were observed in P1 or P2. This means that the larger number of transformations for the texts written in collaboration cannot be explained by the length of the text, but by a higher density of transformations.

Table 2. Number of Words by Experimental Condition and by Product

	Initial text (P1)		Individual posttest (P2)	
	Individual	Dyad	Individual	Dyad
Mean	254	249	222	211
Standard deviation	104	103	72.6	70.9
Range	94 - 438	123 - 494	114 - 391	107 - 419

4.2 Function of Text Transformations

As shown in Table 3, the differences between the experimental conditions are significant both during the initial text production sequence and during the second post-test sequence (statistics respectively $\chi^2 = 23.294$, $df = 2$, $p < .001$; $\chi^2 = 13.377$, $df = 2$, $p < .002$).

During the initial sequence, the proportions of transformations affecting the semantic-lexical dimension are similar under both production conditions. On the other hand, the individuals revise more than the dyads with respect to spelling, whereas the dyads carry out relatively more revisions with respect to textualisation. When we analyze the distribution of the textualisation transformations across the subcategories of this dimension (segmentation/connection, cohesion, modalization), we find that there are no significant differences between individuals and dyads: this means that although dyads carry out more textualisation transformations, they are of the same types as those carried out by individuals.

Table 3. *Functions of Transformations by Experimental Condition and by Product*

Function of transformation	Initial text (P1)		Individual posttest (P2)	
	Individual	Dyad	Individual	Dyad
Semantic / lexical	16	16	21	16
Textualisation	24	40	29	42
Spelling	60	44	50	42

In the second sequence, the individuals' percentage of spelling transformations decreases, while their percentages of semantic-lexical and textualisation transformations increase (+5% in both cases). On the other hand, the distribution of the percentages for the dyads remains stable. It can be noted that, in both sequences, textualisation is a major concern for the children having worked under the collaborative condition, while spelling is the dominant concern for those having worked individually. This preoccupation for spelling revisions by individuals can perhaps be explained by the usual organization of classroom activities linked to writing: textualisation is rarely worked on as a specific focus of revision and therefore needs a collaborative structure of interaction to support it, whereas numerous individual exercises in the classroom focus on spelling.

4.3 Types of Spelling Transformations

Spelling transformations are classified in three major categories. Phonogramic transformations involve phoneme-grapheme transcriptions (correct use of the alphabetic code, omissions, confusions). Morphogramic transformations concern both grammatical and lexical morphemes (agreements, derivation affixes, etc.). The category "other aspects" includes logogramic aspects (e.g., homophones), ideogramic aspects (e.g., capital letters, hyphens) and miscellaneous problems linked to nonfunctional letters (e.g., some cases of double consonants, final letters of historical etymology).

When we examine the details of the spelling transformations (table 4), we find that the differences between experimental conditions which are nearly significant in the initial sequence ($\chi^2 = 5.3656$, $df = 2$, $p = .068$), become significant in the posttest sequence ($\chi^2 = 17.3788$, $df = 2$, $p < .001$). Individuals modify spelling relatively more at the phonogramic and morphogramic levels, whereas dyads are relatively more concerned with other spelling aspects. When the texts are examined, we find that the "other" transformations which explain this difference are primarily ideogramic (i.e., the addition of a capital letter or a period when the other has already been specified). It is not obvious, however, why the dyadic condition would make students more attentive to the ideogramic aspect of spelling than to other aspects.

Table 4. *Type of Spelling Transformations by Experimental Condition and by Product (% By Column)*

Spelling transformation	Initial text (P1) Individual	Dyad	Individual posttest (P2) Individual	Dyad
Phonogramic	32	27	40	28
Morphogramic	44	39	48	41
Other	24	34	12	31

4.4 Optional Versus Conventional Transformations

As shown in Table 5, for the initial text production sequence, significant differences are observed between the experimental conditions ($\chi^2 = 7.46$, $df = 2$, $p = .024$). The students writing under the collaborative condition carry out relatively more optional transformations (28% vs. 23%), thereby showing their ability to transform a text beyond what is required on purely formal grounds. In addition, when they carry out conventional revisions they make fewer mistakes than the individual writers (6% vs. 10%). These trends are accentuated in the posttest sequence of text production, thus showing that the advantage of collaborative writing persists in subsequent individual text production ($\chi^2 = 15.61$, $df = 2$, $p < .001$).

Table 5. Optional vs. Conventional Transformations by Experimental Condition and by Product (% by Column)

	Initial text (P1)		Individual posttest (P2)	
Type of transformation	Individual	Dyad	Individual	Dyad
Optional	23	28	33	35
Conventional	67	67	52	58
Incorrections	10	6	15	7

5. DISCUSSION

In summary, the main effects of the collaborative condition of text production on revision appear to be:
- higher quantity of revisions during the collaborative task;
- relatively more transformations linked to textualization, rather than to spelling;
- relatively more transformations of ideogramic aspects of spelling;
- relatively more optional transformations;
- and relatively fewer incorrect transformations.

The first result is interesting from an instructional viewpoint since teachers often complain about the lack of revisions made by most elementary school students. It might seem obvious that two children working together are likely to make more revisions in a text than a single individual. However, since the length of the initial texts is similar under dyadic and individual conditions, it appears that peer interaction stimulates greater intensity of revision and, as the other analyses show, also leads to different patterns of transformation.

The lack of a significant difference in the number of transformations carried out by the two groups in the posttest does not imply, however, that the intense revision activity during the collaborative interaction could not be reactivated if the students were again placed in dyadic conditions of text production. The work on "situated cognition" (Brown, Collins & Duguid 1989; Salomon & Perkins, 1989) suggests that cognitive competencies are closely tied to the conditions in which they are utilized.

Significant transfer effects are found for textualisation, spelling and optional vs. conventional transformation. Although subjects were closely matched on the basis of their grades in French, this does not fully insure equivalent initial competencies in writing. Thus, further analyses are being carried out to determine the correlations between amount and types of revisions and the quality of the texts both before and after the revisions. These analyses will help us to verify whether the effects can be attributed to peer collaboration during revision activity, rather than to the quality of the drafts being revised.

It is interesting to note that the effects presented here result from a single sequence of collaborative text production. More powerful effects could be expected if such sequences were repeated in school instruction strategies aimed at improving writing.

Two other sources of data need to be considered. First, an analysis of the sequences of peer interactions observed under a dyadic condition of text production is expected to specify their effects on the subjects' writing procedures and, more specifically, on the types of self-regulation involved. Second, the types of metacognitive knowledge verbalized in the interviews conducted after the posttest will shed light on the relationship between this type of knowledge and the types of transformations carried out.

Finally, at least three questions require further reflection. Are peer interactions likely to have a greater effect on metacognitive processes in writing (planning, monitoring, revision) than on the basic cognitive processes involved in writing (translating, linearization, etc.)? In other, more provocative terms, can social interaction contribute to learning to write precisely because of its role in the processes of metacognitive regulation? Concerning the activity of revising, can we specify more precisely the aspects of metacognitive regulation that are responsible for text transformations?

ACKNOWLEDGMENTS

The study presented in this chapter was part of the author's doctoral dissertation, conducted under the direction of Professor Linda Allal, at the Faculty of Psychology and Sciences of Education, University of Geneva.

THE DIRECTIVITY OF TEACHER STRATEGIES IN COLLABORATIVE WRITING TASKS

CHRISTINA DÍEZ */**, JUAN JOSÉ ANULA *, FERNANDO LARA**, & PILAR PARDO*

*Universidad Nacional de Educación a Distancia, Spain & **Burgos University, Spain*

Abstract. The efficiency of the teaching-learning process is closely linked to the level of adjustment between teacher help on the one hand and the process of constructing meanings by the pupils on the other. To attain this level of adjustment the teacher has to use communicative strategies that evolve throughout the pupils' schooling. These strategies also define the teaching style that we studied for two consecutive school years in a Spanish classroom with three to five year old pupils. To be able to analyse the information obtained, we created a multidimensional analysis system which allows us to describe both the quantitative and qualitative evolution of the constructivist teaching style in the literacy progress. Quantitatively, through the percentage variations of teacher participation compared to her pupils, and qualitatively through directivity, understanding this to be the level of information given by the teacher which gives the pupils a greater or lesser degree of freedom when managing their own learning process. Likewise, we have been able to observe how the teacher's and pupils' interactive strategies evolve together in the process through which the latter start to gain greater autonomy in resolving group-writing tasks.

Keywords: literacy, collaboration, strategies, pre-school, constructivist, scaffolding, discourse analysis, discussion, whole-language, process-product.

1. INTRODUCTION

Children, from a very early age, move in a society in which the printed page plays an important role in their daily lives, so they have some intuitive knowledge of written language before they start school (Goodman, 1991). Likewise, Ferreiro and Teberosky (1979) and Ferreiro (1991) demonstrated that children form many hypotheses concerning reading and writing on their own, such as the minimum number of letters needed to make up a word, the necessity of an internal variation in the distribution of letters to make each word different, or the syllabic hypothesis which

---

Díez, C., Anula, J.J., Lara, F., & Pardo, P. (2004). *The directivity of teacher strategies in collaborative writing tasks.*
Rijlaarsdam, G. (Series Ed.) & Rijlaarsdam, G., Van den Bergh, H., & Couzijn, M. (Vol. Eds.). Studies in Writing. Studies in writing. Vol. 14, Effective learning and teaching of writing, 2nd Edition, Part 1, Studies in learning to write, 91 - 103.

makes them represent a syllable with just one phoneme. In line with this evidence, the constructivist perspective of education is to see the child as an active subject, able to create his own hypotheses about writing and to contrast them with the actions and guidelines he gets from adults and other children in a family or school context.

From this perspective, children's learning does not necessarily imply reproducing the words the teacher shows them. By simply using words and opening them up to a teacher-guided debate in the classroom, children draw progressively closer to the conventional system of writing. In these situations of usage and debate, the teacher's role undergoes a radical change, since the child no longer needs the adult as a source that transmits, but rather as a guide through whom he is introduced to the practices of literacy (Bruner, 1996; Olson, 1994). Thus the teaching activity focuses on the pupils' learning process, giving greater relevance to the co-construction process of knowledge than to the teacher's transmission of the solution to a given task. The efficiency of this teaching-learning process is closely linked to the level of adjustment between teacher help on the one hand and the process of building up meanings by the pupils on the other. To obtain this level of adjustment the teacher must use a variety of communicative strategies which should vary during schooling and which will define the teaching style that we analyze below.

There are very few publications that analyze peers interaction in infant education and the communicative teaching style in a constructivist educative context (Teberosky, 1993; Tolchinsky, 1993; Pontecorvo and Zucc</mark>hermaglio, 1991; Orsolini, Pontecorvo and Amoni, 1989; Orsolini and Pontecorvo, 1986; Pontecorvo, 1987). Using these studies as a starting point, especially Orsolini, Pontecorvo and Amoni (1989), as well as Vygotsky's reflections on the function of language (1978), we developed a multidimensional analysis system to observe the evolution in teacher and the pupil interaction strategies when solving writing problems as a group during the two first years of a child's initiation in literacy at school.

This system consists of five dimensions which permit the registering of the intellectual and pragmatic aspects implied in the social construction of knowledge, although we are presenting one of them in this work. Using this analysis system we examined, among other things, the plurality of strategies used by the teacher to encourage a progressive autonomy in the group of pupils aged between three and six. In this present chapter, we concentrate on the analysis of the process whereby the teacher and pupils' strategies evolve together as the latter acquire greater autonomy. Thus, through a longitudinal study over a period of two years, we have been able to see how the pupils not only accumulate knowledge but also acquire learning strategies made visible by the teacher in the communicative situations which accompany the task. This became a central factor in explaining the progressive pupil autonomy. Moreover, the results show that it is possible to create situations where three and five year olds collaborate which are useful when learning how to read and write.

2. OBJECTIVES

The overall objective of our investigation was to study the evolution of the processes of co-construction of writing knowledge through interaction strategies used by a teacher and her pupils in-group learning situations. The specific objective of this chapter is to describe how the *interactive strategies* of the teacher evolve during a process in which the pupils acquire a greater autonomy in resolving group-writing tasks. We describe both the quantitative and the qualitative evolution of the constructivist teaching style in the literacy process. Quantitatively, by means of variations in the percentage of teacher participation compared with that of the pupils. Qualitatively, the evolution of *directivity,* understanding this to be the level of information offered by the teacher which allows the pupil a greater or lesser degree of freedom in managing his own learning process.

3. METHOD

3.1 Procedure

This investigation took place in a Spanish infant school over the two consecutive school years that integrate the children's evolution as they learn to read and write, i.e., between the ages of three and five. We selected a class whose the teacher has a constructivist theory of written language and who also has experience in peer collaboration. During these two years, the research team formed part of the class dynamics, taping and video recording the pupils working in groups of three with the help of the teacher. We recorded 12 sessions each term over the two years of the investigation, gathering a total of 72 sessions which meant transcribing and registering 10,297 conversation utterances related to instructions, decisions about the text to write, the code, the child who was going to write, etc. In this publication we are going to concentrate on those related to the code – the graphic system of the Spanish written language – which represents 6,567 conversational utterances.

As can be seen in figures 1 and 2, our activities not only cover writing but written language as a whole. Children do not write a given text but they discuss what they want to write in different types of texts, e.g., their names, the comic, the calendar, the recipes, etc. The activities videotaped were the most representative of the daily work in each term and were proposed by the teacher and the researchers. These constructivist activities were characterized by introducing the children to significant reading and writing activities right from the beginning of their schooling, the teacher adopting a non-directive role and encouraging peer conversation about the task. To analyze the data we began by transcribing the recordings, writing down word for word the dialogue held between the children, and describing the behavior which indicated what was going on at that moment (e.g., excerpts 1, 2 and 3).

Activities are similar in the corresponding terms of each year as we can observe in the comic of figures 1 and 2: the children have to decide what to write and they write it in collaboration. Both activities correspond to the third term of 3/4 and 4/5 years old respectively, but the resolution corresponds to the children's level of writing: the pupils in their first year write pseudo letters without any conventional value, while in the second year they write in the conventional way, but phonetically (they do not write the letter "h" for the verb "haciendo" – making – which is silent). Other examples of activities can be seen in excerpts 2 and 3, which shows children writing with mobile letters in the corresponding first terms.

Figure 1. Activity resolved by 3/4 years-old children in the third term of the school year.

- I am proud of my little storks! Sniff...
- But, how are we flying to Africa? It's very very far!
- Making nests

Figure 2. Activity resolved by 4/5 years-old children in the third term of the school year.

During the day, the teacher forms peer groups of three children and every one works on a different activity such as literacy, mathematics, construction games, puzzles, etc. Researchers register the literacy group, without interfering in the work, in order to respect the natural situation. Every term we have balanced the sample of situations so that in half of the seventy-two sessions analyzed the teacher's presence was constant in the literacy group, whereas in the other half she attended these children only when they needed her or when she felt it was necessary. The different results of these situations are presented in table 3.

3.2 The Analysis System

For the unit of analysis we decided on *conversational utterance*. We have defined this conversational utterance as the communicative contribution inserted by one participant between two others. To study our transcriptions of the 72 sessions we developed inductively five dimensions of analysis (Díez et al., 1999), revised and extended in Díez (2002). Each dimension has different categories and they are mutually exclusive within each dimension, whereas the categories of the different dimensions are not. The socio-semiotics basis of a discourse multidimensional analytical system are explored and discussed in Anula (in preparation).

We have called the first dimension of analysis "Phase of the task". This perspective registers different stages of the activity such as the instructions to resolve it, the negotiation of the text to write, the writing of this agreed text, the sharing out of who's going to write a letter or a word, etc. Every analytical category determines the type of discourse operations, which we analyze in other dimensions. In this study we centre on the writing of the agreed text and it is analyzed through the dimension *discourse regulation*.

The following two dimensions analyze the writing co-generation and are called "Discourse Regulation" and "Content Management". They cover the dichotomy of communicative functions versus intellectual speech proposed by Vygotsky (1934/1962). The *Discourse Regulation* is the object of analysis in this article. It is formed to study the ways in which the participants encourage the development of ideas during the interaction: asking the participants some questions, giving them cues to facilitate the answer or giving the solution to the task. The *Content Management* dimension covers the discourse strategies and solutions with which the participants perform the task of learning to write.

The last two dimensions cover the argumentative activity registered in the participants' discourse. The dimensions of "Evaluation" and "Justification" are grouped under this criterion, the aim of which is to generate an objective knowledge so long as it is agreed and shared. In this negotiation process the *evaluation* dimension makes it possible to register, in the discourse, the gathering or separating of perspectives through *agreements, total and partial disagreements, doubting* and *invitations to debate*. The *justification* dimension registers the evidence offered by the participant to explain their point of view.

4. RESULTS

According to the objectives and the space available in this publication, we will centre our analysis in the *discourse regulation* dimension. It analyses the educational style of the teacher, characterized by a low directivity which shows more interest in the process of resolving the task than in finding the right solution. We want to describe both the qualitative and the quantitative evolution of the constructivist teaching style in the literacy process. Qualitatively, the evolution of *directivity,* understanding this to be the level of information offered by the teacher which allows the pupil a greater or lesser degree of freedom in managing his own learning process. Quantitatively, by means of variations in the percentage of teacher participation compared with that of the pupils.

4.1 Levels of Teacher Directivity

In order to analyze the teaching style from a qualitative point of view, we used as our starting point the *discourse regulation* dimension shown in table 1. In this dimension, we show how the participants' interventions are connected to encourage the building of a shared knowledge, making requests, offering clues or giving solutions to the task. This dimension, applied to the teacher, allows us to analyze her educational style in a *directivity scale*. Taking directivity to mean the margin of freedom the pupil is given to manage his own activity and learning, we can observe that the teacher moves at three different levels.

LEVEL 0	*The absence of direction* shows the lowest intervention level where the teacher refrains from intervening. The absence of direction is precisely the quantitative measure we are using in the teaching style, which we will see evolve over the two years.
LEVEL 1	*Non-directive strategies* are also fundamentally centered in the process. However, in contrast to Level zero, there is only one question, which guides the children's performance, but no clue giving information to help solve the task (e.g., "Which letter comes now?").
LEVEL 2	*Semi-directive strategies* are those interventions leading the child so that he can find the answer by himself. At this level of directivity, a clue with information is offered to help resolve the activity (e.g., "Which letter comes now?. Say it slowly, Feeeee").
LEVEL 3	*Directive strategies* are those which directly give the solution to a precise problem in the task (e.g., "The letter E").

Table 1 presents the evolution of the teaching style in our study and we can see some relevant results. Analyzing the two years together we observe how the teacher basically uses semi-directive (42.7%) and non-directive (53.6%) strategies, whereas directive strategies are scarce (3.7%). These results demonstrate that the teacher's regulation strategies give a clear primacy to the process (*non directive* and *semi directive* strategies: 96,3%) with regard to the result (*directive* discourse mechanisms: 3,7%). We could see that the teacher's interest in both years is centered on helping the children to solve the task on their own without giving them the solution (as we can observe in excerpt 1 below), even though the initial answers they gave were incorrect (see the pseudo letters written in figure 1 presented above). This implies that the teacher was able to accept that the pupils' mistakes were also an important learning source if submitted to debate.

Table 1. Discourse Regulation Dimension. Percentages per Column (χ^2 85,367; df 2; asymp. sig (2-side): 0,000)

Directivity of teacher strategies	School Year		
	3/4 years	4/5 years	Total
Non directive	44.3	58.7	53.6
Semi-directive	47.9	39.8	42.7
Directive	7.8	1.5	3.7
N	835	1505	2340

Comparing the evolution of the teacher's strategies in each year, we noticed how the non-directive strategies, which ask the question without offering any informative clue on how to solve the activity, increase from 44.3% to 58.7% in the second year. These strategies are the less directive ones. In contrast, the semi-directive strategies, characterized by the clues offered to help in finding the answer, show a marked decrease in the second year (from 47.90% in the first year to 39.8% in the second). Likewise, the directive strategies, which offer answers to the task, drop significantly in the second year (from 7.8% in the first to 1.5% in the second). It shows that each year the teacher offers fewer answers – solutions – and guides the resolution of the activity offering less information than the previous year.

From these results, we can conclude that in our study the teacher's help is parallel to the pupils' needs and that the scaffolding (Bruner, 1984) decreases as the control is progressively handed over to the children.

In excerpt 1 we give an example of the interaction which took place between the teacher and her pupils who, on this occasion are in the first term of the second year at infant school (4-5 year olds). This protocol shows how the teacher concentrates on the process and not on the conventionally correct answer. From this conception of any mistake being a "constructive mistake", we accept that the answer is wrong according to conventional rules, but valid within the child's process of reconstructing knowledge. The group is making up the word "felicidades" with moveable letters, and has as far written "Fel". On arriving at the i, Samuel does not accept that this letter corresponds to its real sound value since his mother taught him the letter "i" as a small letter but not as a capital. So Samuel only accepts letters with a dot on top as representing this sound. (Utterance 4749: "No, because it's got a, a dot here"). In the face of the teacher's mirroring (Lumbelli, 1985; 1988), that is to say, the repetition of the previous statement to dig deeper into it, this participant reaffirmed his position by giving an argument based on maternal authority: "Yes. My mum taught me. Yes" (utterance 4751). The teacher tried to offer him a clue to contrast his position on the letter "i" – the name of his classmate Iván –: "Isn't this the I for Iiiván?" (utterance 4756); this information, familiar to him because of the time spent in the classroom working with the Christian names, conflicted with the information coming from his family, and allowed him to begin to understand the apparent contradiction: on the one hand, he recognized perfectly well the phoneme of the capital "i", but now he cannot understand why "Iván" is written with this letter, something he had never questioned up till then. For this reason he is thoughtful in utterances 4761 and 4763. Samuel understands that this situation means he must justify his contradiction but he cannot form an argument in utterance 4765 ("I think that less than no it's more than...") nor in utterance 4767 ("Yes, but..."). To break out of this situation, the teacher, instead of offering a solution, uses his classmates as a source of information and mutual help. So she asks Alberto, thus giving an interactive model whereby the children build up their knowledge together.

Excerpt 1. Teacher's strategies are centred in the process but not in the product of the activity. 2nd school year, 4/5 year-olds. Infant school, 1st term. Continuous presence of the teacher.

4746 Teacher Come on. Feelii. Samuel says that it isn't an I Is this an I o not? (showing a capital letter I)
4747 Alba   (nods)
4748 Teacher Samuel says it isn't
4749 Samuel   No, because it's got a, a dot here (pointing to the top of the I)
4750 Teacher It's got a dot here?
4751 Samuel   Yes. My mum taught me. Yes.
4752 Teacher So this isn't an I?
4753 Alba   (Can't find an answer)
4754 Alberto (Can't find an answer)
4755 Samuel   No
4756 Teacher Isn't this the I of Iiiván?
4757 Samuel   (Makes a movement of having realised something and nods)
4758 Teacher Iiiván What is the first letter? Iiii
4759 Samuel   The I
4760 Teacher So it isn't written with this?
4761 Samuel   (Thoughtful)
4762 Teacher Yes or no? What do you think? Is it written with this or not?
4763 Samuel   I'm going to see, (thoughtful)
4764 Teacher Let me see. Bring the cards please (to someone in the classroom)
4765 Samuel   I think that less than no it's more than...
4766 Teacher No? Isn't Iván written with this one?
4767 Samuel   Yes, but...
4768 Teacher Hasn't Iiiván got an I? Alberto, what do you think? Let me see. Is this an I or not?
4769 Alberto (Nods)

4.2 Decrease in the Teacher's Intervention

While table 1 lets us analyse the qualitative evolution of directivity (levels 1, 2 and 3), *Level 0* – the absence of teacher intervention – allows us to quantitatively analyze the teaching style, and so highlight the autonomous activity in the pupils. In table 2, we compare the percentage of interventions of both the teacher and the pupils in both years.

Table 2. Percentage of Pupil and Teacher Interventions according to the School Year (χ^2 41,117; df.: 1; asymp.sig (2-side): 0,000)

Interventions	3/4 years	4/5 years	Total
Teacher	41.3	33.1	35.6
Pupils	58.7	66.9	64.4
N	2021	4546	6567

By making a global analysis of the information in the table above, we can appreciate that the average teacher participation is 35.6%, greater in the first year (41,3%) than in the second (33,1%). Nevertheless, it is necessary to distinguish between the two types of videotaped situations in which the teacher participates: in half of the sessions recorded each term, the teacher's presence is constant (36 sessions) and in the other 36 sessions her presence is partial, helping a group only when the participants ask her to or the teacher considers it necessary, e.g., when teacher observes that children do not know how to continue.

By differentiating the teacher's participation according to the work situation, we can see in table 3, as is logical, that it is far greater in the constant presence than in the partial presence situation in both school years. On the other hand, while both situations show a decrease in the importance of the teacher's role from one year to the next, this decrease is much sharper in the partial presence situation. This reveals that the children are more autonomous in this second year and now find it easier to accept the possibility of working alone in groups than they did the year before, and they do not demand the teacher's attention so often. In consequence, and based on the data obtained, we can observe how, in the second year, the children have improved their autonomy as a group and have assumed both a greater level of participation and a greater independence from the teacher.

In a traditional teaching model, the teacher presents the information, the pupil receives it and the teacher then checks if learning has taken place. In such a system, according to Flanders (1962), the teachers speak 70% of the time in the classroom and the pupil is regarded as a knowledge receiver. Other studies contrasting with this teaching model such as those carried out by Cazden (1986) and Pontecorvo, Castiglia and Zucchermaglio (1989) who, working in innovative teaching contexts, demonstrated that conversation in the classroom can forget evaluation as its prime objective and centre on the discussion itself. The above-mentioned authors arrived at an operational definition, which allows *discussion* to be characterized as the situation in which the teacher intervenes in around 30% of the total discussion. Nevertheless, these writers recognize that it is fundamental to make a qualitative analysis of the teacher's interventions and of their repercussion in the children's behavior. We have done this through our analysis system.

Table 3. Percentages of Pupil and Teacher Interventions according to Work Situation (Constant: χ^2 21,304; df.: 1; asymp.sig (2-side) 0,000; Partial χ^2 53,549; df.: 1; asymp.sig (2-side) 0,000)

	Participant	3/4 years	4/5 years	Total
Constant	Teacher	47.2	39.3	41.4
	Pupils	52.8	60.7	58.6
	N	1149	3083	4232
Partial	Teacher	33.6	20.0	25.1
	Pupils	66.4	80.0	74.9
	N	872	1463	2335

We consider that although it does not exactly fit into the 30% of teacher's interventions, which was our initial criteria to discover a discussion according to Pontecorvo, Castiglia and Zucchermaglio (1989), the percentages fell to 39,3% in the constant presence situation and fell as far as 20% in the partial presence situation. On the other hand, it is important to bear in mind the limitations inherent to groups of three/four year olds when it comes to resolving tasks in a group, which means it is possible to suppose that this percentage will continue to fall in a third school year when the children – five/six year olds –, despite their still early age, will continue learning to collaborate in peers.

In order to exemplify the decrease in teacher participation we present two sequences in which we can observe the difference in child autonomy when resolving the tasks. Excerpt 2 below shows a conversational segment recorded during the first term in the first Infant school year (3/4 year olds). On this occasion, the teacher is working with the children throughout the whole session. Here we can see how the teacher tries to create a debate among the students and also the difficulty they have in paying attention to the group resolution. In this session the pupils have chosen which of the Three Wise Men's names they want to write in moveable letters (Melchor, Gaspar or Baltasar, who bring presents to Spanish children at Christmas). For this task and bearing in mind that we are in the first stages of literacy, the pupils have a written model in capital letters (e.g., GASPAR). The pupils have already put the letter A at the beginning of the word and the letter R at the end.

Excerpt 2. The teacher helps the children to resolve the task in collaboration. 1st school year, 3/4 year olds. 1st term. Continuous presence of the teacher.

---

830 teacher (Lorenzo wants to put another letter A without looking to the model). You haven't looked at the model! Wait! Like this (and replaces the letters). See if you can put it now. Look and see if you can put it or not. Let's see where you are putting it. Think.
831 Lorenzo This one goes here (by the other A in already in position).
832 teacher Yes? But it is there, it's there. Can't you see that it is already there? Look it is already there.
833 Lorenzo He doesn't listen and puts the letter were he wants to.
834 teacher Ivan, look and see if you agree (She tries to involve the partners and create a debate, but they aren't interested).
835 Iván (He turns around and without looking, half-heartedly says:) Yeees
836 teacher Is it alright there?
837 Iván (He begins to think and gives the correct answer). No (he points) with both, with both, with both.
838 Diego This goes here (pointing to the letter G and without paying any attention to the teacher's proposed discussion)
839 teacher Look and see which is left over, which is left over (there are two As together)
840 Lorenzo (Meanwhile, Lorenzo wants to leave) See you tomorrow.
841 teacher Wait, wait. Find out which is left over.
842 Diego (He puts the G letter he had pointed out, in front of the letter A)
843 teacher (Once again she tries to involve the partners). Very good!. Let's see if they are all OK. Ivan said they're not. Look. Look and see what you think, Lorenzo. Look and see what you think, we are leaving in a moment. Let's see. Let's see. Ivan, which did you say wasn't OK?
844 Lorenzo This one is OK. This one is OK, but this has an xxx (we can't understand what he means)
845 Iván This one and this one (he points to the G that Diego has just put and the A that was already there.
846 teacher Good. This one (he points to the G) – is the same as this one (she points to the G on the model)
847 Iván (Now Ivan is the one who wants to leave and turns around to go away)
848 Teacher Look and see, Ivan. Ivan!
849 Iván (Leaving) I can see it.

Now, in comparison with excerpt 2 we present excerpt 3 in which we can appreciate how the children can debate autonomously, despite the fact that in this session the teacher is, like in the previous sequence, always present. The teacher does not want to intervene because she considers that the children can interact by themselves. In this sequence 3, the children are using moveable letters to form the words "Feliz Navidad" (Merry Christmas) and have already put the two first letters "FE". After a guided discussion on the letter L and after a unanimous agreement they are going to put it in its place. In utterances 4203-4205 the children argue about the placing of the letter. In utterance 4207 Ignacio picks up the letter I. Throughout the previous year and during this first term of the second year with the same teacher the children have frequently been able to see her interest in reaching an agreement among the pupils. So, two utterances later, Ignacio asks his partners for an opinion (utterances 4209 and 4211). In spite of the fact that Sergio doesn't agree, saying that letter I is the next one, Ignacio explains that this letter has already been put, so Sergio seems convinced and expresses it in a friendly way (utterance 4215: "OK, little kid"). In utterance 4216, it is now David who doesn't agree with the letter they have put, because he is putting a phonetic emphasis on an incorrect place in the word: "feliz navidaaa", instead of "feliiii". But David seems to convince Sergio (utterance 4217), who reacts immediately justifying his change of mind (utterance 4219: "Noo, Feliiz. The I"). In utterance 4221 the teacher intervenes to remind them that the word to be composed is "Feliz" and in this way facilitating the identification of the last phoneme, "z". In this short fragment we have been able to see the autonomy of the pupils in the collective performance of a task, and consequently, the decrease in the teacher's participation in spite of being present in the group during the whole session.

Excerpt 3. The teacher lets the children resolve the task by themselves, without intervening. 2nd. school year, 4/5 year-olds. 1st term. Continuous presence of the teacher.

4203	Ignacio	Now it's my turn
4204	Sergio	He's going to put the letter L
4205	David	(David also intervenes to put it)
4206	Sergio	No. I want to put it (he finishes putting letter L).
4207	Ignacio	Picks up the letter I
4208	David	And then me. Li-ci-da-des
4209	Ignacio	(To David). Which one do you think?
4210	David	The I
4211	Ignacio	(To Sergio). Which do you think?
4212	Sergio	The lll, the lll
4213	Ignacio	We've already put it! Sure the I comes now!
4214	Sergio	Ok, little kid
4215	Ignacio	Okaaay (with letter I in his hand)
4216	David	He has put the I, and it's not right, it's feliz navidaaa
4217	Sergio	Oh, the A
4218	David	Feliz Navidad
4219	Sergio	Noo. Feliiz. The I
4220	David	There's already an I (at the same time he places it)
4221	maestra	Feliz

Excerpts 2 and 3 exemplify the evolution of teacher interventions showed in table 3 above: teacher participation decreases in the second school year when children are learning to cooperate and they become more autonomous of the teacher.

5. CONCLUSION

Children go to school with previous knowledge and hypotheses, both acquired from different written materials they have at hand. They can contrast this knowledge and these hypotheses in interaction with the teacher and their peers in classroom contexts designed by the teacher. We have recorded the information obtained in a multidimensional analysis system made up of five dimensions that reflect the multifunctionality of the discourse and lets us observe the development of communicative strategies between teacher and pupils. Since the objective of this study is the analysis of the teaching style and its repercussion on children participation, we have shown one of these dimensions, specifically, the relative to the joint resolution of the activity, examined in the *Discourse regulation* dimension.

This dimension has allowed us to record the greater or lesser amount of information offered by the teacher when guiding a joint activity. Thus we have classified the teacher strategies on a scale of four directivity levels that reflect the degree of freedom the teacher allows the students in solving their activity on their own. The information obtained has shown that her low directivity level characterizes the teacher's style, since she gives greater importance to the process than to the right answer. This teaching style is in line with the constructivist perspective she ascribes to.

The *Discourse regulation* dimension not only qualitatively analyze the level of adjustment between teacher help and the process of building up meanings. It also allows us to quantitatively examine the percentage of teacher intervention compared to children participation: we observe that the average teacher participation is greater in the first school year than in the second one and, consequently, children assume a greater level of participation and independence from the teacher this second year.

In conclusion, the results reflect a tendency towards fewer teacher interventions that at the same time are progressively less directive, transferring the teacher leading role to the pupils as they advance in the learning process and producing a gradual level of autonomy in their collective literacy process.

We consider that this study can be of interest for those teachers who want to take advantage of the benefits of interaction among equals when teaching how to write. Therefore in this article we offer three of the 46 sequences (Díez, 2002) which show how the writing knowledge is built between a teacher and her Infant School pupils. On the other hand, as we have seen in the different workshops in which we have submitted this work to teachers, the analysis system lets teachers acquire a consciousness of their interactive strategies, increasing the quality and effectiveness of the teaching activity. It also offers some keys for reflection on the amount of information supplied to the pupils, and on how it can be modulated depending on their levels of conceptualization of writing, in such a way that the work takes place in the pupils' Zone of Proximal Development.

MAKING DIGITAL ANNOTATIONS USING THE WORLD WIDE WEB

HENRRY RODRÍGUEZ & SANDRA BRUNSBERG

The Royal Institute of Technology of Sweden, Stockholm, Sweden

Abstract. Initially, only the final product of the writing process (e.g., a document) was presented on the Web. More recently, however, attempts have been made to utilize the shared space for collaborative aspects of writing, such as revision and reviewing. The revision stage of the writing process has to deal with a new element: digital annotations. This chapter presents a longitudinal study in a graduate writing course in which is observed how third-party reviewers produced 276 digital annotations while using the DHS, a Web-based annotation system. We mainly focus on the form of the digital comments and the needs experienced by third-party reviewers when communicating annotations that would lead to a change in the original text. Our study showed that reviewers devise their own strategies to link their comments with the text that may have implications for design. It also revealed the need for the original text to be displayed and readily available for editing.

Keywords: Annotation, Web annotation, revision, comments, collaboration, annotation interface

1. INTRODUCTION

The writing process can be seen as a three-component model according to Hayes and Flower (1980). These components are planning, translating, and reviewing. During the writing process, from its genesis to the final product, annotations are almost certain to be made. In particular, during the reviewing process, a reviewer can make countless annotations; some can be classified as corrective. A corrective annotation aims to instruct or persuade authors to perform a correction (change) in the text in question. It could be as simple as marking a misspelling or suggesting a language style change; making corrective annotations mainly implies suggestions to add, delete, move, or change the text. These kinds of annotations are very important during the process of learning to write.

The reviewer role can be played by the author or by a third party. An annotation by a third-party reviewer demands more elaboration than if the author-reviewer is

---

Rodríguez, H. & Brunsberg, S. (2004). Making digital annotation susing the worls wide web.
Rijlaarsdam, G. (Series Ed.) & Rijlaarsdam, G., Van den Bergh, H., & Couzijn, M. (Vol. Eds.), Studies in writing. Vol. 14, Effective learning and teaching of writing, 2nd Edition, Part 1, Studies in learning to write, 105 - 120.

one and the same person. The third-party reviewer needs to convey his/her ideas to another person, who will typically read the annotations at a different time and place. These annotations can be made on paper or in digital form. The benefits of annotation on paper far outweigh those of on-line tools (O'Hara & Sellen, 1997). However, most documents today are produced originally in digital format and current word processors include features for digital annotation, such as the revision feature, insert comment and comparing documents function, and the change bar of most word processors today e.g., Microsoft Word, and FrameMaker.

The World Wide Web (Web) is a great repository of digital documents. Writing for publication on the Web is becoming increasingly frequent and tools that facilitate the production of documents to be shown on the Web are now very common. In fact, most word processors include the feature "Save for the Web". However, little is known about how third-party reviewers make corrective annotations in digital form using the Web.

In the present chapter, we report on a study of 40 Ph.D. students and two teachers making corrective annotations using the Domain Help System (DHS), a Web-based system introduced as a Web-annotation tool in a writing course. The DHS presents a simple interface and allows comments to be attached to a set of selected Web documents. The interface for writing the comment is also very simple; only plain text is offered.

We are mainly concerned here with identifying the needs experienced by third-party reviewers using a simple, generic Web-based tool when making corrective annotations, that is, how the digital annotation was used to describe desired changes in the text. The rudimentary nature of the system has forced users to make up their own notations, thereby indicating their needs.

2. RELATED WORK ON ANNOTATIONS

In a study, Marshall (1997) focused on the form and function of annotations made in textbooks by students and discussed some issues and implications for the design of annotation tools for a digital library setting. She found that the annotations were made in the text (also called in-situ), or in the margin (also called off-side). They could be telegraphic, namely, using a personal opaque coding, or explicit, usually textual. Finally, they could be removable or not. It was found that "annotation form arises in part from the characteristics of the material themselves, the imprints and the implements used to write them" (p. 134). For example, students that use highlighters wrote fewer marginal notes than those who used pens. Finally, she suggested support for digital annotations:
1) in situ annotation (e.g., interlinear annotation),
2) annotations should be distinguishable from the source (c.f. Neuwirth et al., 1990),
3) non-interpretative marking (e.g., underline, highlight of text) as they are very much used,
4) fluidity of form because annotations on paper were very rich in form,

5) informal coding; several annotators a developed personal system of annotation in which symbols and pen colour meant something to the reader,
6) public and private annotations,
7) annotation should interrupt reading as little as possible.

The most common types of annotation interfaces are the split-screen, interlinear, and aligned interface (Figure 1).

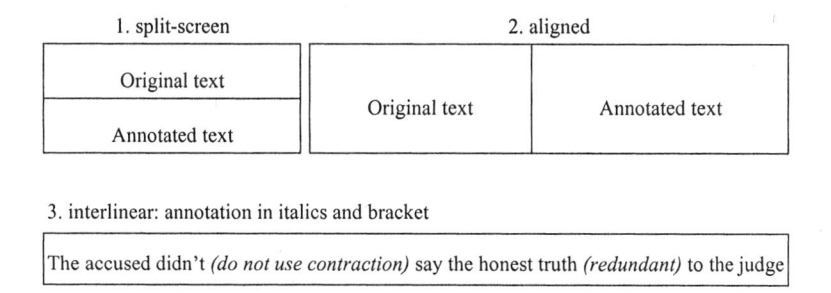

1. split-screen		2. aligned	
Original text		Original text	Annotated text
Annotated text			

3. interlinear: annotation in italics and bracket
The accused didn't *(do not use contraction)* say the honest truth *(redundant)* to the judge

Figure 1. Three annotation interfaces.

In the split-screen, the user's screen is divided into two horizontal adjacent windows and in the aligned interfaces the screen is divided into two vertical adjacent windows. The original text is shown in one of the windows (usually the upper or the left one respectively) and the annotated text in the other. The interlinear interface annotations are differentiated from the original text by using format features (bold-face, italics, parenthesis, capitalization, etc.), see figure 1.

Some studies have addressed the annotation interface. For instance, Neuwirth et al. (1990) has proposed a set of requirements for annotation interfaces: a) there should be a minimum of motion required to start an annotation; b) the primary text should be easily distinguishable from the annotation text; c) the annotations should be visible "at a glance" while reading the primary text; d) the relationship between the primary text and the annotation should be easy to see, that is, authors should be able to see to which part of the text the reviewer is referring; and e) different annotators should be readily distinguishable.

Ovsiannikov, Arbib, and McNeill (1999) pointed out that digital annotation systems are in an underdeveloped stage. They presented an empirical study of annotation and demonstrated that digital annotations are able to perform hypertext-oriented action, such as linking and sharing; they can be synchronized in real time; serve as the basis for conversations, and thus for coordination during planning; searched; and have capabilities specific to the media type, such as soundclip, and reply.

Vasudevan and Palmer (1999) note that Web-based "annotations systems are constrained both in capability and efficiency by the limitation of the Web" infrastructure, and that HTML is limited as a layout language for annotation; for example there is no way to render annotation on the sidelines of a Web page. Thus, annotation features on the Web are very limited compared to stand-alone word processors, like Microsoft Word. For a discussion on currently available and developing technologies for creating and presenting annotations, glosses, and other comments on digital documents, see Wolfe (2002).

3. THE DHS IN BRIEF

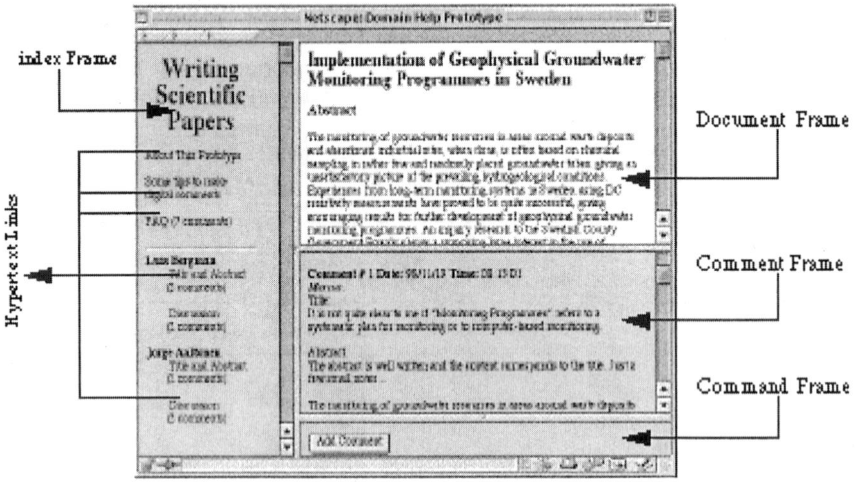

Figure 2. The layout of the DHS in a Web browser's window.

The DHS (see figure 2) is a Web-based tool that uses a standard browser and presents a collection of Web documents to which users can attach comments. The comments and the documents are saved in a shared space that is call a *domain*. The DHS administrates this domain. Figure 2 shows the layout of the DHS in a Web browser in which we can see 1) the index-frame, which displays the list of documents included in the domain in the form of hyperlinks; 2) the document-frame, showing the content of the document (original text); 3) the comment-frame, for adding comments (annotated text) to the document presented in the content-frame, that is, a screen-split interface; 4) the command-frame with the "Add comment" button that pops-up the Add Comment Window (ACW).

The ACW is divided into two vertical frames (see figure 3). The left frame contains a copy of the Web document. In the right frame are the name-input and the comment-input fields. In the latter, the annotation is written, that is, an aligned interface. There is also a "paste" button that attaches the text of the Web document into the comment-input field. This provides users with an editable copy of text to be commented and they can make interlinear annotations while the original text is also right aligned to it.

When a comment has been made and submitted, it is available immediately together with the previous annotations attached to the document. The system sends the owner of the Web document an awareness email containing the message made by the user (Dourish and Bellotti, 1992). Another form of awareness is the "comment counter tag" placed beside every item in the index-list that tells the users how many comments have been made on a document so far.

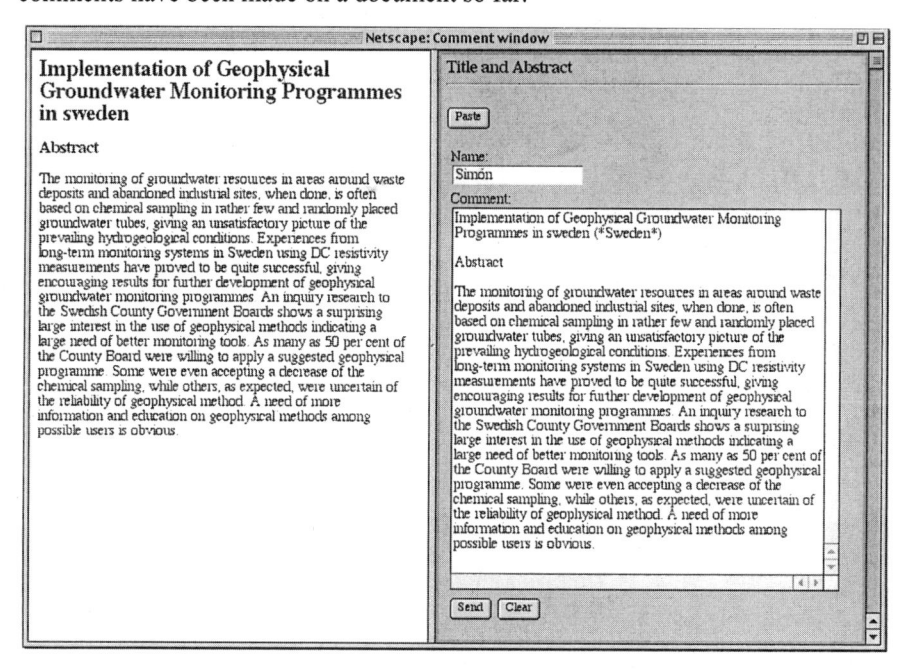

Figure 3. The add comment window with the paste button. Note that the reviewer makes a correction (sweden for Sweden) to the text directly.

The system supports independent reading and writing spaces. Both spaces can be accessed concurrently and they can be manipulated independently. Furthermore, it provides a minimal overlap of the writing space and the reading space. The DHS allows the support of a quick and effortless switch between these two spaces and navigation in them. The DHS has a logging function providing information about the users' actions in the system, which documents they visited, how long they spent on each document, how long it took for a comment to be written, and the duration of each session. For a detailed description of the DHS, see Rodriguez, 1999.

4. METHOD

The DHS was used in three English academic writing courses given in a technical university in Sweden, in the period 1997-2000. The use of the DHS was not mandatory; nevertheless, all the students used it to share their homework and to make annotations on other students' homework.

This environment was suitable for our study because corrective annotations were bound to be made by third party reviewers. In total, 276 annotations made by 40 Ph.D. students and two teachers were recorded by the DHS. HTML tags could also be part of the annotation but no support for editing them was given. In table 1, we show the case studies in which the DHS was used and the number of comments and words produced in every case study by students and the teachers. At the end of the course, the students were asked to fill a Web-based survey. The aim of the survey was to evaluate the use of the system and to obtain relevant information about the participants, such as familiarity with the Web. The evaluation of the tool is not presented here.

Table 1: The Case Studies that Used DHS as an Annotation Tool (Raw Numbers and Percentages)

Case Study	Participants	Comments made by Teachers	Comments made by Students	Words in comment by Teachers	Words in comment by Students
A1997	15	19 (26%)	55 (74%)	5094 (30%)	11625 (70%)
A1998	13	16 (20%)	63 (80%)	2377 (26%)	6850 (74%)
A2000	16	29 (24%)	94 (76%)	5765 (32%)	12208 (68%)
Total	44	64 (23%)	212 (77%)	13236 (30%)	30683 (70%)

4.1 Participants

The students that participated, 13-16 for each group, were non-native English speakers. They were Ph.D. students that had different engineering and scientific backgrounds, e.g., chemistry, metallurgy, and physics. All the participants had access to the Web and they reported that it was the first time they had taken a writing course. The students had all used the Web for at least two years and had communicated with the teacher and, very infrequently, with classmates in other courses by email. The teacher of the course, who took part in the study and wrote several annotations, was also familiar with the Web. Apparatus

The DHS was the Web-based tool we used to collect the annotations made by reviewers. In our case studies (see figure 2), the index-frame displays the student's name and his/her assignments. Each assignment is a hypertext link. The version of the DHS used by A1997, A1998 did not have the "paste" function of the ACW.

4.2 Procedure

Each course took 10 weeks, with classroom sessions once a week. During each class, a new topic was discussed and homework was assigned to the students. The homework normally involved writing a short text, about one page long, using the techniques and writing styles that were discussed during the class. The class was divided into groups of three students, who reviewed each other's texts, so that two others read each student's work.

We included one document in the DHS describing some informally developed conventions that would serve as a model to help the students make interlinear corrective annotations using digital plain text. The convention proposed the use of the following symbols *(,)*, ~, *, *= for adding, deleting, suggesting, changing. These conventions were mainly oriented towards distinguishing the annotation from the original text. This choice was made to prevent students spending an excessive amount of time figuring out how to make a corrective annotation, the danger being that they might perceive the DHS as an obstacle to accomplishing their homework.

We have analyzed all the annotations that were entered by the students in these three case studies. Additionally, we counted words and phrases in the text of the annotations recorded in the DHS.

5. RESULTS AND DISCUSSION

The examples that we present in this chapter are numbered, written in italics and they are taken verbatim from the reviewers' annotations in the DHS.

5.1 Degree of Integration of the Original Text in the Annotation

Almost all the comments made by the participants integrated to some extent the original text. For corrective annotations it is very important that the reviewer has access to the original text and is also able to edit it. This will save time typing (or cutting-and-pasting) the text that will be annotated.

In general, there were three ways in which the reviewers made their annotations: full integration, partial integration, and null integration of the original text.

5.2 Full Integration

One strategy was to copy the entire original text and work on it. This was observed in all the case studies, even those in which the "paste" function of the system was not available.

Copying text from a Web browser window has the inconvenience of adding an extra break at the end of each line relative to the browser window's width[1]. The DHS conserves any line breaks that the user might enter. There is, therefore, no way to distinguish one line break made by the user from another added while copying from the browser. So the extra line breaks added by the reviewer when performing a copy-paste from the browser window were also conserved. The extra line breaks meant that the DHS showed the annotation in a strange layout. An example is shown in figure 4.

Despite the browser window being wide enough to show a sentence longer than it is shown in the previous text (*The aim of the workshop was* ...), the DHS breaks the line where a line break (added by the copy-paste action) is found and does not use the rest of the space. To solve this problem, instructions on how to eliminate

---

[1] *This problem has recently been solved by Internet Explorer 5 and Netscape 7.*

extra line breaks were included in the DHS with the conventions about how to write digital annotations. Only some students followed the procedure. Eliminating the extra line breaks required a great deal of effort on the part of the reviewers.

The origin of the "Paste" feature of the DHS is found in these observations. Pressing only the "paste" button, members of the A2000 case study had the original text copied in the text input area. This eliminates the line break that caused the problem presented in figure 4.

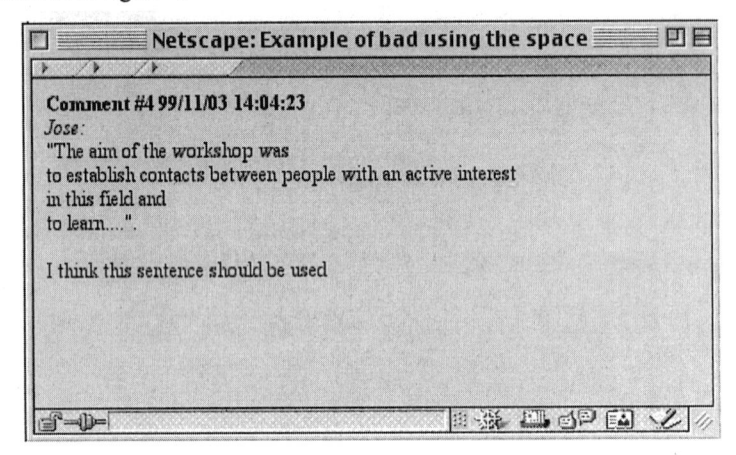

```
Netscape: Example of bad using the space

Comment #4 99/11/03 14:04:23
Jose:
"The aim of the workshop was
to establish contacts between people with an active interest
in this field and
to learn....".

I think this sentence should be used
```

Figure 4. Example of how the system could present a copy-pasted text from the original breaking the flow and bad using the Web space. The arrows show the empty space.

5.2.1   Partial Integration

Reviewers did not always copy-paste the whole original text. Sometimes they copied only the portion they wanted to annotate, for example, a sentence or part of it. We do not know exactly how this was done. They could have copy-pasted the interesting portion or they could have typed it; see example 1:

> "But the most important thing is to change the mentality". I feel this sentence is in the wrong position as the word "but" puts it in the opposite of the previous sentence

5.2.2   Null Integration

In some annotations, the reviewers did not integrate the original text at all. Instead, they went directly to the annotation; see example 2.

> Paragraph 2:
>
> You give some "solutions" here. Could you make sentence 2 clearer by starting with something like "One way is by using.

5.3 Helping the Author to Find the Correction Context

The correction context of the annotation was defined differently, depending on the degree to which the reviewer integrated the original text. For example, when using full integration of the original text the annotations were interlinear so the corrective context was given by the annotation itself. When partial integration was used, the annotation is presented in a split screen interface, which is why the location of the corrective context has to be indicated. We observed:

5.3.1   Quoting the Beginning of the Sentence

We observed that reviewers identified a whole sentence just by quoting the first few words. In none of the cases did we find that the number of words copied by the reviewer was less than five. In example 3 the reviewer indicates to which sentence he/she is referring using this approach.

> Might I suggest a minor change to the sentence starting /Due to the fact that. / Can you reduce this

5.3.2   Topic Related Location

Another way to locate the sentence was by its content or theme, see example 4. Reviewers usually wrote the words "*the sentence about*", but in some cases they just used the structure sentence-topic (see example 5). Observe that this strategy somehow lies between partial and null integration of the original text. For example:

> The sentence about the method could be left out

> The only sentence I don't like is the one with the explanation to why?

On the other hand, when the original text was not integrated, the reviewer clearly felt the need to clarify the correction context. Reviewers used invisible location marks to help the writer enter the context. They used the spatial context to make reference to their annotations. It was very common to find annotations in which the spatial context was very important in understanding the annotation.

5.3.3   Ordinal Position

One common strategy was to use ordinal position to locate annotations. Expressions such as "*the last*", "*the beginning*", "*the next*", "*the sentence before*", and "*the opening*" were adjectives commonly used by reviewers. Example 6 shows the reviewer indicating the position on two levels: sentence level and paragraph level.

> The first sentence in the last paragraph I would write

5.3.4   Numbering Position

Enumerating the sentences or paragraphs was another of the strategies used by the reviewers, see example 7.

> in sentence 2, paragraph 3, your verb describes; you could probably combine it with sentence 3

We have examined the text to see how the participants effected the link between the original text and the annotated text using the ordinal and numbering position approach. We have used four "text markers" words as units of observation: *text, paragraph, sentence, and line* to show the hierarchical structure of the texts. For the sake of validity we have also counted the number of times these text markers appeared in the original text. It is worth mentioning that the word *line* occurred many times in the original text because some of the homework was related to graphics.

From table 2 we can see that the most frequently mentioned word in their corrective annotations was sentence, then text, paragraph, and line in that order. Participants hardly ever used the text marker *text*, or *line* when using numbering position; they referred mainly to a paragraph, and seldom to a sentence. Many would agree that locating a blank line (a common separator for a paragraph) is easier than locating a full stop or period (the separator for a sentence) in the text. Probably that is why numbering position was more used for paragraphs than for sentences. When using ordinal position, participants referred mainly to a sentence, though they also frequently referred often to a paragraph.

The logical sequence used in making a comment (first reading then commenting) is also reflected in table 2. First, participants work on a micro level, that is, on the sentences in a paragraph. As they are closely involved in the task, it might be easier for them to remember the ordinal position or simply comment on the sentence they are reading which is compatible with our results in which participants used *the/this sentence* 105 times. Clearly, participants worked more on a sentence level than a paragraph level (220 and 90 times mentioned respectively). After reading the last sentence of a paragraph, they appear to zoom out and "count" which paragraph they have just read and if appropriate, comment on it using the cardinal number. What is relevant here is not which approach (numbering position or ordinal position) participants used but the fact that they have to perform a "counting task". Numbering the sentences and paragraphs in the original text would alleviate the cognitive load of the revision process in this context.

It was interesting to see that the recency effect and primacy effect are present while reviewers make comments. The *last sentence* was mentioned 32 times and the *first sentence* 22. This might also be because the first and last sentences in a paragraph are typically topic sentences, and therefore contain key information.

Table 2. Use of the Ordinal And Numbering Position Approach for Helping the Author to Locate the Context of the Annotation

	Appeared in original text	Appeared in annotated text	The/this ~	Numbering position		Ordinal position		
				~N°	~ordinalN°	next~	~before	last/final~
			'this sentence'	'sentence 3'	'3rd'	'next sentence'	'sentence before'	'last sentence'
Text	9	111	66	1	1	0	1	1
Paragraph	1	90	14	22 Par. 1, 5x Par. 2, 9x Par. 3, 6x Par. 4, 2x	27 1st par.,16x 2nd par.,6x 3rd par.,5x	4	0	10
Sentence	2	220	105	8 times: Sent. 1, 2x Sent. 2, 5x Sent. 3, 1x	34 times: 1stsent.,22x 2nd sent.,7x 3rd sent.,4x 4th sent.,1x	11	2	32
Line	43	11	1	0	0	0	0	0

Observe that the text marker *line* was not used at all. This is not the case when revision is made face to face on paper. In this context the text marker *line* was not likely to be used because it was too demanding to count the lines, which might significantly vary depending on the Web-browser window.

If the reviewer uses numbering or ordinal position, this also means that authors, when editing the revisions, will probably have to go through the same counting task that the reviewers had performed. The authors' system of counting might be distinct from that previously made by the reviewers, creating confusion and wasting time.

5.4 Distinguishing Annotated Text and the Original Text

When using full or partial integration of the original text, the annotated text is presented in the same space as the original text; therefore it is important to distinguish them. There were several ways to do this.

5.4.1 Space Delimited

Some annotations were put in the line following the text splitting after the original text (example 8), others were aligned with the text (example 9), others were interlinear (example 10). Observe that in these examples the participants sketch the three common annotation interfaces presented in figure 1. When full or partial integration of the original text approach was used, we found no cases in which the annotation was made before the copied text.

It is also difficult to distinguish between the original content and the comment. Different conventions used by different reviewers make this even more difficult. However, the system always shows the original text with no changes in the content frame and the annotations in the comment frame. For the authors of the commented text, however, distinguishing between the original content and the comment might be easier. Observe that in the examples the reviewers use special characters, e.g., /, >>, to distinguish their annotations.

> whether genetically modified (GM) food is hazardous to human health or not.
> /you could leave out "or not", gives a better flow I think but it's not necessary/

> The process are the repeated >> The process is then repeated

> These (*+factors*) include(*+:*) flow velocity of mobile phase,...

5.4.2 Use of Parenthesis to Highlight Annotations

Parenthesis was the commonest sign reviewers utilized to make a distinction between their annotations and the original text. However, the use of parentheses is not a good strategy because it could also be used in the original text and might be confusing. The following example is a case in point:

> (But) Unlike to (omit) the concentrated narrow Web in an I-beam.

In this case, the reviewer suggests some changes but it is not clear which ones. The sentence could be understood in a number of different ways, listed in table 3. Here, words that are struck-through mean "to be deleted" e.g., ~~word~~, and underlined words mean that they should be added to the text e.g., <u>word</u>.

The reader might interpret the word "omit" as a new word to include and not as an action, as is shown in case a) of table 3. On the other hand, if the reader interprets the word "omit" as an action, it is not clear on which word the action should be taken: it might be on the word "to" as shown in case b), or it might be the word "the", a common error for speakers of languages that lack the article, as shown in case c).

Parentheses were used in our conventions, which may explain why they were commonly adopted. Nevertheless, what we want to bring out is how confusing a convention can be if it is not clear what action has to be taken, and on which part of the text.

DIGITAL ANNOTATIONS 117

Table 3. Four Possible Interpretations of Example

	Potential interpretation	It would read
A	But ~~Unlike~~ to <u>omit</u> the concentrated narrow web in an I-beam	But to omit the concentrated narrow web in an I-beam
B	But ~~Unlike to~~ the concentrated narrow web in an I-beam	But the concentrated narrow web in an I-beam
C	But ~~Unlike~~ to ~~the~~ concentrated narrow web in an I-beam	But to concentrated narrow web in an I- beam
D	But unlike to <u>omit</u> the concentrated narrow web in an I-beam	But unlike to omit the concentrated narrow web in an I-beam

5.4.3   Use of Colour and Symbols

In many cases, reviewers explained the notation of their annotations and their meaning as we can see in example 12, in which mathematical signs were used and in example 13, where color was used:

> \+ means adding a word and
> \- means take a way a word

> What is in RED means to delete
> What is in BLUE means to add what is in brackets [] or my annotation
> What is in Violet means that I am not sure if that should be used or could be replaced by something else.

The words RED, BLUE, and Violet were colored with the color they described. The reviewer in this case used HTML tags to achieve the color effect.

As we can see here, reviewers used signs or colors to represent the actions add and delete which are the most common ones used for corrective annotations. In example 13, the reviewer decided to assign a color to those cases in which he or she was not sure whether his/her annotation was valid/right (see section 5.5.2).

5.5   Making Interpersonal Comments

5.5.1   The Reviewer and Author Dialogue

The fragment of example 12 shows that the reviewer is trying to reach a common understanding with the author. The reviewer tries to guide the author on how to read his/her annotations. This explanation was found at the very beginning of the corrective annotation sent by the reviewer.

We found the following situation while analyzing the data. John made his first corrective annotation, used his own change representation (color meaning in example 13), and explained to Mary how to read the annotations. For the next homework,

John revised Peter's work for the very first time. John assumed that Peter had read the explanation of his own change representation (made to Mary), and therefore did not bother to explain it to Peter. This assumption is probably a consequence of the shared space that the DHS offers.

It might be important to support the common actions for corrective annotations, namely: add, delete, change, and change the place of a word to avoid extra effort by the reviewer (see example below):

> in a sandwich structure (I would suggest you add a comma here, and possibly also "however, ") the faces take the place

In this case, the reviewer had to type 65 characters to indicate the changes. Authors and reviewers would benefit from using the same change representation in the text. Using, for example, the annotation conventions that we have discussed above, the same reviewer's annotation would look like:

> in a sandwich structure (~however,) the faces take the place

that is, 53 fewer characters. Unfortunately, reviewers and authors have to learn the conventions, an effort which would be justified for long revisions. However, this solution could have a secondary effect, especially on the author. It does not encourage a dialogue between author and the reviewer because it is impersonal. For example, example 15 does not involve any subject. Observe that in example 14, the pronoun *I* is used. Many readers would agree that example 15 could be interpreted as more remote and cold than example 14. On the other hand, a corrective annotation in which the reviewer addresses the author as is done in example 14, in a more personal and friendly manner, might result in better communication between the reviewer and the co-author, but this topic is outside the scope of this chapter.

5.5.2 *Reviewers Need to Express Uncertainty*

The question mark (?) was the second most commonly used sign by reviewers in their annotations. The question mark was used in the following format: **word**?, see example 16. In this way the reviewer showed uncertainty about the understanding of the context and whether the writer should accept the remark as valid. At the same time, the reviewer is inviting the writer to reflect on the context based on the word marked with the question mark. Here are some examples:

> During (in?) the sixties Sweden was in

>> I don't know if it's right or wrong, but I think it sounds better to say "suitable for mapping, monitoring. "

In some cases, the question mark was repeated more than once in a row (e.g.???), which suggests that probably the reviewers need to express the extent of their doubts. The primary reason for this could be that all the students were non-native speakers of English; the topics in the homework were highly specialized and questions are regarded as more like suggestions for change, rather than instructions (see example 17). They are also typical features of interpersonal communication rather than transactional and could serve as a means of establishing a dialogue between writer and reviewer. Furthermore, they signal respect for the writer and acknowledge that there might be other possible interpretations of the text.

Uncertainty was also manifested, however, when reviewers modified some of the suggested changes with words like *"perhaps"*, *"maybe"*, *"I would rather"*. This can also be seen as a negotiation protocol between the reviewer and the author.

5.5.3 End Comments Appended

Not surprisingly, general annotations were mainly given at the end of the text that the students had reviewed. An interesting observation is that the reviewers clearly labeled these annotations with such word as *"General"*. When the reviewer did not label them, blank lines (two-three lines) were left between the annotated text and the general commentary so that readers could identify the annotation as special. The next example was appended after a full integration of the original text:

> (*General: Clear and easy to understand. Would it be of interest to annotation the shape of the decline in spontaneous polarization with increasing temperature*)

General corrective annotations related to a specific paragraph were also written immediately after it and were delimited by parenthesis.

5.5.4 Justifying the Corrective Annotation

In many cases, the reviewers mentioned not only the error, but also a solution or the rule to be applied.

> Sides come in contact with English in several ways, (I would use colon here instead. You are introducing a series) through movies, TV (here must be a comma,) and recently also over the Internet.

In this example, the reviewer indicates the action and then supports the suggestion made. In the next example, the action to be taken is represented and explicitly indicates the rule that supports the correction:

> Some examples of such words used in Swedish are "site", "mail" (+,) and "freestyle".
> Rule: Use a comma before and, or, nor in a series.

From the annotations presented in this section we could discern the same model as that used in the spelling and grammar checker programs: the error is detected and diagnosed, then a solution is suggested and the rule given.

6. CONCLUSIONS

The main objective of this study was to observe how reviewers devise means to communicate their thoughts to the writer in electronic format using a Web-based tool, the DHS, that supported only plain text.

We found that few change representation artefacts could be satisfactorily expressed using plain text. Furthermore, these representations might be weak and misleading. Thus, a common system or standard for change representation needs to be created between reviewers and writers. For participants in the DHS, the log files of the case studies provide evidence that student regularly visited the model document giving the marking suggestions. Users should have easy and constant access to the convention for the change representation. The DHS fulfils this need by including a link to the conventions in the index-frame.

Reviewers clearly needed to have access to the original text on the screen when making corrective annotations. For example, they frequently quoted the beginning of the sentence referred to; wrote interlinear comments, even when the paste function was not available; invested great effort in cut-pasting using their mouse. In order to locate relevant sentences, reviewers often referred to their position in the paragraph (First, second, third, etc.) Particularly the adjectives "first" and "last" were extensively used, "last" more than "first". It is not clear whether this was because these sentences more often contain key information in a paragraph, or because reviewers found it difficult to allocate the correct number to the intervening sentences.

Tools oriented towards supporting corrective annotation should support automatic numbering of sentences and paragraphs in the original text. This will reduce possible conflict between reviewers and authors. Also, adequately supported line numbering could provide an alternative to the use of text markers.

Participants were using a simple interface. Only plain text was supported by the DHS. It is important to note that the tool imposed a limitation that participants were trying to cope with in order to perform the task in hand. When doing so, they were sketching tools or techniques that are relevant to the revision process in general. For example, using special characters to distinguish the original text and the annotated text, placing the annotated text in relation to the original text that suggested the split-screen and the aligned style of the annotation interface, indicated the need for a common ground on which to interpret the change representation, spelling and grammar checker program and models. We suggest that by presenting an initial prototype that enables users to perform the simplest operations with very simple tools, valuable information could be collected for the improvement of computer systems for writing.

ACKNOWLEDGMENT

This research has been supported by the Swedish Board for Industrial and Technical Development, the Swedish Transport and Ericsson Utvecklings AB. Thanks to Kerstin Severinson Eklundh, Olle Bälter, Ann Lantz, and Uwe Geist for comments on earlier versions of this chapter.

POPULAR CULTURE: A RESOURCE FOR WRITING IN SECONDARY ENGLISH CLASSROOMS

DOUGLAS MCCLENAGHAN* & BRENTON DOECKE**

*Viewbank College, Melbourne, Australia & ** Monash University, Melbourne, Australia

Abstract. This chapter explores how a secondary English teacher working with students aged 14-15 enabled them to use their popular cultural practices as a resource for writing. The chapter provides examples of conventional classroom situations in which this teacher created a space for students to bring their own semiotic resources to bear on the curriculum. It argues the need for English teachers to become sensitised to the complex literacy practices in which their students engage outside school and to the ways these practices are bound up with their social relationships and sense of identity. The discussion challenges conventional understandings of 'reading,' 'writing', 'speaking' and 'listening' as components of the English curriculum, arguing that a more contemporary understanding of literacy must take into account the multi-modal practices in which students engage in beyond school.

Keywords: Writing pedagogy, English teaching, popular culture, cultural studies

1. INTRODUCTION

Recent critiques of subject English claim that the subject has become increasingly irrelevant to the needs of secondary school students, and that 'new times' demand a new kind of English (Sefton-Green, 2000; Luke, 2001; Sefton-Green & Nixon, 2003). With respect to the writing curriculum, this means enabling students to investigate the formal possibilities of a more diverse range of genres than the school essay (or essay text literacy) (cf. Clyne, 1999; Teese, 2000: 17), thereby transcending the division between school literacy practices and the popular cultural practices in which teenagers engage outside school.

In the following chapter we discuss ways of using secondary students' out of school cultural practices as a resource for writing in secondary English classrooms. We argue that the knowledge of popular culture that adolescents bring with them

---

McClenaghan, D. & Doecke, B. (2004). Popular culture: A resource for writing in secondary education.
Rijlaarsdam, G. (Series Ed.) & Rijlaarsdam, G., Van den Bergh, H., & Couzijn, M. (Vol. Eds.). Studies in writing. Vol. 14, Effective learning and teaching of writing, 2nd Edition, Part 1, Studies in learning to write, 121 - 130.

into class, including the information and communication networks in which they operate, provides a framework for developing curriculum which they find both relevant and challenging. The curriculum development that we are proposing does not mean simply importing popular culture into the English classroom, as though anything can be gained by substituting Shakespeare with Kylie Minogue or Eminem. Nor are we suggesting that middle aged teachers should ape the enthusiasms of young people in some last ditched attempt to establish rapport with these 'aliens' in their classrooms (Green & Bigum, 1993). We are arguing for a more sophisticated understanding of the ways in which popular culture mediates the experiences of young people, requiring teachers to reaffirm English language classrooms as sites where students are able to negotiate issues of identity and meaning that are significant to them. To give adolescents a space to explore the formal possibilities of popular cultural practices is to develop a curriculum that equips them for the future.

One of the authors of this chapter is currently working in a government secondary school, and our discussion is based on research that he is conducting into his own teaching practice with two Year 9 classes in the middle school (ages 14-15). The secondary school at which Douglas teaches is located in a middle class suburb in Melbourne (what Australians call a 'leafy' suburb). The school population is moderately affluent, though some families are struggling. By examining some of the texts that Douglas's students have produced, we shall show how the semiotic potential of popular culture can been exploited in English classrooms, and how students' out-of-school literacy practices can become a valid frame of reference for understanding and developing their textual knowledge and literacy practices in school.

Whilst there is a growing research literature that acknowledges the significance of popular culture for young people, comparatively little of this draws on actual instances of classroom teaching. Nor has very much of this literature been written from the point of view of practitioner researchers who are systematically exploring how students might use their knowledge of popular culture within English classrooms. Accordingly, the following chapter comprises theoretical discussion involving the usual protocols for scholarly analysis alongside grounded accounts of classroom situations. The latter will be written in the first person singular and be anecdotal in character. We thereby hope to set up a generative tension between the possibilities opened up by theory and the dynamic of a classroom filled with adolescents. We also hope to point beyond the terms of our analysis and to gesture towards rich complexities that we are only beginning to understand.

CLASSROOM VIGNETTE ONE

DOUGLAS MCCLENAGHAN

Early in the semester I invited my Year 9 Literature class to create their own narratives. This was a special elective class for students with better than average language abilities, in which they enrolled in addition to their usual English class, and my long term goal was to introduce important narrative concepts, such as point of view and genre. Most students decided to write stories, but one group opted to produce a version of the television program Xena: The Warrior Princess and to videotape it. They called their version 'Tina' (which, along with Mandy and Kylie and Sharon and Lisa, is a very popular name in Australia, conjuring up stereotypical notions of growing up as a girl in the suburbs) and – as their title implies – their video was a parody of the original.

Only a few minutes into the tape and you encounter numerous intertextual references to Xena: the video uses the voiceover from the original ('In a time of evil warlords, gods and kings, a land in turmoil cried out for a hero. She was Xena, a mighty princess forged in the heat of battle...') while presenting small excerpts from the upcoming episode. Xena's ululating call is lampooned by Tina who gargles and then spits. When the story begins, the brave Tina and her sidekick are walking alone through the countryside (my school is located in an area where typical suburban dwellings exist on the fringes of large paddocks that have somehow escaped development). They do battle with an evil demon who challenges them, performing cartwheels and martial arts in much the same way that their Amazonian originals fight their way through each episode. All the text – characters, dialogue, action – is only meaningful if you know the original text they are parodying.

The students draw on a range of semiotic resources in their efforts to create a story that their peers might enjoy. They are assuming that their audience has a good knowledge of Xena, and so they freely incorporate imagery and other elements deriving from the original. At the same time they also draw on other conventions of film narrative that we have looked at in class – whenever the evil character appears, for example, eerie music is heard in the background. Xena has clearly been a significant part of their lives, including the ritual of viewing and talking about the latest episode each week. But – just as importantly – through their engagement with Xena and other popular cultural texts, the students appear to have developed a relatively sophisticated understanding of parody as a strategy for making meaning.

When I asked them what they thought they had achieved with the video, one student, perhaps indicating what she thought I wanted to hear, replied, 'We changed the genre from an action adventure into comedy'. Another student said, more matter-of-factly: 'It's a break from the rest of school. We don't get much opportunity to do videos and they're fun'. Another added: 'Working with friends'.

2. COMMUNICATIONAL WEBS

More often than not, teenagers' popular cultural pursuits remain the subject of an unofficial school curriculum, merely the stuff of casual conversations at recess time or breaks during official classroom work. You need only walk around the schoolyard at lunchtime to find teenagers talking about the latest episode of their favorite television show, swapping opinions about movies or CDs, or sms-ing friends at other schools. They are usually engaged in very animated conversations that contrast with the form and content of their exchanges in class. We need to find ways of identifying and using students' out-of-school literacy practices in class, revivifying the classroom as an environment for language and learning.

The concept of 'communicational webs' (Kress, 2000) is one way of naming the complex network of textual practices in which adolescents operate outside of school. The term refers to the different modes, for instance visual or print modes, and media, such as magazine or console, which teenagers use when they communicate with one another and try to make meaning out of their lives. Popular cultural texts – digital media texts, chat groups, the Internet – play a particularly significant role in adolescents' communicational webs. Such concepts are important, not simply because they highlight new forms of communication, but because they sensitize us to the ways in which literacy practices are bound up with the network of relationships in which people find themselves. Individuals do not simply 'read' or 'write' or 'speak' or 'listen' (i.e. the traditional way in which we conceptualize the components of the English curriculum); these acts are social practices, embedded in specific sets of social relationships, which are mediated in technologically complex ways (cf. Bennett, 1984; Frow, 1995). For adolescents, the immediate context for their exchanges is provided by the personal relationships they form at school, where expressions of taste and other preferences play a crucial role in affirming their burgeoning sense of identity and membership of a discourse community (Gee, 1990, 1991; Buckingham and Sefton-Green, 1994; Doecke and McClenaghan, 1998). But it is also important to acknowledge that those relationships – as mediated by new forms of communication – are part of a larger communicational network, involving people they do not know, and heterogeneous layers of (unauthored and unanchored) visual and print texts.

We are not making a technologist fetish of these new forms of communication, as though digital or silicon literacies have radically altered the consciousness of those who use them. The struggle to make connections between language and meaning remains what it has always been (cf. Doecke, 2002). Yet we are doing our students an immense disservice if we refuse to recognize the complexity of the meaning-making processes in which they engage, and fail to connect with what Julian Sefton-Green calls 'the incredible potential' of students' out-of-school cultural experiences (Sefton-Green, 2000). In the first instance, this can simply mean giving students a license to draw on the narratives and imagery that constitute their everyday world, as in the case of 'Tina', the Year 9 girl who became a Warrior Princess. It also means being sufficiently familiar with popular cultural forms to appreciate what students are trying to do when they use them in class and to help them achieve their aims. There can no longer any justification for extolling the value of 'high' culture as opposed to 'popular' culture – both are 'regimes of value' that require equally complex discriminations and judgments (cf. Frow, 1995). Sefton-Green tells the story of a student whose teacher was unable to understand a narrative he had written because its characteristic features (sudden shifts in point of view and an excessively complex plot) were completely foreign to him. Whereas they were not strange to the student, who had consciously set out to emulate the kinds of adventures he experienced when playing computer games (Sefton-Green, 2000). As teachers we need to recognize the complexities of such forms and their meaning-making potential.

CLASSROOM VIGNETTE TWO

DOUGLAS MCCLENAGHAN

James, a member of the same Year 9 class mentioned in the previous vignette, decided to write a film review for his final assessment task. To wrap up the semester, I had invited the class to reflect on the reading and writing that we had done together, taking up an aspect of this work and developing it in some way. This meant that they could write poetry or a short story, create a video – videos had become very popular after the success of 'Tina' – or possibly write a review of a novel or film. James's decision to review *The Ring* (a recent film starring Naomi Watts) was made only after he had seen the film – he did not initially watch the film with the intention of writing about it. We talked about what he might mention in the review and I suggested that he include something about his own response to the film, as well as giving readers an idea of the background and plot. I was interested, however, in seeing the form that his response would take without providing him with too much scaffolding about the characteristic features of movie reviews.

Here is an excerpt from James's review:

> This movie, though I hate to admit to it, got to me. I don't like the idea of a piece actually affecting my thoughts or actions, for that's all it is, acting, but somehow *The Ring* got past my barrier of rational thought and reasoning, and the more I thought about the movie, the more scary, well done and mysterious it seemed to become. I actually ventured back another day with a different friend, and ended up seeing the same film. Even though I'd seen it all before, and knew exactly what would happen where, it didn't stop my heart from racing a little faster and my hands from gripping the arm rests a little tighter. The first time around when I viewed the film the significance of what the story was about didn't quite sink in. I was with a group of friends and was talking to them partially throughout the movie. The complexity of the plot and spooky scenes didn't make an impression on me until I went back the second time. It so happened that when I met up with a friend a week later…. I found myself once again sitting in the darkness watching the same movie I had viewed only a week ago. This time however there was a distinct difference. The normal increased thudding of my heart and sweaty palms begun, yet with a frightfully cold edge. The second time the meaning and absolute psychotic evil behind the storyline came to life, and seemed to tear at me through the cinema screen, grabbing at me. I was whisked away into a land where for a moment I was petrified beyond belief, and for a split second I was there. Tingles of confusion and horror rushed up my spine making me shiver, stunning me, turning me to stone. The deeper the story delved into the realms of evil now awakened, the scarier the implications became. A girl of such wickedness, with thoughts so unimaginably disturbing, with desires so gruesome and horrific they were almost impossible to comprehend...As the movie drew to a bewilderingly disturbing close, I sat numb, with the fears of what had been unleashed in front of my eyes, still playing havoc in my head.

James's review shows a number of levels of response to the text (Thomson, 1987; Wilhelm, 1997). He foregrounds the fact that the film is only an artefact – 'for that's all it is, acting' – but then explores how he was nonetheless drawn into the narrative, in much the same way that the story itself turns on the ways in which people become transfixed by mysterious images and forces over which they have no control. James appreciates that there are multiple dimensions to the story, and that those dimensions only become available to readers in the process of viewing and then re-viewing the text. He understands that reading involves an interaction between readers and texts, and – what is more – that each reading is a product of the social context in which it occurs. It is noteworthy that when he 'actually ventured back another day' it was with 'a different friend', and so although his deeply felt emotions are intensely personal ('the meaning and absolute psychotic evil behind the story line came to life, and seemed to tear at me through the cinema screen'), they are also implicitly experiences that he has shared with his companion. Indeed, his written review might be read as the outcome of a shared experience, involving not simply viewing the film together, but the conversations that he had with his companion after the event. Writing the review is yet another attempt to construct a meaning out of his interaction with the text, whereby he is able both to relive the way he became totally immersed in the film and to reflect on the way the text worked. His review is itself a kind of performance, in which he relives the film's visceral effects.

3. TROUBLING BOUNDARIES

Writing of the quality that James has produced reminds us of the important role that schools play in providing students with a space in which to reflect on their cultural practices and thereby make the criteria that they apply when judging films, videos and other popular forms available for scrutiny. James does not name the textual dimensions that he explores in his review – indeed, there are surely good reasons why we would not encourage him to use literary theoretical language, as this would run the risk of conflating a capacity to mime a certain discourse with genuine understanding – but he nonetheless reveals a relatively sophisticated appreciation of the complex ways in which texts are 'framed' (MacLachlan & Reid, 1994)) and how readers construct meaning through their engagement with texts. Sefton-Green argues that despite the differences between school literacy and out-of-school literacy practices, there are 'huge areas of overlap, where popular culture and schooling actually reflect back on each other' (Sefton-Green, 2000: 15). James's work reveals a very powerful way in which schools can 'reflect back' on the world in which teenagers live, providing them with an opportunity to develop a meta-critical awareness of the cultural practices in which they engage. He would not have produced this writing if he had not been required to do so.

We do not, in short, wish to idealize popular cultural pursuits in comparison with the dull routines embodied in school knowledge. We think it is lamentable that students in Victorian schools are currently obliged to sit for pen and paper tests, and to demonstrate their literacy abilities by writing essays according to a narrowly prescribed formula that fails to do justice to the rich semiotic environment they inhabit (cf. Teese, 2000). But this is not to deny that students benefit from making their informal knowledge of popular cultural practices explicit in relatively formal ways when they are given this opportunity by their English teachers. James is simultaneously drawing on his out-of-school knowledge and producing what is, after all, an example of 'school writing' to be assessed by his teacher (Sheerin & Barnes, 1991). To be sure, James's review was also read and enjoyed by his peers – Douglas typically emphasizes the value of writing for real purposes and real audiences (cf. Langdon, 1961; Graves, 1984) – but he also had no difficulty in assessing this writing as a form of school knowledge. Indeed, it is a knowledge that James is only able to construct through school, through his interaction with his peers and a knowledgeable and an interested adult (Wells, 1999).

By crossing the boundary between school writing and students' out-of-school pursuits, we are also challenging other boundaries that currently shape English curriculum in Australian schools. The old notion of setting aside a discrete period of time for 'composition' was supposedly swept aside by Australian schools in the early 1980s, when many teachers (most notably primary school teachers) integrated writing with reading, speaking and listening and began to run their classrooms as writing workshops. This was part of the 'writing revolution', which also promoted the importance of allowing students time to draft their writing on topics of their own choice (Walshe, 1981) and to 'publish' their work for their peers and even larger audiences. Since then, the English curriculum has once again been segmented, with the specification of a range of 'outcomes' for reading, writing, speaking and listening, and an increasing emphasis on written exams in which students are required to produce formulaic pieces that supposedly reflect the totality of their literacy abilities. The notion of the classroom as a social space in which students are able to engage in the joint construction of knowledge (Mercer, 1995) has been rudely displaced by a narrowly psychologistic view of learning and a competitive academic curriculum that positions students as isolated individuals who simply swallow and then regurgitate information (Renshaw, 1998: 85).

James's writing has not, however, sprung fully formed from his head, but is the product of talk (both classroom talk and the talk in which he engaged with his companions after viewing *The Ring*). It is also noteworthy that his writing is something that he has been prompted to write in response to a film, and is therefore an excellent example of what can happen when we combine reading (or viewing) with writing. But we especially wish to emphasize the ways in which a productive writing classroom allows students to engage in small group discussions and thereby benefit from sharing their ideas and making their knowledge public. Recently, Australian English teachers, in an attempt to develop professional standards for accomplished teachers of English in primary and secondary schools, have affirmed that 'talk is at the centre of English curriculum and pedagogy' (see www.stella.org.au). This sounds like a brave statement within the context of the utterly sterile policy and curriculum environment in which Victorian English teachers are currently obliged to operate, but nonetheless remains an eloquent attempt to affirm the importance of providing students with classrooms that are interactive and democratic, a site for the exchange of ideas and the joint construction of knowledge.

Such classrooms promise to provide a space in which students can engage in literacy practices that match the complexities of the practices in which they engage outside school. It is not simply a matter of setting up an environment in which students can freely engage in speaking and listening and reading and viewing in an effort to produce writing, but of recognizing that their 'writing' itself is likely to take a multi-modal form. The literacy practices in which they engage outside school are typically multi-media texts involving juxtapositions of written text, images and sound. The 'writing' they produce in school should likewise take a diverse range of forms and combine a diverse range of modes.

CLASSROOM VIGNETTE THREE

DOUGLAS MCCLENAGHAN

I am sitting with my Year English 9 class in the Textiles room (great place for teaching English!) period five on a Friday afternoon. This is a compulsory English class, consisting of students with a wide range of abilities who evince varying degrees of engagement in schooling, not the special elective class that I have described in previous vignettes. We have managed to shoehorn a TV and VCR in between some tables and have re-arranged the room so that everyone can see. Three boys are about to play us a video of their 'crime story'. The class has been writing crime stories for several weeks and today is the day for submitting them. All the other students have submitted written pieces but these three boys decided to make a video: David, who does little but talk to his mates and wander around the room – his parents despair of him; James, who is clever, wants to do well, and will work at home, but mainly socializes in class; and Georgi, who is irritatingly garrulous and inattentive, bugs other students about what they're doing, and only ever partially completes tasks. The boys had filmed their video on weekends, while their class time was used to 'plan' and 'script' (their words, not mine) the piece and to reflect on the previous weekend's filming adventures.

The video is loosely modeled on the Arnold Schwarzenegger film *Predator*. The boys play three soldiers who are in the jungle on a secret mission to find and destroy a drug baron's hideout. Along the way they are ambushed, have to struggle against the harsh elements and the terrain, and suffer wounds inflicted by their enemies. The twist in the plot is that Georgi's character is a really a traitor who is leading them into a trap. The climax happens when he is eliminated and the drug baron (played by a student in another class) is killed. At the end the two remaining comrades limp away, bloodied but victorious.

Ostensibly the video portrays a very limited and stereotypical masculinity and a simplistic, predictable plot. The boys are dressed in army gear, they brandish weapons and most of the action involves stalking, shooting, screaming, flexing muscles, with the goodies finally triumphing over the baddies. At first sight an outside observer might deplore the video, the students, and their teacher for such superficial and unenlightened educational practice.

But a glance around the room while the video is playing suggests other possible readings. The class are all watching intently and laughing. The video's creators provide a running commentary. There is plenty of self-mockery as well as 'insider' observations on the making of the video. Everyone is involved in the experience; authors and audience alike are part of a community event. Far from passively watching the video, the audience is jointly constructing meaning. They are reading the video as a parody: David does a good Arnie accent, the toy guns are hilariously inadequate in size and sound. One could easily mount an argument that the video is subverting a sexist stereotype, and that the boys have exploited familiar generic conventions to comic effect.

I am especially impressed by the manner in which the three boys have stuck to this task – a first for Georgi and David. They've found a way to engage with the English curriculum on their terms, making use of a particular textual form to create and present a sense of self. Their work is as much about social identity as it was about telling a crime story. They have effectively explored a popular stereotypical notion of what it means to be a male and opened it up for public scrutiny.

4. CONCLUSION

It would be a very limited kind of sociological analysis that tried to explain the nature of school by focusing on the personal relationships enacted there. We know that historically schools have played a key role in maintaining the existing class structure, and that our relationships with students are shaped by larger social determinants. We know that there is often a difference between what teachers imagine they are doing and what they actually achieve, and that the 'hidden curriculum' continues to produce unequal social outcomes even when teachers consciously espouse social democratic values. Students, too, experience a complex interplay between their values and aspirations and the situations in which they find themselves when they go to school.

Images of schools as bureaucratic and uncaring institutions proliferate in popular culture, often as material for parody or satirical comment. We need only think of the jaded old hands who teach Bart and Lisa Simpson, or the caricatures of teachers in movies like *Clueless*. When teachers are portrayed as caring and concerned about the welfare of their students, they often seem naïve and out of touch, as with the hippy teacher in *Beavis and Butthead Do America*, who imagines that he can create a warm and caring environment by strumming his guitar and singing folk songs to his students.

However, English teachers in Australia and elsewhere can still legitimately claim that historically they have been committed to an ethic of pastoral care and that they have experienced some success in implementing it – indeed, in significant respects this has been their special province. Over the years, their classrooms have provided places for students to clarify their values and beliefs in a way that other subjects do not necessarily permit. As Ian Hunter argues, English teachers have traditionally given students an opportunity to fashion a sense of identity under their careful surveillance (Hunter, 1988; cf. Patterson, 2000; Reid, 2003; Doecke 2002; Doecke and McKnight, 2003). Hunter's analysis is flawed, because this is all that he sees happening, at the expense of acknowledging the social conflict occurring both within and around schools as ideological state apparatuses (cf. Althusser, 1971). He is locked into a Foucauldian analysis that focuses on the production of a citizenry without giving due weight to the complex ways in which individuals resist the forms of subjectification or interpellation they experience in schools and he is completely blind to the role that schools have played in 'making a difference' with respect to the distribution of wealth and the maintenance of existing class relations (Connell et al., 1982).

These contradictory accounts of schooling mean that the image of a classroom community that we have presented in the last vignette should not be taken at face value. We have, indeed, built in detail (the fact that the lesson is taking place in the Textiles room and that some of these boys usually behave in a fairly distracted and disruptive manner) which gestures towards social issues that we do not pretend to have resolved. The challenge remains as to whether the boys' satisfaction in making their video will motivate them to embrace other dimensions of the English curriculum (McClenaghan, 2001). We are also mindful of the fact that confronting issues of gender or racist stereotypes can never be straightforward, especially when you are working within a community which embraces those stereotypes.

Nonetheless we wish to conclude by noting that all the creative work we have been reviewing is the product of social relationships within the classroom as exemplified by the way in which the boys' video was completed by their audience's response to it. Those relationships extend beyond school where they are mediated by the popular cultural pursuits and literacy practices in which students engage in their daily life – you obviously need to have seen Arnie Schwarzenegger in *Predator* to understand the text which the boys have produced. However, leaving aside the need for everyone – teachers included – to be culturally literate, the focus of our energies as English teachers is firstly to ensure that the social relationships between students provide a context for them to participate in class and to produce 'school writing' (Sheeran and Barnes, 1991) that is meaningful to them. In saying this we are not really saying anything radically new, but situating our own work within the rich tradition of 'growth' pedagogy to which we have just alluded, which emphasizes the need for English teachers to be 'totally accepting' of the experiences that students bring with them into class (Britton, 1971), and to break down the barriers between what Barnes calls 'school knowledge' and 'action knowledge' (Barnes, 1976; cf. Doecke & McClenaghan, 1998).

But it also seems important for us to finally reiterate that the texts which these students have produced are indeed a form of 'school writing', and that this is not necessarily a negative description. Much of the discussion about school writing over the past couple of decades – from Dixon's account of the way in which students are able to draw on their experiences as a resource for writing to Graves' arguments about treating students as 'real' authors – is structured around a binary opposition between the artificial and conventionalized nature of schooling (where 'shades of the prison house' begin to close around us) and the 'natural' pursuits and relationships that people otherwise enjoy (Dixon, 1967; Graves, 1984; Reid, 2002, 2003; Wordsworth, 1950). When we reflect on the work which these Year 9 students have produced, we judge it to be a legitimate extension of the cultural practices in which they engage outside school and a form of 'knowledge' that might be validated in conventional terms.

We feel that we have much to learn from these students, as they try to make school into a congenial space. This is not to deny that sometimes they find themselves in conflict with the regulatory purposes of the adults who are in control, or that for some of these students school remains a profoundly alienating experience, but generally speaking they embrace the opportunity that school provides them to meet and talk and collectively make sense of their lives. Douglas's vignettes show students operating with a degree of autonomy that enables them both to meet accepted learning outcomes and to engage in tasks that are meaningful and relevant to them. This points beyond simple binary oppositions between school literacy practices and out-of-school literacy practices, and constructions of adolescents as 'digiteens' or 'aliens in the classroom' (Green & Bigum, 1993), as though an unbridgeable gulf exists between teachers and these new creatures of a postmodern age. Teachers and students alike can jointly commit themselves to enacting curriculum that is a meaningful form of communication (Barnes, 1976).

THE GARDEN OF THOUGHT – ABOUT WRITING POEMS IN UPPER SECONDARY SCHOOL

PER-OLOF ERIXON

Umeå University, Sweden

Abstract. This chapter takes as its starting point a 10-year-project in the upper secondary school in the north of Sweden, called "The Garden Of Thought", which involved students in creative writing such as poetry, as part of the ordinary school curriculum. One of the main questions was whether the students accept creative work of this kind as part of their schoolwork, since a poem can be highly personal, involving love and the deepest feelings.
A recent study of mother tongue teaching in Sweden shows that students mainly practise what the author calls "internal schools genres", i.e. genres that are constructed for the purpose of the school alone (Nyström, 2000). It also shows that many students write in their free time. Students outside the boundaries of the school use more creative genres, such as poetry and song lyrics. It is suggested that creative writing activities should be a part of the ordinary school curriculum. The question I pose in this chapter is, thus, how do young people themselves feel about these forms of creative writing in school? Are they prepared to break down existing borders between their schooling and their private lives?
In my study it is evident that writing poetry could become a common part of mother-tongue teaching. At the same time there are evident differences between writing in the privacy of home and in the public space of school. Students, it seems, develop a range of strategies to deal with this dualism.

Keywords: teaching poetry, upper secondary school, private, public, teaching writing and reading, Habermas, Ziehe, Sweden

1. BACKGROUND

The Swedish National Curriculum of 1994 (The Ministry of Education and Science, 1994) states that teaching in mother tongue at upper secondary school will increase students' ability to speak, read, and write Swedish as well as improve their knowledge of literature. Language and literature constitute the core of the school subject,

---

Erixon, P.-O. (2004). The Garden of Thought: About writing poems in upper secondary school.
Rijlaarsdam, G. (Series Ed.) & Rijlaarsdam, G., Van den Bergh, H., & Couzijn, M. (Vol. Eds.). Studies in writing. Vol. 14, Effective learning and teaching of writing, 2nd Edition, Part 1, Studies in learning to write, 131 - 140.

Swedish. In order to obtain these skills, it is proposed that all students should be able to read and write texts of different genres.

Nyström (2000) studied the teaching of writing in today's Swedish upper secondary school (16-19 years old). Although it is not compulsory only a small percentage of the youngsters of this age do not attend the Swedish upper secondary school, which is currently organized into different three-year-programs. In one sense all the programs prepare students for university studies. Practically, only two of them are university-oriented. The other programs are more or less vocational. Nyström's study indicates that writing in all programs is dominated by a small number of "internal school genres", i.e. analyzing essays and factual texts, all in prose.

Nyström shows, however, that more that 50 percent of students also write texts in their free time. From a genre perspective, these text types differ from texts produced in school. The out-of-school material is dominated by other genres, such as poems and song texts. From these results Nyström claims that increasing private written genres such as poems in schooling might develop students' ability to write.

This notion, however, is not unproblematic. Chaib (1996) studied students involved in amateur theatre activities in their free time. More than half make clear that amateur theatre activity is strongly connected with leisure activity and therefore not possible to include in ordinary school activities. The reason given, as one of the students says, is that it would "destroy" much of what the amateur theatre activity symbolizes for them.

This chapter takes its starting point in Nyström's conception, i.e., that poems and songs written by students in their leisure time offer a potential which could be taken up by schools. The question I pose is, how do young people themselves feel about this? Are they prepared to break down existing boundaries between their schooling and their private lives?

The focus of the chapter is a 10-year-project in the upper secondary school in the north of Sweden, called "The Garden Of Thought", which involved students in creative writing such as poetry, as part of the ordinary school curriculum.

2. THE GARDEN OF THOUGHT

A school priest originally initiated The Garden Of Thought project. His purpose was to break down the walls, as he saw it, between the church and the school. The essence of the project was to give students at upper secondary school (for 16-19 year olds) the opportunity to express their existential thought in the form of poetry. That was in the year of 1991 and the title of the first published poetry collection from the project was *About life, about death, about love, about meaning.*

Results from my own study, on which this chapter is based, show that the project, however, never became the platform for existential issues as originally intended (Erixon, 2003). Issues more closely related to life and love have dominated the material over the years.

Generally girls, as compared to boys, have been more successful in getting their poems published. The process of selection has been carried out with the intention of enabling different categories of students to get their poems published, in terms both of gender and program. During a particular year, girls may dominate the collection. In another year, there may be more contributions from boys. In one year students may predominate from academic programs; in another year, more contributions may come from students on vocational programs.

There seems to be a strong consensus among the teachers in the project group. Emphasis may be different in different aspects of the project, but generally there is agreement on basic issues, such as that the word should be in the centre of the project and also that all students should be involved and able to express themselves. As an example, a poem, by a boy, "Varför" [Why], from the first collection is quoted below:

<blockquote>

Varför...   [Why...

Vi föds   We are born
Mognar   Mature
lär oss   we learn
frågar   ask
Varför   Why
Varför lever vi?   Why do we live
Arbete   Work
Kärlek   Love
Äktenskap   Marriage
Ett barn föds   A child is born
Det frågar...   It asks
Varför   Why
Vi säger därför   We say because
det växer   it grows
vi åldras   we grow older
det utvecklas   it develops
pension   pension
vi dör   we die
de frågar varför   they ask why
Varför...   Why...]

</blockquote>

As a part of the study, a questionnaire was distributed to approximately 900 students, which showed that more than two thirds of students have a fairly positive attitude to reading poetry. Gender differences are, however, significant. Girls tend to prefer reading poetry more than boys. Approximately 50 percent of girls and only 21 percent of boys claim a positive attitude towards reading poetry. More girls write poetry also. 50 percent of girls, and only 14 percent of boys, claim to write poetry either in school or in their own free time.

This chapter is, as a part of the study, based upon individual interviews with eleven students that participated in the project in the year of 2000-2001. I met these students when they just had handed in their contribution to the project. I was interested in their views and opinions about the project. Sometimes our conversation became a little too personal. The students sometimes hesitated when it came to more personal perspectives and when questions about their participation focused, more precisely, on what type of poem they had written etc. Despite these obvious methodological difficulties, it was possible to complete the interviews more or less successfully.

The students' attitudes towards poetry can be divided into three different groups or categories: girls on university oriented theoretical programs, girls on vocational programs and boys. In order to identify the students and what category they belonged to I gave them Shakespearian names that start with the first letter of the words theoretical, vocational and boys, i.e., t, v and b. The girls' names are thus Tamora, Thaisa and Titania, Valeria, Viola, Violenta, Virgilia and Volumnia, altogether eight girls. The boys' names are Brandon, Bates and Benvolio. Of these three boys, only Brandon is on a theoretical program.

3. POETRY AS A GENRE

One of the most important subjects for poetry is love. It is as impossible to imagine poetry without love, as it is to imagine love without poetry (Bergsten, 1994). The first and perhaps most famous poet in ancient Greece was a woman, Sapho (600 AD) (Bergsten, 1994).

However, it is a man, Orfeus, who has come to embody poetry in the western history of literature. The "Orfeus ideal" stresses the poet's extraordinary function as a medium of unknown dimensions of reality. Algulin (1977) studied the retreat from this poetry ideal during the 20th century in Swedish history of literature. The "Orfeus retreat" could be described as a climb down from those high notions that have been given to the poet in western culture. This retreat includes a transformation from a vertical to a horizontal notion of the world. One consequence is that the metaphysical and divine forms of apprehension are transformed into more human forms of apprehension. Algulin identifies this transformation as a "literary democratization process".

At the same time as poetry to a certain extent and with a post modernistic vocabulary is connected with the "high", of which the Orfeus ideal is an example, there is also another side that connects poetry with the natural and the "low" (Boëthius, 1990). In this latter respect Tjukovskij (Cukovkij) (1976) argues that the verse or the poem is normal for children's language and a natural way of expressing feelings and thoughts. Even before a child is a year old and still not able to talk, you can see how he/she enjoys listening to poetry. When it comes to the upbringing of a child it is therefore important to make use of this "poetic period" in a child's life.

The embryo of the rhyme is, according to Tjukovskij (1976), the two infant words "da" and "ma". The two words mummy and daddy become an "archetype for all dualities and all forms of symmetry". When children write poetry it should not be regarded as nonsense. The tendency to have one's head turned by melodious sounds has been expressed in nursery rhymes all over the world.

In summary, poetry is considered to shape or present a personal experienced reality. It conveys a message that cannot be conveyed in other ways. Conceptually, poetry can only be understood intuitively, associated with the language of emotion and regarded as a natural expression of feelings. It is a fusion of experience and reflection, established by an associative process under the conscious level.

This notion is formally connected with the idea that poetry conveys knowledge that nothing else can convey. Each element affords a unique semantic loading, due to the restrictions that are laid upon a poetic text. The poem expresses ideas in an indirect way by displacements in the text. The intuitive and immediate side of poetry is not far from Tjukovksij's idea that verse is a natural expression for children's feelings and thoughts.

The eleven students in this study appear to have an intuitive opinion about what a poem is, in terms of both content and form. Their definitions are close to definitions in dictionaries. Poetry is the direct expression of the feeling and the thought. Poetry delivers knowledge and experiences that are difficult to clothe in other literary forms such as short stories etc.

Generally, girls stress that poetry is a tool for expressing feeling and thoughts. Girls on theoretical programs express this opinion using a general and abstract language. In that respect they express a distance to writing poetry. Girls on vocational programs tend to take as their starting point, definitions from their own experiences. Their language is less elaborate. There are also clear differences between girls and boys. Girls tend to take notice of the content of poetry, while boys focus on the formal side of poetry.

4. POEM WRITING IN SCHOOL

Theoretically, it is possible to locate the project *The Garden of Thought* within Habermas' (1998) work on different types of models for the public sphere. During the twentieth century the border was dissolved between what he calls the public sphere and the intimate sphere, meaning that it in modern society is difficult to tell the difference between what is private and what is public.

Ziehe (1989) claims that during the modernization of society in the late twentieth century schooling moved from one point as "cold", i.e., a dehumanized body, to another point as "made hot", i.e., more personal and subjective. This leads to a paradox: teachers who want to improve the dehumanized situation are compelled to develop their personal side and ability. They thus become "relation workers" (p 128). The project *The Garden of Though* could be understood also in this context, since the students as well as the teachers, are expected to focus on the personal.

To write poetry in school is, in itself, a social activity that can be explained in linguistic and pragmatic terms. A prerequisite for a communicative action, if it is to be experienced as meaningful, is that the action is not carried out by compulsion, but with free will. Meaningfulness is necessary for motivation. Teachers are naïve, Berge (1988) claims, if they think that students primarily want to express something that is personal, important and meaningful to them. Students write in school because they are obliged to do so, not necessarily because they want to. Within a more enlarged socio cultural context, students also practice certain social roles when they write. To have competence in a school genre means also having a competence in certain social roles.

According to Habermas (1996) the active subject intervenes in the world in order to obtain a certain goal: strategic, ritual or communicative. A "strategic" act aims at obtaining a specific condition. The way this is reached is subordinated to the goal, such as in the case of most students getting high grades. A second type of action is the "ritual", which is an action for its own sake. The purpose is to participate for the sheer joy or benefit. The third type is the "communicative" action, which focuses on the medium itself. An act of communication aims at getting the receiver of the action to understand. To talk or discuss is not always a communicative action. Politicians, for example, may sound as if they are communicating, while they actually are acting strategically.

5. THE PRIVATE AND THE PUBLIC

It became clear that the students were very positive about *The Garden of Thought* project, even if some were more enthusiastic than others. This is also the case when it comes to the issue of privacy. Superficially, students seem to think that it is a good thing to introduce private things into schooling, but after some thought it becomes evident that students are not unconditional about this.

Tamora describes the relation between students and teachers today as quite "tight". Students and teachers have a close relationship with each other in today's Swedish upper secondary school. This is positive, she maintain:

> Man måste ju kunna diskutera med en lärare och lärare måste samtidigt kunna ha förståelse för en elev när han kanske inte har lyckats så bra. Jag tycker det är bra med en tight relation. Det är positivt.

> [You must be able to discuss with a teacher and the teacher must at the same time be able to understand when a student perhaps does not manage that well. I think it is a good thing having a tight relationship. It is positive.]

As a student, she continues, you are prepared to give of your best if you get a response. If not, you withdraw into yourself. The student's attitude appears to depend much on the teacher. If the aim is to elicit emotional poems, teachers need to be more intimate themselves. If a teacher just "stands there", as Tamora expresses it, there will be no "deep" poems. There are certainly differences between poems, and this depends much on the teacher, Tamora claims.

According to Tamora most students seem not to be aware of how "serious" many poems are. Since poems within the project are sent in anonymously, neither school friends nor teachers know or seem to care. It sounds quite mean, she says, but that is the way it is.

Tamora also considers that certain themes are taboo, for example suicide poems or poems about homosexuality or racist poems. Where poems about suicide and homosexuality are concerned, self-censorship is active. In regard to racist poems, teachers censor what should be published or not.

Thaisa thinks that students feel the same whether poems are written at school or in free time. Perhaps, she says, students are more careful when they write in school; they are more aware of how and what they write. They work harder with the poems; they think more about what words to choose etc.

Hemma kan man skriva och om man inte tycker om dikten kan man slänga den. I skolan ska man själv tycka om det också. Jag tror man kan vara lika ärlig och privat i skolan som på fritiden.

> [At home you can write and if you don't like the poem you can throw it away. In school you should also like it. I think you can be as honest and private in school as in your free time.]

Therefore, she finds it positive to incorporate some parts of her private life in ordinary school activities. She finds this more interesting than, as she expresses it, "doing grammar all the time". Students get to know themselves better as well as their school friends.

Emotions, Thaisa suggests, should indeed be incorporated into school activities. Privacy and school are "intertwined". It is, however, not necessarily so that a good relationship with a teacher automatically leads to an honest poem. It depends on the person who writes the poem as well, Thaisa says.

When Titania writes a poem, she wants other people to read it. She wants to share it with others in order to know how they perceive different things. It is a natural thing for her to do, she explains. She argues, however, that students do not write poems at school as private as those written at home.

> Jag tror inte det handlar om vad man skriver om, utan det är väl mer hur du skriver och vad du säger. För det är ju mycket du kan säga om det mesta. Och det är ju bara hur personlig prägel man sätter på det egentligen och hur utelämnande man är. Det är ju som lättare, de flesta dikter, det som är skönt när man har skrivit, men man kan låta dom ligga ett tag. Så kan man läsa igenom den sen och okej, det var så och så då. Då är det som lugnt. Då kanske det inte alls är så längre. /.../ En personlig dikt är lättare att lämna ifrån sig om man har distans till den. Innan man har fått distans känns det som fortfarande att det ligger för nära och säger för mycket om en själv.

> [I don't think it is a matter of what you write about, rather how you write and what you say. Because, there are a lot of things you could say about many things. And it is just a matter of how personal you are and what you leave out. It is like easier, most poems, it is good when you have written, but you can leave them for a while. So you can read it through later and ok, it was like that then. It is cool. Then it is perhaps not like that anymore./.../ A personal poem is easier to hand over if you have a distance. Before you have distance there is still a feeling that it is too close and that it says too much about you.]

Titania claims that she feels more sensitive when she has just finished a poem. After a while, it matters less. Therefore it is not a matter of *what* you write about in your poem, but rather *how*, she says. The crucial thing is the personal mark that is set on the poem.

It is easier to hand over a personal poem, according to Titania if students are able to see the poem in perspective. Otherwise, it is too close and it reveals too much. There has to be a period of time between writing a poem and its publication. It is only after a couple of months, Titania suggests, that a poem is "ready" to be published.

One of the girls studying on a vocational program, Valeria, expresses enjoyment at writing poems in school. Then you learn how people feel, she says. There is a "chance" that you feel less alone when you get the opportunity to read other people's poems. In addition to giving students the opportunity to express themselves, poetry writing in school also gives the teachers an image of how students think.

Valeria claims that there are certain differences between writing poems at home and school. At school, students tend to write more generally; they are happy or sad, in love or not in love etc. At home, students might write about certain experiences, such as their experience of bullying. Apart from bullying, she says, writing about serious issues such as racism and phobia, homosexuality, is not very appealing.

When it comes to content and form, Volumnia, another girl on a vocational program, does not think that there are differences between poems written in school and poems written in free time. You can always be anonymous, she says. Her best friends have already read her poems, as have people that she does not know or who do not know her, she says.

Violenta claims that she is never satisfied with poems that have been selected for publications. She finds those poems _too_ personal. "You certainly do not want to reveal things to people you do not know". In that respect *The Garden of Thought* was terrible for her. She argued that if students write good poems from their hearts and manage to get them accepted for a poetry collection, it is "hard". In school she would rather not write 'mean' poems or "suicidal" poems, or even love poems. 'It is to leave out too much', she says. Violenta continues:

> När man skriver för nöjes skull, privat, tänker man inte på om det är rätt till exempel. Det blir lätt att man blir lite manisk när man ska skriva för skolan, men i skolan sätts ju betyg och därför vill man att det ska se bra ut! Man kan därför sitta och jobba länge med en och samma dikt.
>
> [When you write for pleasure, you are not aware if the content and form are right. You can easily get "manic" from writing poems in school. In school you get grades and therefore you want it to look all right. You therefore work harder with a poem in school.]

One of the three boys, Benvolio, has a more neutral attitude to the project. He says that he cannot write about love because he is not on the "front line" when it comes to girls. "You must have experienced it before you write about it", he claims. Even if he was lucky enough to be in the front line, he thinks that he would probably not write love poems in school. His strategy is to be "partly serious" about the project. His only poem is therefore about a motor scooter.

Brandon occasionally writes poems in his free time. Poetry writing is a means of self-expression. The project, he suggests, could help students to see that poetry writing is not difficult. It is just a matter of practice. It is clear, he suggests, "that you are more private in those poems you write in your free time." At the same time he places restrictions on himself when he writes poems in school.

> Jag försöker inte att vara så djup som möjligt. Man kan få intrycket av dikter att de ska vara väldigt djupa och känslomässiga.
>
> [I try not to be too deep as is possible. You easily get the impression that poems should be deep and sensitive.]

Both Brandon and Benvolio imply that they are not attracted to writing "deep" or serious poems. The best thing about the project, according to Benvolio, is that students get an opportunity to practise writing, not that they share their thoughts and feelings with other people.

To Bates, however, it is clear that poem writing is deeply personal. He argues that it is up to each individual how "deep" he/she wants to go. He finds anonymity helpful. It is then possible for students to write better poems and perhaps more honest poems. "There are certain things that you do not write about when you write poems in school". He suggests that someone who is a little bit more retiring than he is, may find it hard to express himself or herself in the form of a poem.

6. SUMMARY

Students' experiences from a project in the north of Sweden, *The Garden of Thought*, provide the basis for this chapter. A key issue is what attitudes students take to writing poems, in their free time as compared to in school.

The study confirms that love is an important subject for poetry. The girls are in general more positive about the project. The boys are more expectant. The more academic girls tend to focus on the formal side of poetry. Girls with a vocational orientation, in contrast, tend to focus on poetry and its expressiveness.

The students generally indicate that there is a difference between writing poetry in school and in their free time, and in particular that there are subjects which are not acceptable when writing poetry in school, such as suicide, sexuality and racism. Writing poetry in school also involves more effort.

Nevertheless, both girls and boys seem positive about introducing private issues into school life, but they have different perspectives and stress different things. Academic girls stress the relationship between teachers and students, and place the responsibility on teachers for the quality of student poetry. According to the students', their openness implies that teachers are also prepared to draw on their private experiences. Lack of intimacy in school, according to this point of view, is dependant not primarily on the students', but rather on the teachers' lack of will.

Girls on vocational programs draw more on their own experiences such as if they are "in love" or if they are sorry about something etc. Poetry writing in school tends to be more private for these girls. Boys distance themselves from poetry projects such as *The Garden of Thought*. They seem less willing to expose their inner feelings in poetry and not being "serious" is one aspect of this.

What conclusions can be drawn from these findings? Are poetry projects like *The Garden of Thought* a potential for teaching about writing in school? It is clear that schools could become an arena where writing poetry is a common part of mother-tongue teaching. At the same time there are evident differences between writing in the privacy of the home and in school. Students, it seems, develop a range of strategies to deal with this.

We have seen that students already when they start at upper secondary school, or even earlier, are socialized into a culture that we may call the culture of *The Garden of Thought*. The students know well before they become involved into the project in their second year what they are expected to do; what types of themes are available, what they are expected to write about and not least what they are not supposed to write about.

There are consequently "presuppositions" in those themes that are presented to the students each year. As members of a communicative community they are expected to agree to them. If students do not accept these "presuppositions", they do not participate in the activity.

Participation in the project should partly be regarded as a ritual activity. Sisters, brothers and friends have participated and therefore certain individuals are expected to participate. There is no other way. Students simultaneously perform ritual action and strategic actions. They know that the project is a part of a course, which affects their grades. From another perspective the students also perform a communicative action – they want to communicate.

Students thus participate in different actions when they participate in *The Garden of Though*. They communicate not only with their classmates and teachers. Some of the poems are published in a book. Therefore the students also strive to communicate with an anonymous audience.

The Garden of Thought is oriented towards communication. Students are expected to communicate with other students, teachers and an audience outside the school. Participation also involves other sorts of actions, ritual as well as strategic. Generally these are the circumstances in which students participate in the project, even if they are not totally aware of this.

The students make it clear that they each have a special place of their own, to which nobody has access, least of all the teachers. Despite this they seem willing, to some extent, to tear down existing divisions between the private and the public, of which school is a part.

Similar projects in other schools might therefore use expressive writing as a potential for teaching writing in school. We have, however, to accept that genuine communication between students may be less easy to establish. As a result of projects like *The Garden of Thought* ritual activities are expressed alongside elements of communication. That is certainly a step in the right direction.

AUTHOR'S NOTE

Thanks to the students interviewed: Brandon, Bates, Benvolio, Tamora, Thaisa, Titania, Valeria, Viola, Violenta, Virgilia, and Volumnia.

USING A STRUCTURED WRITING WORKSHOP TO HELP GOOD READERS WHO ARE POOR WRITERS

RONALD L. HONEYCUTT & RUIE J. PRITCHARD

Wake County Public School System & North Carolina State University Raleigh, North Carolina, USA

Abstract. This study explores the influence of a Writing Academy on the strategy applications, perceptions, and emotions that good readers who are poor writers experience when writing narrative text on-demand. Eleven fifth grade students (12 years old) were identified as good readers who are poor writers based on their academic history of passing the state-required End-Of-Grade Reading Test when they were in the third and fourth grades, but failing the state-required Fourth Grade Narrative Writing Test. Each subject participated in a specially-designed 16 week Writing Academy. Special Needs students who exhibited an identified behavioral or learning disability participated in the class but not in the study. This qualitative study included individual in-depth interviews and focus group discussions. Data for each student consisted of interviews, teacher annotations from conferences, writing portfolio, self-assessment writing, and scores on the *Writer Self-Perception Scale*. These data were systematically analyzed using the constant comparative method, and classified according to their relationship to two construct categories that emerged (a basic profile of good readers who are poor writers, and the impact of the Writing Academy), and/or to a theme category (strategies, common experiences, and emotions). Results indicate that good readers who are poor writers (a) lack knowledge and application of both prewriting strategies and story grammar schema to plan and generate narrative texts; (b) do not employ self-regulation strategies to evaluate and to revise the texts they compose; (c) are inhibited in their writing by strong, negative emotions coupled with the perception of themselves as poor writers; and (d) benefit from participating in a structured writing workshop aimed at addressing the above mentioned problems.

Keywords: Writing self-perception scale, special needs education, writing workshop, prewriting strategies, story grammar schema, self-regulation strategies, negative emotions

1. INTRODUCTION

Researchers and practitioners have been intrigued by the seemingly paradoxical inability of good readers who have no learning or behavioral disabilities to master basic writing skills and demonstrate proficiency when completing on-demand writ-

---

Honeycutt, R. L., & Pritchard, R. J. (2004). *Using a structured writing workshop to help good readers who are poor writers.*
Rijlaarsdam, G. (Series Ed.) & Rijlaarsdam, G., Van den Bergh, H., & Couzijn, M. (Vol. Eds.). *Studies in writing. Vol. 14, Effective learning and teaching of writing, 2nd Edition, Part 1, Studies in learning to write,* 141 - 150.

ing tasks. A typical example of writing from such a student is provided below. The student, whom we shall call Jim, had successfully passed the state-mandated Reading Tests in third (approximately age 8) and fourth (age 9) grades, yet failed the state Narrative Writing Test in fourth grade. His story is written in response to the prompt to "Write a story about a time that you had fun." The prompt was designed to elicit a personal narrative response in 50 minutes. Because two raters scored his paper below passing, Jim became a participant in the Writing Academy. Following is the transcription of Jim's story, with errors intact.

> "Nice job." I told my friend Matt as I slapped him on the back. We all looked up at the scoreboard where a strike sign had just come up under the fifth collum for Matt. I was at 45 points and Matt was at 60 with his strike. It was my turn to bowl and I got a spare that made me excited and took my points to 57. On the sixth frame I bowled a spare and so did Matt which took me to sixty eight and Matt to seventy two. Seventh frame I got a 9 total and Matt got a 9 which took me to seventy seven and Matt to eighty one. Eighth frame I got a 6 and Matt a 5, Me 83, Matt 86. Nineth frame I got a strike and Matt got another strike. Matt 115, Me 103. Last frame I got a 6 and Matt got a 5. I had finished with 109 and Matt 120! "Yeah" Matt and Me exclaimed as we took off our bowling shoes. Matt and Me played a game called Dynomite Cop before we left. When we left the bowling alley at 12:35 a.m. I thought about the fun time we had had in that one bowling alley for a long time. "Thanks Edd and Mom" Me and Matt exclaimed as we got in the car and left.

2. THE WRITING ACADEMY

2.1 Description

Research (Pritchard & Marshall 1994; 2002a; 2002b) has concluded that children produce better writing when their teachers have been trained in the writing-as-process instructional model. The Writing Academy was developed by one of the researchers who had been trained in a summer institute of the National Writing Project (NWP), a network of funded programs across the USA that endorses the process approach. The premise that guides the Writing Academy is that students more easily learn to improve their writing if they are provided developmentally appropriate instruction and assignments where they are allowed to experiment with their writing while simultaneously being provided specific, supportive feedback. Students in the Writing Academy receive direct small group and individualized instruction in the writing process, narrative structure, conferencing, and Six Traits assessment (Ideas, Organization, Voice, Word Choice, Sentence Variety, and Conventions). Additionally, they identify and learn to overcome emotional factors that inhibit their writing, and are provided explicit instruction in schema and self-regulation (meta-cognition) strategies related to the production of narrative text. Mini-lessons are designed to address such narrative features as story structure, character development, and key concept. The instructor models self-regulation strategies during whole class demonstrations with applications and illustrations provided during one-on-one conferencing. The teacher-researcher (TR) who designed the Writing Academy set these specific goals for students to attain by the time they completed the 16 week program: Each student will: (a) learn to feel emotionally in control when writing, (b) engage in writing for long periods of time on a regular basis, practising the writing process at every stage as it relates to the creation of narrative text, (c) learn to assess and revise his/her own writing using the Six Traits rubric and story grammar, and (d) learn to transfer and use the skills and strategies practiced in the Writing Academy to writing assignments in the regular classroom.

By the end of the Writing Academy, each student is required to have completed at least three narrative stories that the student has revised at least three times after conferencing with the instructor. Students are also required to have a minimum of one individual conference with the teacher and to lead one peer conference each week. During track-out times when students are not in school, students practice composing stories in their journals and sharing their writing with their parents, siblings, and friends. At the end of the Writing Academy, the students submit a writing portfolio and take a retest of the fourth grade Narrative Writing Test. After the instructor scores each student's writing samples and the retest, two independent raters read and score the writing samples and the retest in order to protect against bias.

The original Writing Workshop, as conceptualized by the National Writing Project (NWP) approximately 25 years ago, is grounded in part in the work of Carl Rogers (1969), who stressed that the role of an effective teacher is that of facilitator, not conveyor of information. Moreover, the stages in the writing process were derived through interviews with real writers who acknowledged that they did not employ textbook methodologies when composing; rather they engaged in considerable prewriting in their head and on paper, and varied in how much structure they initially impose on writing and in how and when they revise. Furthermore, they did not know all of the specifics of their texts prior to writing their first words. They wrote in order to discover meaning.

Graves (1983) modified these ideas for elementary students by organizing the teaching of writing into five categories: (a) brainstorming, (b) drafting, (c) revising, (d) editing, and (e) publishing. In a writing workshop, the teacher creates a non-threatening environment that encourages students to take risks, to experiment with their writing, and to foster a supportive relationship with the other participants. Other researchers and practitioners (Atwell, 1987; Calkins, 1997; Murray, 1987; Pritchard, 1993) have extended the concept of Writing Workshop to include applications to literature study, student-teacher conferencing, peer conferencing, self-evaluation, and self-reflection on one's writing process.

Six basic principles guide the daily procedures in the Writing Academy. First, students are provided regular, significant portions of time to write each day. A minimum of 40 out of 60 minutes is set aside each class period for students to engage in the recursive process of writing; this includes completing a self-reflection sheet for each completed piece of writing. Second, students are provided numerous prompts for writing and for journal topics in order to gain practice in writing-on-demand; however, students also follow their own topics of interest in additional assignments. Third, each class begins with a mini-lesson on a skill or strategy. Fourth, students meet regularly with the teacher individually for conferencing and instruction and to learn how to conference, as well as in small groups of 2 – 4 students to gather responses to their writing and practice providing feedback to peers. During these activities, students are introduced to a composing vocabulary, e.g., *freeze frame, key concept, voice, story grammar, cohesive tie, WOW! moment, honor the process,* and *make a promise to the reader.* Fifth, at appropriate times, students gather in response groups to read aloud their pieces, and afterwards the peers share what they liked about the piece and offer suggestions for improvement. Selected pieces are shared with the whole class in the Author's Chair. Finally, a certificate of achievement and a bound copy of each student's writing are presented during a celebration and author's signing.

2.2 Students in the Writing Academy

To participate in the Writing Academy, students must meet the following criteria: (a) they must have taken and failed the fourth grade Narrative Writing Test during the previous school year, and (b) they must meet with the instructor prior to the beginning of the Writing Academy to personally explain to the instructor why s/he wants to be in the Writing Academy and what his/her goals are. For the purpose of this study of good readers who are poor writers, only those students who do not have any identifiable behavioral problems or written language disabilities that would require the expertise of a Special Educator, and those who had passed the state Reading Test and failed the Writing Test were scrutinized.

Good readers who are poor writers have been relatively neglected as a focus in most of the professional literature. Only two formal studies have been devoted to them. Thacker (1990, 1991) and Jordan (1986) have both found that good readers who are poor writers tend to compose texts that do not make sense. They omit important details that help the reader in understanding the text, producing writer-based rather than reader-based prose, even when they have a defined public audience.

Palmer (1986) suggests that good readers who are poor writers and who have no learning or behavioral disabilities are by several unique characteristics. He summarized the current literature as follows: Regular education students who are good readers but poor writers utilize four basic strategies when reading: (a) they plan, (b) they translate or interpret, (c) they read, and (d) they reflect upon and/or evaluate what they read. Conversely, when writing, these same students: (a) make scant use of planning, (b) limit the use of reading what they produce during the creation of text, (c) revise only after the production of text, and (d) devote little or no time for reflection or evaluation of text after its production.

The authors of this chapter undertook a study to confirm/refute, and elaborate on Palmer's general characteristics of good readers who are poor writers, and to investigate the impact of the Writing Academy on the emotions, strategies, and overall writing performance of participants. Eleven participants in the Writing Academy who were identified as good readers who are poor writers were the focus of study. One of the researchers served as teacher-researcher (TR) in the data collection; the other is director of the NWP site that provides staff development in the process approach.

3. METHOD

3.1 Individual Student Interviews

As the primary method of data collection, the researchers designed and used an individual, in-depth, piloted interview with the eleven students. The questions were open-ended to ensure that the students would have an opportunity to elaborate on their responses.

In order to develop a context for understanding the participants' perspective, the first several questions in the interview focused on students' experiences with reading and writing, particularly their perceptions and feelings about writing on-demand. The second phase of the interview asked the participants to reflect on their experiences in the Writing Academy and whether or not they made any connection between the writing they did in the Writing Academy and the way they later approach writing tasks, especially on-demand writing assignments.

3.2 Writer's Self-Perception Scale

During the individual student interviews, all the subjects mentioned that prior to attending the Writing Academy, they lacked confidence in themselves as writers. As a result, the TR administered the *Writer Self-Perception Scale (WSPS)* to evaluate the subjects' overall change in their self-perception as writers as a result of attending the Writing Academy.

The *WSPS*, developed by Bottomley, Henk, and Melnick (1997/1998), consists of 37 items in a Likert-type format, each with five possible responses ranging from *strongly agree* (5 points) to *strongly disagree* (1 point), and 1 general item, "I think I am a good writer." The *WSPS*, designed to be administered to fourth, fifth, and sixth grade students, yields five general areas of information: (a) General Progress, GPR, refers to the student's perception as to whether or not s/he perceives that s/he has improved in his/her overall writing over a specified amount of time and as to his/her perception concerning the effectiveness of instruction; (b) Specific Progress, SPR, refers to how well the student perceives his/her ability to revise text based upon explicit dimensions of writing such as focus, clarity, organization, style, and coherence; (c) Observational Comparison, OC, measures how a student perceives his/her performance in relation to peers; (d) Social Feedback, SF, examines how a student perceives the feedback s/he receives from teachers, parents, and peers; (e) Physiological States, PS, measures the internal feelings a student has when writing.

3.3 Focus Groups

After the completion of the individual student interviews, and after all the interviews had been transcribed, coded, and analyzed, the TR offered two focus group sessions, and all interviewed students were invited to attend one or both sessions.

The groups met for approximately 45 minutes. The discussion topics were designed to query the students further about their perceptions of writing and the impact of the Writing Academy. Further, the discussion was also designed as member checks to confirm, modify, or refute the researchers' initial findings and interpretations based on the interviews.

3.4 Teacher Focus Group

The TR met with seven teachers for a focus group discussion after the data from the focus group with students had been compiled and analyzed, and he had confirmed or modified the initial findings from analysis of the individual interviews. The study was conceptualized this way in order to balance the students' perceptions with those of teachers and to compare and contrast them.

3.5 Document Collection

Document collection refers to the collection of written documents produced by the students, teachers, and the TR involved in this study. Anderson, Herr, and Nihlen (1994) argue that documents, "provide the researcher with facts pertaining to the subject and give insight into the organization, its history, and its purposes." In this study, the researchers used: (a) students' portfolios, a collection of three stories that each student completed going through the entire writing process; (b) four self-reflection forms per student; (c) TR conference notes transcribed in each student's portfolio; (d) TR notes transcribed in the lesson plans for the Writing Academy; (e) transcripts of the individual student interviews and TR notes from the interviews; (f) notes made during the teacher focus group discussion; and (g) the discussion sheets that regular classroom teachers completed prior to attending the focus group.

4. DATA ANALYSIS

The qualitative approach used in this study is analytic induction whereby the researchers sought to generate and develop categories in order to produce delimited theories grounded in the data. The researchers read across interviews, noting similarities and differences, and used pattern coding to identify themes. This approach balanced the analysis of samples of the students' writing from their portfolios and the notes that the TR had previously transcribed during and after conferencing with each student during the Writing Academy. Using the "constant comparative method," the researchers constantly and recursively compared data gathered from the interviews and focus groups, the analysis of student writing from the portfolios, the transcriptions of conferencing notes, and the teacher commentary recorded in student portfolios.

5. RESULTS

Three types of procedures (Denzin, 1989) were used to verify the data: across collection methods (document analysis, scores on the *Writer Self-Perception Scale*, individual interviews, and focus groups), across data sources (students and teachers), and across investigators (two researchers, one serving as TR and the other as "critical friend;" formal member checking in focus groups; and informal member checking with individuals). Data were systematically classified according to their relationship to the two construct categories (a basic profile of good readers who are poor writers, and the impact of the Writing Academy), and/or to a theme category (strategies, common experiences, and emotions)

The overall results of this study reveal that good readers who are poor writers lack fluency in writing because they have a flawed understanding of both the writing process and the features of narrative text to the extent that they are unable to compose narrative text on-demand. These findings confirm those summarized by Palmer, but also add to a fuller understanding of good readers who are poor writers. Specifically, good readers who are poor writers are plagued by emotional factors that impede their writing because they do not have the schema for prewriting strategies and/or self-regulation/monitoring strategies necessary for composing. Additionally, they have not had sufficient quality conferencing experiences with teachers or peers to improve their writing and internalize features of good writing evident in the work of their peers.

All students in this study acknowledged that they benefited from participating in the Writing Academy. Specifically, they mentioned learning prewriting and monitoring/self-regulation strategies, and learning how to identify and employ strategies to deal with negative emotions that interfered with composing.

Prior to attending the Writing Academy, student Jim exhibited several characteristics typical of many good readers who are poor writers. In his interviews, he revealed that when composing, he: (a) attempted to engage in prewriting, such as using a flow map, but never referred back to his prewriting or considered the elements of story grammar schema to guide his composing; (b) was skilled at using metacognitive strategies to monitor his comprehension when reading texts, indicated by making predictions and verifying them, but only had a few, ineffective self-regulation strategies to rely on when composing; and (c) experienced the emergence of negative emotions when faced with writing tasks as indicated by admitting he was "scared" about adequately addressing specific topics in his writing when he exhibited no such fear while reading.

A review of Jim's portfolio indicates that throughout the Writing Academy the TR conferenced with him about creating stories that had a clear beginning, middle, and end. Notes in his portfolio indicate that initially the conferencing focused on creating a scene where the student had to describe what happened in slow motion. The TR used this cinema analogy of *freeze frames*, teaching the student to report the events that he wanted to describe in his story as if he were watching a scene in a movie in slow motion. The student had to describe the characters, their physical movements, facial expressions, and important verbal statements or thoughts. Jim conferenced and revised his first story eight times before he agreed with the TR that the story was ready to be part of his portfolio and submitted to the school's Writing Committee to be scored.

Mini-lessons addressed several schema strategies that Jim lacked: (a) using story grammar as a prewriting strategy, (b) creating effective introductions and reflective endings that tie the story together, (c) consistently employing basic self-regulation strategies, and (d) composing text using various sentence structures.

A review of conference notes reveal that while student Jim attended the Writing Academy, teacher conferences centered on teaching him how to determine when and how to create paragraph breaks and how to combine sentences to improve syntax and semantics. Jim conferenced and revised his second paper four times prior to submitting it to be scored; he only revised and edited his third and final story two times. Both of these stories were included in his portfolio.

After completing the Writing Academy, Jim retook the fourth grade Narrative Writing Test in one 50-minute session. The prompt, which called for an imaginative narrative, was "Imagine that your mom bought you a small rug to put in your room. When you got home and stepped on the rug, it turned into a magic carpet. Tell a story about what happened next." Following is a typed version, with errors intact.

> "Thanks for the rug Mom" I yelled as I sprinted upstairs to my room. I crashed through my door, hurled my new red rug next to my bed and stepped on it. All of a sudden I was hovering in the air on a majic carpet, clinging to it for all I was worth. After a while I got the confidence to say one word, "Forward." That was probably one of the things I regretted most in my life, thanks to that word I shot out of my window like a mad bullet on what I thought was a joy ride, but boy was I wrong.
>
> All of a sudden I was soaring over the buildings and houses of [the neighborhood] gazing at the ground far, far below. Moments later I was past [the neighborhood] in the country, then something really bad happened. I started plunging downwards! I thought I was a goner, little did I know I was right over a lake. There was an earsplitting splash as I landed on the water. Lucky for me the rug was able to float on the calm lake water. Then the water wasn't calm anymore, a huge freshwater shark came speeding towards me!! I grabbed the nearest thing I could, a floating stick and hit the shark a stunning blow to the nose just in time. It disappeared into the lake depths to find a "less aggressive" prey. I swam with all my might to the nearest bank so I wouldn't have to worry about any other hungry fish. With water dripping from me I dragged myself ashore with the sopping wet rug behind me. With my last efforts I wrong out the rug and stepped on it. As I had hoped the water hadn't hurt the rug and I was in the air. With renewed spirit I said, "Home" and I was off back the way I had come.
>
> I zipped through the still open window, crashed against the wall and landed on my bed just in time. My mom came through the door and looked at me laying on my bed. She asked, "Do you like the rug," I smiled and managed to gasp out one sentence, "Yeah, it's a real lifesaver." When she left the room I feel asleep of weariness, thinking to myself, "Nobody will ever know."

During the retest, Jim composed a rough draft in cursive, made some minor revisions, and then rewrote his story on the test form within the allotted 50-minute test time frame. This paper was scored a 4.0 (above grade level) by the local school system graders.

In contrast to the unelaborated "listing" which comprised Jim's writing before taking the Writing Academy, this post-Academy story has a strong personal *voice*. It is a creative and exciting narration of a fantasy experience with a magic carpet. Jim shows audience awareness. In the first paragraph he makes a *promise to the reader* that he will explore why his ride was not a "joy ride." He fulfills this promise by building and maintaining suspense by creating a *Wow! moment* and by using humor throughout the story. The narrative evidences that Jim understands *story grammar*, for it is well sequenced with a clear beginning, middle, and end. It clearly addresses the prompt. He includes relevant details that support and add to the story. Additionally, his sentences are varied and complex. Finally, he creates a *cohesive tie* with words that frame the tale: it begins with the narrator's command, "Forward" and ends with his command, "Home."

In terms of the impact of specific activities he experienced in the Writing Academy, Jim's writing provides evidence of specific *story grammar* schema being applied when he: (a) sets the scene and sequences the events in a clear, logical order, (b) employs dialogue, thoughts, and sound effects throughout the tale to build and support the interwoven theme, (c) creates a plot, which includes a problem, attempt and outcome, and (d) provides an insightful reflection as the resolution to the story – "It was a real lifesaver."

An analysis of Jim's portfolio and a comparison/contrast of his writing when he first took the fourth grade Narrative Writing Test and later the retest, indicate that Jim's overall writing improved in several specific ways, representative of the students who attended the Writing Academy. As a result of his time in the Writing Academy, Jim (a) increased the quantity and quality of the texts he composed, b) included all the necessary features of *story grammar* – characters, setting, plot, attempts, and resolution, (c) engaged in substantial revision after composing an initial draft, (d) reported that he learned to *honor the process* by reminding himself that writing is difficult for many people and thereby "trained" himself to persevere in the writing task, even when it was difficult, and (e) reported that he frequently entered a state a *flow* when composing, and even when composing on-demand. Jim's four self-reflection papers evidence his increasing metacognitive awareness of the processes of writing and the effects of feedback. They illustrate how he employs the self-regulation strategies of (a) pausing to reread the text and visualize the characters, setting, and scene to determine whether or not he included sufficient information, (b) making notes on the margins of his drafts as he reread them, marking places where he needed to elaborate or go back to work on tone, rhythm, or stylistic features, and (c) revising and editing using the 6 Traits. Furthermore, analysis of the *Writer Self-Perception Scale* clearly indicates that Jim's perception of himself as a writer improved over the period of time when he attended the Writing Academy. He rated himself the highest of the group in terms of general progress, and second highest in specific progress. Finally, in the teacher focus group, Jim's teachers testified to his applying writing strategies to assignments in the content areas.

6. CONCLUSION

In this study, the researchers examined a group of students who are typical of students at all levels in the educational system, good readers who are poor writers. The findings in this study suggest that good readers who are poor writers display pervasive limitations in their understanding and application of the various schema strategies for story grammar and self-regulation when applied to writing. Furthermore, the data presented in this research point to the role and impact of students' emotions on their writing performance, particularly with respect to the students' negative emotions and perceptions of themselves as writers. Moreover, as the students in this study themselves attest, good readers who are poor writers benefit from an intensive remediation program – a writing workshop program combined with focused instruction, such as the Writing Academy.

DEAF WAYS OF WRITING NARRATIVES: A BILINGUAL APPROACH

MARIA KOUTSOUBOU

City University, London

Abstract. This chapter investigates the writing process in narratives by Greek deaf students in two different conditions: a) translation from Sign Language into written Greek from video stimuli and b) direct composition in written Greek from picture stimuli. Following language assessments, the deaf students were divided into three language groups according to their differing abilities in Greek Sign Language and Greek. Two parameters were manipulated: language skills and source material used for writing. The study aims to answer the questions: a) How do the different groups make use of the source material (which students benefit from the use of sign language?) b) Which material produces better written texts? Four qualitative analyses have been undertaken on the texts: amount/type of information given, organisation of information, grammatical characteristics of the text, and error analysis. The results show that the use of sign language in the writing process has positive effects only on specific groups and on specific aspects of writing.

Keywords: Deaf students, writing, narratives, bilingualism, translation, direct writing.

1. DEAF EDUCATION AND BILINGUAL EDUCATION

Deaf education has been an area of dispute in relation to methodology and communication mode for over a century. It is still the case that the majority of deaf students finish school with literacy skills equivalent to the $3^{rd} - 4^{th}$ year of education (Turner, 2000). According to standard measurements of literacy, skills below $4^{th} - 8^{th}$ years of schooling represent functional illiteracy (Albertini, 1993).

In the last decade deaf education has been approached in the context of bilingual education. This development has been based on the application of research findings that deaf students' written language resembles second language learners' errors more than it does deviant language. The literacy development of deaf children, as well as their development of spoken language, shares the characteristics and developmental pattern of second language (L2) acquisition (Lightbown & Spada, 1993; Slobin, 1996). The outcomes of a bilingual approach to deaf education have not been widely reported, as this approach has been applied only recently (Paul, 2001; Turner, 2000). With the introduction of a bilingual framework for deaf education, it is necessary to explore current issues in bilingual approaches to education generally. The most prominent issue is the place of the first language (L1) in second language (L2) teaching. There is a general acceptance of the positive role of L1 in teaching another language (Bialystok, 1991; Hakuta, 1986; Krashen, 2001; Mayer & Akamatsu, 1999). This L1 facilitative role is less related to learning the form of L2 than it is to support a metacognitive level, including constructing meaning in thought, negotiating meaning via meaningful communication, deciding on how much information, what kind of information and how to transmit the information (Cook, 2001; Wang & Wen, 2002). Nowhere in L2 teaching are the above metacognitive abilities manifested better than in the activity of writing. By extension then, L1 use in teaching L2 writing can actually assist the process.

The arguments against L1 use (or use of any other language than the target L2 language) mainly concern interference issues. Structures from one language may interfere with the target language unless the two languages are kept apart. It has also been argued that using two languages in the same setting may make it more difficult for the child to separate them into independent linguistic and communication systems (Cook, 2001). Apart from this, there has been dissatisfaction with the outcome of bilingual approaches to the education of Hispanic children in United States. In this group, bilingualism has not resulted in an improvement of literacy skills compared to other minority groups (such as African-Americans) even though bilingual approaches have been used for decades (Noonan, 2000; Porter, 1998)

The relevance of this debate to deaf education lies in the use of sign language in the classroom. It has been argued that introducing sign language provided by deaf native signers into schools will improve deaf students' reading, and especially, writing abilities where they mostly lag behind hearing peers (Gregory, 1996). Sign language has been argued to be the most easily acquired language for deaf children because its structure is visual. Its use can promote communication within peer groups and with teachers. In addition, the grammatical rules of the L2 can be explained via sign language, with sign language used as a teaching tool and as a medium of instruction (Mayer & Akamatsu, 1999; Rodda & Eleweke, 2000). Finally, sign language can serve social, political and cultural purposes if introduced formally in the class. Deaf students will have signing deaf role models to relate to, which will enhance their positive self-identity. This is of importance, since literacy failure in bilingualism is connected to attitudes about the first language. If the first language is highly esteemed then, it has a positive effect on the overall academic process whereas the opposite happens if the L1 is considered a "poor" language (Lightbown & Spada, 1993).

The application of bilingual approaches to the use of sign language in the classroom is not wholly straightforward, however. The different language acquisition experiences of deaf children mean that sign language is not always the deaf child's L1. Ninety per cent of deaf children are born to hearing parents and therefore sign language is heavily influenced by the attitudes of the family to language, deafness, early intervention and other factors, which are absent in typical language acquisition (Paul, 2001). The relevance of the use of L1 in the bilingualism debate about deaf education, therefore, is specifically connected with whether in teaching a target language another language should be involved.

2. WRITING IN L2

Writing is a very complex activity because many processes occur at the same time: decisions on information, meaning construction, language formation, editing the product and constant monitoring of the process (Silliman, Jimerson, & Wilkinson, 2000). The whole activity is even more complicated when writing occurs in a L2. Some of the above processes are facilitated by the writer's knowledge of the L1 and other processes only from the existing L2 skills. The less proficient an individual is in one of the languages, the more use is made of the other, since the writer is forced to pass on the message even where the correct forms are not known. Resorting to the L1 is one strategy of L2 learners as well as other strategies such as guessing, avoidance, or overgeneralization (James, 1998; Lightbown & Spada, 1993; Mayer & Akamatsu, 1999).

As far as bilingualism and writing are concerned, there appears to be a connection between literacy in the L1 and literacy skills in L2 (Cumming, 1989). Other factors that correlate are oral skills in L2 and literacy skills in L2 (Kobayashi & Rinnert, 1992). Such links are not the case for the majority of deaf students. First, for those whose L1 is sign language, there is no written form. So there can be no transfer of planning processes and thinking strategies for writing from one language to the other. Secondly, the overwhelming majority of deaf people do not have skills in the spoken form of their L2. Research has shown no relationship of "oral" (i.e., conversational) skills in a sign language to written skills (Mayer & Akamatsu, 1999).

Despite the difficulties with the application of models of bilingualism devised for spoken languages, in practice we can investigate which materials improve the writing performance of deaf students. We can investigate if manipulating the linguistic input (i.e., sign language input vs. no linguistic input) results in improvement in writing, and thus how the teachers can use the available linguistic systems for better results. We also can research how linguistic input interacts with different degrees of fluency in both L1 and L2 – a case unique to deaf people, as it is rare for hearing children to commence learning to write an L2 before fully mastering an L1.

The present study considers the following areas:
- Deaf students' bilingualism (their abilities in sign language and written language) and
- Manipulation of input material in order to see the effect on performance.

This study seeks to answer three questions:
1) Do deaf writers with different bilingual skills make different use of sign language input?
2) Can we influence the process of writing by using different materials?
3) Do the patterns of errors change when we change material or do deaf students always go via the same route?

In order to answer the first question, we need to assess the bilingual skills of deaf students. In order to answer the second question, we need to compare the effects of different input on deaf students' writing. Finally, in order to answer the third question, we need to analyze the patterns of errors and see whether they change in the context of different stimulus material.

3. THE DESIGN OF THE STUDY

3.1 The Tasks

Twenty Greek deaf students participated in the study. The two variables considered were the stimulus material and the bilingual language abilities. Two sets of stimulus materials were designed. The first was a story presented on video in Greek Sign Language. The second was a picture storybook without printed text. In both tasks the requirement was to write the story down. The aim was to compare the stories elicited by the different material and to decide which was more elaborated in information, organization and language use.

These specific tasks were chosen because they replicate features of either a bilingual approach in the classroom (video) or a traditional approach to teaching deaf children (picture book). In the video task, sign language is explicitly involved in the writing process, as it is a translation task. In the picture book task, there is no explicit source language involved in writing. The video task may therefore be expected to show more interference from sign language. If similar errors are found in the picture task, it may indicate that in both situations sign language is used to create meaning and to facilitate the process of writing in Greek.

3.2 Participants

The second variable – bilingual language abilities – was determined by assessing the two languages involved in the writing process i.e., Greek Sign Language (GSL) and written Greek. Although several sign language assessment tests have been developed for British Sign Language (Herman, Holmes, & Woll, 1999) and American Sign Language (ASL) (Mounty, 1993) there are no standardized assessments for GSL. The researcher therefore constructed a scale with four levels, each defined in terms of general linguistic and pragmatic characteristics. Teachers were asked to rate each student's performance in GSL and written Greek. For a full description of the assessment see Koutsoubou, in preparation. Deaf teachers assessed the GSL and deaf and hearing teachers assessed written Greek. The assessment procedure resulted in the division of the sample into three groups:
1) Sign Language Dominant group (GSL high, written Greek low) 6 subjects.
2) Weak balanced bilingual (GSL low, written Greek low) 6 subjects.
3) Strong balanced bilingual group (GSL high, written Greek high) 8 subjects.

3.3 Materials

The materials used, were two picture stories without words of about the same length. The "Frog, Where are you?" (Mercer, 1969) and the "The Grey Lady and the Strawberry Snatcher" (Bang, 1986). Both were signed by a deaf native signer of GSL. The stories were piloted with a bilingual GSL and Greek hearing subject and both stories elicited a similar length and a similar degree of grammatical complexity. Half of the participants received the Frog Story in GSL and the Strawberry Lady in pictures and the other half received them the other way round, in order to control for story effects.

3.4 The Analysis of Texts

The texts have been analyzed in four levels:
1) *Information* (amount and type of information revealed) (see appendix A). This is measured in two ways: (a) the *basic structure* of the story. This consists of the setting, the reason, the action, and the closure. This is applied to both stories. The terminology used is the researcher's but the approach is based on previous research (Bamberg, 1997; Labov, 1997; Yoshinaga-Itano & Downey, 1998); (b) the *basic story lines*, which are specific to each story.
   The type of information is also measured in two ways: (a) *descriptive information* – any state or action in the story; (b) *affective information*, any information about the thoughts of the characters, dialogues, monologues, comments, attributes, or evaluations by the narrative writer.
2) *Organisation* (how the information is structured) (see appendix B). This is measured through the use of tree diagrams (Langer, 1986). The deeper the tree grows, the tighter the structure of the story. The wider the tree is, the more information is present. Finally the greater the variety of relationships found in the tree, the better elaborated the story is. Langer's original model has been modified to some extent, since the language produced here is quite different – due to its bilingual nature – from that for which the tree diagrams were designed.
3) *Text characteristics*. These are standard measurements of the complexity and well-formedness of written language. The measures used here are: number of words, number of T-Units, number of clauses, clauses per T-Units, T-Unit length, Subordinate clauses, Co-ordinate clauses and T-Unit complexity (Fraser, 2001; Silliman et al., 2000).
4) *Error analysis* (see appendix C) (James, 1998). This is focused on language form, with a particular focus on the weaker parts of the texts

3.5 The Hypotheses Tested

Comparisons between the three groups and within each group have been made to see whether there are differences in the *information level, organization level* and *grammatical level* between the tasks and among the groups. There are two hypotheses:
1) The different bilingual groups will produce different texts in quality and quantity with different characteristics in organisation, grammar and information.

2) The picture and video material will produce different texts in quality and quantity of organisation, grammar and information revealed.

4. RESULTS

Data were analyzed using general linear model-repeated measures with SPSS. The model used was repeated measures. The within-variables were the video and picture material (two levels) and the between-variables were the three groups (three levels). The graphs are boxplots, which show the median (the thick black line), the 25th & the 75th percentiles of the values and the largest or smallest values (indicated by the whiskers). Small circles also indicate outlying and atypical values. The level of significance was set on 0.05 for all the analysis in this study.

4.1 Main Effect of Groups

The strong balanced bilingual group (the group defined as having good written Greek skills) performed consistently and significantly better than the other two groups in most of the measures. Of interest, however, are the differences between the SL dominant and the weak bilingual group as well as their relation to the strong bilingual group.

4.2 Results: Information Level

On the *story grammar* information the only significant difference between the groups was between the strong-balanced and the weak balanced group ($p = .045$) with a main effect of $F(2, 14) = 4.784, p = .026$ (see Table 1).

Table 1. *Differences among the Groups on Story Grammar Production*

Compared groups	Mean Difference	Standard Error	Significance
Strong balanced Weak balanced	*.372	.134	.045
Strong balanced SL dominant	.283	.125	.119
Weak balanced SL dominant	-.089	.147	1.000

The SL dominant group does not differ significantly either from the bilingual group or the weak balanced group. This makes the SL dominant group a middle group, representing bridge between the high achieving strong bilingual and the low achieving weak bilingual group. Figure 1 presents data on the groups in greater detail. The strong balanced group performs better in both conditions than either of the other two groups. The weak balanced group produces the lowest scores in both tasks and the SL dominant group is located in the middle – although it should be noted that this group exhibits more variability in scores. This distribution is also found in other analyses.

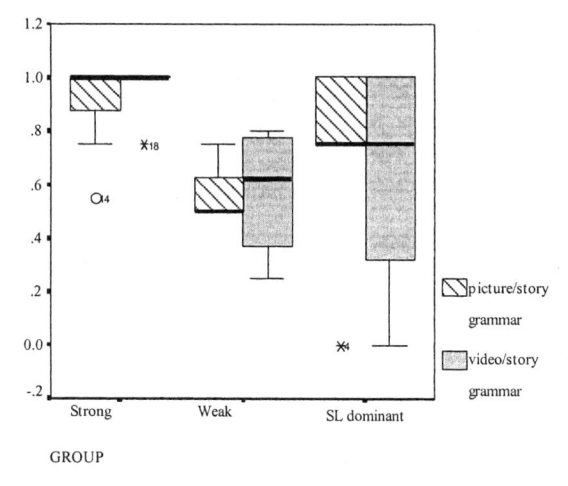

Figure 1. Performance of the three groups on story grammar production in the video and picture task.

On the *basic story line* information the main effect of group is $F(2, 14) = 7.570$, $p = .006$ and the pairwise comparison between the strong-balanced group and weak-balanced group was significant ($p = .008$). Again the SL group's scores are between these two groups with no significant difference from either (Table 2). Figure 2 shows the wide distribution of scores within the SL dominant group.

Table 2. Differences among the Groups on Basic Story Line Production

Compared groups	Mean Difference (I-J)	Standard. Error	Significance
Strong balanced Weak balanced	*.502	.137	.008
Strong balanced SL dominant	.325	.128	.070
Weak balanced SL dominant	-.178	.150	.773

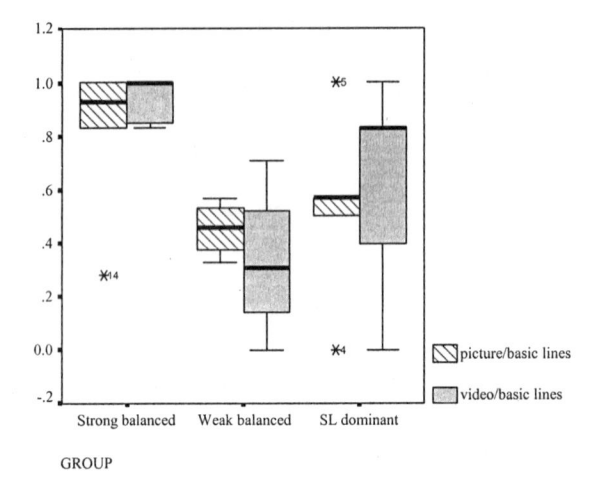

Figure 2. Performance of the three groups on basic story line production in the video and picture task.

4.3 Results for Analyses of Organization

On the *variety of relations* produced in narratives the main effect of groups is F (2, 14) = 6.646, p = .009 and the pairwise comparison between the strong-balanced and weak balanced groups was significant (p = .014). In this analysis, the SL dominant group more closely resembled the weak balanced group than the strong balanced group, although results were not significant (Table 3). This can be seen more clearly in Figure 3 where the medians of the two groups are almost on the same level.

Table 3. Differences among the Groups on the Variety of Relationships Production

Compared groups	Mean Difference (I-J)	Standard. Error	Significance
Strong balanced Weak balanced	*2.625	.783	.014
Strong balanced SL dominant	1.850	.729	.071
Weak balanced SL dominant	-.775	.858	1.00

Figure 3 shows that the weak balanced and the SL dominant groups perform at a similar level, although they react differently to the material: writing from video is better for the SL dominant group and writing from pictures is better for the weak bilingual group.

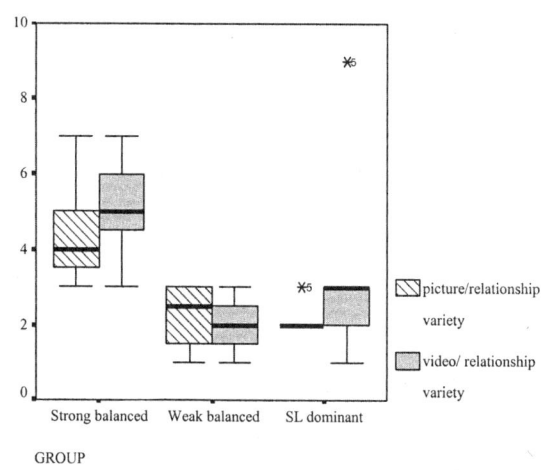

Figure 3. Performance of the three groups on the variety of relationships in the video and picture task.

4.4 Results for Analyses of Text Characteristics

On this measure, the strong bilingual group performed significantly better than either of the other groups. The text characteristics were similar for the weak balanced and the SL dominant groups.

4.5 Results for Error Analysis

There were no significance differences on error analysis between any of the groups, with all groups having approximately the same amount and type of errors.

4.6 Main Effect of Material

There was a main effect of the material on the organization level and the error analysis. The relevant results for *organization of the stories* relate to the 2nd and 4th level of the tree diagrams (see appendix B). The video produced significantly better results than the picture book on the 2nd level [$F(2, 14) = 7.363$, $p = 0.017$] (see figure 4) and the 4th level of the story diagrams [$F(1, 14) = 5.924$, $p = 0.029$] (see Figure 5).

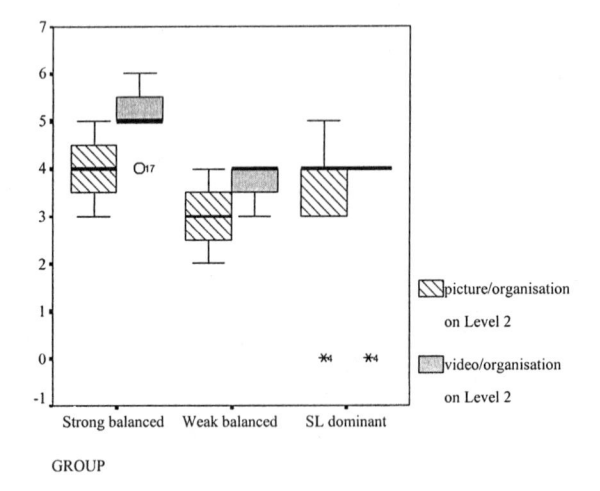

Figure 4. Performance of the three groups on the 2ⁿᵈ level of story organisation within the video and picture task.

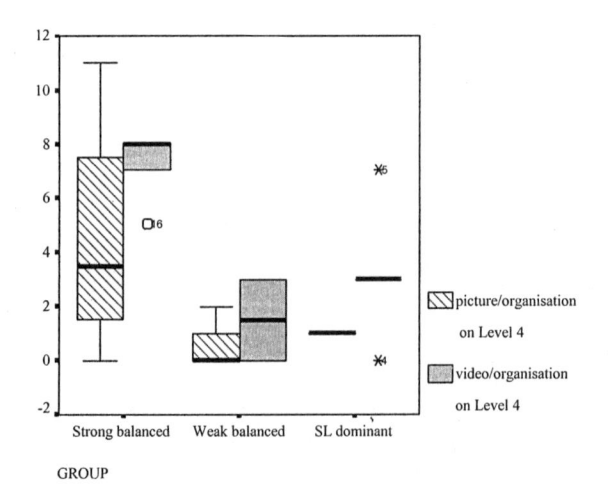

Figure 5. Performance of the three groups on the 4ᵗʰ level of story organization within the video and picture task.

As for *error analysis* (see Appendix C) the type of stimulus material produced only one effect that was close to significance: the "grammar - omission" category [F (1, 14) = 4.348, p = .056]. "Grammar-omission" means that the writers omitted various grammatical words from the text. The video produced more omission errors in the strong balanced and the SL dominant but there was no effect on the weak balanced group (see Figure 6).

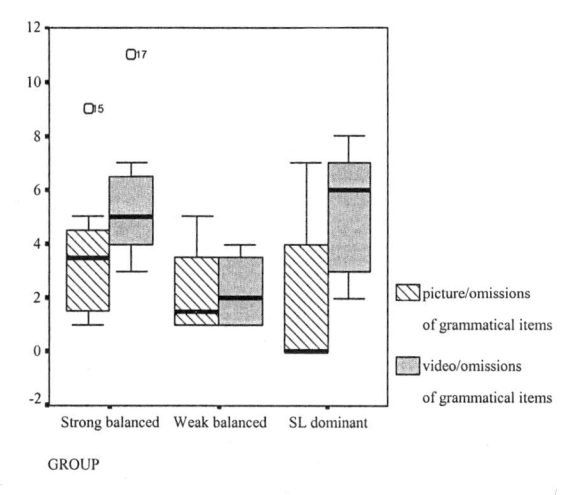

Figure 6. Performance of the three groups on errors of omission within the video and picture task.

Some of the omission subcategories yielded results approaching significance: "omission of preposition" [F (1, 14) = 4.178, p = .060] (see Figure 7), and "omission of verb" [F (1, 14) = 5.149, p = .040] (see Figure 8). More omissions were found in the video condition than in the picture condition. These finding are in accordance with previous studies of the writing of deaf students. Deaf students frequently omitted many function words and verbs. Most often state and existence verbs are omitted (e.g., "to be", "to have", "to appear"). This is probably due to sign language interference, as these omissions are noted only in the two groups with good sign language skills: strong balanced bilingual and SL dominant. The scores for the weak balanced group, although showing a tendency in the same direction (i.e., producing more omissions in the video task than the picture) were not significantly different from the picture task (see Figure 6 and 7). Verbs were significantly omitted from all the groups (see Figure 8).

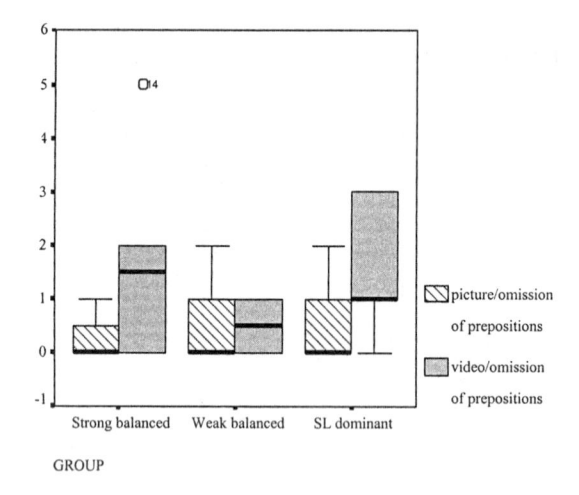

Figure 7. Performance of the three groups on errors of omitting prepositions within the video and picture tasks.

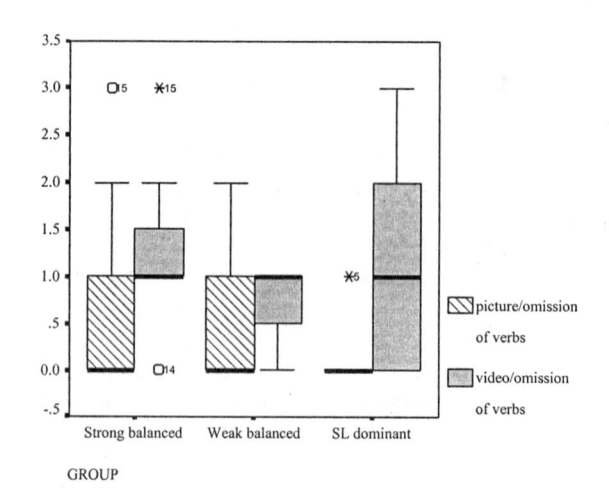

Figure 8. Performance of the three groups on errors of omitting verbs within the video and picture tasks.

4.7 Interaction Effect between Group and Material

The only significant difference of interaction between groups and material occurred at the information level – affective type [$F(2, 14) = 4.124$, $p = 0.039$]. The video *significantly improved* the strong balanced bilinguals' performance, *significantly impaired* the weak balanced bilinguals' performance and had *no significant effect* on SL-dominant performance, as seen in Figure 9.

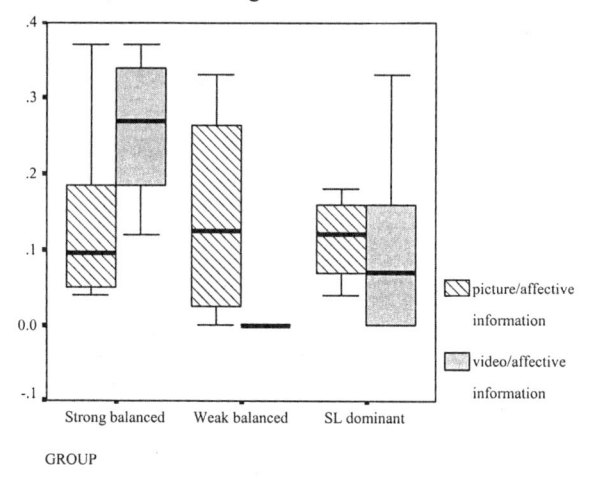

Figure 9. Performance of the three groups on the production of affective information within the video and picture task.

5. DISCUSSION

Writing is a complex activity, which starts with decisions about how much information and what type of information a text should have, progresses to organizing the information and finally to decisions about how everything will be linguistically expressed. The type of input – in the present case, sign language input – facilitated different aspects of writing and interacted in different ways with various levels of bilingualism.

At the higher levels of writing (i.e., decisions on information and organization of the story) the availability of sign language and language fluency have a significant effect on deaf students' writing. The strong balanced bilingual group improved its performance in the sign language condition, whereas the weak balanced bilingual group and the SL Dominant group showed more limited effects. In general, sign language source material improved the structure of the texts in terms of organization (Figures 3, 4 and 5). In relation to text characteristics, the source material caused no significant effect. The only negative effect of sign language was found in the error analysis and that occurred only in omission of function words such as prepositions, and verbs of state/being. This can be interpreted as an effect of transfer from one linguistic system to the other. It has also been described in the literature as one of the characteristics of deaf writing (Paul, 2001). Apart from omissions, the two types of materials produced text of more or less the same quality. This is evidence that the language used in thinking for writing in the context of the pictures was similar to that used in the translation (video task): Greek Sign Language.

The effect of sign language on writing demands attention to the issue of how to use it most effectively in schools. Even if sign language has been accepted as a language for use in deaf education, deaf students' sign language skills are not formally assessed or even scrutinized. Deaf students should be treated as bilinguals with varying skills in sign language. Such an approach may lead to consideration of grouping deaf children in classes according to their language skills and not according to their age. This of course will only be fully feasible when assessment tests for sign language are developed and standardized.

A second conclusion from the results is that teachers need to consider what types of source materials can be used in order to improve specific aspects of deaf students' writing. A third conclusion is that error analysis provides the only evidence of sign language material having a negative effect on all groups. In all the other levels of analysis, the strong balanced bilingual group significantly outperformed the other two groups. Even though errors are present, the texts with the greatest number of errors are not necessarily the worst texts. Error counting is a fairly low level of analysis, and meaning can be passed on even in the absence of correct grammatical form. What makes for a good text is the provision of all necessary information, good organization and good discourse manipulation. These were best with the sign language source material.

In conclusion, this study has provided us with answers to the questions posed at the beginning:

1) Do deaf writers' of different bilingual experiences make different use of the linguistic input? With the exception of one result (differences on affective information, see Figure 1), the groups do not differ very much in terms of use of linguistic input.
2) Can we influence the process of writing by using different material? We can influence some aspects of writing but not all. For example by using sign language, we can influence information and organisation of written stories but not necessarily the text characteristics.
3) Do the patterns of errors change when we change material or do deaf students always go via the same route? Since – as indicated by the answer to Question 1 – the groups do not react differently to the materials, they are likely to be using them in more or less the same way. With the exception of omission of words, both materials produce the same kinds of errors. It is obvious that the video task – as a translation task- was more vulnerable to sign language interference. But it may be concluded that the picture task – which was free from language input – produced similar types of errors. This may indicate that deaf students, regardless of their sign language skills, resort to sign language to form their texts.

One final comment may be made on the allocation of groups. The fact that the SL dominant group is always placed between the best performers and the weakest performers indicates that the development of a high degree of fluency in a sign language can facilitate literacy in deaf students.

APPENDIX A

TABLE FOR MEASURING AMOUNT AND TYPE OF INFORMATION: THE STRAWBERRY LADY[1]

Story Grammar	Basic story lines	Descriptive information (action, events, descriptions)	Affective information (manner/characters' interaction/inner state, thoughts)
SETTING	Lady buys strawberries	Time/character introduction/ Place/ At grocer's shop/ Scene (grocer prepares the box)	Lady- careless/ happy/ Grocer-friendly
REASON	Man follows her Man tries to snatch box	Time (while she was walking/after she left) Place (street/ shops/ out) Scene a strange man follows her/ woman ignorant/ says hello to flower lady/ lady senses him/ man tries to snatch the box but fails	Lady- careless, friendly, talks to flower lady Flower woman- friendly, talks to lady Man- strange look/ strange clothes, bad, poor, homeless, hungry, wants to eat strawberries
ACTION	Man starts chasing woman She always manages to escape	Time Place (bus/ woods) Scene Lady runs to bus/, another lady was coming on a roller-skate/ Man missed lady/ Man falls on other lady/ Bus leaves/ Bus arrives to woods/ Woman gets off but man comes with roller-skate/ Man chases woman into wood/ Woman escapes/ Man always behind/ Woman hides behind tree/ Man spots her/ Woman climbs tree/ Man spots her/ Woman swings away from tree/ Man spots her/ Man looses her/	Lady- frightened/ in hurry Woman relieved/ Strange atmosphere/ Lady- scared Man- puzzled/ unhappy/desperate
CLOSURE	He eventually finds raspberries and forgets her She arrives home and gives strawberries to her family	Time Place Scene Man finds a raspberry bush/ Starts eating and forgets the lady/ Time (after/ eventually) Place (home) Scene Woman arrives home/ Gives all family the strawberries/ Box empty/	Man-happy/ excited Lady- relieved Family members have good time/ happy
Total:	Total:	Total:	Total:

---

[1] *The table for "The Strawberry Lady" is given as an example in the Appendix. The same structure was applied for "The frog Story".*

APPENDIX B

FRAGMENT OF A TREE DIAGRAM FOR STORY ORGANISATION

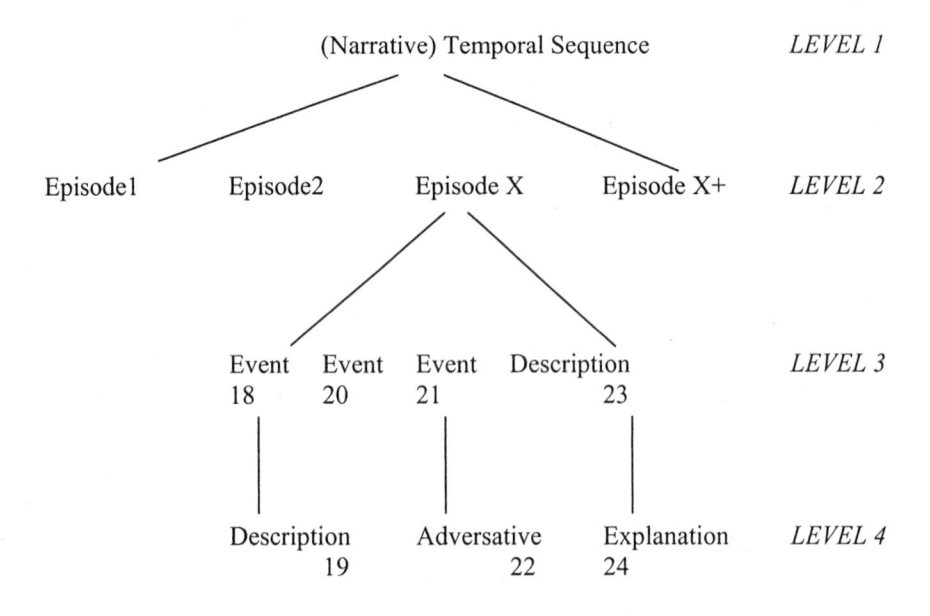

```
                    (Narrative) Temporal Sequence         LEVEL 1
                   /         |         \
        Episode1  Episode2  Episode X  Episode X+        LEVEL 2
                           /    \
                  Event Event Event Description          LEVEL 3
                   18    20    21      23
                         |           |           |
                  Description   Adversative   Explanation  LEVEL 4
                      19            22            24
```

This is a fragment of a tree diagram, indicating the structural relationships in a story. Four levels are represented, the deepest has three clauses (clause number 19, 22, 24) and there are four different types of relationships presented (Event/Description/Adversative/Explanation). The numbers under the relationships refer to clauses in the narrative. The written text it refers to and the clause segmentation are following:

> [...] Some other time again he saw a lady who has the strawberries was running and followed but lady disappeared in the wood But is boy disappointing because not is-found the strawberries [...]

Clause segmentation:
18) Άλλη φορά πάλι αυτός είδε μια κυρία = *Some other time again he saw a lady*
19) Που έχει τις *φραουλες* = *who has the strawberries*
20) Έτρεχε = *was running*
21) Και ακολούθησε, = *and followed*
22) Άλλα κυρια εξαφανίστηκε μεσα στο δάσος. = *but lady disappeared in the wood*
23) Όμως είναι αγορί απογοητευτικός = *But is boy disappointing*
24) Γιατί δεν βρίσκεται τις φραουλες. = *because not is-found the strawberries*

APPENDIX C

ERROR ANALYSIS TABLE ADAPTED FROM JAMES (1999)

Level	SUBSTANCE	TEXT		DISCOURSE
	Grapheme Spelling Punctuation	GRAMMAR Class: noun/verb/adj/adv/ prep/conj/article/ pronoun	LEXIS Sense relations Collocations	Cohesion Coherence
Modification				
Omission Overinclusion Misselection Misorder Blend Random				

STYLISTIC IMITATION AS A TOOL IN WRITING PEDAGOGY

UWE GEIST

Roskilde University, Denmark

Abstract. In this article I reintroduce and discuss imitation as a tool for the learning and teaching of writing. I begin with some overall reflections on teaching and learning. Then, I focus more closely on imitation as a dimension in teaching and learning, arguing for its use. In this connection I refer to theoretical treatment of imitation, mostly in Piaget's work. Thus prepared I then describe how imitation can be used meaningfully as a tool for the learning and teaching of writing, without contradicting modern pedagogical principles like motivation toward self-activity and creativity. Finally, I present some reflections on the writing process which are not derived from the traditional coding metaphor for writing and reading texts.

Keywords: Linguistic features, style, imitation, active learning, induction, observational learning, experimental learning, acquisition of rules

1. INTRODUCTION

Language is the material texts are made of. Being able to handle language is consequently essential for writing. In this article I want to argue that stylistic imitation can be one of the pedagogical tools to make the student develop a practical knowledge of language use, and I want to show how stylistic imitation can be practised.

I will use the concept of style in the same sense as Leech and Short in their book *Style in Fiction*. Style for them is not a matter of singular, more or less well defined stylistic figures. It is the "way in which language is used" (Leech & Short, 1981: 38) in a certain text.

And when I say "imitation", I do not mean "parodying" (though that can very well be part of working with imitation), and I certainly do not mean slavish imitation of canonized models. My aim is to raise the students' sensibility towards the linguistic expression, and to make it clear for them that everything can be said in many

---

Geist, U. (2004). Stylistic imitation as a tool in writing pedagogy.
Rijlaarsdam, G. (Series Ed.) & Rijlaarsdam, G., Van den Bergh, H., & Couzijn, M. (Vol. Eds.). Studies in writing. Vol. 14, Effective learning and teaching of writing, 2nd Edition, Part 1, Studies in learning to write, 169 - 179.

different ways, but once said it has taken on the special meaning inherent to just this formulation.

I have practised imitation in writing courses at the university, but in my opinion the method I want to present functions most optimally at high school level. I have never made systematical experimental checks of the method described in this chapter, but I have received very positive responses from high school teachers about it. And in the last three years a presentation of imitation as a method in writing pedagogy has been part of the curriculum in the pedagogical courses for coming teachers of Danish in Denmark.

Beyond the scope of the chapter, but maybe interesting in connection with it, I could add that the method with its extremely practical and concrete focus on the use of language in texts has proved also to be a good instrument for dealing with literature. The close observation of the way language is used in a text – as it is implied by working with imitation – is a useful tool, too, for opening literary texts for interpretation.

2. THREE MODES OF TEACHING AND LEARNING

Writing, formulating a text, is problem solving. The problem to be solved is manifold: e.g., there is the problem of thinking the ideas, sensations, emotions, etc precisely enough to be able to formulate them, and of finding words and sentences to express them; there is the problem of how to understand and how to fulfil the demands of the genre; the problem of deciding what picture the text should give of itself and of how to make the text do that. Teaching writing is making others learn how to handle these problems. Learning is something the learner must do on his own. The problem of teaching thus is to bring teaching in accordance with learning and thus help the learner. Learning to write – as all other human learning – has three dimensions:
- the acquisition of techniques and skills, often by observation and imitation,
- the gathering of experience, often by experimenting and trial and error,
- the acquisition of knowledge of rules, a vocabulary and a systematic understanding, often by verbal explanation or instruction.

Accordingly, teaching has three dimensions:
- showing the learner how to do something and adjusting it,
- making the learner carry out the task and reflect on it,
- telling the learner how to do something and evaluating or correcting it.

A pedagogy of writing – as all other pedagogy – must integrate and make room for all three dimensions. Obviously, language is the specific human tool for learning and teaching. It is what gave the human race its evolutionary advantage. But that does not mean that the other modes should be neglected. They are related to language and to a certain degree formed by it, and practised in accordance with language. But they still are obligatory dimensions in teaching and learning. A human being cannot learn everything merely through the verbal communication of instructions, advice etc. Evolution is not a process of replacing something by something else, but a process of differentiation and of rearrangement in a more complex form.

3. IMITATION: THEORETICAL BACKGROUND

In the history of writing pedagogy, we can see all three dimensions represented. Ancient Greek and Latin writing pedagogy was dominated by imitation (Quintilian, 1961). In more modern times, starting in the late 18th century, writing pedagogy was dominated by rules of proper writing and instruction. And in the late 20th century's dominating paradigm of writing pedagogy the writing process and the writer's activities and experiences are in focus. But even though process oriented writing pedagogy is the dominating writing pedagogy today, other methods are still practised, pointing towards other dimensions in the learning process. Thus, the teaching and learning of more scientific and technical writing seems to be dominated by a mixture of instructing and imitating methods – by rules of how to do things and by models. And although the individual paradigms of writing pedagogy give priority to certain dimensions, they themselves still incorporate other dimensions. In this connection I will merely draw attention to the element of stealing, an imitating element in process oriented writing pedagogy (Healy, 1982). The stealing strategy, in fact, was the point of departure for my ideas about imitation. When writing, we all steal – we cite, we parody, we imitate – and in our postmodern times these practices have become a more crucial part of our culture.

I think we ought to use and teach this form of 'stealing', not necessarily more extensively, but more deliberately and more systematically. The unreflected, casual and random use of imitation we practise all the time is uncontrolled, e.g., it often becomes an imitation of the 'ends', and not of the 'means', as Dewey formulates it, and imitation thus loses its element of analysis, of 'close observation and judicious selection' which makes it 'an intelligent act' (Dewey, 1916: 42). The potential in imitation I want to activate is precisely this semi-conscious analytical component of observation and selection. In its semi-consciousness, it provides access to funds of techniques which are commonly shared, but which are too subtle, too varied, too contextually determined to be formulated in common rules or instructions. They may be found by trial and error, but more or less by chance and to a very limited degree. But the potential of imitation lies also in the fact that it is a drive. Human beings are able to, like to and in a way are forced to imitate. Imitation is biologically grounded: 'As a species we are strongly imitative' (Morris, 1977:18). It is an evolutionary inheritance, 'an essential and unique capacity' for vertebrates (Maturana & Varela, 1987:196), but leading up to mental representation and thus directly preparing for language (Bruner 1966; Yando 1978; Sloate & Voyat 1983).

In accordance with psychoanalytical theory, we identify ourselves with – and therefore to a certain degree imitate – both our worst enemies (Anna Freud, 1942) and those who are closest to us, our primary objects. Imitation is a fundamental trait in building up our identity out of elementary social settings. Thus the ability and the drive to imitate is deeply rooted in man, and imitation as a method is fundamental in many ways for our functioning, both in a social context and as individuals.

Imitation should therefore be used in modern writing pedagogy, too. Imitation is not a new idea in the pedagogy of writing. It was practised and discussed in Greek-Latin antique rhetoric and throughout the Middle Ages. To be a good rhetorician one not only needs theoretical knowledge, knowledge of the rules of style and grammar, and one needs an 'assured facility' (Quintilian, 1961: X.i.1) in the practical use of this knowledge as well. As in the modern conception of expertise (Dreyfus, 1986), the crucial point for experts is not the rules, but the assured facility. The 'rules which are taught in the schools' (Quintilian, 1961: X.i.15) lay the foundation. But then examples, practical demonstration and imitation take over and prepare the orator really 'for the contests in which he will have to engage' (Quintilian, 1961: X.i.4). Imitation thus is a solid and important ingredient in classical rhetoric. But at the same time Quintilian emphasizes that it should be used selectively and critically. "The greatest qualities of the orator are beyond all imitation, by which I mean, talent, invention, force, facility and all the qualities which are independent of art" (Quintilian, 1961: X.ii.12).

Throughout the Middle Ages imitation had a dominant position (Carruthers, 1992). Then, with the increasing confidence in scientific explanations and the growing belief in individuality and originality, imitation was downgraded. One of the most inspiring modern theorists who takes imitation up again is Piaget (Piaget, 1969). To Piaget, the individual's acting or functioning is bound to schemata, patterns of behavior. Development is: to differentiate, revise or change one's schemata in order – to a higher degree – to adapt to reality. The individual's adaptation to reality consists of both accommodation (the individual's adjustment of his own functioning to the way reality functions) and assimilation (the individual's making reality function in the way he himself functions). In this framework, imitation is a tool for the adjustment of one's own functioning to the way reality functions (accommodation). Play, on the other hand, is a tool for making reality function according to one's own way of functioning (assimilation). Playing is pretending. It means making up one's own conditions and handling something not in accordance with its real nature, but exclusively in accordance with one's own schemata and in accordance with what one can do and likes to do.

Imitating, however, means trying to do something which seems to be useful out in reality, but which one's own schemata are not yet prepared for.

However, to be able to imitate, one must be aware of what is to be imitated and how it can be imitated. Thus, imitation is closely connected with observation and analysis ('exploration' as Piaget calls it). Working with imitation it is therefore important to be aware of and make available the analytical resources surrounding imitation – observation and exploration. At the same time, it is necessary to combine imitation and play. Just playing, the individual will lose his sense of reality; just imitating, he will lose the sense of his own identity.

4. WHAT WILL I USE IMITATION FOR?

Imitation can be used for changing the learner's often naive attitude towards stylistic form. To him style can have good or bad elements, but beyond that it is more or less invisible and thus unimportant and unchangeable. I want the learner to supplement the personal-intuitive attitude with a technical-problem-solving one. This means that the learner must become aware of the stylistic form, must learn to focus on it and to see stylistic features as technical ways of solving certain problems which also could have been solved in other ways.

In imitation, form is separated from content, and the focus is on form. When imitating, the writer is free of the responsibility for or of existential involvement in the content. Content does not disappear. By manipulating stylistic features, the writer can bring up new content, triggered by changes in form. But content nevertheless is not the leading factor in imitation. Of course, content in an overall perspective is the main point of writing. For that reason imitation must not become especially extensive. The worst that can happen is that learning to write becomes emptied of content. But now and then it is productive to concentrate on form and on being able to work technically with form, undisturbed by content, and at best in a playful atmosphere. The moment of play in imitation is engaging and thus important as a provisional substitute for content.

But imitation should not bind the learner to ideals which have to be imitated in every detail. Learners should not imitate ideals, but single stylistic features. What is important is that they learn to work with a number of possible stylistic features, not that they learn to write the way, say, Hemingway did.

5. PRACTISING IMITATION

Following the reflections above, it is important to handle imitation in a proper way. I will describe the way I practise imitation in the teaching of writing, in five steps.

5.1 Step One: The Teacher Chooses Texts and Prepares an Analysis

In order to open up for formal observations, I try to build up clusters of 3-4 texts that differ in one or a few dimensions. For example, I have worked with argumentative texts that differ with respect to the dimension of rhetorical appeal: logos – the factual mode of arguing, concentrating on the matter; ethos – the trustworthy mode, concentrating on the image of the sender; and pathos – the emotive mode, concentrating on the arousal of the receiver's feelings.

I try to find texts which differ from each other markedly, and where each of them to a high degree and quite consistently and clearly represents one type of appeal. The texts should not be longer than half a page each. Then I try to find out for myself how the writers have managed to present the respective types of appeals. This is not always an easy task, but it is necessary, because it is also quite difficult for the students, who are to do the same thing in step two.

It is difficult, because of the way we are trained in textual analysis is not the optimal way to do this. We are not accustomed to analyzing texts from a productive point of view. We categorize the stylistic phenomena we meet and conclude something quite abstract about the content or the possible effect of the text. But we are not used to working the other way around: starting out from a special effect – e.g., the factual form for arguing – and then showing in detail how the writer works with his language in order to produce this special effect, and showing it in a way that facilitates imitation. In this connection it is important not only to name the phenomena, but to find as many examples of these techniques as possible in the texts and to show them, e.g., on overhead slides.

Beside these model texts, I have to find something that can help the students write their own texts. This for example could be an interesting controversial claim they could argue about.

5.2 Step Two: The Students Analyze the Texts

The first phase of their work is to 'observe' the three texts, one by one. The students are asked to describe briefly their impression of the individual text, and then we discuss the various impressions in plenum. After this the students are asked to describe in detail how the different writers have used the language to bring forth these particular impressions. They are asked to give very technical descriptions of three or four different dominating features of the use of language in each text.

It is important not to ask for more features than four, at the most five features, because it is difficult in the writing phase in step three (see below) to control more than a rather limited set of features. Often, in connection with small and quick exercises, inexperienced students can only handle two features. It does not really matter that they only work with two or three stylistic features, because the aim is not to imitate the style in another text as a whole. The aim is to become aware of certain stylistic features as technical possibilities and to get a chance to try them out and to become familiar with them. The students are to describe the features as technically and precisely as possible so that the descriptions can be used as instructions, and they, too, are to find examples.

The students work in small groups. When they are finished with a text, we discuss it in plenum and decide which three or four features we will concentrate on.

In our example with argumentative texts, depending on the texts, we will probably end up with the following features:

Logos-appeal: Many sentence connectors, primarily causal, adversative and conditional ones; only the third person is used (he, she, it, they); often passive voice; a lot of data, names and places.

Ethos-appeal: The first-person is used a lot (I, we); references to the first-person's experiences, position, considerations and actions ('I know from my frequent journeys to these islands that ...'); adverbs, adverbials and sentences marking the sender's attitude to what is being told ('naturally', 'to my great relief', 'I doubt whether ...').

Pathos-appeal: The second person is used a lot (you); frequent use of questions and exclamations; frequent use of adjectives, adverbs or nouns clearly marking something as positive or negative ('terrible', 'delightfully', 'scoundrel').

5.3 Step Three: The Students Write a Text

The students are now asked to write or rewrite an argumentative text, using one of the three sets of features – either logos, ethos or pathos. The teacher decides who writes according to which set. All sets should be used. The text can be written in small groups because writing here is explicitly technically oriented and not existentially. My own experience is that the groups have great fun, and the result is often very exaggerated. I have even asked for more exaggeration.

The problem, of course, is that the students use the features in such an exaggerated way that they can by no means identify with the text and thus emotionally reject the stylistic features in question. When writing in groups and really having fun – a quality in itself – I therefore usually continue with step four in its second variation (see below).

The texts the students have produced can be shown on an overhead, and we can discuss in plenum whether the sets of features that should be imitated are represented in the texts and how.

5.4 Step Four: The Students Rewrite

Further work can be structured in different ways. One version of step four is that the students rewrite the 'same' text using another set of stylistic features than those used in step three. The advantage of this version of step four is that the students can experience how other stylistic features will change the text fundamentally, not only on the surface, but in its motives, priorities, function and meaning. Using 'I' instead of 'you' in argumentative texts, they are also simultaneously forced to look after new arguments that fit into a text where the writer talks a lot about himself. They also have to establish another textual relation to the receiver of the text with consequences for other parts and elements of the text than the ones originally in focus as a set of features – only to mention some of the textual consequences of the shift from "you" in focus to "I" in focus.

The drawback of this version is that the students get tired of writing the 'same' text twice. This is especially dangerous when working with imitation. There is no problem in being negative with respect to specific stylistic features – which happens quite often ('This just isn't me!'). Here I am not afraid of pushing them and telling them to just try. A negative attitude can be an emotional drive, just as a positive one is.

Rewriting the same text once again with another set of stylistic features is one version of step four. Another version is rewriting the exaggerated text with the same set of stylistic features, but with a lower intensity of their use. The task is to try to use the same set of features as in step three, but now only to use them to a degree and in a form which the student thinks is appropriate and not parodic, and which he can back up and maybe even like. This time each student should write his own text. It still is not quite the student's own choice of how to write, but my general experience is that the students now – having the opportunity to minimize and modulate the features according to their own taste – are quite serious about it.

5.5 A Variant of Steps Three and Four

I have used the second form of rewriting (i.e., using the same set of features, but lowering the intensity of their use) especially when teaching people who have certain writing habits they want to change – like people in bureaucratic settings who are used to writing their texts in a very formal manner, and who want to change to a more free and flexible style. In this connection I have used pairs of texts in step two consisting of a text in a bureaucratic, formal style of writing and a text with the same function, but on quite a different stylistic level. Depending on the type of the formal text, the other text could be a recipe from a cookbook or an article from a tabloid newspaper or from a popular science magazine.

I do not have much experience with this variation, but I did practise it in the following way. In step two the students find three or four characteristic features in the popular text. In step three they are then asked to use these features in rewriting a formal text of the type they are used to producing themselves. In this connection it is really necessary for the teacher to make sure that the three or four features are fundamental features, e.g., including a device for the composition of the text. This is necessary because the rewriting should not only consist of superficial changes in the text's stylistic make-up. I also can recommend encouraging the students to make very strong changes, to overstate, to parody, because they will be very reluctant to change the style in which a great deal of their professional identity is bound up. Consequently, in the beginning they must have the opportunity to distance themselves from their new text as something they do not need to take seriously, in order not to offend them, thereby blocking the writing. It is the new text, written using other features than the ones these professionals are used to, that should be laughed at.

Having laughed, they are asked to rewrite the text according to the instructions for step three in its second version: Try to retain as many of the new features as possible, but boil them down to a level where you feel comfortable with the text and can take responsibility for it.

5.6 Step Five: Varying and Recombining Different Sets of Features

As a last variation, the students can be asked to mix some of the stylistic features from different sets derived from different texts. Thus, the stylistic features of logos, ethos and pathos can be mixed – as they usually are mixed in real-life texts. Or – if they have worked with different modes of representing speech in a text – they can be mixed: referring, indirect speech, normalized direct speech, idiomatic direct speech with its hesitations, self-corrections and breakdowns.

Having imitated these single features, the students are asked to combine them in a text in a way they are satisfied with and one they think would work. Here the teacher could also introduce new texts showing different ways of mixing the various features. I did not use these texts as imitation objects in the narrow sense I use in this chapter, with an elaborated analytical step, but only in a broader sense, as examples and inspiration.

Discussing the products, the students have to explain why they chose the dominating feature they did, and what effect mixing it with other features has.

6. DISCUSSION

My experience in using imitation is limited. And I have not tried to prove the method in a scientific way, e.g., by trying to test its results. I have simply tried it out and reflected on it. I have seen it work, and I am strongly convinced that imitation, practised in the way I have described it, is an important tool in the teaching and learning of writing. Of course, it only is one tool among many, and maybe a tool with quite a narrow scope, but still an important part of a comprehensive and varied writing pedagogy.

Following Piaget, imitation has to be connected with observation and analysis, and it has to be practised playfully. Following Quintilian, it is not to be practised uncritically, but selectively. And – more on my own account – it has to be imitation of single features, to be combined freely. When imitation is practised in this way, it should be possible to combine it with imagination, analytic energy and creativity.

Nevertheless, I will point out three main problems which I have already mentioned in the presentation of imitation as a pedagogic method.

The three problems are:
- the difficulty of detecting and describing stylistic phenomena,
- the risk of ideals,
- the deficit of content and the danger of emptiness.

6.1 The Difficulty of Detecting and Describing Stylistic Phenomena

Analysing stylistic features is a crucial point for imitation as a method. The first step is to detect them. Here, contrasting texts like I have used are very helpful.

The second step is to describe them. Style in connection with imitation does not refer to a narrow traditional definition of style, but to a broad one as described by Leech & Short: 'Style is a way in which language is used .... (t)herefore style consists in choices made from the repertoire of the language' (Leech & Short, 1981: 38). In this definition 'stylistic categories are ... complex phenomena which are often difficult to define' (ibid. 64). To define them often requires a level of linguistic expertise that is beyond that of many learners. Of course it is not necessary to describe the features scientifically. A great deal of the identification can be done by examples, functioning as models, but there must be the possibility of talking about them, too. The problem is very much the teacher's. It is his task to categorize the students' observations (step 2) and to give them a comprehensible form as well as workable rules.

6.2 The Problem of Ideals is a Problem Of Goals

Imitating models, ideals, or working according to a manual is not my goal. If style is choice (Leech & Short, 1981: 38) – to me it is – then the students must become able to choose and not to copy whole patterns. Imitation thus must not become an end, but it must be a means, as Dewey said (Dewey, 1916: 18) – a means to becoming able to choose. But it is difficult to mark and maintain the dividing line. One solution may be to make the students imitate many different (sets of) features and combine them in many ways. It probably is very helpful to integrate imitation with variation – changing style by varying single stylistic elements or clusters of them, and thus producing parallel and counter-texts (Pope 1995).

6.3 The Deficit of Content

The most severe problem is that of the deficit of content. I have dealt with it above, under step four. It is problematic, because it is a threat to the students' engagement and satisfaction, and thus to the learning effect. It is a strong argument for practising imitation often, but only as a short term activity and one clearly subordinate to activities where content is much more in focus.

7. PERSPECTIVES

My work with imitation both originated in and has been reconfirmed to me through an understanding of the writing process different from the traditional one, which rests on the coding metaphor. The coding metaphor means that a meaning or intention is transformed or coded gradually from thought into language (Beaugrande 1984: 87ff).

I would prefer another model showing the work of formulating or writing as a back and forth between intention and meaning on the one side and its realization in language on the other side.

The process of text production is a double one: working out a meaning and working out a linguistic expression. When it starts, more or less vague ideas and intentions and more or less accidental and fragmentary wordings are beginning to interact. The interaction is not an interaction between single elements, but between more or less fuzzy wholes, which are more or less consistently structured. The writer works on both meaning and expression, in connection with each other, trying to match the structures for the two lines of production. And through this interaction, both meaning and linguistic expression become more complex and more structured and consistent within themselves, and at the same time more in accord with each other. The writer decides when there is enough consistency within and accordance between meaning and expression to stop the process, thus deciding when the process of text production has been completed. The writer does not code one line into the other. The writer works on both lines at the same time. He is matching them, not coding.

Sperber and Wilson wrote about comprehension that "verbal communication is never achieved merely by the automatic decoding of linguistic signals" – nor by automatic coding of them, we could add from the perspective of text production. Because "if comprehension is defined as a process of identifying the speaker's informative intention [and so it is – UG], linguistic decoding is not so much a part of the comprehension process as something that precedes the real work of understanding, something that merely proceeds an input to the main part of the comprehension process" (Sperber & Wilson 1986: 177). Correspondingly, coding is not really part of the formulation process, but something that makes the provisional and final results of an ongoing formulation process explicitly available for the mind.

Expressing oneself is not at least scanning huge amounts of words, word combinations, etc, selecting them, trying them out, listening to them so as to find out whether they correspond with something the writer has in mind, whether they support it or derail it, specify, evolve, clarify or distort it.

The stock of words, word combinations, etc is built up on the basis of experiences with other texts. It is gathered by stealing. And the larger the stock is, the more sensible, creative and precise the writer can be towards his own intentions, thoughts and assumptions, when formulating them in words.

Writing, formulating texts thus always also is a means of understanding, i.e., of developing the content through working with the expression (and vice versa). Expression can be manipulated, because language is a sign system, and as such language is different from reality and partly independent of reality. That is why everything can be said in lots of different ways. That is the real strength of language, because that makes it possible to see reality in different ways, and thus to become able to change it.

To do this, you have to be aware of the possibilities that language provides. And a rather effective way of becoming acquainted with the possibilities in language is to try them out through imitation. Every child does it.

IMPROVING ARGUMENTATIVE WRITING BY FOSTERING ARGUMENTATIVE SPEECH

SERGIO CRASNICH & LUCIA LUMBELLI

University of Trieste, Italy

Abstract. The present investigation tested the effectiveness of an educational project aimed at improving the ability to take the addressee's stance into account and to apply it to the planning of argumentative discourse and text. This aim is derived from the assumption that the ability to make argumentation suitable to the addressee's stance (Perelman & Olbrecht-Tyteca, 1958) is an important condition for conceiving effective claims, arguments and counter-arguments and for expressing them both in oral discourse and in written compositions.
The educational methodology adopted can be characterised as a route from oral to written expression of argumentation (Lumbelli & Camagni, 1993). In 9 experimental sessions 30 high school students (a) first discussed upon topics selected by themselves, observed and evaluated their own transcribed utterances (b) were presented with a problem-solving situation, in which they were given the task to detect the most effective route to make a hypothetical addressee change his/her point of view into an opposite one, (c) were presented with a special kind of modelling in which there was the experimenter who talked aloud while reading a few argumentative texts which had been in advance evaluated as significant instances of argumentation and counterargumentation.
The argumentative competence was assessed by a test specially tapping the ability to take the addressee's point of view into account in the choice of the best argumentation (among four ones) and by the evaluation of written compositions according to categories based on the same criterion. 30 students matched on both these argumentative ability tests worked as control group. Experimental students significantly outperformed the control ones as to their sensitivity to audience's needs and their ability to adjust the arguments and counter-arguments to the addressee's stance.

Keywords: argumentation, observational learning, problem solving, speech, teacher-student interaction, text, writing

1. THEORETICAL FRAMEWORK

Planning an argumentative discourse requires that the speaker/writer engages in two different activities, i.e., (a) the justification of his/her position by means of argu-

---

Crasnich, S. & Lumbelli, L. (2004). *Improving argumentative writing by fostering argumentative speech.*
Rijlaarsdam, G. (Series Ed.) & Rijlaarsdam, G., Van den Bergh, H., & Couzijn, M. (Vol. Eds.). Studies in writing. Vol. 14, Effective learning and teaching of writing, 2nd Edition, Part 1, Studies in learning to write, 181 - 196.

ments, and (b) the negotiation of the discourse elements in order to take the addressee's viewpoint into account. Negotiation becomes crucial, but also more difficult, in written argumentation, as the audience must be constructed by the writer in his/her own mind. This is one of the main reasons why adolescents and adults do not frequently produce elaborated argumentative text (Coirier, Andriessen, & Chanquoy, 1999).

The two elements of argumentation mentioned above have been connected to each other by Chaim Perelman in his *nouvelle rhétorique*, aimed at defining the discourse mechanisms best suited to triggering or increasing audience adhesion and agreement (Perelman & Olbrechts-Tyteca, 1958: 5). In Perelman's theory, as in Aristotle's rhetoric, the pivotal concept is that each element of strong argumentation is tailored to the audience (*l'auditoire*: Perelman and Olbrechts-Tyteca, 1958: 7). The strength of the argumentation depends on two conditions, i.e., (a) the speaker/writer's knowledge of the audience (Perelman & Olbrechts-Tyteca, 1958: 26) and (b) the speaker/writer's ability to bring about a process of adaptation to the audience (*adaptation à l'auditoire*: Perelman and Olbrechts-Tyteca, 1958: 31). This means that effective argumentation contains premises (*prémisses*) and other negotiated objects (*objets d'accord*) such as facts, truths, values worthy of consideration by the specific audience to which it is addressed (Perelman and Olbrechts-Tyteca, 1958: 36).

Argumentation is thus considered as the result of an individual thinking process in which the speaker/writer deliberately interacts with a mental representation of the addressee. This interaction plays a crucial role in Perelman's evaluation of the strength of the arguments (*force des arguments*): the speaker/writer's ability to conceive objections to an argument supporting his/her thesis is indeed the necessary condition for formulating a counter-argument, which can be either a predictable rebuttal (*argument prévu*: Perelman & Olbrechts-Tyteca, 1958: 621) or the resumption of an argument accepted by the addressee, so as to reach a conclusion which is quite different and even contrasting with the ones s/he had drawn originally (Perelman & Olbrechts-Tyteca, 1958: 622).

This emphasis on the interaction between the speaker/writer's argumentation processes and his/her representation of the addressee characterises Perelman's theory and distinguishes it from other theories about argumentative production. For example, Toulmin (1958) considers argumentation as an individual activity in which the speaker/writer organises a discourse justifying the position asserted. Although Toulmin proposes a precise and exhaustive description of the way in which information must be arranged in order to obtain a correctly structured argumentation, he fails to attribute the strength of the arguments to the speaker/writer's adaptation of data, warrants and backing to the addressee's point of view. Hence, his theory only concerns monological argumentation and does not consider the representation of the addressee's possible reactions as a criterion for evaluating argument strength, namely as a criterion relevant to dialogical argumentation.

More recently, pragma-dialectics (Van Eemeren & Grootendorst, 1992) which is based on speech act theory (Austin, 1962; Searle, 1969) has maintained that the phases of argumentative dialogue should follow some rules in order to help resolve differences of opinion reasonably and avoid risk of 'fallacies' (Van Eemeren &

Grootendorst, 1999a). Indeed, this approach strongly emphasises the dialogical aspect of argumentation, since pragma-dialectical rules refer chiefly to the interaction between the speaker/writer and the addressee. Moreover, in their educational suggestions, Van Eemeren and Grootendorst (1999b) have directly focused on writing, i.e., on some *analytic* and *presentation transformations* (e.g., deletion, addition, substitution) which should make an argumentative text acceptable to the intended reader. Unlike Perelman's approach, the main point here is the writer's revision of a previous version of his/her argumentation, rather than the thinking process which must be performed in the planning phase in order to construct a complete representation of the addressee/reader.

The present educational project is based on the *nouvelle rhétorique* precisely because this theory emphasises the planning phase of an argumentation and assumes a close link between the speaker/writer's thinking and his/her representation of the constraints arising from the audience. Perelman's theory is taken as a useful premise for an instructional project aimed at fostering the cognitive abilities needed for the planning of good argumentative discourse and text.

This stress on the representation of the audience's viewpoints, goals and attitudes implies highly significant assumptions regarding educational strategies aimed at improving the ability to write effective argumentative texts. One main assumption is that planning argumentative texts involves thinking first of all: namely (a) exploring our own representation of the addressee in order to continuously check whether it is complete and reliable enough, and (b) searching in our own mind not only for ideas in support of our own claims but also for ideas which are counter-arguments and thus addressee-centred, and not egocentric in the sense defined by Piaget (1926).

If planning argumentative text is made effective by the writer's ability to discover routes suited to lead the addressee from his/her present stance to the writer's one, this planning can be considered as involving that specific way of thinking which Gestalt psychologists called *productive thinking* and consists of viewing a given problem-situation in a way which allows us to detect new relationships between its elements and, thus, to obtain a change of problem perception which makes the path to the solution emerge (Duncker, 1935; Wertheimer, 1945)

The task of writing down is only to be faced once a cognitive representation of the goal-solution (changing the addressee's mind) has been reached and a suitable route to that goal has been mentally planned.

We do not mean to deny the importance of transferring into written text, but only to emphasise the importance of a preliminary phase in which the thinking task is tackled by speakers/writers, free from the constraints and the additional difficulty of a writing task.

This preliminary phase is based on the interesting assumption that argumentative discourse is fruitful material for research on productive thinking. According to Mosconi (1978: 15-16) 'argumentative discourse can be seen as a problem-solving process', 'the attainment of listener's adhesion to a given viewpoint is the solution to the problem' and 'the listener's initial thinking and the information available about the issue under discussion' are the 'data' which the speaker must elaborate in order to persuade the listener, namely in order to solve the problem. Argumentative discourse is therefore 'the route which must be found in order to lead the listener from his/her initial standpoint to the goal represented and targeted by the speaker'.

From this definition of argumentative discourse Mosconi draws some methodological considerations pertaining to research on productive thinking. Its advantage is that here the process of searching for a solution is made completely explicit unlike other kinds of problem-solving tasks, in which it is very difficult to obtain complete and reliable verbal protocols on the participants' attempts to solve the problem, because the problem solving process only occurs 'in the solver' s mind' and can only very partially become verbal protocols. Mosconi's definition leads us, on the other hand, draw educational conclusions which are the core of our project.

If the ability to plan argumentative discourse is a sub-category of the problem solving ability, it has to be targeted by presenting students with problem solving tasks, in which

- changing the addressee's mind is the solution or goal,
- the addressee's initial standpoint is the problem-situation or problem-space,
- the arguments and counter-arguments are moves towards the solution and are either to be identified in the information available or inferred from it.

Our educational strategy is an *indirect approach*, which can be characterised as a special kind of *Umweg* or *detour* openly and directly working on the students' ability to search in their own minds in order to detect the most suitable arguments which are then to be written down. The writers must first learn to free themselves from their own point of view and evaluate arguments from the stance of their addressee, and only then (as a consequence of this learning) cope with the transfer into written text.

The emphasis on the productive thinking elements in planning argumentative discourse also confirms the educational suggestions derived from the results of a previous study (Lumbelli & Camagni, 1993) in which written texts were improved by working on the corresponding oral version. There, the goal was to monitor the micro-planning processes to make them more suitable to the addressee as regards local coherence and comprehensibility. Written texts were made locally more coherent through the revision of their oral reformulation. That investigation showed (1) that the detour from writing to speech can be effective in improving writing, and (2) that two types of shortcoming are to be distinguished in written texts: gaps which can be traced back to insufficient communicational ability and can so be repaired through the experimented strategy of working on the oral planning and gaps which were not merely due to low verbal ability but to corresponding gaps in the writer's cognitive representation itself and therefore could not be treated educationally simply through the revision of speech planning.

In the present investigation, the detour strategy implies that the ability to write argumentative text is fostered by using the analysis of oral discourse. This analysis concerns a set of verbal protocols on those cognitive activities which consist of (a) detecting the ideas which can work as premises for new argumentation suitable to the addressee, and (b) noticing useful connections between the information retrieved from long-term memory and the information upon which the addressee's statements are based.

Cognitive processes thus become the core of the educational treatment, and the only features of argumentative competence taken into account are the ones based on those cognitive processes, while the linguistic aspects of argumentative competence are to be tapped only once the students have already acquired effective cognitive strategies of argumentation-seeking.

Other premises of our educational project are concerned with two principles of educational procedure. First, we decided to exploit the advantages of both self-regulated learning and observational learning (Couzijn & Rijlaarsdam, 1996; Couzijn, 1999; Braaksma, Van den Bergh, Rijlaarsdam & Couzijn, 2001; Braaksma, Rijlaarsdam & Van den Bergh, 2002) so as to both enhance students' motivation and provide them with well-defined criteria for identifying suitable argumentation. Secondly, we adopted two forms of instructor communication corresponding to those forms of learning.

In the self-regulated learning, i.e., when commitment to the tasks had to be encouraged, we decided to give the students a feedback consisting of accurate reformulation of their statements (Lumbelli, 1996). In the observational learning, in which the experimenter acted as an expert model, we decided to present the students with verbal protocols focused on the correct comprehension and evaluation processes for the argumentative written texts used as instructional material (Lumbelli, Paoletti & Frausin, 1999).

2. HYPOTHESES

The following main research question was drawn from those assumptions: Can the ability to write elaborated argumentative texts be improved by encouraging high school students to take into account the addressee's viewpoint, and search for and find suitable arguments while tackling problem-solving activities? Can conscious focus and reflection on our own representation of an addressee, through problem solving activities, improve the ability to write argumentative text?

Since considering the addressee's stance is assumed as a chief feature of the ability to write argumentative texts, the measure of this ability was based on the presence of two kinds of communicational act in writing:
- argumentation of one's own claims,
- counter-argumentation suited to contesting the addressee's claims.

Another measure was related to the specific ability which the instructional treatment was focused upon, namely to the ability to distinguish an argumentation tailored to the addressee's stance from an argumentation which seems to ignore it.

3. MAIN PHASES OF THE INSTRUCTIONAL TREATMENT

The first phase of the treatment was principally aimed at providing the motivational ground for the successive phases, i.e., at providing students with the conditions assumed most likely to enhance their autonomous, self-motivated attitude towards any instructional activity which they would be asked to participate in subsequently. They were invited to choose a few issues which they would be interested in talking about; they were then presented with the transcription of those sequences which were judged most suitable to be examined according to the principle of relevance to the addressees' viewpoint. In this phase, any instructional artefact was avoided. The only instructional goal was to make all students likely to store in their episodic memory both the items of communicational experience which they reflected upon and the outcomes of their self-evaluation, so that the later phase activities could be founded on them.

The following example illustrates how this stage encouraged the students to monitor their argumentation in order to adapt it to the addressee's viewpoint. In a class discussion about whether it is acceptable to allow a homosexual couple to adopt a child, two students express their position (against and for, respectively) in a fragmentary and unclear way.

(1) Katja: Does it seem to you that a child... who lives for example with two women or with two men, and goes to school... then you see... but mum and dad, why does that one have a mum and dad of different sexes, and I have two of the same sex?
(2) Kim: But you can make him understand...
(3) Katja: No! You see?... Because when the child goes out of his home, he'll go to school and he'll be the one who's different, he'll be... in my opinion this child will also suffer some psychological damage

The information presented as argument is not linked to the students' claims, and the information presented as counter-argument is not explicitly referred to the addressee's opposing viewpoint. In the collective analysis in the classroom, the students, encouraged by the experimenter's responses, realise that their utterances prevented reciprocal comprehension of their viewpoint and complete them by making their respective discourses more relevant to each other's arguments.

(1) Experimenter: Here, Katja, you respond to Kim
(2) Katja: Yes, I respond to her alright!... In short, I shut her up
(3) Kim: Yes, because she didn't let me speak
(4) Experimenter: She didn't let you speak
(5) Kim: Yes, I meant that you can make the child understand... by talking to him, you see... that there's nothing strange if two people of the same sex live together, and that he doesn't have to feel different because of that
(6) Katja: I wanted to say that for me that's not the way it is, since the child will feel different from other children because his parents are homosexuals, and he won't be able to understand
(7) Experimenter: You don't think he'll understand
(8) Katja: No, and maybe the other children will sneer at him too because of his parents and he'll suffer

In her analysis, Kim (utterance 5) completes her discourse by referring explicitly to her idea of talking with the child, which she had not explained in the previous discussion: this statement is a rebuttal of the addressee's viewpoint, as it implies that the child can understand and accept the relationship between his/her parents. Katja (utterance 6), on the other hand, supports her own claim about the psychological damage suffered by the child adopted by a homosexual couple by presenting it as a consequence of the other children's reactions.

The second phase, too, was centred on the oral production of argumentation. Here too, we applied the approach defined and proved by Lumbelli & Camagni (1993) and based on the assumption that a more direct and effective influence on thought strategies can be obtained by focussing on oral production and postponing the passage to writing. Students, divided in small groups of three or four, were invited to plan an argumentative oral discourse suited to an addressee with an opposing stance on a determined topic, chosen by the students themselves in the first phase and reformulated by the experimenter in the initial instruction. They were then asked to find possible arguments and counter-arguments and evaluate them by applying the criterion of their suitability to that addressee's viewpoint. The problem-situation was enriched with further elements which could be processed in order to find the possible path to the solution, i.e., counter-argumentation suited to the addressee's stance. These elements consisted of a set of short texts on that specific issue which could be skimmed through for possible premises of suitable arguments and counter-arguments. The students were invited to think aloud and were encouraged to further complete their spontaneous initial think-aloud protocols by experimenter feedback systematically centred on those protocols (Rogers, 1951; Lumbelli, 1996). The small number of students enabled the experimenter occasionally to pay attention to each of their thought efforts as much as in an individualised session.

The following example illustrates how this stage of the project encouraged the students to conceive their argumentation taking into account the addressee's opposing viewpoint. Katja argues that the USA offers more opportunities for social mobility than European countries, but she has just found information about the inequality of job opportunities between WASPs and other ethnic groups.

(1) Katja: It's true... that the WASPs have all the power and so on... but in my opinion it depends on the individual, despite the fact that there are some conditions that may help or not
(2) Experimenter: If I've understood you properly, you're saying that you think it depends on the individual whether he has opportunities or not
(3) Katja: As I've already said, I accept most of what my addressee says, but he has not considered the individual in himself, he has always considered the masses
(4) Experimenter: You say that he has always considered the masses
(5) Katja: Because what emerges from the passages is that it's true that the lower classes have few opportunities for social mobility
(6) Experimenter: So what you're saying is that you agree with some of the things he says but it seems to you that they haven't considered the individual, but the masses
(7) Katja: Yes, in my opinion, there are some factors that may or may not help the individual but it depends a lot on him
(8) Experimenter: What you're saying is that there are some factors that limit the individual, but that a lot still depends on him
(9) Katja: Yes... I think that if someone from a lower class really wants to change his social position he can... even though he won't make much progress, but most people think it's very difficult to change and so they stay in the same class

After a moment's hesitation, the student spontaneously proposes a distinction between the masses and individual (utterance 1). The experimenter's feed-back (utterance 2) encourages the student to better formulate the distinction in order to use it as a counter-argumentation more suited to the addressee's standpoint (utterance 3).

Then, the student takes the opposing viewpoint explicitly into account (utterance 5) and supports (utterances 7 and 9) her counter-argument by defining the conditions suitable for making her position acceptable. By the end of the interaction, she was able to autonomously adapt her argumentation to the opposing viewpoint, just by being encouraged by the experimenter to keep thinking.

In the third phase, a special form of *observational learning* was provided (Couzijn & Rijlaarsdam, 1996) in which the experimenter became a reader model (Schriver, 1992) of argumentative text processing. The main function of this phase was to help students organise the knowledge stored in the previous phases, and make explicit all that which was likely to be implicit and/or not consciously monitored. The emphasis shifted from learner self-regulation to the acquisition of rules and principles for correct and effective argumentation. Newspaper articles written by expert authors were used as instructional material. The experimenter read each successive piece of text and verbalised both his own comprehension processes and his evaluation of the suitability of arguments and counter-arguments expressed there; at the end, he recapitulated the argumentative strategies used in the text, the evaluation outcomes and supplied a formal definition of the criteria already introduced less formally in the previous stages.

4. ASSESSMENT INSTRUMENTS

Two dependent variables were distinguished: the general ability to write an effective argumentative text, and the specific ability to recognise the arguments' suitability to the addressee's stance.

The *argumentative composition* checked the students' ability to plan an argumentative written text which contains both argumentation of their own claims and counter-argumentation relevant to the addressee's claims. The students were invited to write an argumentative text designed to make an addressee change his/her standpoint on a determined issue, a standpoint which was assumed to be completely different.

A topical issue was selected from those proposed in the IEA written composition test (Gorman, Purves & Degenhart, 1988): *Does watching TV for a long time cause people be less likely to think in an autonomous way?* The instruction explicitly asked the students to assume that the addressee's point of view was radically opposed to their own and to write arguments and counter-arguments designed to change his/her mind. This is the scoring procedure:
- Score 0 for texts containing only claims without any argument.
- Score 1 for texts containing at least one claim and one argument, but no counter-argument.
- Score 2 for texts containing at least one claim, one argument and one counter-argument.

We will present some examples to make the evaluation procedure explicit we adopted and so counterbalance the following methodological limitation: after a first pilot phase, in which both the authors evaluated a sample of written compositions independently without any disagreement, only one of the two authors analysed and evaluated the written compositions.

The following text is an example of a composition which received score 0. The text contains some claims together with further information that is not used to support these claims, and the opposing viewpoint is not considered.

> In my opinion, watching television for a long time influences people's behaviour. Whereas sometimes it makes us think with our own head. According to some people, watching TV makes people incapable of thinking independently; whereas according to others watching TV helps growth. I think that TV can also help, if people don't watch it for a long time.
>
> Some parents leave their children alone at home, and the children begin to watch TV and exclude themselves from the external world. I think that it would be better to watch TV very little and spend time taking a walk or doing something else.
>
> I don't think that TV makes it difficult to think independently, as long as a person watches TV just for the pleasure of it and doesn't identify himself with it.

Next text is an example of a composition which received score 2. The text presents one claim and supports it with a few arguments. The addressees' opposing viewpoint is also presented and supported by means of two arguments. The student's first counter-argument maintains that the programmes that do not influence the audience are rare. The second counter-argument is introduced by a concession, and consists of stressing the partiality of television comments about facts.

> I think that watching television for a long time makes it more difficult to think with one's own head. For example, television succeeds in bewitching middle-aged women by promising a fast improvement in their physical appearance by the use of beauty creams. However, nothing really happens, because they can't become as attractive as the girls in the advertisements.
>
> Another example concerns children. They learn models and roles by watching TV programmes. A lot of research has pointed out that children are very violent nowadays, because that's what children are taught by cartoons and films. These cartoons show fighting, shoot-outs, and destruction, and hence children become more and more aggressive.
>
> A lot of people might disagree with me, and claim that there are a lot of television programmes which don't influence viewers either positively or negatively. I believe that such programmes are like "a needle in a haystack" since they are very rare. Another criticism might be that television provides information about things that happen in the most remote areas of the planet. I think this is the only advantage of television. However, I also think that television doesn't allow people to have a personal opinion, because the journalists' comments often don't present all the facts, but only some of them.

The *test of the ability to recognise argumentation suitability* was specifically prepared for the project by means of a two-step try-out in which 89 secondary school students (mean age 17.3 years) participated. In the first step, 30 items were presented in three sessions lasting 45 minutes each; the presentation order of the booklets containing the items was counterbalanced. Ten items were discarded by means of an item analysis, obtaining a set of 20 more homogeneous items (Cronbach's α= .753) which were ranked by difficulty and divided in two parallel forms comparable as to difficulty index (mean .427 and .397 respectively) and as to Johnson upper-lower index (mean .393 and .341 respectively). In the second step, we controlled the reliability of the parallel forms by presenting them in one session and in counterbalanced order; a reliability coefficient of .80 was obtained.

As to the structure of the multiple-choice test, each item was divided into two parts. The first part describes the addressee's interests, motives and values; the second part lists four arguments only one of which is suited to the addressee; the respondents have to choose the argument they think best satisfies the conditions described in the initial piece.

This is an example of one item from the multiple-choice test.

> An ecological movement is preparing a referendum designed to obtain the closing of nuclear power stations, which currently produce a very low quantity of electric energy and require expensive maintenance operations.
>
> A recent survey has discovered that many voters are undecided. In fact, people are worried about the possible consequences of an accident, but at the same time consider closing of the plants would be a waste of public money, and they want this kind of waste avoided.
>
> From the following four discourses, choose the one that seems to you suited to convincing referendum participants to vote in favour of closing nuclear power stations.
>
> (1) Closing down the power stations will show that a flourishing economy can do without dangerous and harmful sources of energy; if the majority vote in favour of closure, the politicians will understand that this is necessary in order to avoid damages to public health.
>
> (2) Closing down the power stations is a responsible choice, because in case of war they would make a country more vulnerable; moreover, it is very easy to transform the uranium used in these power stations into a nuclear weapon.
>
> (3) Closing down the power stations is a good thing, even though this will cause an energy shortage. In fact, we may have to use more expensive energy sources in order to produce the same amount of energy, but these will be less dangerous for our health.
>
> (4) Closing down the power stations the plants will eliminate the risk of terrible disasters and also save all the money required for their maintenance, which would still not eliminate the risk of accidents.

Finally, after every item there is an open question, in which respondents are asked to explain briefly why they chose a given answer. Their responses were used to check whether they were able to give a clear reason for their choices.

This is the scoring procedure:
- Score 0 for a wrong answer.
- Score 1 for choosing the correct argumentation.
- Score 2 for choosing the correct argumentation and explaining their choice correctly.

These are some examples of explanation of the correct choice (number 4) that were considered adequate: in these cases, the students received a score of 2.

(1) It mentions two worries of the population: more safety and less waste of public money
(2) The citizens consider the nuclear power stations to be dangerous and want to avoid wasting money. If the power stations are closed, the risk of accidents can be eliminated, together with the waste of the money spent on avoiding that risk

These are some explanations of the correct choice that were considered inadequate: in these cases, the students received a score of 1.

(1) It's more convincing
(2) Nuclear power stations are a great danger from every point of view and if they were closed down this would also eliminate the risk of serious accidents which could cause the disappearance of mankind

5. PARTICIPANTS AND PROCEDURE

Sixty students, attending the 11th and 12th grade of two high schools ("Ginnasio") for the Italian minority in Slovenia, participated in the study. The curricula of the two schools were the same. Moreover, the same teachers worked in both schools due to their small size. Hence, the students can be considered comparable as to the teaching styles and the school curriculum which they were exposed to.

The students were divided into two groups matched on both dependent measures in the pre-test phase. One group was assigned to the experimental treatment, while the other group worked as control. The experimental subjects' mean age was 17.6 years, while the mean age of control subjects was 17.5.

In the multiple-choice test (range 0-20), the mean pre-test scores were 9.50 (SD 3.01) for the experimental group, and 9.20 (SD 3.03) for the control group. An ANOVA applied to the pre-test scores confirmed that the difference between the groups was not significant ($F = .148; p = .702$).

In the pre-test written composition (range 0-2), the percentages of students who scored 0, 1 and 2 were 56.7, 36.7 and 6.6 for the experimental group, and 53.3, 43.3 and 3.4 for the control group. Due to the ordinal nature of the scoring, a Wilcoxon test was computed. This difference between the groups was not significant either ($z = .126; p = .899$).

Throughout the study, the control group was only exposed to the school lessons; the experimental group was exposed to both the school lessons and to the treatment. As to L1 curriculum of the Italian schools in Slovenia, its main aim is to provide the students with an overall knowledge of Italian literature. Hence the teachers do not deal with argumentative texts, but devote their attention to narrative texts and poems. In their writing assignments, the students are invited to adopt an expository rather than an argumentative perspective in dealing with the authors and texts studied.

Every experimental student was presented with 9 sessions. Every initial and final treatment phase session took around 90 minutes weekly and involved 15 participants. In the middle phase sessions, smaller groups of students (3 to 4) received the treatment in order to help everyone interact with the experimenter as much as possible. All the experimental sessions of the treatment were audio-recorded. After the treatment, both groups were presented with the same written composition test and the parallel form of the multiple-choice test.

6. RESULTS

The analysis of the results confirmed that the instructional project was effective in fostering the ability to take into account the addressee's viewpoint.

As to the multiple choice test, the post-test mean scores were 13.93 (SD 4.79) for the experimental group, and 9.33 (SD 2.60) for the control group. The ANOVA confirmed that the difference between the post-test scores of the experimental and the control group was significant ($F = 21.343$; $p = .001$). The same analysis applied to the gain scores confirmed that the improvement in the performance of the experimental group was also significant ($F = 25.260$; $p = .001$). Hence, the instructional project was effective in fostering the ability to evaluate arguments and counter-arguments from the addressee's point of view.

The following table (Table 1) shows the overall results and the mean gain scores in the multiple choice test.

Table 1: Multiple choice test: pre-test, post-test and gain scores with standard deviations

	Experimental M	Experimental SD	Control M	Control SD
Pre-test	9.50	3.01	9.20	3.02
Post-test	13.93	4.79	9.33	2.60
Gain	4.43	4.52	.13	1.25

Similar results were obtained in the written composition, which measured the ability of the student to write an elaborated argumentative text. In the post-test, the percentages of students who scored 0, 1 and 2 were 23.3, 26.7 and 50.0 for the experimental group, and 66.7, 30.0 and 3.3 for the control group. The following table (Table 2) shows the overall results in the written composition.

Table 2. Pre- and post-test written compositions: Proportions of subjects scoring 0, 1, 2

Score	Experimental Pre-test	Experimental Post-test	Control Pre-test	Control Post-test
0	.567	.233	.533	.667
1	.367	.267	.433	.300
2	.066	.500	.034	.033

Due to the kind of dependent measure, in which an ordinal scale is adopted, the scores were submitted to a two-way rank ANOVA using the Friedman test. The analysis applied to the overall data showed significant differences between the groups' pre- and post-test written composition scores ($\chi^2 = 31.005$, $df = 3$; $p = .001$).

In the post-hoc comparisons, the improvement in the post-test scores of the experimental subjects was significantly greater than that of control subjects (mean rank difference 1.35; $p = .0004$). The difference between the experimental group's pre- and post-test scores was also significant (mean rank difference 1.13; $p = .0036$), while the difference between the control group's pre- and post-test scores was not significant (mean rank difference .23). Thus, the results of the analysis confirmed that the instructional project was effective in fostering the ability to write an argumentative text.

Finally, the correlation between the two dependent measures was computed. Spearman's rho correlation coefficient between the post-test scores was .726 ($p = .001$).

7. DISCUSSION AND CONCLUSIONS

The educational project proved to have a positive effect. This effect concerned, firstly, the specific ability to recognise the argumentation suited to the addressee distinguishing it from argumentation which fails to take the addressee's stance into consideration, and secondly, the general ability to support one's own claims when writing an argumentative text and referring to the argumentation of others by means of counter-argumentation.

These outcomes were obtained in the course of just 9 instructional sessions and can be attributed to the influence of the treatment as a whole; i.e., a treatment
- characterised by a main phase where the acquisition of argumentation ability is pursued by helping students solve the problem of identifying a route which starts from the addresses' stance and leads to the one of the speakers themselves;
- in which the students' involvement in this problem-solving activity is encouraged by a previous free conversation activity about topics they selected themselves, and therefore based as much as possible on their own interests;

- in which observational learning is inserted as a teacher's modelling aimed at presenting students with formal and explicit reference to those rules and principles of argumentation theory which in the previous phases were only introduced indirectly and applied unconsciously.

Further experimental investigations are obviously needed in order to ascertain whether one phase influenced the positive outcome more than the others. However, some qualitative observations are already possible since all educational sessions were audio-recorded. Some fairly clear empirical evidence can be anticipated: it seems that in the main problem-solving phase, the less successful participants were more likely than the more successful ones to have received less initial encouragement from the experimenter and were therefore less active in exploring the material made available and searching it for argumentation.

The following excerpts taken from two sessions of the central treatment phase provide some preliminary insights into the effect of experimenter's feedback. In both excerpts, the students are preparing a discourse plan to support the claim that capital punishment is not justifiable.

In the first example a student receives suitable feedback by the experimenter.

(1) Experimenter: You said before that you wanted to talk about justice
(2) Tea: Yes, because my addressee talks about justice and claims... that capital punishment in the United States satisfies people's desire for justice
(3) Experimenter: That is the first thing he said
(4) Tea: Yes... and then he said that the death penalty is perfectly legal if the defendant doesn't succeed in proving he is not guilty...
(5) Experimenter: That is the second thing
(6) Tea: Yes... I would say that justice is connected to the equality before the law, and I would start from that... in my opinion, a criminal should be punished, and justice must be done to the victims of crime, but it's also important to guarantee that defendants are judged under identical conditions
(7) Experimenter: It is right to punish criminals and it is right to ensure identical conditions for all defendants
(8) Tea: That's it... well... if we consider the social status of people condemned to the death penalty, we see that the majority of them are black... but we have seen that black people can't be defended by a good lawyer the same way as the members of other social classes
(9) Experimenter: So you would say that a great number of black people are on death row because they can't defend themselves like the other social classes
(10) Tea: Yes, because good lawyers don't defend them and they are judged by a jury that tries to apply the death penalty whenever possible, and that's easier if a person is not well defended, and so I think that a black defendant doesn't have the same defence opportunities as another person, with a good lawyer... since our premise was that justice is an important... fundamental point, but that equality is just as important and fundamental an element of justice, we see that the equality principle is violated because there is no equal treatment between a white and a black in a criminal court in Texas for example
(11) Experimenter: Two defendants... a white and a black don't get the same treatment
(12) Tea: That's it... and for that reason, even though I agree that it is right to punish the criminals so that they can't be a danger, it seems to me that the death penalty is not a just punishment because it effects the poor people and the drop-outs more that the real murderers

In this excerpt, the experimenter's feedback manages to encourage the student to go on thinking and speaking at the same time. In her argumentative plan (namely, in utterances 6 and 10), the student conceives an argumentative scheme defined *rule of justice* (*règle de justice*: Perelman and Olbrechts-Tyteca, 1958). Moreover, the addressee's claims are submitted to concessions (utterances 6 and 12, first part) and to counter-arguments (utterances 10 and 12, second part), while the premises of the student's argumentation are explicitly and clearly stated (utterance 10, second part).

In the following example, the experimenter managed to encourage only one of the two students involved in the interaction. While the encouraged student goes on verbalising his argumentative thinking process, the student who was not encouraged reduces his commitment to the activity.

(1) David: If new evidence for the defence is found after a sentence is passed, the defendant should be brought to trial again, but in Texas this does not happen...
(2) Experimenter: Now we have to decide if this information can be used
(3) David: Yes (break)
(4) Experimenter: From this information we can say that it depends a lot on the lawyer because someone may have committed a lot of murders but not be sentenced to death
(5) Marko: While someone else may only have killed once and if he is black or poor he might be defended by a lawyer who doesn't pay attention during the trial, so that he is sentenced to death
(6) Experimenter: If a person is poor then he may be defended by a lawyer who doesn't defend him so he is found guilty... now I wonder how this information about the lawyers can be used
(7) Marko: I could use it to say that the sentence doesn't depend on what the defendant has done, but only on who his lawyer is
(8) Experimenter: It doesn't depend on the defendant but on the lawyer whether
(9) Marko (interrupting): Whether someone is sentenced to death, in practice, if I'm poor, I'll be defended by a bad lawyer and I'll be found guilty, while if I am rich, I'll be defended by a good lawyer and I won't be found guilty
(10) Experimenter: If someone is defended by a good lawyer he won't be condemned to death
(11) Marko: Yes, so it doesn't matter what he has done but only who his lawyer is
(12) David: And that is not right
(13) Marko: No, because if I'm rich I can save myself, whereas if I am poor I can't
(14) Experimenter: If I am poor I'm sentenced to death, if I am rich I'm not
(15) David: Yes
(16) Experimenter: You said that it's not right and, if I've understood you properly, it is not right that a person is sentenced to death because he is poor or rich... and it seems to me that this information can be useful for the discourse
(17) David: Yes!
(18) Experimenter: And it can be useful because
(19) Marko (interrupting): Because you can see that if I am rich I'm not sentenced to death
(20) Experimenter: The death penalty is applied to the poor ones and not to the rich ones
(21) Marko: And that is not right because the poor ones and the rich ones don't have the same opportunities to be defended by a good lawyer

David's first spontaneous utterance (1) is not reformulated by the experimenter, and this is probably the reason why David only says "yes", and is then reduced to silence for several minutes. Instead of trying to enhance David's involvement, the experimenter goes on with his suggestion. The interaction with Marko which follows is similar to the previous one with Tea. David's poor communication efforts later (12 and 17) are ignored by the experimenter, who continues instead to pay attention to Marko's lines of thought and discourse.

These observations seem to support the hypothesis that encouraging participants' involvement in the problem-solving activity might actually have worked as a crucial condition for the effectiveness not only of this activity itself but also of the subsequent observational learning stage.

MONITORING LOCAL COHERENCE THROUGH BRIDGING INTEGRATION

From text comprehension to writing revision and planning

LUCIA LUMBELLI & GISELLA PAOLETTI

University of Trieste, Italy

Abstract. Two experiments are reported, which are aimed at verifying a main prediction: since the monitoring of the processes that are necessary for correctly maintaining or restoring text local coherence is a significant feature of both text comprehension and writing, educational treatment can improve this type of monitoring in writing. The treatment works directly on reading comprehension and/or on the writing revision phase that consists in detecting incorrect text gaps. The independent variables in Exp.1 were three educational sessions that focused on text gaps requiring inference from both prior knowledge and previous text information in order to restore coherence. In Exp.2 as many sessions focused on a revision task concerning peers' written texts containing impossible-to-bridge gaps. The common dependent variable was a local coherence measure applied to written texts produced by participants (18 approximately-12-yr-old children) These experimental participants were matched, based on their writing pre-tests scores, with 18 controls of the same age, and they outperformed the controls on the written post-test. In Exp.2 a writing revision post-test was also used, where experimentals again outperformed controls, but no correlation between the two dependent measures was found. New hypotheses were drawn from this datum.

Keywords: Local coherence, inference, comprehension monitoring, audience, writing, metacognition, revising, thinking aloud, observational learning, ecological validity.

1. INTRODUCTION

The pattern of cognitive processes required by a text to guarantee a locally coherent representation has been identified and analyzed by experimental researchers using 'testoids' (Graesser, Millis & Zwaan, 1997). However, this pattern can be easily found in natural text comprehension, where it is likely, however, to be more complex and difficult to perform. This very fact takes on significance, from an educa-

Lumbelli, L. & Paoletti, G. (2004). *Monitoring local coherence through bridging integration: From text comprehension to writing revision and planning.*
Rijlaarsdam, G. (Series Ed.) & Rijlaarsdam, G., Van den Bergh, H., & Couzijn, M. (Vol. Eds.). Studies in writing. Vol. 14, *Effective learning and teaching of writing, 2nd Edition, Part 1, Studies in learning to write,* 197 - 208.

tional perspective, when we make the switch from the experimental and abstract occurrences of this set of cognitive processes to the real ones required in concrete, social contexts, where it can be used as an important unit of analysis.

In the present work, we shall, first of all, describe the pattern of processes in question. Secondly, we shall show its relevance, not only to text and discourse comprehension, but also to the revision and even to the local planning of writing; thirdly, we shall report the results of two investigations where we verified the effectiveness of instructional projects aimed at improving local coherence monitoring in writing, by using educational activities that concern text comprehension as well as writing revision.

Let us shortly justify our basic methodological option. Thanks to our previous observational evidence, we are able to assume that our experimental investigations actually tapped real problems which real learners encounter in text comprehension and written text revision. It is true that they took place outside of real classrooms and in a brief period of time; it is therefore true that the issue of interaction with the more complex factors of the social context (Gubern, 1999; Milian Gubern, this volume) as well as the question of long-term effects (Espèret, 1999) were temporarily set aside. However, this was a temporary, provisional choice. We thought it right to carry out a preliminary and "abstract" verification of our predictions in order to make further, more costly, applications to real social contexts more likely to be effective. In other words, our assumption is that the experimental data on the short-term effectiveness of our treatments spare us the risk of implementing rather complex instructional experimental designs in vain.

1.1 A Special Pattern of Processes

We shall briefly summarize here the identifiable steps of every correct inferential integration of a sentence sequence in a text: (a) a gap or incoherence between the meaning of two adjacent sentences is detected; in other words, the decoding of explicit information proves to be insufficient for assuring local coherence between the two items of information; (b) prior knowledge, stored in long-term memory, is searched for information items that function as a premise for the inference required for restoring local coherence; and (c) the exploration of prior knowledge is also constrained by previous text information, since the solution of the local coherence problem must be compatible with global text coherence and must, therefore, run parallel with previous text exploration. This is necessary in order to ascertain whether the required local integration can also be obtained by drawing inferences from previous and relatively separate text information items. The more easily detectable the gap or coherence problem and the more easily retrievable the knowledge required, the more likely the single correct inference will be drawn (Clark, 1977).

All these steps are usually carried out automatically and therefore, unconsciously; indeed, the required problem-solving performance is out of the reach of readers' metacognitive monitoring, and thus they are not able to self-evaluate comprehension errors, which consist of inadequate inferences.

In this regard, a important difference emerges between texts usually used as experimental material and most natural texts: in natural texts, comprehension coherence problems, requiring solution by inference, are less likely to be noticed and are therefore less likely to be correctly solved.

The following is an example of easy integration required by experimental material: "The road was frozen. The truck was running very fast. Several people were hurt." (Abbott & Black, 1986). The bridge between the two initial sentences and the last one can be sketched out as follows: since frozen roads and fast vehicles are very likely to cause accidents (very common and available knowledge) the injured people are to be considered the consequence of the occurrence of an accident, which must be inferred from the explicit antecedents. Although the accident is not explicitly expressed, it is very easily inferred by explicit information.

Let us now consider an example from a natural text (genre: instructional; subject: history of science; target: high school students), where the required integration can be considered difficult and, therefore, unlikely to be made: "The phrase 'precision geometry' and 'demonstrative geometry' were used as equivalent; a clear-cut distinction was *therefore* made between natural sciences founded on observations and exact sciences, founded on reason (on the logic deduction)". The consequential link marked by *therefore* can be understood only by readers able to process the initial sentence, so as to draw the inference that, if the quality of 'precision' coincides with 'demonstration', this quality is denied to those sciences *based on* exclusively observational methods. Only if this inference is drawn from the initial sentence, can the connective *therefore* and the following reference to the 'clear-cut distinction' be coherently linked to it. Since that condition depends, in turn, on the possession of knowledge about inductive versus deductive methods, the target of the text is very unlikely to draw such an inference and is, therefore, unlikely to correctly comprehend that passage.

Concerning natural text comprehension, therefore, we assume that the main difference between poor and good readers is the difference between readers who integrate gaps in the very way required by accurate decoding of sentences that must be linked and readers who draw their inferences from insufficient exploitation of explicit information and/or incorrect use of prior knowledge.

Two chief instructional goals can be derived from the pattern of cognitive processes heretofore described: (a) increasing mental effort, activation, or attention to any single text information item, thereby preventing readers from skipping over incoherent explicit items that require bridging by inference, and (b) improving metacognitive conscious monitoring of retrieval processes, in order to avoid over-hasty inadequate identification of knowledge items from which inferential integration is drawn.

Readers should learn (a) to accurately and systematically monitor the perception and decoding of explicit text information, in order to continuously evaluate its coherence and thus to detect any gaps requiring bridging, and (b) to consciously and intentionally monitor retrieval processes, which work as necessary conditions for inferring integration relevant to information gaps or to local coherence problems.

1.2 From Reading to Revising and Writing

Our further assumption is that participants who acquire these forms of monitoring should also be effective revisers of their own and others' written texts, as long as the revision is aimed at verifying and detecting the coherence problems caused by writers assuming that the addressed audience is in possession of knowledge, of which it is not.

Research on writing has highlighted (a) the importance of the revision phase that consists in *detecting* problems, which are then to be *diagnosed* and *solved* (Bartlett, 1982; Bereiter & Scardamalia, 1987; Flower et al., 1986; Galbraith, 1996; Klein, 1999), and (b) the revisers' difficulty (Flower, 1979; Witte, 1987; Black, 1989) of adopting a reader-oriented perspective and therefore, of also detecting passages that require inferential integration that should be drawn from knowledge that the target of the text is unlikely to possess. This difficulty, concerning coherence problems, can be traced back both to difficulty in noticing glaring inconsistencies in texts – exhibited not only by children and poor readers, but also by highly educated adults (Baker, 1985; Barton & Sanford, 1993; Johnson & Seifert, 1999) – and to the general trend to process explicit text information in an inaccurate way, with an insufficient amount of mental effort. Both of these aspects confer validity to the above-described educational goals (improving attention to a text's explicit information as well as conscious monitoring of inferential integration processes), not only for readers but also for writing revisers. Furthermore, they help us appreciate *observational learning* (Bandura, 1977; Schunk, 1991; Schunk & Zimmerman, 1994;Couzijn & Rijlaarsdam, 1996; Couzijn, 1999; Braaksma et al., 2002) and its special application to writing, named the *reader protocol method* (Schriver, 1992), which we modified only partially.

Schriver's basic assumption is that "feedback from real readers might enable writers to build a mental model of readers and more effectively represent readers' understanding processes" (Schriver, 1992: 182). From this assumption and from the evidence that "examples can be powerful ways of teaching perceptual knowledge", she derives the hypothesis that "extensive experience in interpreting readers' feedback provided through transcripts of thinking-aloud reading protocols would help writers to become more aware of how readers construct texts" (*ibid*). This hypothesis was experimentally verified with college juniors and seniors as participants, who were selected from "writing in the professions" courses. The participants were presented with "problematic texts", which caused "comprehension difficulties for the intended audience" and the transcripts of think-aloud protocols produced by "a person trying to understand the text"(p.185). The experimental participants showed greater improvement than controls in their ability to anticipate readers' problems while revising problematic texts. In Schriver's work, a wide range of comprehension problems was considered, such as "incomplete forecast or preview statements, poor definitions, unclear procedures, missing examples, misleading headings, ambiguous goals statements, weak summaries" (p.184). These problems chiefly concerned the *results* of readers' comprehension processes rather than the processes themselves. Indeed, the think-aloud protocols contained very little reference to the processes by which the protocol authors reached their conclusions. e.g., "This text needs an example here", "This section here makes the idea too hard to understand" (p.186)

In our opinion, instructional treatment should, instead, directly target the pattern of processes to be consciously monitored. If revisers must increase their attention to explicit text information, and if the conscious monitoring of inference is to be encouraged, the aloud-thinking protocols (which work as to-be-observed models) should clearly refer to (a) every explicit information item in a systematic way, and (b) the reasoning that ensues from gap detection and, subsequently, the reasoning that takes information retrieved from long-term memory into account, as necessary conditions for the integration of the detected gap.

All these processes must be explicitly and intentionally made observable, so that learners become able to consciously imitate them while revising written texts. Our modification of Schriver's method, therefore, consists in analyzing the *processes* that produce the *outcome* of perceiving comprehension problems and selecting only the processes that can be rendered conscious and than can therefore also become the content of think-aloud protocols.

Finally, if the kind of problem detection described here is an important component of revising, and if revising is an important component of writing ability, we can also assume that this educational approach, which is aimed at improving abilities in detecting coherence problems in written texts, is also effective in improving written text planning. This can be assumed, at least on the micro-structural level, where the connection between the meaning of adjacent sentences is monitored, so as to avoid the risk of requiring integration readers cannot provide.

2. EXPERIMENT 1

The purpose of Experiment 1 (Lumbelli, Paoletti, Camagni & Frausin, 1996) was to verify whether it is possible to improve local coherence in writing by improving monitoring of the previously described integration processes. Our prediction was that increasing readers' attention to explicit information, as this is a crucial condition both for text processing and for planning written text, would positively influence the ability to achieve local coherence in writing. In other words, if writers become careful explorers in reading, they are more likely to accurately heed what they are actually writing and to distinguish what they have written from what they intended to write; in particular, they should become more able to avoid the gaps that make written text incomprehensible.

2.1 Method

2.1.1 Participants and Design

From 150 elementary and junior school children (grades 5-8) we selected 36 participants: those who, during a pre-test, had written texts requiring integration from readers. Comprehension scores were assessed by the MT reading test (Cornoldi, Colpo & MT group, 1981) before and after treatment. Participants were distributed into four groups. The design was a 2x2 between participants with two age levels (elementary and junior). After four weeks, both experimental and control participants completed post-test tasks. Experimental treatment began one week after the initial assessment.

2.1.2 Pre-Test and Post-Test Writing Tasks

In order to obtain comparable outputs from participants and to improve the likelihood of their coping with coherence problems, all participants listened to the experimenter read a text out loud while examining a set of pictures illustrating the text information. They were then requested to write down the text for a classmate who had been absent during the reading. Four texts were used: two each in the pre-test and post-test sessions. The younger participants (grades 5-6) were presented with two short stories and the older ones with a procedural description of a simple physics experiment.

The experimenters analyzed collected texts independently, and points demanding integration impossible to infer from the local context were identified. Written texts containing at least one gap that could not be bridged by drawing inferences from text information were negatively evaluated. Namely, written texts with no demands for inferential integration were scored 0; written texts with anaphors or ellipses that could be univocally processed by means of a bridging inference were scored 1; and written texts demanding integration that could be derived only from previous knowledge items that the target readers may not have necessarily possessed were scored 2.

The following is an example of a text scored 1:

> There are two mice, they follow the cheese smell, they arrive in a big kitchen and they see some cheese on the table. The table leg is very slippery and only the taller one can go up because he has longer paws and the shortest one cannot climb up and waits while *he* is eating and *the other one* who is eating has fallen asleep.

It contains two cohesion errors, which can be repaired by means of an inference from the text as a whole. Both anaphors can be co-referred to the taller mouse and less severe inadequacy is therefore attributed.

The following is an example of a text scored 2:

> We take a balloon and a puppet cut out of paper, blow up the balloon, rub it against a wool cardigan. Now the balloon has a negative electric charge. Then we bring it near the puppet, which has a positive electric charge, and we see that the balloon attracts the puppet until they stick together. Then, *since* they are stuck, the puppet will gain a negative electric charge and *therefore* the balloon will push it back.

In the second example we can find two integration demands, introduced by the connectives *since* and *therefore*. They imply a specific piece of knowledge the written text itself should communicate but does not provide.

2.1.3 Training Procedure

Experimental treatment consisted of three individual sessions with each participant. In each session the participants read an approximately-four-page-long narrative text, step by step. The texts consisted of three stories from Italo Calvino's book entitled *Marcovaldo*. We followed our standard procedure, described here below:

1) In each narrative text we single out one or two paragraphs requiring rather complex integration processes.
2) We then conduct an individual interview, centred-on-the-reader-thinking-aloud, instructing each participant to say everything that comes into his/her mind while reading each piece of text. When the critical paragraphs are encountered, the initial verbal protocols are rendered more complete and accurate by means of the interviewer's *reflection responses* (Rogers, 1951; Lumbelli, 1996). This stage concludes with either comprehension or incomprehension. If comprehension takes place, treatment does not continue. Incomprehension, in turn, may be either unconscious (due to automatic, over-hasty gap repair with uncontrolled top-down processes) or conscious, viz. incomprehension with awareness of a coherence problem that cannot be solved. Treatment proceeds only in the last two cases. If the reader is aware of the comprehension difficulty, the problem situation arises on its own. If the reader has already bridged the gap unconsciously and inadequately, it is the experimenter who identifies the problem by pointing out the inadequacy of the participant's integration and asking him/her to look for another one that fits the contextual information;
3) the participant is invited to re-read the text in order to find the information items required to solve the problem, i.e., to fill in the gap in a coherent way,
4) when text exploration is not adequate for solving the problem, the experimenter formulates the solution by telling the participant which cognitive processes are needed to fill in the gap appropriately.

2.2 Results

A Manova analysis was applied to scores, and as no significant interaction was found between age and the other variables, we placed all participants into either a single experimental group, or a single control group. Table 1 shows the pre-test and post-test writing and comprehension mean scores of both groups.

Table 1. Pre-Test and Post-Test Mean Scores

	Writing (range 0-2)		Comprehension (range 0-10)	
	Pre-test	Post-test	Pre-test	Post-test
Experimental	1.6	0.5	7.2	8.6
Control	1.6	1.1	7.3	7.9

While no significant difference between groups was found in writing pre-test scores ($F(1, 36) = 2.36, p = .1339$), a significant difference emerged between experimental group pre-test and post-test writing scores ($F(1, 18) = 32.66, p < .00001$) and between experimental and control group gain scores ($F(1, 36) = 4.70; p < .05$).

Both groups' comprehension scores improved, but the improvement was significant only for the experimental group ($F(1, 8) = 8.9, p < .01$. The results confirmed our prediction that the text explorations used in our experimental treatment would help participants become more sensitive to textual gaps and would thereby induce participants to exhibit this kind of sensitivity while planning written texts, leading them to avoid making impossible integration demands on readers. Consequently, insofar as the correct integration of text information is concerned, we can assume a certain similarity between the cognitive processes involved in comprehension and production. In fact, an improvement in written production was obtained by working on the very integration processes that must be tapped while reading a text.

As to the interaction between instructor and learner, the effectiveness of our training procedure is based on a combination of feedback encouraging the learner's active and autonomous text exploration and the teacher's modeling of the cognitive processes a text requires. In fact, the participants who failed in autonomous, active text exploration, and who *then* needed to observe the experimenter's modeling of protocols regarding necessary integration processes, also showed an improvement in the final written test.

3. EXPERIMENT 2

The purpose of Experiment 2 (Lumbelli, Paoletti & Frausin, 1999) was to test the hypothesis that (1) the ability to consciously monitor inferential integration while revising a text written by others can be improved through treatment that calls the participant's attention to usually automatic and unconscious text elaboration processes, and (2) this kind of revision ability can be transferred to the planning of writing itself.

Our treatment made use of the previously discussed think-aloud protocols, which systematically focused on the integration processes that must take place in order to detect comprehension problems in a written text.

We used texts written by poor writers, containing critical points that required difficult, or even impossible integration from readers, either because the necessary bridging inference required concurrent processing of different, often rather far-apart text sections, or because the inference was impossible for a reader who did not share the relevant knowledge with the writer. These critical points were identified through a specific kind of text analysis aimed at detecting gaps that could not be bridged unambiguously. The revision processes concerning these points were made explicit in the think-aloud protocols, which work as *reader models* and were audio-recorded by the experimenters themselves.

The following is a text used for treatment, written by the junior school pupils:

One game I play with my friends is called animal steps. 1/ Five boys or girls stand against the wall while a girl or boy stands against another wall 2/ and says, for instance, Lucy a kangaroo-step, Laura a frog-step, and so on. 3/When someone gets close to the wall and touches it, the one who was there before goes to the place where the other was, and so on.4/.

Let us now examine an example of the experimenter's protocols. It concerns section 3 and refers to the required inference and to the prior knowledge from which it must be drawn. The person who stands against one of the two walls, who is alone says (the sentence is reread). The examples of animal steps make it clear that there are different steps, depending on the animal named, because I know that a kangaroo moves in a way that is different from a frog. So I think these children make different kinds of steps trying to imitate the steps of different animals.

We predicted that just a few sessions of such treatment would have been sufficient for participants to acquire standards useful for detecting comprehension problems consisting of hard-to-bridge gaps, when revising written work, and to avoid these kinds of gaps when planning written texts.

3.1 Method

3.1.1 Participants and Design

The participants were 28 students from junior school (6th grade), selected from a sample of 200 participants on the basis of their scores on a standard reading comprehension test (MT Reading Comprehension Test, by Cornoldi, Colpo & gruppo MT, 1981), and on the Raven's Progressive Matrices (Raven, 1938, first series), for the purpose of obtaining a group that could be considered homogeneous, with respect to linguistic and intellectual abilities.

All 28 participants were then given a writing test (already described for Experiment 1) and were matched on the basis of their results. The paired participants were randomly assigned to one of two conditions: 14 students received the experimental treatment and 14 served as the control group.

The experimental treatment began one week after the pre-test and lasted three weeks, with one weekly individual session for each participant. A post-test was given to both groups, in order to assess the comprehensibility of their writing.

The design has two conditions (treatment vs. no treatment) as between-participants variables, and the results on comprehensible writing as the within-participants variable. A further comparison between participants was based on scores from a test aimed at evaluating revising ability.

3.1.2 Training Procedure

Each individual session lasted about one hour. A short written text was first read aloud by the experimenter, while the participant followed along, reading silently. Then the participants were asked to read again, while listening to the audiotaped thinking-aloud protocols, which were produced by the experimenters and which chiefly referred to difficult- or impossible-to-bridge gaps. Participants were encouraged to stop the tapes and listen again if they felt they needed to. Task instructions were to look for either unclear or missing information and to either correct the text or write a question that could be of help in obtaining the necessary information. Both types of performance were considered as indicators of success in detecting problematic gaps. We put a great deal of effort into creating as natural a situation as possible, into guaranteeing the ecological validity of our procedure. For example, the aloud-thinking protocols were not written, but were unrehearsed, oral, and produced spontaneously at the time of recording and thus contained all the flaws and redundancies of oral language; the expert reader's uncertainty had been fully verbalized, so that uncertainty about the possible different interpretations of the same passage could be traced back to uncertainty about which processes would most adequately integrate the explicit information, as read and decoded.

3.1.3   Pre-Test and Post-Test of Writing Ability

The writing ability test was previously described in the corresponding session of Experiment 1: Participants heard a story-text being read and then had to write a text for an absent classmate. Consequentially, connected pairs of statements were assumed to be indicators of control of local planning processes, and the written texts were therefore evaluated by counting the number of consequential connections made completely explicit, i.e., how many times both the antecedent and the consequence were mentioned in each written text. Since a preliminary text analysis showed that there were seven possible consequential connections in the two texts, to be reported by participants, the range of scores was 0-7 for both pre- and post-tests.

3.1.4   Revision Ability Post-Test

Participants were asked to revise a text by identifying gaps demanding integration to be inferred from participants' own prior knowledge, and they were presented with both the definition and a few examples of the kind of errors to detect while revising the text.

Participants' annotations (questions for the writer or integration proposals) were assessed by using the critical points identified, by means of a preliminary analysis, as standards. Since 5 critical points resulted, the score range was set at 0-5.

3.2   Results

A summary of the results obtained by experimental and control participants in the Writing test and the Revision test is represented in Table 2. Writing scores on the pre-test were the same for the two groups, while the experimental group outperformed the control group in the post-test. In the Revision post-test the experimental group's performance was superior.

Table 2. *Effects of Condition on Writing Ability and Revision: Pre- and Post-Test Means and Standard Deviations*

	Writing test (range 0-7)		Revision test (range 0-5)
Condition	Pre-test	Post-test	Post-test only

	M	SD	M	SD	M	SD
Experimental	3.6	1.1	5	1.8	3.6	1.4
Control	3.9	1.3	3.8	1.8	2.4	1.6

As to writing ability, no significant difference was found between groups on the pre-test scores. However, the three individual sessions were successful in improving participants' ability to write comprehensible text. In fact, a significant difference emerged from a Manova analysis applied to the pre-test and post-test writing scores ($F(1, 28) = 6.36$, $p = .018$), because the scores of the control group had slightly decreased, and the scores of the experimental group had increased substantially.

Concerning the revision test, an Anova analysis of the scores, obtained by detecting text errors with treatment conditions as the between-participants variable, showed a main effect for treatment ($F(1, 28) = 5.33$, $p = .029$), with experimental participants outperforming controls: experimental participants were better at detecting incomprehensible statements in written texts.

No correlation between the two dependent measures was observed: the revision dependent measure was related to the writing measure, but the relationship ($r = 0.331$) was not statistically significant.

Group scores on both post-tests were subjected to analysis of covariance, with MT scores, Raven scores and the pre-test writing scores as covariates. The analysis demonstrated that the effects of treatment on the two dependent variables was significant, even when the pre-test measures were used as covariates: the experimental group performed significantly better than the control group on the writing test ($F(1, 28) = 4.67$, $p = 0.041$) as well as on the revision test ($F(28, 1) = 5.15$, $p = 0.033$).

Since the experimental participants wrote clearer, more accurate texts, and since they detected more errors than the control participants, we can conclude that our data support the hypothesis that our treatment targeting revising ability has positive effects, on that ability and on the ability to write locally coherent texts as well.

4. CONCLUDING REMARKS

The idea of focusing on the pattern of processes that solves natural coherence problems in natural texts proved to be educationally fruitful. In both experiments, learning tasks that encouraged and facilitated the conscious monitoring of these processes were effective in improving writing, as far as the aspect of writing identified as local coherence and/or comprehensibility is concerned.

The positive effect on writing was measured by means of two partially different procedures, both of which are centered on one aspect with the following methodological advantages:
- it can work as a well-defined category for the observation and analysis of writing,
- it is related to the significant quality of writing as both process and product,
- it can be assessed independently from other interwoven variables, such as the amount of prior knowledge; text length; relevance of contents, argumentations, and concepts expressed; and other variables, which are likely to affect writing quality without being a relevant indicator of it.

All results of both experiments were clearly positive. Only one datum, from the second experiment, requires discussion, i.e., the relatively low and statistically insignificant correlation between revision test and writing test scores.

We hypothesize that in this case, better monitoring of local coherence in writing was obtained, thanks to processes partially different from those that brought about better monitoring of revision. Our treatment may have fostered two different kinds of important cognitive abilities: (a) the type of *text sensitivity* that consists in paying the greatest attention possible to every explicit piece of text information, in order to detect natural coherence problems that must be solved by inference, and (b) a kind of mental effort which consists of consciously monitoring the processes triggered by that detection, i.e., the searching of both prior knowledge and previous text for information concerning the gap and the inference of the very integration the gap requires.

Observational learning about the processing of local coherence problems and their correct solution might have worked in two different ways on these two types of ability and, consequently, on the written *versus* revision test outcomes.

Since the modeling of revision processes facilitated an increase in attention paid to explicit text information, it might have positively affected both revising and writing. Insofar as the processes by which gaps (once detected) are to be bridged were modeled, revising was more likely to improve than writing. In fact, when writing, learners do not need to repair other writers' hard-to-bridge gaps, but just avoid them when communicating their own thoughts. This hypothesis obviously requires verification through further research.

LEARNING TO WRITE INSTRUCTIVE TEXTS BY READER OBSERVATION AND WRITTEN FEEDBACK

MICHEL COUZIJN*/** AND GERT RIJLAARSDAM*/***

*University of Amsterdam, the Netherlands, **Pieter Nieuwland College, Amsterdam, the Netherlands, & ***Utrecht University, the Netherlands

Abstract. Can young writers enhance the quality of their texts by observing real readers trying to comprehend them? What do these writers learn from such observations? In this chapter the authors suggest that writing instruction can be made more effective by making communication failures and successes observable. To a certain extent, writers are blind to the communicative failures in their texts since they have all the prior knowledge to fill in the gaps. On-line observation of readers may help them in detecting these gaps, and in learning to repair or avoid them.

An experiment is carried out in which four groups of students write an instructional text and receive different types of feedback for revision: self-evaluation, reader observation, reader observation with written comments from the reader, and reader observation of an unknown text. Effects are assessed on revision quality and on learning (knowledge of criteria for successful communication). Results show that all three observation conditions were more effective than the self-evaluation condition, and that observation supported by written comments was most effective with respect to both text quality and learning. Moreover, the readers who formulated these comments outscored the other readers on writing a first version of a similar text; they also could recall more criteria for successful writing.

Keywords: learning by observation, instructive text, audience awareness, peer feedback.

1. INTRODUCTION

This experimental study deals with learning to write manual texts for a physics experiment. The question addressed is which of four types of readers' feedback is most profitable for writers. Profits may be twofold: an improvement of textual quality after revision, and increased knowledge of criteria for good manual texts. In other words, readers' feedback may contribute to both writing and learning-to-write. Be-

Couzijn, M. & Rijlaarsdam, G. (2004). Learning to write by reader observation and written feedback.
Rijlaarsdam, G. (Series Ed.) & Rijlaarsdam, G., Van den Bergh, H., & Couzijn, M. (Vol. Eds.). Studies in writing. Vol. 14, Effective learning and teaching of writing, 2nd Edition, Part 1, Studies in learning to write, 209 - 240 .

cause (the perception of) readers' behavior is used as input for writing or revision activities, this study also addresses the question of transfer from reading to writing. Four instances of readers' feedback were distinguished and experimentally put to the test. The first instance is made up of comments from the writers themselves, re-reading and using their own manual texts three weeks after having written it. A second instance consists of observation of readers thinking aloud while using and evaluating the text in a realistic situation. The third type of feedback consists of observing readers as well as receiving written comments on what these readers consider to be weak spots in the text. Lastly, the fourth feedback type is similar to the second type, but now writers observe readers using someone else's text instead of their own.

It is our idea, as we will explain further on, that purposeful observation of communication processes may allow language users to discover criteria for more or less successful communication, and to incorporate these criteria into their own communication behavior. We write 'language users' instead of 'writers', because in theory the beneficial effect could extend to the observing writers as well as to the observed readers. For this matter we added hypotheses concerning the writing skill acquisition of the observed readers.

Several theoretical considerations have awakened our interest in feedback by means of reader observation. We will first point out which part of the writing process can be affected positively by reader observation.

1.1 Writing as a Recursive Process

From a communicative or pragmatic perspective, writing is considered a goal-directed activity. By writing a text, a writer tries to satisfy his need to inform and/or the need of his audience to be informed. On a pragmatic-linguistic level, most texts cover various modes of information which are related to various needs. For example, in one and the same text factual knowledge can be transferred as well as personal opinions, questions can be asked, requests, promises or statements can be made, explanations can be given and amusing stories can be told. Speech-act theorists work on a taxonomy of various types of verbal information conveyed in communication (Austin, 1975; Searle, 1979).

The quality of text production is determined by the extent to which the various needs for information are actually satisfied. Not only should the information in the text provide for the needs regarding content, it should also be presented in a way that enables the reader to comprehend it. For instance, a promise that is not recognized as such ('Anne will come tomorrow') will not function as a promise. Therefore, within speech-act theory certain conditions are made for recognizability as well as for soundness of content of the information transfer.

When writing a text of any substance, the writer must thus fulfill various needs for information, and each in a recognizable way. Because it is impossible for the writer to realize all these needs synchronically (the *cognitive load* would exceed human capacity), most of the work is done sequentially (Hillocks, 1986). Writers aim their conscious attention alternately at each of the various needs until they consider the text finished. In between, they evaluate their realizations and alter them when necessary.

For this matter, *writing* has often been described as a *recursive* or *iterative* process. The text or product-thus-far is continuously under reconstruction. What has been written is repeatedly adjusted to other 'needs', be it for content or for comprehension, or realizations of former 'needs' are reconsidered. This complex, recursive character of writing makes it a difficult, but interesting activity to learn or teach.

Learning to write a certain text type does not have a physical goal (creating a text), but a mental goal (acquiring a skill). It encompasses getting to know the communicative needs connected with this type of text, certain ways to meet these needs, and developing the ability to regulate a writing process with sequential and recursive qualities monitoring these needs. The regulation is aimed at delivering a product that meets the needs in an organized way. Like writing, learning-to-write is a recursive process, and its effectiveness relies heavily on the quality of self-regulation (Vermunt, 1992).

In educational contexts, writing processes are often framed *within* a learning process. Students doing a writing assignment in a learning situation – the standard situation in schools – can be considered to have a 'double agenda'. They must work according to one set of goals with the physical aim of producing a text with certain qualities, and subsequently – or simultaneously – they must work according to another set of goals with the mental aim of acquiring writing skill. Monitoring one set of goals is difficult already, let alone monitoring two interrelated sets of goals. Nevertheless, we think that in learning-to-write, the one (set of goals) cannot go well without the other (set of goals). Reflection on one's writing behavior is a necessary precondition to reflection on one's learning-to-write behavior (cf. Rijlaarsdam, 1993, Rijlaarsdam & Team, 2003).

Although process studies on learners' capabilities of attending to both agendas are desirable, this study does not offer such research yet. As a preliminary study, it focuses on a part of the 'executing agenda' which theoretically seems to be closely connected with the 'learning agenda': the self-evaluation by writers and the informational input for this activity.

1.2 Learning to Write by Reader Feedback

The pedagogy of learning by reader observation is best explained by planting it in learning-psychological soil. The basis for effective monitoring and learning of complex skills like writing is feedback on one's behavior. In general, the importance of feedback in task execution and learning can hardly be overestimated. Without knowledge of the consequences of one's behavior, it is impossible to modify it in another way than by trial and error. In any situation people will learn from their successes and from their mistakes. More specifically, they will learn from distinguishing their successes from their mistakes, and from discovering how to turn mistakes into successes.

At least two types of information are required for learning by experience: information about one's strategic behavior and information about its consequences in relation to the goal. An evaluation of the consequences allows the learner to determine whether the behavior should be maintained in similar situations or should be modified. In both cases the learner ought to construct a mental concept of the behavior or strategy to which the results are attributed; only if such mental concept is stored in memory can it be activated if necessary.

In individual learning processes, the source for the two types of information is usually the learner's own perception. It is the learner who attributes perceived consequences to his/her perceived behavior and who may integrate the new cognitive construction in memory. Thus the quality of these perceptions (of behavior and consequences) is decisive for the quality of the resulting learning. This is why we stress the importance of feedback on executive processes. Learning processes use the result of feedback processing as input. Without adequate feedback, or with inadequate feedback (such as biased perceptions), the effectiveness of learning by experience will be limited.

How are these viewpoints related to the domain of writing? In which ways can a writer, who has the objective of communicating with one or more readers, collect feedback on the adequacy of his writing performance (and thus on his being on track with respect to learning)? Getting feedback is very difficult for writers, since usually a considerable distance in time and/or space keeps them separated from their genuine test case: the reader. This is a serious problem for writing instruction because in many domains, feedback is known to be mainly (or even: only) effective if it follows directly after the task. If a writer has to wait for days or even weeks before getting information about the adequacy of his task execution, it will be very hard for him to link concrete writing strategies to (evaluations of) their real consequences.

In many writing and revision theories it is suggested that the writer should counter this problem by creating his own feedback: he should compare an 'intended text' with the 'text written-thus-far', taking the differences as a basis for revision (Hayes et al., 1987). But there are other ways for writers to collect feedback for revision. This study deals with one of those ways, viz. feedback from authentic readers.

It should be noted that the abovementioned 'text written-thus-far' is also a mental representation of the writer. He will read his own text (*after* as well as *during* the writing process) and will try to construct a text representation as if he were a normal reader. The problem here is that the writer is nothing like a normal reader. He is a very special reader, since he has all the necessary prior knowledge to interpret the text just like it was meant by 'the writer'. Obviously this prior knowledge can hardly be neglected. Therefore the writer will easily pass over many unclear, vague, incorrect and otherwise inadequate passages. In short, the writer himself is not the best person to identify possible readers' problems, i.e., to supply feedback for his writing or learning process (cf. Bartlett, 1982).

The writer can tackle this problem in two ways. First, he can ask authentic readers to assist him, like asking colleagues to give comments on his text. In writing instruction, this commenting task is usually done by the teacher who detects and diagnoses weak spots and may even give hints for revision. Second, he can try to read the text himself 'with the eyes of a stranger', trying to detect possible communication difficulties. Some people try this by abandoning their text for some days, expecting to re-read it with a fresher view. They suppose that the renewed mental representation will better resemble the representation of authentic readers, resulting in a higher capability to detect deficiencies.

These types of feedback (authentic or virtual readers' evaluations) can be used as input for the writing process as well as the learning process. The feedback is likely to be used for text revision. Consequently, it is up to the writer to make inferences about the adequacy of the previous writing activities in order to establish learning that may transfer to future writing tasks. It is hard to predict to what extent the writer will make such inferences. In comparison with the extensive study of writing processes in the past two decades (Hillocks, 1986; Faigley et al., 1989; Van den Bergh & Meuffels, 1993), learning processes in the domain of writing have received much less attention.

When supplying these types of feedback, the 'readers' will function like external evaluators who identify flaws rather than performing functional reading tasks. In this respect, the writer is not offered direct insight in the communicative consequences of his writing: the evaluators will necessarily offer a subjective selection, evaluation and verbalization of their reading experiences. This is a weak spot of indirect post-reading responses.

Schriver (1991; 1994) notes that writers may profit more from confrontations with responses of genuine readers, because it helps them to build mental models of comprehension processes and readers' needs. These models can then be invoked in the writing process as input for self-evaluation. Schriver investigated the effect of a particular type of readers' responses, viz. on-line responses to text recorded in readers' protocols. In an instructional experiment, students learned to analyze these reader protocols, resulting in a higher capability to predict potential readers' problems in texts compared to a control group. The writing pedagogy based on this idea, known as 'reader-protocol teaching', is one of the few tested pedagogies which explicitly teach students to anticipate readers' comprehension problems.

1.3 The Present Study: Observation of Readers Responding to an Instructional Text

One may infer that on-line readers' responses are superior to post-reading comments (by authentic readers or self-generated ones) as input for revision and, as a consequence, for learning. In the present study, we compare the effect of self-generated comments with the effect of observing on-line readers' responses. We will investigate effects on text quality after revision and acquired knowledge for students both in the role of writers and of readers.

In order to evoke many and literally visible responses from the readers, we chose a highly appellative text type for the experiment: instructional texts, i.e., texts conveying instructions to the reader to perform one or more actions. In this study, subjects are asked to compose a manual for a physics experiment. It is the reader's task to perform the physics experiment on the basis of the writer's manual text. The experiment will be explained in detail in section 3.

With respect to writers, we want to answer the following questions. Do writers profit more from observed on-line readers' responses than from their own responses to their text? If so, does the profit concern only the quality of the text after revision, or also the writers' learning about specific criteria for good communication? To what extent should the profits be attributed to the observer's authorship of the text in question? And to what extent can the effects be amplified by adding written comments from the reader?

To answer these questions, we investigate three variants of reader observation. In the simplest variant, a writer observes a reader who is thinking aloud while reading and commenting on his text. This reader thus supplies on-line information about the comprehensibility of the text. A difference from Schriver's protocol-teaching pedagogy is the fact that the writer is confronted even more directly with verbal and visual information from the reader than by studying verbal protocols.

In a second variant, the reader's observations are accompanied by written evaluative comments from the reader. Although we expect that evaluative comments in themselves will be less profitable for the writer than on-line observation, the comments may have additional value if they are combined with the observations. Learning usually implies abstraction from particular experiences. We therefore expect that more learning will occur if the writers have an abstract or 'condensation' of the reader's experiences at their disposal, which may help them to categorize the communicative failures they run into during observation.

The third variant is identical to the first, with the exception that the observed text is not written by the observer. In the first variant, the writer can 'test' the communicative quality of his own text, and use the 'test results' for revision and learning. It would be interesting to know to which extent potential benefits are sanctioned by the observer's authorship. Would the same benefits occur if the usage of someone else's text were observed? If so, this type of learning would come close to *modeling* (observing imperfect models). It is, however, not likely that alien texts would lead to the same results. A cognitive counterargument is that the observed feedback would not be tuned to the individual flaws in the observer's performance, and that it would be difficult to translate the observed feedback to observers' writing; and a motivational counterargument explanation is that the observer would be less personally involved because it is not his own performance that is at stake – he is not part of the communication between the observed reader and an unknown writer.

Although much research has been carried out to determine effects of *receiving* feedback on writing, the opposite is true for learners *giving* feedback (Hillocks, 1986: 166-168, 219-221). Only in studies concerning peer response groups or collaborative writing, the act of giving critical comments is part of the learning activities. In these cases, however, the resulting learning effect has rarely been isolated from the effect of receiving feedback, since the students are usually part of write-and-comment rounds (cf. Rijlaarsdam, 1986).

In our study, we also expect beneficial effects for the readers supplying feedback by reading and commenting. These tasks can have preparatory value with respect to their writing skill. For this reason, we have set up the experiment in such a way that this effect can be determined in isolation.

The expectation of transfer from the reading and commenting task to the writing task can be accounted for by the – almost age-old – concept of common elements (Thorndike & Woodworth, 1901). In this case, the elements shared by the two tasks are cognitions about criteria for good manual texts. The writing process is partly guided by normative ideas – or even a model – about content and organization of a certain type of texts. A writer may for instance have the idea that manuals mainly consist of instructions, or that they should contain pictures as well as text, or that explanations must accompany the instructions. Such cognitions can be activated in the orientation phase and can be used in planning, monitoring and revision. A reader on the other hand will make use of similar schematic knowledge as a reference for comprehension. For instance, readers trust that the order in which the instructions are given will be chronological or that the goal will be specified in the beginning of the text. They will also invoke such cognitions when commenting on the quality of the text, adapting them as norms when criticizing the order of the information or the absence of a goal description.

It is possible that readers, having activated or constructed such cognitions during their reading and commenting task, will transfer these cognitions to a subsequent writing task. If this is so, the commenting task can be part of a learning-to-write curriculum; no student time would be sacrificed to have the students participate in the feedback task, since the feedback activities would be beneficial for their writing skill. Sonnenschein & Whitehurst (1984) showed empirically that commentary tasks can in fact transfer to performance of the commented activities. So we have good reasons to expect potential benefits for the readers, especially for readers who reflect on the detected deficiencies and arrive at a stadium of 'condensation' by writing down their comments.

In all, four groups of writers and two groups of readers take part in the experiment. The experiment is mainly inspired by Schriver's work (1991), although it differs in two significant aspects. First, our experiment is aimed at high-school students (15 y.) instead of college undergraduates (19 y.). Second, the writers did not observe readers' responses by analyzing typed protocols, but by looking at videotaped readers-at-work who thought aloud while using the text.

Of all experimental groups, the effect of the treatment on 'writing' is determined by assessing the textual quality of manuals written immediately after receiving or supplying feedback by reader observation. The effect on 'learning to write' is determined by assessing the declarative knowledge about criteria for manual texts. This declarative knowledge was assessed by asking the students to write down as many pieces of advice as they could for a classmate who would have to write such a text (De Glopper, 1986; Braet, Moret, Schoonen & Sjoer, 1993).

One could wonder why we do not determine learning effects by letting the students write another manual and assessing its quality. The main reason is that a gain in conceptual or declarative knowledge does not automatically lead to a gain in performance or procedural knowledge. The construction of declarative knowledge is a first stadium of acquiring skillfulness in a new domain (Anderson, 1987), but students differ in the readiness with which new cognitions are used in new task situations. Of two students who have learned the same criteria for good manuals, the one may be better able to transfer this cognition to the new writing task than the other. In our opinion it makes more sense to assess the precondition to better writing: better knowledge about how to write. We can visualize the variables as in figure 1.

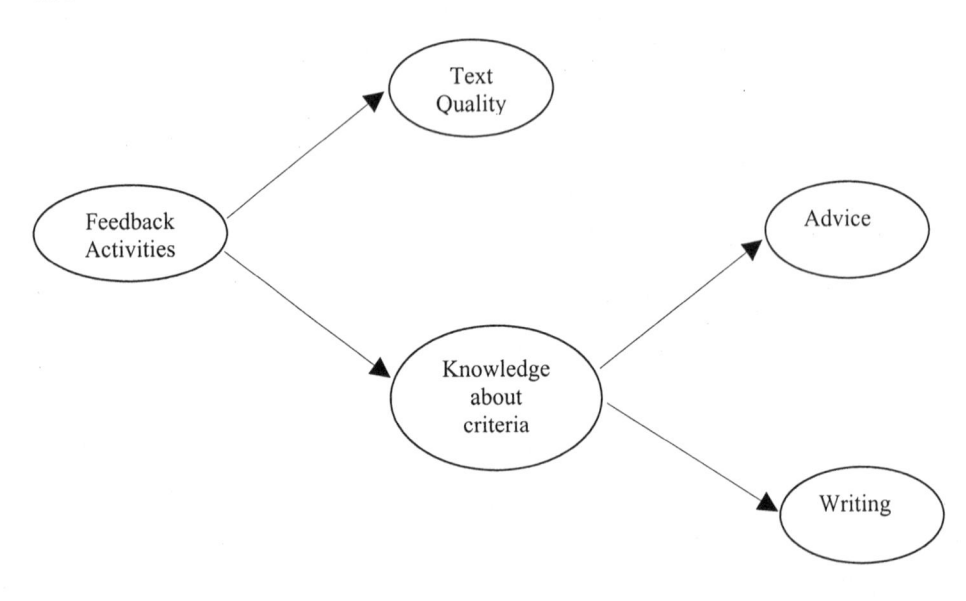

Figure 1. Causal relations between key variables in this study.

The declarative knowledge about criteria is a precondition to better writing. With our posttests we try to assess the extent to which the feedback activities have caused better writing (1) and learning (2). Causal link (3) is supposed to come close to mere reproduction of a purposeful memory search, while causal link (4) requires application and a facultative memory search. Therefore we suppose that knowledge about criteria can be better assessed by the ability to give advice than by another writing task.

2. RESEARCH QUESTIONS AND EXPECTATIONS

2.1 Research Questions, Variables and Operationalizations

The theoretical considerations explained in the previous part led to the following research questions:
1) What are the relative effects of *four types of readers' feedback* on the *text quality* after revision, and on the writer's *knowledge about instructional texts*?
2) What are the relative effects of the *two types of reading and commenting tasks* on the *text quality* of a subsequently composed text, and on the reader's *knowledge about instructional texts*?

Independent variables. The four types of readers' feedback consist of: (1) Self-generated comments by the writer reading his text after three weeks, (2) observation of readers who think aloud while using the text written by the observer, (3) as (2),

with the addition of written comments from these readers on the quality of the text, and (4), as (2), but the observed text has not been written by the observer.
The two types of reading tasks consist of (5) reading and using the manual text while thinking-aloud, and (6) as (5), with the addition of producing written comments on the text quality.

Dependent variables. Text quality refers to the quality of the manual text, rewritten after receiving one of the four types of feedback (question 1) and to the quality of the text written by the reader directly after having read and commented on a manual text (question 2). Text quality is operationalized as the number of necessary and adequate information elements in the manual. This will be explained in detail in the 'method' section.

The knowledge of instructional texts mentioned in questions 1) and 2) refers to declarative knowledge about criteria for good manual texts and about strategic activities for writing such texts. This declarative knowledge is operationalized as the number of adequate pieces of product- and process-oriented advice which a student will give when asked to inform a fellow student on how to write this specific type of text.

2.2 Theoretical Expectations

We will briefly state our expectations as to answering the research questions. It is assumed that writers will fail to identify ambiguities, vagueness and missing information in their texts because they will compensate textual deficiencies with their prior knowledge. Thus, the detection of such deficiencies by authentic readers will be more comprehensive. From these assumptions it follows that authentic reader responses will form a broader and more adequate basis for revision than self-generated comments. We therefore expect the effect of feedback types 2-4 on text quality to exceed the effect of type 1, assuming that writers can and will take advantage of these comments during revision. It is expected that feedback of type 3 will be most powerful, since it is expected that written comments and authorship of the observed text will strengthen the use of the feedback. Feedback types 2 and 4 are likely to set off the effect of type 3.

It is further assumed that learning to write from revision is stimulated by a generalization across the detected deficiencies. If writers receiving feedback of type 1 fail to identify many deficiencies, there is not much to generalize across, and they are likely to learn less than the other writers, resulting in less knowledge about instructional texts.

Identifying causes of the deficiencies may enhance generalization, a process known as diagnosis. Generalizations (like categorizations) and other diagnoses will take place when writing general comments on the quality of a text. Thus writers receiving written comments from their readers have more generalizations at their disposal than writers lacking these comments. We therefore expect the effect of feedback of type 3 on the writer's declarative *knowledge about instructional texts* to exceed the effects of feedback types 2 and 4.

It follows that for readers, the activity of writing comments on the text quality also contributes to their generalization across the difficulties and thus to their knowledge about criteria for good instructional texts. We expect that feedback of type VI will result in a higher knowledge gain than feedback of type V.

If we assume that this extra knowledge is acquired during the production of written comments, we expect the text quality of readers giving feedback type VI to exceed the text quality of readers giving feedback type V.

3. METHOD

3.1 Design

An experiment was set up to test our hypotheses. Table 1 shows the distinctive features of the seven conditions.

Four experimental activities of writing students are compared and two activities of reading students. Students in condition 0 serve as a base-line or control group, writing only 'first versions' of manuals and showing their resulting declarative knowledge about manual texts. All other conditions are experimental conditions to be compared with condition 0, on the two dependent variables of text quality and declarative knowledge.

Experimental writing students work in three sessions: creating and revising a manual text in the first two sessions and generalizing about their experiences in the third. The reading students take part in two sessions: using and commenting on a text and creating a new text in the first session, and performing the generalization task in the second.

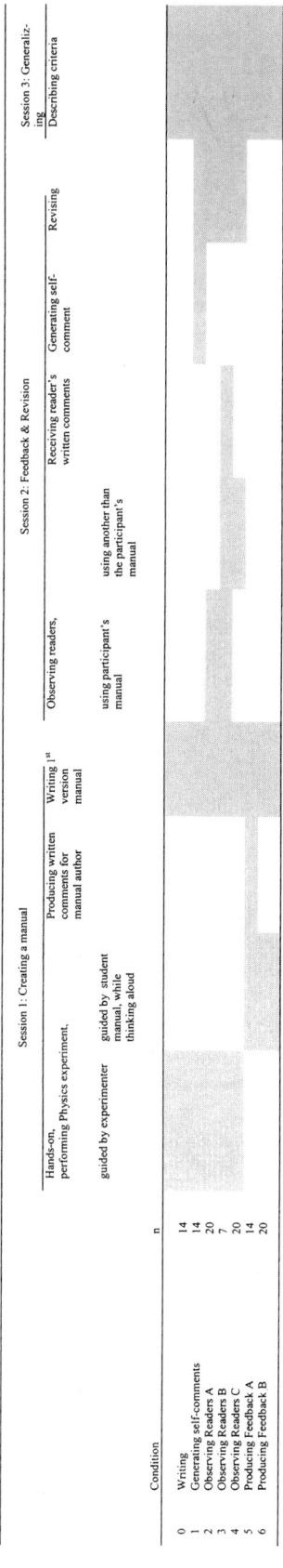

| | Condition | n | Session 1: Creating a manual ||||| Session 2: Feedback & Revision ||| Session 3: Generalizing |
			Hands-on, performing Physics experiment, guided by experimenter	Hands-on, performing Physics experiment, guided by student manual, while thinking aloud	Producing written comments for manual author	Writing 1st version manual	Observing readers, using participant's manual	Observing readers, using another than the participant's manual	Receiving reader's written comments	Generating self-comment	Revising	Describing criteria
0	Writing	14										
1	Generating self-comments	14										
2	Observing Readers A	20										
3	Observing Readers B	7										
4	Observing Readers C	20										
5	Producing Feedback A	14										
6	Producing Feedback B	20										

Table 1. Design of the Study; Shaded Cells indicate Participation in a certain Activity

3.2 Subjects

In all, 109 students from the 9th grade of two different schools (intermediate and high level) took part in the experiment. The average age was 15 years old. The students were randomly selected from nine student groups and randomly assigned to the experimental conditions, after removing from each student group the five lowest achievers and the five highest achievers in writing skill (recent school assignment). The reason for this homogenization is that the study focuses on *typical* student behavior, not on differences between more or less skilled students. It is assumed that the within-group variance on writing skill would decrease as a result.

3.3 Procedures

All writing and reading assignments were administered individually. Each student worked privately in a room with a research assistant giving standardized information and answering questions. The assignments were given orally, and were read from paper.
We will describe the procedures in the following order: (1) session 1 for conditions 0-IV, (2) session 1 for conditions V-VI, (3) session 2 for conditions I-IV, and (4) the 'generalizing session' for all conditions 0-VI.

3.3.1 The Initial Writing Task and Materials

The writing task for conditions 0-IV was the composition of a manual for a simple physics experiment. Each writer was told that this manual should serve two goals: it should enable a classmate to *perform* the experiment without problems as well as to *understand* it. This formulation of goals should stimulate the writer to take several needs for information into account (see 1.1): it should contain instructions as well as explanations.

Before being given the writing assignment, each writer received explanations from the research assistant about the physics experiment and did the experiment him/herself until he/she understood and performed it faultlessly. Thus it is assumed that between-group differences in comprehension of the physics experiment were minimized. This is a necessary precondition for an equal start of each experimental group.

In order to fully understand the writers' task, it is necessary to know the physics experiment in detail. The aim of this experiment is to prove that *air takes up space*. Three figures were shown to the writer in order to explain the experiment. The research assistant read out the accompanying text. The student did not receive any written explanation, because we wanted to avoid his or her using them as a 'model' for writing.

> "This little experiment will show you that air takes up space. This means that boxes or bottles which are commonly called empty, in fact contain air – and as long as the air is

inside, nothing else can go in. If you fill an empty box with books, the air has to go out at the same time.

So, at first sight, air may seem equal to 'nothing'. But in some cases the existence of air is something that should be seriously taken into account."

Construction with bottle, cork and funnel....

'To see for yourself that air takes up space, we will do the following experiment. In figure 1 you see a construction that you can make with some objects on the table (one bottle, one cork and one funnel). You have to choose the objects well so that the construction fits exactly, i.e., so that no air can escape.'

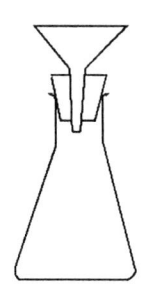

Water poured in the funnel will not run in the bottle...

'If water is poured into the funnel, this will not run into the bottle. The reason for this is that the air is still inside and cannot escape. You may say that the air 'obstructs' the water.'

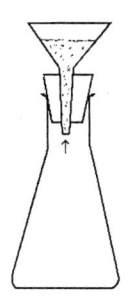

A straw helps the air escape ...

'Figure 3 shows how this problem is solved. A straw that is stuck through the funnel creates a passage for the air, just like a chimney. The escaping air will free up space within the bottle, which is immediately occupied by the water. Therefore you will see that the water starts flowing into the bottle'

'Now you must put your finger on the top of the straw. Then the air cannot escape any longer and the water will stop flowing. As soon as you lift your finger, air and water will continue to flow: the air out of the bottle and the water into it.'

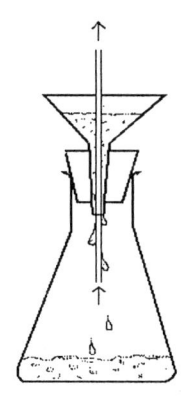

Figure 2. Three steps in experimental procedures: OHP transparencies showed to participants, and text spoken by experimenter.

After these explanations, the student had to perform the physics experiment. Several problems had to be overcome in performing. First, the choice of the necessary objects. At the student's disposal were the following objects: 3 bottles (one too small, 150 ml; one too big, 400 ml; and one exactly right, 250 ml), 4 corks (one too small with a hole; one too big with a hole; one the right size but without a hole; one the right size with a hole), 3 funnels (one small but fitting; one a size too big; one two sizes too big) and 3 straws (thin and red; too big and red; too big and blue). The students spent a considerable time finding the one fitting combination, i.e., the medium-size bottle, the medium-size cork with a hole, the smallest funnel and the thin red straw. All other combinations did not fit. In their manuals, the students had to identify exactly which objects they used, or the experiment was doomed to fail.

A second problem consists of the airtightness of the construction. This could only be obtained by pushing the objects really firmly together. As long as the construction was not hermetic, the experiment was guaranteed to fail. As soon as water was poured into the funnel, the construction would show whether it was hermetic: if not, the water would run immediately into the bottle and not stand in the funnel.

A third problem arose when the straw was put into the bottle through the water in the funnel. This would fill part of the straw with water, which had to be removed (by carefully blowing or sucking the straw) before the air could pass through.

The student had to overcome these and a few more problems to bring the experiment to a successful conclusion. Only when necessary, e.g., if the student got stuck and could not resolve the problem him/herself, the assistant gave advice.

Directly after the experiment, which took about ten minutes, the writing assignment was given. The instruction was as follows:

> Suppose that in the afternoon one of your fellow students has to do the same experiment. He or she enters the room, and all these objects (bottles, corks etc.) are on the table. No one is there to give instructions or explanations (like I gave to you) and there are no figures (like I have shown you).
>
> What this student needs is a good *manual* for this experiment, in which it is exactly stated what he/she should do and know in order to *perform* the experiment without problems and to *understand* what it is about. Now it is your task to write such a manual on the basis of your experience with the experiment.
>
> You may only use words. You are not allowed to draw any figures.
>
> Be aware that your text is meant to be used by one person who has to do the same experiment you have done. You should try to write a manual that will ensure a quick and unproblematic execution of the experiment and clear understanding. Use as many details as you consider useful. Again: don't draw any figures."

The writing task was usually completed within twelve to fifteen minutes. After finishing, every student was prompted to read the text aloud and correct any errors that he or she detected.

3.3.2   Reading & Commenting Procedures for Conditions V and VI

Peers used the manuals written by experimental groups II and III. The research assistant gave no explanation and no figures were shown. The students or 'readers' were only instructed to perform a physics experiment as described in the manual, using the objects on the table in front of them. They had to think aloud during the experiment and were prompted to continue talking whenever they fell silent. The readers were also instructed to give on-line comments on the quality of the manual. The reader's performance of the experiment and the oral comments were recorded on videotape. The following instruction was given:

> You will need some of the objects on the table in the following physics experiment. To execute the experiment, you will have to use the manual. In this manual, someone has tried to describe for you what you should do in order to perform and understand the experiment.
>
> Your task consists of two activities:
>
> First you should *precisely* follow the instructions in the manual. Try to do exactly what is written: no more, no less. Don't start working according to your intuition, follow the instructions literally.
>
> Whenever the manual is not clear to you, say it *immediately*. Also point out missing or incorrect information. Think aloud continuously while doing the experiment, so I can follow your line of thinking."

In this way, defects in the manuals would become visible and audible in the execution of the experiment. Readers would run into many problems due to missing, incorrect and unclear information, leading to observable confusion and imperfect task execution. The video recordings serve as 'reader protocols' in which speech and images of the reading process are combined.

For condition IV, the reading task was followed by an assignment to write general comments about the quality of the manual. The instruction was:

> 'One of your fellow students has tried to write this manual as clearly as possible, so that it would cover all the necessary information for you to do the experiment well and to understand it. Now I ask you to write down your comments on this text. Do you think it is a good manual? What are its weak points, what was unclear or incorrect, what was missing? And what are its strong points, which helped you to do the experiment well? Look it over thoroughly and give as many comments as possible."

Writing a short list of comments took about three to four minutes.
The second session ended with a writing task for both reading groups. After having used and commented on an imperfect manual, the students were asked to write their own 'first version'. Using the manual they had seen as a model was not allowed.

> "Now write your own manual for another student who has to do the same experiment. Think of your experiences with the manual and your comments on it."

The average time for writing their version was twelve minutes. When finished, the students were prompted to read their text aloud and correct any mistakes.

3.3.3 Feedback Procedures for Conditions I, II, III and IV

This part of the study focuses on the various feedback and revision activities that were part of the second session for conditions I to IV. The four types of feedback all consist of 'readers' comments', although the nature of these comments differs considerably.

In condition I, the writer becomes his own reader. Three weeks after having written a first version of the manual, the writer receives it again and is asked to redo the experiment. The same collection of objects is at his disposal. The instruction focuses the student's attention on revising the manual text:

> "Many people discover problems in their texts when they read them after some time. While you are using your own manual, you may get useful ideas for improving it. You will probably find that it contains some good points, but it may also be susceptible to improvement.
>
> So your last task will be: think of as many points as possible that may cause problems for another student who has to execute and understand the experiment without problems. Revise your manual so that all shortcomings are corrected."

First the students were asked to read their text aloud. Secondly, they had to use the text in redoing the experiment. While doing the experiment and after having finished, they had to generate as many comments as possible on the quality of the text. The student wrote down these comments. The last task was to rewrite the manual, using the first version as a model.

Students in condition II and III did not have the opportunity to redo the experiment themselves. Instead of acting as their own reader, they were confronted with authentic readers. After rereading the first version aloud, they were shown videorecordings of students from the reader conditions who had used their manual. The video observations lasted for ten to twelve minutes and contained nonedited recordings of one or two students using and directly commenting on the manual texts. The instruction was as follows:

> "Some fellow students tried to do the experiment using the manual that you wrote. You will see on video what has come of it.
>
> What should you look for? While looking at the video, you may get useful ideas for improving your text. You will probably find that it contains some good points, but it may also be susceptible to improvement. Try to concentrate on information that will help you in improving your manual. Does the student you see understand your intentions? Does he/she perform the experiment well? What are his/her comments on your text?
>
> Take notes while looking at the video. Whenever you want, the tape can be stopped so you can write or ask something."

After having seen the video recordings, only the students of experimental group III were given the written comments of the observed reader(s), as a supplement to the notes they had taken themselves. Directly after, the students were instructed to rewrite their first version:

> "You have seen one or two students who used your manual. You may have gotten ideas for the improvement of your text. So your last task will be: revise your manual so that all shortcomings are corrected. Make good use of the information you received by looking at the video recordings."

The revision of the manual took fifteen minutes on average. The students had to write a revised version and could use their old text as a model.

The feedback and revision procedure for writers in condition IV was similar, with only one difference. The manual that the observed reader used was not written by the observer, but by an unknown writer. As a consequence, the observer was confronted with communicative failures of someone else's text and had to determine whether they could also be repaired in his own manual:

> "Some fellow students tried to do the experiment using a manual that was written by one of your classmates. You will see on video what has come of it.
>
> What should you look for? While looking at the video, you may get useful ideas for improving your own text. You will probably find that the manual that is used contains some good points, but it may also be susceptible to improvement. Try to concentrate on information that will help you in improving your own text. Does the student you see understand the writer's intentions? Does he/she perform the experiment well? What are his/her comments on the manual?
>
> Take notes while looking at the video. Whenever you want, the tape can be stopped so you can write or ask something."

These students also had to revise their text after having seen the video recordings. They did not receive written comments from readers.

3.3.4 Generalization task for all conditions

Four weeks after the revision session, all students were given a writing assignment which was supposed to tap their declarative knowledge about manual texts. With declarative knowledge, we mean knowledge in the form of assertives that can be verbally reported by the student, such as facts and opinions. Declarative knowledge, as opposed to procedural knowledge, is supposed to be the first stadium of knowledge expansion when learning in a new domain (Anderson, 1987).

We assume that in this experiment, learning takes place at least in the form of expansion of declarative knowledge about instructional texts. By writing and revising, students become aware of specific criteria discerning good manuals from weak ones. If knowledge about these criteria can be reported, it can be assumed that the first stadium of learning has taken place.

We use this rather cautious definition of learning here, because transfer to other writing tasks often fails to take place for other reasons than mere failure to learn declaratively (e.g., failure to invoke the declarative knowledge when possible). In other words, we consider declarative knowledge not as learning per se, but as a good indicator for possible learning. If declarative knowledge about criteria for good manual texts cannot be reported by a subject, it is assumed that learning has been poor.

All students were asked to write a letter to a fictitious fellow student, who needs advice on how to write a manual text for a physics experiment. We assume that the number and quality of the pieces of advice that were given are an indication of the student's knowledge about criteria for writing good manual texts. The following instruction was given by the research assistant:

> "Imagine the following situation: one of your classmates comes to ask you for advice. He or she has to write a manual for a physics experiment, and has heard that you have some experience in writing such texts.
>
> Although you do not know what sort of experiment your classmate has to write about, still you think that you can explain what points he/she should pay attention to when writing a good manual text. The manual should be used by students your own age.
>
> Write a friendly note to your classmate and give *as many pieces of advice as possible*, clearly stated, that would help him/her to write a high-quality text."

The students were given twenty minutes for writing this letter of advice. The research assistant stated explicitly that a manual text should not be written, but described.

4. RESULTS

4.1 Instrumentation and Scoring

For the assessment of 'text quality' a standard manual was constructed which could function as a scoring model. This model consists of an introduction, three episodes called Construction, Water, and Straw, and a conclusion. For each of these parts, a list of standard information elements is stipulated. See Appendix A for the list of standard information and two examples.

Each text was scored on the occurrence of each of the 29 information elements. That is, for each element it was checked whether the writer had realized it in the text. If so, the element was scored with a full point. If not, the score was zero. If serious doubt existed, the element scored a half point. Scoring was done by independent and trained scorers. Their inter-scorer reliability was .86 (Cohen's Kappa).

It was possible to interpret almost every textual element written by the students as a realization of one of the 29 elements in the standard manual. The object descriptions were scored positively if the description referred *unambiguously* to one of the objects on the table, because unambiguity is the essence of referential communication (Sonnenschein & Whitehurst, 1984). 'Take a bottle' is therefore scored as inadequate (score: zero) while 'take the medium size bottle' is considered adequate because only one object answers this description (score: one).

The reliability of the scale, made up of all 29 elements, is 0.64 (Cronbach's alpha). If low-contributing items 1, 9 and 19 of the standard manual are left out, reliability increases to 0.70, which can be considered sufficiently high. Leaving these items out has no consequences for the reported between-group differences.

4.2 Effects On Writing

4.2.1 General Text Quality

For answering both research questions A and B, the effect of the independent variables on text quality must be determined. A one-way ANOVA of the total score of all elements followed by a post-hoc comparison yields the following results for *text quality*.

Table 2. Mean Scores, Standard Deviations and Post-Hoc Comparisons (Duncan, $p < .05$) for 'Text Quality'

	Condition	M	SD	Comparison
0	Writing	9.79	2.93	
1	Generating self-comments	10.11	3.43	
2	Observing Readers: Video own text	14.31	1.67	2 > 0, 1
3	Observing Readers: As cond. 2, plus receiving written comments	17.43	3.14	3 > all
4	Observing Readers: Video other text	12.85	3.11	4 > 0, 1
5	Producing Feedback: performing the manual, thinking aloud	11.97	3.16	
6	As cond. 5, plus producing written comments as feedback	13.54	2.55	6 > 0, 1

Revision on the basis of self-generated comments yields no significant improvement of text quality (condition I equals condition 0). Revision based on observation of readers (conditions II, III and IV) is effective, and observation supported by written comments is even more effective than observation without written comments or observation of someone else's text (condition III surpasses conditions II and IV). Observing readers performing the viewer own text or observing readers performing a text not written by the viewer, has an equal effect on text quality (no difference between condition II and IV).

The kind of critical reading activities exercised in conditions V and VI does not automatically lead to a better preparation for writing. Only when the commenting activities are immediately 'condensed' by writing the comments down, the students write a better first version. Remarkably, the quality of this first version is even higher than the quality of revised texts based on self-generated comments (condition VI exceeds condition I).

4.2.2 Specific Text Quality

The question arises how to account for the increase of text quality by reader observation. To understand this increase, we assigned all 29 elements of the standard manual to four categories, related to speech acts (Searle, 1979). These are: Instructions, Object descriptions, Theoretical explanations, and Precautions. In the standard manual at the beginning of this chapter they are marked I, O, T and P.

Instructions are the heart of any manual text. They describe (or better: commission) the actions to be undertaken. They should be ordered chronologically, so the reader can follow the manual step by step.

Object descriptions supply the reader with the necessary information about the materials to be used. Many constructions or experiments will only succeed if the correct materials are used, like with this physics experiment. Without knowledge of the correct materials, the reader is likely to waste much time and energy.

Theory and explanations support readers in understanding what they are doing. It is not useful to just 'go through the motions' when performing a physics experiment. The writers had received sufficient explanation helping them to understand the aim of the experiment and to interpret their observations, so they should be aware of the need for such information.

Finally, Precautions make up a very useful category of hints within manual texts. In every experiment, some things are guaranteed to go wrong. The writer has experienced some of these misfortunes, such as air leaking from the bottle, water entering the straw, etc. In good manuals, these misfortunes are anticipated, pointed out, and remedied.

Table 3 gives the quantification of the qualitative differences between the manuals written in the various conditions. Categories are transformed into 10-point scales to enable direct comparisons. Asterisks indicate a significant post-hoc comparison (Duncan, p<0.05) when compared to condition 1 (for the writing conditions I-IV) or condition 0 (for the reading conditions V and VI).

Table 3. Mean Scores, Standard Deviations and Post-Hoc Comparisons for Four Types of Speech Acts (* = p < .05)

Condition	Instructions M	SD	Objects M	SD	Theory M	SD	Precautions M	SD
0	6.43	1.24	2.23	2.60	1.64	1.66	1.64	2.46
I	6.50	1.63	3.21	3.76	1.89	1.29	0.86	1.35
II	7.18	1.15	4.86	4.58	3.18 *	1.26	3.00 *	2.30
III	7.14	1.21	8.57 *	2.33	4.29 *	1.38	5.14 *	2.61
IV	7.60	1.38	3.25	4.06	2.77	1.32	2.35	2.62
V	7.17	1.50	3.18	3.92	2.35	1.66	1.15	2.10
VI	6.68	1.59	7.14 *	3.72	2.93 *	1.59	2.14	1.83

The number of instructions is equal across the conditions. As concerns the four groups of writers, the increase in general text quality is mainly due to an increase in object descriptions, theoretical explanations and precautions. The reading groups have improved the quality by inserting better object descriptions and theory for the reading conditions.

The essential speech acts in instructional texts are, of course, instructions. The writing proficiency of the 15-year-old students is at such a level that they have no problems with writing these essential parts. They do not try to improve their text by adding more instructions, but they include information that supports the reader in following these instructions: about the tools to be used, about the meaning of the experiment and of their observations, and about possible pitfalls. Only writers who were confronted with the fact that readers need such information improved the quality of their texts according to these needs.

4.3 Effects on Learning

Reader observation seems to offer a useful basis for revising instructional texts. But is the beneficial effect limited to the revision of a text, or do observers learn something from their observations that contributes to their writing expertise in general? By having the students write a 'letter of advice' about manual texts (see 3.3.4), we tried to tap potential knowledge gains about criteria for good and weak manuals. Between-group differences in the quantity or quality of the pieces of advice can be attributed to the type of feedback that each group processed or supplied.

First we will explain the scoring of the advice. Next, the results for the experimental groups are presented. Finally, relations between experimental effects for writing and learning are discussed.

4.3.1 Instrumentation and Scoring

The students could demonstrate their declarative knowledge about criteria for good manual texts in a 'letter of advice'. The request to give as many pieces of advice as possible and the open formulation of the task served to evoke a non-selective memory search and unimpeded writing.

In all, 108 letters of advice were collected. The number of pieces of advice in each letter as well as their nature was assessed. This was done by means of a score form that contained a categorization of possible pieces of advice. In the construction of this form, it was assumed that the pieces of advice were either *process oriented* or *product oriented*; and if they were product oriented, that the advice concerned either *style* or *content*. Each of these classes was further subdivided, resulting in a system of quite specific and recognizable categories. See appendix B for scoring information.

Two scorers categorized the pieces of advice according to this scoring form. Their interrater-reliability (Cohen's kappa) varied from .82 (main categories) to .70 (sub categories). This reliability is sufficient to make between-group comparisons.

Two letters may illustrate the variety of responses:

Comparatively weak letter:

> Dear someone,
> I am happy that you asked for my advice.
> If you want to write a good manual, you should mind these points:
> - Write neatly and precisely, or the person who has to do the experiment won't be able to read it.
> - Don't write too much nonsense.
> - Write everything in detail.
> - First write down all the important things you can think of.
> I hope this helps. If you still have problems, do call me.

This letter contains some very general product advice regarding style, which applies to many types of texts. The last piece of advice is process oriented: a suggestion to brainstorm before starting to write.

Comparatively good letter:

> Hello, here is my promised letter with advice for your manual for the physics experiment:
> It is very handy if you start by thinking <u>really well</u> about the things that you need and that you don't and about what has to be done (If you don't make such a plan, it is better to not write at all.)
> Next: keep the order of the activities in mind and also the moments when some tool has to be used.
> Then it is time to start writing: Emphasize the most important things, such as:
> How to do it! And: <u>which</u> object to use.
> You must not forget that children your age must be able to understand your manual.
> So when you are finished, you check it yourself and correct mistakes. Check if you would be able to do the experiment with your own manual (faultlessly!)
> Only if you are certain that you've done everything to keep your classmate from running into problems, you can hand the manual in to the teacher.

This letter of advice is longer and shows more variation in pieces of advice. The writer seems to have followed the course of the writing process: advice concerning orientation, writing and revision is present in a natural order. The letter contains three content-oriented pieces of advice concerning the use of instructions, objects and precautions, albeit not very precise. Also three style-oriented pieces of advice are given.

All the advice from all advice letters was categorized by using the score form. Some phrases contained more than one advice, such as in:

> 'Describe chronologically all the things that need to be done.'

This advice would get a positive score on B.2.1 (instructions) and B.1.6 (organization).

If some experimental groups had acquired more knowledge about manuals than the others, this should result in a higher score in the category 'product-oriented pieces of advice - content'. In order to increase the sensitivity of our assessment, the pieces of advice assigned to this category were rated on quality. In this way, justice can be done to differences between advices like:

> 'Write down what to do with the tools'

and

> 'Describe very accurately which of the available objects must be used, so that the reader doesn't have to guess and try for a long time; also tell him which precise acts must be performed with the objects'.

Two raters rated each content-advice as '½' (content advice given, but in a very general wording, or implicit) or '1' (content advice given, precisely formulated, with motive or example). Interrater-reliability was 0.80 (Cohen's kappa).

Table 4. *Mean Scores, Standard Deviations and Post-Hoc Comparisons (Duncan, $p < .05$) for Total Number of Pieces of Advice and for Number of Pieces of Advice for each Subcategory*

	Condition	Mean	SD	Comparison
	Advices: Total number			
0	Writing	4.93	1.73	
1	Generating self-comments	5.14	2.11	
2	Observing Readers: Video own text	5.47	2.22	
3	Observing Readers: Cond. 2, + receiving written comments	10.86	2.73	3 > all
4	Observing Readers: Video other text	5.50	2.33	
5	Producing Feedback: performing the manual, thinking aloud	4.45	2.11	
6	As cond. 5, plus producing written comments as feedback	7.50	1.70	6 > all but 3
	Advices: Process			
0	Writing	0.57	0.85	
1	Generating self-comments	0.71	1/07	
2	Observing Readers: Video own text	1.15	1.30	2 > 4, 5, 6
3	Observing Readers: Cond. 2, + receiving written comments	1.71	1.38	3 > all but 2
4	Observing Readers: Video other text	0.50	0.76	
5	Producing Feedback: performing the manual, thinking aloud	0.30	0.57	
6	As cond. 5, plus producing written comments as feedback	0.29	0.47	
	Advices: Style			
0	Writing	1.43	1.16	
1	Generating self-comments	1.50	1.16	
2	Observing Readers: Video own text	1.79	1.47	
3	Observing Readers: Cond. 2, + receiving written comments	3.43	1.71	3 > all but 6
4	Observing Readers: Video other text	2.00	0.79	
5	Producing Feedback: performing the manual, thinking aloud	1.25	1.16	
6	As condo. 5, plus producing written comments as feedback	2.71	1.06	6 > 2, 4, 5
	Advices: Content			
0	Writing	2.93	1.77	
1	Generating self-comments	2.92	1.64	
2	Observing Readers: Video own text	2.53	2.17	2 > 0, 1
3	Observing Readers: Cond. 2, +receiving written comments	5.71	1.50	3 > all, but 6
4	Observing Readers: Video other text	3.00	2.49	
5	Producing Feedback: performing the manual, thinking aloud	2.90	1.68	
6	As cond. 5, plus producing written comments as feedback	4.50	2.11	6 > 2, 4, 5

4.3.2 Knowledge about Criteria for Good Manuals

In order to answer the second part of research questions A and B, an ANOVA was performed on the advice-letter data. The ANOVA was followed by a pair-wise post-hoc comparison. The results are presented in table 4.

By far, most pieces of advice are given by students from condition III: writers who observed readers and received written comments for the purpose of revision.

This can be concluded with respect to the total number of pieces of advice (which is twice as high as in most of the other groups) and each of the subcategories of advice. The lead with respect to content-oriented advice is most significant, because this category represents cognitions that are specific for the type of text that was written.

Readers from condition VI, who not only used the text but also commented on paper, appear to have learned more than the comparable condition without written comments. The lead they take is respectably large, if we compare it to the other writing conditions II and IV.

It has not yet been determined whether the feedback and revision activities have allowed these students to acquire *more* knowledge about instructional texts, or that these activities have resulted in knowledge that is *more readily retrievable* from memory (which in itself is a quality of learning as well).

5. DISCUSSION

5.1 Writing Effects

In the first place, we had several expectations concerning the effectiveness of four different types of feedback. Our expectations were based on the idea that a writer is 'necessarily' blind to the communicative handicaps in his texts, because even when he tries to read his text like an authentic reader would; he has the advantage - and curse - of access to the writer's mind.

The consequence is that writers had better make use of authentic readers' responses as a means to detect possible flaws in their texts. We chose to experiment with the more direct method of observing readers' responses (rather than indirect post-reading commentary) because we expected that on-line detection of comprehension problems through observation may lead to a better understanding by the writer of readers' needs; needs that the writer may not be aware of. By observing comprehension processes and difficulties, the writer may become better prepared to adapt his writing strategies to these processes and difficulties.

The implicit hypothesis that the three types of feedback by reader observation (cond. 2, 3 and 4) would prove more effective in revision than feedback by self-generated comments (cond. 1) was not rejected. The text quality after self-revision did not exceed the quality of non-revised texts (cond. 0).

Differential effects with regard to text quality could be found with the three feedback conditions: when reader observation was supplemented by written comments from the reader (usually a summary or selection of the experienced problems, along with advice for improving the text), the quality of the text after revision was significantly higher than when no written comments were given: cond. 3 outscored conds. 2 and 4.

An unexpected result is that it does not make a difference whether the observed reader uses a text written by the observer, or by an unknown person. Although it could be expected for motivational or cognitive reasons (see 1.3) that an observer-outsider would not profit as much from the observations, this did not turn out to be the case. There was no difference between conditions II and IV with respect to writing.

We expected the readers who were observed while reading aloud, using the text and commenting on it, to profit from these activities. They had not been observing, but personally experienced the comprehension problems and sometimes voluntarily gave advice on how the writer could overcome them. As a consequence, they ought to be better prepared for writing a manual text if they could translate their reading experiences into writing behavior. This expectation was confirmed only in the condition where the readers were asked to write their comments down. Possible explanations for this phenomenon are that formulating the advice requires investing time and effort in the topic (which the other group did not do), and that writing the comments down is a means to conceptualize and generalize, so that the comments could be more easily transferred to the text they had to write.

The students wrote and improved an instructional text. It was remarkable that the improvement of the texts was not due to more or better instruction; the students included enough instructions already in their first versions. Improvement was found in adding more explanations, precautions or warnings, and in repairing ambiguous descriptions. In this way, the students discovered that instructional texts have to meet more readers' needs than only the need to be instructed.

5.2 Learning Effects

Regulation of learning is meaningless without regulation of the task to be learned. Similarly, feedback in the learning process depends on feedback in the task execution. If writers never discover whether their writing is understood or not, they have nothing to go on in evaluating their learning process. That is why feedback by observation, which offers a window on the comprehensibility of text, may not only be beneficial for improving writing, but also for improving learning-to-write.

The learning effect of the four types of feedback was measured by a test of declarative knowledge, the 'letter of advice'. It was found that the conditions which had scored highest in the writing assessment also scored highest in this 'knowledge assessment': condition 3 for the writers and condition 6 for the readers. It again seems that the production and reception of written comments are the active elements: they may well affect the construction of knowledge or at least the condensation of experiences into more general cognitions.

There are a few factors that possibly influence the internal validity of the results. One might say that we make unfair comparisons, since the time-on-task differs between the conditions. This is true. The difference is largest *between* the writers' and the readers' conditions: the readers work in two sessions, and the experimental writers work in three sessions. *Within* the collection of writers' conditions, the differences between conditions are comparatively small. The written comments added to condition 3, for instance, did not prolong the session with more than five minutes. Generating self-comments lasted, due to the method of brainstorming and elaboration, not much shorter than observing the readers on videotape. The experimental effects we found cannot very likely be attributed to the differences in time-on-task. It should be added here that we are not interested in making all the possible comparisons between the conditions on every possible variable. We have limited ourselves to only answering the research questions.

The data for conditions III and VI was collected one year before the other data. The procedure was standardized (read from paper), the test assistant was trained only to stimulate and not to assist the student, and the scoring procedure was anonymous; therefore we consider it unlikely that a significant part of the effects found ought to be attributed to between-group differences. We already mentioned that an ANOVA did not yield any significant difference in the quality of the first versions written for each writing condition.

We have partly discussed the topic of concept validity concerning the assessment of 'learning'. We have chosen to do this indirectly, by trying to measure the declarative knowledge. Of course having such knowledge at one's disposal does not guarantee a successful implementation in a new writing situation. We have only tried to determine to what extent the first step of learning has been taken.

Some objections against the external validity of the study concern the generalizability of the results. Over which population can the results be generalized? By means of selection we had excluded the very good and very weak writers from the experiment. This means that it has not been decided whether this pedagogy would be equally effective for these groups. Only new research can answer that.

Secondly, one may wonder to which other types of texts the results may be generalized. We specifically chose a manual text for a physics experiment because of the appellative function of the text and the literal visibility of potential comprehension problems. With more cerebral types of texts such as essays or letters of application, it would be harder or might even become impossible for the observer to detect communicative weaknesses.

We would respond that much depends on the reader's task. In the present experiment, the reader was supposed to read and think aloud, and was prompted to keep talking whenever he or she fell silent. Once readers have gotten used to this activity, they disclose many of their thoughts, concrete or abstract, certain or intuitive, to the observers. It is also very important that the reader has to perform a well-defined task with the text. Not just 'read and comment' but a less comprehensive assignment. When reading an essay, it could be a reader's task to search the main viewpoint of the author and the two (three, four) main arguments. Or the reader could be asked to draw a schematic structure of the text. Or, when letters of application are to be read, it could be the reader's task to compare two texts on their respective strong and weak points. Feedback by reader observation, in our opinion, like any other type of feedback, is well served by well-defined tasks and criteria to comment on. If these are absent, the observing may even become boring.

Another point of discussion concerns the most suitable mode of communication between reader and writer. As was pointed out before, there are several possibilities for the reader to convey his or her comments to the writer. Each of these modes will have its own advantages and disadvantages. It may be interesting to find out how practical (dis)advantages correlate with the conveyed content. Since we chose to depart from Schriver's method by using videotapes instead of typed protocols, we would like to discuss the benefits of a few methods here. We can place the methods on the dimension direct vs. indirect. Indirect modes of communication suffer from a time delay or a distortion of the responses by the selection of reformulation; post-reading comments, oral or written, are the best-known example of indirect reader feedback. The communicative advantage is that the reader can more easily help the writer with diagnosis and correction of textual problems, because he/she is not under pressure of time. Also, responses that need a certain amount of (re)consideration can better be given afterwards.

Reader protocol analysis (Schriver) is a more direct method, although the writer does not listen to the reader but reads his text from a typed protocol. The advantage is the naturalistic recording of genuine readers' responses and the option of looking back in the original text, which makes it very suitable for intensive studying. It is a pity that the writer cannot see or hear the reader working with the text, which leads to a loss of information.

More direct again is listening to (and looking at) the reader by means of audio (or video) tapes. Little information about the oral responses is lost and the writer can experience a time dimension. Like with protocol analysis, this method requires much preparative work.

The ultimate confrontation with readers is a live confrontation. But there are some disadvantages which must not be underestimated. First, the writer cannot 'look back' like he can do when reading written comments, protocols or tapes. Second, it is very difficult for a writer to not interfere with the reader. Very short interruptions in the reading task, for instance if the reader asks for a simple clarification, can lead to a change in the nature of the reader's task: the reader will probably step back from his naturalistic reading and will fulfill the role of evaluator.

We think that the mode of communication we have chosen in this experiment, a very direct, non-interactive, interruptible, and multi-mode (sound and vision) method, is a good compromise between all the (dis)advantages. It would be interesting to experiment with one writing/reading task and several modes of reader-writer communication.

This brings us to our plans for future research. In order to bring clarity to some aspects of the present study, it would be wise to add a few conditions. To assess the separate contribution of observation activities and written comments to writing and learning, there should be one condition of writers who only receive written comments and try to revise their text.

Just as interesting would be a study of knowledge construction about the evaluation criteria by writers and readers, when more than one text is evaluated. Can the model function of the texts be exploited by contrasting them and evaluating the differences?

This study can definitely not say the final word about reader observation as feedback for writing students. In fact, this study is among the first words to be said about the subject. Schriver deserves the credit for bringing this pedagogy into the scientific lab; we hope that more laboratory workers will find themselves attracted to investigating its merits so that it may one day leave the lab.

APPENDIX A: SCORING MANUALS

Communicative utterances in a 'good manual'.

Manual items	Explanation
Introduction 1. (T) What is the experiment about? 2. (I) Notice the initial situation.	Readers want to know what they can expect. Therefore, in the Introduction information should be given related to the *subject* or *aim* of the experiment, and the reader should be prompted to *familiarize* himself with the initial situation with the many objects on the table before him.
Construction episode 3. (O) Which bottle should be used? 4. (O) Which cork? 5. (I) Put the cork on the bottle. 6. (O) Which funnel? 7. (I) Put the funnel into the cork's hole. 8. (P) Push everything tightly together. 9. (T) because no air may escape.	With these objects a construction must be made during the Construction episode. Unambiguous descriptions of the necessary objects are of great value to the reader, who would otherwise become lost in construction problems (not knowing what the intended construction looks like). The reader should be instructed to make a firm assembly; if not, the construction is guaranteed to leak.
Water episode 10. (I) Put water into the funnel. 11. (I) Check if the water stays in. 12. (T) that is because the air in the bottle stops it. 13. (P) If it does not stay in, press everything together more tightly. 14. (T) that is because air is leaking somewhere.	A first observation is done in the Water episode, when the water – counter-intuitively – does not run into the bottle. An ignorant reader would not be alarmed by the water running in the bottle due to a leak in the construction, so a preventive warning is very useful here. Also, the reader wants to understand this unusual phenomenon, so an explanation is suitable. A hint must be given on how to correct an undesirable situation.

Straw episode
15. (O) Which straw?
16. (I) Put the straw into the funnel's hole.
17. (P) Make sure the straw's one end is pushed into the bottle.
18. (P) The straw's ends mustn't be put into the water.
19. (T) The straw is needed to remove air from the bottle.
20. (I) Check if the water is running into the bottle now.
21. (T) that is because air can go out now.
22. (P) If the water doesn't run, blow, suck or move the straw;
23. (T) that is because the water in the straw must be removed.
24. (I) Hold your fingertip on top of the straw.
25. (I) Check if the water stops flowing,
26. (T) that is because air can't escape any longer.
27. (I) It will go on flowing if you lift your finger again.

In the Straw episode the relation is observed between escaping air and flowing water. Readers will run into several problems in this episode, which can all be overcome by correct descriptions, precautions and explanations.

Conclusion
28. (T) This experiment proves that water occupies space,
29. (T) because the water cannot go into the bottle as long as the air cannot go out.

Finally, a concluding part should supply the reader with information on what inference to make from the observations, because 15-year-old readers cannot be expected to make such an inference themselves.

Two examples of a comparatively weak and a good manual will illustrate the scoring method.

Manual for the physics experiment

You take a bottle. You put a cork in it. You put the funnel in the cork's hole. You put water in the funnel and then you see that no water comes into the bottle and that's why you put the straw in and then the air can go away and the water in.

(7 points: 5, 7, 10, 11, 16, 19, 20)

Readers using this text would most probably run into problems choosing the correct materials. It is very hard for readers to find the correct combination if they are completely unaware of what construction should be made. The semi-causal links 'and then you see that...' and 'and that's why you...' are not really informative. A reader probably would not understand what the experiment is about, because the aim is not mentioned explicitly.

Manual for the physics experiment

- You see 3 bottles and 3 corks on the table.
- Take the middle bottle and the cork without marks or spots, with an opening.
- Put the smallest funnel in the cork's opening.
- Push the funnel in really well (no air may escape).
- Pour water into the funnel.
- You'll see that the water stays in the funnel (if you have pushed everything really well together, so no air can escape).
- In order to let the water run through, it must be made possible for air to escape.
- Put a straw (the thin one) through the funnel until halfway the bottle.

- You may not leave the straw in the funnel itself, there's water in there which stops the air from flowing out.
- If the water still doesn't run through, there must be water inside the straw, so the air can't go through. (Suck if necessary.)
- The water will run through now.
- Put your finger on top of the straw, then the water will stop, because no air can escape.

(21 points: 2-4, 6-11, 13-17, 19-20, 22-26)

This text exceeds the first in length as well as in quality: it contains more detailed descriptions, explanations and hints for readers.

APPENDIX B SCORING LETTERS OF ADVICE

A. Process-oriented advice (advice on how to organize the writing process)
A.1 Orientation
    'start with doing the experiment yourself'
    'first examine all the objects on the table'
A.2 Text production
    'while you write, repeat the experiment in your mind'
    'write down all you can think of'
A.3 Revision
    're-read the text when you are done'
    'finally, check if your little sister would understand the text'

B. Product-oriented advice (advice on desirable properties of the text
B.1 Style-oriented, regarding:
B.1.1 - Clarity   'what you write must be very clear'
B.1.2 - Length   'keep the text as short as possible'
B.1.3 - Accuracy   'don't forget small details'
B.1.4 - Completeness   'make sure you mention all the objects'
B.1.5 - Correctness   'beware of mistakes'
B.1.6 - Organization   'give the instructions step by step'
B.1.7 - Accent   'pay special attention to the theory'
B.1.8 - Audience   'someone your age must understand it'
B.1.9 - Goal-directed   'don't over-emphasize the details'
B.1.10 - Spelling   'check for spelling errors'
B.1.11 - Other   'make a drawing if you want'
These general pieces of advice can be applied to many types of text
B.2 Content-oriented, regarding:
B.2.1 - Instructions   'everything the reader must do'
B.2.2 - Objects   'also which tools you should use'
B.2.3 - Theory   'and what the whole thing is about'
B.2.4 - Precautions   'if things go wrong, what to do'
B.2.5 - Other   'tell them to clean up afterwards'
These categories are more specific for one text type: manuals)

To illustrate the use of this score form, we present two letters of advice and their scores.
Comparatively weak letter:
score:

    Dear someone,
    I am happy that you asked for my advice.

	If you want to write a good manual, you should mind these points:
B.1.3	// - Write neatly and precisely, or the person who has to do
B.1.8	the experiment won't be able to read it.
B.1.5	// - Don't write too much nonsense.
(B.1.3)	// - Write everything in detail.
A.1	// - First write down all the important things you can think of.
	I hope this helps. If you still have problems, do call me.

This letter contains some very general product advice regarding style, which applies to many types of texts. There are two pieces of advice from category B.1.3. If the second one seems to be just a paraphrase of the first, like in this case, they are counted as one piece of advice. The last piece of advice is process oriented: a suggestion to brainstorm before starting to write.

Comparatively good letter:
score:

	Hello, here is my promised letter with advice for your manual for the physics experiment:
A.1	// It is very handy if you start by thinking <u>really well</u>
B.2.2	about // the things that you need and that you don't // and
B.2.1	about what has to be done // (If you don't make such a plan, it is better to not write at all.)
B.1.6	// Next: keep the order of the activities in mind // and also the moments when some tool has to be used.
A.2	// Then it is time to start writing:
B.1.7	// Emphasize the most important things, such as:
(B.2.1 B.2.2)	// How to do it! // And: <u>which</u> object to use.
B.1.8	// You must not forget that children your age must be able to understand your manual.
A.3	// So when you are finished, you check it yourself and
(A.3)	correct mistakes. // Check if you would be able to do the experiment with your own manual (faultlessly!)
B.2.4	// Only if you are certain that you've done everything to keep your classmate from running into problems, you can hand the manual in to the teacher.

This letter of advice is longer and shows more variation in pieces of advice. The writer seems to have followed the course of the writing process: advice concerning orientation, writing and revision is present in a natural order (A.1, A.2 and A.3). The letter contains three content-oriented pieces of advice concerning the use of instructions, objects and precautions, albeit not very precise. Also three style-oriented pieces of advice are given.

LEARNING TO READ AND WRITE ARGUMENTATIVE TEXT BY OBSERVATION OF PEER LEARNERS

MICHEL COUZIJN & GERT RIJLAARSDAM

University of Amsterdam, the Netherlands

Abstract. This chapter offers a theoretical and empirical comparison of 'learning by doing' and learning-by observation, applied to the field of reading and writing. Participants are fifteen-year old high school students, who followed one of a series of experimental courses on composition and/or comprehension of argumentative text.
The effect study focuses on observational learning, as opposed to a more traditional 'learning by doing' pedagogy. In two experimental groups, students (15 y.) observed either writing or reading activities performed by age-group students. Observations were made by means of authentic videotape recordings. It was the observer's task to compare and evaluate the activities of the observed students. These two instructional programs were compared with two more conventional (control) programs in which participants learned to read or write by applying theory in exercises. Intra-modal learning as well as inter-modal transfer results were assessed for both writing and reading.
Results show that this type of observational learning was more effective than 'learning by doing'. Learning effects for the observation groups surpassed the results for the matching 'learning by doing' groups. Moreover, learning to write by observation appeared to be more efficient since the experimental writing subjects more readily transferred their increased writer's knowledge to reading tasks.

Keywords: argumentative texts, observation, reading.

1. INTRODUCTION

> For most academic skills like reading, writing and arithmetic, there simply is no substitute for repeated practice. Only with much practice will these habits become automatic and be performed rapidly and effortlessly (Bower & Hilgard, 1981: 539-540).

In the above citation, the authors stress the importance of practice for learning complex skills. Their position is that extensive practice is a necessary condition for the acquisition of expertise in the domains of reading and writing. It would be very dif-

Couzijn, M. & Rijlaarsdam, G. (2004). Learning to read and write argumentative text by observation
Rijlaarsdam, G. (Series Ed.) & Rijlaarsdam, G., Van den Bergh, H., & Couzijn, M. (Vol. Eds.). Studies in writing. Vol. 14, Effective learning and teaching of writing, 2nd Edition, Part 1, Studies in learning to write, 241 - 258.

ficult to find a teacher, educator, or educational psychologist who disagrees with this viewpoint. Even more, looking at current text books and teaching practices for language skills education, one will find that many teachers and educators have adopted this *necessary* condition as a *sufficient* condition (Hillocks 1986; cf. De Glopper 1988). *'Learning by doing'* is the dominating pedagogy in the everyday practice of language skill education, leaving little room for essentially different pedagogies. The effectiveness of practice as a learning tool, so widely relied on, can however be questioned. In this study we want to compare the effects of a 'learning by doing' approach to reading and writing with a pedagogy which we will call 'learning by observation'. We will also pay attention to the transferability of learning outcomes of each pedagogy.

At least two arguments oppose the idea that 'learning by doing' deserves its status of unassailability. In the first place, the learning output of practice is not equal for every student. Some learners, so-called 'good novices', manage to profit more from practice or exercises than others, even within the same IQ subclasses (Elshout & Veenman 1992). Apparently effective skill acquisition is induced by more factors than practice alone. The development of effective instructional methods requires insight into these additional factors that modify the effect of practice on skill acquisition.

In the second place, 'learning by doing' alone does not always and automatically result in a 'rapid and effortless' skill execution - to speak with Bower and Hilgard. Particularly in more complex task domains, such as mathematics, literature, or essay composition, the expertise to be acquired is made up of more than only of knowledge proceduralized by practice. Automatic activities are strategically alternated with mental activities of a different kind: the systematic error detection of one's own solution to a problem, the deliberate reflection on one's habits or attitudes towards a topic, or conscious self-regulation of otherwise less systematic and effective behavior. In short, learning in complex domains often calls for the learner's *self-reflecting* ability, with the aim of enhancing their *self-regulating* activity during task execution.

Learning psychologists have called attention for the crucial role of self-monitoring (perception of one's activities during task execution), self-reflection (processing the output of monitoring by evaluation, abstraction and attribution) or self-regulative activities (controlling the task execution for the sake of its effectiveness, on the basis of information from self-monitoring and self-reflection) (Kuhl & Kraska, 1989; Pieters & Beukhof, 1991; Vermunt, 1991; Ng & Bereiter, 1992; Schunk & Zimmerman, 1994). Many of them placed their theory in the context of *learning* processes. However, it is important to note that regulation of learning a certain skill requires – in theory – regulation of the *executional processes* of that particular skill. Task regulation conditions the regulation of the learning process for that task (Ng & Bereiter, 1992). By comparing these processes of *executing* a task and *learning to execute* it, we want to clarify the key mediating function of self-observation and evaluative activities.

1.1 Writing Versus Learning Activities

Taking writing as an example, a skill that has often been conceived of as a problem-solving activity (e.g., Hayes & Flower 1980a&b, 1986), we can divide the cognitive activities aimed at resolving a writing problem in three clusters of activities. *Executional* activities aimed at text production (orientation, writing and rewriting activities), resulting in a solution to the set task, i.e., a text which is a proper reflection of the assignment (Kellogg, 1994). *Monitoring* activities which consist of observing (i.e., monitoring), evaluative and reflective activities (Hayes, 1996) and aimed at on-line knowledge of one's actual task behavior. These activities are guided by the goals the learner-writer set at the beginning and during the execution of the writing task. *Regulative* activities aimed at strategic control of the former types of activities, dependent on their evaluation; they control the effective temporal organization of the monitoring and executional component, and create new strategies based on learning outcomes (See Figure 1).

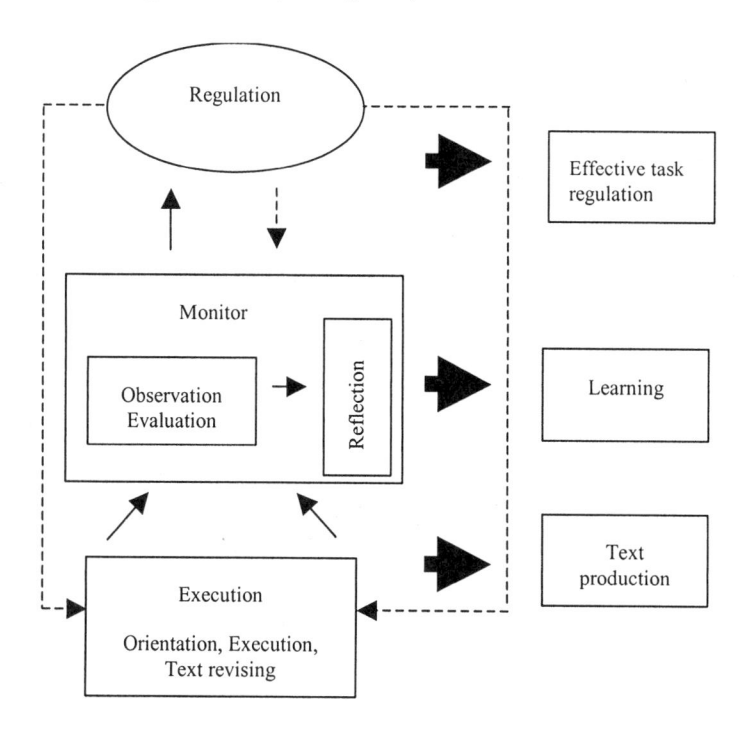

Figure 1. Three components of performance of writing (based on Couzijn, 1999: 111)
Note. Straight arrows indicate the flow of information between activity categories, and dotted arrows indicate activation prompts. Adapted with permission from Braaksma, Van den Bergh, Rijlaarsdam & Couzijn, 2001).

In figure 1 executional and monitoring activities are placed on levels I and II respectively. An effective temporal organization of these activities is governed by regulative activities placed on a third level. Straight arrows indicate the flow of information between activity categories and curved arrows indicate activation prompts. In this representation we gave a central position to monitoring and evaluative activities, since they supply the knowledge base for skilful regulation and thus execution of the entire writing process. Being self-aware of one's writing activities and their consequences is an essential step towards detecting possible flaws in, and enhancement of one's writing. Thus good writers invest in being aware of their activities during the course of the writing process.

How is this viewpoint related to learning? Writers in a learning situation, like students at school, will consider a writing task as being part of a learning task. They will execute a writing process (with a physical aim: producing a text) simultaneously with a learning process (with a cognitive aim: acquiring skill in producing such texts). This 'parallel' learning process can be represented as having the same morphology as the writing process, including executive activities (orientating, establishing learning goals, practising, remembering and storing writer's knowledge), monitoring activities (self-observation and evaluation of learning activities) and regulation of learning.

The connection between these processes lies in the writing experiences from which students can learn. To be instructive, writing rules, techniques, strategies must not only be executed by the writer; they must be monitored, conceptualized, experienced, along with their positive or negative effects. Writers may use their 'writing awareness' (the output of the monitoring processes on level II) as input for their learning. This awareness consists of conceptualizing writing behavior (what am I doing now? how should I call it? which strategy must I choose? have I done anything similar before?) and evaluative labeling (this strategy has been very time-consuming; the brainstorm was, or was not, successful). Writers who both realize and evaluate their working-method while writing invest in the meaningfulness and effectiveness of their learning.

In sum, learning-to-write by performing writing tasks appeals strongly to the students' self-observing and self-regulative capacities. Writing students follow a 'double agenda' with activities aimed at text production and other activities aimed at learning. They need to regulate executional and monitoring processes for each of the agendas. And last but not least, they must orderly control a variety of executional activities for the composition of text.

Obviously such learning demands a lot of the writer's self-monitoring and self-regulative abilities. We suggest that a 'learning by doing' pedagogy for reading and writing may not be supportive enough for many students. While some students do succeed in finding instructive aspects in even simple writing assignments, others will just 'go through the motions' and fail to observe, let alone improve, their writing behavior; mostly because a strategic distribution of attention across learning and writing levels is beyond their capacities. Such students need a type of process-oriented instruction that assists them in their monitoring or observation of writing activities, and evaluating their effectiveness.

In this chapter, we will focus on *learning by observation* of writing and reading activities, performed by others instead of by the observer. For the observer it is no longer necessary to simultaneously perform, observe and regulate writing as well as learning activities: he can more conveniently concentrate on the observed writing activities.

1.2 Learning To Read and Write by Observation

Learning by observation has been extensively studied by Bandura (1977, 1986) and more recently by his colleagues Schunk and Zimmerman (1989, 1991, 1994). Bandura has set himself to the explanation of social, cognitive, learning, and strategic behavior by mechanisms of *observation* and *imitation*. He has stressed that many human behavior patterns and skills are learned not learned by instruction or external conditioning, but by observing and imitating other people, specially if the observed behavior is valued positively for its results. Similarly, observed behavior which does not lead to desirable results is 'unlearned'.

Bandura uses the term 'observational learning' for a type of modeling in which completely new behavior must be observed and acquired. In various experiments this type of learning activities have show to be more effective than direct instruction or step-by-step instruction (Schunk, 1991, ch. 4). Bandura's social cognitive theory holds that the observing student constructs symbolic mental representations of the observed acttivities/strategies, and stores these representations as the basis for his own behavior.

Models that are suitable for observation fall into two groups: *mastery models* who show a faultless skill execution and thus serve as a 'good example', and coping models who are openly hesitating, make faults etc. and thus serve as 'natural examples'. In empirical studies each type of models has shown to be effective, especially if more than one model was observed.

In sum, the 'learning by doing' pedagogy is very common in language education, while there are reasons to doubt its effectiveness. These doubts concern the potentially little attention for observing, evaluative and reflective activities. The presented 'learning by observation' pedagogy on the other hand relies to a great extent on observing and evaluative activities, and has shown to be effective in empirical studies.

We want to answer the question whether 'learning by observation' is more effective than 'learning by doing' in the domains of reading and writing. Sonnenschein & Whitehurst (1983, 1984) already provide some evidence. They found that learning effects of young children observing either speaking or listening models were very high, and surpassed the corresponding 'learning by doing' groups. They also tested for transfer between writing and reading, but found none.

Transfer between productive and receptive language skills can however be expected, since these skills rely partly on the same knowledge (cf. Shanahan & Lomax, 1986). In order to assess the effectiveness of the two pedagogies, we must to measure both their intra-modal learning effects (gain in writing skill after observing writes) and their inter-modal transfer effects.

2. RESEARCH QUESTIONS, VARIABLES, AND EXPECTATIONS

2.1 Research Questions and Variables

The research questions concern 'learning' and 'transfer' effects. With 'learning' we mean progress within the same mode as within the student exercised, or observed others making exercises. With 'transfer' we mean progress in the complementary mode. So for a student who has done or observed writing exercises, his increase in writing skill is called 'learning' and his increase in reading is called 'transfer'. We thus formulate four research questions:

With respect to (intra-modal) *learning*:
1) Is learning to write by observing students doing writing exercises more effective than learning to write by doing these exercises?
2) Is learning to read by observing students doing reading exercises more effective than learning to read by doing these exercises?

With respect to (inter-modal) *transfer*:
3) Does learning to write by observing students doing writing exercises lead to higher transfer to reading than learning to write by doing these exercises?
4) Does learning to read by observing students doing reading exercises lead to higher transfer to writing than learning to read by doing these exercises?

The theoretical considerations allow for explicit expectations. Such expectations allow for one-tailed testing of null hypotheses, thus enhancing the power of the statistical tests. Since observation of reading and writing exercises done by others is supposed to result in more meaningful learning of communication rules compared to individually performing these exercises, we expect OW > DW and OR > DR for both dependent variables.

3. METHOD

3.1 Design

An experiment was set up in order to test our hypotheses. The research design can be schematized as in table 1.

Table 1: Research Design

Condition	N	Intervention	Post tests
DW	30	Executing Writing tasks/exercises	Reading & Writing
DR	30	Executing Reading tasks/exercises	Reading & Writing
OW	30	Observing Writers' exercising	Reading & Writing
OR	30	Observing Readers' exercising	Reading & Writing

In this posttest-only control-group design, 'learning by doing' conditions are denominated as control groups. The experimental treatments differ with respect to the 'modal content' or skill that is practiced (writing or reading) and to the type of instruction (aimed at learning by doing or learning by observation & evaluation). The posttests, however, are the same for all conditions: measurements of both reading and writing skill. The writing posttests thus constitute *intra-modal learning* measurements for the DW and OW conditions (training and testing within the same mode), and *inter-modal transfer* measurements for the DR and OR conditions (training and testing in opposite modes). Similarly, the reading posttests are *learning* tests for DR and OR, and *transfer* tests for DW and OW.

3.2 Subjects

In all, 120 students who finished the 9th grade (intermediate and high level) took part in the experiment. The average age was 15.5 years. Of about 30 % of the students, Dutch was not the language spoken at home, although all students were fluent in Dutch. Twice as many girls participated in the experiment as boys. The students came from 8 different city schools and participated voluntarily in the experiment. For their participation they received a modest financial reward.

Assignment of subjects to the 4 conditions was semi-random. That is, stratification was applied first with respect to level of education (intermediate vs. high); further assignment within the strata was random. As a result, in each condition precisely 12 students took part from intermediate level and 18 students from high level.

3.3 Training Materials: Experimental Courses on Argumentative Texts

A communication course was required dealing with one text type, which could be adapted for both writing and reading instruction, by means of adding exercises. It was necessary that in the theoretical part of this course, properties of the text type be treated 'neutrally', i.e., with a modest and balanced attention for application in reading and writing (because the real focus on reading or writing would be made in the exercises). Moreover, the text type had to be relatively new to the students. Lastly, the level of the course had to be sufficiently high to avoid ceiling effects, so that potential experimental effects would become observable.

For these reasons we decided to develop a four-lesson course on 'argumentative texts'. These are texts in which a speaker or author defends a standpoint by supplying argumentation. In the Netherlands, the ability to analyze or compose argumentative text is obligatory for secondary students of intermediate and high level. Although third-grade students have already had some experience with verbally expressing and explaining their opinions, they have not yet received formal instruction on the composition or analysis of argumentative text. The subject matter is generally abstract in nature, since it calls on the ability to invoke complex speech acts and thinking skills, such as arguing, refuting, comparing and contrasting, selecting main ideas and paraphrasing.

3.3.1 Learning Contents

In selecting subject matter for the argumentation course, we chose to join the pragma-dialectical perspective on argumentation that Van Eemeren and Grootendorst advocate (Van Eemeren & Grootendorst 1992). The advantage of this perspective is the explicit framing of argumentation within the social situation of a (critical and problem-solving) discussion. We expect that this social perspective with its distinct communicative roles will allow for integration of receptive and productive skills in a meaningful way (see Table 2).

Table 2: Learning Contents of the Course on 'Argumentative Texts'

Unit 1: Argumentative texts and discussions
Introduction of five main concepts:
- Standpoint (opinion)
- Argument (reason)
- Argumentative text
- Issue
- Discussion

In an inductive fashion, the concept 'argumentative text' is explained by means of its constituting elements: standpoints and arguments (opinions and reasons for having these opinions). The genre is placed in the social context of discussions aimed at resolving a dispute, which centers around the acceptability of a certain proposition (the 'issue').

Unit 2: 'The structure of argumentative texts'
Presentation of a rhetorical model, consisting of:
- Introduction: Request for attention; issue at stake; parties and standpoints
- Body: Author's standpoint, pro-argumentation, refutation of counter-argumentation
- Ending: Conclusion; most important arguments; consequence.

The well-known global text structure (introduction, body and ending) is specified for argumentative texts. The function of each subpart is discussed in relation to the discussion goal. Various examples help to give meaning to the concepts.

Unit 3: 'The argumentation in argumentative texts'
Presentation and discussion of several types of argumentation:
1) Singular argumentation
2) Compound argumentation
3) Subordinate argumentation

and the complex argumentative structures of which these are the constituents. Moreover, a simple notation system for schematization of complex structures is taught.

Unit 4: 'The presentation of argumentative texts'
Presentation and discussion of three means for clarifying the text structure
1) Paragraphing and the rhetorical model
2) Using verbal structure markers
3) Argumentative connectors

It is demonstrated how each of these means is helpful in recognizing or expressing the global text structure, the parts that make up this structure, or the complex structure of the pro-argumentation.

The complete course consists of four lessons and is self-instructive: all subjects work individually without a teacher's help. Each lesson lasts one hour. There is a workbook for each lesson, containing theory and exercises. The theory is divided in small parts of 1 - 1½ page and is illustrated by many examples. The construction of the course is cumulative, so that in each consecutive lesson the theory from the previous lessons is repeated and extended. In order to stimulate the cumulative acquisition of knowledge by the students, each lesson starts with a summary of previous theory which must be actively studied and completed by the subject. The learning objectives for the four writing lessons are related to those of the reading lessons (table 3):

Table 3. Learning Objectives for the Reading and Writing Minicourses

Reading	Writing
Recognition of the social parameters of the discussion: issue, parties, standpoints, communicative goal	Explicitizing the social parameters of the discussion
Analyzing the text structure on the basis of a model	Composing a well-structured text on the basis of a model
Analyzing complex argumentation and its simpler constituents	Writing on the basis of complex argumentation structures
Identification of means for the presentation of text elements	Applying various means for presentation of text element

3.3.2 Instructional Sequence

The theory on argumentative texts forms the backbone of the four different courses that are developed for the experimental conditions. Nevertheless, the subjects spend about 70 % of the time on the exercises in which the theory must be applied. The nature of a course as a 'reading' or 'writing' course is therefore not so much determined by the theory as by the type of exercises. Figure 2 shows the similarities and differences between the four courses with respect to the instructional sequence of theory and exercises.

The chronological order is from the top downward. Subjects in all conditions study the same theoretical part, and subsequently answer one or two 'control questions'. These questions ask for the gist of the part that has just been studied and are intended to stimulate active reading of the theory.

Next, subjects apply the theory in *one* of four different types of exercises: either individual writing (DW) or reading (DR) exercises, observation and commenting of writing (OW) or reading (OR) exercises. After completing one or more exercises, subjects continue with the next portion of theory, the next exercise, and so on.

The reading and writing lessons can thus be considered mirror-images: the subject matter presented in two matching courses is identical, but the nature of the exercises differs: the theory must be applied to the construction (writing) or analytical reconstruction (reading) of argumentative text.

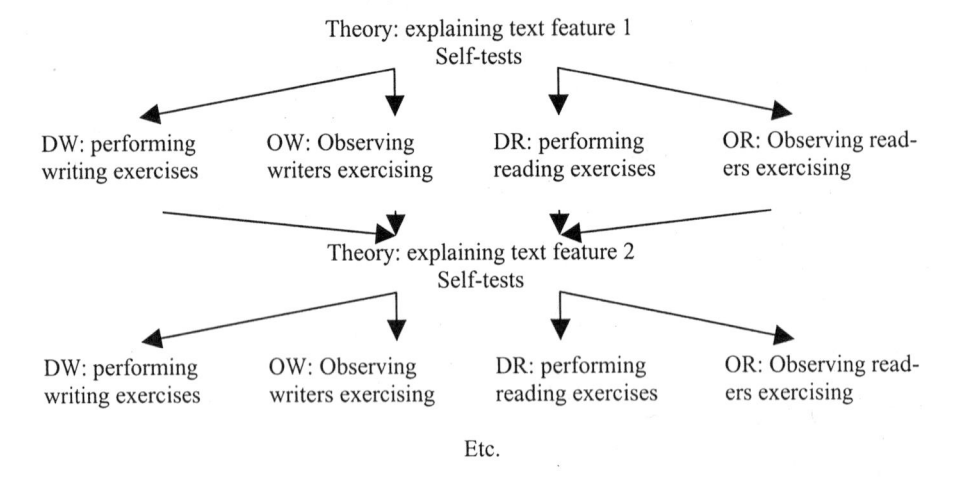

```
              Theory: explaining text feature 1
                         Self-tests
      ↙         ↙              ↘            ↘
DW: performing  OW: Observing   DR: performing   OR: Observing read-
writing exercises  writers exercising  reading exercises  ers exercising
      ↘         ↘              ↙            ↙
              Theory: explaining text feature 2
                         Self-tests
      ↙         ↙              ↘            ↘
DW: performing  OW: Observing   DR: performing   OR: Observing read-
writing exercises  writers exercising  reading exercises  ers exercising

                          Etc.
```

Figure 2. Instructional sequence of the courses.

3.3.3 Exercise Types

We will describe the differences between the types of exercises by means of an example from the first lesson. In the theoretical part, the two characteristics of argumentative text have been introduced: an opinion is stated, and one or more reasons for having this opinion are supplied. Some examples are given:

> 'I think we should go to Italy for our holidays, because the whether is always fine and the food is great.'

> 'You must really put the volume of your music down. I cannot work with all that noise in my ears.'

The learning that takes place is a form of concept learning (Mayer, 1983). Subjects learn to identify a text as belonging to a certain subclass of texts, according to a conceptual rule:

> < (text type X) **is characterized by** ((characteristic A) and (characteristic B)) >

A 'receptive' formulation (cf. Anderson's 'production rule') of this conceptual rule would be:

> < **if goal** (typify text as X)
>
> **then action** ((check for characteristic A) **and** (check for characteristic B))

Such formulation is aimed at the identification of properties of characteristics from which class membership is inferred. In this form, the conceptual rule can be used in identification tasks and for self-checking in writing tasks. Its counterpart, the productive form, can be used in writing tasks for generating activities:

< **if goal** (produce text type X)

then action ((realise characteristic)

and (realise characteristic B)) >

After the subjects reproduce the characteristics on paper (control question), they start the first exercise.

DW (learning by doing writing exercises). The subjects from the DW condition do the following assignment:

Check again the three examples on page 2 and then *write three new examples of argumentative texts.*

1. ....
   ....
2. ......etc.

Figure 3. 'Writing' assignment: production of simple argumentative text.

The DW subjects must use the rule productively. In the workbooks a limited space is reserved for the answer, so they must confine themselves to application of the rule. More specifically, they must inductively give meaning to the characteristic concepts 'opinion' and 'reason for having this opinion', aided by the examples. Secondly, they must understand that *both* characteristics are necessary to meet the rule, so that opinions only, however floridly presented, will not suffice. Finally, they must generate new instances of the characteristic concepts.

DR (learning by doing reading exercises). Assignments of the following type are done by the DR subjects:

Jackie says to his father: *'We haven't been to the cinema for ages. So I think it is high time that we go and see 'Jurassic Park' with Christmas*
1. Question: Is this an argumentative text?
O NO!
O YES, because I can find the following characteristics of argumentative texts:
2. Opinion:
reason for having this opinion: ....

Figure 4. 'Reading' Assignment: Analysis of simple argumentative text.

The DR subjects must use the rule in the analysis of given texts. They must check for the occurrence of each characteristic, and then determine if the text matches the rule. Answering 'yes' is not enough: in order to check if subjects mix up opinions and arguments, they must write down their analysis.

OW (observation of writing). OW subjects do not do the writing exercises themselves. Instead, they observe age-group students doing these exercises. Authentic videotape recordings of the age-group students are used for the observations. The observed students think aloud while writing, so the observer can closely follow the writing activities. The assignment runs:

Read the following assignment, and imagine how you would answer it.

'Check again the three examples on page 2 and then *write three new examples of argumentative text*'

You are going to see two students doing this assignment.
It is your task to find out what they do well, and what they do wrong.
When you have observed both students, you may advance to the next page.

(...)

(next page):
You saw two students doing the assignment. They wrote the following texts:

Student 1   Student 2
"I don't need a dog any more   *"Dogs are more fun than cats,*
because I already have three"   *but they need much more attention"*

===>>> Which student did better, according to you? Student .....

===>>> Explain briefly why you think the other student did worse.

Student ..... did *worse*, because ....
....

The subjects orientate on the observation exercise by reading the writing assignment. Next they are explicitly instructed to aim their attention at evaluating the observed students' task performance, which should stimulate engaged and therefore instructive observation. Observation thus holds that the subject checks the application of the rule by the observed students.

After having observed two different student writers (see section 'Procedures') the subject must determine if one did worse than the other, and explain what exactly made this performance less successful. In this way the subjects are forced to designate 'good models' and 'worse models'.

It should be noted that subjects in this condition, along with observing writing processes, also perform comprehension activities: in order to evaluate the texts of the observed writers, they must analyze them in terms of the argumentative characteristics.

OR (observation of reading). The observation exercises for the OR subjects are similar, with the exception that reading processes are observed (such as the DR subjects perform) instead of writing processes. The observed students think aloud as well. OR subjects received the following exercise:

Read the following assignment, and imagine how you would answer it:

"Read the following example:

Jackie says to his father: *'We haven't been to the cinema for ages. So I think it is high time that we go and see 'Jurassic Park' with Christmas'*

Question: Is this an argumentative text?
O NO!
O YES, because I can find the following characteristics of argumentative texts:
opinion:
reason for having this opinion:

You are going to see two students doing this assignment.
It is your task to find out what they do well, and what they do wrong.
When you have observed both students, you may advance to the next page.

(....)

(next page:)
You saw two students doing the reading assignment. Their answers were:

Student 1:   Student 2:
'Yes, because   *'Yes, because*
opinion: "That it is time to   *opinion: "that it was too long*
go to the cinema again"   *ago that he was in the cinema".*
reason for opinion: "He has not   *reason for opinion: "that he wants*
been there for a long time"   *to go by Christmas".*

===>>> Which student did better, according to you? Student .....

===>>> Explain briefly why you think the other student did worse.

Student ..... did *worse*, because

Figure 6. 'Observing Reading' assignment: analysis of simple argumentative text.

OR subjects are also prompted for orientation and task definition, and go through the same stages of observation, comparison and evaluation. It is important to note that, as in the OW condition, the subjects were not allowed to read the written answers by student 1 and 2 *before* the observations had ended. This is because the experimental pedagogies are aimed at observing *processes* rather than *products*. If the subjects would have had the final 'solutions' at their disposal before or during the observations, it is well imaginable that they would evaluate these products only and not be patient enough to observe the complete process that led to each product.

It is the OR subjects' task to evaluate the use of the conceptual rule by the observed readers, who try to analyze the text. In this example it is clear that the second observed student has mixed up standpoint and argument. The observer must detect the differences in the analysis, and can attribute them to differences in working-method of the two readers.

3.4 Test Materials

Six posttests were administered: three for the measurement of reading skill and three for writing. Each of the four learning objectives for a certain mode (see section 3.3.1) corresponds with each of the four variables measured in the posttests for that mode.

For the measurement of post-experiment *reading skill*, two comprehensive text analyses had to be made, including: identifying the parties and their standpoints, and the proposition at stake, identifying the nine functional components of an argumentative essay, and writing down the argumentation structure (c). Lastly, the student had to mark all argumentative connectors and markers (d). The third reading test measured the analysis of singular, compound and subordinate argumentation types (Oostdam, 1991; Oostdam, this volume). Students had to identify argumentative relations between short sentences and find the direction of argumentative support. The number of items varied from 4 to 43. Internal consistency indices (Cronbach's alpha) ranged from .51 (4 items for Identifying means of presentation) to .83 (19 items for Reconstructing complex argument structures from texts) and .91 (48 items for Identifying singular, compound and subordinate complex argument structures from texts).

Measurement of post-experiment *writing skill* took place by writing one comparably large text on the basis of a given complex argumentation structure, which was scored on the four learning objectives; writing smaller assignments which could serve as only the 'body' of an argumentative text, and a validated test for the ordering of argumentation (adapted from Oostdam 1991). Reliability indices ranged between .62 (7 items for Adhering to a textual model for argumentative texts) to .86 (10 items for Ordering and connecting arguments in a text structure) and .92 (32 items for Constructing complex argumentation structures).

3.5 Procedures

Participation in the experiment took place in two sessions during two consecutive mornings or afternoons. On the first day, students followed lesson 1 and lesson 2. On the second day, the course continued with lesson 3 and lesson 4. After lesson 4, the posttests were administered during the last two hours. All subjects in all conditions worked individually from a workbook, in which theory and exercises were combined.

Sessions of the *learning by doing* conditions were rather straightforward. Subjects had a workbook and a pen at their disposal and could work individually in a normal tempo until the hour was over. Due to the fact that the course had been pretested, the time estimation of one hour appeared to be sufficient.

The *learning by observation & evaluation* sessions were more complicated. Subjects had a workbook and pen at their disposal, and were seated facing a videoplayer. Each subject had a 'private' videoplayer and headphones. At the start of each lesson, a tape would be inserted and started. By means of an on-screen timer and on-screen messages the subject was informed about how much time was left for each activity: reading a piece of theory in the workbook, answering a control question, and doing a reading or writing exercise. The students to be observed on tape were announced in plenty of time by means of short beeps; this to make sure that the observer would not miss the fragments.

After two or three fragments of students doing an exercise, there was ample time for the subject to write down the comments on the observed performances. In this way, the time spent on the various parts of the lessons was highly controlled. However, because the tempo was not too high and the tape could be stopped if necessary, the time control appeared not to entail more stress for the subjects than in the 'learning by doing' conditions.

4. RESULTS

4.1.1 *Effect on Learning*

'Learning' is defined as the acquisition of skill in a communication mode that corresponds with the mode of practice or observation. Table 5 shows the posttest results. Differences between groups are assessed by MANOVA procedures, since several variables from the posttests are analyzed together as a simultaneous representation of the dependent variable 'reading' or 'writing'. The effect of the observation condition proved to be statistical significant for both modes (for Writing F 6.33, $p < .02$; for Reading F 5.21, $p < .03$). Both in the reading mode and in the writing mode, the learning-by-observing is more effective than 'learning by doing'.

4.1.2 *Effect on Transfer*

Here 'transfer' refers to the acquisition of communicative skills in a mode different from the one in which practice took place. The two 'outsider observation' modes OW and OR can together make up an experimental successor to the Sonnenschein & Whitehurst (1983, 1984) series of experiments described earlier. These researchers had found that transfer from practice in the productive mode to the receptive mode (or vice versa) had mostly held off. It can be seen now if this finding is repeated with another age group, and a very different task.

MANOVA procedures were again selected to determine between-group differences. When the two writing conditions are compared on the resulting reading scores, the observation condition outperformed the practice condition (F 6.25, $p < .02$); the same holds for the two reading conditions, compared on their resulting writing scores (F 3.97, $p < .05$). Transfer from writing practice to reading appears here to be extra promoted by observing writers, compared to doing normal writing assignments. On the other hand, extra but to a smaller amount transfer to writing can be obtained by observing readers.

Table 5. Means and Standard Deviations (in Italics) of Post-Test Data

Condition	Writing		Reading	
	\multicolumn{4}{c}{Communicative parameters}	
	Rendering the communicative parameters of the writing task		Identifying the communicative parameters in texts	
DW	1.51	*2.11*	5.72	*3.25*
DR	2.22	*2.30*	6.68	*3.19*
OW	4.13	*2.32*	8.06	*2.64*
OR	3.03	*2.36*	8.89	*3.06*
	\multicolumn{4}{c}{Textual Model}	
	Adhering to a textual model		Identifying Parts of a textual model	
DW	7.51	*5.82*	8.97	*5.69*
DR	8.16	*7.69*	9.03	*5.85*
OW	9.34	*5.63*	17.26	*4.59*
OR	8.06	*4.91*	16.57	*4.72*
	\multicolumn{4}{c}{Argumentative structures}	
	Ordering and connecting arguments in a text structure		Identifying singular, compound and subordinate argumentation	
DW	21.51	*8.52*	23.32	*8.15*
DR	20.87	*9.74*	23.58	*8.24*
OW	27.44	*8.06*	27.65	*10.05*
OR	27.37	*6.58*	28.03	*10.30*
	Constructing complex argumentation structures		Reconstructing complex argument structures from texts	
DW	16.55	*7.17*	8.58	*5.50*
DR	15.06	*9.36*	14.92	*7.15*
OW	22.65	*5.82*	24.27	*4.62*
OR	21.03	*6.01*	23.34	*4.84*
	\multicolumn{4}{c}{Textual Models}	
	Use of paragraphing, markers and connectors in text		Identifying means of presentation: paragraphing, markers, and connectors	
DW	4.13	*2.85*	5.36	*1.85*
DR	4.58	*2.88*	6.86	*2.03*
OW	8.89	*3.53*	12.08	*2.17*
OR	5.27	*4.19*	12.79	*2.98*

5. SUMMARY AND DISCUSSION

The aim of this study is to make an empirical comparison between two types of learning activities for reading and writing argumentative text. We expected 'learning by observation' to promote both within-mode learning and between-mode transfer.

The supposed cause for within-mode learning is that purposeful observation and evaluation would stimulate reflection, conceptualization of the observed processes and meaningful learning of criteria for correct and incorrect task behavior (Schunk, 1991). In the traditional 'learning by doing' paradigm learners would not be able to keep control over executional as well as metacognitive processes, specially not in complex task domains, such as reading and writing, which call for extra monitoring.

The supposed cause for between-mode transfer is that reading and writing partly feed on the same knowledge about the coding or decoding of text, and that reading activities are integral part of the writing process.

A multivariate analysis of variance was used in order to test the hypotheses. The main findings are that 'learning by observation' was more effective than 'learning by doing' (research questions I and II), both for learning to write and learning to read. A second main finding is transfer to another mode of communication is stronger in the observation conditions (research questions III and IV). Remarkably, writing-reading transfer is so large that it exceeds the learning effect of learning-to-read-by-doing. The ultimate consequence of such a phenomenon is the advice to observe others constructing a text, if you want to learn how to comprehend such texts.

A possible explanation for the large transfer from writing to reading is that reading and writing processes are not perfect mirror-images. This is reflected in the organization of these processes: reading processes are comparably much more linear than writing processes. Writing processes include many reading activities, whilst the opposite is not true. In addition it must be noted that the thinking activities of the experimental students who *observed* writing, probably resembled more co-reading and comprehending processes than writing processes.

A serious problem is the difficulty to provide any backup for the possible explanations of the findings. Observational learning theorists (Bandura, Schunk) as well as developmental theorists (Sonnenschein & Whitehurst) have provided for the hypotheses around which the study was built, but we cannot confirm yet that the learning processes took place exactly as was described by these authors and had their origin in a more reflective, critical, conceptualizing behavior.. Only posttest product data have been collected from the students. Neither can we combine the results with data on students' thought processes while executing the writing or reading tasks. We consider this the major handicap of this study and at the same time the most interesting point of application for more profound studies.

Some threats to the external validity of the study must be mentioned. Due to the organization of the experiment, the posttests were administered very soon after the training had taken place. We can therefore not be certain about the durability of the results. On the other hand, it was not our aim to develop long-lasting skills with the students, but to have our questions answered in an experimental setting. Durability is important, but not yet top priority.

We consider it a very important point that the observator's task is clear and meaningful. With clarity we mean that the aim and means of the observation task are delimited and understood by the student. It is probably not sufficient to instruct students to 'look at what is happening'; the precise aim of the observation must be specified. Should they check for certain errors? Should they describe the solution to a problem? Which qualities of the process or product should be specially checked for? 'Meaningful' refers to the relation between observation and the learning goals the student is supposed to attain: the observation aims should be chosen such that they are clearly instrumental to the observer's acquisition of reading or writing skill.

In the past, observational learning has mostly been studied with respect to the acquisition of social behavior and skills. We believe that the recent attention for 'learning by observation', which is more than before focused on (meta)cognitive tasks and strategies, (Schunk, 1991; Schunk & Zimmerman, 1994) can provide important contributions to the development of process-oriented instruction. The accent shift in skill education from product-orientation to process-orientation is generally considered important and promising with respect to effectivity (De Jong & Van Hout-Wolters, 1993). The precise learning and thinking activities that can make up such process-oriented pedagogies in cognitive domains, need to be studied and empirically tested.

It must be understood that the results of this study do not discredit 'learning by doing' in general. We believe that 'learning by doing' remains indispensable in, and essential to language skill education, but that it is not the 'only true pedagogy'. We have only tested this type of learning in contrast to two types of observation in the field of reading and writing argumentative text, and only with students for whom the subject was comparably new and difficult. In such a situation, the students can be considered in need of good examples (models) who demonstrate what the behavior-to-be-acquired is like, along with examples demonstrating the pitfalls to avoid; pitfalls they are likely to make since they are novices to the task. In this situation, 'learning by observation' showed to be advantageous. However, once a basic cognitive level of knowledge and skill has been acquired, the need to proceduralize and flexibilize arises (Salomon & Perkins, 1989; Anderson, 1990). This calls again for 'learning by doing' activities. These activities can now profit from the observation experience because criteria for self-evaluation have become more explicit.

In the end, we expect most of a well-balanced interplay of 'learning by observation' and 'learning by doing' activities. Each of these pedagogies has its qualities and drawbacks. It is up to the educator to compose learning programs in which the qualities are combined and the drawbacks compensated. That the qualities of 'learning by observation' deserve to be studied in close detail, is what we hope to have demonstrated.

THE UPTAKE OF PEER-BASED INTERVENTION IN THE WRITING CLASSROOM

EVA LINDGREN

Umeå University, Sweden

Abstract. This chapter presents and discusses a method, peer-based intervention (PBI), in which conscious reflection of key-stroke logged writing sessions is used to improve written composition. Multiple writing opportunities are used together with discussion and observation of the writer's own and a peer's text. The method entails the theoretical assumption that the release of cognitive resources in working memory helps writers to focus the attention towards deeper structures of the text under construction as well as towards the writing process *per se* and thus assist in raising writers' metacognitive awareness of writing. The chapter reports on a study of Swedish 13-year-olds composing descriptive and argumentative texts in their first language (L1), with and without PBI. The texts were graded and all revisions undertaken during the writing process were analysed according to their impact on the text product. Further, text quality and frequency of revisions were tested statistically in order to delimit the impact of the PBI treatment. The results indicate that the method was generally successful for low L1 ability writers, while high L1 ability writers benefited from the treatment in the argumentative assignments. The treatment further raised writers' awareness of contents features involved in writing by increased frequency of text-based revisions.

Keywords: L1 Swedish, keystroke logging, revision, PBI, noticing, metacognitive awareness, working memory, social interaction, input at the right level, 'zone of proximal development'.

1. INTRODUCTION

Learning to write is a truly multi-levelled activity. Like the writing process *per se*, learning to write is influenced by a number of internal as well as external variables. The vast range of influences on the writing process (Flower & Hayes 1981; Hayes 1996) provides a vast amount of possible areas of improvement. Important fields in learning to write are research on working memory capacity and metacognitive awareness. Methods, such as observational learning (Braaksma et al., 2001, 2002; Couzijn et al., this volume) and multiple writing opportunities (Chanquoy, 2001),

---

Lindgren, E. (2004). The uptake of peer-based intervention in the writing classroom.
Rijlaarsdam, G. (Series Ed.) & Rijlaarsdam, G., Van den Bergh, H., & Couzijn, M. (Vol. Eds.) Studies in writing. Vol. 14, Effective learning and teaching of writing, 2nd Edition, Part 1, Studies in learning to write, 259 - 274.

have been developed that release working memory capacity in order for the writer to be able to notice new features in the writing process and thereby enhance metacognitive awareness and learning of writing. This chapter addresses the question whether multiple writing opportunities together with peer-based intervention (PBI), that is reflection on and discussion of the own and a peer's writing process, can enhance awareness and noticing processes, as a result of released cognitive space, and improve the quality of first language (L1) Swedish texts, written by thirteen-year-olds in a high-school environment.

2. BACKGROUND

In order to improve in writing one needs to become aware of and able to control the processes involved in writing: "...if students are not even aware of their writing strategies and their results, they can hardly be expected to evaluate – and thus deliberately change maintain or abandon – them." (Rijlaarsdam & Couzijn, 2000: 176). Successful writers need to be self-regulated and thus able to take charge of and organise their own writing processes (Graham & Harris, 2002). Deborah McCutchen (2000) described the skilled writer as someone who is in possession of "...fluent text-generating and transcription processes as well as extensive knowledge about topics, text genre, and routines for coordinating writing processes" (p.15). This demands maturity, well developed linguistic as well as motor skills, knowledge about the writing process and a considerable amount of self-regulation. In general, young, or novice, writers do not possess these diverse writing skills but use knowledge telling strategies when composing text (Bereiter & Scardamalia, 1987). They plan in a 'listwise' manner, translate their thoughts directly into text and revise mostly surface features, such as spelling and punctuation. Somewhere between the age of twelve and fourteen children start shifting from knowledge telling to knowledge transforming strategies, in which goal setting, planning and audience adaptation are central

The limited capacity of the working memory is a restraining factor in the writing process (McCutchen, 1996, 2000). When a writer, for example, struggles with a demanding topic, or is composing in a second language, the working memory capacity might not be enough to consider linguistic and content demands simultaneously. The cognitive overload forces the writer to focus attention on some writing aspects, for example spelling and punctuation, while other aspects, such as planning and contents are left on a basic level. In a study of 3rd, 4th, and 5th grade children, Lucile Chanquoy (2001) found that multiple writing opportunities and postponing of the revision process led to increased frequency of revision and more text-based revisions. She drew the conclusion that "Postponing the revision seems a powerful strategy, allowing the children to free cognitive resources and to focus on the text to be corrected." (Chanquoy, 2001: 36). Another method, in which effective learning to write is achieved by the reduction of cognitive overload during writing, is observational learning (Braaksma et al., 2001, 2002; Couzijn et al., this volume). In observational learning the learner's attention is focussed on a model writer and the learner can devote more cognitive resources to the reflection on, and evaluation of, the writing process and product of another writer.

In both studies the released cognitive space in working memory enables the writers to become aware of and notice features in the writing process, "...noticing is necessary for the acquisition of metalinguistic knowledge..." (Truscott, 1998: 103). If one raises the writers' meta-cognitive awareness of, for example, topic, genre or the different processes involved in writing and helps them to develop these in their own writing, their writing is likely to develop positively (Galbraith & Rijlaarsdam, 1999; McCutchen, 2000). One way of enhancing metacognitive awareness is to "...offer students the opportunity to 'step out' of the writing process in order to *observe* their activities and results, and to learn from this by *verbalising* what they observe." (Rijlaarsdam & Couzijn, 2000: 176). This didactic methodology could also make already existing meta-cognitive knowledge more accessible to the writer. According to Vygotsky (1998) collaboration and social interaction, in which verbalisation forms a central part, are core elements of a learning situation.

In a study of adult writers Sullivan and Lindgren (2002) found that collaborative reflection on computer key-stroke logged writing sessions (Severinson Eklundh & Kollberg, 1996; Kollberg, 1998) enhanced awareness of a range of features that included knowledge of the writing process, language, task or motor skills, that the writers experienced that they needed to improve in order to achieve higher quality text.

Furthermore, in order to be able to notice features in the writing it is important that the working memory release is combined with input on the right level for the individual learner (c.f. 'readiness' in second language learning, Pienemann, 1998). Observational learning, for example, has proven most effective when the learner focuses on a model at the same competence level (Braaksma et al., 2001, 2002). However, for the teacher, or the individual learner, in the writing classroom it is a difficult task to find optimally levelled input for each individual learner. Revisions can provide useful information about, for example, a writer's linguistic level and "...can to some extent show where the writer is on the ladder of learning, i.e what he/she is about to learn and, therefore would need help with and be receptive to learn" (Pålson, 1998: 8). A revision of, for example, a grammatical feature reveals an awareness of that particular feature even if the revised version is incorrect. By using one's own writing process, including revisions, as input in the learning situation, one would be provided with input at a suitable level; one's own output has become input for learning (Rijlaarsdam & Couzijn, 2000). One's own writing process coupled with social interaction and verbalisation could, thus, assist in targeting the individual learner's 'zone of proximal development' (Vygotsky, 1998) and thereby support the learning process.

In the exploratory study presented here key-stroke logs and peer-based intervention have been used as tools to direct the learner's attention primarily towards the text production process rather than towards the final text prouduct. Multiple writing opportunities have been combined with peer observation of and comments on the writing process in order to release working memory capacity. The use of the learner's own on-line output, now used as new input, was investigated as a method to provide the learner with input at 'the right' level, enabling noticing of various writing features and promoting a raised awareness of writing.

3. AIMS AND METHOD

The study was carried out at a junior high school in Sweden and is a part of a larger project in which both L1 and EFL texts are composed under PBI conditions. Here the analysis of the L1 Swedish data is reported[1].

3.1 Key-Stroke Logging and Peer-Based Intervention (PBI)

The writing process data was collected using the key-stroke logging software JEdit (Severinson Eklundh & Kollberg, 1995; Cederlund & Severinson Eklundh, n.d.). The key-stroke logging software registers every key-stroke and all pauses a writer undertakes during a writing session. The program includes a replay facility, which enables the entire writing session to be replayed in slow, real, or fast time. In the PBI treatment used in this study the participants use the software as a stimulus to recall the reasons and thoughts behind the revisions and pauses during the writing process (c.f. Gass & Mackey, 2000).

The PBI sessions are undertaken in pairs together with a teacher. The writers replay their texts one at the time using the key-stroke logging software. While replaying the text's evolution, the writer describes and explains as carefully as possible what went on during writing, including thoughts during pauses and reasons for revision. The peer is encouraged to intervene positively in the discussion, ask questions and give comments. The role of the teacher is to prompt talk when necessary by, for example asking the writer 'What are you doing now?' or 'Why did you revise that?'. All discussions are initiated by the students and the teacher only intervenes in the discussion when it is necessary, for example, to focus on, explain or confirm a particular language or writing feature that has already been initiated by the students.

An example of a discussion during a PBI session is given in Table 1. Two female writers, Annika and Kajsa, have written their first versions of a descriptive text and now they are discussing a revision undertaken by Annika. The topic was to describe her house to a pen-friend in Australia. Annika and Kajsa are discussing Annika's text with the teacher. Annika has described her room and revises a typical difficulty in Swedish writing, compounds (1-2). The words 'skriv bord' (desk) and 'bok hylla' (bookshelf) should be written as compounds. When the computer replays the end of the sentence (3-4), preeceded by a 24-second pause both girls react, 'Oops' and laughter, to the fact that she has yet another table in her room or to the fact that she wrote 'natt bord', when the correct word would be 'nattduksbord'. The focus on tables in the discussion of Annika's description made Kajsa realise that she forgot to mention her desk in her text and the discussion during PBI induced her to revise her text on a second writing occasion.

In her first version Kajsa wrote "My room has green wall-paper in two shades and an edging. I also have green curtains and a white cupboard." (translated into English). During her second writing session she inserted 'a desk' into the second sentence: "My room has green wall-paper in two shades and an edging. I also have

---

1 A case study of two EFL learners from the project is reported in Lindgren and Sullivan (2003).

green curtains, a white cupboard and a desk.". She explained this insertion as a result of the PBI of the first version of her peer, Annika's text on the same topic.

Table 1. Discussion of Annika's Writing Process during a Passage in which she describes her Room on the First Version of her Descriptive Text

	Swedish text	English translation	Discussion
1	I mitt rum har jag en stor säng, två skriv bord en	In my room I have a large bed, two desks, one book-	R. Desk...right...What are you doing here?
2	bok hylla...<revision> ...två skrivbord, en bokhylla...	shelf...<revision of compounds>	A. I wrote desk and book case together. R. That's a typical difficulty, I think, in Swedish. Whether to write the words together or separately. But that is correct! But not in English, there it's the other way around.
3	...fyra garderober, ett stort fönster	... four closets, a large window	R. Now you have written that you have one bookshelf, four closets, a large window
4	<paus 24s> och ett natt bord	<pause 24s> and a night table.	A. laughter K. Oops R. Tell us! Something is happening A. Yes...but there weren't that many....'night table'? K. I forgot to write that I have a desk (laughter).

Annika and Kajsa are discussing Annika's text with the researcher. Annika has described her room and revises a typical difficulty in Swedish writing, compounds (1-2). The words 'skriv bord' (desk) and 'bok hylla' (bookshelf) should be written as compounds. When the computer replays the end of the sentence (3-4), preceeded by a 24-second pause both girls react, 'Oops' and laughter, to the fact that she has yet another table in her room or to the fact that she wrote 'natt bord', when the correct word would be 'nattduksbord'. The focus on tables in the discussion of Annika's description made Kajsa realise that she forgot to mention her desk in her text.

3.2 Research Questions

The aim of the research that this chapter forms a part of is to answer the question whether PBI can improve young writers' text quality and enhance awareness of revision. Here three specific research questions are addressed:

1) Is the uptake of PBI similar across learners?
2) Is the uptake of PBI similar for descriptive and more cognitively demanding argumentative assignments?
3) Is there a long-term effect of PBI?

3.3 Participants

Ten native 13-year-old Swedish children, six girls and four boys, from the same school year seven class participated in the study. None of them had any known reading or writing problems. All parents/guardians had been informed about the project and given their consent to participation. All participants follow the ordinary Swedish curriculum although the school has a focus on reading. At the time of the study, all pupils had started every school day, for four months, with a 30-minute reading session, in which all pupils engage in individual reading of a book of their own choice. In the writing classroom they had worked with, among other things, book-reviews, letters to fictive editors and ghost stories. According to a questionnaire about their spare time writing habits all the participants write three, or more, times a week. The most common purposes for spare time writing are e-mails and homework. Five of the writers, all girls, also write letters and three keep a diary. Other spare time writing activities that the participants engage in are chatting on the Internet, writing lyrics and computer games.

When using key-stroke logging methodology the participants' computer skills is a factor that may influence the writing process. Differences between pen and paper and computer writing have been shown in several studies (i.e., Haas, 1989, 1996; van Waes, 1992; Severinson Eklundh, 1992)[2]. These studies examined the writing processes of subjects who learned to use the computer as adults. The massive focus on information technology over the past few decades has developed the computer from being an advanced typewriter for the few into being a multi medium for the masses. In Sweden today, most families have a computer at home and all the participants in this study have grown up with the computer as a normal and familiar medium for both writing and communication.

The ten participants of the study presented here were asked which medium, the computer or pen and paper, they preferred when composing a text. Six writers reported that they would rather use the computer than pen and paper; two use both but for different purposes and only one prefers pen and paper. Nine of the ten participants use the computer at least three times a week. In their spare time the most common purpose for using the computer is surfing the Internet and playing computer games. In school they use the computer for word processing and for information search on the Internet. At the time of the study they were being taught touch typing[3] once a week in their computer lessons. The participants thus had highly developed key-board skills.

3.4 Experimental Design and Variables

All pupils at this school undertake a Swedish language test at the beginning of school year seven. The results of the test were used in this study as a pre-test to ascertain the participants' L1 Swedish abilities. Prior to writing, the class teacher divided the participants into pairs according to which pupils would feel comfortable

---
[2] *For a review of the influence of the medium on writing see Kollberg (1998: 9-12).*
[3] *Learning to use the key-board without looking at the hands.*

with each other. It was believed that a pair that does not trust or know each other very well are not likely to produce text in their normal behaviour knowing that another pupil, whom they do not know, is going to read the text. Further, the pairs were divided randomly into two groups (group 1 and group 2) and the writing sessions were divided into two periods in order to study possible sequencing effects of the treatment. During period one group 1 received PBI. During the second period group 2 received PBI. During each period the participants wrote two texts in two different genres, descriptive and argumentative. Each text was written on two occasions, with or without PBI treatment in between. The variables used are thus PBI (PBI/noPBI), Topic (Descriptive/Argumentative), Version (Version1/Version2), Sequencing effect (PBI-noPBI/noPBI-PBI) and L1 ability. Table 2 shows an overview of the experimental design.

Table 2. Experimental Design

		Period 1				Period 2			
PRE-TEST	Group 1	PBI				NO PBI			
		Descriptive Text		Argumentative Text		Descriptive Text		Argumentative Text	
		Version 1	Version 2	Version 1	Version 2	Version 1	Version 2	Version 1	Version 2
	Group 2	NO PBI				PBI			
		Descriptive Text		Argumentative Text		Descriptive Text		Argumentative Text	
		Version 1	Version 2	Version 1	Version 2	Version 1	Version 2	Version1	Version 2

3.4.1 Topics

The descriptive topics were addressed to a familiar audience with the instruction to describe something with which the writer was familiar. One example of a descriptive topic is "You have a pen-friend of your own age in Australia. Write a letter to him/her and tell him/her about your home and your room". The argumentative texts were addressed to an unfamiliar audience with the instruction to persuade the reader. An example of an argumentative topic is "Your school needs more activities for the students in the breaks. Write to the municipality to convince them to give your school more money for activities". Similar topics have been used in current writing research involving young subjects (Schoonen et al., 2002; Sullivan et al.,1998). The writing topic order was balanced.

3.4.2 Procedure

All participants were informed that their writing sessions were being logged and that they were given two writing opportunities for each text. Each participant wrote one text every other week for a total of eight weeks, a total of four texts. The writing took place in a separate classroom and the participants left their ordinary lesson, two or four at a time to write the texts. On the first writing opportunity for each text they were instructed to write as usual, write around half a page of text and use around thirty minutes to complete the text. The approximate text-length and writing time instructions were given in order to encourage the writers to decide for themselves when their text was finished. On the second writing opportunity for each text the participants were instructed to improve their texts in whichever way they preferred. They were given an approximate time limit of fifteen minutes to perform their revisions and were explicitly told that they themselves had to decide when the text was finished.

During the period with PBI the treatment, i.e., replaying of the logs and peer-discussion, followed directly upon the writing sessions. All PBI sessions were tape-recorded for later transcription. During the period without PBI, the writing sessions were not followed by any treatment and the day 2 writing sessions were, thus, undertaken without intervention. Two independent and qualified Swedish and EFL teachers graded all texts. The maximum grade given was 45 marks, divided between contents (15 marks), audience adaptation (10 marks), language (10 marks) and vocabulary (10 marks). Correlation tests (Pearson's) showed that the two judges' grades correlate significantly ($p < 0.01$) in all the four sub-grades[4]. The final grade for each text is the average of the two judges' grades.

3.5 Analyses

3.5.1 Revision Analysis

All revisions[5], a total of 4723, have been analysed according to the on-line revision taxonomy presented in Lindgren and Sullivan (2002). The taxonomy is based on Faigley and Witte's (1981) model, which divides the revisions into categories depending on the effect the revisions have on the text. The three main categories in the taxonomy are surface changes, text-based changes and balance changes. Surface changes include changes that do not affect the contents, for example spelling, grammar or punctuation. Text-based changes affect the contents either locally in the text or on a macro level. In the latter case the entire summary of the text is altered. Balance changes include revisions that balance the text either towards the reader, by for example changing the register, or towards the topic itself by, for example, adding modifiers. Balance changes further include one revision category that is typical for

---

[4] The r-values are: Contents $r = .78$, Audience adaptation $r = .65$, Language $r = .45$ and Vocabulary $r = .69$.
[5] As defined by Trace-it, a computer tool used to assist in the manual revision analysis. Trace-it defines revisions as deletions or insertions of text (Severinson Eklundh & Kollberg, 1996; Kollberg, 1998).

on-line writing, discourse juncture revisions. These revisions occur at the end of the on-going text and as they do not have any full context they are difficult to define as surface or text-based changes. However, the text-elaboration at the point of inscription positions the writer at a juncture in the discourse, where she is trying to make up her mind about where to go with the composition. In the literature these revisions have been defined as, for example, "pre-text revisions" (Witte, 1985) or "shaping at the point of inscription" (Matsuhashi, 1987).

All typographical revisions have been excluded from the analysis[6]. In the categorisation of typographical revisions the definitions from Stevenson and Schoonen (2002) have been used. The remaining revisions have been divided into the categories described above and standardized by the total number of typed characters in each text.

3.5.2 Analysis

A statistical analysis was carried out in order to delimit the effect of the various writing conditions on both Text quality and Revision. Each text was composed under different conditions depending on intervention (PBI or no PBI), type of text (Descriptive or Argumentative) and text Version (1/2). This leaves eight different writing conditions[7]. Sequencing Effect is included in order to study any possible transfer effects of the PBI. For example, if the writers who started in the PBI condition receive higher marks on the texts composed without PBI during the second period, a possible transfer effect could be the explanation.

Repeated measures analyses of variance (ANOVAs) were chosen for the analysis. The dependent variables are *Text quality*, *Surface changes*, *Text-based changes* and *Balance changes* respectively. The inter-variable correlations between the dependent variables are shown in Table 3. *Surface changes* correlates significantly with both Grade and Text-base changes, which could justify the reduction of this variable. It was, however, considered important for the study to examine the three revision categories separately as they can provide different answers to the question whether the PBI had any effect on awareness of revision.

Three within subject variables were used in all four ANOVA models defined by the different writing conditions the writers had to undertake: *PBI*, *Text type* and *Version*. One between subjects variable, *Sequencing Effect*, was used in all four ANOVAs. Finally, one co-variate *L1 ability* was used. L1 ability was considered a factor that was likely to influence all writing conditions.

---

[6] *Revision of typographical errors could have an effect on text quality. Writers with poor typing skills would have to focus much of their attention on motor activities and a result could be that less cognitive resources are left to focus on, for example, language or contents; a poorer text quality could be a consequence. In this study, however, no significant correlation between typographical revisions and text quality was found (Pearson, r = .347).*

[7] *1) PBI-descriptive-version1, 2) PBI-descriptive-version2, 3) no PBI-descriptive-version1, 4) no PBI- descriptive-version2, 5) PBI-argumentative-version1, 6) PBI-argumentative-version2, 7) no PBI-argumentative-version1, and 8) no PBI-argumentative-version2.*

The α-value has been adjusted to compensate for the four different ANOVAs and the small number of individuals included in the test. Results with a $p < 0.01$ will be considered as significant, but results where $p < 0.05$ will be reported as they can hint at trends in the material.

Table 3. Correlations (Pearson) between the Dependent Variables.
(** = significant at the 0.05 level)

	Grade	Surface	Text-based
Surface	-.706**		
Text-based	-.410	.802**	
Balance	.197	.294	.258

4. RESULTS

To interpret the results of the repeated measures ANOVAs the descriptive statistics of the dependent variables have been used (see Table 4).

Table 4. Descriptive Statistics of the Dependent Variables. Mean Frequencies and Standard Deviation (between brackets). N = 4 for Group 1 and N = 6 for Group 2

		PBI Descriptive Day1	PBI Descriptive Day2	PBI Argumentative Day1	PBI Argumentative Day2	No PBI Descriptive Day1	No PBI Descriptive Day2	No PBI Argumentative Day1	No PBI Argumentative Day2
Grade	Group1	55.63 (5.81)	57.00 (6.45)	59.38 (3.45)	60.25 (2.63)	55.25 (7.04)	58.88 (10.49)	59.00 (9.26)	59.63 (9.11)
	Group2	66.75 (8.07)	67.17 (7.55)	63.50 (7.15)	64.75 (7.97)	66.17 (6.06)	67.08 (6.07)	67.25 (9.62)	68.08 (8.71)
Surface changes	Group1	1.17 (0.60)	0.65 (0.59)	1.52 (0.67)	0.86 (0.16)	1.30 (0.93)	0.42 (0.20)	0.79 (0.54)	0.15 (0.12)
	Group2	0.48 (0.25)	0.11 (0.14)	0.49 (0.37)	0.29 (0.39)	0.58 (0.27)	0.23 (0.13)	0.47 (0.22)	0.22 (0.28)
Text-based changes	Group1	0.21 (0.27)	0.16 (0.20)	0.16 (0.11)	0.17 (0.13)	0.05 (0.05)	0.19 (0.11)	0.11 (0.05)	0.05 (0.06)
	Group2	0.07 (0.06)	0.10 (0.07)	0.02 (0.06)	0.08 (0.05)	0.13 (0.06)	0.10 (0.14)	0.12 (0.10)	0.05 (0.10)
Balance changes	Group1	0.92 (0.26)	0.13 (0.16)	0.64 (0.22)	0.26 (0.15)	0.97 (0.41)	0.32 (0.16)	0.84 (0.35)	0.17 (0.19)
	Group2	0.74 (0.46)	0.14 (0.10)	0.42 (0.37)	0.16 (0.13)	0.80 (0.49)	0.11 (0.06)	0.63 (0.51)	0.07 (0.09)

4.1 Text Quality

Two significant interacted effects and three trends were found for *Text quality*, all the results are presented in Table 5. One of the interactions includes the variable *Sequencing Effect*, which indicates that the sequence of the *PBI* would have an effect on the *Text quality*. More specifically, it would mean that Group 1 improved their descriptive texts more from Version 1 to Version 2 in the no PBI condition as compared with the PBI condition. These results could be interpreted as a transfer effect of the PBI treatment; Group 1 were able to use the positive effects of the PBI during period 2, when they wrote texts without the PBI treatment. However, a close analysis of the individual results revealed that the interactions with *Sequencing Effect* were due to one Group 1 writer's exceptional improvement of his descriptive text from Version 1 to Version 2 in the no PBI condition. Although it might be possible that this is actually an effect of the intervention, the opposite may well be the case; it is not possible to draw any conclusions from one exceptional result. It could be argued that this writer should be considered an outlier. After careful consideration, however, I decided to include him in the analysis and the main reason for doing so is that it is actually possible to write a very good text on one occasion.

*Table 5. Results of the Statistical Analysis for Text Quality and Surface, Text-Based (TB) and Balance Revisions. Only Significant Results and Trends are included. + = Variable included in Test; ** = p <0.05, *** = p <0.01*

PBI	Task	Version	L1-ability	Sequencing effect	Quality	Surface	Text-based	Balance
+		+			13.44***	0.43	0.50	0.02
+		+	+		13.77***	0.41	0.46	0.00
+		+		+	6.19**	0.01	10.24***	0.62
+	+	+			7.95**	1.77	3.45	0.04
+	+	+	+		8.25**	1.72	3.20	0.06
		+			0.61	2.45	5.95**	2.29
		+	+		0.47	1.70	5.91**	2.93
+			+		1.61	0.01	0.01	5.27**

The remaining four interactions are not affected by this one result. Two of the results are significant *PBI*Version* and *PBI*Version*L1 ability* and two of the results show trends *PBI*TextType*Version* and *PBI*TextType*Version*L1 ability*. Taken together the results indicate that the interactions *PBI*Version* and *PBI*TextType*Version* varies across levels of *L1 ability*. In the Descriptive assignments the low L1 ability writers improved their texts more in version 2 in the PBI condition as compared with the no PBI condition. The opposite was found for high L1 ability writers. In the Argumentative assignments all writers improved their texts more in the PBI condition as compared with the no PBI condition. Figure 1 shows the grade difference between Version 1 and Version 2 in the different conditions of *TextType* and *PBI*. Here the writers have been divided into two groups, according to their results on the pre-test.

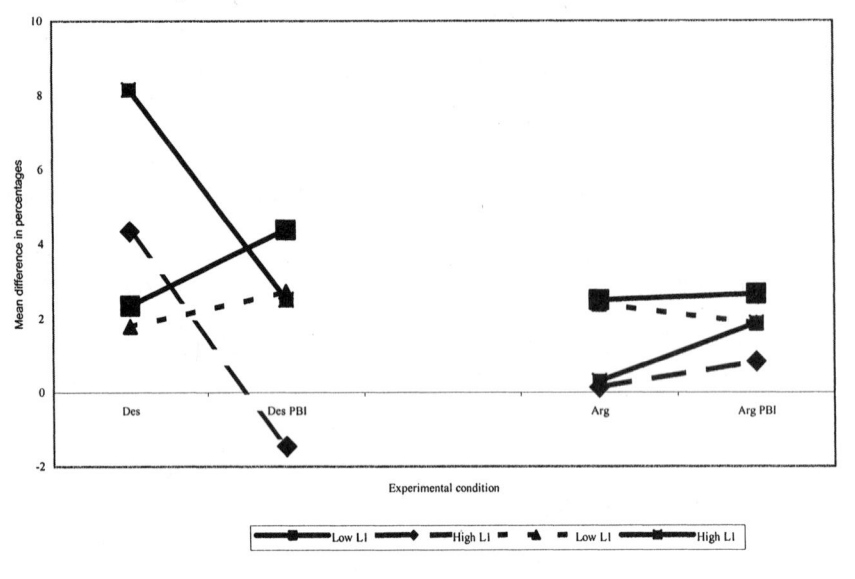

Figure 1. Low and high L1 ability writers' differences in text quality between Version 1 and Version 2 in the experimental conditions TextType (descriptive or argumentative) and PBI. Standard deviation values for the Low L1 group are Des 1.79, DesPBI 2.72, Arg 2.40 and ArgPBI 01.87. Standard deviation values for the High L1 group are Des 8.17, DesPBI 2.51, Arg 0.31 and Arg PBI 1.88.

4.2 Revisions

The participants' revision strategies has been measured by the frequencies of revisions at the three levels *Surface*, *Text-based* and *Balance*. For example, if a writer revises more on a *Text-based* level in the *PBI* condition this would indicate that the intervention was successful in raising writers' awareness of text-based features in writing. The results of the repeated measure ANOVA of *Surface* revisions showed neither any significant results nor any trends. The results for *Text-based* and *Balance* revision are presented separately. The writer whose grade on one text skewed the results of text quality and Sequencing Effect did not affect the analysis of revisions.

4.2.1 Text-based Changes

One significant effect and two trends were found for *Text-based changes* (see Table 5): *Version, Version*L1 ability* and *PBI*Version*Sequencing Effect*. Figure 2 illustrates the significant interaction, *PBI*Version*Sequencing Effect*. The effect of *PBI* varied across levels of *Version* and *Sequencing Effect*. Group 1 revised more text-based features in Version 2 than in Version 1 in the no PBI condition, as compared with the PBI condition. The opposite was true for Group 2, who revised more in Version 2 in the PBI condition.

The results of *Version, Version*L1 ability* shows a trend that the frequency of *Text-based changes* is higher in Version 2 than in Version 1 on the whole and this difference varies across levels of *L1 ability*. The lower L1 ability writers revise more text-based features in Version 2 while the opposite was shown for the high L1 ability writers.

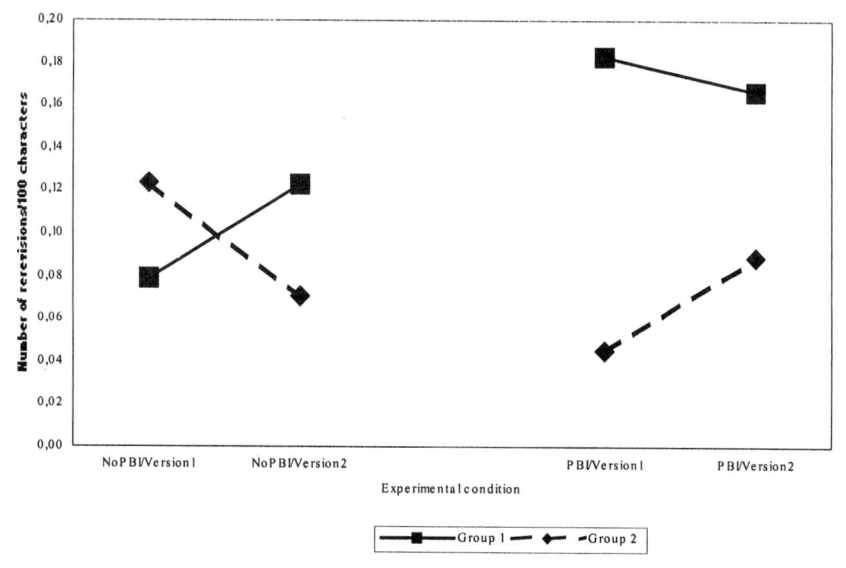

Figure 2. Average frequencies of Text-based revisions in Group1 and Group 2 in the experimental conditions PBI and Version.

4.2.2 Balance Changes

One trend was found for *Balance changes*: *PBI*L1 ability* (see Table 5). These results indicate that the effect of *PBI* varies across levels of *L1 ability*. The low L1 ability writers revise balance features more in the PBI conditions while the high L1 ability writers revise more balance features in the no PBI conditions.

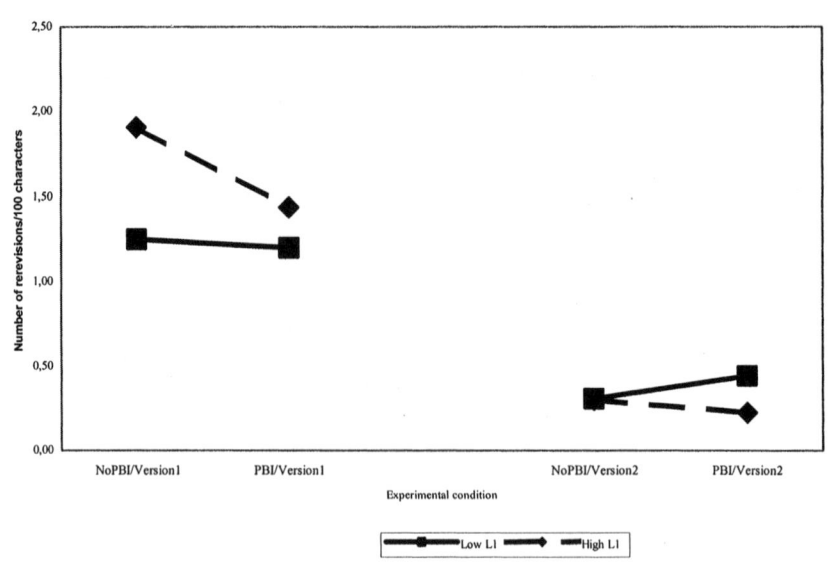

Figure 3. Average frequencies of Balance revisions in the experimental conditions PBI and Version. The writers are divided according to L1 ability.

5. DISCUSSION

In terms of text quality the uptake of the PBI differed between the writers and L1 ability turned out to be an important factor in the understanding of the results. The low L1 ability writers improved their texts in the PBI conditions in both the argumentative and the descriptive assignments. The high L1 ability writers, on the other hand, seemed to benefit from the PBI, in terms of higher text quality, only in the argumentative assignments. During the Version 1 writing process a high L1 ability would imply a high level of automatisation of linguistic skills. Automatisation of linguistic and/or motor skills can result in less surface revisions and higher text quality, when the writer can move the focus away from the surface structure in the text to planning and construction of meaning (McCutchen, 1996, 2000; Graham et al., 1997; Graham & Harris, 2002; Alamargot & Chanquoy, 2001). A descriptive assignment would demand less cognitive resources from the writer than an argumentative one. While the descriptive one is straightforward and knowledge-telling in structure, the argumentative one would entail more structuring of arguments and audience adaptation. One possible explanation is that the high L1 ability writers in this study had working memory capacity enough to fulfil the descriptive assignment on one writing occasion, but benefited from an extra writing opportunity in the cognitively more demanding argumentative assignment.

The results of Surface revisions did not show any significant effects. This result is not surprising. Most surface level revisions are changes of spelling and grammar and as the writers in this study used their L1 when composing their texts they did not need to revise surface features to any considerable extent. It is interesting to note, however, that both groups revised more surface features during Period 1. This could be interpreted as a learning effect of the experiment. They wrote eight texts and perhaps they managed to automatise some of the surface level features during the process, leading to less need for revision of surface features during the second period.

The results of Balance changes indicate that the low L1 ability writers revised more on this level in the second Version in the PBI condition as compared with the no PBI condition. A closer analysis of the frequencies of the sub-categories discourse juncture, topic orientation and audience orientation reveal that the frequency of audience orientation revisions in the PBI condition was 0.12 as opposed to 0.02 in the no PBI condition. Apparently, the PBI helped in raising the writers' awareness of audience.

The analysis of the PBI recordings further showed that 42 per cent of Balance changes in version 2 in the PBI condition were directly induced by the PBI in version 1, thirty-three per cent by the discussion of the own text and eight per cent of the revisions were inspired by the peers' texts. Similar results were found for text-based changes. Thirty-two per cent of the Text-based revisions were undertaken as a direct result of the discussion of the writer's own text in version 1 and eight per cent of the revisions could be directly connected to the peer's text.

The sequence of the PBI appeared to have an effect on Text-based revisions. Group 1, who undertook the PBI treatment during the first period, revised more Text-based features during the second period, when they wrote their texts without PBI. It is possible that this group transferred positive effects of the PBI into the second writing period. Group 2, who undertook the PBI treatment during the second period, revised more Text-based features during the second period. It is likely that an awareness of more cognitively demanding contents revisions was stimulated by the PBI treatment.

Multiple writing opportunities, with or without PBI, would appear most effective for the low L1 ability writers, resulting in higher text quality increase as well as more text-based changes than the high L1 ability writers. This result concurs with the findings of Chanquoy (2001), who concluded that by postponing the revision process cognitive space would be released, enabling the writers to focus on the contents of their text. The fact that most surface features were revised on the first writing day further indicates that the cognitive load during day one, when most of the contents and text structure had to be generated, made the writers focus on surface rather than text-based features.

6. CONCLUSIONS AND IMPLICATIONS

In this exploratory study the uptake of PBI was most effective for the low L1 ability writers, both in terms of increasing text quality and revision. These writers increased their text quality from day 1 to day 2 after the PBI in both descriptive and argumentative assignments. They revised more on both text-based and balance levels after the PBI treatment, which probably had a positive effect on text quality. Revisions were undertaken as a result of observation and discussion of both the writer's own and the peer's writing process. High L1 ability writers improved their text quality in the cognitively more demanding argumentative texts after the PBI treatment. The PBI appeared to lighten the cognitive load and helped the writers to notice features in the text that needed improvement. Further, the method seemed to raise the participants' metacognitive awareness of writing, particularly concerning text-based and audience orientation revisions.

In terms of revision one possible transfer effect was found in the study. The group that started with the PBI treatment revised more Text-based features in the second versions of their texts composed during the second period (no PBI) than in the first period (PBI). However, considering text quality all those writers, except one, wrote texts of higher quality during the first period (PBI) than during the second period (no PBI). Future studies of this kind should take into consideration the possibility that a longer period than eight weeks of PBI could be needed in order for the writers to transfer the positive effects of the method. Regular post-testing should also be included in order to try to ascertain whether PBI can generate sustainable writing improvement.

Finally, as Tynjälä (this volume) points out it is important for both learners and teachers to employ multidimensionality and diversity in learning. In order to become self-directed the learner has to be provided with a vast range of different learning methods: "...it is useful for students to reflect upon the processes they have employed in a differentiated way." (Galbraith & Rijlaarsdam, 1999: 97-98). Key-stroke logging together with PBI provides learners and teachers of writing with a process oriented method for the improvement of writing.

ACKNOWLEDGEMENTS

The author thanks Kirk Sullivan for his advice throughout the writing of this chapter, Gert Rijlaarsdam for his constructive comments and helpful advice on the statistical analysis and the reviewers for their comments on earlier versions of this chapter. This research was undertaken as a part of the grant *The Use of S-notation to Study Writing in a Second Language* (Dnr. F1130/97) from HSFR (The Swedish Council for Research in the Humanities and Social Sciences).

TEACHING WRITING

Using Research to Inform Practice

ROGER BEARD

University of Leeds, UK

Abstract. Recent years have seen several centralising initiatives in the English education system, including statutory curriculum content and assessment arrangements and regular school inspections. The chapter briefly sets this centralisation in its historical context. The latest initiative, the National Literacy Strategy, has encouraged greater use of teaching objectives, dedicated literacy teaching time and increased use of shared and guided teaching approaches. However, a recent increase in reading standards has not been matched by a similar rise in writing attainment.

A recent report from Her Majesty's Inspectorate has highlighted some recurring weaknesses in the teaching of writing in English primary schools: an over-reliance on duplicated worksheets and stimuli for writing; an inappropriate balance between reading and writing; and insufficient transfer of skills learned in literacy lessons to work in other subjects. Research studies are identified that will inform practice and help to address these weaknesses. These studies include research into composing processes; meta-analyses of effective teaching approaches; and genre theory, particularly in relation to non-fiction texts. The chapter ends with a discussion of the possible role of grammatical reference in the teaching of writing and the need for more classroom-based studies of children's writing development.

Keywords: Centralisation, grammatical reference, guided writing, National Policy, shared writing.

1. INTRODUCTION

This chapter will discuss how the outcomes from research may be used to inform classroom practice. The main focus of the chapter is on the primary years of schooling (7-11). The issues raised in the chapter will be illustrated by reference to a national literacy initiative in England. The UK government's National Literacy Strategy (NLS) is aimed at raising standards of literacy in English primary schools (5-11 year olds) over a 5-10 year period. The short-term success of the Strategy in raising reading standards, as indicated in the attainment of 11-year-olds in annual national tests, has not been matched by a similar rise in writing attainment. A number of ad-

Beard, R. (2004). Teaching writing. Using research to inform practice.
In G. Rijlaarsdam (Series Ed.) and Rijlaarsdam, G., Van den Bergh, H. & Couzijn, M. (Vol. Eds.), Studies in writing. Vol. 14, Effective learning and teaching of writing, 2nd Edition, Part 2, Studies in how to teach writing, 275-289.

ditions have been made to the NLS in response to the slower rise in writing attainment. These include *Developing Early Writing* (DfEE, 2001) which encourages greater use of shared and guided teaching approaches than has been evident in English primary schools in the past; another is *Grammar for Writing* (DfEE, 2000) which encourages the judicious use of grammatical terminology in the teaching-learning dialogue. The wider significance of the latter initiative will be discussed later in the chapter.

The use of research to inform classroom practice raises many issues, not least of which is the mediation of any recommended research-based practices by teacher-based factors, including teacher beliefs, knowledge and habituated practices. There is not space in this chapter to examine this mediation in detail. Instead, the focus will be on the research-based recommendations for practice that are embodied in government-mandated curricula. The content and pedagogical aspects of these curricula provide parameters for the evolution of teachers' practices. In the UK in recent years, these parameters have taken on particular significance because of the increasing centralisation of educational provision.

1.1 Increasing Centralisation in UK Schools

The NLS is part of an increasing centralisation in UK education policy in recent years. This centralisation will be briefly discussed first, in order to contextualise what follows in the remainder of the chapter. British primary education has had a long tradition of teacher autonomy in deciding the content of the curriculum, assessment arrangements and teaching methods used. In 1976, the primary school curriculum was described by the Prime Minister, James Callaghan, in a speech at Ruskin College, Oxford, as a 'secret garden'. This was a phrase that reflected the teacher autonomy of the time and the fact that central government had relatively little say in what was taught or the teaching methods that were used. In fact, for much of the last 30 years of the twentieth century, 'good practice' in English primary schools has often been associated with individualised approaches, in which classes of children have tackled several different subject areas at the same time in various kinds of 'integrated day'. Thus one group of pupils might be working on a Mathematics task (perhaps following a commercial Mathematics textbook); one group might be engaged in art or craft work; another group might be undertaking some writing or a sentence completion exercise, and so on. Science was rarely taught in English primary schools at the time of Callaghan's speech (DES, 1978) although some schools tried to link much of the curriculum together in theme-based termly topic work (e.g., 'Transport' or 'Animals') and some elements of Science may have been included in the theme.

One explanation for this open-ended view of the curriculum was that a government commission chaired by Lady Plowden in 1967 (whose report was indicatively titled *Children and their Primary Schools*, my emphasis) seemed to conceptualise good practice by projecting the informality and the more child-centred curriculum provision of early years education upwards into older age-ranges (CACE, 1967; Peters, 1969). In the intervening years, a succession of research findings have included caveats about the related quality control issues of the integrated day approach: it is very difficult for teachers simultaneously to monitor so many different aspects of learning across several subject areas. These findings also raise questions about how an individualised approach is translated into practice: the approach tends to generate substantial amounts of worksheet tasks and the teacher is likely to spend a substantial amount of time in an administrative and supervisory role (Mortimore et al., 1988; Alexander, 1992). As will be seen later, for many years worksheets may have been used disproportionately for the teaching of writing in many English primary schools.

In the years after 1967, a variety of influential approaches for helping children to write in continuous prose were published in England. At the time of the Plowden Report there was much interest in the use of 'creative writing', typically encouraging the use of poetic prose, perhaps celebrating natural phenomena such as sunsets or misty winter mornings and often encouraging the use of sensory experiences encapsulated in vivid vocabulary (e.g., Maybury, 1967).

The creative writing approach ran the risk of teachers artificially exhorting pupils to write in ways that only superficially reflect the desired outcomes. A government inquiry into the teaching of English in the mid-1970s was concerned that such an approach may result in writing that is 'divorced from real feeling' (DES, 1975: 163). A few years later, a national inspection survey went as far as to applaud the absence of this kind of stimulus-driven approach to teaching writing in its findings (DES, 1978). Instead the 1975 government inquiry adopted the model of writing functions that had underpinned a research project at London University into *The Development of Writing Abilities 11-18* (Britton et al., 1975). The model identified three main functions of writing: the 'poetic' (e.g., literature and poetry), the 'expressive' (informal writing used by intimates in a shared context) and the 'transactional' (the language of 'getting things done', as in explanations or persuasion); it underpinned these by also stressing the importance of a sense of audience. Subsequent influential publications built upon this model by giving even greater attention to varieties of writing purposes, audiences and the social contexts of which purposes and audiences are part (e.g., Beard, 1984; Hall, 1989).

English primary education was also distinguished at this time by longitudinal studies of how children's writing develops over time: according to various linguistic indices (Harpin, 1976); and through different aspects of the 'communicative individual' (Wilkinson et al., 1980). There were also major studies on children's spelling (e.g., Peters, 1985). However, as will be seen later in this chapter, there was surprisingly little attention in research and publications to how writing as a whole was *taught* and whether some teaching approaches might be more effective than others.

In general, then, in the 1970s and 1980s, the teaching of writing in English primary schools, like much of the rest of the curriculum, lacked consistency and direction. It could be said that the 'secret garden' was growing in on itself. Moreover, as curriculum commentators such as Richards (1982) pointed out, there is a fundamental tension between the inconsistency that results from teacher autonomy on curriculum provision and a comprehensive system of education. Until the late 1980s, few central government initiatives had been targeted on curriculum or pedagogy. Any related central government publications had largely comprised the discussions and recommendations of committees of inquiry. Sometimes such reports were published without the commitment of any additional resources to support implementation (e.g., DES, 1975). This situation was substantially changed in the years following Prime Minister Callaghan's speech. His words triggered a series of central government reports and reforms that eventually culminated in a national curriculum, a national testing programme, regular school inspections and advice on teaching methods. Each of these will now be briefly discussed in turn. Particular attention will be paid to the implications of each of the reforms for the teaching of writing.

1.2 The National Curriculum

The first major centralising initiative was the introduction of a national curriculum in all four UK countries in 1989, although the actual content varied from country to country. The first version of the England and Wales national curriculum was devised by the quasi-autonomous organisation set up by national government, the National Curriculum Council (later to become the Qualifications and Curriculum Authority). The working party appointed by the Council to decide on content of the national curriculum in English divided the English curriculum into three components: one for talking and listening; one for reading; and three for writing ('conveying meaning', 'spelling' and 'handwriting'). Programmes of study were then provided for each, as well as for another eight subjects in primary schools, several of which were also sub-divided into different components. The precise details of the programmes of study were an eclectic mix that reflected the knowledge, judgement and values of the working party, in the context of extensive consultation and feedback. However, the first version of the national curriculum as a whole proved to be overcrowded and it was generally slimmed down in 1994, following an independent review (Dearing, 1994). In English, the three profile components for writing were merged into one and grouped into 'key skills', 'range' and 'Standard English and language study'. These sub-divisions were further modified in 1999. 'Range' was incorporated into 'Breadth of study'. 'Key skills' and 'Standard English and language study' were incorporated into 'Knowledge, skills and understanding' (DfEE, 1999).[1]

1.3 Assessment

The second initiative was in some ways an extension of the national curriculum. The initiative was an annual programme for all British primary schools of national testing for seven, eleven and fourteen year old pupils that began in 1991. Again, arrangements vary among the four countries. The tests have a higher profile in England because the results of the tests for eleven year olds are published in annual league tables of schools' performances. In England, pupils' attainments in the criterion-referenced tests are equated to 'level descriptions', from level one (the lowest)

---

[1] *The underlying rationale for these categories has broadly addressed (i) skills, (ii) contexts for using these skills and (iii) ways of reflecting upon this use. The changes in wording and emphasis have been pragmatic ones, based on evaluations of the National Curriculum in practice.*

to level eight.[2] When the tests were developed, the modal attainment for eleven year olds was level 4. Since then, the government body delegated to oversee curriculum and assessment has equated level 4 with the notion of 'national expectation', as a part of a broader target-setting culture that central governments of both main political parties have adopted.

1.4 Inspections

The third initiative is that, since 1992, the 19,000 publicly-funded English primary schools have also been subjected to a programme of school inspections every four years. The inspections are undertaken by specially trained inspectors, co-ordinated by the central government's Office for Standards in Education (OFSTED) that was set up in that year. Inspections normally last a week and currently cover: the standards achieved; teaching quality; curricular and extra-curricular activities; pupil care; partnership with parents; and the school's leadership and management. Before 1992, schools were inspected by Her Majesty's Inspectorate (HMI), although the small size of the inspectorate (about 300) meant that individual schools were only fully inspected on an average of every 30 years or so. The new national data-base of inspection evidence is now used to produce annual reviews and other subject-specific publications. Meanwhile, the size of HMI has been reduced to about half of what it was. Its new role includes monitoring the training of inspectors and school inspections and undertaking special investigations, for instance an evaluation of the National Literacy Strategy that is discussed later in the chapter.

Through the 1990s, accumulating inspection evidence provided indications of the strengths and limitations of practices in the teaching of writing in English primary schools. Some key factors associated with effective practice were suggested from a HMI survey of 350 classes in 1990: 'The most effective writing....was often preceded and supported by discussion, so that children began...with a clear idea of what they wished to communicate, the conventions they should follow, and how they might gain further support (HMI, 1991:15). However, the following year, a survey of 1134 primary school classes reported that 'high attainment in writing was infrequent and that [in the 7-11 age-range] it was clear that opportunities for writing were often too constrained (HMI, 1992: 14). In 1994 a survey of 112 primary phase schools reported that 'Good standards of writing are evident in only one in seven schools' and went on to note that [in the 7-11 age-range] 'There is too much use of decontextualised and undemanding exercises' (OFSTED, 1995: 8). By 1998, the Chief Inspector's annual review of inspection evidence from 5864 primary phase

---

[2] *The level description for level one includes the criteria that 'Pupils' writing communicates meaning through simple words and phases...pupils begin to show awareness of how full stops are used. Letters are usually clearly shaped and correctly orientated'. The criteria for level four attainment include 'lively and thoughtful' writing in a range of forms, 'adventurous vocabulary choices', some use of complex sentences where appropriate, correct spelling of regular words (including polysyllabic ones) and correct use of full stops, capital letters and question marks (full details can be found on* http://www.qca.org.uk).

schools expressed the growing unease about the teaching of writing in primary schools that had been profiled by the rapidly accumulating inspection evidence from the greatly expanded inspection programme: 'Too many pupils are unable to produce sustained, accurate writing in a variety of forms. This has been a pervasive weakness in many primary schools, which should be addressed more urgently' (OFSTED, 1998: 19).

The increasing centralisation through these different elements is viewed ambivalently or critically by some educational professionals. The inspection regime, in particular, has been subjected to recurrent criticism (e.g., Fitz-Gibbon, 1998; Fitz-Gibbon and Stephenson-Forster, 1999). At the same time, the mutually supportive elements of the increasing centralisation have also created a heuristic device for use when examining the relationship between research and government-mandated curricula practices. The potential of this device is highlighted when a fourth element in the centralising process is considered – the pedagogical advice from the National Literacy Strategy.

1.5 Teaching Approaches

As referred to earlier, 'good primary practice' in English primary schools has often been associated with individualised and 'integrated day' approaches, in which classes of children have tackled several different subject areas at the same time. This kind of curriculum provision may have led to an over-reliance on duplicated worksheets and stimuli, reported in the school inspection findings that are discussed later in this chapter. Alternative approaches to this individualisation have been slow to gain status, even though the growing evidence from international studies of school effectiveness have indicated the possible gains from alternative teaching arrangement (Scheerens, 1992; Creemers, 1994). One of the most influential school effectiveness studies was a three year investigation of 50 London junior schools [7-11 year olds] that identified the factors that most significantly contributed to pupil progress (Mortimore et al., 1988). Among 12 factors that were characteristic of 'effective' schools, were the following:

- structured sessions, involving a teacher organised framework but allowing pupils to organise a degree of independence;
- intellectually challenging tasks, with teachers using higher-order questions and statements and with pupils using creative imagination and problem-solving;
- a work-centred environment, with high levels of pupil industry and low levels of noise;
- a limited lesson focus, on one curriculum area (or, at the very most, two) with some differentiation, as needed;
- maximum communication between teachers and pupils, with some whole-class teaching.

Despite this accumulating literature, local policy makers sometimes continued to associate good practice in English primary schools with pupil 'busyness' and with curriculum provision for several subjects to be tackled simultaneously (see, for example, Alexander, 1992). However, it was not until the late 1990s that English primary schools were encouraged to consider other notions of good practice by central government – with implications for the teaching of writing that took some time to be realised.

2. THE NATIONAL LITERACY STRATEGY IN ENGLAND

The National Literacy Strategy (NLS) was established in 1997 by the incoming UK government to raise standards of literacy in English primary schools over a five to ten year period.[3] The main strands of the Strategy were as follows:
- A national target that, by 2002, 80% of 11 year olds should reach the standard 'expected' for their age in English (National Curriculum Level 4). The proportion reaching this standard in 1996 was 57%.
- A *Framework for Teaching* (DfEE, 1998a) which (i) sets out termly teaching objectives for the 5-11 age range, based on the National Curriculum, and (ii) provides a practical structure of time and class management for a daily literacy hour.
- A programme of professional development for all primary school teachers, centred on a Literacy Training Pack (DfEE, 1998b), comprising study booklets, overhead transparency slides, video and audiotape material. The Pack was designed for the teaching staff of each school to work through over several training days, led by the teacher who had subject leadership responsibility for English in the school.

These strands have been subsequently supplemented by other initiatives, in the light of issues arising during the Strategy's implementation. These initiatives have included additional published materials, including some to support the teaching of phonics and the teaching of writing, as well as to assist pupils who need greater support in literacy learning (see also Beard, 1999, 2000a, 2000b).

The literacy hour is the core of the Strategy. The recommended structure of the hour is as follows: approximately fifteen minutes of whole class 'text-level' work (comprehension and composition, often using shared reading or writing); approximately fifteen minutes of whole class 'word-level' or 'sentence-level' work (vocabulary, phonics and spelling); approximately twenty minutes of differentiated group work; and a whole class plenary session. The Strategy recommends that every primary school should adopt the *Framework* unless it can demonstrate through its action plan, schemes of work and pupil test performances that its own approach is at least as effective as that of the use of the literacy hour. The indications from inspection evidence are that the literacy hour was adopted in virtually all schools, although sometimes in a slightly modified form (HMI, 1999).

---

[3] *The definition of literacy in the NLS is essentially an instrumental one, focused on the skills of reading and writing. The definition is extended into eleven aims for pupils, including: understanding the sound and spelling system and using this to read and spell accurately; planning, drafting, revising and editing their owm writing; using, understanding and being able to write a range of genres in fiction, poetry and non-fiction; and developing their powers of imagination, inventiveness and critical awareness (DfEE, 1998a: 3).*

Understandably, discussion of the implementation of the National Literacy Strategy has often been primarily concerned with the progress of pupil attainment towards the national target[4]. As can be seen below in Figure 1, there has been significant progress in raising standards of literacy over the first four years of the NLS, as measured by pupil performance on national tests, even though the 2002 target was not achieved. However, the combined data mask the relative underachievement in writing and this is shown in Figure 2.

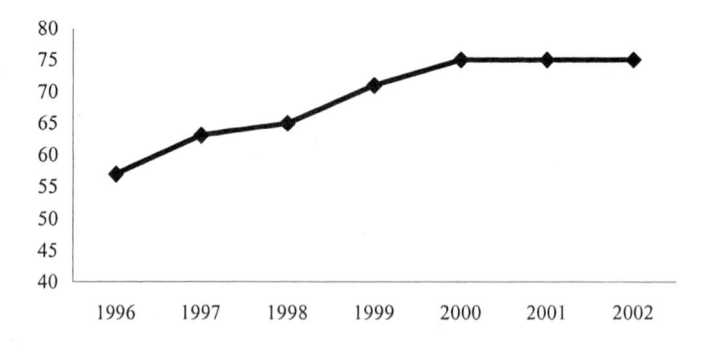

Figure 1. National test results for 11 year olds in England 1996-2002: Percentage of pupils scoring Level 4 or above in English.

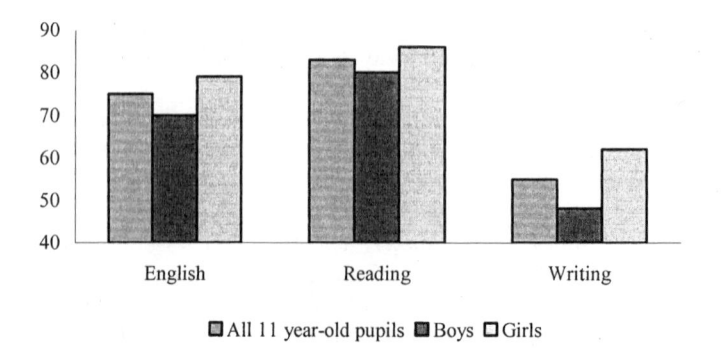

Figure 2. English national test results for 11 year olds in 2000.

Some qualifying comments need to be added to these Figures. The levelled scores in English are composites, incorporating speaking and listening, reading and writing.

---

[4] National interest was fuelled by the 1997 Education minister's pledge to resign if the 2002 target was not achieved. In the event, this minister moved to another government department in 2001 and it was his replacement who resigned in 2002, albeit in rather confused circumstances that seemed only partly related to the failure to achieve the target.

The annual criterion-referenced national tests for reading and writing are devised by the quasi-autonomous organisation that now oversees the national curriculum and assessment arrangements, the Qualification and Curriculum Authority (QCA). The QCA commissions test material from external agencies such as universities or the independent National Foundation for Educational Research (NFER).

The completed test papers are assessed by specially trained markers. In addition, pupils' attainments are informally assessed by their own teachers and these assessments are also published. Teacher assessments are generally slightly lower than the test results.

2.1 Differential Progress in Achieving National Targets: Inspection-Based Explanations

Due to the speed of implementation of the NLS, few independent research studies have yet been reported that shed light on the national attainment data reported above. Nevertheless, relevant information has been provided by inspection evidence. In 2000, a discussion paper was published by HMI that drew attention to some explanations based on the inspection evidence that had accumulated since the implementation of the NLS. The discussion paper was titled *The Teaching of Writing in Primary Schools: Could do Better* (HMI, 2000). It notes the occurrence of the following in a significant number of schools:

- an over-reliance on duplicated worksheets;
- an over-reliance on a stimulus to inspire pupils to write without the necessary teaching in the form of modelling or other forms of scaffolding. HMI suggest that the cost is insufficient high quality sentence work.
- in many schools, the NLS had not been introduced with an appropriate balance between reading and writing. In 300 literacy hours observed by HMI in the autumn term of 1999, for example, there was no shared writing in three-quarter of the lessons;
- while pupils were being given opportunities to write in subjects other than English, the skills learned in literacy lessons were being insufficiently transferred to work in other subjects. More could be done to use these lessons to teach the genre features of writing which are commonly used in other subjects.

Each of these points will now be discussed in turn, as each provides an example of how research can be used in order to inform practice. Furthermore, the research sources used are drawn from several countries, thus illustrating the benefits of a global approach when addressing the research-practice interface.

2.2 An Over-reliance on Duplicated Worksheets

The use of duplicated worksheets may reflect a teaching approach in which pupils are allocated practice or small-scale tasks in writing, perhaps focused on a particular linguistic structure or other component of writing. The finding that such approaches are sometimes over-relied upon has been a recurrent one in English primary school inspection findings. As long ago as 1978, a survey of a nationally representative sample of primary [in this case 7-11] schools reported that books of English exercises were used in nearly all classes of 9 and 11 year olds (DES, 1978). The authors of the survey added that the use of such exercises do not necessarily help pupils to write fluently and with purpose [the exercises typically being short tasks, involving little 'authorship'].

Nearly all the research studies discussed below offer empirical findings that may be used to address the issues raised by writing being taught piecemeal rather than as a holistic process in which several component skills have to be integrated in the pursuit of a communicative goal. It is understandable that teachers try to help pupils improve their writing by using various kinds of exercise. Such small scale activities may appear to provide the building blocks of subsequent writing of continuous prose, for example listing word families, filling in gaps in sentences or inserting punctuation marks. However, psychological research into the composing process suggests that whole text planning is an important aspect of 'local planning' – the choice and ordering of particular words in a particular sentence (Bereiter and Scardamalia, 1987, ch. 3; see also Galbraith and Rijlaarsdam, 1999). This suggestion is linked to differences between 'conversation and composition'. Bereiter and Scardamalia's research in Ontario has been underpinned by a recognition of a profound difference between much speech and writing: that writing has visible genre features which shape the emerging text. Accomplished writing is characterised by abundant planning, not only in advance of writing, but also during writing, as plans are realised and then further elaborated in response to 'discoveries' during the writing itself (Bereiter and Scardamalia, 1987: 69). The implication of this research is that any attempt to improve writing competence is likely to benefit from extensive attention to the attributes of continuous prose and sustained experience of composing it.

2.3 An Over-reliance on a Stimulus to Inspire Pupils to Write without the Necessary Teaching

The over-reliance on a stimulus to inspire pupils to write reflects specific assumptions about the nature of writing processes and how they are learned. George Hillocks at the University of Chicago has undertaken major reviews of research on the teaching of writing and has identified three broad teaching approaches (Hillocks, 1984, 1986, 1995). Their particular features are set out in Table 1 below.

Hillocks reports a meta-analysis of research that compares the three approaches, using specific linguistic indicators of pupils' learning. From 73 comparable studies, Hillocks reports that the 'environmental' teaching approach (also known as a 'guided' approach) was two or three times more effective than the natural process approach and over four times more effective than the presentational approach.

The use of a stimulus to inspire pupils to write appears to reflect the use of a presentational approach. The relative ineffectiveness of this approach is particularly noteworthy in the light of the suggestion in the HMI report discussed above. HMI suggest that the excessive use of this approach may be related to the more modest gains in standards of writing during the early years of the National Literacy Strategy. This suggestion appears to be in line with the findings from Hillocks' meta-analysis.

Hillocks goes on to discuss why the presentational approach only minimally effective. It involves telling pupils what is strong or weak in writing performance, but it does not provide opportunities for pupils to learn procedures for putting this knowledge to work. As an example, a teacher might ask pupils each to write an information text and then fastidiously to mark the resulting pupil errors, but would not actually teach procedures to help pupils write such texts.

Table 1. Features of Three Teaching Approaches

Approach	Published Example	Teacher's Role	Writing Topics	Particular Teaching Strategies
Presentational	Many English course books	Imparting knowledge prior to writing	Assigned by teacher	Setting tasks and marking outcomes
Natural Process	Graves (1983); Calkins (1986)	Engaging pupils in writing and fostering positive dispositions	Chosen by pupils	Providing general procedures e.g., multiple drafts and peer comments
Environmental or guided	Scardamalia et al. (1981); Martin (1989)	Inducing and supporting active learning of complex strategies that pupils are not capable of using on their own.	Negotiated	Developing materials and activities to engage pupils in task-specific processes

2.4 Beyond the Use of a Stimulus to Inspire Pupils to Write

Hillocks reports on the effectiveness of two alternatives that go beyond the use of a stimulus: the natural process approach and the environmental/guided approach. The former involves the teacher prompting ideas and plans for incorporation into particular pieces of writing. However, it does not ensure that pupils develop their own ideas and plans autonomously. This is especially so in the organisation of different kinds of writing. As an example, a teacher might encourage pupils to draft, discuss and receive feedback on information texts, but not use procedures for correcting or avoiding problems.

The environmental/guided approach was identified in the meta-analysis as the most effective. Hillocks describes it as involving the presentation of new forms, models and criteria and facilitating their use in different writing tasks. Problems are tackled in a spirit of inquiry and problem-solving. As an example, a teacher might draw pupils' attention to information texts, help them to identify the distinctive features of such texts and provide tasks in which they can apply this knowledge in their own independent writing.

Some cautions need to be added to these conclusions. They are drawn from carefully designed research studies rather than ongoing classroom contexts; teachers may use a combination of the three approaches. Moreover, given the current drive to raise standards in English schools it is understandable that teachers gravitate towards a presentational approach when this is closest to the mode used in the national test assessments.

2.5 An Appropriate Balance between Reading and Writing

HMI express concern that, in 300 literacy hours observed in the autumn term of 1999, for example, there was no shared writing in three-quarter of the lessons. There may be several reasons why shared writing appeared not to be widely used in the early years of the National Literacy Strategy. As was discussed earlier, it was uncommon in England before the late 1990s. The emphasis of the NLS may also have been widely perceived as primarily concerned with raising reading standards, with the assumption that improvements in reading would feed through to improved writing attainment.

The effectiveness of shared writing, the joint construction of a text by teacher and pupils, is difficult to assess in research studies because of its interactive and diverse nature. Nevertheless, shared writing builds upon psychological research that has revealed the complexity of the writing process and the potential value of teachers modelling writing and incorporating children's suggestions into the text that is jointly constructed. Generalising the implications of their many experimental studies into the compositional aspects of writing, Bereiter and Scardamalia (1993) make a number of recommendations that are built around the possibilities of shared writing:

- pupils (and teachers) need to be made aware of the full extent of the composing process;
- the thinking that goes on in composition needs to be modelled by the teacher;
- pupils will benefit from reviewing their own writing strategies and knowledge;
- pupils need a supportive and congenial writing environment, but will also benefit from experiencing the struggles that are an integral part of developing writing skill;
- pupils may also benefit from using various 'facilitating' techniques to help them through the initial stages of acquiring more complex processes (e.g., listing words, points that may be made, the wording of final sentences etc.), in advance of tackling the full text.

As was referred to earlier, there have been a number of additional elements in the National Literacy Strategy since its inception in 1998. These include a finer distinction within the shared writing teaching approach: teacher modelling – supported composition – teacher transcription (DfEE, 2000, 2001). This provides a continuum for the changing locus of teacher-pupil dialogue, each of which is worthy of further systematic research, particularly in relation to the varying demands of different genres of text. Overall, though, the novelty of shared writing within the teaching repertoire, and its demands on professional knowledge, currently makes this teaching approach an issue for sustained professional development in many English primary schools.

2.6 Skills Learned in Literacy Lessons are Insufficiently Transferred to Work in Other Subjects

This reported finding may in part reflect the increase in setting (attainment-related pupil grouping across classes for specific subjects) that has occurred in English primary schools in recent years. The increase is likely to be related to an unintended consequence of the national 'trickle-down target-setting' that has become very influential in the light of the government-led drive to raise literacy standards. The use of setting is likely to mean that pupils may be taught literacy for an hour or more each day but be taught by another teacher, or in a different pupil group (or both), for much of the rest of the day, making cross-reference and explicit skill transfer more difficult. However, data on the extent to which setting is used is not easily available.

Furthermore, curriculum development models that focus on reading-writing links have only become influential in England in the last ten years or so, particularly through publications related to 'genre theory' non-fiction projects in Australia (Callaghan and Rothery, 1988; Cope and Kalantzis, 1993). Such projects aim to make visible what has to be learned in factual writing genres. In the model put forward by Callaghan and Rothery, shared reading is used to model the uses and features of factual genres (e.g., reports, explanations, procedures, discussions and recounts). Discussion focuses on what the text is for (purpose), how the text is organised (text level structure) and the way the texts 'speaks' (sentences and words). A new text in the same genre is then constructed in shared writing (supported composition) by teacher and pupils. Pupils then construct another new text in this genre independently, using individual drafting, consultation with teacher and peers, editing and publishing, evaluation and future planning. In the UK, the model has been further developed by Lewis and Wray (1995) in highlighting how pupils' factual writing can be supported by the use of 'frames': sentence starters, connectives and modifiers, which are typically found in certain genres.

3. THE POSSIBLE ROLE OF GRAMMATICAL REFERENCE

Explicit teaching of grammar in England declined rapidly in the late 1960s and in the early 1970s, partly because of the legacy of a highly influential book published by Andrew Wilkinson. Wilkinson (1971: 32) drew upon a range of studies to conclude that the claims for the benfits of grammar teaching are nearly all completely without foundation. In 1994, this conclusion was systematically challenged by David Tomlinson. Tomlinson published a paper that drew attention to various weaknesses in the studies which Wilkinson considered and concluded that these studies did not support the conclusion that the teaching of grammar had no value in schools. Tomlinson's paper has been followed up by discussion papers from the Qualifications and Curriculum Authority (QCA, 1998, 1999). The papers point out that the routine discussion and teaching of language is something that seems to

have been lost in English schools. This loss includes discussion of syntactic structure and rules, as part of preparation for and feedback from writing. The QCA's tentatively conclude the following:
- discrete teaching of parts of speech and parsing in de-contextualised exercise form is not particularly effective;
- there is evidence that experience of the syntactic demands of different types of tasks is a key factor in pupils' writing performance and development;
- drawing explicit attention of the syntactic features of pupils' writing can increase pupils' awareness of how language works. This may in turn increase their control over their writing.

The response of the NLS has been to develop an innovative package for schools, *Grammar for Writing*, comprising a teacher booklet, C-D Rom and videotape, that supports the teaching of sentence-level objectives by the use of shared writing and selective use of grammatical terminology (DfEE, 2000).

Typical extracts include the following:
(For 8-9 year olds, Summer Term, with the objective of helping children 'to understand how the grammar of a sentence alters when the sentence type is altered, e.g., when a statement is made into a question...noting the order of words, verb tenses, additions and/or deletions of words, changes to punctuation' and with a group of pupils standing at the front of the class):

'Hand five children the [provided] cards for the sentence "Mr Bloggs is going to the library." Hand another child a question mark and ask him or her to rearrange the children into a question and take up the right position. (Ask the child with the full stop to sit down.) Repeat with "Mr. Bloggs has been to the library." and then with "Mr. Bloggs went to the library." Note that the last statement cannot be made into a question using the same words.' (The teacher's guide includes photographs of children taking part in a similar activity.)

(For 9-10 year olds, Spring Term, with the objective of helping children to 'use punctuation to signpost meaning in longer and more complex sentences'):

'Write four or five sentences, e.g., "The man was waiting in the queue. He was a sailor. He wanted to buy some stamps. He needed stamps to send his parcel. He hadn't any money." Discuss the best way to combine these sentences into one to retain the same meaning.' (The use of easy-wipe whiteboards and felt pens by children is recommended.)

These extracts reflect some of the main features of the NLS. Specific aspects of sentence-level learning are expressed as objectives. The full range of termly objectives allow these aspects to be linked to a range of texts used for shared reading and writing. The emphasis is on interactive teaching methods. However, in the light of the demise of grammatical reference in English education in recent years, such suggestions do make demands on teacher's subject knowledge. The accompanying training materials include a range of technical terms that teachers may be meeting for the first time as teachers or as former pupils, such as some basic elements of sentence grammar: subject, verb, object, complement and adverbial; as well as the various word classes, such as nouns, conjunctions, adjectives and verbs. However, the rationale for the materials makes it clear that their primary aim is not the study of grammar in its own right, but as a means to improving children's writing. The rationale argues that grammar provides a link to ways of investigating, problem-solving, and language play and a growing awareness of an interest in how language works.

It is too early to judge whether *Grammar for Writing* will act as a lever for raising standards of writing in English primary schools or indeed as a catalyst for re-energising professional interest in the structure of written language. A recent inspection findings report of the fourth year of the National Literacy Strategy (HMI, 2002: 13) notes a small improvement in the quality of teaching of sentence-level work, but adds that there are still too many lessons where the sentence-level work is not integrated effectively into the 'increasingly good' shared writing.

4. WIDER ISSUES IN THE RESEARCH-PRACTICE INTERFACE

Some commentators (e.g., Wyse, 2001) have reiterated the difficulty in identifying the research evidence that supports the teaching of grammar, although he accepts that some highly significant findings from the use of sentence-combining activities were reported some years ago in the USA (e.g., O'Hare, 1973). More importantly, though, *Grammar for Writing* reflects a wider issue in the research-practice interface. Many of the research studies discussed above are based on relatively pure contexts, representing the parameters of quasi-experimental design. What is needed now, especially in the light of high-profile national initiatives such as the National Literacy Strategy in England, are sustained classroom-based studies, so that pupils' writing may be related to the communicative contexts which have given rise to it. Such classroom studies would also provide opportunities to investigate the mediation of government-mandated curricula by the teacher-based factors that were referred to at the beginning of the chapter. Such studies are likely to illuminate the many complex issues raised when research is used to inform the teaching of writing.

IMPACT OF REGULAR PHILOSOPHICAL DISCUSSION ON ARGUMENTATIVE SKILLS

Reflection about education in primary schools

EMMANUÈLE AURIAC-PEYRONNET*/** & MARIE-FRANCE DANIEL***

*University of Nancy 2, France, **University of Clermont Ferrand, France, & ***University of Québec, Canada*

Abstract. The aim of our contribution is to expound the relationship between philosophy and argumentation. We propose to circumscribe the effects of philosophical oral teaching/learning on the writing abilities of young pupils. The central hypothesis is that the original, moral, social or cultural values discussed in philosophical oral workshops develop the capacity to better generate ideas, because philosophical practice produces more complex thinking than ordinary co-operative conversation. Within this framework, the activity of argumentation focuses on ensuring that young writers can transfer their oral abilities to manage the process of negotiation when writing. A study conducted during a two-year period with four experimental groups supports our presentation. The results illustrate the positive transfer between philosophical activity and predisposition to write argumentatively. The conceptualisation process was quantitatively improved as soon as children reached the age of seven. Hence, philosophical dialogue with its complex characteristics should be considered as focus of activities in teaching and learning to write.

Keywords: planning, philosophical dialogue, elementary school, complexity, conceptualisation, teaching and learning.

1. INTRODUCTION

Philosophical dialogue is a practice of critical thinking, supported by and participating in the edification of a thinking community of inquiry (Lipman, 1991) that enables the emergence of generic characteristics. Structurally, philosophical dialogue (contrary to argumentation) reveals an absence of univocal orientation: the discussion is non-linear, favors doubt, and fosters creativity and interdependency (see Beausoleil & Daniel, 1991). The argumentative figures, locally present, serve the progressive edification of criteria for judgment that are essential to the construction of reasoning. The latter is socially structured and contextualized rather than purely logical. Argumentation can be planned while, in contrast, it is impossible to plan a philosophical dialogue. So why cross philosophy and argumentation? Is it possible? After illustrating a philosophical oral activity, we will present an analysis, conducted in a primary school context, studying the impact of oral philosophical practice on the development of written argumentative skills.

2. PHILOSOPHICAL DISCUSSION IN ELEMENTARY SCHOOL

Philosophical dialogue is a particular language behavior (Espéret, 1989) that must be studied within the framework of this specificity (see Auriac-Peyronnet & Daniel, 2002). Theoretically it combines three interdependent dimensions: 1) dialogical form (Jacques, 1988), 2) argumentative abilities (Golder, 1996), and 3) critical reflective behavior (Lipman, 1991).

2.1 Type of Discussion

This excerpt illustrates a type of interaction, among 7 years olds, regarding the difference between humans and animals.

Pupil:	I agree with Yohan but there, there is a difference, not all the same because they are animals but not us, there are cycles, like grandfathers, animals have different cries
Pupil:	Small animals they also learn cries, but small ones because they are smaller. They don't have much voice, then they cry louder when they are older.
(...)	
Pupil:	Also we don't have to hunt, we buy. There aren't any supermarkets for animals.
Teacher:	Why?
Pupil:	Well, because they don't know how to talk, they don't have any money, they don't go to school, they don't know how to count.
(...)	
Pupil:	What I don't understand is they eat the hair?
Pupil:	How do they do that, do they peel them?
Pupil:	I saw the fox, they left the skin.
Pupil:	My grandpa takes the peel off then my grandma takes the inside and the core and all that out.
Teacher:	And the animals?
Pupil:	No, they er don't have hands?
Teacher:	And what else does your grandpa have?
Pupil:	A knife.
Pupil:	Those that live in the wild, well I think that with their nails they cut the peel.
Teacher:	It depends on the animal.
Pupil:	Do animals eat the core?
etc.	

Philosophical dialogue is an interactive or collaborative activity: Thinking within a group in order to think better. It reflects Vygotsky's theoretical logic of passing from *inter* to *intra* (see Brossard & Fijalkow, 1998). The *praxis* of dialogal activity increases in pupils the ability to integrate an opposite point of view and, in doing so, the ability to diversify perspectives. Thought is no longer individual, but common or social. Theoretically, it breaks away from a "dialogue of the deaf" and from "daily conversation" (Daniel & Pallascio, 1997).

2.2 The Notions of Dialogal vs. Monologal and Dialogical vs. Monological

To understand the cross between the two dimensions of *dialogal* and *dialogical,* we have to consider this distinction. Roulet explains:

> "to the traditional distinction between a discourse generated by a single speaker/writer, called *monologal,* and a discourse generated by at least two speakers/writers, called *dialogal,* we suggest adding the distinction between a discourse with a structure of speech in which the constituents are linked by interactive functions, which we call *monological,* and a discourse with a structure of exchange in which the immediate constituents are linked by initiative and reactive illocutory functions, which we call *dialogical.*" (Roulet et al., 1987: 60).

Table 1. Dialogal vs. Monologal vs. Dialogical vs. Monological (Adapted from Roulet et al. 1987)

Discourse	Monologal One speaker/writer	Dialogal Two speakers/writers
Monological (Intervention)	*Soliloquy*	*Dialogue of the deaf*
Dialogical (Exchange)	*Argumentative text*	*Philosophical dialogue*

Dia-logic defines the manner and the objective of the philosophical discursive practice. Both fundamental cognitive operations of argumentation – justification – *giving support to one's point of view* – and negotiation – *taking into account the point of view of another so as to integrate it into an acceptable presentation of one's own point of view* (Golder, 1996) – are involved in this language behavior. To have a dialogic perspective means to be able to adopt, through dialogal space, the possibility of appropriating the reactive sentences of peers. During the writing process the dialogal space cannot be used: there is a single speaker in the text, which is necessary monolingual. But the monolingual text can integrate dialogic perspectives or orientations related to past dialogal experiences from a philosophical dialogue.

2.3 The Impact of Discussion on Argumentative Abilities

The practice of philosophical dialogue in classrooms is recent in France. We do not actually have much literature available on the subject. However, Caillier (2001) presents an emblematic example that enables one to specify the impact of regular philosophical discussions on argumentative abilities. In a class of pupils aged ten to eleven, the proposed topic for written and oral productions was "Is man an animal?". We now suggest taking a closer look at a young girl's statements from both, before and after a philosophical discussion. Cindy's first opinion, prior to the philosophical discussion, was as follows (Caillier, 2001: 65):

> "I think so because we come from monkeys. Almost all animals are like us, they have a nose but we don't necessarily call it a nose for a dog or a horse, a mouth, eyes, and especially a heart, they breathe and they also walk, they do their business and also they have children just like us".

Her second opinion adopts a dialogical perspective, as seen in the following excerpts (Caillier, 2001: 66):

> Yes and no.
>
> Yes, man is an animal because they have the same manner of living that we have, they eat, they drink, they sleep. The physical aspect is not very useful when trying to find out if man is an animal. You have to look at the moral aspect at a moral level, man is sometimes a man and sometimes man has an animal behaviour..."
>
> And no, because man creates, invents machines because we, we need them while they can manage on their own. [...]

So it appears that a philosophical discussion improves the ability to distance oneself and avoid producing a thesis that is limited to a single opinion, to a single orientation. Philosophical dialogue aims at integrating controversial perspectives. To illustrate this process, here are some interventions from Cindy, during a workshop where pupils were stimulated to think better (Caillier, 2001, 66):

> **1.49**. Cindy: I don't agree with Julien because he says we don't know / that we have no proof that man "er" that animals are not intelligent / but yes look / cats manage to catch mice / foxes to "er"...: **1.58**. Cindy: Sometimes we kill in pairs.. . well yes [... ?] and the dog that hunts (big smile to her classmate): **1.66**. Cindy: I agree with Oliver because we have many versions / some say that that we "come from" others that we come from monkeys and there you go: **1.88**. Cindy: Those that say that man isn't an animal / animals don't get dressed "er" / they don't / they don't speak [. .. ?]:

3. PROCEDURE

For the past three years, we offered teachers specific training in philosophy. Ten teachers are now involved in philosophical practice with their pupils. However, within this context, there is a lack of experimental groups, therefore, it will take some years for the exploratory protocol we have established to be completed.

3.1 Protocol

Our protocol comes from research-action[1]. Our perspective is not strictly experimental, and we had at our disposal several classes that practiced during one or two years, and several control groups from various classes to control the teacher effect.

Table 2. Levels of Schooling and Number of Participants

Age Group	Control group	Experimental group
7-8	Ce1: 39	38
8-9	Ce2: 61	21
9-10	Cm1: 75	35
7-12	C.l.i.s[2]: 6	9

N.B.: Each class practiced philosophy during a one-year or a two-year period.

The experimental group was formed of six classes (see table 2) that experienced philosophical discussions at a rate of one hour per week, during the entire school year, from October to May. The teachers conformed to the specificity of philosophical dialogue. In other words, the eleven dimensions of non-linearity, interaction of discourse levels, doubt, creativity, wandering, inquiry, emergence of criteria, importance of question, self-effacement, intellectual adventure, critical judgment and verification of hypothesis (Beausoleil & Daniel, 1991).

Our main hypothesis is that philosophical discussions, when regularly practiced, foster in pupils the ability to generate many original ideas within a dialogical perspective, in both oral and written argumentation.

3.2 Methodology

From October to May, pupils practiced oral philosophical argumentation. At the end of the school year, in order to verify if argumentative verbal abilities were transferred to written argumentation, we asked the pupils to write an argumentative text.

To compare these texts, we used the classical approach inspired by Brassart (1985, 1887, 1988, see Peyronnet, 1998, 1999, Peyronnet & Gombert, 2000). A first text presupposed writing a proposition related to moral positioning between the pupils' parents and themselves (see Peyronnet & Gombert, 2000, Peyronnet in press).

---

[1] Thanks to Mrs. Cataneo, Chaucot, Loubet, Milien, and Mr. Martinet for their participation.
[2] For more information see Auriac-Peyronnet, Martinet, Peyronnet, Torregrosa & Tressol, 2002 and Auriac-Peyronnet, Martinet & Peyronnet, in progress.

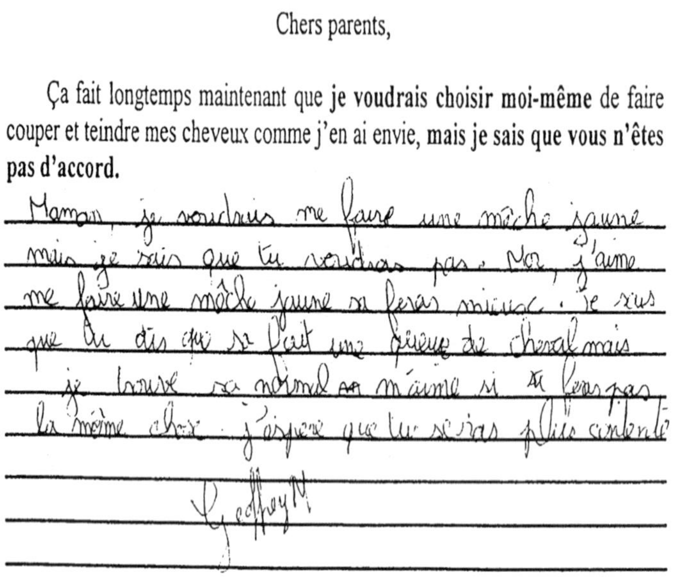

Chers parents,

Ça fait longtemps maintenant que **je voudrais choisir moi-même** de faire couper et teindre mes cheveux comme j'en ai envie, mais je sais que vous n'êtes pas d'accord.

Maman je voudrais me faire une mèche jaune mais je sais que tu voudras pas. Moi, j'aime me faire une mèche jaune ça feras mieux. Je sais que tu dis que ça fait une queue de cheval mais je trouve ça normal on m'aime si ça feras pas la même chose. j'espère que tu seras plus contente?

Geoffrey

Dear parents,

For a long time now, I have wanted to be the one to choose my haircut and the color of my hair, but I know you don't agree.

Mom, I would like to have a yellow streak in my hair, but I know you won't want me to. I would like to have a yellow streak it would look better. I know you say it would be like a pigtail but I think it would be normal even if it weren't the same. I hope you will be happier.
Geoffrey.

Figure 1: Geoffrey's original text.

Conform our hypothesis, it is important to ensure that the philosophical discussion has a significant impact on the generation of ideas. For this reason, in order to anticipate the written work (Pouit & Golder, 1996; 1997), a preliminary planning task was required of the pupils, as shown Figure 2.

The pupils complete this grid, which consists of two columns: one for their own point of view and the other for their parents'. The word "because" is used to guide the pupils towards argumentative ideas. Then the pupils are asked to expand each idea and, doing so, to write their text. There was no time limit for the two tasks. It took the pupils approximately twenty minutes to generate ideas and thirty minutes to write the texts.

Write down all your ideas to convince your parents.

Choosing by myself is normal because:
- I want a yellow streak in my hair...
- Having hair.

My parents don't think it is normal because:
- They say it doesn't look good...
- They won't allow it in the summer because they say it's too hot...

Figure 2. The pre-planning task. Production example (Geoffrey, 10 years old).

4. QUANTITATIVE RESULTS

In this first exploration, the variable taken into consideration is the global number of ideas that are produced in two categories: ideas that support the children's points of view and ideas related to controversial arguments. Respectively, these two variables concern the cognitive operations of justification and negotiation used to convince the parents. If children show good argumentation skills, they will generate ideas in both categories.

4.1 Impact of Philosophy

The ideas were extracted from each pre-planning grid. Two independent judges analyzed the responses and eliminated repetitive ideas. In figures 3 and 4, post-test results (established in June) are presented.

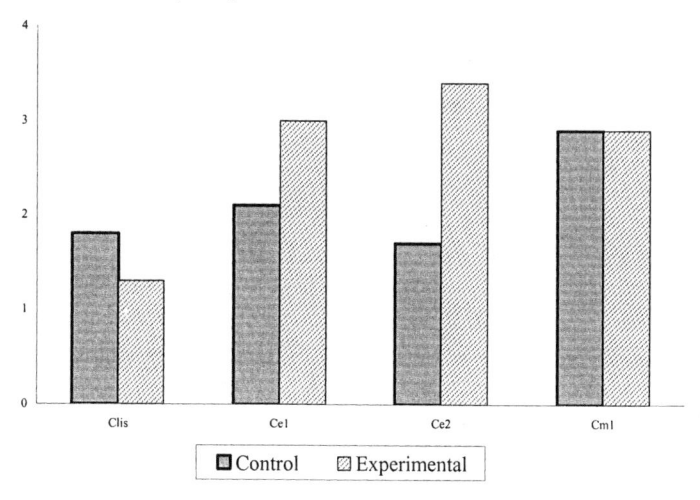

Figure 3. Justification. Number of ideas that represent justifications, i.e., opinions in favour of the children's point of view.

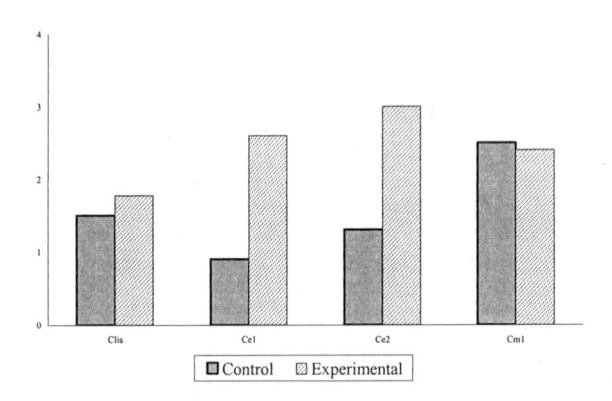

Figure 4. Negotiation. Number of negotiation ideas that take into consideration the adult's point of view.

Based on the results of these post-tests, the practice of regular philosophical discussion has a positive impact on the pupils' generation of ideas (all classes groups experimental>control: $F(1, 280) = 18,93; p <. 001$). Our hypothesis is confirmed with the Ce1 and Ce2 classes (ce1 justifications experimental>control: $t(68, 37) = -3,08; p <. 01$; ce1 negotiation experimental>control: $t(56, 39) = -6,73; p <. 001$; ce2 justifications experimental>control: $t(23, 42) = -3,13; p <. 01$; ce2 negotiation experimental>control: $t(80) = -4,34; p <. 001$). Especially with the Ce1 subjects since they generated an average of three ideas per planning in their second production compared to an average of one-and-a-half during the first production. The quality of the second planning is also more balanced. The production of counter-ideas, which take into consideration the adult's point of view, is, first in Ce1 and then in Ce2 greatly improved. It is also important to note that during this progress, between ages 7 and 10, the average number of 3 ideas per plan is consistently respected. Usually, the standard level is an average of 3 or 3,5 ideas per text (as presented by Gérouit, Roussey & Piolat, 2002). Therefore, the impact of regular philosophical discussion actualizes (meaning acceleration of development abilities, as in Vygostkian's theoretical zone, see Brossard & Fijalkow, 1998) the ability to generate ideas. It is to be noted that the overall ability, in the process of idea generation (creativity), is better in Ce1 than in Cm1. Indeed, philosophical discussions are particularly rich in Ce1 classes: participation levels in debates are very strong with children aged 7 or 8. Is this the main reason? It is probably a factor of influence but not the only one.

The lower results obtained in Cm1 (Cm1 justifications experimental *vs.* control: $t(106) =. 09$ not significant; Cm1 negotiation experimental *vs.* control: $t(86, 56) = .51$ in significant) give rise to questions. Should we interpret this phenomenon in terms of a developmental threshold attained by pupils in this age group or adopt the idea that there is an absence of teacher impact in these classrooms? However the experimental group was from an under-privileged social group (educational priority sector – Z.E.P. –). Additional research with other classes is necessary before confirming any hypothesis.

4.2 Theoretical Experimental Graph

Having studied a number of classes enables us to generate a theoretical graph to determine principal standard levels (within the framework of our study, of course). The following figure is meant to illustrate the development of argumentative skills with – experimental classes – or without – control groups – philosophical- practice.

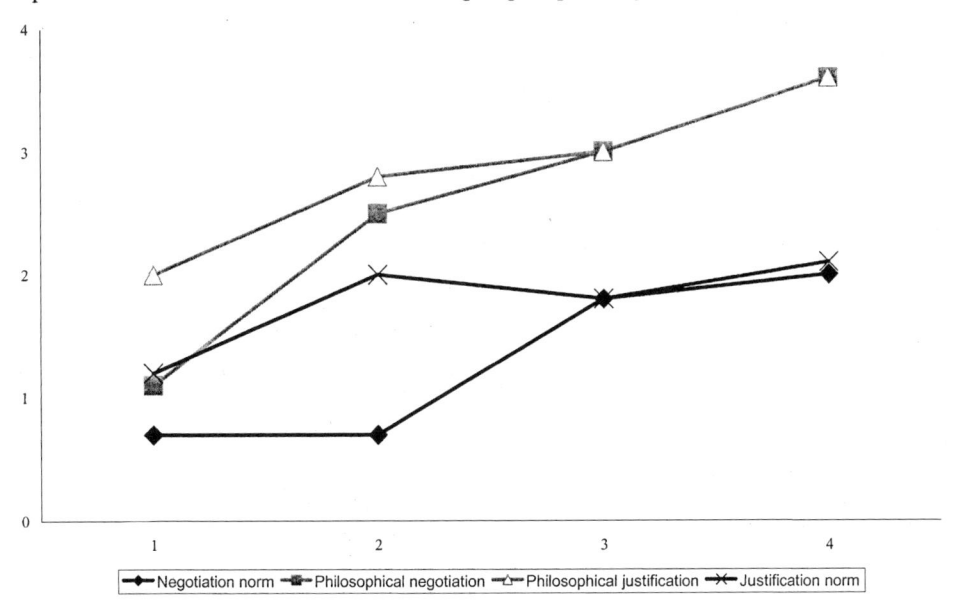

Figure 5. Theoretical graph of normal vs. experimental philosophical pattern. Theoretical impact of the practice of philosophy on each dimension: justification and negotiation on 4 levels. 1= beginning ce1, 2= terminal ce1, 3= beginning ce2, and 4= terminal ce2.

The ability to equilibrate justification and negotiation exists in normal development for the Ce2 age group (ages 8 to 9). Before this, at the beginning of the school year, Ce1 children (aged 7) could not generate as many negotiated points of view as justifications. Afterwards, it seems that normal development corresponds to this balance. Teaching philosophy has, in this instance, a positive impact on the ability to maintain (Ce2) or increase (Ce1 and Cm1) a high level of conceptualization with adjustments between justification and negotiation. The principal result resides in the fact that some pupils aged 7, after a single school year, obtain results that are comparable to the Cm1 with regards to the ability to manage both these dimensions interdependently. What can we conclude from this impressive fact? It should also be noted that children, in the C.l.i.s. special class obtain good results because they are mature enough to better adjust negotiation and justification, enough to be compared to theoretical level 2 (see previous data in comparison to theoretical level 2: 1,5 ideas is less than 2 for justification, but average 1,77 is more than 0,7 for negotiation.).

In the next section, the qualitative studies of the relationships developed by the pupils between their own point of view and the adult's controversial position will complement the quantitative view.

5. QUALITATIVE RESULTS

Dialogical exchange – or monolingual – sole intervention – links connect the child's and the adult's points of view. Which qualitative links stand? As it is more often the case in the control group, ideas are proposed without connection or exchange between justification and negotiation. Ideas of adults and children are presented face to face but the underlying chain of reasoning is not necessarily connected. In the control group, ideas are presented separately and are sometimes non-existent.

Table 3. Conceptualisation in a Ce1 Control Group (7 year olds)

15	Long hair	Curly hair
16	Squared off	They like my haircut
17	I like it	Afraid I won't do something nice with my hair
18	Stay a bit long	They want to cut it (tautology)

In this class, the ideas suggested are reduced to a minimum. In contrast, in the experimental group of young children aged 7, the transfer mechanism from dialogal thinking to dialogism is clearly in progress (table 4).

Table 4. Conceptualisation in a Ce1 Experimental Group (7 year olds)

6	It's to be pretty I will be a star I will break my piggy-bank I will win the lottery at 1000009999 €	⋈	No, you are ten times prettier like this You need money But you don't have enough (O.K. but 5 years)
7	(I want to cut it) (Please) I will be better looking (Please)	⋈	No I don't want you to I said no No and no (Well yes)
8	(I know you don't like it but) I still want to cut and dye I think I will be better looking (if I do all that) Yes, I promise	⋈	No you won't look good And so we don't agree But if it will make you happy As long as you promise to wash your hair every day

The transfer from the discussion sessions is obvious. Sometimes the ideas remain in a dialogal form (as in number 7 of table 4, for example): the opposite point of view is instead marked with a dialogal indicator (no, no, no and no!). However in other cases the links are more dialogical than simply dialogal (as in number 6 of table 4, for example). In fact the qualitative results of Ce1 confirm the previously studied tendencies in which the experimental level would simply fall into line with the theoretical level of spontaneous and natural development of abilities (see table 5 and 6, below).

Table 5. Process of Natural Conceptualisation in a Cm1 Control Group

9	Because I am big I am old enough to choose I do what I please I won't do anything stupid Everybody got some colour at school I'll give you a night (to think it over)	We created you We're the ones to decide whether or not to cut it I don't care about the others: you're the one that counts We'll see We'll think about what you've said

Table 6. Process of Conceptualisation in a Cm1 Experimental Group

15	We're big We don't always like the way we are We'd like to change	*We aren't big enough* We're always pretty just the way we are We mustn't change
16*	I am 10 years old I will soon be a teenager I could take the colour out	Yes, but we are still your parents Yes but not an adult (No!)

The perspective of bonds or links is perhaps dependent on the thematic of the idea. Ideas are not equal. We may or may not have some reasoning underlying an idea. Three dimensions appear in the productions (table 7). In the first dimension, the children explore some esthetical ideas that give some indication as to their individual and personal choice. The second dimension is rather moral: the subject is required to take a stand through the emergence of a background (example 16 in table 6). At times, some ideas suggest other preoccupations through consequences.

It is a fact that the developmental level is an important factor that interferes on these dimensions. Ce1 children – 7 year-olds – are unable to develop much the idea of morality. Whereas in Cm1, the subject can better explore this dimension by using more references (example 20, table 8). The idea of "it looks gangsterish" seen in a

Ce1 production is the same as the one developed under the "gypsy" or the "gang" theme (table 8).

Table 7. Background Idea in the Text

Dimensions	Examples
Esthetical	Esthetical ideas are shaving, a short haircut, colors (Ce1, 7 years especially)
Moral	Moral ideas regard responsibility, autonomy, age . . .
Social	Ideas of extrapolation or generalization (consequences/causes): find me beautiful, because it is a great world cup, my friends, my sister too...

Table 8. Process of Conceptualisation in a Cm1 Control Group

20	All my girlfriends do it	I don't care
	If not, my girlfriend is going to kill me	Speak to the principal
	I'm going to my girlfriend's	I would tell them "no" and you are under my care
	I'll be kicked out of the gang	Those aren't good friends
	I'm old enough	Until you are an adult, I decide
	They say I'm a gypsy	Drop them

The final question leads us to the possibility of studying the transfer between a pre-planning task and real writing. Is good planning a good way to write better? (see Ambroise, Auriac-Peyronnet, Jandot, & Rage, submitted).

6. CONCLUSION AND PERSPECTIVES

The advantage of our studies lies in the long-term examination of the argumentation dimension. Often argumentation, studied under experimental laboratory conditions, for example, results in standardized sequences that short-circuit the possibility to really examine the development of the mechanism of dialogism. In our protocol, the links developed with philosophical oral workshops offer the possibility to verify that very young children, who don't have much opportunity or ability to write, could benefit from this specific type of teaching and transform the conceptualization process. How, why and in which manner should we pursue new research in this field?

How? In the past few years, research has explored the categorization of the developmental level integrated within the overall dimension of argumentative discourse abilities. This field has in fact been well covered by Golder since the 90's (see Golder, 1996). Actually, new research oriented towards case studies (see Peyronnet, 2001) could prove of interest, for comparison, as well as other studies involving classroom reality.

Within the context of the present study, it appears necessary to define the links between the generation (emergence of ideas) and linearization (finding the appropriate linguistics tools to write) processes (as explored by Coirier et al., 2002). Our position is that this perspective must be pursued in constant relation to studies in ecological conditions through analysis of real classroom situations This last form of research is especially useful -in our point of view- to help researchers extract the various limits and links between writing processes. In fact, have we, in the psychological community of inquiry, sufficient and appropriate tools to interpret the developmental level of texts, and to characterize productions in terms of quality of performance? As Denis Alamargot says: *"What is a coherent text? What is great quality? This last indicator needs to be carefully used because it is very global. Tests of same quality could be composed with different strategies, with activation of different processes or different sequences of processes".* (Alamargot, Synthesis paper, Verona, 2001). According to us, the possibility of characterizing a good text must be in interaction with the characterization of the teaching that leads to it. Apparently less structured lessons, closer to real teaching conditions, should be further explored for comparison with excessively controlled teaching situations (as Dolz & Pasquier, 1994, or Peyronnet, 1998, 1999).

Why? The interest of research related with real practice of teaching (at the frontier of research-action and experimental research) is a different approach that compels us to consider the local constraints that act upon the different writing processes: this perspective could complete the theoretical definition of the planning processes as often simulated in models (Hayes & Flower 1980, Bereiter & Scardamalia, 1987, see Fayol, 1997 or Alamargot & Chanquoy, 2001). In fact, the difference resides in the overall manner in which the teaching activity can be evaluated. Can we reflect only on short-term teaching or on long term as well? Thinking about the pupils' progression during the argumentation learning/teaching on a scale encompassing schooling from ages 4 to 17 is a question of utmost importance. The central question would be: What place do argumentative skills have in the overall development of man and mankind? Introducing philosophy from the beginning of elementary school (Lipman, 1991, Daniel, 1992/1997, see Conche, 2000, Tozzi, 2002) is not an innocent choice. Forming pupils to the possibility of managing, in oral workshops, their specific human ability to reflect on subjects related to life, through philosophical discussions, is certainly a strong education approach on humanity, which transcends the field of argumentation (see François 1981, François et al, 1984). Conversely, it is probably necessary for the argumentative field of research to integrate philosophical dialogue and to specify the impact of long-term teaching to circumvent Taylor's conception, which could lead to consider learning solely as repetitive sequences, and therefore reduce the possibility of organizing authentically human teaching. Here, the results of our exploratory studies in French classrooms, in the continuity of other studies (Daniel, 1992/1997, Daniel & Pallascio, 1997, Pallascio & Lafortune, 2000), favor the integration of this type of oral philosophy in teaching, while pursuing the more refined characterization of its impact in further years.

Finally, which new perspectives of research? The most important suggestion resides, for us, on focusing on and studying intermediate writing (rough copy, see for example Grésillon, 1994, Feneglio, 2003) and rely second improved texts with teaching experiences (see Bucheton & Chabannes, 2002, Dolz, 2002) to better and more largely circumscribe the process of articulation between thinking and writing. The analysis focused on the manner in which change or adaptation operate during the complex process of writing between different phases of comprehensive planning, specific planning, control activities, linearization competencies, etc. could be an important contribution to research in future work. Within this framework, about the pursuit of our own study researches, about transfer from oral to write, characterizing the transition between the cognitive plan and the written text, could be conduced. For example, does a well-negotiated plan necessarily result in coherent and well-written texts? For us, the merging of various dimensions that qualify the knowledge of references used as the basis for exploring ideas – conceptualization – could be used to specify the pupils' strategies to explore good texts – linearization.

ACTION RESEARCH

A Study on Using an Integrative-narrative Method to Teach L2 Writing in a Hong Kong Primary School

ANITA Y.K. POON

Hong Kong Baptist University, China

Abstract. To date writing has not received sufficient attention at the primary level in Hong Kong albeit numerous initiatives in the current curriculum reform launched in 2001. Typically writing is taught based on a prescribed textbook in Hong Kong primary schools. The traditional approach to teaching writing is mechanical and rigid. Learners are forced to follow a prescribed pattern to write. The content is standard and banal. Language-wise it is far from being rich because everybody uses the same vocabulary and sentence structure. In terms of teaching methodology it is not in line with the current approach of integrating various skills as advocated in Communicative Language Teaching.

This chapter reports an action research conducted in a Primary 5 English classroom. The research question is how to make an English writing class interesting and stimulating. An entirely new method is adopted. Stories are used as the teaching materials, and integrated skills of listening, speaking and writing are adopted.

Qualitative research methods are employed. The following methods are used to collect data: pre- and post- interviews with the students, pre- and post- interviews with the teacher, journals written by the teacher, class observation reports written by the researcher, the stories written by the students.

The findings of this study affirm the belief that using an integrative-narrative method is an effective way to teach L2 writing in Hong Kong.

Keywords: teaching writing in Hong Kong, teaching writing in primary education, action research in writing, teaching writing, narrative method in teaching writing, integrative method in teaching writing,

1. INTRODUCTION

Research in L2 writing emerged in the 1960s. Substantive research in writing started only in the 1980s (Ferris & Hedgcock, 1998; Grabe & Kaplan, 1996). There are

---

Poon, A. Y.K. (2004). Action research. A study on using an integrative-narrative method to teach L2 writing in a Hong Kong primary school.
In G. Rijlaarsdam (Series Ed.) & Rijlaarsdam, G., Van den Bergh, H. & Couzijn, M. (Vol. Eds.), Studies in writing. Vol. 14, Effective learning and teaching of writing, 2nd Edition, Part 2, Studies in how to teach writing, 305-322.

some issues that need addressing in the writing research field. The first issue pertains to the contents of the studies. Recent research indicates that the topics are mostly on writing *per se*, such as writing strategies, writing assessment, different genres of writing, process writing, grammar in writing, cohesive devices, reading and writing, L1 and L2 writing, CALL and writing (Silva & Kapper, 2001a, b; 2002). Research in writing from a pedagogical perspective is scant. There are some on error corrections, instructors' feedback and peer feedback (Ashwell, 2000; Ferris & Roberts, 2001; Huang, 2000; Zhu, 2001), but very few on methods of teaching writing.

Integration of skills is another issue of concern. Reading and writing are typically perceived as related skills, so research in this area proliferates (Belcher and Hirvela, 2001; Morino, 1998; Peregoy and Boyle, 2001). By contrast, little work has been done in the writing literature to link listening and speaking skills to the development of writing skill. According to Second Language Acquisition theories, acquisition of a language including L1 and L2 follows a natural route: listening – speaking – reading – writing (Krashen & Terrell, 1983). Sufficient and comprehensible input of listening, speaking and reading will facilitate writing. In the same vein Communicative Language Teaching advocates an integrative approach to teaching the four English skills because language is acquired holistically rather than discretely (Brown, 2001; Littlewood, 1981; Widdowson, 1978).

A further issue is about the sample of subjects. There has been a tendency to select subjects for research from the tertiary sector, probably because researchers are usually based at universities and university students naturally become their convenience samples (Cohen & Manion, 1994: 88). To date school students especially primary school students have not received sufficient attention in this area of study.

If research in L2 writing is 'little' compared with that in L2 reading in English speaking countries such as the U.S.A., Canada, the U.K. and Australia (Ferris & Hedgcock, 1998; Grabe & Kaplan, 1996), it is even 'less' in Hong Kong. L2 writing research in Hong Kong centres around the areas of process writing, feedback, coherence, teachers' beliefs and practices in writing and the like (Cheung, 1996; Hyland & Hyland, 2001; Lee, 1997, 2002; Tsang, Wong, & Yuen, 2000). Very little attention has been given to writing pedagogy in L2 classrooms in primary and secondary schools. However, problems abound in the area of teaching writing at school in Hong Kong, and particularly so at primary level. This chapter is an attempt to fill that gap.

This chapter provides a report about an action research project conducted in a primary school in Hong Kong between September and October in 2002. As the research adopts a multiple-angle design, the study encompasses different layers of meaning. For instance, from the perspective of the teacher: how can the writing class be made more interesting and stimulating? From the perspective of the researcher: how is it possible to improve the current situation in teaching writing in Hong Kong? What is the alternative method? From the perspective of the teacher educator: how can we help the teacher to develop the skills of teaching writing? How can we help the teacher to become a reflective English teacher? From the perspective of the curriculum designer: which is better – the traditional method or the narrative method? how can we compare the products that emerge from different methods?

Given the constraint of the chapter, I will give a general report of the present study from the perspectives of the teacher and the researcher only.

2. RESEARCH PROBLEM AND RESEARCH QUESTION

2.1 Problems in Teaching Writing at the Primary Level in Hong Kong

The teaching method is the first and foremost issue worth probing into. Typically writing is taught based on a prescribed textbook in primary schools.[1] Most teachers simply stick to the textbook and adopt a very traditional method. A typical composition lesson goes as follows: the teacher teaches the class a sample of writing in the unit, which usually consists of several sentences describing a person or an object. Then, with the help of some guiding questions, the teacher asks the class to do parallel writing, which means to write a similar text by changing simply the names, pronouns, numbers or some details of the original text. Finally, the students copy the answers to the guiding questions in their exercise books, and submit their 'composition'.

The English teachers demonstrate their traditional method also through the way they treat the four skills in English. The writing skill is taught separately in the assigned composition lesson, which does not integrate with other three skills – listening, speaking and reading. Interaction between the teacher and students, and among students is minimal. Students are required to work on their own and compile the answers to the guiding questions into a piece of 'composition'. Hence the writing class is rendered boring, and students are not motivated to learn writing.

Over-reliance on the textbook and the guiding questions restricts the minds of the students. Students are not given any room for exercising their creativity both in terms of the content and language use in the composition. The composition produced is thus rather 'standard' and poor in ideas and expressions. To my knowledge, some teachers even provide answers to the guiding questions and ask students to copy the answers, which are then claimed to be a piece of composition. Such a traditional method to teaching writing is far from being challenging because the input is not pitched at the right level as postulated in Krashen's input hypothesis (Krashen, 1982). Acquisition of the writing skill is thus affected.

2.2 Problems in ELT in Hong Kong

The above issues of teaching writing in Hong Kong are just the tip of an iceberg. They reveal some serious problems in the field of English Language Teaching (ELT) in Hong Kong. Policy-wise Hong Kong follows the ELT methodology developed in the west quite closely. In the 1983 English syllabus (Curriculum Development Council, 1983) the previously used Oral-Structural Approach was replaced by the Communicative Approach. In the 1999 English syllabus (Curriculum Development Council, 1999) task-based language learning was introduced along side the Communicative Approach. However, in real practice most English teachers still

---

[1] *Worksheets are more often used in secondary schools.*

stick to the traditional grammar and structural approach. English skills are not taught integratively. Emphasis is placed more on grammar and English usage exercises. Practice in listening and speaking is minimal. The situation in primary is worse than in secondary.

Medium of instruction is a further problem. English is taught mostly through the target language – English – at secondary level, but rarely so at primary level. That is why primary students do not have much chance to expose themselves to the target language. The issue of medium of instruction is, in fact, related to a bigger issue of teacher qualifications and training. Because of a high demand in the supply of English teachers, to date quite a large number of them are not subject trained. Some may even have problems with their English proficiency.[2] The situation is more adverse in primary than in secondary.

2.3 Research Question

Based on the analysis of the current situation in the ELT field in Hong Kong in general, and in the teaching of writing in primary schools in particular, it is found that the writing class is boring and thus students are not motivated to learn writing. Something ought to be done to change the methodology in practice rather than at the mere policy level. The present study attempts to address this problem. The research question is: How can the English writing class be made more interesting and stimulating?

The study focuses on the pedagogical level of the issue in question from the perspectives of the teacher and the researcher. By 'pedagogical' is meant the overall approach to teaching writing. The current approach draws on the structuralist view that writing is taught separately from other skills, and that the writing skill can be acquired through the drilling and modelling of sentence patterns and vocabulary. The present study aims at exploring a new approach to teaching writing in Hong Kong primary schools with a view to stimulating students' interest in writing, which is lacking in the current classroom. The theoretical underpinning of the 'new' approach will be further elaborated below. Given its limited time frame and the nature of the study as qualitative action research, it would be unrealistic to expect a marked improvement in students' writing proficiency. An attitudinal and/or behavioral change in the subjects (e.g., students like writing classes more than before, students participate more actively in class than before) is, therefore, a more realistic objective of the present study.

---

[2] *The Language Benchmark Test was launched by the Hong Kong government in March 2001 to assure the English proficiency of English teachers. Serving English teachers are given five years to upgrade their English. It is estimated that a certain number of English teachers, primary teachers in particular, will not be able to pass the benchmark test.*

3. RESEARCH DESIGN AND METHODS

3.1 Research Design

Action research seeks to enhance the teacher's understanding of classroom teaching and learning and to improve practice through participation, reflection and evaluation (Kemmis & McTaggart, 1988; Nunan, 1990; Richards & Lockhart; 1996). It is a useful means to try out new methods of teaching in the classroom. I, therefore, adopt action research as the framework for the present study, which addresses the issues raised previously pertaining to teaching writing in Hong Kong at primary level.

Action research is normally initiated by the teacher, who at the same time plays the role of researcher. In the present study the situation is a bit different. The author is a teacher educator and researcher. I am actually the one who initiated the action research based on my previous experience as an English schoolteacher and my current informed knowledge of the ELT field in Hong Kong as a teacher educator. Bearing the research problem in mind, I approached the teacher who is involved in the present study. I was happy to find that the teacher also shares my view that something is wrong with the local ELT field. She wants to improve her own teaching but does not know how to achieve this end. It is this shared goal that brings the two strangers together.

As mentioned in the introduction, the research design is a multiple-angle one. The study can be viewed from the perspectives of the teacher, the researcher, the teacher educator and the curriculum planner. This chapter selects only the perspective of the teacher and that of the researcher. Additionally, the students' perspectives are included as student interviews are built in the design of the study.

3.2 Research Methods

This is a qualitative study. Interviews, observations, journals and post-lesson conferences are employed to collect data. An additional source of data is the students' compositions.

Semi-structured interviews are conducted by the researcher on both the teacher and her students before and after the study to solicit their views on writing lessons and the use of narratives (for details of questions asked in pre- interviews and post-interviews, see Appendices 1 – 4). Each interview with the teacher lasts 30 minutes, and each interview with the student lasts 10 minutes. Altogether three students have been selected for both pre- and post- interviews based on their English standards: one high, one average and one low. There are both male and female students. The interviews are audiotaped.

Lesson observations are also conducted by the researcher. Four lessons have been observed during the research period. Each lesson is a double period comprising 70 minutes. The teacher's teaching methods, interaction with the class, students' responses, and the like are observed (for details of the observation plan, see Appendix E). Field notes are taken by the researcher.

The teacher is asked to keep a journal and record her reflections after each lesson. There are altogether four journals.

A post-lesson conference is held between the researcher and the teacher after each lesson observed. There are altogether four conferences, and each lasts 25 minutes.

The same instruments of interviews, lesson observations, journals and post-lesson conferences are used to verify how much has been achieved as stipulated in the research question – i.e., 'how can the English writing class be made more interesting and stimulating?'

4. PROCEDURES

4.1 The New Method

The structuralist view of language is still prevalent in the English teaching profession albeit the introduction of communicative approach to Hong Kong two decades ago. The traditional method of teaching writing in local primary schools as described previously poses problems for teachers and students. Students do not appear to find such classes very stimulating and enjoyable, and some conscientious teachers – sensing a lack of engagement on the part of their students – are keen to find ways in which to make L2 teaching relevant to them.

The method being tried out – an integrative-narrative method – draws on the communicative view of language. Using stories to teach children language is nothing innovative (Grainger, 1997; Grugeon et al., 1998; Howe & Johnson, 1992). Neither is the use of integrative skills such as integrating listening and speaking, reading and writing new. But a combination of both the integrative and the narrative methods is not often used in the teaching of L2 writing, especially when writing is integrated with listening and speaking, and not with its commonly perceived related skill – reading. In the writing class students are given a chance to practise not only their writing skill, but also their listening and speaking skills. Students' attention is explicitly drawn to the listening skill first, then to the speaking skill, and lastly to the writing skill. Students will not be able to complete the task in the absence of one of these skills.

The teaching and learning materials used in the writing class are stories rather than the prescribed textbook. The four stories selected are: Goldilocks, Peter Pan, Aladdin and The Emperor's New Clothes. Only an excerpt of three to four minutes' recording of each story is used in each lesson. Students are asked to listen to the stories recorded in the CD-ROMs only. They are not allowed to see the images on the computer screen. Their task is to listen to the excerpt of the story and then construct an ending to it.

English – the target language – is used by the teacher throughout the lesson. The students are also encouraged to use English throughout the lesson.

4.2 Procedures of a Lesson

The proposed procedures of the writing class are as follows: (1) the teacher plays to the class the story recorded by a native speaker of English, and there is no ending to the story; (2) the teacher discusses the story with the class and helps them to understand the gist of it; (3) the teacher brainstorms some possible endings of the story with the students orally; (4) the students write up individually the ending of the story with some new vocabulary and sentence structure provided; (5) the teacher invites some students to share their endings with the class.

The above procedures have been modified throughout the study. Starting from the second lesson, the students are asked to work in groups of four and write up the ending of the story together. In the third lesson, the groups are given the choice to draw some pictures in the story. Towards the end of these lessons, the groups take turns to present their endings to the whole class.

During the process of the lesson, the teacher plays a key role in helping students to understand the story through asking them questions, soliciting ideas from them, providing clues and explaining some vocabulary and expression, and the like. The teacher knows that getting the gist of the story through listening is a new challenge for her class. Knowing what the story is about is just the first step to the writing task. In the second stage of students constructing their own endings of the story, the teacher's role relaxes a little bit. Nevertheless, she still needs to walk around and attend to individual group's questions, mostly on how to express an idea in English and how to spell some words.

4.3 Background Information of the Participants

The participants of the study include both the teacher and the students. This is a Band one primary school[3] in the New Territories[4]. Like most primary schools in Hong Kong, this school adopts Chinese as the medium of instruction.

The teacher is a female teacher graduating from the Hong Kong Institute of Education[5] with Social Studies as her major subject. She has taught in this primary school for six years, but she started to teach English only two years ago. She admitted that she had not had any training in English language teaching. She is learning on the job. In addition to teaching full time, she is now attending a part-time Bachelor in Education course at a local university.

The class to be observed – 5A – is the top class in Primary 5. There are 38 students in the class. According to the teacher, most students of this school come from a lower socio-economic background, so they cannot get as much support pertaining to English learning from their parents as their middle-class counterparts in other districts.

The background information of the three students selected for interviews is as follows:

---

[3] Schools used to be categorised into five bands. Starting the academic year 2001 – 02, the number of categories of schools has been reduced to three, Band 1 being the top school, and Band 3 being the bottom.
[4] The suburban area.
[5] A teacher training college.

Table 1. Background Information of Student Interviewees

Student	Gender	Age	English standard	Family support for English learning
A	F	10	High	Some support from parents and brother
B	F	10	Average	Some support from mother and private tutor
C	M	10	Low	Some support from parents, uncles and cousins

5. RESULTS

The following aspects of the writing class were observed during the period of research: student participation, classroom interaction, classroom dynamics, the product (i.e., the composition produced), and language use. Findings are reached drawing on the data collected from the perspectives of the researcher, the teacher and the students.

5.1 Student Participation

Both the teacher and the researcher found that students had more participation in the later stage of the research than in the initial stage. In the post-observation conference with the researcher immediately after the third lesson observation on 15 October 2002, the teacher said to me,

> " I'm glad that this time I see more hands up, especially those weaker ones who seldom respond. In the previous two lessons it was always those few bright students who answered my questions. I hope next time even more students will put up their hands."

My observation affirms that the participation rate is even higher in the fourth lesson. Apart from responding to the teacher's questions, students' willingness to present their stories is another sign of increased participation. Student C confessed,

> "My English is poor. I dared not utter even one sentence in English in front of the whole class before. I was afraid folks would laugh at me. Now in these lessons all groups are asked to go out and present their endings of the story to the class. Since the group mates accompany me, I feel more comfortable to speak in English."

The teacher corroborates what Student C said. In fact, students are seldom given a chance to present what they have written in a traditional writing class.

5.2 Classroom Interaction

Comparatively speaking, the first lesson observed was much quieter than the other three. In the first lesson, the teacher did a lot of talking to prompt students to understand the gist of the story, for instance, through asking comprehension questions, encouraging students to infer the meaning of words, explaining the meaning of words and expressions, helping students to find out the sequence of events. There was some interaction between the teacher and those few students who answered the questions. However, there was practically none between students.

Starting from the second lesson, the interaction pattern began to change. As the teacher modified some procedures and asked the class to work in groups rather than individually, interaction between students began to emerge. This change in turn ignited the interaction between the teacher and the class. That is why interaction in the classroom was improving during the course of research. All three students interviewed shared the same view that group discussion was the part that they enjoyed most because they could have a chance to create their own endings and draw pictures. This is indeed the component that is lacking in the traditional writing class. The teacher wrote in the journal of 15 October 2002 (the third lesson):

> "The response of the students this time is very good. They all participate in the group discussion. They enjoy discussing with their classmates. I did not realize until now that the element of interaction is so important in the English class ... I think both students and I enjoy this lesson tremendously."

5.3 Classroom Dynamics

The dynamic of the class depends on how the class is conducted, the participation of the students and interaction between the teacher and students. As mentioned in the previous two sections, the class was not as dynamic as it ought to be in the first lesson. The flow of the lesson was quite smooth. The teacher tried hard to solicit responses and engage students in the process of understanding the story and constructing the ending. However, the atmosphere of the class was not relaxed, and it took time for students to adapt to the new integrative-narrative method used in the writing class, which is much more demanding than the traditional method of asking students to answer several questions and write down the answers. Students' participation in class discussion was confined to several bright students only.

The second lesson started off with some technical problem – the computer broke down. The class resumed after ten minutes. It took the teacher some time to gather momentum. Luckily the change of strategy – i.e., replacing individual work by group work in the writing part – ignited more student participation and interaction, which contributed to the building up of a more relaxed atmosphere and a better classroom dynamic.

The atmosphere in the class became more and more lively in the third and fourth lessons. Students were relaxed as they were more familiar with the new integrative-narrative method, and thus much more eager to participate and contribute ideas about the stories. At certain points they became rather excited and noisy, and the teacher had to stop them from making too much noise.

5.4 Products

Although some students may have heard some stories such as 'Aladdin' and 'The Emperor's New Clothes' in Chinese, they were encouraged to use their imagination and create their own endings of the story. For each story, different endings were produced by different students or groups of students (students were asked to do

Story 1 individually and Stories 2 - 4 in groups of four). The quality of content varies, some being rich and imaginative while others being average and commonplace (for samples of composition, see Appendix F). On the whole stories created by groups are more interesting than those created by individual students. The laughter of the class in the sharing session suggests that students enjoyed the stories. All three students interviewed agreed that working in groups had more fun than working individually. They could get mutual support and inspiration from the peers in-group work. They also enjoyed listening to stories and writing their own endings. It was the freedom to exercise their creativity that they loved most.

The endings to Stories 3 and 4 are on the whole more creative because students were allowed to supplement their stories with drawing. Some groups produced very beautiful and colorful drawing (see Appendix F). Both Student B and Student C said that they loved drawing and drawing could help them to express their ideas. They could not imagine before that drawing could become a component in the writing class.

Nonetheless, if we judge the products from the point of view of language, it is far from satisfactory. They are full of grammatical and spelling errors (see Appendix F). Grammatical errors like tenses, subject-verb agreement, pronouns, sentence structure, and the like are not uncommon. There is little sign of progress in this aspect throughout the entire period of study.

5.5 Language Use in Class

The teacher conducted the writing class in the target language throughout all four lessons observed. She occasionally used a few Chinese words or sentences when students did not understand. She always encouraged students to speak in English, and managed to make students answer her questions in English. However, when students split into groups and discussed their endings of the story, most of them automatically switched back to Chinese.

6. DISCUSSION

The findings in the previous section indicate that there are changes pertaining to classroom dynamics, student participation and interaction between the teacher and students in the process of the study. Such changes are due to three possible contributing factors: the teaching method, strategies and techniques.

The integrative-narrative teaching method employed in this writing class – i.e., use of narratives and integration of listening, speaking and writing skills – is new. According to the students interviewed, their English teachers in Primary 1 to 4 used the traditional methods as described in Section 2.1 in teaching writing. That is why they find this writing class particularly interesting and enjoyable. The approach – i.e., assumptions and beliefs about language and language learning (Richards and Rodgers, 2001) – and theories underpinning such methods are those of Communicative Language Learning. Language is a system for the expression of meaning, and using language which is meaningful to the learner promotes learning (Brown, 2001;

Littlewood, 1981; Widdowson, 1978). Stories embed meanings, so students are readily encouraged to use the language in the process of decoding the meaning of the story and reconstructing it.

Along side the narrative method, "integration of skills backed up by meaningful experience is essential to second language learner" (Lo, 1992: 34). Students said in the pre-interviews that the writing class that they had before was boring because they were asked to write only. The integrative method allowed them more chance to hear and speak the target language. "That explains why the students are more engaged in my writing class now," said the teacher in the post-interview.

One may of course argue that the effective intervention may not be so much 'using narratives and the integrative skills' as it is 'simply allowing children to cooperate, interact and discuss'. The latter pertains to general teaching methods whereas the former is subject-specific. 'Cooperation', 'interaction' and 'discussion' should not be dealt with in vacuum, but rather in the context of teaching a specific subject, which is English Language Teaching in our case. As mentioned above, 'using narratives' and 'using integrative skills' are informed by theories of Communicative Language Teaching, which by default incorporates the concepts of cooperation, interaction and discussion. The findings of the study indicate that there is increased student participation, classroom interaction and thus classroom dynamics. It is the story that motivates students, particularly young children of this age cohort, and provides a context for them to practise their listening, speaking and writing skills. It is the use of both narratives and integrative skills that permit cooperation, interaction and discussion in the classroom.

The changing strategies used by the teacher are another contributing factor. Flexibility in adjusting the research methods or processes of the research is a merit of action research (Kemmis and McTaggart, 1988). In each of the post-lesson conferences the teacher reflected on the strategies used in the lesson with the support of the researcher. It was found that asking students to construct the ending of the story individually as originally planned was not effective in terms of student participation and interaction, so the teacher changed her strategy and used group work in the second lesson. After more reflections, the teacher decided to add one new element to the third lesson – drawing – to give students more room for creativity. It is this constant search for suitable strategies that contributes to the improving dynamics in class.

Good teaching techniques are a further contributing factor. The teacher has very good solicitation skills. She was able to guide students to get the gist of the story after listening to it twice. When students had difficulty in understanding it, the teacher would modify her questions or give more hints in order that students could get the answer. Through such skills student participation and interaction could be maintained, and thus classroom dynamics could be enhanced.

The fact that the teacher keeps changing her teaching strategies and techniques indicates that she is conscious of the role that the teacher should play in this writing class. As mentioned previously, listening and speaking skills are not emphasized in the traditional English classroom in Hong Kong primary schools. Neither is the writing skill taught integratively with the listening and speaking skills in the writing class. Students find it very difficult to understand the story through listening. So the teacher needs to play an active role in providing students with sufficient scaffolding and support (Grabe and Kaplan, 1996; Ormrod, 2003), especially to weaker and more passive students, and in involving as many students as possible in the entire process. Very often the teacher needs to give specific instructions to influence the way in which students learn from the lessons, for example, asking students to guess the meaning of words from the context in order to get the gist of the story.

Having explored some possible factors that contribute to the changes pertaining to classroom dynamics, student participation and interaction, I will now examine the significance of such changes. From what the teacher and the three students express in the pre-interviews, the writing class taught in the traditional way is boring. Except some bright students who are intrinsically motivated (such as Student A), average students (such as Student B) would not like the writing lesson in particular, and the English lesson in general. Below average students (such as Student C) would even hate it. Poor teaching methods would demotivate learners. Motivation is, in fact, the most crucial factor in learning (Maehr & Meyer, 1997). Successful second language acquisition depends on whether teachers can stimulate students' intrinsic motivation (Brown, 2001; Dornyei & Csizer, 1998). In the context of teaching writing, "the first processing step would be to activate goal setting for writing", and using stories is "a situation-initiated activity" (Grabe & Kaplan, 1996: 230). The attitudes of three students interviewed have undergone some changes. In the post-interview Student A said that she likes English even more than before. Student B said that she begins to like the English writing class. Student C, who was reluctant to be interviewed before the study started, said that he did not realize the English writing class could be fun. Moreover, the changing classroom dynamics, student participation and interaction depicted in the present study suggest that students have already been motivated in learning writing specifically, and English language learning generally.

In addition to classroom dynamics, the findings about the products are equally important. It is found that students produce different endings to the same story. Heterogeneity of the content suggests that students really 'think' when they write, unlike their practice in the past. In the traditional writing class, they were provided with a model passage and asked to do parallel writing, which requires merely some changes in vocabulary and pronouns. The old products are naturally standard and banal. By contrast, the new products are *different*. The quality of some may be commonplace, but at least they vary in content. The quality of others is, nevertheless, rich and imaginative. The rich content is primarily due to the narrative method, which can easily arouse students' interest and free their imagination. I talked to the whole class for a short while immediately after the fourth lesson. I asked them what they liked most in the entire lesson. Their response was unanimous: "Freedom and creativity!" This corroborates the answers of the three students in the post-interviews. Student A said, "I really feel free to express myself when we write the story." Student B said, "I love drawing very much. I'm glad I have a chance to exercise my creativity." Student C said, "If I were given a choice, of course I would opt for this kind of method. I have never felt so free before."

Along side all the positive findings reported above, there is, however, something that remains unchanged throughout the study. That is, language proficiency of the students. It is found that the language produced by the students is far from satisfactory. The stories are full of grammatical and spelling errors. As mentioned previously, given the time constraint, the nature and the scope of the study, the aim of the study is to find out how the English writing class can be made more interesting and stimulating in the primary school. Arousing students' interest in English learning is the first and foremost task. Hence, the measurement of English proficiency is not built in the research design.

A further finding that the students automatically switch back to Chinese when they discuss their stories reveals that the students do not have sufficient proficiency in speaking and writing. This is, in fact, a fundamental problem in English language teaching in Hong Kong schools, especially in the primary sector – i.e., not paying sufficient attention to listening and speaking, and learning English in the same way as learning Chinese (Poon, 2001). That is why literacy scaffolding is needed especially for young learners, such as vocabulary, language structures and discourse routines, which "should be incorporated gradually into ongoing student interactions while they are writing, and thus become part of their own active writing over time" (Grabe and Kaplan, 1996: 274). Of course, Grabe and Kaplan also argue that attention to form should be paid at the later stages in writing (Grabe & Kaplan, 1996: 267). In a way insufficient language skills do not necessarily stop students from creating their stories despite many errors, as evident in the 'compositions' produced by the students. After all, the research question addressed by the present study is: how can the English writing class be made more interesting and stimulating?

To sum up, the findings suggest that the use of integrative-narrative method in teaching writing is effective in this Primary 5 class, albeit the undesirable language output.

7. LIMITATIONS

The limitations of the present study are three-fold. First, the focus is more on the content of writing than on the language aspect. After motivating students, what is the next step in helping them to acquire the writing skills? Second, only the listening, speaking and writing skills are emphasized. Reading should also have a role to play in the acquisition of writing. Third, narrative is only one genre of writing. How can primary students be motivated to write other genres?

8. SUGGESTIONS FOR FURTHER RESEARCH

The following are suggestions for further research:
1) The study can be replicated at different levels (e.g., Primary 4 and 6, and even Secondary 1) in different types of school (e.g., lower band schools)
2) More focus should be put on the language aspect in writing.
3) Reading should be incorporated as a component in the teaching of writing.

9. CONCLUSION

I have reported an action research conducted in a Primary 5 English writing class in Hong Kong. This study addresses some fundamental problems in teaching writing at the primary level in Hong Kong specifically, and in ELT in Hong Kong in general. Sticking to the textbook and treating the writing skill independently from other skills render the writing class boring, and limit the minds of the students. An alternative method of using narratives and integrating listening and speaking skills in the writing class has been tried out and proved to be effective. The advantages of using this method are fourfold. First, stories can easily arouse students' interest and thus remove their psychological block to a second language. Second, constructing the ending to a story can free students' imagination. Third, integrating various skills enhances interaction in the classroom. Fourth, writing stories encourages rich content and expressions.

The new method of teaching writing proposed in this study is in line with the current curriculum reform in Hong Kong since creativity and greater use of literary/imaginative texts in English language learning are the major themes highlighted in the new English curriculum (Curriculum Development Council, 2001).

ACKNOWLEDGEMENTS

I would like to express my heartfelt thanks to the participants of this study, and particularly the teacher, without whose support the study would not have been possible.

APPENDICES

APPENDIX A: PRE-INTERVIEW WITH THE TEACHER

How do you usually teach writing?
Is this the standard approach adopted by other English teachers in your school?
Is writing taught as a separate skill in the English curriculum of your school?
What do you think of the idea of using narratives to teach writing in primary school?
What made you agree to participate in this study?
What outcome do you anticipate upon completion of the study?
What is your view of ELT?

APPENDIX B: PRE-INTERVIEWS WITH THE STUDENTS

Do you get support from the family regarding English learning?
Do you like the English subject?
How was writing taught last year?
How was English taught last year?
How was writing taught in P.1-3?
Do you like stories? Do you want to learn writing through stories?

Do you think writing should be learnt through listening, speaking and writing? Do you think you can learn English through English only? Do you think there will be any difficulty?

APPENDIX C: POST-INTERVIEW WITH THE TEACHER

What do you think is the outcome of this study?
Do you think you have achieved what you anticipated in the pre-interview?
What problems/difficulties did you encounter throughout the study?
Is the use of narratives feasible in your class? How about applying it to other classes? What are the greatest advantages of this approach?
Is the use of integrative method feasible in your class? How about applying it to other classes? What are the greatest advantages of this method?
Will you recommend the narrative method to other colleagues?
Will you recommend the integrative method to other colleagues?
Have you changed (or modified) your view of ELT?

APPENDIX D: POST-INTERVIEWS WITH THE STUDENTS

Did you enjoy the writing class? Why?
How do you compare the writing class like this with what you had before? Which one do you like best?
What do you think of the use of stories to learn English?
What do you think of using listening, speaking and writing to learn writing? Is it more effective than having writing only in the class?
What problems/difficulties did you encounter in this writing class?
Would you like to shift back to the writing only method?
Are you now more interested in English learning?

APPENDIX E: OBSERVATION PLAN

The teacher able to help students to comprehend the story? Questioning techniques? Solicitation skills? Provision of vocabulary and sentence patterns?
The teacher able to solicit ideas from students about the ending of the story? Responding to student initiatives? Stretching students' imagination? Helping students to express in English?
The teacher able to arouse students' interest in the lesson? Motivation skills?
Teaching methods? Communicative? Integrative? Innovative? Inductive or deductive? Able to strike a balance between accuracy and fluency?
The teacher's ability to communicate?
Students' response? Willing to participate? Interested? English proficiency? Confidence in using English?
Interaction? Between the teacher and class? Between the teacher and students? Between students?
8.Students' written work? Interesting? Imaginative? Accurate?

APPENDIX F: SAMPLES OF COMPOSITION

Then the two tailors went out and bought some cloth and thread, but they forgot to bought the thread, so, they used the gold to ~~make~~ the thread. The emperor knew this and fell this is very luxury, and kill them.

Then, three mosters are ~~go~~ come in ~~out~~, they see Goldilocks is eating their porridge. So, they are very angry, they want to kill Goldilocks. This, a dog come to the house and help her. His name Billy, he is a good time dog, he is very kind to other. Billy take Goldilocks ~~go~~ home and say "good bye". three mosters want to kill Goldilocks, but have Billy, they can't kill her.

Goldilocks ~~is~~ was very hot. Suddenly, the cloud cover the sun. Goldilocks ~~is~~ was not hot. She continued to walk, ~~so~~ she ~~saw~~ saw a helicopt She can fly back to home.

There had many treause. He wanted a lamp. But he knew this is a trap. So he went out. suddenly, a beautiful girl ran out. But the girl is the monster. She kill him.

LO Tsz-yan (Kitty) P.M.5A (26)

She eat the ~~medium~~ porridge in the medium bowl. She felt very bad. She eat the porridge in the small bowl. She felt very good. ~~She eat all the por~~ porridge in the ~~small~~ small bowl.

~~B~~ Goldilocks ~~felt~~ want to sit down on the chair, ~~&~~ she sit on the great big chair, she ~~felt~~ felt ~~hard~~ hard. She on the medium, ~~&~~ she felt very soft. She sit on the small chair, she felt very ~~softly~~. But ~~&~~ she is heavy, the small ~~chair~~ chair ~~is~~ was ~~&~~ broken.

~~Sh~~ Goldilocks felt very tired. She go in to the bedroom. There are three bed. She sleep on the small bed.

Then they saw a very beautiful gril in the beautiful garden. And her pet a bird took a lamp from the garden.

then, Peter Tam was very happy, Beacuse his shadow can stay with him forever. Then, Peter Tam will go to Wendy's home and stay with them. Two days later, Wendy's parents go home. They stay forever!

And then

Amy, Winnie
Andy

The king very happy when he saw the clothes. Suddenly, he was flew in the sky. Then the other people were died, because they were so afraid Then the king in the sky for a long time, so he was died. Then the country was disappear.

Kittu, Vivian, Winnie, Aron

TEACHING HOW TO WRITE ARGUMENTATIVE TEXTS AT PRIMARY SCHOOL

MILAGROS GÁRATE & ANGELES MELERO

University of Cantabria, Spain

Abstract. This chapter describes a classroom intervention working with 16 pupils in 5th grade Primary Education (11 year olds). The objective was to ascertain whether written argumentative abilities could actually be improved through teaching, to investigate what this improvement consisted of and to analyse the relationship between production and comprehension of this type of text. Two classes were involved: one was the experimental class and the other, of the same educational level and from the same school, served as the control class. The pedagogic intervention was carried out over several one-hour sessions. Different procedures were used: direct instruction, modelling, participative learning and microinstruction, basically. The pupils were also given a series of six help-cards, which showed them the steps they had to take as they progressed towards autonomous text writing. Both a pre-test and a post-test were carried out, and these included a test of text production and another of comprehension, both based on an argumentative text. Statistical analyses relating to the production test reveal a significant difference between the experimental class and the control class in the post-test, and also between the pre-test and the post-test of the experimental class. From a qualitative point of view, the principal achievement of this group was the construction of counterarguments, which were totally lacking in the control group. However, although the results concerning the relationship between production and comprehension were significant, they are not so clear. Some of the implications of these results are looked at in greater detail in the discussion.

Keywords: Argumentative writing, writing teaching, primary school, argument and counterargument, argumentative scheme.

1. INTRODUCTION: THE IMPORTANCE OF ARGUMENTATION IN PRIMARY EDUCATION

Despite there being a considerable amount of educational research in which writing is regarded as a tool for the development of thought and for in-depth learning in curricular domains (Boscolo & Mason, 2001; Rijlaarsdam, Van den Bergh & Couzijn,

---

Gárate, M., & Melero, A. (2004). Teaching how to write argumentative texts at primary school.
In G. Rijlaarsdam (Series Ed.) & Rijlaarsdam, G., Van den Bergh, H. & Couzijn, M. (Vol. Eds.), Studies in writing. Vol. 14, Effective learning and teaching of writing, 2nd Edition, Part 2, Studies in how to teach writing, 323-337.

1996; Sheridan, 1995; Tolchinsky & Simó, 2001), it is our opinion that the same amount of attention has not been given to the teaching of writing in itself, especially argumentative writing, in Primary School education. Sometimes it is rather naively and optimistically assumed that as a result of pupils being taught a limited number of genres, they will then be able to produce any kind of text whenever they so require.

We believe that there are indeed many reasons to support the petition calling for the teaching of oral and written argumentation to be considered a teaching goal in Primary School education. As Camps (1995), Cotteron (1995) and Dolz (1995) have indicated, children, the same as adolescents and adults, are embedded in a persuasion oriented society where an attempt to influence their opinions and beliefs is made via the many different oral and written mass media messages. In a subtle way the child is exposed to a kind of message in which demonstration, explanation and argumentation are being replaced by reiteration (Ramonet, 1995). These points, among others, together with the virtual absence of objectives aimed at developing argumentative abilities at Primary School level, have led us to investigate the possibility of improving these aspects in Primary Education 5° graders.

We wish to make a brief reference to research work that has been carried out in Primary and Secondary Education classrooms, where there has been a planned teaching of argumentation (Camps, Dolz, Cotteron). All of these research studies share common aspects such as the following: the efficacy of this kind of intervention in the classroom setting; the possibility of working with and developing argumentation from the very first school years as long as the proposed tasks conform to the pupils' abilities; the need for the subject content to stem from polemic situations, controversies or conflicts of interests which are recognizable for the pupils and the convenience of working on reading and writing at the same time.

It is our firm belief that learning to present arguments is difficult but that it helps to build up complex linguistic and cognitive abilities and leads to pupils' having more tolerant attitudes, thereby giving citizens a more enlightened moral code.

2. THE NATURE OF WRITTEN ARGUMENTATION AND DEVELOPMENTAL ACQUISITION

Argumentative texts present a number of specific characteristics which, as a whole, means that it takes longer for their developmental acquisition to come about than for other kinds of texts and also that there are very few pupils who are able to come to terms with all the requirements demanded by these particular texts (Coirier, Andriessen & Chanquoy, 1999). These characteristics are as much cognitive as linguistic, although both kinds can, at least in some cases, be interrelated or interdependent. Some of these characteristics are:

- The audience acquires greater presence and gains importance: in the case of argumentative texts it is not a question of "only" looking on the audience as a receiver, but rather that the audience itself has to have a stronger presence than for other types of texts in order for the objective to be achieved: convincing them.

- Despite the fact that the prototypical argumentation is oral debate (Cuenca, 1995), a complete argumentative text is much less similar to oral work than other types of texts, such as narrative, which rely heavily on the same formal structure as oral dialogues[1]. Children from a very early age understand the scheme of conversation as a succession of taking turns to talk (Bereiter & Scardamalia, 1987), but this scheme has to be reconstructed in written argumentation so that it will become autonomous rather than interactive. In contrast, the spontaneous developmental trend is simply to transfer oral language to written language (Brassart, 1995).
- This very transfer of the fluid chain of thought to the "frozen" structure of written language and the fitting into each other of both processes means that argumentation has additional difficulties, since planning has now become threefold: planning one's own ideas, planning the other's, and a logical linking framework for both sides.

Synthesizing, it can be stated that, from a cognitive perspective, written argumentation implies:

- a logical activity, one of reasoning (Voss, Wiley & Sandak, 1999)[2],
- a social perspective-taking which will allow the emissor to represent the receptor without the latter being present and to be in his/her place, and
- a dialogue activity (Camps, 1995), since in argumentation it is not merely a question of defending a thesis, but also, and at the same time, refuting that of the other person (Adam, 1995). This means that there has to be a simultaneous intellectual coordination of both movements that should result in an articulation between arguments and counterarguments. That is to say, with argumentative texts it is necessary to coordinate the mental representations of one's own opinion and the representations of the opinions that the author attributes to the audience.

Parallel to this, what has to be taken into account is the fact that each one of those cognitive operations has a linguistic correlate that is also difficult to acquire, and which functions on a syntactic, semantic and pragmatic level, both at local level (sentence or paragraph) and overall (the whole text). See for a detailed description Cuenca (1995).

There have been numerous occasions when research has focused upon determining the age at which children clearly possess an argumentative scheme that is capable of controlling the production of his/her texts. The results reveal serious discrepancies which are due, amongst other things, to a lack of agreement between the researchers over the operationalization and definition of the argumentative scheme, and on account of the different character and difficulty of the experimental tasks

---

[1] *In this respect, Campos & Dolz (1995: 6) state that "although narration can be seem to have an argumentative orientation, in this type of text [narratives] the arguing is done indirectly without, in general, the author explicitly taking responsibility for the opinion s/he is defending".*

[2] *Argumentation has been related with the notion of demonstration and also with logical structures of formal and informal reasoning (Cuenca, 1995).*

used in the research studies (Piolat, Roussey & Gombert, 1999). Some researchers set the age of the appearance of this ability in an oral format at three years old (Stein & Bernas, 1999).

Basing our opinion on the work by Toulmin (1958), Adam (1995), Brassart (1995) and Piolat et al. (1999), what we want to emphasize here is that the requirements as regards the criteria for determining whether a text can be considered argumentative varies. The minimum criterion would be the existence of arguments in favor of or against an opinion (Toulmin). This minimum criterion would be followed by others that are more demanding such as the sequential linking of arguments that leads to a conclusion, since natural argumentative texts are rarely limited to being supported by one sole point, such as the convergence of arguments and counterarguments towards a conclusion, and the coordinated and integrated handling of opposite points of view (Adam 1995; Brassart, 1995, 1989). The coalescence of all these elements in one comprehensively coherent written text would give rise to an EAT (elaborated argumentative text) (Piolat, Roussey & Gombert, 1999). Our research has led us to consider that it is EAT, with our Adam's model (1992) being the one we fit into. It is not surprising that the chronological discrepancy in argumentative abilities that appear in the existing research, and which we will look at now, reflect the varying concepts of the argumentative scheme on which the research is based. In the review by Piolat et al. (1999) on the age at which children are capable of coordinating a complete argumentative scheme, the following data are offered. Akiguet (1997) and Akiguet et al. (1996) found that at the age of 10 children are capable of using an argumentative scheme. At 11, thanks to a better knowledge of how connectors work, their texts improve in overall coherence.

Brassart (1989) finds differences in the age depending on the type of task set. With open tasks children 9–10 years old are capable of justifying their positions (a minimum condition for argumentation), but until they reach the age of 11 to 12 they are not capable of writing coherent argumentative texts in tasks that correspond to the alpha-omega pattern. Finally, Schneuwly et al. (1989), Coirier and Golder (1993) and Feilke (1996) conclude from their research studies that it is necessary to wait until the age of 13 to 14 years in order for the pupils to be able to adapt their writing to the complete argumentative scheme.

The second source of discrepancy concerning the age at which a pupil controls the argumentative scheme is, as we have already indicated, to be found in the characteristics of the task (how open the task is, instructions, familiarity with the subject...). The tasks used here have been extremely varied, ranging from closed to quite open. Our research has taken a different direction: we chose an ecological situation, a real classroom, and offered a very open, yet no less complex, task: our pupil subjects had to construct a complete argumentative text, for which they were given only the subject matter and the audience. To compensate for this complexity, we gave the pupils an important piece of help: a series of cards which, as a whole, represent the external argumentative scheme, and which are directed more towards conceptualization processes rather than those of textualisation. These latter were dealt with using the modeling technique carried out by an expert, thereby making, from a Vygotskian perspective, the passage from the interpsychological to the intrapsychological easier.

3. AIMS OF THE INTERVENTION

These were the goals we set ourselves:

A) During the writing process:
1. To improve the writing of argumentative texts by means of teaching planning.
1.1. Learn to support one's own opinions with arguments.
1.2. Look at the question from the audience's point of view and anticipate their ideas and opinions on the subject.
1.3. Produce arguments bearing in mind the opinions of the audience.

2. To produce the argumentative written text from the planning notes.
2.1. Learn to organize and articulate different arguments present in the planning.
2.2. Learn to introduce the audience's ideas into one's own written text so as to be able to counteract them with one's own arguments (counterarguments).
2.3 Learn to use linguistic resources in order to make the connection between different arguments and these arguments and the conclusion possible.

B) After the writing of the text
3. To revise and possible rewrite the text.
3.1. Think about and be aware of the arguments used in the writing.
3.2. Think about and be aware of the ideas that correspond to the person who has written the text and those which correspond to the audience.
3.3. See if the arguments used can be improved.
3.4. See if further arguments can be added.
3.5. See if all the arguments to appear in the planning have been used.

C) Study the effects that an intervention of these characteristics has upon reading comprehension.

4. METHOD

The intervention was carried out in a full 5th grade class at a state school in a Spanish city. The other 5th grade class at the same school served as the control group. The experimental class was made up of 16 boys and girls aged 11. The control class had another 16 boys and girls of the same age and, as we have already said, from the same school[3].

The independent variable was the intervention both in the planning and in the writing of argumentative texts. The dependent variable was the quantity and quality of the arguments used and their articulation within the produced text. Comprehension of an argumentative text was also measured.

---

[3] *It is frequent to find fewer than 20 children per class in the Primary levels in Spanish state schools, at least in our city (Santander).*

4.1 Experimental Design

A pretest–posttest design was used. There were two pre-test measurements, one for writing and the other for reading. For the first the children in both groups were asked to produce a written text asking the Environmental Officer on the local Council to supply every street with a paper bank, a bottle bank and a used battery drop-off point. They were encouraged to think first about what they wanted to say and to make notes on these points on their note-sheets before actually starting to write. What they wrote in their text had to based on the notes they had previously made.

The second pre-test assessment involved reading a text that we had prepared specifically for the purposes of our research, and answering a questionnaire that measured the pupils' understanding of it. (See appendix). No differences in the comprehension and writing of argumentative texts were to be found between the experimental class and the control class in either of the pre-test assessments.

4.2 The Intervention

Twice a week for a period of four weeks we carried out our intervention in the planning and writing of argumentative texts in the experimental class focusing on the following subjects: healthy eating, men's work around the house, keeping the streets clean, aid for the Third World, the advantages of having a longer school morning but no classes in the afternoon, and the need for leisure centers in suburban districts. The methodology used in the teaching was varied: direct instruction, modeling and participative learning were all used. Other activities and procedures, such as how to differentiate between descriptive and argumentative texts, group writing and micro-instruction were also brought into play. We will now give a description, albeit brief, of the procedure that was followed so as to allow readers to better appreciate what the intervention involved.

A. *Direct instruction.* This activity consisted in explaining the different stages of a planning process. The instruction at each stage was supported by six "help cards" on which the planning would be based and the efficacy of which had been tested out in previous research studies (Gárate & Melero, 2000). The cards were the following:
1) Think and write down the ideas you have on this subject, and above all what you know about this subject.
2) Think and write what you want to achieve with this written text.
3) What ideas do you think those who read this written text have on the subject?
4) Taking into account the ideas they have, what would you say to convince them? Find reasons that support your ideas. The more you find, the better.
5) What is the most important idea that you want to get across?
6) How would you organise all these ideas in your written text? Where would you start? How would you finish?

This direct instruction (explanation of each one of the cards) only required the first day. Each pupil had a set of cards from the beginning of and for the entire duration of the intervention. Each card brought into play a kind of mental activity that we consider necessary in any planning process. As we have already indicated, these cards, as a whole, externalize the main steps in the writing of an argumentative text, especially those related with conceptualization processes.

B. *Modeling*. The planning process and the production of the argumentative text (textualisation) were modeled by means of thinking aloud. At the same time as the instructor made comments aloud following the instructions given on each card, she wrote the result on the blackboard in the form of short notes. Then the argumentative text itself was written upon another blackboard, where the step from planning notes to written text was made explicit.

The modeling technique was used primarily on the first day and was returned to specifically when the difficulty of the task set the children so required it. During the first day, therefore, the decision taken was that the production of the text was basically the instructor's responsibility and that the children would not take an active part so that they could pay closer attention to the process of converting thought into text.

C. *Participative learning*. From the second day on of the intervention, participative learning took over from modeling. In each session the children were presented with a subject of interest to them, with which they were familiar, and of psychological, and occasionally also moral, relevance. The planning linked to the help-cards was carried out by all the children, with the instructor acting as moderator. The instructor wrote up on the board in note form what the children told her to from the use of each card. The writing of the text from those notes was also carried out in the same fashion. Mention must be made here of the fact that this second process turned out to be rather complex and required more help from the instructor, with actual modeling being used in some cases. Each session produced a single text, which everyone had helped to elaborate, and which the instructor gradually wrote up on the board as a result of the pupils' interventions. Participative learning was used on a daily basis.

D. *Differentiating between descriptive and argumentative texts*. Our aim was to make the children become more aware of the meaning of argumentation and of the arguments they were actually using in their writing. For that reason, we decided to present them with a task oriented towards their acquiring the notion of argument, which, although not necessarily explicit, would help them to recognize arguments wherever they were and to use them in their own writing. As a result, the pupils were asked to analyze two different texts, one clearly descriptive, "the duck-billed platypus", and the other clearly argumentative "the time to go to bed". Their task was to establish as many differences as they could between the two texts.

We feel that the way in which this particular task was carried out is of interest. The children started by focusing on only the superficial differences and then little by little they started to establish deeper and more significant differences by themselves. For example:

> "One of them has got paragraphs and the other hasn't". "One of them is on one subject 'the duck-billed platypus' and the other is on another 'the time to go to bed'" "One is directed at children, it's like a newspaper article, and the other is the description of an

animal". "One is directed at children to convince them of something and the other is a description".

When asked which of the two was more similar to the texts we were working on in the intervention, they answered unhesitatingly "the time to go to bed". They then immediately began to pick out one by one all the arguments that existed in the text, with pupils highlighting those arguments which they considered the most convincing and the best elaborated, and giving reasons for their choice.

When this session drew to an end, the children dared to define what arguing is and to point out a series of clues to identify an argumentative text.

> "Arguing is giving reasons in order to convince", "it is giving a big explanation so that someone realises something important", "an argumentative text is one in which lots of reasons are given", "in an argumentative text it is not enough to say you are for or against something, you have to say why".

E. *Group writing.* In this session a written text on aid for the Third World was planned, following the usual procedure of all the pupils participating with the help of the cards. What was new here was the fact that each child was given a note sheet so that s/he could write down on it the results of the joint planning just as the instructor was doing on the blackboard. Also new was the fact that the text was not to be written by the group as a whole with the help of the instructor and on the board (only notes were written here), but instead four groups were formed and each one of them was asked to write a text from the notes taken collectively.

Several things in this session are of note. Firstly, the quality of the planning lessened. The children, instead of writing down in their own words on the note sheets the result of the joint planning, merely spent their time copying the notes that had been written on the board by the instructor. We believe that, because the intervention took place in a classroom, there was transference of the "routines" that so often accompany schoolwork. The children forgot to some extent the order that had been given and did nothing more than to copy out what the instructor had written up on the board (the notes based on the ideas that the boys and girls had put forward).

Regards the question of group writing, it is important to make clear here that, overall, it was a somewhat difficult task for the children. Once their main idea had been brought out, as suggested by help card nº 2 "Write what you intend to achieve with this written text", it then became very difficult for them to coordinate amongst themselves and to turn the notes they had taken into a written text. The constructed texts were characterized by the following:

- The use of arguments that revealed little inter-coordination.
- A lack of lineal coherence between either the arguments or clauses used, e.g., "they haven't got education or food or where to live and that poor people here can find a job".
- A lack of overall coherence between the clauses, usually the non-argumentative ones, and the aim of the written text, e.g., "people think that they could also develop, but they haven't developed".
- Unsuccessful attempts to construct counterarguments, e.g., "we know that you think that those countries could have recovered sooner and they haven't taken advantage of this".

Some of the paragraphs in which the above inaccuracies pointed out by us appeared and some others were subsequently used by us as material to work on and improve and, wherever necessary, to rewrite (that is to say, revise) in the two following sessions and which we have called "microinstruction".

F. *Microinstruction*. This stage of the intervention was carried out in two sessions that were shorter than any of the others. Five paragraphs were chosen to serve as a kind of sample of those characteristics in the children's writing that we wished to improve upon via our intervention and which we had already noticed in the pre-test.

1) They construct a paragraph by placing together two clauses (one usually argumentative and the other not) that have nothing to do with each other.

   "If we were in their shoes we'd like to be helped, there are also poor people here and in other countries".

2) They attempt to construct an argument by repeating their opinion more emphatically, giving rise to some kind of tautology:

   "We should help because we have to".

3) They move off the point or even forget what their written work should be focusing on. We believe that the process of seeking arguments in their long-term memory means that the discovery of one idea leads them to another or others that have little, if anything at all, to do with the objective of their piece of writing. The result of this is an overall loss of coherence in the text. This form of behaviour corresponds, we believe, with the model described as "Knowledge Telling" (Bereiter & Scardamalia, 1987; Van Wijk, 1999).

4) There is an unsuccessful attempt to construct a counterargument. At this point we believe it is important to highlight the absence of counterarguments in what the children wrote in the pre-test and in those texts that were the result of group work. It is for this reason that the paragraphs used in those microinstruction sessions were those from their written texts which incorporated audience opinion (readers of a local newspaper), in order to "model" the counter argumentation. E.g.:

   "People think that they could also develop, but they haven't developed", and "I know that you think those countries could have recovered sooner and they haven't taken advantage of this".

Furthermore, when improving these paragraphs, emphasis was placed upon the usage of those connectors and linkers that favor the use of counter argumentation. We believe this to be a way to work in the Vygotskian "zone of proximal development": the instructor takes those ideas of the children that refer to an audience opinion and reproduces them at a higher level of complexity (Newman, Griffin & Cole, 1989). Those audience ideas become part of the counter argumentation thanks to the instructor's help. In this way the child is helped to gradually take as his /her own this procedure which is more complex than his/her own, producing "execution before competence" (Cazden, 1988), or with the function changing from interpsychological to intrapsychological.

4.3 Post-Test Tasks and Correction Criteria

Three days after the intervention had ended the post-test assessment was carried out on both the experimental class and the control class. The children were asked to do the following:

> "Write a text defending your own point of view on whether you are for or against animals being held in captivity. You must try to convince those who do not agree with you, making use of the greatest number of reasons or arguments that occur to you. Your piece of written work should be in the form of a letter sent to a newspaper in your town, so that any citizen can read it".

They were also asked to plan their work and for the results of this planning to appear on the note sheet. To measure the pupils' comprehension the same text as was used in the pre-test was once again used, and comprehension was assessed by means of a questionnaire (See appendix A).

A) In the argumentative text writing
- Presence of objective (0-1).
- Presence of audience (0-1).
- Presence of argumentative scheme (0-5).
- Presence and quality of arguments (3 for each one).
- Presence of counterarguments (5 for each one).
- Organization and structuring of the text:
    - Straying from the subject under discussion (penalization: ranging from -1 to -5).
    - Listing of arguments (penalization: ranging from -1 to -3).
    - Overall coherence evaluation (0-5).

As can be seen, this last criterion is expressed via three specific subcriteria. Straying from the subject and the mere listing of arguments means penalization in the overall mark. As regards overall coherence, we understand that this occurs when there is coordination between the different arguments used and that these are oriented towards the conclusion, thereby producing the close of the argumentative scheme. We consider that the resulting overall coherence should, above all, be semantic. Nevertheless, we do assess positively the presence of inter-clause connectors (both argumentative and non-argumentative) and also those intra-clause connectors at the service of well-elaborated arguments. In short, we believe that the appropriate chain of arguments that leads to the conclusion is one of the signs of the writer having and using an argumentative scheme, and that a supported opinion is not by itself sufficient. It is for this reason that considerable weighting is given to the chain process in the correction.

B) In the argumentative text comprehension
- Recognition of the author of the text by means of a process of inference (0-1).
- Recognition of the audience (0-1).
- Recognition of the objective that the author-writer is pursuing (0-2).

ARGUMENTATIVE WRITING IN PRIMARY SCHOOL

- Identification and construction of the main idea in own words (0-2).
- Differentiation between the author's arguments and those that the latter attributes to third persons (0-6).

The correcting was undertaken by two judges, who coincided in their awarding of marks in 80% of the cases on a first reading and then later, after some rechecking and revising, agreed in 100% of the cases.

5. RESULTS

5.1 Argumentative Text Production

We observed a double result: 1) the comparison between the experimental group and the control group in the post-test; 2) the pretest–posttest comparison for the experimental group. Regarding the first, the Mann-Witney test revealed a significant difference in favor of the experimental group (Tied P-value: .022). With regard to the difference between the text produced by the pupils in the pre-test and the one they later produced in the post-test, the T-test revealed a significant difference (.012). In contrast, when the Wilcoxon test was given to the control group, there was no significant difference between the pre-test and the post-test for the control group (.45).

We feel that we can, therefore, say that the intervention in writing argumentative texts by means of training in planning, argument awareness, microinstruction and rewriting, resulted in an improvement in the argumentative text writing of the pupils in the experimental class.

These statistical results tell us nothing at all, however, about certain important characteristics of the texts produced by the experimental group's pupils. The principal qualitative difference (which was, of course, reflected in the quantitative marks that were awarded) is the inexistence of counterarguments in the control group's work, whereas they were present in that of the experimental class. Let us look at some examples:

> "You might say that they are properly fed in zoos but there are animals that need to get their own food".

> "I also think that you believe them to be better off in their natural habitat but in zoos the newly born can be given greater assistance, so the species will grow in number".

> "We know that you think that if there weren't zoos our city would lose tourists that pay to get in, but it's not about money".

There were even cases in which, possibly as a result of the child's focusing all his/her attention on bringing in the counter argumentation, the arguments supporting the child's own opinion only appear in the counterarguments. There were also other cases in which there were incomplete attempts at counter argumentation, which consisted in, for example, offering an explicit point of view and a particular argument from the audience, but this was then not refuted by one of his/her own:

> "I know you think that in the zoo they will be locked up in a cage for ever and that they will not be able to return to their families".

> "We know that some of you think that it is good [for them to be in captivity], because if they are loose they might kill somebody, but others of you will think that it is an injustice because they are not allowed to live in peace, although they are properly fed".

On other occasions the counter argumentation was introduced, but "weakly", in the sense that although the syntactic form was there, what was missing was the semantic content necessary to refute or weaken the audience point of view:

> "We know that you think that this does not harm them but it does".

In other cases the inference supporting the counter argumentation elaborated by the children is not made explicit: "We know that there are a lot of poachers, but animals need to be in their natural habitat too". We see that the child who wrote this does not make the inference given by her/him explicit because s/he does not write what appears in bold:

> "We know that there are a lot of poachers, *["from whose pursuit animals would be free if they were placed in zoos]*, but animals need to be in their natural habitat too".

5.2 Argumentative Text Comprehension Test

The difference between pre-test and post-test in the experimental group, calculated with the Wilcoxon test, reaches significance (.043). In contrast, when the same test was given to the control group there was no significant difference between the pre-test and the post-test.

6. DISCUSSION

In this report on the intervention that we have carried out what is evident is that it is possible to improve the writing of argumentative texts of children aged 10-11. At this age children are capable of producing complete argumentative texts by themselves once they have been shown how and with an autonomously used external argumentative scheme as support. In this way the results ratify those of other researchers such as Brassart and Veevaert (1992) and support the idea of researchers, such as Camps and Dolz (1995), that insist that the teaching of argumentation can be taught at Primary School level. We would like to mention some of the more important changes that took place as a result of the intervention.

Prior to the intervention the children were capable of supporting their opinions with arguments but were not able to integrate and coordinate argumentative and non-argumentative clauses in a coherent manner. Their arguments appeared "listed" with barely any articulation. At no moment did they include in their writing the opinions of the audience and we do not find, therefore, counter argumentation in any of the pre-tests. According to the work by Piolat, Roussey and Gombert (1999), the argumentative scheme that would control the writing of those pupil-subjects participating in our research would be close to the one by Toulmin (1958) since the children confined themselves to supporting their opinions with arguments. Similarly their argumentation schemes were not consistent with Adam's criterion (1992), because our subjects did not manage to integrate all the elements of their production so as to create one coherent comprehensive piece of work.

After the intervention the improvements made were to be found in two different, but related, fields. Firstly, what the children wrote was now more coherent, there was better coordination between the arguments, and the style of the text ceased to be a mere listing. From the syntactic point of view, there was some subordination and use of argumentative connectors, basically "but", after the not always successful attempts at introducing the opinions of the audience clearly. Likewise, they also used another type of connector within the arguments themselves, which made these more compact and more skillfully produced, and use was also made of phrases that made counter argumentation easier ("I know that you think..." and other similar expressions). Secondly, as we have already stated in the "Results" section, the children constructed not only better-elaborated arguments but also counterarguments.

This study makes it clear, therefore, that in spite of the already pointed out limitations, children aged 10-11 do respond to the intervention we have carried out and do indeed reap great benefits from it. This preparedness to profit from the teaching received could also be observed in the two microinstruction sessions in which, between everyone and with some help, they managed to correct the lack of coherence in the written texts and to improve them. This confirms for us the advisability and possibility of including correction and rewriting of paragraphs in teaching processes for this age group.

One aspect that we consider interesting to emphasize is, as Gombert has already shown (1997), the influence that familiarity with the subject matter and personal agreement with the thesis to be defended have on argumentative writing. With regard to this last point, we would like to describe what happened during one of the sessions in our intervention. In this particular session the children had to write a letter to the parents of all the pupils at the school, convincing them of the advantages of having a longer school morning but with no classes in the afternoon. What we discovered was that the fact, unexpected by us, that quite a few children were not in favor of the longer school morning (which meant being at school from 9 till 2, and then not returning after lunch). These children found it difficult to set themselves apart from their own point of view and to find arguments in favor of an idea that they did not share, not even simulating that stance. In fact, those who were not in favor of there being a longer school morning elaborated reasons typical of an educational psychologist against the longer school morning.

This confirmed for us the importance of writing in general and of argumentative writing in particular in order to favor and improve thinking and knowledge-production in children. We are certain that those children would not have arrived at those profound thoughts as they did if they had not been faced with task of seeking arguments in favor of and in support of an idea, of a particular subject that aroused great interest in them.

Closely related to what we have just shown is what happened when the children did not really know which opinion to defend. "On one hand" they supported one idea and "on the other hand" the opposite. This is what happened to some children when they were asked to do the following task: "Do a piece of written work defending your own point of view on whether you are for or against animals being held in captivity. You must convince those who do not agree with you". The lack of decision on the part of some children as to which opinion to defend led them to mix up the arguments in favor of living in freedom and those in favor of living in captivity. What is not so clear is why they are not aware of the lack of coherence in the resulting text. Our interpretation is that their work memory was not capable of keeping the objective to be defended active, by dedicating explicit attention to it, at the same time as confronting that objective with the arguments found (Alamargot & Chanquoy, 2001; Lea & Levy, 1999). This would have led them to maintain the arguments in favor of the chosen objective and to cast aside those of the rejected objective, which is an excessive item load for the work memory at that age.

We should like to add a comment here from the developmental point of view. We have seen the difficulties involved in "splitting into two" for children aged 11, in the sense here of being able to argue in favor of a point of view that is not one's own. Nevertheless, given their age, and according to Selman (1980), it is highly likely that they are in stage 3 (mutual adoption of perspectives), which allows them to get off centre cognitively, or in other words, to consider simultaneously their own point of view and another's and, therefore, see it from the audience's point of view. It is clearly unthinkable that a short intervention, such as ours was, could help to build that structural ability in so little time. Yet what the intervention did achieve was to allow that ability to materialize linguistically. What we would like to mention, on any account, is that in previous research carried out by us in 2000 with Primary School 6° graders (12 years old) we found that the number and quality of counterarguments was far greater, as was their ability to handle coherently ideas corresponding to opposite points of view.

Finally, some words on the effect that teaching how to write argumentative texts had on the comprehension of this kind of text. As has already been stated in the "Results" section the difference between the pre-test and the post-test for the control group was not significant, whereas a level of significance is attained in the pretest–posttest comparison for the experimental group, albeit borderline. On making a qualitative analysis of the protocols, we found that in the scoring system we applied to the answers in the comprehension test we had given a very high weighting to the criterion "s/he differentiates between the author's arguments and those that the latter attributes to third persons". Quite a few children failed to score well on this question. Without our going any more deeply into this question, what we can state now is that the transference of writing generated abilities towards comprehension, and vice versa, seems to be somewhat more complex than we first felt it to be and, quite clearly, in order for a more definite result to have been produced, a longer intervention would have been necessary.

APPENDIX A: COMPREHENSION TEST

FAMILY NAME AND FIRST NAME.............

Dear Council Environmental Officer:

A few days ago, taking advantage of the good weather, I went for a walk at the Magdalena beach with my three children aged 10, 14 and 16. While we were playing paddle tennis there I saw three people with jet skis riding close to the beach. My two older children stood there admiring them and said to me excitedly: Isn't that really cool, Dad! Aren't they having a really great time! It was wonderful to see the happiness on their faces, but the terrible noise that the jet skis made ruined the peace and quiet of our walk along the beach. It is true that that young people really do enjoy themselves with their jet ski acrobatics in the water, but I also think that riding jet skis in the water has some negative consequences, such as, for example, the following: they are a danger to bather safety, besides guzzling petrol and being a source of pollution. It is also true, though, that Jet Ski riding can be a sport, like motocross for example, and like this young people develop their sports skills. However, it mustn't be forgotten that there are ways of enjoying yourself that are more ecological and which disturb other people less. I would like you, as the person responsible for the safety of people on beaches and for the environment, to take some kind of measure to prevent these consequences.

QUESTIONS:

1) Who is the person that is writing the letter?
2) Who is s/he writing to?
3) What does s/he want to achieve with this letter?
4) What does the person writing the letter think of jet skis?
5) Underline those of the following sentences that the person writing the letter agrees with:

   It is all right for young people to use jet skis although they pollute the sea.
   Using jet skis is a danger to bathers.
   Young people really enjoy using jet skis and it is all right for them to use them although they make a lot of noise.
   When the jet skier parks his jet ski on the sand he endangers the bathers' safety.
   Jet skis pollute seawater and fish.
   It is all right for young people to develop their sports skills by using jet skis on the sea.

TEACHING WRITING – TEACHING ORAL PRESENTATION

SUSANNE MUNCH

Frederiksværk Gymnasium, Denmark

Abstract. This study describes the benefit of teaching writing in a combination with teaching oral presentation. For two successive years, two different classes were taught writing and presentation individually and in groups. The classes worked with three interdisciplinary projects in addition to their schedule and integrated IT in written as well as oral work. To measure and to improve the results the criteria of the four dimensions of a text were used and an extra dimension was added with special reference to oral presentation. The examination forms were oral group presentation and the writing of an individual essay with a preceding group work.

Keywords: Writing, oral presentation, interdisciplinary teaching, projects work, group work.

1. INTRODUCTION

In 1999 a reform was introduced in upper secondary education in Denmark. Soon it turned out that the total amount of written work was a burden on the students. The extended use of the computer also had a share in this, and more and more products tended to be written products. It was necessary to consolidate oral presentation.

The Danish Ministry of Education invited teachers to research in project work, in various forms of examinations, and in working with IT. In the years 2000 – 2002, I worked as a Danish teacher in two teams of teachers. We focused our research on project work with IT and group examinations.

The Danish primary and lower-secondary school does a lot of project work, and so it would be natural to continue this method of working in the upper secondary education. To reflect the methods of the daily work the examination form must consequently be a group examination. The computer is integrated in the everyday teaching, practically all papers are written on computers, and so we decided to include the use of it for information retrieval and power point presentations in project work as

Munch, S. (2004). Teaching writing – Teaching oral presentation.
In G. Rijlaarsdam (Series Ed.) and Rijlaarsdam, G., Van den Bergh, H., & Couzijn, M. (Vol. Eds.), Studies in writing. Vol. 14, Effective learning and teaching of writing, 2nd Edition, Part 2, Studies in how to teach writing, 339-347.

well as in group examinations. The computer was a meeting point for all products, and so writing could benefit from the methods of oral work and vice versa.

Furthermore I decided to combine teaching writing and teaching oral presentation. The idea was that the writing style would benefit from the more personal spoken style and that it would be easier to work with structure when doing written and oral work in combination.

Danish students are taught literature and writing in their native language. When they graduate after three years, they sit an oral examination (30 minutes) in literature and a written examination (five hours) where they write a classic essay based on material provided, a total of five or six texts: a short story, one or two poems, an article, an extract from a controversial book etc. The question paper has a number of texts five assignments to choose from, e.g., a literary analysis or a text to sum up and to discuss. To inspire the students all the texts are about one theme.

Instead of sitting a completely individual examination the class can choose to start in groups for the first one and a half hour in which they read and discuss the material with each other. After this they have four and a half hour to write individual essays. The students and I decided to prepare for this examination form as it corresponded to the oral group examination.

2. DESIGN – 2000/2001

In 2000/2001 I worked in a team with another Danish teacher and two History teachers. In pairs we taught a class of twenty-eight 16-year-old students of mathematics, called 1z, and a class of twenty-four 16-year-old students of language, called 1b.

In 2001/2002 I worked in a team with two English teachers and a History teacher. One English teacher and I, the Danish teacher, taught a class of twenty-six 16-year-old students of mathematics, called 1y, while another other English teacher and a History teacher taught a class of twenty-four 16-year-old students of mathematics, called 1x.

The classes had traditional lessons with their teachers, but also three times two or three days in a year without fixed lessons in which the four teachers taught fifty students in groups of five students chosen from both classes.

2.1 The First Step

The first step – one month after start of school in August – was a video recorded session in which students gave a two minutes speech on a topic of their own choice.

We rated the students on a scale from 1 to 5 according to the criteria of a writing study 1995 – 1999 under the Ministry of Education (see appendix). The criteria are based on the four dimensions of a text:
1) Language
2) Structure and presentation
3) Treatment of subject
4) Originality

To this we added a fifth dimension, namely
5) Body language

The students were then given marks from the traditional marking scale ranging from 00 to 13 (00, 03, 5, 6 (= passed), 7, 8, 9, 10, 11, 13). At the same time each of the five dimensions was evaluated on a scale from 1 to 5, and plotted into a figure (see appendix). In this way the students were able to diagnose the strong and weak dimensions of their presentations so they could work on their weak points and develop their strong points even further. Some students were very good, a few more were rather bad, and the rest was divided between the middle marks 7 and 8. The average was 7.3. The students also commented on their own performances. This together with the figures showed us where to concentrate on teaching oral presentation. (See step 2).

At the same time the students wrote a paper in which they were to discuss a topic of their own choice. These papers were rated according to the criteria for the four dimensions of a text. Each dimension was evaluated and shown in a figure illustrating the weak and the strong points of the paper that the mark given was based on. The marks fell within the range of 6 to 9, and the average was 7.1. The students had problems with language, structure and presentation, and treatment of subject (dimensions 1, 2, and 3), partly because they had not sorted out their ideas, partly because they did not focus sufficiently on form. They scored 3 and 4 in dimension 4, being original and personal in handling the chosen subject.

2.2 The Second Step

The second step was a program in which the students were taught body language[1], story telling[2], rhetoric[3], and project work[4]. This program was taught in special sessions and followed up by exercises in the daily work. The students told jokes, learned fairy tales, legends, and myths by heart and told them to an audience. They learned, explained, and applied the basic rules of rhetoric and made improvised speeches and debates. The different stages in project work were studied, and the students had exercises in-group work and in the mechanisms and roles of a group.

2.3 The Criteria

These were the criteria that the student were taught to apply to their oral work:
Do you speak in a loud voice? Have you got eye contact with your audience? Does your body language enhance (or at least not disturb) your message? Is your style

---

[1] *Nils Gunder Hansen: Etik I 90'erne, s 38 – 46, Gyldendal 92; Torben Jetsmark: Sig det så det ses, s 9 – 52, Gyldendal 95.*
[2] *Ulf Arnström og Peter Hagberg: Fortæl – igen!, Dansklærerforeningen 94; Vigga Bro: Orkanens øje, Drama 96; Kirsten Thonsgaard: Drømmenes Torv, Klim 98.*
[3] *Bent Pedersbæk Hansen: Retorik for gymnasium og hf, Sydvest 83; Charlotte Jørgensen og Merete Onsberg: Praktisk argumentation, Ingeniøren/bøger 99.*
[4] *Stig Püschl m. fl.: Projektarbejde, Gads forlag 2000.*

precise, vivid, and personal? Is your language correct, subtle, and interesting? Is your speech focused, structured and coherent? Is there a balance between level of abstraction, generalization and concrete examples? Is your speech original as well as personal?

2.4 Writing Tasks

Except for the first three the same criteria were applied to the written work. The four dimensions of a text (see appendix) were trained both separately and jointly. The students had short writing exercises:
- Text summaries in which they focused on language (sentence structure, punctuation, spelling, inflection, and phraseology).
- Fiction and non-fiction in which they focused on structure and presentation (composition, coherence, focus, the balance between level of abstraction, generalization and concrete examples, and compliance with the chosen genre and style).
- Text interpretations and discussions in which they focused on subject treatment (understanding, analysis and interpretation, documentation, argumentation, precision and subtlety).
- Character sketches and reports in which they focused on being original and personal.

During the two semesters the students were given six major writing tasks in the form of essays in which they had to concentrate on all four dimensions at the same time. The students worked in permanent groups in which they read and discussed the material and took notes for their individual essays.

3. THE PROJECTS – 2000/2001

In 2000/2001 the two classes did three cross-disciplinary projects:
1) Speeches (in October)
2) The power point presentation (in December)
3) The annual examination (in May)

3.1 Speeches

For two weeks before the project days all three subjects, Danish, English, and History, analyzed famous speeches (among these: Martin Luther King, John F. Kennedy, the Queen's and the Prime Minister's New Year speeches). In the two projects days each student prepared a synopsis and gave a ten minutes' speech of his or her own. The written assignment was also a speech, but on a different, though still optional, topic. This session was videotaped and evaluated along the same lines as the speeches in August.

This time the average of the two classes was 7.9. The scatter was bigger than the first time. This time only two students got 6; the majority was divided between 7, 8, and 9 while five students got 10 and 11. The evaluation of the written work showed an average of 7.2. The majority got 7 and 8, but there were more weak writers getting 6 than good writers getting 9 and 10. Though the speeches were well structured and original (dimensions 2 and 4), there were problems with language, style, and subject treatment (dimensions 1 and 3). These dimensions were now particularly brought into focus in the period up to the next project. (See the above-mentioned writing tasks.)

3.2 The Power Point Presentation

In the week before the two and a half project days the school librarian gave both classes a course in information retrieval. The two classes trained group dynamics, the synopsis was re-introduced, and they had several exercises in composition. One class was taught how to make a (simple) power point presentation; the other class was introduced to the Middle East crisis.

The two classes were divided into six person groups with three members from each class. They had to cooperate and to make use of their different expertise. The groups were given one and a half day to work out a power point presentation on an important aspect of the Middle East Crisis. They were to find a focus, to delimit their subject, to find, sort, and select information, to present their ideas in a proper order, and finally to make good use of power point.

Sixty students are quite a handful, so after a session of brief lectures they were left to work on their own and to consult their teachers whenever they had problems. And they had a lot of problems, but also got many suggestions for solutions. On the whole they needed very little help with power point, which turned out to be a tool appealing to their imagination.

On day two we had invited a large audience. The groups made their presentations, and after each presentation there was a round of criticism summed up by a teacher. At the end of the day the best three presentations were nominated. We had asked three external teachers to evaluate the groups. Two groups got 5 and 6; three groups got 10 and 11, while the rest was divided between 7, 8 and 9. The average was 8.3.

The next day we had a class discussion in which we worked out a list of the most important principles for power point presentations. We discussed composition and line of thoughts.

The students then wrote a homework paper in which they turned their power point presentations into essays. The average was 8.5. They wrote about a thoroughly prepared subject, and the weak groups had learned from the others and elaborated on their subject. It varied from student to student, but the general picture was that structure and presentation, subject treatment, and originality (dimensions 2, 3, and 4) had been improved while language (dimension 1) was still a problem for some students. In the spring semester, there was a special focus on language and on handling all four dimensions at the same time.

3.3 The Annual Examination

In the end of each of the first two of the three years the classes sit for one or two final oral examinations and two or three annual oral examinations in continuing subjects to prepare them for the third year in which they sit for a total of four or five final oral examinations. They sit for the same number of final written examinations.

One of the first year annual examinations was turned into a project with group examination and 24 hours of preparation. The class was divided into 5-person groups, and Danish and History gave each group a set of unknown as well as familiar texts to analyze. They were to find additional material by information retrieval. After the 24 hours the group had one hour in which to make a presentation in front of external examiners. They were to write and follow a synopsis, and they were each to take their share of the presentation, so they could have individual marks.

The awarding of marks was one point above the Danish average; there were more high marks and fewer low marks and this resulted in an average of 9.1 against 8.1 for the whole country. This must be due to the fact that students have a long preparation phase in which they can help each other. The students stress the importance of this, the training from the many projects and the fact that they do not feel alone in the examination situation. The external examiners pointed out that the students were very confident for a first year class. They ascribed this to their training in presentation.

The class sat a traditional written examination with group work and wrote fine papers. The average was 8.6 and above the Danish average of 7.9. Compared to the other classes they were good at expressing themselves in well-composed essays with a lively style. There seemed to be less low marks but also less really high marks. Top and bottom seemed to have disappeared. Some students still had problems with language, some were too superficial in their treatment of subject but in general the students did well (between 3 and 4) in all four dimensions.

4. DESIGN – 2001/2002

In 2001/2002 I continued my work with 1z, but now on my own. The students wrote traditional essays with a constant focus on the four dimensions of a text, and they gave oral presentations individually and in groups.

At the same time I started a new class, 1y, in teamwork with the English teacher. We worked with another class, 1a, and two of their teachers, the English teacher and the History teacher. This time we trained individual presentations in class and focused three projects on project work and group presentations. In 1y we focused on literary methods, while the teachers of 1a focused more on putting literature into perspective. So the classes could benefit from each other when working in groups across the classes.

The schedule and the criteria were the same as the previous year, but this school year the subjects were given.

5. THE PROJECTS – 2001/2002

1) The Danish emigration to America
2) Witches
3) The annual examination

For the first two projects the project groups were given a new text material each time: 10 pages Danish (letters, poems, photos, pictures, and short stories), 10 pages English (extracts from a novel, poems, and short stories), and 10 pages History (historical sources; mainly in Danish). For the annual examination they were given a combination of familiar and unknown texts. In all three projects they had 24 hours to work with the material and prepare a synopsis and a presentation in which they contributed individually and as a group. They were given individual marks.

The written work was intensified as the text analysis was combined with creative writing exercises. The class wrote e.g., songs about the land of dreams, propagandistic ads for travel agencies, socialist realism about smallholders, reports from the workhouse, letters home from America.

The students also wrote 6 major essays: two in connection with the America project and the witch project, one traditional examination paper (at the annual examination), and three essays in the form of the traditional examination paper. The four dimensions of a text were used as criteria to instruct the students individually. One after the other the weakest points were focused on. They varied from student to student but this class had problems with language and punctuation in common. In the beginning their average was 7, that is almost one point below the Danish average. The average of the examination papers was 8.1 which is 0.2 points above the Danish average. At that time the students were either at the top or near the bottom of the marking scale. Very few were in the middle. The good students gradually got the skill of the four dimensions while the weak students continued having problems mastering all four dimensions at the same time. Again the students worked in permanent groups but this time there was a tendency to polarization.

The oral presentations gradually improved throughout the three projects, and the class average changed from 6.7 at the first project to 9.3 at the examination project. The five dimensions were used for individual guidance and differed very much from student to student.

6. CONCLUSION

The writing benefits from the oral presentations depended on the complexity of the writing tasks and the degree of integration between oral and written work. The more complex the task, the more dimensions to handle on a high level. In the learning process a high degree of integration between oral and written work resulted in high quality written work. Not surprisingly the benefit depends on the starting skills of the individual student. It is difficult to see how much the group preparation influences the results as the two pictures differ. Does it result in the disappearance of top and bottom or in polarization? Or is this simply the results of the difference between two classes? The four and five dimensions of a text and of an oral presentation respectively are valuable as learning tools. They give the students a very precise picture of their strong and weak points and a possibility to improve one point at a time.

APPENDIX A: CRITERIA OF ASSESSMENT – THE FOUR DIMENSIONS OF A TEXT

1) Language: Correct, appropriate, and clear:
    - sentence structure
    - punctuation
    - spelling
    - inflection
    - phraseology, accuracy and variation
    - this includes linguistic economy and use of narrative effects.
2) Structure and presentation: Relevant, focused, well-ordered and clear:
    - composition (introduction and conclusion)
    - coherence (within and between paragraphs)
    - focus
    - this includes level of abstraction, specification and generalization
    - observance of the chosen genre and style.
3) Treatment of subject: Reading, selection, relevance, and thoroughness in:
    - handling of assignment
    - analysis and interpretation
    - documentation
    - argumentation
    - accuracy and variation.
4) Originality:
    - personal approach
    - engagement
    - originality
    - independence
    - versatility in choice of perspective and attitude.

APPENDIX B

This figure shows the four dimensions of a text. 5 is the highest mark, 1 is the lowest. The four axes are: language, structure and presentation, treatment of subject, and originality. When an essay is evaluated, each dimension of the text is marked with a number on the axis in question, e.g., language 2, structure and presentation 3, treatment of subject 3, and originality 4. In this way the figure clearly shows the strengths and the weaknesses of the text.

TEACHING WRITING & ORAL PRESENTATION

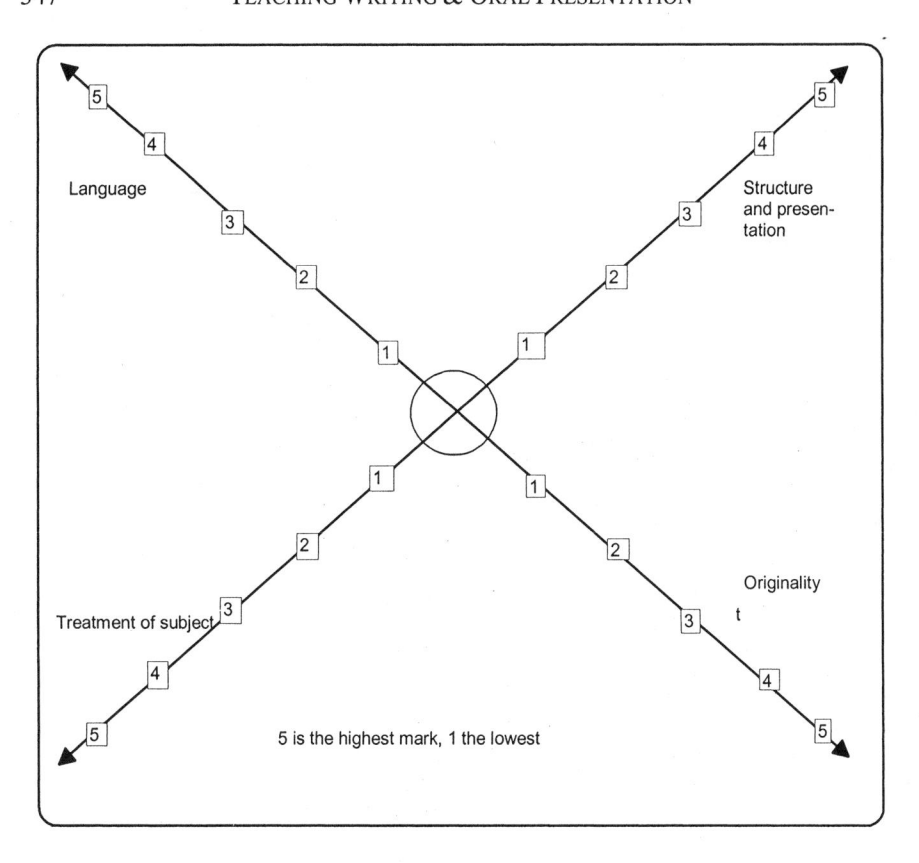

Language

Structure and presen-
tation

Treatment of subject

Originality

5 is the highest mark, 1 the lowest

WRITING TO LEARN: CONSTRUCTING THE CONCEPT OF GENRE IN A WRITING WORKSHOP

MILLY EPSTEIN-JANNAI

Kibbutzim College of Education, Tel Aviv, Israel

Abstract. For those working on writing, genre can be a suitable framework for stressing the complex web of relationships between the reader in a personal, idiosyncratic role and the socio-cultural conventions, which involve both text and reader. The concept of genre – with all its wide and heterogeneous background – may prove to be fertile when working on reading and writing with different learning populations, in order to discuss and understand literary, linguistic and cultural topics as integral forces.
In this chapter, I would like to relate to some theoretical ideas about reading and writing and their influence on the organization of a writing workshop. I will emphasize the idea of genre as a "framework" for meaning construction and simultaneously as an analytical tool.
I shall focus my discussion on writing within a generic framework as a way of clarifying the reader's role and deepening his/her awareness of the genre's constraints and its role in enabling personal innovation.

Keywords. Writing workshop, reading and writing processes, creativity and its development, learning and teaching processes.

1. INTRODUCTION

The purpose of this chapter is to describe educational practice as it is determined by theoretical ideas about reading. Specifically, the aim of this chapter is to point out these theoretical influences on the approach to the writing process and its products. My assumption is that writing constitutes a personal testimony to various reading processes. It follows from this that the individual's sharpened awareness of the reading process is made possible by intensive and critical writing experience (Epstein-Jannai, 2001). This assumption has given rise to a teaching vehicle – a writing workshop –, which will be described below. Experience of such a workshop can serve to emphasize for the writing reader the formulation of writing as a "network" created

---

Epstein-Jannai, M. (2004). Writing to learn: constructing the concept of genre in a writing workshop.
In G. Rijlaarsdam (Series Ed.) & Rijlaarsdam, G., Van den Bergh, H. & Couzijn, M. (Vol. Eds.), Studies in writing. Vol. 14, Effective learning and teaching of writing, 2nd Edition, Part 2, Studies in how to teach writing, 349-365.

among different texts, a "network" that at times creates even him – the reader – as a writing subject (Juranville, 1994). The space in which writing and reading exist is imprinted, among other things, by the stamp of other reading that had been done in the past. Simultaneously, these traces mark future writing and reading. In other words, writing is one way of *uncovering* previous readings and examining their presence in the new text. As an example of the close relationship between reading and writing, I chose the term "genre" in order to emphasize this relationship in a framework whose purpose is educational.

The question that links the topics I have outlined above is whether writing in the framework of a defined genre can develop writers' awareness of the complex nature of the reading process, which is unique and biographical, but at the same time grounded in a cultural, social and historical framework. In other words, can writing experience within the "boundaries" of a specific genre – through coping with its characteristics and conventions from a thematic, narrative and linguistic point of view – contribute to writing novices' deeper understanding of the reading process and the way the text is created through it?

The aim of this chapter is therefore dual. On the one hand, it seeks to point out the nature of the text from the point of view of genre as a literary and cultural issue. On the other hand, it aims to emphasize the contribution of theoretical ideas to teaching-learning practice. In accordance with these aims, the discussion is based on actual work in writing workshops for elementary school and kindergarten teachers and speech therapists, which usually take place in the framework of teachers' refresher courses.

The chapter is divided into four major sections: remarks about reading, remarks about the concept of genre, a description of practice in the writing workshop and examples of them, and implications of the workshop for constructing participants' new knowledge about writing (revealing non-formulated knowledge and its processing).

2. REMARKS ABOUT READING

In the present chapter, I will relate to the reading process as an internal experience (Poulet, 1986) that permits an "imagined" encounter (Mannoni, 1979, Epstein-Jannai, 1996) between the reader/subject, the text and variegated previous experience – including previous reading. This experience is unexpected and its unpredictability facilitates the more revolutionary and significant aspects that reading can evoke (Freire, 1987; Hadot, 1997). In the course of reading, the reader activates patterns and decoding conventions that are appropriate to what he sees as proper to being a reader. The reader, then, fulfils this role[1] in order to actualize the kind of reading he considers suitable to the text being read (Culler, 1982; Rabinowitz, 1987).

The cumulative memory of the reader and the writer is what allows them to conduct a kind of "dialogue" between texts. It may thus be stated that the text when it is read reflects the "polyphonic" (multi-voiced) dialogue that the famous critic of cul-

---

[1] *"Playing a role" (for the reader) includes an acting element that is clearly expressed in other languages such as French, Spanish and German (for example* jouer, jugar, spilen*).*

ture Michail Bakhtin (1978) identified in his discussion of the novel. The dialogue between texts points to the relationship between readers and reading, but not necessarily to a direct or deliberate influence[2]. Hypothetical or well-grounded relationships between readers and readings are reflected in the text being read, and they leave traces in the "tapestry" of the text and the way it is written as well as in the experience of reading it. The written text appears to be made up of heterogeneous fragments, some new and unknown, some that "have been read before" (Barthes, 1970). The polyphonic nature of what is written is activated and "concretized" by the reader (Iser, 1974).

The relationship between texts from a rather wider point of view is indicated by the concept of inter-textuality (Foucault, 1969; Kristeva, 1971). As Bakhtin (1978) has stated, every text relates in one way or another to other texts. As a result of this relationship, each text belongs to a specific tradition of readers and their ways of understanding and interpreting, thus weaving a kind of "web" whose strands embrace ways of relating to what is written (Tompkins, 1986). Personal memory is interwoven into what culture "bestows" upon us and is marked by it.

3. GENRE AS A FRAMEWORK FOR CONSTRUCTING MEANING

The concept of genre can help us better understand the complex, convoluted relations between texts and those who write and read them. This is due to the fact that although one can study it formally, genre is one of those concepts whose existence can be sensed intuitively and identified in a text inadvertently. That is, the concept of genre actually allows one to activate and examine non-formulated and tacit knowledge (Caspi, 1985) that may be revealed through the writing process. Knowledge regarding the concept of "genre" crystallizes into a kind of internal compass that guides readers and writers, while determining their way of approaching different textual utterances since they belong to a definite class of texts. Thus genre appears to be an ever-changing socio-cultural way of shaping readers and guiding writers (Cope and Kalantzis, 1993; Martin, 1989). It may be assumed that intensive experience in writing and writing analysis can expose novices to the concept of genre as a kind of abstraction of previous readings. Each genre has unique qualities that allow it to be intuitively classified as a different text type that fulfills different social and cultural goals (Martin, 1989).

Genre arouses expectations in readers, since it organizes in advance what is read as a significant construct (Bakhtin, 1985), thus allowing the reader to anticipate what is coming. Genre supplies types of "scenarios" for organizing events, thus directing

---

[2] *What is under discussion is a socio-cultural state of mind in which reading and writing take place. Concepts such as "story," "motif" (for example, the stepmother), and "literary language" (for example, "sparse," "rich," "symbolic") are formulated by reference to a variety of texts that make up the reader's and writer's repertoire. In each of the concepts mentioned above, the inter-textual phenomenon will be revealed to the reader that recognizes it, but this phenomenon can also not be discovered, remain invisible or become blurred in the textual weave.*

readers and writers alike. For example, in a fairy tale there is a tendency to "expect" a happy outcome of complicated events.

Bakhtin (ibid.) claimed that readers and writers, acting in a changing social environment, learn to shape the dialogue that is orchestrated between them in generic forms. The individual perceiving the words of his interlocutor, whether verbally or in writing, usually identifies the genre organizing them from the opening words of the expression (ibid.: 268). Bakhtin also emphasized that the private discourse of each and every speaker is filled with others' words, with things that were said in the past, similarly or differently. Each text appears as a fabric of other texts, while at the same time underlining the social and cultural horizons that allow its creation. A genre is a broad ideological phenomenon that is present in various socio-cultural fields, such as classroom discourse, psychoanalytic discourse and ritual encounters.

Genre is generally learned and examined by relating to texts that are included in a specific group (Martin, 1989). It appears therefore to have a dual nature. On the one hand, its existence is experienced as a general framework including different text types (for example, fairy tales, detective stories, adventure books, etc.). On the other hand, its existence *partially* disappears when discussing a specific text that "creates" the genre anew, while at the same time being created by it (Epstein-Jannai, 2001). In this way, as stated above, the concept of genre is formulated as an abstraction of readings. Consequently, genre appears as a special socio-cultural way of allowing the organization of various kinds of expression as a whole. In a more focused way, it is a "framework" within whose boundaries – and even beyond them – it is possible to refer to, understand and interpret a certain text, thus constructing its meaning.

One can thus summarize and say that the concept of genre not only indicates text types but also the *processes that make it possible to create texts.* Genre acts as an agreed cultural framework that allows the shaping of a certain meaning and the fulfillment of certain social and cultural goals in a specific situation with the help of certain linguistic tools. In addition, genres *stimulate an examination* of the possible ways of creating this meaning as a kind of social exchange (Cope & Kalantzis, 1993). The examination of such ways is the core of the discussions taking place in the workshop I will describe. The central question is: In which ways does genre as a framework for constructing meaning combine more or less permanent constraints (the qualities that allow the identification of the genre) and unique, creative and changing realizations (the special form of each and every text) that reflect individual style?

My assumption is that consciousness of the reading process develops through the sharpening of generic principles and by paying attention to the restrictions that genre dictates to readers and writers alike. The subsequent discussion will attempt to show how theoretical issues relating to literature, linguistics and culture may be applied when analyzing the texts written in the course of a writing workshop.

4. THE WRITING WORKSHOP AS A TYPE OF WORK: FROM THEORY TO PRACTICE

4.1 Description of the Workshop

The decision to name a program for teaching and learning about writing through writing tasks a "workshop" stems from viewing the writing process as a working and creative one. A workshop is *a place where one works* and creates products. In this case, the material is language that is used according to culture, imagination, personal associations and conventions dictated by the choice of genre, etc. The workshop allows those working in it an authentic "encounter" with various textual phenomena while they are being created (for example, the symbolic dimension that may be identified in the course of an apparently trivial plot, the choice of a certain syntactic organization to increase tension and canonic creation as the object of intratextual critical dialogue).

I will briefly describe the principles of the workshop and the way it is taught. (Epstein-Jannai, 1996.) The permanent framework of the workshop is comprised of the following:

1) Every week, each participant receives a new writing task. This is the skeleton structure of the workshop. The number of tasks varies according to circumstance.
2) The participants fulfil the writing assignments, usually as homework.
3) A class discussion takes place regarding the texts that were written in fulfillment of the task. The discussion revolves around participants reading the texts and analyzing them.

The program is thus constructed from writing tasks that combine a certain "constraint" and a certain "possibility" (terms borrowed from Caspi, 1985). The constraint is an invitation to unconventional writing (for example: "Present yourself 'using' the letters of the alphabet.") and it involves the possibility of examining language and discovering it afresh (for example, using writing conventions that are not "fashionable" today, such as writing poetry according to alphabetical order, in an "acrostic"). In the course of the workshop, no exact explanations are given regarding the way to fulfill the tasks (for example: How should one "present" oneself? What is the meaning of "presenting"? Before whom and why should one present oneself? What is the meaning of "using the letters of the alphabet"?). Sigalit, a student in one of the workshops[3], expresses a typical dilemma presented by the tasks:

> "The course presented me with a challenge in the way a variety of tasks were given to us, but not in an entirely clear way, which on the one hand made me rather apprehensive during the writing process and anticipation of the final product, and on the other hand made me curious to see how I would succeed in coping with the task. There was difficulty at times in the way it was done when questions arose during work: Is this the right

---

[3] *All the students' quotations are presented as translations from Hebrew without syntactical corrections. These quotes are taken from their comments regarding the workshop and the processes they underwent in its course. Some of the quotes, while they are presented regarding a certain topic, shed light on additional topics mentioned in the general discussion, so I decided to include them.*

way, or is there another one? How will my ideas appear? The same task was given to everyone, but each expressed it so differently. It was enjoyable to observe, listen, differentiate and compare between different participants' work."

The tasks are perceived as an invitation to practise, investigate, play, and learn. They are intended to activate supposed "literary," "linguistic" and "cultural" knowledge, so they are formulated in an extremely open manner. In the framework of the workshop, writing and reading are examined as phenomena that are not obvious, but arouse deep inquiry. Therefore, the tasks sharpen awareness of the different elements that are interwoven in texts, emphasizing the recursive relations between theory and practice. This kind of awareness contributes to improving the reading methods of participants in the workshop. Lilach and Shany refer both to the tasks themselves and the ways they were analyzed in the classroom:

> Lilach: "The tasks that were given in the lesson were a challenge for me. The tasks were given in an interesting way …and demanded of us to use imagination, thought and our world of associations. [...I will] refer to the analyses and the attention that was given to each work written in the classroom. I felt that everything I wrote would receive attention and a professional analysis in the classroom, as though it was a work of classical literature. I feel that the classroom climate and the attention I received allowed me to embark on the writing process. They created in me a feeling of security in bringing the result to class…In addition to this I feel that these things gave me the ability, as well as the possibility, to analyze others' texts …"

> Shany: "The workshop contributed a lot to me. I feel that thanks to the theories I was exposed to, I improved my skills as a reader, and therefore also as a writer… The workshop got me to write. The tasks were a basis and a springboard for me, an interesting and surprising starting off point. I liked the lack of clarity of the tasks. The definitions were clear, but within them there was a large degree of freedom. I was amazed to learn each time anew how many ways there were to interpret the same instructions."

The participants are asked to complete the tasks from one lesson to the next. The class discussion arises as a result of students being engaged in writing; this encourages them to read critically and analyze texts with the help of the instructor. The discussion focuses on questions that one may "ask the text" in order to broaden understanding and the conditions that gave birth to it. Writing analysis thus emphasizes for the writer the place of the reader and reading conventions in text construction. Anath writes thus:

> "I always accepted my ability to read as something I took for granted. During the workshop, I suddenly realized what a complex process this is, and I felt glad like I did in first grade that I know how to read and how wonderful this is … I would say that I underwent a process of 'being opened and freed'. This is expressed in my desire to continue writing and the feeling of freedom to do this."

As it is possible to appreciate from previous citations, students' testimonies regarding processes of writing, reading and re-writing are part of the methodological framework of the workshop, and they are considered as "facts" presented by the students. These testimonies permit students to re-organize personal feelings, experiences and ideas that arise during the workshop and after it, and they constitute important raw material when evaluating learning processes, although a "certain skepticism" is necessary when reading these testimonies.

The discussion of texts that are written in the workshop is guided by a varying number of questions, an example of which may be seen in the task I will analyze below. The aim of these questions is to encourage thinking about what is being done and emphasize intriguing aspects of topics that seem "natural" and obvious: what constitutes a story, how meaning is constructed, who speaks in a text. The tasks impel, encourage the workshop participants to depart from a routine attitude to language, and this occurs in a humorous, relaxed and "playful" atmosphere (Lieberman, 1977).

The discussion about writing that take place during the workshop is recursive and spiral and its purpose is to learn about the text, its texture and its way of demanding a certain kind of "work" on the part of the reader. The instructor relates to what was written using tools taken from literary text analysis. Various theoretical references to the reading process, narrative building and the relationships between culture, society, literature and language are made according to the type of discussion.

Over the years, about 300 teachers and education students have taken part in these workshops[4]. The participants were elementary school and kindergarten teachers, teachers in non-formal education and speech therapists. In all these frameworks, the length of the workshops ranged from 15 to 30 meetings (a course lasting either a semester or a year). When the workshop spans an entire year, it generally includes the reading of theoretical material – whose purpose is to deepen the understanding of processes taking place in the workshop – as well as tutelage in running writing workshops for children.

4.2 Choice of Genre: The Story

Between 1998 and 2001, I decided to focus on the story in its widest sense as one of the genres to be used as a framework for writing. This choice mainly stemmed from the familiar and "taken for granted" nature of the genre, the high incidence of the story in daily life and the indisputably natural way in which school children are repeatedly asked to tell stories of all kinds[5].

The story is an ancient genre, and children in many cultures around the world are exposed to it as they grow up. This is a genre that is used for purposes of learning, religion, entertainment, as well as healing and self-expression (Schank, 1998; Bruner, 1986). The social and cultural goals of the story are as wide and varied as the aesthetic forms it may take. We get involved in the story and unthinkingly activate the automatic cultural mechanism by means of which it "works" as a result of its misleading naturalness and its always being "close at hand". Thus, a series of events are accepted as "expressing" something. This naturalness invites questions

---

[4] *The workshop took place for two years in the Experimental Creative Education Program of the School of Education of the Hebrew University of Jerusalem (1991-1993), in the framework of the Teacher Enrichment Program at David Yellin College (1993), in teacher's refresher courses at the Center for Language Development at Bet Berl College (1994-2000) and in the Creative Education Program and the Early Childhood Education Program at the Kibbutzim College of Education (2000-2002).*
[5] *For a broader discussion of this topic, see Peled, 1996.*

regarding the changing conventions that allow its existence. This is due to the fact that a folk tale, a detective story or a biography of the painter Picasso each activate conventions of their own, while at the same time telling us "something" about people, the ability to discover truth, the social order, emotional life, the mysteries of art. In the framework of the workshop as a learning environment, this naturalness also invites an examination of the "laws," "syntax", language and ideologies that shape the story (Derrida, 1967; Martin, 1989, Baudrillard, 1994).

In the course of the workshop, text analysis focuses on three aspects of the story: plot structure, characters and perspective. Each aspect is connected to one particular writing task. The tasks thus encourage an examination of those common concepts in order to uncover the conventions that "build" the supposed naturalness of the generic textual framework in general and of the story in particular.

Texts written by the workshop participants are examined in light of four major perspectives or contexts. These perspectives or contexts function on two parallel levels and allow a transition from theory to concrete realization in practice and vice versa. On the one hand, they constitute a "framework" for building meaning on the part of writer and reader. On the other hand, they provide "tools" for sharpening awareness and analysis. These perspectives therefore emphasize the interaction between reading and writing and between various conventions and any specific performance guided by them. The four contexts are listed below:

1) The cultural context reflects the cultural canon that determines "what is printed," "what is learned," "how to evaluate," "what is considered good, fresh, daring, old-fashioned, etc.". This context allows an examination of the interaction between accepted culture and marginal culture, and also points out the ideological reflections that shape the text and the social institutions of which it is a part.

2) The literary context emphasizes inter-textual relationships (at times following in the wake of other texts and at times going against them). It focuses on the aesthetic dimensions of special ways to organize information and create characters through the use of repetition, deletion, description, allusion and a whole range of devices that build the story.

3) The theoretical-critical context tends to identify a symbolic dimension in the examined text that departs from the representative-referential aspect of the writing. For example, I emphasized in the past (Epstein-Jannai, 1999) that through the fabric of its plot, the detective novel raises problems regarding "reading" and "decoding". It does so by presenting at its core an interpretive mystery while undergoing a reading process[6]. Similarly, the journeys through geographical space in the pastoral novel symbolize the emotional journeys of its characters.

---

[6] *In the detective novel, the story involving a detective and a murderer is the referential aspect of the writing. It is possible to identify in this relationship a kind of "reference" to a discussion of the relationship between reading and readers, since the detective identifies/ reads "clues" of the murderer's activity that allow him, as an expert reader, to reconstruct the plot of the murder. This is an unusual understanding of the referential level of the story in order to identify a symbolic dimension.*

4) The linguistic-organizational context focuses on linguistic, syntactic and narrative elements, and also on a set of conventions that indicate that the text belongs to a genre as a framework for creating meaning for a certain audience. This includes ways of creating tension and delaying resolution, the choice of action verbs or stative verbs, the decision to concentrate action or present it to the reader in detail and the creation of a salient semantic field that is utilized throughout the story. The organization of the story plot is what keeps it open-ended and "impels" the reader to read on to the end.

I will describe below one of the three tasks, in which the workshop participants were required to write a short story in their own way. While confronting the writer with constraints that represent various writing possibilities, each task "pulls" language and its conventions in different directions, thus allowing an examination of both language and those who use it. The theoretical background presented above generates lively discussion in the course of analyzing participants' work.

For the sake of clarity, the task presented in this chapter includes only one story-example and focuses on only one theoretical topic. However, the actual questions that were discussed in class covered a wider range of topics. These will not be presented here in full, but it is worth mentioning that each text written in the workshop might arouse various questions regarding generic conventions due to the language used, the dialogue between the text and its models and other topics regarding generic form. The questions accompanying the task afforded an opportunity to expand the discussion to topics beyond the range of the major issues I focused on.

5. AN EXAMPLE OF A WRITING TASK[7] DESCRIPTION AND DISCUSSION

I will describe below a task that the workshop participants were required to perform. This description will include the task itself, one example of a student's work, the questions that aroused discussion and finally my analysis of literary, generic and didactic aspects related both to the writing task and to students' commentaries. The task is as follows:

Write a short story (about 20 lines long) whose starting point is the description presented in a horoscope for one of the Signs of the Zodiac.

EXAMPLE

(The text of the horoscope is from a newspaper and was chosen by Hava, the writer of the story)

---

[7] The other two tasks are enounced like this: A. Write a short story in which the following are the names of the characters taking part in the plot: Urganda, Melisanda, Archesileus Santander, Bastian, Franz, Ugolino, Doriana. B. Rewrite the story of the Tower of Babel (Genesis 11) from a different point of view.

PISCES 21.2 - 20.3

A stormy and tense mood will accompany you this week in meetings with others, conversations that turn into arguments, and even casual meetings with people at work, in the street, in the bus or while driving on the roads. It is important to beware and avoid this, since arguments, on the roads for example, are liable to be dangerous.

Money: The subject of money is also liable to be a cause of argument and struggle. Money payments that are definitely owing to you will be delayed, and transactions such as selling or buying a car are liable to get stuck or blow up due to a lack of agreement about a minor point. If you weigh up the gain and loss involved, you might discover that it is worthwhile giving in and compromising with other people.

Love: A relationship you're involved in will become deeper in the next few weeks, and will play a significant role in your life. For those of you who are unmarried, a relationship that begins in the near future will differ in its early stages from other relationships you have had.

Good days to go out and do things together – Tuesday and Wednesday.

"A stormy and tense mood will accompany you this week in meetings with others, conversations that turn into arguments, and even casual meetings with people at work, in the street, in the bus or while driving on the roads. It is important to beware and avoid this, since arguments, on the roads for example, are liable to be dangerous."

"These horoscopes always predict bad things. Check with other people: it says the same thing for everybody," I said to my sister. "And anyway, I don't believe in all that nonsense."

"I don't want to argue with you," my sister said. "If you think like that, then that's fine." She went over to the telephone and lifted the receiver. "Who are you calling?" I asked her. "Ruthie," she answered. "Oh, please be quick. You know that your conversations with Ruthie go on for hours, and I'm waiting for an important call." "An important call?" asked my sister rather sarcastically. "Since when do you wait for important phone calls?" I tried to get out of answering her by slightly shrugging my shoulders and lifting my eyebrows. "You won't get off that easily," my sister said with her usual stubbornness. "Who is it?" "Well, you know, just someone I met two weeks ago." My sister broke out in a giggle. "Just someone...you character! Just a minute ago you said you were waiting for 'an important call' and now you say 'just someone' ?!?"

I gave in. "It's the most amazing guy I ever met in my life," I told her. "We decided to go out somewhere this evening."

"I knew it," my sister crowed. Suddenly the phone rang and broke the silence. I ran to the phone. "Hello?" I said nonchalantly. When I heard what the caller had to say, my face fell. "Okay, we'll do it some other time. Bye."

My sister looked at me sympathetically. "Don't say a word! I have no patience for your sorrowful speeches," I barked in her direction. B-r-r-r-r...another phone call. My sister answered it: "For you." She handed me the receiver. It was my friend Yael. The longer I listened to what she had to say, the angrier I got. "How do you dare?" I shouted at her and slammed down the receiver. My sister looked at me and didn't say a word. She was already acquainted with this kind of mood. "I'm going to bed before something else makes me angry," I roared at my sister. She didn't answer. From experience she knows it's worthwhile keeping quiet until the storm blows over.

"Tomorrow is Tuesday," she suddenly said. "What? Don't you think I remember the days of the week?" I answered in a belligerent tone. "Sure. Look what it says: 'Good days to go out and do things together – Tuesday and Wednesday.' "

"That horoscope again? I don't want to hear anything about horoscopes!! Until you started with that horoscope, I was a happy person. Leave me alone!" I shouted and slammed the door of my room. Hours passed until I fell asleep, hours of tossing and turning and angry and annoying thoughts.

A knocking on the door woke me up. I glanced at the clock. Seven o'clock. "Who could that be, for Heaven's sake?" I thought. I looked out of the peephole. Outside stood the most amazing guy (that's right, the one from yesterday) with a huge bouquet of flowers. I opened the door and also my mouth...I stood there and stared at him open-mouthed. "Pretty flowers for a pretty girl," he said. "I'm sorry about yesterday. Maybe you could take the day off and we could go out together?" "What day is it today?" I muttered in confusion. "Tuesday," he laughed. "You mean to say you don't know?"

Questions for discussion
- On which details of the horoscope was the story based?
- What place was given to the horoscope in constructing the plot? Was it a background for the events or part of the story's opening, or did it justify the chain of events?
- How was the transition made from the language of the newspaper to the language of the story? What was added to the text and what was left out?
- Is there a clear inter-textual connection between the horoscope (the source) and the story (a quotation, a reminder, a paraphrase, other)?
- What was the attitude to the horoscope (amused, skeptical, serious)?
- How was the horoscope integrated into the text organization from the point of view of the plot and its place on the page?
- How did the details of the horoscope shape the nature of the text?
- What types of readers are reflected in the stories written by each person?

Analysis. If the first task (see footnote 7) facilitated many stories that took place in faraway times and places, the second task – writing based on a horoscope – yielded stories taking place in the cultural "here and now" of our era. These are stories that in various ways transform the future predicted by the horoscope into a plot nucleus that propels action and includes an emotional dimension or psychological observations. Varda expressed it thus:

> "The first thing I did was to change it [what was written in the horoscope] into first person, so that there was much more identification with the events. I worked line by line according to the topic [of the horoscope]... I thought about what I needed to change in order for the details to become important and give some depth to the text itself...I included a certain problem that moved the plot forward...an external problem: being late for work ...and an internal problem: the heroine is alone and wants to be together with someone else."

The horoscope gives value to "units of time" (according to the days of the week) or "thematic units" (love, money, friends, etc.). This stems from the hidden assumption that these units must be used critically, economically[8]. Therefore, the horoscope can be accepted as a chain of signifiers having significance for the character involved in them. What is being discussed is a *possible, hypothetical plot* that must translate the potential dimension of horoscopes into the actual one. Here, a theoretical-critical context (which I described above) that tends to identify a symbolic dimension in the text may reveals itself as useful in emphasizing a non-referential vein present in the temporal organization of plot. Therefore, "units of time" may appear as presenting social values related to the concept of "change" in personal life or of success as perceived in a "developed society". Moreover, this type of plot encourages the writers to "give human shape" to an anonymous succession of events that comprise the horoscope, or to "impose" some kind of causality that impels the actions or part of them. As a result, this task is suitable to a broad discussion of the topic of plot, since it affords a clear distinction between the "succession" of events and the causes that link them and the linguistic "form" that is actually employed while writing. Classical distinctions between *fabula* and *sujet* may also be made to enrich the discussion of this task[9].

In addition, coping with this task presents problems regarding the literary perception of time in the story (Genette, 1972). Thus, synthetic description as opposed to detailed presentation and the relation between actions and feelings and ways of designing and organizing the plot may appear as interesting topics for the elaboration of non-formulated knowledge. In particular, it allows us to deal with the topic of suspense and the ways it is developed in the story, since the horoscope "tells" us what will happen, raising the question: should one make it happen in the story or not, surprising the readers by the characters' choices? Such a reading of the stories

---

[8] *See Lakoff & Johnson (1981) about metaphors of time in our modern culture.*

[9] *The terms "fabula" and "sujet" were suggested by the Russian formalists at the beginning of the 20th century, in order to describe the "intuitive" relationship between the story (the form of the content) and the aesthetic form of this story, and there is no agreement regarding the question whether this division can actually be carried out in practice. Todorov's distinction between "histoire" and "discours" and Chatman's between "story" and "discourse" are additional examples of attempts to map these distinctions.*

written in the workshop emphasizes the context of analysis that focuses on linguistic and organizational devices (context four) and permits participants to become aware of various narrative conventions. Regarding her text, Hava, the author, says:

> "Personally, I don't believe in horoscopes...I especially remember from the writing process that I was careful to select different words that would express the angry mood of the character. I made sure that I didn't repeat the same words all the time. To my surprise, a text resulted that proves that horoscopes come true...Regarding the end of the text, it is important to mention that at the beginning I thought the text would end badly, and only when I got to the end did I write the present ending."

This task allows the articulation of cultural voices through a text that is obviously peripheral to the cultural canon. Thus, it rises for discussion beliefs and opinions that shape popular culture and are also reflected in canonical culture, issue related to the cultural context (context one) and its impact on shaping the ways different kinds of texts are received. It is also possible to examine different types of inter-textual relationships with the workshop participants, using the horoscope as the starting point for the plot (context two). These range from exact quotations (as is true in Hava's example) to general influence that influences both the nature of the plot (what will happen to the character) and the nature of the character (his or her psychological traits). It is possible to demonstrate in a simple manner using a "non-canonical" text such as the horoscope the complex convoluted nature of "dialogue" among texts, a phenomenon I discussed above.

In addition, this task uncovers the variety of values and feelings that a text can evoke, thus raising them for discussion. For example, though most of the writers declare that they do not believe in horoscopes, they generally tend to choose their own Sign of the Zodiac as a starting point. They also tend to write in the first person or with the aid of a narrator who elaborates on the character's feelings, using extensive inner discourse or positioning himself very close to the main character. Ariella and Varda wrote the following regarding choosing the Sign of the Zodiac:

> Ariella "This task was relevant in my opinion as an opportunity to be critical and cynical about the horoscopes that appear in the newspapers. I actually chose my own sign – closeness and distance. First of all I read the horoscope and tried to create a character whose personality is as is predicted in the horoscope, while also meeting up with events mentioned in the horoscope. I wanted to create the absurd situation of people who act according to the horoscope in order to believe in it."

> Varda "When I looked at my horoscope, something I especially like to do, I noticed that when I read it I actually choose the good things, and about the bad things I say, 'Nonsense, it's not true what they have written. Who needs this anyway?'...This was my opportunity to write my own personal horoscope, to supposedly animate the written text into something live... I introduced the breath of life into my horoscope."

This task permits the "construction" of causal relations between events and states of mind as suggested by the horoscope, simultaneously answering questions generated by it: How can one understand the transition between different events? Who undergoes the suggested changes? What causes these changes to occur? The choice of specific factors as the cause of the shift between a starting circumstance and its resolution at the end of the story is what allows "a story" to be constructed, having different laws than the original text – the horoscope itself. Therefore, the task allows novices to cope with one of the most important and complex topics referred above that arise in theories of narrative (Rimmon-Kenan, 1983). Language and tone are developed accordingly, as is apparent in the story I chose as an example, and are discussed in the course of the workshop in accordance with the stories that are produced.

The analysis of the texts written by the participants also stresses the fact that the meaning we construct out of the text is a result of negotiation between the text and its readers, which is characterized by a certain amount of blindness to some of the aspects of the text (De Man, 1971). The narrator, his voice and viewpoint are uncovered as rhetorical mechanisms that allow the "non-naïve" organization of the plot in such a way as to impel the reader to continue reading (Genette, 1972). The narrator's point of view is what determines the order that was chosen to relate the events suggested by the horoscope "categorization" of items in order to achieve a specific effect: an interesting, seductive story.

6. CONCLUDING REMARKS

The workshop experience stresses the concept of genre as a delicate combination of "constraints" as determined by the tasks and by previous uses of genre and of "possibilities" of creating a personal statement that grows from the ongoing struggle of the writer with the meanings he wishes to shape. Therefore, the reference in the text to what was previously written makes obvious the fact that the various generic conventions define the framework within whose boundaries meaning can be created. Characters, point of view and plot were among the theoretical topics that came up for discussion in relation to the story as a type of generic framework within whose boundaries it is possible to create meaning. I chose these topics due to the fact that much has been written about them from a theoretical point of view, and they constitute part of the terminological repertoire that guide text interpretation in schools. It was thus important to re-examine them in the workshop. In addition, regarding the stories that were written in the workshop, the grammar of the text makes it possible to actually describe the relationship between a specific text (story, letter or article) and *abstractions* regarding texts. It also affords an examination of the transitions between practice and theory about practice as a way of learning and constructing knowledge about text as fulfilling a wide range of socio-cultural goals. This transition between actual texts and abstractions regarding texts is what facilitates personal – but socially grounded – learning.

Students' testimonies regarding processes of writing, reading and re-writing, in addition to the discussions that took place during the workshop regarding the kind of work "demanded" of the writers by each task, confirm the assumption I presented at the beginning of this chapter. The workshop framework has the ability to satisfactorily impart to participants a deepening understanding of reading and the way the text takes shape in the course of "textual" activities such as reading, interpreting and writing. Nevertheless, I must limit this statement in two ways. First, by suggesting that a relativistic point of view in relation to students' testimonies has to be assumed, because in a certain way, the students are "conditioned" by a very specific style of working and learning in class[10]. Secondly, one must add that the story as the generic framework proposed here may allow some of the participants to "skim" and write in an uncommitted and unengaged way. This is "acceptable," as long as there is a "temporary continuity" among events that sustains an "apparently" coherent continuum. However, other participants may develop the abilities and the sensibilities necessary for profound, valuable reading and writing that examines and "reinvents" its conventions, as well as the writer who does so. It is clear that these two attitudes regarding the activities in the workshop yielded different results, from the point of view of personal knowledge constructed in the course of the workshop and developing awareness regarding reading and writing processes

Throughout the dialogue in the workshop, attention was given to the recurring and changing characteristics of genre in light of the completed tasks. *Tacit knowledge* regarding writing and reading conventions was gradually revealed through careful examination of the written results and a discussion of their characteristics. This knowledge was expressed in the written texts and the writers' concrete decisions regarding questions that bothered them while writing, such as: Does writing in the first person generate identification? Does the elimination of details raise tension? What is the relationship between various gaps in the plot and further reading? What type of language should be used? Uncovering this knowledge and examining it in the classroom are the added value of the activity in the workshop. It allows participants to bring to light "knowledge we were unaware of, but that was there all the time" in a special and unexpected way. This knowledge is especially obvious in discussions and analyses in class, which examine the mechanisms and assumptions that allow the text to exist as an interaction between reader and writer[11].

In this process of searching, writing is a testimonial of readings that took place in the past, but it can also testify to the writing subject as the "inventor of himself" and creator of his own uniqueness[12]. This is due to the fact that *each time anew* he must

---

[10] *I can add from my personal experience during a post-doctoral research, that this kind of work in class also "influence" the way children in secondary school "think" and give testimony about the process of reading and writing. That is way it may be perhaps suggested that the use of workshops could help to learn to write and understand text's characteristics also in school. But this is another story. I would like to thanks to Emmanuele Auriac-Peyronnet that in her fine comments to this paper remember me these facts.*

[11] *Evidence of this may be seen in one of many examples: Na'ama: "The fact that the group talked about my texts, gave their opinion and "interpreted" the form of the text and its content – made me see my writing from another standpoint, understand things in a deeper way and understand what was conveyed to the readers and what was not... The barriers fell and the world of writing opened before me. I would have liked more opportunities for discussion, analysis, reading of the texts that were written by the workshop participants: because the actual reading of the texts and afterwards the response to the texts created in me as a writer learning of a different kind, very important learning. Learning takes place also from another angle – an angle that hears and responds to texts – I learned a lot about different writing styles through the texts that were written... The process still has not ended. It is still at the beginning and I hope to use the tools I have been given and the powers inherent in me in order to continue and never stop. I want to know more."*

[12] *This topic is my present spot of interest in analyzing texts created in the workshop during "automatic writing".*

place himself opposite the language and its conventions so that a certain text can be created. This is obvious, for example, in many students' texts and appeared "between the lines" in previous examples and in different testimonies[13].

The reference to texts in the workshop makes it possible to transform phenomena that seem obvious and "natural" on the surface – such as an understanding of continuity and coherence, drawing conclusions and creating symbolic connections between characters and ideological attitudes – to phenomena that uncover intense interpretive activity and reading habits. The activities in the workshop intend to de-automatize reading, and in this way create a space where *reading exists as an art,* an art that inquires about itself and its nature. De-automatized reading has an obvious affinity with contemporary plastic art, cinema and literature, which also "examine" their expressive tools. This affinity with art is not accidental, and is bound up with my perception of the writing workshop. The non-automatic approach to the written text was emphasized in analysis in the classroom, since this critical aspect contributes to a development of consciousness of the reading process in the framework of a specific genre. In addition, this aspect uncovers novices' writing in the workshop as a testimony of themselves, their methods of reading and constructing meaning, their ways of saying things and shaping them, their ways of being positioned in sociocultural environments. These elements emerge at various levels in the above quotations from participants' testimonies.

---

[13] *Here two testimonies:*

> Anath: "I would like to discuss the psychological aspect of writing. How in fact do the things I write, which are not necessarily based on fact, touch my personality, my internal world – at which point does everything intersect, and why? Why, someone else writes about the same thing in an entirely different way, from within his own personality. More than once I have met up with a strange incident: I wrote something and only afterwards understood that I didn't choose this form of writing randomly…Some kind of wish that was buried deep in my soul…burst onto the page while I was preparing my tasks."

> Yarden: "The goal of the course was in my opinion…the transition from randomness to significance…This influenced the fact that today, when I write, I also ask myself: Why did I write like that and not otherwise, and what is the significance hiding behind those words?"

The workshop activities presented in this chapter require ongoing experience. They also require study and a willingness to examine the cultural-linguistic surroundings in which we find ourselves, an activity that is liable to produce a certain *discomfort*. This is however a fertile discomfort, as it is a means of stimulating learning about written texts and the frameworks that affords their construction. Simultaneously, it seems to me that this is a type of investment that promises a unique yield for each and every reader and writer – both teachers and learners.

ACKNOWLEDGEMENT

My thanks to Prof. Elda'ah Weizmann for her useful comments on a previous version of this chapter and her help in its preparation. Thanks also to the students who took part in the workshops I have held over the years. The examples in this chapter are from their work.

WRITING "IN YOUR OWN WORDS": CHILDREN'S USE OF INFORMATION SOURCES IN RESEARCH PROJECTS

ROB OLIVER

University of London

Abstract. In this chapter I examine how a group of primary school children used sources of information in individual research projects on the subject of alternative energy. The chapter focuses on some of the strategies adopted by the children to make use of reference sources, in both book and electronic formats, and the ensuing transformations of source material, both verbal and visual, observed in the children's work. The study proposes that working with sources involves the project writer, here envisaged as a "text-maker", in a range of semiotic and inter-textual relations with other texts. These material relations, it is suggested, cannot be fully understood by a view of research which emphasises the extraction and re-use of "information" as content detached from textual form. Moreover, the traditional distinction between "copying" and "your own words" obscures these inter-textual relations and, consequently, a full picture of children's learning activity as composers of research genres. Instead, an understanding of how children both borrow material from existing texts and, at the same time, re-contextualise and innovate as a result of new communication may prove more helpful. The study points to the value of extended research projects in early literacy education, especially given the importance of independent research skills in later years.

Keywords: Writing from sources, research, semiotics, inter-textuality, multi-modality, genre.

1. INTRODUCTION

Doing an extended research project is a common learning experience for many children in the later years of primary school when working with multiple sources of information – reference books, encyclopaedias, CD-ROMs, the internet – begins to play a role in writing and oral presentations. Based on curriculum topics in, for example, science or history or on personal topics such as hobbies, projects typically involve children in the research of content information and its re-presentation in

---

Oliver, R. (2004). Writing 'in your own words': Children's use of information sources in research projects.
In G. Rijlaarsdam (Series Ed.) and Rijlaarsdam, G., Van den Bergh, H. & Couzijn, M. (Vol. Eds.), Studies in writing. Vol. 14, Effective learning and teaching of writing, 2nd Edition, Part 2, Studies in how to teach writing, 367-380.

texts of their own. The resourceful moving-between-texts required in this activity, prefiguring the more complex research tasks faced in secondary school and beyond, becomes evident in the projects produced by children. They can be distinctive in terms of how diverse materials are brought together (Ormerod and Ivani, 1997; 2001), how different genres are juxtaposed (Romano, 2000) and how semiotic modes such as writing and drawing are combined (Kress et al, 2001; Kress and van Leeuwen, 2001).

Work on children's research has tended to focus more on reading than on writing and how textual sources are used in projects (Wray, 1985; Wray and Lewis, 1993). As a result, it is not often acknowledged how reading and writing activities interact in research processes. In an attempt to reach some understanding of this interaction – how composition of a project text does not necessarily *follow* acts of reading for information, but is often closely integrated with them – I focus in this chapter on how a group of ten-year-old children used published sources of information while composing projects on alternative energy in an international school in the Netherlands.

The school in question had recently adopted a new curriculum which explicitly links "research skills", "enquiry learning" and "communication"[1]. Such a curriculum raises many questions about the role of research in children's literacy learning and its possible outcomes. How, in particular, may already-composed sources of information, available in electronic as well as print media, be re-used in ways which enable the active re-presentation, as opposed to the mechanical reproduction, of forms of knowledge? The seemingly innocent request to write "in your own words" masks the complex material processes involved in such transformations, the work of *project-ing* from other texts. How does the genre of the research project facilitate this learning by creating links between the reading/viewing of information and the activity of producing a new text?

Dianna Bradley, the teacher of the group featured in this chapter, expressed similar questions about children's research:

> The term "research" can be broadly used. What does it effectively mean for children? It seems ludicrous for children to know where to find information and how to get it if they can't interpret their information. When does information become their own and how can they use this skill to their own benefit? (Personal communication).

2. WRITING FROM SOURCES AND "YOUR OWN WORDS"

Wray and Lewis report a frustration commonly expressed by teachers about children's research-based writing: "How can I stop my children copying from reference books?" (Wray and Lewis, 1997: 3). They claim that

---

[1] *The International Primary Curriculum (IPC) was founded in 2001 and is currently followed by a number of schools in the Netherlands and elsewhere. The curriculum is based on a series of topic units through which "learning goals", broken down into "subject, personal and international goals", are pursued. See www.internationalprimarycurriculum.com.*

most junior children are quite aware that they should not copy from reference books, and can usually give a cogent set of reasons why not, but when they are actually engaged in the practical tasks of locating and selecting information in books will revert to copying behaviour with little demur. (Wray and Lewis, 1997:3)

However, the term "copying" appears far from straightforward in the learning of source-based writing where writers are in the business of making texts from other texts. A sharp distinction between what is "copied" and what is "original" conceals not only the transitional challenges of learning to write from sources, but also the kinds and degrees of textual borrowing and appropriation which are a feature of research genres, where our own words and the words of others combine and interact in multiple ways.[2]

Behind the doors of the copying/original distinction lie important issues in writing education at all levels. In her study of university student writing, Angèlil-Carter found that often "the student learning a new discourse is unable to do anything other than use the words of the texts she is reading in her writing, as a way of 'trying on' the discourse" (Angèlil-Carter, 2000: 103). This "trying on" means reproducing chunks of source language by a form of mimicry or "ventriloquation" (Wertsch, 1991). Far from being "copying", this adoption of already-phrased "voice types" (Wertsch, 1991:59) through the texts of others may function developmentally as part of a normal language learning process – an initial step towards more independent participation in disciplinary discourses, where one can make "one's own voice speak through the voices of others" (Angèlil-Carter, 2000: 37).[3]

There is a link between these observations and the work studied in this chapter. Children's research projects can be seen as an early encounter with the source-based, citation-rich, multi-layered composing which later becomes "academic writing". At the same time, children's projects typically draw on visual as well as verbal modes, a material feature which the appeal to write "in your own words" obscures.

3. CHILDREN'S WRITING AS SIGN-MAKING

The view of children's composition adopted in this paper draws on that developed by Kress et al. (2001) and Kress (1997; 2003) which sees children's texts as part of *"a dynamic process of sign-making"* (Kress et al.: 27, italics in original). In this social semiotic view, children are seen as active participants in the re-shaping and re-animation of knowledge rather than passive recorders of pre-established accounts. Their texts are one "sign" of this participation.

Sign-making, however, does not have a purely expressive or psychological bearing. It has a "double social motivation", reflecting both "who the sign-maker is, and

---

[2] *This recalls recent research from sociocultural and sociohistoric perspectives which has pointed to powerful myths of originality and individualism underlying western views of language. Such myths, it is argued, serve to obscure the social, cultural and institutional contexts in which* different kinds *of authorship and text production are shaped and mediated (Scollon, 1995; Pennycook, 1996; Prior, 1998).*

[3] *Taking this a step further, Sherman (1992), Pennycook (1996) and Price (2002) give examples of how textual borrowing in language learning also varies according to cultural factors and traditions.*

what her or his history has been" and "what the sign-maker assesses the communicational environment to be" (Kress, 1997: 93). The making of the sign depends on both orientations at once. The interests and motivations of sign-makers interact with the constraints and resources of contexts where signs are made in certain, conventional ways. Though already culturally pre-formed, these resources are still "unstable" in that they are constantly re-shaped "through the interests of social actors engaged in interaction with others" (Kress et al., 2001: 19). Children compose as "active decision-makers", drawing on the "semiotic affordances" of different genres and modes in their learning (Kress et al., 2001: 144). Writing can be understood as a prestigious but nevertheless changing *mode* which makes available *designs* for texts, for "conscious and creative communication *with* and *through* materials to achieve a human effect" (Sharples, 1999: 71; see also New London Group, 1996).

Close to this view of texts as sign-making is the idea of *transformation* as a normal feature of semiotic activity. A text ("sign") can not emerge from nothing or take place against a blank backdrop. Signs come from (other) signs. All texts, to some extent, emerge from, respond to and anticipate other texts and in doing so enact different types of *inter-textual* relations (Kristeva, 1984; Bakhtin, 1986; Fairclough, 1992). According to Kress, transformative activity is not a feature of specialised or elite creativity, but of everyday practice:

> Against notions of copying, imitation, acquiring, however implicitly they may be held.....I would like to propose the idea that children, like adults, never copy. Instead...we transform the stuff that is around us – usually in entirely minute and barely noticeable ways. (Kress, 1997)

This transforming work can be further understood as negotiation or dialogue between our own sign-making and the signs we come into contact with. Our own discursive experience and history is unique and individual but it is nevertheless "shaped in continuous and constant interaction with others' individual utterances" (Bakhtin, 1986: 89):

> Our speech.....is filled with others' words, varying degrees of otherness or varying degrees of "our-own-ness", varying degrees of awareness and detachment. These words of others carry with them their own expression, their own evaluative tone, which we assimilate, re-work, and re-accentuate. (Bakhtin, 1986: 89)

This re-accentuation, which makes sign-making both indebted and responsive to prior signs, and yet constantly pulling away from them, geared to new expressions, does not always come easily. As Bakhtin reminds us, "not all words for just anyone submit equally easily to this appropriation, to this seizure and transformation" (Bakhtin, 1981: 294). Many words "resist,.....sound foreign in the mouth of the one who appropriated them....as if they put themselves in quotation marks against the will of the speaker":

> Language is not a neutral medium that passes freely and easily into the private property of the speaker's intentions; it is populated with the intentions of others. Expropriating it, forcing it to submit to one's own intentions and accents, is a difficult and complicated process. (Bakhtin, 1981: 294)

Bakhtin here recognises that our making of signs is a struggle of thought and action to work in increasingly independent but at the same time increasingly responsive ways, not to free us from the influence of other signs – for that is impossible – but to see and hear and experience "otherness" as a resource for meaning rather than a force of authority and imposition (Bakhtin, 1981).

In the context of children's project-writing, information sources contribute to "the stuff that is around us". Information does not arrive as fluid raw material but as already-shaped, designed texts, culturally-laden, often radiating an aura of authority or prestige. Transforming the already-shaped into new shapes is not a matter of assimilation and recall, nor a matter of complete innovation, but of learning to *work with* information-bearing texts in creative and transforming ways – to draw from them, but also to draw away from them in the light of new understanding and communication. It is to set up increasingly dialogic relations with sources as *re*-sources and to turn the act of research into a purposive, situated sign-making – a form of communication and interaction rather than location and storage.

4. CONTEXT AND METHOD OF RESEARCH

The research on which this chapter is based took place over a four-week period in an English-medium international school in the Netherlands. I observed a group of twenty ten-year-old children engaged in research which culminated in individual written projects and oral presentations. The children come from a wide range of cultural and linguistic backgrounds, with many speaking at least one other language apart from English.[4]

As part of a unit of work on energy the children were asked to research one alternative source of energy such as solar, wind or tidal power using resources available in the classroom (reference books, children's encyclopaedias and CD-ROMs) and any other resources from home, including the internet.

Children carried out their research and project-writing in class and at home. They worked in pairs or small groups, typically for sessions of about one hour, often collaborating on the initial designs of projects and finding useful information together. At the outset of the project, the teacher used two plenary sessions to discuss what was already known about alternative energy and to model some outlines for projects. Useful resources on energy were also identified. Children were shown examples of basic bibliographies and asked to show evidence that they had used at least three different sources in their work.

These preparations included discussion of generic features of projects (title pages, contents, introductions, bibliographies) but little explicit demonstration of research techniques. The teacher, working closely with me as a researcher, wished to create a supportive but relatively free space for the production of the children's projects precisely to see how children went about doing research on an individual basis and particularly to study how they used sources. The nature of the topic meant children engaged with predominantly non-narrative genres.

---

[4] *This multi-lingual factor was not studied in this investigation but could become a focus of future research. There was evidence that some bilingual children used more than one language in their research, even though projects were written in English.*

I carried out classroom observations of children doing their research and interviewed a number of children as they worked and after the completion of their projects. The children's texts were analysed in terms of use of sources and how children had changed the material they had selected. Elements of the children's texts, both visual and verbal, were traced to book, internet or CD-ROM sources wherever possible, and the different types and strategies of transformation were described.

The following account describes, firstly, some strategies of individual project design in relation to sources which emerged during observation and interviews; and, secondly, some more general types of source appropriation observed in the children's texts.

5. CHILDREN TRANSFORMING INFORMATION

As with the projects studied by Ormerod and Ivani, this sample gave evidence of "children's intertextual processes" (Ormerod and Ivani, 2001: 86). It confirmed that children make active semiotic choices about material resources, modes and technologies in making project texts. Through these choices they make the "otherness" of information their "own" whilst at the same time recognising, and sometimes struggling with, the already-made nature and referential authority of their sources. Interview responses illuminated some of this struggle[5]:

> I found it hard to put things in my own words. Mostly the worst thing was....there's a lot of in information right in front of you...but you know, I mean, just how easy it is to copy it out – done! – and nobody will know but......no......basically then it's not your work. (Brandon)

> It's hard because once.....the internet usually says it in the good way of saying it, and you have to put it, like, even better....kinda hard. (David)

> We have a lot of information down....this is from there [*points to screen*] but kind of in our own words...but we look at something like [*reads from CD-ROM screen*] 'The Kaplan turbine was designed by Viktor Kaplan in 1913'.....and we can't really put 'Viktor Kaplan' in our own words. (Suny).

While drawing on and using sources of published information children were also trying to *draw away* from their sources, to get informed distance from existing formulations and designs in order to transform them within the context of a classroom event. Most children in the group expressed a desire to make information their own in some way, but at the same time felt the urge to "copy" word for word or to trace or import pictures unchanged from sources which appeared to have "the good way of saying it". This sometimes led to excessive printing-out from the internet or blanket-highlighting of photocopied sections from reference books. In these cases, the already-composed, packaged, authoritative appeal of "good" sources tended to re-

---

[5] *Names of students have been changed in this account.*

duce the transformative work of children unless this overload was resisted in some way.[6]

This resistance, by which children made space for their own thinking and action in relation to sources, took many forms. One child, Angelina, spoke of how she gained physical and compositional space from her sources:

> I get all the information, but I can't put it all together....I thought, I can't put that in my own words, what should I do? Put the book away. Just like not seeing it....I just don't look at it, and remember some of the information.....and write what I remember. It was tempting to copy....but I just put the papers down.

Other children described similar material strategies of leaving time-gaps between their reading and their writing or creating space by actually going to another room, switching off a computer or holding a conversation with a family member to see what they could remember from a source.

Several children used highlighters to indicate important points in sources, but as a consequence sometimes marked or saved unmanageably large sections. Strategies designed to overcome this overload included: highlighting or underlining only key-words or phrases; "chunking down" sources by transferring words or phrases, not whole texts, by "cut and paste" or manual transcription to another site, such as an exercise book or a word-processing document, thus effectively leaving sources "behind"; and using notational forms such as flow diagrams to produce new versions of technical processes, such as how a turbine works, rather than printing out diagrams from source.

These interventions tended to increase transformative work by "loosening up" the already-composed nature of published sources. They rendered information more fluid for re-use in texts. Inroads were made into source texts' designs, fragmenting them into usable elements or "chunks", both verbal and visual.

In this way children tended to think about the design and layout of their projects from the beginning of the research episode rather than at the end. At an early stage they drafted cover pages and illustrations, made provisional decisions about page design (borders, headings, use of colour), began to plan out where bits of verbal text and illustrations would go, or drafted possible chapter headings for their sections. Frequently they used questions as structuring prompts ("What is solar energy? Where do we get it from? Can we use it anywhere?") which clearly drew on prior knowledge about energy. These prompts were often changed in later drafts.

In these cases, the act of research merged into the semiotic event of making a new text. Reading and composing were in constant interaction. Instead of amassing information and then doing something with it, children tended to work on their

---

[6] *This dilemma is perhaps made more difficult by the abundance of information available on the internet. Many of the resources on alternative energy on the web seem targeted to meet the needs of children doing school projects (such as those offered by the US Department of Energy at www.eren.doe.gov). The comprehensive packaging and authority of these resources can leave children with the feeling that all has been said and done on the topic unless the research task requires them to take a particular* stance *towards the resources, designed to remake them in some way.*

sources from the outset, looking for particular things by reference to the task or by activating existing knowledge. In her project on tidal energy, for example, Alison knew something about the influence of the moon on tides and used her initial search for information to improve this knowledge base, approaching the subject of tidal energy from that angle.

Another strategy adopted by children to open up a creative space from sources, whilst at the same time drawing on them materially, was to adopt particular communicative roles to filter the research process. Imagining themselves as writing for peers, or for a younger audience, or as an editor of a fact-sheet gave some children a platform to help them read sources dynamically, with an eye to their transformation. Their reading became a forward-looking, interpretative activity as decisions about how and where to use specific source elements took place against gradually unfolding designs for new texts. Such roles helped children to see that in terms of genre the classroom project is not the same as a web-site, a reference book or an encyclopaedia. Therefore the forms of "information" must undergo change.

Angelina's decision to write her project "for younger children", for example, gave her a role which shaped her whole research activity. She used her knowledge of story-writing to construct her project on hydro-electric power as "kind of like a story….in a story you make people's hearts beat faster. In this one (the project) you have to make their brains beat faster, and make them understand". Angelina gathered information, but found the sources at odds with the "child language" she wished to use in her project. She learned early on in her research that hydro-electric power originated in ancient water wheels. This became the "roots" of her story. She then added pages on water ("hydro") and energy ("electricity") to structure the narrative:

> I had 'water' and 'electricity' – which makes 'hydro-electricity' – and I had the roots in water wheels, the past of it…I had the water, the electricity…all the ingredients needed to make hydro-electricity. The sugar, the flour, the milk.

She read and edited her reference book sources guided by these three projected elements or "chapters". The cover page of her project indeed resembled a child's picture story, showing a water wheel by a stream. The overall project design and the metaphors sustaining it guided her reading and her composition in a transforming way, loosening the hold and authority – the "composed-ness" – of source information. Her generic choice helped her to engage actively with the sources she had located.

The cooking metaphor is apt for the research-based writing process itself, where "other" texts are mixed and transformed into a "new" text. In this case the metaphor seemed to play a role in the whole project. Reading that the early water wheels were used to grind flour, Angelina decided to make some biscuits to give out during her presentation. This decision can be seen as part of her overall *design* to communicate the knowledge she had gained in a situated way, linking scientific information about energy to the daily business and pleasure of eating. Her pride and sense of achievement in this designing of a whole project is clear:

> If you think about it. Wow! I made a book, nobody ever wrote it. I didn't copy it. I did it by myself, with some help, books and things. You have that feeling...I really did it.....This was the first one, not really the first one, but the first one with those words.

A strong sense of the project as an event and the child's text as a unique but at the same time inter-textual sign comes across strongly in her words. In addition to these transformations through metaphor and genre, some children tapped their personal experiences in relation to the topic to motivate their projects and change the shape and phrasing of sources. On the first page of her project under the title "What is Tidal Power?", Alison combined personal experience, additional knowledge and newly-acquired scientific knowledge to frame her work:

> If you have ever been water rafting, then you have felt a little bit of the power of water. A tidal wave (tsunami) can destroy an entire city.
>
> Tidal power is energy that is made by machines which get their energy from the movement of water with the tides.

Here she answers her title question on two levels, the first based on personal experience, the second on scientific knowledge (establishing "Tidal power" as a subject). The combination of two contrasting "voice types" (Wertsch, 1991) shows her designing her project to make the "new" scientific information accessible in relation to more everyday experience. Below the piece of text given above, she manually pasted a colour aerial photograph of a tidal power station, giving the reader an initial panoramic orientation to the topic before the more technical drawing of a generating system later in the project. She ended her project on tidal power with a paragraph beginning "I love water" and giving details of a marine biology camp she had attended. She also used prior knowledge of the Japanese *tsunami* to illustrate the natural power of tides, and in interview explained how a disaster movie had roused her interest in the topic.

Similarly, some children made links between source material and other areas of knowledge. Working on geothermal energy, one student imported into his project a painting by Frederick Church of the volcano Cotopaxi which he had found on the internet. Brandon introduced the volcano alongside more topic-specific material because volcanoes exist in countries where the earth's crust is thin, and these are also the countries which can use geothermal energy. In designing this page of his project he combined the painting with a map taken from the NASA web-site showing the "ring of fire" of volcanoes. A scientific and an artistic source from different locations were here brought together to make a single new text.

A final feature of this "loosening" of source information to enable transformation was the role of talk in re-formulation. Two children, Suny and Angelina, were using a CD-ROM to find out how turbines work. At one point they were making use of two diagrams and a piece of written information. One sentence caused them particular trouble:

> A nozzle converts the kinetic energy of high-pressure water into a powerful jet, and the buckets extract the momentum. ('Hydraulic Turbines', Encarta, 1994)

Using the diagram and their own talk, the children worked towards an understanding of this process:

Suny: We'll try to put it into our words....a nozzle is....um....something like.....pressure or something...like pressure...

Rob: Why not just use the diagram? The water comes in.....

Suny: ..the water comes in, it's pushing itself in with the nozzle...//.it hasn't become a jet yet, this is just going round good,...so...these are the wheels with buckets, so they carry the water...

Angelina: ..and when it turns, that's when they're heavy...it makes energy.. that's in the olden days they had a wood stick or something, a really big one, attached to (inaudible)....and they made cookies that way..//

Suny: ....so it goes in...the water pushes itself in, with the nozzle...into the buckets, and then it goes, it's flushing itself....so it has to go faster so it can keep going into the buckets, so now it becomes a jet...// ..it's gonna move.....the pressure of the water is quite high...//...so it turns the wheel faster for electricity to come out.

By jointly narrating the events depicted in the diagram the two children moved towards their own formulation of the turbine process. Their understanding of words like "converts", "extracts" and "momentum" unfolded the densely-packed source in a new way. The order of grammatical subjects, with "high-pressure water" recast in a subject role firstly as "water" and then "the pressure of water", mirrored the temporal sequence of events in the diagram. Two sentences from Suny's final project echo this sequencing, first rehearsed in this conversation, with active process verbs replacing many of the passive forms used in the original source whilst retaining some of the technical vocabulary:

> High pressure water forces itself through a sluice and makes the blades on the turbine spin faster. A nozzle is like a force of high-pressure water or kinetic energy into a powerful turbine jet.

Her first sentence projected the passive construction of the source sentence ("Broad, swivelling blades on the turbine are spun by high pressure water as it is released through a sluice") into a more active formulation. Her second sentence was, similarly, an attempt to explain the process in order of temporal occurrence. In a small but significant way, the researcher was here making sense of what she had read "in her own words", trying to re-shape the information for a new purpose. She was also "trying on" a new discourse by using technical vocabulary and phrases ("high-pressure water", "sluice", "turbine", "nozzle", "kinetic energy") probably for the first time.

Her final description was accompanied by a simplified version of the turbine picture, placed at the head of her text. The design concept of the page appears to have taken root with the conversation above. The two children were engaged in an active dialogue with their source, not a passive reproduction of it. The sign in the original published source was refracted, through reading and speech, into a new sign in the child's text.

These examples give some idea of how children were becoming aware of the need to both exploit and resist information sources in their own research projects. In no case did children depart completely from source representation. Indeed, the projects gave many examples of directly imported material. However, in most cases the children's projects showed various kinds of blends: imported formulations blended with newly-composed ones. As signs, children's projects bear multiple traces – of personal decisions and interests, of other texts, of classroom events and interactions, and of broader generic designs.

6. SIGNS OF TRANSFORMATION IN CHILDREN'S PROJECTS

This section briefly summarises five different kinds of transformation of published sources observed in the children's projects. This is not presented as a hierarchy of skills but as an open inventory of the semiotic moves used by children as text-makers in this sample. These descriptions are not designed to typecast research behaviour in a closed typology but to outline practices of appropriation through which individual pathways of composition were seen to emerge in this particular genre.

Direct Importation. The text-maker imports wholesale a chunk of text or an image from a source using a replicating technology ("cut and paste", manual *verbatim* transcription, scanning). The transformation involves acts of selection and importation, but also a certain amount of composition in that the imported chunk or image becomes part of a new text and is, therefore, re-contextualised. This may involve, for example, inserting the imported element into a sequence. One child in the sample produced a project made up entirely of pages printed from different internet sites. He had, however, selected the pages from a potentially vast source and arranged material in a chapter sequence which showed at least some degree of transformative design. Most children in the group imported at least some material, mostly images, directly from the internet or electronic picture libraries into their project texts.

Selective Importation and Arrangement. The text-maker imports a chunk of text or an image, but changes the spatial or compositional arrangement of the source material in the light of a new design. This may involve, for example, putting two imported passages of (written) text from different sources side by side, cropping a section of imported text, or placing an image in a new relation to writing. In these kinds of transformation the material and modal design decisions of the text-maker begin to play a part. For example, choice of fonts and typefaces as well as decisions about borders and colour may all influence the ways in which imported material is rearranged.

Amended Importation. The text-maker imports pieces of text and image, but intervenes in them in editorial ways. This may involve, for example, altering particular words. In this sample, a number of children appropriated chunks of source material directly but made lexical changes. One child, for example, changed the word "incandescent" to the word "fiery" in an otherwise transcribed short passage from a reference book about volcanoes. Other examples included: removing subordinate clauses from sentences to simplify them or to distribute clauses across a number of sentences; editing out sentences completely or changing their order; using italics or colour to highlight keywords for a glossary; reducing or enlarging images; producing a simplified version of a drawing; changing the font of a label on an imported image.

Re-shaping of a Source. The text-maker draws on a dominant focal source but reshapes it in significant ways. Transformations of this kind include some of those featured in the previous section where metaphorical, generic and experiential perspectives re-cast source material in selective ways. Children in the sample often took words or phrases from their sources, but did not take whole sentences or paragraphs. Sometimes they re-shaped information by applying other styles of language, for example by changing a scientific account of a process into a dialogue. In this kind of work with sources skills of editing, note-taking and paraphrase play an important role, but also the transfer of information from one mode to another, for example from a diagram to a verbal account, or vice versa. Three children, for example, made three-dimensional models to accompany their texts. Other examples of this kind of transformation involve the re-casting of source material in new genres. In a similar research episode observed in the same school factual information from encyclopaedias was transformed into quizzes, mock interviews, cartoons and narratives.[7]

Synthesis and Re-shaping of Multiple Sources. The text-maker draws on a range of sources and absorbs them, with different degrees of explicitness, into a single, designed text. Phrases and images may still recall specific sources but there is no dependence on a single or dominant source. One child, for example, combined material from four different sources on one page of her project, bringing together scientific information in different modes on hydro-electric power and linking it to geographical information on Niagara Falls. These complex, allusive transformations are characterised by a strong sense of overall design, with highlighted, saved or imported source texts used as a spur at the beginning of the research episode but soon abandoned or back-grounded in favour of the researcher's own notes or drafts. Sources become grafted onto other sources. Children who transformed information in this synthesising way tended to visualise and constantly update their project designs while researching. They also introduced material and ideas from their own experience and made textually-supported links with other topics.

Together, these transformative moves could be seen as a repertoire of semiotic activity, as resources for action in relation to other texts in this particular genre, the information research project. It is likely that other genres of children's school writing, such as narrative or report writing, will draw on different ways of using and transforming other texts. A project writer may make creative use of all of the above resources in a single project. He or she may compose, for example, a piece of verbal text by synthesising chunks of information from two different sources and combining the resulting text with an image imported directly from an internet site, but with the latter given amended annotation, a new frame or a new caption. In the projects in

---

[7] *Kress et al (2001) give examples of secondary students re-shaping information about blood circulation using a range of narrative and media genres, including fairy tales, spy-action movies, and 'Dear Diary' formats (Kress et al, 2001: 143-152).*

this sample, these operations were performed in both electronic and manual ways. Indeed, one striking feature of several of the projects was the integration, *frequently on the same page*, of electronically-generated material (for example, a written passage imported from an internet site and then edited) with hand-drawn or handwritten material (for example, a labelled, coloured-pencil diagram adapted from a more complex original in a reference book).

7. CONCLUSIONS AND IMPLICATIONS FOR TEACHING

The research confirms the material diversity of young children's projects found by Ivani and Ormerod (2001) and their typically "multi-modal" composition (Kress and van Leeuwen, 2001). It also reveals a diversity in the resourceful ways in which children use published sources of information and employ strategies to appropriate them. The research suggests that these strategies are artisanal and individual, but also draw on shared practices of textual transformation.

The appeal to write "in your own words" is in many ways misleading. It masks the materiality of research-based writing and its inter-textual and multi-modal qualities. From the evidence of this study, children work on source material in multiple ways, all of which involve some degree of re-contextualisation and some degree of preservation. They *work with* information as it is textually articulated through modes and genres rather than as a neutral essence of fact which is extracted (through reading) and then reproduced (through writing).

Seeing children's composition in this way implies an interactive and contingent view of authorship in the midst of textual practices, a view based on transformation rather than origination. This emphasis on practices does not, however, annul individual creativity, engagement and imagination.

The most transformative work on sources seems to take place when children understand and share the communicative aims of a task and use this understanding to motivate, jointly, their research and their text-making. "Writing" and "reading" both then entail "sign-making", with much productive shuttling between them. There is evidence from this research episode that engagement with the *overall* visual design of a project, however sketchy, at early stages of research encourages children to use sources with more transformative agency.

Further research could look at how interaction, for example spoken dialogue between peers at a computer, plays a role in the research process by contributing to the "loosening up", the making-available, of source texts. One limitation of this study is that I have concentrated on *textual* sources and transformations by individuals, as if they are working alone but still projecting a communicative strategy. In reality, research activity and design might draw on a wide range of "sources" arising from different social genres – a class discussion, a TV programme or magazine, a family discussion or outing. Such "sources" might range from a single word or phrase to a whole passage of written text or a series of images. Transformative activity on these appropriated elements might work across modes (for example, extracts from a classroom conversation about volcanoes might be visualised in a drawing) or across genres (the scenes, images and voice-over of a video about volcanoes might be imaginatively re-worked as the written account of someone visiting an active volcano). Future research could take these broader communicative transactions into account by considering project-making not as a purely textual activity but as a fully multi-modal and social-interactive event of learning.

Research projects, I suggest, have a role in the teaching of content knowledge, but also a role in children's textual education. Through active work on sources children can become aware of the multiple constructions of knowledge, and their own involvement in those constructions. Through their own texts they can come to participate in knowledge-making and, in small ways, break down assumptions that information is fixed, corporate, author-less, and "already-said".

A teacher could model approaches to the transformation of sources, and thus show design as materially changeable and not just a surface feature, by showing how a sentence in a reference book can be re-shaped in alternative grammatical forms, or how an image can be re-presented in alternative formats. In these changes "information" does not remain neutral or static but takes on new meanings. Critical literacy can take shape in such hands-on experiments with texts, as well as open up ways of evaluating the usefulness of sources.

Research projects require space and time, often a luxury in literacy environments dominated by testing and the need for short-term results. Taking the longer view, independent research skills are in demand and highly valued in later phases of education. These skills must begin somewhere, in early acts of reading, viewing, appropriation and design.

ACKNOWLEDGEMENTS

I would like to thank the children and staff at the Haagsche Schoolvereeniging, the Hague, especially Dianna Bradley and Dave Porter. Thanks also to Helen Martin.

METACOGNITION TO LEARN HOW TO WRITE TEXTS AT SCHOOL AND TO DEVELOP MOTIVATION TO DO IT

ANNE-MARIE DOLY

Auvergne University, Clermont-Ferrand, France

Abstract. This chapter presents a study carried out in four several final year elementary school (for pupils of 10/11 years old) and two college classrooms (12 to 14) during a period of six years and its different theoretical references. The aim was to teach pupils how to write narrative texts while developing motivation for this task. Metacognition was chosen as a tool for learning because it is at the same time: (1) an efficient strategy to manage a task throughout, by the pupils using self-control over their own activity (through the processes of forward planning, autoregulation/monitoring and evaluation) which requires awareness of activity, meta-knowledge of the task and especially a knowledge of the "evaluation criteria" (which describe *what* is the aim to be achieve) and of the "procedural criteria" (which describe *how* one can manage to write narrative texts)., and (2) a good way to develop motivation, throughout the development of self-concept, the knowledge of oneself as a learner, the feeling of self-efficacy and internal locus of control.
This study is a 'design' study: after trying out a first model, it was tested and review as many times as necessary for its fit (feasibility for teachers, fitting the national program, stimulating motivation for teachers and students, etc.). The model is theoretically validated, and empirically tested and reviewed, using questionnaires, interviews and student outcomes, during a period of five years.
We think that: (1) this metacognitive learning needs several conditions we explain and describe; (2) using metacognitive strategy will be really possible for pupils if they can construct themselves the two types of criteria, and (3) one of the main condition is that this work can't be done by the pupils alone, they must be help systematically to do it by the teacher. So we had to define this sort of help (i.e. what she has to aim and how) by the reference to the notion of mediation and tutoring.
After an account of the research – theoretical references, work hypothesis, action plan and conditions of implementation, modalities and content of evaluation – we present the different steps we carried out after six years of practising in several forms.

Key-Words: Metacognition, writing text, self-regulation, evaluation, assessment, procedural criteria, motivation, locus of control, self-efficacy, tutoring.

Doly, A-M. (2004). Metacognition to learn how to write texts at school and to develop motivation to do it.
In G. Rijlaarsdam (Series Ed.) and Rijlaarsdam, G., Van den Bergh, H. & Couzijn, M. (Vol. Eds.), Studies in writing. Vol. 14, Effective learning and teaching of writing, 2nd Edition, Part 2, Studies in how to teach writing, 381-392.

1. INTRODUCTION

In such a written cultural tradition as ours, knowing how to write is essential for the appropriation of a culture. Actually, writing is useful for the handing down of the culture and for its construction. At the same time, it enables us to acquire a freedom and citizen's behavior for which critical and reflective reason is essential. We know, with J. Goody (1979) the connection between the emergence of the reason, the scientific thought and writing. We can understand that learning to write has always constituted the major goal of schooling since its origin.

Learning to write has become much more difficult, particularly when pupils had to write not only isolated sentences or paragraphs but real texts. Psychological and psycholinguistic researches (see the Hayes & Flower model, 1980; Fayol 1985; Gombert 1991), resumed by teaching methodology (Garcia-Debanc, 1984; Charolles, 1984; Rosat, Dolz, & Schneuwly, 1991; Roussey, & Piolat 1991; Rémond, 1999) have emphasized the different cognitive processes – planning, putting in text ("mise en texte"), revision. Now, for these mental processes, metacognitive control is indispensable, so the cognitive cost is important, especially for novices.

These difficulties, intrinsic to the task, are not the only ones. Writing is less and less used. Its meaning may get lost in our society as oral language and visual signs tend to be preferred: they are less cognitively demanding especially as for metacognitive work required for writing.

Writing is thus both difficult and depreciated: it neither represents a motivating activity nor a motivating learning curve for pupils, particularly for those who are underprivileged. Actually, metacognitive abilities, (mainly for language mastery), which require distance, reflection, and awareness, which are also necessary to the individual's internal control, are analyzed by Lahire (1993) from pupil's written productions as one of the essential abilities lacking in those who are identified as failure in school. Now, these pupils come in the main, from underprivileged social classes which are dominated by types of oral tradition, even when school, which hands down writing tradition, requires metacognitive capacities without learning it (Rochex, 1995).

We can understand the importance and the benefit of metacognitive work about these two aspects of efficiency and motivation mainly for these underprivileged pupils. And teaching them metacognitive skills, through learning to write texts, could be very useful in a society where they are indispensable tools for constructing social and cultural identity.

2. THEORICAL FRAMEWORK FOR THE TEACHING MODEL

2.1 About its Definition

Metacognition consists of two elements (Flavell, 1985; Yussen, 1985; Doly, 1998; 1999). First element is *metacognitive knowledge* – true or not – that the individual has about "cognitive processes" (Flavell, 1985): cognitive functioning – particularly one's own – about strategies – those he's got, those he's not got – about task – writing for example – and about "cognitive products": what he knows – and does not know – about knowledge. Second element is the *control processes*: predicting, guessing, planning, monitoring (self-regulation) and evaluation. These processes are carried out by sudden awareness ("prises de conscience") on what one is doing to reach the aim; this awareness enables him with two things: (1) they stimulate metacognitive knowledge useful for monitoring and (2) they put procedure and aim in relation in order to execute self-regulation.

It will thus be advantageous for teaching writing text, that pupils learn how to control their writing activity by self-regulation with true metacognitive knowledge which has been constructed by them with the help – but a special one – of the teacher.

2.2 About its Role and Efficiency

2.2.1 Metacognition and Success and Transfer

The main results of studies on metacognition show that using metacognition promotes success in managing tasks and transfer of their results. Many researchers (Yussen, 1985; Gaveleck & Raphael, 1985; Paris & Winograd, 1990; Ostad, 1999) show connection between metacognition and:
- progress in learning (Paris & Winograd) and success in problem solving task;
- transfer of strategies and knowledge (learnt with metacognition);
- school achievement and more precisely, attainment of skills to learn. Good pupils are labeled as "learning experts", "transferors" and "self-regulated" (Bouffard-Bouchard, Parent, & Larivée, 1991a; 1991b). In point of fact, they are metacognitive in their way of managing their tasks – they anticipate, guess, plan, self-regulate, self-evaluate, whereas schools less able pupils throw themselves into task without any awareness or self-regulation.

Studies on L.D. (Learning disabled) (Cullen, 1985; Wong, 1985) show that their deficiency is mainly metacognitive – they could have knowledge and strategies but they are not aware of it and they don't know how to use them when necessary.

These studies also show that the learning of metacognitive skills is possible – with some necessary conditions- and it improves the performances (Mélot, 1991, Mélot & Corroyer 1992, Cauzinille-Marmèche 1991, Doly 1998, 2002).

If several researches are cautious about the correlation between metacognition and transfer because of the difficulty to assess it – what we meet with in our own work –, correlation with metacognition is much more reliable.

2.2.2 Metacognition and Motivation

A very frequent result of metacognition studies, especially those on the LD, is that metacognition stimulates motivation (Cullen, 1985; Paris & Winograd, 1990; Van Kraayenoord & Schneider, 1999; Bråten & Olaussen, 2000; Doly, 1996 & 1998). Motivation can be particularly seen in involvement into tasks and in perseverance despite failures. This is what mainly appears in our own work in the classroom

(2.2.). What is necessary for pupils to develop motivation? and what is noted as developed by motivated pupils?
1) They must find sense in their task; and in order to do that, they need to have a representation of the task by its goal and/or it's finality (to be able to control their activity).
2) They must have metacognitive knowledge: motivated pupils know themselves as learners and they know what knowledge they possess (about strategies, task and knowledge) *("they know what they do know and what they don't know yet"*, Rochex, 1995).
3) They must attribute their performances to their own control (internal attribution): *"their actions are indeed what is responsible for their performance"* so " *their failure is never inescapable and uncontrollable "* (Paris & Winograd); so, effort is always possible and stimulating for pupils because they *"are aware of their power of control and monitoring".*
4) They must develop "self-efficacy feeling" (Bouffard-Bouchard & Co, 1991 b), that is the ability to perceive oneself as efficient and to construct a positive self-concept throw the different school activities, performances and assessments.
This feeling is linked with metacognitive activity:

> "the perception of oneself efficiency plays a role of mediation between one's current capacities and his ability to use them adequately. ... It could have higher effects on self-monitoring than cognitive skills themselves (...)" (Paris & Winograd, 1990).

So, motivation is closely connected with metacognition: on one hand, metacognitive pupils show these motivational behaviors, and on the other hand, making pupils use metacognition requires and develops those motivational behaviors (Bräten & Stokke Olaussen, 2000): that constitutes one of my main hypotheses of work.

2.3 About the Conditions of Practising Metacognition

Conditions for improving metacognition in classroom work stem from my own work in classrooms as necessary conditions to practise metacognition in class and from other studies reported in literature about metacognition (Cauzinille-Mamèche 1991; Mélot, & Corroyer, 1991; Fayol & Monteil, 1994; Doly, 1998 & 2003 in press).
1) Pupils need some previous available metacognitive knowledge in the concerned field to enter the task.
2) They must be able to activate this knowledge when necessary: this ability depends on age, but mainly on the method of training, on the way of helping, and on the way this knowledge has been acquired and put in the memory for transfer, which implies three other conditions:
- Pupils must have a representation of the goal (especially by evaluation criteria which describe the final situation) and keep orientated to it.
- They must be aware of parts of their activity while it goes on, and at its end, in order to understand what they are doing, in order to assess the benefit of this way of coping by making the relation between procedure, goal and performance.

- "the key of the transfer would consist in the ability of the individual to work out the particular solutions into an abstract level, what requires abstracting the properties and the fundamental connections of the situation." (Cauzinille-Marmèche, 1991).

So, the individual has to "decontextualize" knowledge and procedures, and to conceptualize them in order to make them able to be generalized (see work in class about criteria cards made by pupils). This work to abstract is close to the three levels of abstraction of Piaget (1974) ("empirique", "réfléchissante" and "réfléchie" that the individual has to get over from "intelligence sensori-motrice" to "intelligence opératoire" using sudden awareness.

3) This re-working out ("ré-élaboration"), very often made by writing prepared by oral communication between pupils and teacher, has to be executed by the pupils themselves and not by the teacher, even if she has to help them to do it.

4) Metacognitive behaviour is not spontaneous for pupils and we do not note it in the forms where the teacher has not anticipated and prepared it precisely. Thus, the "mediation" of the teacher is indispensable and it is essential to define it (Doly, 1998; 1999; 2000).

The mediation of the teacher must be understood as a tutoring. This concept comes from Bruner (1983: 261) who refers to Vygotsky's thought on intellectual development and his idea of child social and cultural development by "internalization" (interiorisation) (1985: 111). The whole literature on this point (Day & Co, 1985) refers to this Vygotski-Bruner frame. These references as well as my work in classes allowed me to define this sort of mediation. It means that the teacher has several things to do:

- to construct a conceptual organization of knowledge, didactic and pedagogical objectives,
- to prepare the lesson in order to make pupils use metacognitive abilities,
- to choice an adequate situation for learning,
- to use a particular way for his intervention which must neither be sanctioning, nor prescribing but questioning, helping to and asking for re-formulation on what the pupils are doing to attain the goal.

Tutoring has to help pupils become aware and make different cognitive operations necessary to execute the metacognitive control of their own activity (and the decontextualisation/conceptualization) without doing this instead of them. This way of helping must be internalized by pupils so that they will be able to "help themselves" (Bruner, 1983; Doly, 1998 & 1999).

These references, to which it should be added pedagogic knowledge about narrative writing text not exposed here, constitute the background knowledge of my work in the classrooms.

3. PUT IN PRACTICE

How to enable pupils to learn writing text using metacognition and what does it mean?

We have to teach pupils to write narrative texts with metacognition abilities in its two aspects of knowledge and of internal control: the teacher has to make pupils to construct metacognitive knowledge about tasks, strategies and their own skills and difficulties in this area, that they will be able to use in order to monitor their own activity of writing.

3.1 Methodology

The hypotheses of this work are based on researches about metacognition in its connections with task management and conditions for self-regulation, and with motivation:
- Using metacognition makes training and progress in writing texts easier for pupils;
- It is possible, if the four conditions stated formerly are respected, especially the way of tutoring, to make pupils construct metacognitive knowledge, particularly the one concerning evaluation criteria (which define the goal) and the one concerning proceeding criteria to control their writing activity;
- This metacognitive way of learning develops motivation for writing texts: it develops a self knowledge about the task, procedures and strategies, what is easy- what is difficult for him, it develops internal attribution, and the feeling of self-efficacy and, at least a positive self concept.

In other words, this metacognitive way of learning develops both the pleasure of writing and the ability to do so (see further the interviews), which widely helps learning.

Device and Evaluation. Our method is qualitative. I tested a model in four different classrooms (age: 9-11) and two classrooms in college (12-15) during a period of five years; Progressively I developed a pattern to stimulate metacognition at school with pupils. The assessment of this work has been made in several ways: (1) the teachers made regular assessments (required by school); (2) we analysed answers to questionnaires and interviews systematically carried out on the pupils and on the teachers; (3) we compared pupil's answers of different classrooms, especially with those without metacognitive work.

Some difficulties still remain. There has been only one comparison with a classroom without metacognition work (as control group). The study of starting data was made only through teacher's and pupils reports. Evaluation of transfer and its connection with metacognition is very difficult in natural classroom situation. This way of teaching requires a special training for teachers as much on theoretical basis as on the question of tutoring which is not a usual way of teaching.

3.2 Modelisation: Description of the Process in Nine Steps

This work required an important work to prepare the lessons: it must concern didactic objectives (which knowledge and skills in the subject are aimed? and how?) and pedagogical objectives about metacognitive abilities and motivation.

1) Didactic objective: learning to write narrative text; operational objective: making pupils construct evaluation criteria (which describe the goal) and procedure criteria.
2) Pedagogical objectives: (1) teaching pupils self knowledge about themselves in writing activity in order to better control and monitor it in connection with its criteria; (2) developing self efficacy feeling and motivation to write concurrent with ability, and a positive self concept (helping pupils to become aware of being able to write narrative texts in order to like it and do it).

Step 1. The teacher advises the pupils of the work's modalities and objectives.

Step 2. She stimulates pupils to set up a first list of basic evaluation criteria: it is to generate meta-knowledge on the task allowing them to monitor to a minimum their writing output. Then each pupil writes a text on a subject chosen by the teacher who only helps those in difficulty to allow them to take part in following sessions. The teacher assesses texts on a separate card, notices difficulties and errors found for each pupil and for the whole form according to the most frequent and to its didactic objectives, those she will use to choose evaluation criteria that she wants pupils to find and use to write at other times. She then selects two or three texts: one represents a good text (according to the criteria), the others show, the most clearly, the errors she should like the pupils to become aware of, in order to have them find the criteria which will be used for the re-writing of their texts. The teacher types these texts and eliminates irrelevant variables.

Step 3. She distributes these texts to pupils, who are put in pairs. They are asked to assess them on a separate card, writing: "what goes well and what does not"; "what could it be written for the writer to help him to improve his text". During this work, the teacher helps systematically and by tutoring (as described above) if anyone needs: she helps them to pass out of an intuitive and global assessment into a precise and explicit one (Vygotsky, 1985): *"school makes pupils pass from unconscious to conscious and willful");* to make them progress in the representation of the goal by criteria to re-write in a better controlled way. At the end, she starts to question them about their procedures to help them to understand the question (new for them) to come back to it afterwards.

Step 4. The teacher gathers these assessment cards, assesses them to know who perceived what in the texts, which criteria have been found and which have not, and makes a synthesis. She wants to know two things: who are the pupils who have the greatest difficulties in evaluation, that is to say to perceive what must be done to write well, that is to say again to perceive and use the evaluation criteria; which difficulties have been perceived by the pupils in the texts and those which have not, to be able to prepare and conduct the next collective oral lesson that must be allowed to set up the list of criteria.

Examples of pupil's evaluation:

> your beginning is too short
> the beginning does not go with what goes next
> there's no action
> your text is too short
> here, we don't know whom you are talking about
> whom are you talking about with all your "he (s)"

your ending is too short" or "not clear"
have your characters speak
make your ending longer
say more about your characters
describe them more
your characters have disappeared. Where?
remove the repetitions
add adjectives
put capital letters after full stop.

The hypothesis retained there (Bruner, 1983: 263-264) is that the capacity to evaluate comes before and allows production:

> "the understanding of the solution (that is also to say, of the goal) must come before its production. (...) That is to say that the learner has to be able to recognise a good solution (...) before being able himself to produce the processes which lead to it without help"

and the progress can only be done with help of an expert tutor. That is why we make pupils practice evaluation before re-writing and in order to do it with better chance of progress. And they evaluate not only before writing and to help their re-writing, but they also construct for themselves the evaluation-criteria necessary to write: we are much more certain that they may be able to use these criteria to control their own writing activity (criteria are in their "proximal zone").

Step 5. The teacher guides an oral and collective lesson of assessment which must lead pupils to a decontextualization/ conceptualization of evaluation-criteria: the teacher gets pupils to do for themselves this work of abstraction and explicitation of criteria by tutoring. The pupils set out the criteria they found, discuss to keep those more pertinent, according to the didactic objectives and to formulate them precisely. The teacher writes the criteria on the board, classifies them in local aspect (microstructure: word and sentence level, style,), and in total aspect (macro-structure level, narrative organization and marks) so that the pupils have a double card. For example:

Card for local criteria:

> Mind repetition of words – mind punctuation (full stop and capital letter after it, inverted commas when somebody is speaking) – mind not changing tense without reason – we must know who/which/what we are speaking about when we write 'he", "she" "it", "her", "his" "its" – find attractive words to describe.

Card for total criteria (example taken after two lessons):

> In the initial situation, we have to present the characters, to say where and when the story takes place, to tell pertinent details for story – there is a hero and other characters, and something happens to him (there is a problem) – the hero sets up a plan – there may be sudden changes of fortune – the story must have an ending and we must know what happened to the characters introduced in the beginning – be aware also of spare texts: it is possible to make the text longer with descriptions or dialogues – we have to find a title in connection with the story.

These criteria evolve as pupils learn and have developed their abilities: some disappear, new ones appear. During this oral lesson, pupils already show that they become aware of their own mistakes (the teacher helps them to realize that because she knows their texts and their errors). The teacher saw the evaluation cards of pupils and knows who is having difficulty, who has to take part in the discussion to understand better, plus what was difficult for all of them: so, she intervenes to focus attention on some points, to encourage some pupils to speak. His purpose is to make pupils go beyond the local and empirical level towards a more conceptual and generalized level. This guidance by tutoring requires from the teacher, listening, availability, and trust in the capacity of pupils to discover what the teacher would like them to learn. So, at the end of this lesson, pupils have a double card of evaluation criteria.

They frequently asked for another card for resistant errors. This card has generally been called "mind!" and it can be different for each pupil (we can note that we very often came across the same difficulties in the different classrooms): Example for card "mind":

> Not too many sudden changes of fortune – no explosion of things or characters into text or their sudden disappearance – no changing tense – no use of familiar or rude words – use "pretty" words to describe – do not copy the TV series (we read a text which made changes of fortune by copying every sentence from TV script)

Step 6. At the end of this first work and more in following sessions (after re-writing), the teacher questions the pupils about their *procedures: "how have you managed writing your text?" "how did you start writing?" "is there anything which helped you?" "which has been the most difficult?" "how do you know you have done what is right according to criteria?"*

This reflection of the pupils, which is first oral and collective then individual and written (as described for the other card) leads to a card for proceedings (" proceeding criteria") used for the re-writing.

Four goals are aimed for this work: pupils must become aware (1) of their own procedures); (2) that there are other procedures than their and which ones they are; (3) that there are some more efficient than others; and, (4) of the benefit of changing if necessary, and how to go about it.

Example: (we can note here again that we find generally the same procedures in the different classrooms): The pupils who have generally done their text well or re-written it says:

> " I go through the story in my head before writing"; "I imagine all the story in my head and then I write it"; "after, I find the words to write"; "I only need to write; "in my head, I imagine a "narrow" text, and when I write, I widen it. "I think very quickly of the ending"; " when I start, I ask myself how my story is going to end"; "I write first in my rough book, I've seen things which did not fit right with the card, so I put it right in my head" "I first think of what should happen to my hero"; "yes, but it's difficult to get the beginning started!" "I think of the characters very quickly"; "I choose a hero"; " I remember other stories I've read, it helps me". "I remember a R. Dahl story, I use it as a model" "I choose the title after writing the text"

They actually planned their text, some of them enter writing via the characters. The pupils who have not succeeded in writing say:

> "I've done my text small bits after small bits"; "I write as ideas come in my head"; " I write as and when required"; "I choose title at first".

Once, after we noted that "small bits after small bits" could not be an effective way, a pupil said after his own assessment:

> "I've done small bits after small bits but my text is not so bad"; the teacher asked:" How did you do it?" -"I re-read after every new small bit to see if it went with the others, it is necessary that all pieces go together".

Another pupil said:

> " I add special words to connect the sentences or the paragraphs", (that made occasion for a lesson about transition).

So, after it's been written on the card of procedure criteria:

> "it's better to first set up (or imagine) all the story in one's head"; "we can first of all imagine the characters";" we can think of the end before the beginning"; "it is often better to get the title after writing the story"

We added:

> "if we write small bits after small bits, we must think of the links between them together with the beginning"; "we must re-read to see if all the pieces go together"; "it is necessary to remember the beginning while writing"; "it's good to re-read aloud one's own text to be sure it is coherent" (this last concept had been worked);"we must take care of transitions"

Cards are tools: the pupils use these cards as they find necessary for them, with the help of the teacher.

Step 7. The pupils individually evaluate their own text with the cards: the teacher helps them (still by tutoring) to see what needs putting right in their text still in accordance with the criteria they know now. Moreover, they ask for the teacher's help in connection with their cards:

> "I can't make a sudden change in circumstances which looks true"; "I' can't find a good ending for my story"; "I can't find a good word which avoid the repetition of "he"; "I can't get a title which goes with my story".

A pupil answers the questionnaire:

> " it's often me who calls R. (the teacher), I ask her to help me to write with the card"?

The teacher has to help the pupils who are having difficulties to select the criteria (three or four) they will have to use for re-writing in order to avoid over cognitive load.

Step 8. Pupils re-write his text: the teacher helps them when they need it. We noted that they never again said "I can't do anything" or "I've no ideas what to write": they always ask for precise questions connected with criteria.

Step 9. The teacher evaluates this re-writing annotating the paper itself: she shows what is better, what is not (still in connection with criteria), what should be put right if the pupils re-write one more time. He avoids negative comments and prefers something like "find a more attractive word" or " one that is less familiar", "re-write this sentence, it's not very clear", "add a sentence to give a better explanation", "re-write your ending", "find a title which fits better with your text", "find an other end which goes better with your story", etc. Most of the pupils want to re-write their text again without requiring help from the teacher: this is a good sign of motivation.

3.3 Some Results of Questionnaires Analysis

We note that there is not a pupil who does not make any progress in the writing of narrative text according to teacher's didactic objectives. Most of the pupils wanted to re-write their text twice because they had become sure that they could do better than the time before: this behavior is very characteristic of motivation, which is seen in the answers to the questionnaires. This way of working in the classroom was used in other branches of learning (mathematics, spelling, English learning, in secondary forms (16/17): we noted that this behavior of motivation is *always* shown. The pupils showed clearly self-efficacy feeling and internal attribution, which are explicitly linked with the pleasure of working in that way.

This way of teaching uses systematically and at each steps, the communication between pupils: it promotes metacognitive behaviors and it also allows the avoidance of subjective and negative judgments on texts, pupils use technical ones only; I never saw a pupil afraid of the evaluation of his text; on the contrary, they are not pleased if their text is not chosen for collective assessment *("after collective evaluation of our text, it is much easier to re-write",* said a pupil).

Examples of answers. The answers show a connection between better capacity and knowledge about the task of writing, a better meta-knowledge of oneself as learner in this task, and the pleasure of writing; pupils clearly develop motivation by doing the writing task itself. A pupil lists all what he could not do before. We can find criteria through the meta-knowledge he shows: and he adds:

"now I know what I have to do when I have to write a text ".

An other pupil in failure said:

" I know why I did not succeed at the first time, it's because I wrote small bits after small bits; now, I try to imagine the whole story in my head before writing".

An other:

"in the beginning, I did not like to write at all, and now, I know how to do, so I write more and I like it much more" "what remains just as difficult for me, it is the conjugations and tenses of verbs, and telling a story with "I" as the subject ""I like working like that very much because it's a bit as if we were the teacher"

About the role of the card as a tool and meta-knowledge:

" I look at the card to remember what is necessary for me – about spelling, presentation of the characters, etc., but I don't use it anymore for "structure", I have it in my head now". We found the same sort of answers in all the classrooms.

4. CONCLUSION

J. Y. Rochex (1995), in his research about pupils who are failing, notes that the "project pedagogy" (doing a video, making a film, etc.), often used in these schools to motivate pupils for school work, may distract them from what they must really learn at school (i.e. academic subjects), especially those who are in failure who think that school is made for doing these projects and not to learn math or grammar. Then, they don't understand what they do at school; they mix up motivation – the means – and the knowledge – the aim. It is so necessary to look for a way of motivating which could sustain pupils academically, which does not mix up means and aims. We think that the way of learning shown here is a possible answer to this problem: pupils have both learnt and developed how to write texts along with the motivation to do so. They constructed a positive concept of themselves and at the same time, a part of their social and cultural identity.

FOSTERING NOVICES' ABILITY TO WRITE INFORMATIVE TEXTS

LIEVE VANMAELE & JOOST LOWYCK

Catholic University Leuven, Belgium

Abstract. In a design experiment, it was investigated whether explicit instructional support enables youngsters to articulate, organize and apply their content knowledge when writing a coherent informative text about a well-known topic.
Participants were 36 eighth graders, divided in three levels according to their language competency, and spread over one experimental group (E) and two control groups (C). They all received an identical assignment: writing an informative text about 'my school'. In all conditions the initial text was written without any instructional support. In control group 1 (C1) all participants wrote the text individually, sitting together in a classroom with the researcher watching them. Control group 2 (C2) and the experimental group (E), however, performed the task in one single (C2) or a series (E) of individual writing sessions. Instructional support offered in a series of individual writing sessions, was provided for the experimental group only. It aimed at improving the initial text about 'my school'. Participants were coached in improving and organizing content knowledge about that topic in a coherent informative text in line with the criteria (concerning content and structure) fixed by the researcher.
The writing performance was assessed for (a) the initial text (C1, C2, E), (b) the final text of the individual writing sessions (E) and (c) a transfer text about a different topic written by all participants (E, C).
From the empirical data, it is evidenced that the final text of the experimental group met the criteria very well. Their achievement clearly differentiated along language skill: high level pupils performed better than low level ones. As to the transfer text the results showed only a significant condition effect on text structure.
This study revealed some problems novices experience with meeting the criteria and which require additional support. One important finding is that novices experience difficulties with the transformation of experiential reality in concepts, the identification of the right term and the construction of this 'abstracted reality' in a transparent text. 'Abstracting' is nevertheless crucial to construct and communicate meaning in a coherent informative text.
The *discussion* highlights some salient findings and it outlines future research needed to offer some realistic recommendations for the teaching of writing. Attention is paid to the further translation of instructional support, exclusively validated in individual settings, into real, ecological classroom-settings.

Keywords: didactic sequence, informative text, content planning, differentiation, design experiment.

Vanmaele, L. & Lowyck, J. (2004). Fostering novices' ability to write informative texts. Rijlaarsdam, G. (Series Ed.) & Rijlaarsdam, G., Van den Bergh, H., & Couzijn, M. (Vol. Eds.) (2004). Studies in writing. Vol. 14, Effective learning and teaching of writing, 2nd Edition, Part 2, Studies in how to teach writing, 393 - 415.

1. INTRODUCTION

Results from a pilot study on seventh and eighth graders' writing (1986-'89) revealed the poverty of their initial text content. However, when the researcher questioned the participants about some aspects of the topic, they could tell a lot about it (Lowyck & Vanmaele, 1992a, b). Bereiter and Scardamalia (1982) already reported that gap between novices' sufficient prior knowledge and the limited quality of their writing product. In research literature on writing a clear mutual relationship between writing and knowledge has been signaled repeatedly. While knowledge may influence the quality of writing, writing itself may enhance the quality of knowledge as well (Scardamalia & Bereiter, 1987). Indeed, since language articulates and organizes content knowledge, schools need to support learners in assimilating and integrating knowledge from different domains through 'writing as knowledge transforming' (Scardamalia & Bereiter, 1987). In order to understand why students neglect to link prior knowledge to their writing, both a literature study and an empirical research were carried out. More specifically, it has been investigated whether explicit instructional support enables youngsters to articulate, organize and apply prior knowledge when writing a text about a well-known topic. Emphasis was laid on writing as conceptualization (Van der Aalsvoort & Van der Leeuw, 1982). The empirical study started from a blueprint of optimal support in line with the findings of the literature, which was gradually validated and refined in an iterative way.

Section 2 sketches the theoretical background. Section 3 deals with the empirical design, while Section 4 reports the empirical findings. A discussion will be found at the end of this chapter.

2. THEORETICAL BACKGROUND

This investigation aims at fostering learners to relate their knowledge and writing through intensive instructional support. In our literature study three topics have been elaborated separately: knowledge, writing and instructional support.

2.1 Knowledge

The interaction between knowledge and writing is most salient in an informative text in which knowledge classification and organization play an important role. As to *knowledge classification* conceptual knowledge is distinguished from method knowledge. Conceptual knowledge contains both content and discursive knowledge in order to construct reality in written language (Alexander, Schallert & Hare, 1991; Feilke, 1993; Hillocks, 1986; McCutchen, 1986). Content knowledge refers to an individual's knowledge about a writing topic. Discursive knowledge is linguistic (lexicon, syntax, text structure) and rhetorical (tuning content and language to writing goals and audience) in nature (Alexander, Schallert & Hare, 1991; Feilke, 1993; Hillocks, 1986; McCutchen, 1986). Method knowledge is necessary to perform a task and it points to strategic knowledge and metacognition (De Corte, 1990; Snowman, 1986; Van der Pool & Van Wijk, 1995).

Knowledge organization refers to an individual's knowledge structure that applies to a particular context. A suitable framework to describe that knowledge structure is the schema theory (Anderson, 1978; Norman & Rumelhart, 1975; Rumelhart, 1980; Rumelhart & Ortony, 1977; Thorndyke & Hayes-Roth, 1979).

Any schema depicts the structure in which an individual organizes his or her knowledge as a set of interrelated concepts. It contains slots for singular concepts and their relationship. Slots are essential topical categories, in which singular knowledge elements can be embedded. It facilitates person-reality interaction since it supports the interpretation of a real context (an event, an object, a situation) by means of interrelated concepts. In line with the schema theory the term 'information unit' will be used in this chapter, which refers to a specific topical category in a text. A topical category or an information unit stems from the grouping of concrete factual information elements into a more abstract category or concept. The topic 'school', for instance, may contain information units, like 'study areas', 'staff members' and 'infrastructure'.

2.2 Writing

Writing can be described from different points of view. We limit our study to two approaches that are situated in the interlinking field between knowledge and writing: the socio-semiotic approach (Halliday & Hasan, 1989) and the speech act theory (Austin, 1962; Searle, 1969), which both conceive of writing as a meaningful, functional act. In addition writing is conceived of as being both product and process.

2.2.1 Writing Product

The evaluation of writing products requires at least the definition of language functions, like expression, artistic creation, conceptualization and communication, that all influence discursive components and text organization (Britton et al., 1975; Bühler, 1934; Halliday & Hasan, 1989; Jakobson, 1960; Van der Aalsvoort & Van der Leeuw, 1982). Exploration of discursive components (Breetvelt, Van den Bergh & Rijlaarsdam, 1994; Brossell, 1983; Halliday & Hasan, 1989; Huot, 1990; Pander Maat, 1994) and of text classification enables the identification of the salient parameters of a writing assignment (writing goal, topic, audience) and of the writing criteria as well (see: Bochner et al., 1992; Breetvelt, Van den Bergh & Rijlaarsdam, 1994; Pander Maat, 1994; Rijlaarsdam, 1986, 1987; Van den Bergh, 1988; Van der Geest, 1990).

2.2.2 Writing as a Process

Writing as a process can be described either as a problem solving or a knowledge-constituting strategy. Problem solving consists of finding and analysing the gap between an initial state and an intended goal, and of carrying out subsequently a set of goal-oriented, systematic cognitive activities to bridge that gap. This includes both a reflective use of cognitive strategies and self-regulation for process control

(Duncker, 1935; Frijda & Elshout, 1976, Newell & Simon, 1972; Voss et al., 1983). As to problem solving our study only highlights the Hayes and Flower model (1980a, b; Flower & Hayes, 1980, 1981), which seems most useful in clarifying writing processes.

In the *Hayes and Flower model* the following cognitive processes constitute the writing process: planning, editing, and revision, of which only planning and revision are elaborated. Planning refers to rhetorical, content and process planning (Hayes & Flower, 1980a, b). In rhetorical planning writing goals and audience are defined in order to orient further content and process planning. For content planning important information units and their corresponding text structure are outlined, while process planning refers to all decisions necessary to reach the writing goal. During the revision process it is controlled whether the text meets the criteria, through: (1) text reading, (2) problem finding and problem diagnosis, (3) defining a revision strategy and (4) carrying out a solution (Flower et al., 1986; Hayes et al., 1987). However, as validation studies by Hayes and Flower reveal, this systematic problem solving for writing is only found with experts, not with novices. Scardamalia and Bereiter (1987) enlarge this Hayes and Flower model in a substantial manner. Firstly, they elaborate a novice model of writing. Secondly, they conceive of writing as a knowledge transforming activity (Scardamalia & Bereiter, 1987; see also: Vanmaele, 2002).

The *knowledge-constituting strategy* (Galbraith, 1999), rooted in the former research of Elbow (1973) and Wason (1980) with youngsters, holds a different approach. Galbraith's basic assumption is that new ideas emerge during writing, while problem solving activities, like planning and revision, lead to the reorganization of existing ideas. In that strategy the writer starts with generating ideas through free writing, whereas problem solving afterwards consists of evaluating and revising text content, structure and language use.

2.3 Instructional Support

We opted for an instructional support that takes into account content, discursive and strategic knowledge necessary to write a coherent informative text, in accordance with novice's characteristics. In our study novice's characteristics refer to their inherent limitations lacking both necessary knowledge and self-regulation. In that line Couzijn and Rijlaarsdam (1996a) plead for the explicit teaching of writing at school. In their approach writing activities need not only to be executed by the learners, but also to be continuously made explicit, articulated and linked with the kind of (content, discursive, strategic) knowledge involved. This is in line with the 'cognitive apprenticeship' of Collins, Brown & Newman (1989), stressing the close interaction between the learner's activities and the articulation (by teacher and/or learner) of each step carried out. Through modeling (demonstrating each step needed by a model), scaffolding (strongly supporting the learner executing each step needed), and coaching (supervising the learner, providing feedback) the learner acquires the necessary knowledge by means of experiences. These experiences are linked with conceptualization and articulation that make the learner aware of his or her cognitive activities. This is clearly documented in 'Learning by observing' (Couzijn & Rijlaarsdam, 1996a), in which the continuous interplay between experiencing and articulation is predominant.

From the theoretical framework described above, an explicit relationship between content knowledge, writing and instructional support has been evidenced. However, some problematic issues deserve further study. They deal with designing learning activities that support novices writing, taking into account the knowledge needed to produce an informative text, in accordance with the peculiar learner's characteristics.

2.4 Research Questions

Our study, from an instructional design point of view, intended to understand if and to which extent explicit, systematic support fosters learners to articulate, organize and represent content knowledge in a coherent informative text. This led to the following research questions:
1) To which degree does explicit, systematic instructional support foster novices to improve their text in line with the specified criteria?
2) Which kind of problems do novices experience in writing an informative text?

3. RESEARCH DESIGN

The study focuses on understanding why novices do not apply full prior knowledge when writing informative texts. Lack of content knowledge cannot be the reason since they were able to express their prior knowledge during an oral conversation. As a consequence, other explanations seem to account for this insufficiency. Lack of discursive and strategic knowledge might be a first candidate, and the ill-structured nature of their available knowledge another one. The latter seems a fair candidate since in our former pilot study youngsters who were questioned about some particular information units of a topic, such as 'a profession', could provide much more information during their writing afterwards: Our questions, pointing to information units, like 'training' and 'spheres of activity', seemed to help the youngsters to retrieve the necessary information when writing. This finding made us suppose that, in this early stage of writing, youngsters' prior knowledge was not yet organized in a schema with slots that contain the most relevant information units (2.1). This unstructured prior knowledge hindered the retrieval of all necessary information to be put in a text.

With these possible explanations in mind, we carried out a design experiment with eighth graders. This is an empirical study in which instructional support is outlined to be validated and revised in an iterative, recurrent way (Brown, 1992; De Corte, 2000). In order to do so, we elaborated a scenario, in which instructional support was designed in a series of individual and group writing sessions in accordance with the learning goals and the novice's writing processes. A 'draft scenario' was tested in a pilot study with eighth graders, which resulted in a 'revised scenario' for the main study.

Characteristics of this empirical research are the following. Firstly, neither hypothesis testing nor comparison of teaching methods was intended. We mainly aimed at (a) looking at problems novices experience when writing an informative text in line with the criteria defined, and (b) exploring to which extent instructional support might foster learners to articulate and organize their fuzzy content knowledge for representation in a coherent informative text. Secondly, the study was carried out in a semi-experimental context with individuals, outside the classroom, though the writing assignment itself was 'ecological' for school context. This design was needed to observe and analyse youngsters' writing closely with explicit control of the intermediate variables. Thirdly, criteria for writing a coherent informative text were defined for the design of instructional support. The number of individual writing sessions was however not fixed in advance, but was dependent on the participant's initial state to meet the criteria.

3.1 Participants

Thirty-six eighth-graders participated in the study. They were allocated to three levels of language competence: high (H, N = 10), medium (M, N = 17) and low (L, N = 9), and spread over one experimental group (E, N = 14) and two control groups (C1, N = 11; C2: N = 11) (see: 3.3.1). Their language competence was measured by the language competency part of the 'Wapso intelligence test' (Mager, Bos & Vander Auwera, 1991/1993) and a writing test of De Glopper (1986). The youngsters were not taught yet about the informative text[1]. The writing assignment was, however, connected with the participants' 'zone of proximal development', a term that refers to activities that a learner can carry out with instructional support only (Vygotsky, 1978; see De Corte, 1996).

3.2 Writing Assignment

The writing assignment consisted of writing an informative text that provides factual information about the participants' school to be published in a magazine addressed to the local community. The audience consisted of non-informed people.

The writing criteria drew on literature on writing. Goal-orientation was the main criterion. Text content, structure and language all need to reflect the writing goal of informing people about the topic at hand ('my school'). Additional criteria for content and structure were delineated at the macro-level of the text (paragraph, section and whole text).

Criteria used for content evaluation were completeness and accuracy of the written information. Completeness pointed to the amount of relevant information units, dealt with in the text, and to the quality of each information unit. As to the structure, each text had to provide a coherent representation of the information units in distinct paragraphs and sections and to articulate the relationships as well. In addition, a

---

[1] *Handbooks 7th and 8th grade were explored in the initial stage of our study. Content to be taught was not covered at the moment of the design experiment.*

suitable introduction and conclusion were required. A more detailed description of these text criteria is presented in Appendix A.

To evaluate text content in terms of completeness and accuracy, we made a hierarchical information structure of the most relevant information units. That information structure served as a landmark for supporting learners in building a well-organized content schema (Appendix A).It drew on texts written by university freshmen in educational sciences and by eighth graders.

3.3 Instructional Support

External support was aligned with the individual's activity (2.3). It was a combination of a criterion-referenced and structured design with a process-oriented, interactive and incremental one. Participants started to write a first draft and all subsequent learning activities aimed at improving each former draft in line with the criteria for content and structure. Instructional support took place in both individual and group sessions.

3.3.1   Individual Writing Sessions

The individual writing sessions took place between October 1995 and April 1996. The instructor was the researcher herself.

In all conditions participants received an identical assignment: writing an informative text about 'my school'. They were told their final text was intended for publication in a magazine for "people who wanted to be informed about your school". In each condition (E, C) writing was preceded by the learner's scrutiny of the assignment in terms of text type (informative text), topic ('my school'), writing goal (informing people) and audience (readers of the magazine). Writing criteria were communicated in terms of completeness, accuracy and coherence (Appendix A). This assignment control in each condition was needed in this study. A too idiosyncratic interpretation of the writing assignment by these novices would indeed hamper a criterion-referenced assessement of the writing products.

In all conditions the initial text was written without any instructional support. The eleven control group 1 participants (C1) wrote the text individually, sitting together in a classroom with the researcher watching them. Control group 2 (C2) and the experimental group (E), however, performed the task in one single (C2) or a series (E) of individual writing sessions. So, C1 resembled the 'ordinary' classroom setting, and C2 the experimental one. This difference was created to control possible effects of the individual approach during the sessions.

Instructional support, offered in a series of individual writing sessions, was provided for the experimental group only (N = 14: 4 H, 7 M, 3 L). Participants were coached in organizing their topical knowledge in a coherent informative text in line with the criteria for content and text structure (Appendix A). Each writing session resulted in a new intermediate text on which further learning activities were carried out in the next session in order to improve the text quality.

The scenario for instructional support was designed around learning activities and instructional interventions.

3.3.2   Learning Activities

The writing process was structured around the following learning activities: (1) topic elaboration, (2) text structuring and (3) refinement of language use. Evaluating and revising were embedded in each phase. Dependent upon the individual needs of the learners, the number of writing sessions varied from 5 to 9, with a modus at 6. Each session lasted 50 minutes.

The organization of support relied on both the knowledge-constituting and the problem solving strategy (2.2.2). In line with the former strategy, generating ideas through free writing was important during the initial writing process. However, according to the problem solving strategy, free writing was in all conditions (E, C) preceded by an assignment analysis for topic, writing goal(s), audience and writing criteria.

During the *topic elaboration* all participants (E, C) wrote a first draft. They all had the choice between either generating ideas in keywords (a simple way of content planning) or writing the text immediately. Afterwards, learning activities (for E only) were provided aiming at refining the participant's content schema. Improving content was enhanced by an external reader, who asked questions on information that was either not dealt with or not elaborated. After the external reader's intervention participants wrote a second draft, on which further structuring activities were carried out.

Two characteristics of that intervention are worth mentioning. The introduction of an external 'reader' is a first one. The external reader might provide support given by a partner in an oral conversation and in that function he or she represents the audience (Bereiter & Scardamalia, 1982; Feilke, 1993; see: 1). This intervention resembles the introduction of collaboration with a supportive partner-reader as was the case in other research (Brakel Olson, 1990; Clifford, 1981; Couzijn & Rijlaarsdam, 1996b; Rijlaarsdam, 1986, 1987). The second characteristic refers to the type of the reader's questions. When asking a question the reader had to use the appropriate slot of the information unit systematically (2.1, 3.2). For instance, slots, as 'identification', 'study areas', 'staff members', were articulated intentionally by the reader, who had been trained in advance.

As to *text structure*, building a content schema was enhanced by the following activities. At first, participants were supported in grouping the information elements into information units to be represented in distinct sections and paragraphs. After that, they were coached in articulating the relationship between the information units as represented in sections and paragraphs, and in writing an introduction and a conclusion. Grouping and articulating relationships were supported by the learning activity 'outlining a hierarchical text schema', in which the structure of content had to be represented clearly. This often challenged learners to formulate the content on a higher level of abstraction, including a clear demarcation of the topic and the search for the exact wording of the higher-level slots. Internalization of the new slots was continuously stimulated. During all structuring and writing activities the participants were challenged to use the appropriate slot.

At the end attention was paid to *language use*: sentence construction, wording and spelling (see Appendix B for a more detailed description of the individual writing sessions).

3.3.3   Instructional Interventions

The interaction between the learner's activities and the teacher's or learner's articulation (2.3) was structured in terms of orientation, performance and review.

Orientation consisted of (a) retrospection of the former writing process and product and tuning writing to the criteria, (b) elucidation of the actual writing task and (c) instruction. *Performance* was supported by (a) initial scaffolding, (b) coaching, (c) co-writing and (d) instruction. *Review* consisted of (a) evaluation (comparing the intermediate text with the criterion), (b) retrospection (reconstruction of the writing phases) and (c) anticipation on the next writing activity. Instruction was embedded in the various writing activities.

3.3.4   Group Instruction

In the individual writing sessions each participant of the experimental group received content, discursive and strategic information about informative texts. However, in order to achieve a transfer effect, each participant should be given the opportunity to internalize the newly acquired knowledge. Therefore the individual writing sessions were followed by a series of systematic instruction sessions on the articulation of the newly acquired knowledge, and on applying that knowledge in new writing contexts. Five sessions took place, each in small groups. The materials, developed by the researcher, consisted of one booklet with the information needed and one with the writing assignments.

3.4 Writing Performance Assessment

The assessment of the individual writing performance aimed at (a) diagnosing participants' initial state, (b) defining whether and to what extent texts written with instructional support (E) met the criteria for text content and structure, (c) measuring whether and to what degree the instructional support enabled youngsters to write a transfer text in line with the criteria and to outperform the control condition participants. Writing performance was assessed for the initial text (T1, E, C), the final text as a product of the individual writing sessions (T2, E) and the transfer text (T3, E, C). Initial and final text both dealt with the same topic 'my school'. The transfer text was an informative text about another topic 'a profession of my choice'. Results of the initial text (T1, E, C) enabled us to assess the initial state of the participants. The final text (T2, E) only assessed the effectiveness of the instructional interventions. The transfer text (T3, E, C) measured the instructional effect on the learner's ability in writing a new informative text in line with the criteria for content and the structure.

All three writing products were assessed by two independent reviewers, with a strict procedure for analysing content and structure. On a checklist the reviewers had firstly to indicate whether a criterion was met. Content and structure received a score on a 9 point scale, with a caesura fixed at 4 (See: Appendix C). In addition, the researcher herself carried out a score analysis and a more in-depth text analysis to confront content and structure with the criteria. For score analysis nonparametric statistical techniques were used because of (1) no normal distribution of scores, (2) the small group size and (3) the use of an ordinal measurement scale (De Jonge & Wielenga, 1973; Siegel & Castellan, 1989). As an index of the interscorer-agreement Cohen's weighted coefficient kappa was chosen (Cohen, 1968). Significance was tested with the sign test, the Wilcoxon rank-sum test and the Kruskal-Wallis test. For computation the software-package Statistix, 3.1 (1989) was used.

In order to avoid misinterpretation, it was controlled whether and to what extent topic and discursive information, provided during the writing sessions, had been taught at school during the research period. These additional data were gathered by questioning each participant about several topics on writing, by the analysis of handbooks seventh and eight grade and by interviews with the teachers of the participants.

4. RESULTS

The empirical findings refer to writing products and writing processes pertaining to problems novices experience with meeting the criteria.

4.1 Writing Products

The assessment of writing performance was based on (1) the initial text (T1, E, C), (2) the final text (T2, E) and (3) the transfer text (T3, E, C). Concerning the initial text (T1, E, C), the quality of content and structure showed no significant differences between the three conditions. This allows us to consider the three conditions to be equivalent in the initial phase. For want of space only the results on the transfer text (T3) will be reported here, because of their closest connection to Research question 1 (2.4): "To which degree does instructional support enable youngsters to write an informative text independently, in line with the criteria, outlined for text content and structure, and with a quality exceeding that of the initial text (T1)?" In other words, does the experimental group perform significantly better than both control groups?[2] This question contains three subquestions: (a) Does the transfer text (T3) reach a sufficient quality? (b) Does its quality increase compared with the initial text (T1)? (c) Might group differences be ascribed to either language competence level (across

---

[2] *Henceforth Condition 1 (C1, N= 11) and Condition 2 (C2, N= 11) will be combined (C, N= 22). This combination will facilitate the analysis of the condition effect and is acceptable since the initial text scores show no significant differences between the conditions.*

condition) or condition (E versus C)? Since two learners (1E, 1C) did not participate in writing the transfer text, group size decreased from 36 to 34 (13 E, 21 C).

4.1.1 Content

In the total group two thirds of the subjects (23/34; 67%) scored at least sufficiently (Md = 4). A progress of T3 compared with T1 was observed. Indeed, most pupils' scores increased (n = 22/34; 64%); less pupils' scores remained status quo (n = 7/34; 20%) or decreased slightly (5/34; 14%). As the sign test proved, for the whole group the progress was significant (n' = 27 en n+ = 22, p = 0.0008). As was evidenced through an in-depth analysis, the content of most transfer texts met the criteria.

The research group (E+C, N = 34), however, differed at the language competence level: A sufficient performance was found for all H (n = 9/9), for most M (n = 13/17) and only for one L (1/8). These differences were all significant (H = 0.16.09; p = 0.0003).

The progress in text quality from T1 to T3 revealed a moderate language competence level effect (Wilcoxon rank-sum test). High and medium level learners made a significant greater progress than low level learners did (H: p = 0.0001; M: p = 0.0009). Between high and medium level, however, no significant differences were found (p = 0.059). The boundary was between the combined high and medium group on the one hand, and the low level one on the other.

Though these results revealed a progress for the total group, only *condition differences* might sustain an instructional support effect. At a first glance no condition effect appeared (Md. C = 4, E = 4; z = 1.284, p = 0.0978; mean ranks: E = 20.3; C = 15.7). However, a more detailed analysis showed condition differences between H en L. Higher scores of E were located in the H-group and lower scores of C were found in the L-group (see Table 1). The Wilcoxon rank-sum test sustained the observation of condition differences along language competence level.

Table 1. Content: Mean Rank and P-Values for Experimental (E) and Control (C) Group- Values of Wilcoxon Rank-Sum Test: Comparison between Experimental Group and Control Groups along Language Competence Level for T1 and T 3 (High, Medium and Low). (Two Sides Testing for T1, One Side Testing for T3)

Text	p	H E	C	p	M E	C	p	L E	C
T1	.629	4.9	5.9	.457	10.4	8.1	.744	5.5	4.8
T3	.048	7.3	3.8	.422	9.9	8.4	.036	6.5	3.3

Experimental H and L participants outperformed control H en L. This was not the case for the medium groups. Indeed, an instructional support effect occurred for high and low level, but not for the medium one. These findings need, however, to be considered as tentative, especially because of the very low number of participants and the skewed distribution of participants over the three levels.

As the researcher's analysis showed, criteria set for content evaluation were sufficiently met by most participants. Texts dealt with a limited number of information units, be it the most relevant ones. These topics were more elaborated than in the initial text.

4.1.2   Text Structure

The analysis of the text structure shows different results. Salient condition differences occurred (Md E = 5, C = 2). Indeed, while most experimental subjects scored at least sufficiently (n = 10/13; 79%), only few control subjects did so (n = 4/21; 19%). The Wilcoxon rank-sum test showed the experimental group to get significant higher scores than the control groups (z = 3.367, p = 0.0004; mean ranks: E = 24.8; C = 13). Condition effect was confirmed by linking condition with language competence level, although these findings need to be considered as tentative too.

For each condition differential outcomes were found. In the experimental group (N = 13) differentiation along language competence level was observed (Md: H = 6, M = 4, L = 3). All high level subjects (N = 3) scored more than sufficiently (> 4). In the medium group (N = 7), only one subject scored less than 4, while in the low group (N = 3) two learners performed insufficiently. In the control groups (N = 21) this differentiation was absent (Md: H = 3; M = 3, L = 2). Condition differences along language competence level were indeed significant, as is shown in Table 2, including a comparison with T1.

Table 2. *T3, Text Structure: P-Values of Wilcoxon Rank-Sum Test: Comparison between Control Groups and Experimental Group along Language Competence Level (High, Medium and Low), in Comparison with Text 1 (Two Sides Testing for Text 1, One Side Testing for Text 3)*

Text	H	M	L
T1	.800	.539	.548
T3	.012	.0048	.036

Our in-depth analysis confirmed these results. Grouping of information units as a structure criterion was realized by most subjects (n = 30; 88%). Condition differences appeared, however, for use and quality of topical passages, introduction and conclusion.

In sum, for content no clear condition effect was observed, since it only appeared in the high and the low language competence group. For text structure, on the contrary, condition effect occurred, which is clearly documented by the significant score differences and our in-depth analysis.

Nevertheless, one important shortcoming needs to be mentioned. Although the text structure of the experimental participants met the criteria in an excellent way, this structure did not consistently reflect the real content organization. For instance, topical passages exclusively referred to the former information unit and only mentioned the next one. This did not always cover the real content and the 'deep' structure of that former or coming section or paragraph. Another example is the introduction, that contained the right elements, but in which the information units, mentioned with their slots, did not represent clearly the main topics in the text. In other words, participants were undoubtedly able to meet the formal criteria for structure, but it is unclear to which extent they were proficient in representing a content schema in a coherent text. Similar findings have been reported by Crowhurst (1987) and Overmaat (1996).

4.1.3 Interscorer-agreement

As an index of interscorer-agreement Cohen's weighted coefficient kappa was used (Cohen, 1968; Flack et al., 1988). Due to the small group size (T1: N = 36; T2: N = 14; T3: N = 34) interscorer-agreement was difficult to obtain. The definition of the acceptability of a weighted coefficient kappa is crucial. A .60 kappa coefficient is not strictly required. Flack, et al. (1988) consider .40 to be sufficient. Since a weighted coefficient kappa, however, provides more accurate information, less than .40 may be accepted (Flack et al., 1988; Landis & Koch, 1977).

The interscorer-agreement was moderate (Landis & Koch, 1977), with exceptions for T1 (structure: almost perfect) and T2 (content: fair). Qualitative analysis by the researcher (see 3.4) identified in which aspects reviewers disagreed. Interscorer-disagreement was due to both interpretation of some criteria and differences when awarding the higher scores (>6)

4.2 Writing Processes

This section on writing processes pertains to problems novices experience with meeting the criteria. Process analysis was carried out on audiotape protocols and intermediate writing products. The observations revealed several problems, concerning both conceptual (content and discursive) knowledge and method (strategic) knowledge.

4.2.1 Conceptual Knowledge: Content and Discursive Knowledge

In this chapter content knowledge refers to the topical knowledge needed to write an informative text in accordance with the criteria for content: completeness and accuracy. Discursive knowledge points here especially to the knowledge needed to write a well-structured text in line with the criteria.

During the writing sessions novices experienced problems with applying both kinds of knowledge when meeting the criteria for content and structure. When novices revised text content, they were not proficient in using the accurate terminology, especially in labeling aspects of the education system, such as 'streams' and 'study areas'. In that stage frictions occurred between persistent inaccurate prior knowledge and the new information provided by the researcher (Vermunt, 1995; Vermunt & Lowyck, 2000).

Problems with text structure mainly pertain to the inability to reach sufficient abstraction and to misconceptions.

'Abstracting' seems crucial to construct and communicate meaning in a coherent informative text. Indeed, in line with the schema theory (2.1), writing may be considered as representing a well-organized schema with slots for singular concepts referring to essential topical categories. In that way, abstracting means transforming experiential reality into concepts, finding the right term and constructing this 'abstracted reality' in a transparent text (see: Taba, 1966). The latter means grouping information in discrete sections or paragraphs and naming those. At a higher level, the elaboration of relationships between sections and paragraphs in suitable titles and topical passages is required. In order to do so, text passages need to link, with one or more sentences, the previous section to the next one, by means of the appropriate term.

At each level problems have been observed. Transforming experiential reality into concepts was a first problem, however appearing only in low competence level pupils, which may be proved by an example.

> Researcher: Which topic did you deal with in this passage?
>
> Participant: Everything is allowed at school, except smoking.

This boy did not understand the necessity to transform a cluster of concrete information elements (things that are allowed and not allowed, like smoking) into one concept. Labeling that concept, such as 'rules', seemed to be a second problem, for each competence level. Thirdly, the elaboration of relationships between sections and paragraphs in suitable titles and topical passages, be it at a higher level of abstraction, seemed very difficult, even for high competence level writers. Participants were successful in articulating the relationship between two (small) paragraphs but in case of larger sections, they only expressed the link between the last paragraph of the former section and the first paragraph of the next section.

Some *misconceptions* from the part of the pupils came to light, especially when writing an introduction, a topical passage and a conclusion. One misconception was conceiving of a topical passage as merely 'word chaining'. Instead of expressing the essential relationship between two sections, some youngsters linked two sentences with the same word (domino strategy). For instance, in switching from 'education system' to 'staff members', a high achiever wrote: "*In the ninth grade the curriculum contains some new subjects. Each subject is taught by a specific teacher*".

A quite unexpected finding relates to the writing processes of both low and high achievers. We expected high achievers to need less writing sessions and to experience fewer problems than low achievers did. This was, however, not the case at all.

First, the high achievers needed more writing sessions (about 7, 8) than some low language competence writers did. Secondly, writing problems were not exclusively experienced by low level writers but even frequently by high achievers. There was a difference, however. While low achievers experienced difficulties during the first writing phases, high language competence participants struggled in the later phases, when more complex learning activities like writing topical passages occurred. A plausible explanation might be that high achievers created a higher task complexity due to the sophisticated text content and structure, along with higher standards for language use.

4.2.2 Strategic Knowledge: Planning and Revision

In our study strategic knowledge was limited to planning and revision, as is emphasized in problem solving models (2.2.2). Our question was whether our participants were proficient in planning and revising without any support.

Planning. Three kinds of planning have been distinguished: rhetorical, content and process planning. In our empirical study explicit rhetorical planning by the youngsters was not required. Since the assignment parameters were defined by the researcher, the participants only needed to analyse the assignment. After the assignment analysis all participants (E, C) got the opportunity to carry out content planning. To elaborate content all pupils had the choice between either generating ideas written down in keywords (a simple way of content planning) or writing the text immediately. No learner of the control group chose the first strategy. Only three participants of the experimental group chose it (n = 3/14, 1 H, 2 L), but their performance was not successful. Most learners (E, C) (33/36) built information units during writing, which resulted in a first draft (see: knowledge-constituting strategy).

For the experimental group an opportunity for *process* planning was offered as well. After termination of the hierarchical text schema each participant was asked the following question: "We still have four or five writing sessions. Which learning activities should we still carry out?" No single learner was able to plan further learning activities, like 'linking text passages', 'writing an introduction and a conclusion'. In the best case, high-level writers proposed to refine their language use.

Revising. As to revision differences between the language levels were observed. When high-level writers were requested to read their former draft, they spontaneously mentioned content and grouping problems and they were able to revise. As to the higher level criteria, however, they were not successful in detecting and revising shortcomings independently. Low-level competence participants needed support for all kind of revising activities.

How can this insufficient planning and revision be explained? Lack of strategic knowledge is, in our opinion, an acceptable but not a sufficient explanation. Difficulties with content planning may be due to the lack of a well-organized content schema that could enable writers to represent the main information units in advance.

Process planning and revision may be hampered since the criteria for writing an informative text were unknown to these novices.

5. DISCUSSION

In line with the aims of our study to better understand the relationship between prior knowledge and writing, four important conclusions can be drawn.

At first, a highly important writing problem seems to be 'abstracting', which means transforming experiential reality into concepts, using the right term and representing this 'abstracted reality' in a transparent text. This finding makes us understand why novices are not successful in outlining a hierarchical schema of the intended text before or during the first phases of their writing activity. That kind of representation always requires a certain degree of abstraction and consequently some preparatory activities, like grouping information elements into information units and, on a higher level, building a suitable hierarchical text structure. In writing research and practice that 'abstracting' problem needs much attention.

A second conclusion is that the representation of a well-organized content schema in a coherent text is not fully realized by the youngsters, in spite of intensive instructional support. The participants are indeed able to meet the formal criteria for structure, but they seem less proficient in representing a content schema in a coherent text.

A third conclusion is that the support of planning and revision can only be effective under certain conditions. The teaching of content planning requires, in our opinion, fostering youngsters in building a well-organized content schema. Instructional support for process planning and revision only seems to be successful if learners have been initiated into the essential criteria of informative texts. In sum, teaching writing strategies should, at least in our opinion, be prepared by introducing content and discursive knowledge.

Last but not least, the unexpected finding that higher-level writers experience difficulties as well deserves attention. The difference between low and high achievers' problems reveals the need of a differentiated instructional approach for both groups.

Since many questions remain unanswered, *further research* is needed. A first issue concerns the usability of the instructional support, exclusively validated in individual settings, in a real classroom. Therefore, a new study has been carried out in a tenth grade classroom (September 2002-June 2003). That study left, however, many questions untouched. To begin with, the lack of correspondence between formal text structure and 'deep' content structure remains problematic. Building a content schema during an individual writing session lacked a transfer effect, which indicates that the participants needed intensive instructional support to reach that goal. Such kind of support might contain the explicit teaching of a strategy for building a content structure for any topic, which was indeed impossible in this short-term study. A further study should therefore aim at the development of a strategy that learners can apply to (1) identify the main information units of a topic, (2) determine the sub-information units of each main information unit, and (3) select the most essential information units to be dealt with and elaborated.

In sum, our study revealed salient problems with youngsters linking content knowledge and writing, in order to produce a coherent informative text. It also contains some landmarks for designing a classroom scenario to support novices in doing so.

APPENDIX A

CRITERIA SET FOR INFORMATIVE TEXTS

Goal-orientation is the main criterion, which means that content, text structure and language all fit the topic, the writing-goals and the audience (Pander Maat, 1994; Rijlaarsdam, 1986, 1987; Van den Bergh, 1988; Van der Geest, 1990). An informative text aims at an accurate and transparent representation of well-organized knowledge on a writing topic (Bochner et al., 1992; Rijlaarsdam, 1986; Van den Bergh, 1988). In line with goal-orientation, criteria are outlined for unity, and further for content and structure, with a stress on the macro-level. The macro-level points to paragraph, section and overall text.

1. UNITY

Unity means that text content and structure both relate to the writing assignment. The text deals with the topic, it is oriented to the writing-goal and the audience and it reflects the essential features of an informative text. Since participant's assignment analysis is controlled by the researcher, this criterion will not play an important role.

2. CONTENT

Criteria are completeness and accuracy.
- Completeness
    Range: dealing with a fixed amount of relevant information units
    Elaboration: describing sufficient relevant aspects of each information unit
- Accuracy: preciseness of the information given. 'Information unit' points to a specific topical category. A topical category or an information unit stems from the grouping of concrete factual information elements into a more abstract category or concept, like 'education system'[3], 'staff members', 'infrastructure'.

---

[3] Subordinate information units may be: 'levels' (elementary, secondary, higher education'), 'structure of secondary education', 'streams' and 'study areas'. Belgian secondary education is structured into three levels: first (seventh, eight grade), second (ninth, tenth grade) and third level (eleventh and twelfth grade). In the second and the third level three streams are distinguished. General secondary education stresses a broad theoretical education. In technical secondary education attention is paid to general and to technical-theoretical subjects. In secondary art education general education is coupled with the active practice of art. Vocational education is a practice-oriented education in which youngsters study a specific trade.

3. TEXT STRUCTURE

The text structure is measured at the macro-level (paragraph, section, whole text). The text contains three parts: introduction, nucleus and conclusion.

3.1 Introduction

The introduction functions as an advance organizer. It at least mentions the topic but it may contain much more elements, like stating the writing-goal, mentioning the main information units that will be presented in the text, and addressing the audience.

3.2 Nucleus

The nucleus meets following criteria
- Coherent representation of the isolated information units, by representing the information units in distinct paragraphs and sections
- Articulating the relationship between the information units as represented in paragraph and sections, by means of (1) titles and subtitles, (2) topical passages
- In addition: reflecting the hierarchical structure of content

3.3 Conclusion

The conclusion mentions the main information units, highlights the most salient findings and addresses the audience.

4. LANGUAGE USE

At the end of the writing sessions attention is paid to sentence construction, wording, orthography and spelling, which will however not be part of the explicit evaluation. To evaluate text content in terms of completeness and accuracy we made a hierarchical information structure of the most relevant information units of the writing topic. This information structure will serve as a landmark for supporting learners in building a well-organized content schema. It draws on texts written by university freshmen educational sciences and by eighth graders and it is represented below.

1. Identification		2. System			3. Daily life		
1. Name, location	2.1 Level of schooling Primary, secondary, higher	2.2 Stream(s)-tracks	2.2 Levels within secondary 1st, 2nd, 3rd level	2.4 Domains of study	3.1 Schedule	3.2 Rules	3.3. Students' participation
4. Student guidance in		5. Infrastructure		6. Extra curricular activities		7. Staff	
4.1 Developing learning strategies	4.2 Building a school career						

APPENDIX B INSTRUCTIONAL SUPPORT IN INDIVIDUAL WRITING SESSIONS. PHASING WRITING PROCESS INTO LEARNING ACTIVITIES

In all conditions the participants receive an identical assignment: writing an informative text about 'my school'.

Every day a lot of people pass your school. They want more information about it. So, we like to make a magazine about your school. You can help us by writing a text. For the experimental group was added: *we'll work at it during several writing sessions.*

Give a full description of everything you know about your school. Mind very well: people who don't know your school at all, should be informed as much as possible. Consequently your description needs to be: (1) complete, (2) precise and (3) coherent.
Mind the things that are not allowed
- no story about when and how you arrived at your school
- no mere shallow description of your school; your text needs to describe much more aspects of it
- no advertisement text fostering people to choose your school
- no text mere expressing your personal feelings and judgment about your school.

---

1. ASSIGNMENT ANALYSIS

In each condition participants are invited to articulate the assignment parameters (topic, goal, audience, criteria) orally, while this wording is consciously controlled and if needed corrected by the researcher. In this initial phase only content criteria are commented briefly. A gradual criterion analysis will take place during the phase in which that criterion needs to be met.

2. ELABORATING CONTENT

2.1 Writing a first draft

In each condition the participants have the choice between two strategies: either generating ideas in keywords (a simple way of content planning) or writing the text immediately. After having finished the first draft the control participants leave the stage, be it after a brief oral reflection on their personal experiences with this writing session. Following sessions are individually attended by the experimental participants only.

2.2 Outlining a first (elementary) text schema

After finishing their first draft, the (experimental) participants are asked to outline a first text schema, grouping concrete factual information elements into information units and naming these information units.

2.3 Improving content

Improving content refers to both criteria for content evaluation: completeness and accuracy, that are analysed more in depth by the researcher and the learner in a conversation at the beginning of the second writing session. Two learning activities take place: (1) interventions aiming at broadening and elaborating text content and (2) revising it.

For broadening and elaborating content a virtual reader of the intended magazine appears on the stage: a master student educational sciences, who read the draft in advance and who received a training beforehand. She raises questions on information units that are either not dealt with or not elaborated and she systematically uses the appropriate slots. Each question is noted by the participant, if needed with an additional clarification by the 'reader' or the researcher in a conversation. As a result of this session the participant gets a list of information units to be dealt with and/or to be elaborated.

When the reader has left the room, the participant reads over the information units, as being listed, and answers the following questions: (1) Which of these aspects did you already deal with in your text? (2) Which didn't you deal with at all? Those questions enable the participant to make a distinction between information units to be elaborated, on the one hand, and information units to be introduced, on the other hand (range). Moreover, the researcher questions the first draft as to the accuracy of the information and of the terminology. After that, the learner starts revising content by broadening and elaborating the information units, which results in a second draft. This revising takes the last part of Session 2, together with Session 3 as a whole

3. TEXT STRUCTURING

Each session starts with the revision of the former draft, in this stage only as to content. The participant is invited to read and revise it independently. If he is not succesful in performing this task, the researcher supports him by giving some cues.

When text content has been completed and refined, the transition can be made to next phase: *text structuring*, firstly focusing on the nucleus of the text. In line with the criteria outlined, two substages are provided, aiming at the coherent representation of the isolated information units in sections and paragraphs, on the one hand (3.1), and the articulation of the relationship between the information units as being represented in sections and paragraphs, on the other hand (3.3). However, a bridging activity is inserted: outlining a text schema (3.2).

3.1 Aiming at the coherent representation of the isolated information units

Two learning activities are provided: grouping concrete information elements into an information unit and building a more hierarchical text structure. Grouping contains: (1) identifying groups of information elements, (2) articulating each group's community, and (3) searching for the right term (slot) to label each group or information unit (Taba, 1966). Building a hierarchical text structure entails subsuming a cluster of smaller information units under a more inclusive one (Ausubel, 1962, 1963). The more inclusive unit 'education system', for instance, may subsume smaller information units as 'study level', 'streams', 'study areas' and 'subjects'. Building a hierarchical text structure requires about the same subphases as grouping does, be it at a higher level of abstraction. The former learning activities enable the participant to revise his draft in line with the criterion: representing the information units in distinct sections and paragraphs.

3.2 Outlining a text schema

Outlining a schema aims at offering novices a clearer insight into the text structure, which is needed to articulate relationships and to write an introduction and a conclusion. This learning activity entails representing a clear overview of the most inclusive information units and of the smaller information units.

3.3 Articulating the relationships between the information units as represented in sections and paragraphs

Articulating the relationship between the information units, and in particular writing topical passages is a hard job to do, since the transparent verbal representation of a hierarchical text structure is expected. Consequently, it requires a lot of time and instructional support.

3.4 Writing an introduction and a conclusion

An introduction states the topic and the writing-goal. It addresses the audience and expresses the core of the text. So it requires the identification of the most inclusive information units and their articulation with the appropriate slots. Therefore a high instructional investment is spent to it. This is also the case for writing the conclusion.

4. REFINING LANGUAGE USE

At the end attention is paid to sentence construction, wording and spelling.

It has to be noticed that each writing session starts with the revision of the former draft as to content and structure. Revising means confronting the text with the criteria outlined and it contains several substages: (1) reading text, (2) identifying problems: (a) problem detection (where do I notice a problem?), (b) problem diagnosis (which is the problem exactly?) and (3) delineating a revision strategy: (a) searching for a solution (which one?), (b) describing that solution (which criteria should it meet?) and (4) executing the solution.

APPENDIX C. WRITING ASSESSMENT BY THE EXTERNAL REVIEWERS SCORING PROCEDURE

On a checklist the reviewers have firstly to indicate whether a criterion has been met for content and for structure. After that, content and structure have to be scored on a 9 point scale, with a caesura fixed at 4. Score 4 is allowed for texts meeting the minimum criteria. Scores 5 to 9 refer to a higher quality. Scores 1 to 3 may be chosen if the minimum criteria have not been met at all. Beforehand the reviewers receive a booklet in which (1) the features and criteria of an informative text are explained and illustrated and (2) the assessment procedure is clarified. In addition they get an assessment training by the researcher at the hand of a virtual writing protocol. Next brief description concerns *content scoring*.

> Score 4 is only allowed if (1) the text contains at least three relevant information units, (2) these information units are at least slightly elaborated and (3) the text mentions the information unit 'education system' (streams or study areas), which needs not yet to be elaborated.

A further illustration for assessing *text structure* is presented.

| I | ANALYSIS AND ASSESSMENT OF CONTENT |

……..

| II | ANALYSIS AND ASSESSMENT OF TEXT STRUCTURE |

As you did for text content, you assess text structure in two stages. Firstly, you analyse it at the hand of the checklist below. After that, you score text structure by using the 9 point scale.

ANALYSIS [4]

Next questions concern text structure. You answer the questions by the appropiate number. 0 means 'no' and 1 means 'yes'.

1. Introduction

1.1 Presence of an introduction

Here you have to state if the text contains an introduction. To state that you only need to take into account the minimum criterion for an introduction (stating topic or mentioning the information units to be dealt with in the text). You need not yet to investigate its correspondence with text content and text structure.

	NO	YES
The text contains an introduction	0	1

If NO, go to 2.
If YES, go to 1.2

1.2 Quality of introduction
Here you have to consider the quality of the introduction. This means at which degree it contains the elements of a good introduction. However, if that element does not correspond with text content as such (nucleus), you cannot assess it as satisfactory and you have thus to choose Score 0.

	NO	YES
The introduction		
(1) States the topic very clearly	0	1
(2) States writing-goal (giving information)	0	1
(3) mentions the information units that will be dealt in the text	0	1
.not in an appropriate order	0	OR
.in an appropriate order		1
(4) addresses the audience	0	1

After having analysed the nucleus and the conclusion in a same way, the reviewer has to go to Stage 2.

SCORING

---

[4] *In this illustration the analysis is limited to the introduction.*

In this second stage you score text structure by using the 9 point scale. The directives refer only to Scale Points 1, 4, 5 and 9.

SCALE POINT 1 should be awarded if

No criterion is met

SCALE POINT 4 is *only* allowed if

at least all information units are grouped appropriately in the text. You need not yet state if this grouping appears in distinct paragraphs

A text that deserves more than Scale Point 1, but does not meet the minimum criterion mentioned, may get Scale Point 2 or 3.

SCALE POINT 5 is only allowed if

(1) at least all information units are grouped appropriately in the text. (You need not yet state if this grouping appears in distinct paragraphs)
(2) the text contains an introduction meeting the minimum criterion (stating topic clearly or mentioning information units to be dealt in the text)

SCALE POINT 9 is allowed if
the text meets all structure criteria; in other words: if you gave each element Score 1 (versus 0).

A text, that deserves more than Scale Point 5, but does not meet ALL criteria, may get Scale Point 6, 7 or 8.

# ADAPTING TO THE CLASSROOM SETTING: NEW RESEARCH ON TEACHERS MOVING BETWEEN TRADITIONAL AND COMPUTER CLASSROOMS

KATE KIEFER & MIKE PALMQUIST

Colorado State University, USA

Abstract: Following a brief review of key results from an earlier study of teachers who taught the same course in both a computer classroom and a traditional classroom, we discuss the results of a follow-up study of teachers who continue to move between these instructional settings and consider how our results have led us to reshape our teaching-training program. We argue that teacher training should be seen as a critical element shaping the complex interplay among teachers' knowledge, experiences, and perceptions as they move among classroom settings.

Keywords: synchronous discussion forums, classroom setting, computer classrooms, in-class writing, teacher training, technology critics

1. INTRODUCTION

Researchers have long studied the complex questions of how the best teachers succeed and how weaker teachers can improve. The history of these studies is too lengthy to address in detail here, but we can note that researchers have consistently studied – and continue to study – teachers' knowledge and practice (Darling-Hammond, 1994; Hativa et al., 1999; Turner-Bisset, 1999; Hativa, 2000; Wray et al., 2000). A related focus on teachers' personal histories, beliefs, and values shows how these factors affect their performance in the classroom as well (Holt-Reynolds, 1992; Holt-Reynolds, 1994; Berliner & Calfee, 1996; McGhie-Richmond et al., 2002). When we look specifically at the ways these factors have been studied in relation to writing instruction in computer classrooms, we note a similar history – albeit one with fewer detailed studies of teachers' decisions as they adapt to various classroom settings. Rodrigues and Rodrigues note that "teaching strategies vary ac-

---

Kiefer, K. & Palmquist, M. (2004). Adapting to the classroom setting: New Research on teachers moving between traditional and computer classrooms.
In G. Rijlaarsdam (Series Ed.) and Rijlaarsdam, G., Van den Bergh, H. & Couzijn, M. (Vol. Eds.), Studies in writing. Vol. 14, Effective learning and teaching of writing, 2nd Edition, Part 2, Studies in how to teach writing, 417-426.

cording to the ability of the teacher to continue learning and adjusting to both the changing students and the changing technology" (Rodrigues & Rodrigues 1989: 16), while Kiefer argues that "writing teachers especially need to be open to new ways of using all the tools at hand" (Kiefer 1991: 119) for developing the critical thinking and writing skills of students in all disciplines.

Unfortunately, relatively little sustained research examines the specific changes teachers make as they move from traditional to computer classrooms. Moreover, the existing scholarship in this area is limited either by its scope or by its focus on students rather than on teachers. For instance, Gruber's (1995) study of a graduate seminar, in which she calls for changes in teaching practices so that students can discuss and resolve conflict situations, reports results from observations of a single classroom. Similarly, Kent-Drury's study, which provides advice on specific strategies for encouraging students "to develop an awareness both of technologies and of the new demographic stratifications they imply" (Kent-Drury 1998: 406), is based on observation of a small number of classrooms. And LeCourt's critique (1998) of the computer classroom as a writing space, while providing valuable insights into how teachers can use technology to enhance their instruction, is based on the author's experiences rather than on empirical study. Other studies focus primarily on student learning outcomes rather than on pedagogical practices. Harris & Wambean (1996) report the results of a "pedagogical experiment" linking classes in Pennsylvania and Wyoming through synchronous and asynchronous communication tools, but the focus of their research is on outcomes for students, not specific changes in teaching behavior. Similarly, Douglas concentrates her comparison of two writing classrooms on student attitudes and writing and concludes that the interrelationships among "computer, pedagogy, and social context" (Douglas 1994: 281) hold the key to incorporating technologies, improving student teaching, and enhancing student performance.

Of those studies that look specifically at teachers in both computer and traditional classrooms, Klem and Moran's is most significant. They report their observations from "a semester-long naturalistic study of two writing teachers teaching for the first time in newly-equipped, networked computer classrooms" and conclude that

> ...each teacher brings a pattern of behavior – one cultivated by past experience, and by beliefs about what writing is and how it is best taught – into a classroom. Making the change to a computer-equipped classroom environment may challenge a teacher's models more deeply and more subtly than we have heretofore recognized. (Klem & Moran 1992: 19-20)

When Moran himself moved back to the traditional classroom after eight years of teaching writing in a networked computer classroom, he further argued that "the presence of computers in a writing classroom does make a difference, that technologies are not transparent, and that the change in moving from a traditional classroom to a computer classroom (or back!) is substantial and ... expensive" (Moran 1998: 9).

When we began our study of specific changes teachers made as they moved between traditional and computer classrooms in 1993, we expected that the classroom context itself would dominate the decision-making of teachers. But as Schoenfeld (1998) and others point out, teaching is such a complex decision-making process that any one component is unlikely to account for all the immediate choices teachers make in light of shifting priorities and goals in the classroom.

Below, we provide a brief review of our study of four teachers in 1993-94 as they taught the same course in both a computer classroom and a traditional classroom. We then report results of follow-up interviews with one of the teachers from the original study and three teachers, each of whom regularly moves between traditional and computer classrooms. We consider how the results of our studies have shaped our continuing efforts to prepare teachers for the two classroom settings, using excerpts from our interviews to flesh out the ways in which training becomes one more part of a complex set of interactions among teachers' knowledge, experiences, and perceptions as they move among teaching contexts.

2. SUMMARY OF INITIAL STUDY

In the fall of 1993, as part of a large-scale study of eight classrooms, we began tracking daily changes that four teachers made as they taught the same course in both a computer and a traditional classroom. We used multiple data-collection methods to capture as much information as possible about adaptations to the teaching environment. Teachers, of necessity, adjusted materials and activities based on the classroom setting, but all data-collection techniques were the same in both settings.

- Teachers were interviewed three times during the semester to elicit their perceptions of differences between classes taught in traditional and computer classrooms.
- Each class was observed three or four times during the term. Although classroom observations focused on student/teacher interactions, the observers noted the classroom activities completed in the paired computer and traditional classes.
- Teachers kept a log of their teaching activities. The teacher logs were designed to capture as much information as possible about the planning and execution of classes, about contacts with students, and about teachers' perceptions of class progress.

To provide a quantitative counterpoint for teachers' self-reports, we also asked students to fill out weekly surveys (contact sheets) noting the number of times they talked directly with teachers, either face-to-face before, during, or after class, or via telephone or email. We also correlated teachers' self-perceptions of student contact with tallies made during our classroom observations.

The four teachers[1] in our study were selected because of their proven teaching strengths. We had also observed each of these teachers on several occasions before the study and knew that their classroom demeanor, their ability to interact with stu-

---

[1] *All interviewees are referred to by aliases throughout this text in accordance with conditions specified by our University's Human Research Committee.*

dents, and their ability to adapt would help them feel positive about this research project.

We identified five key differences between the computer classroom and the traditional classroom that were noted by all four teachers in the study. For these teachers, the computer classroom fostered 1) more time for writing during class, 2) greater ease in encouraging revision, 3) greater student control, 4) a shift away from large-group discussion, and 5) more frequent student-student interaction. Our interviews with students confirmed these differences. In addition, in our classroom observations and analysis of contact sheets, we discerned not only the student-student interaction teachers noticed but also 6) more frequent teacher-student interaction in the computer classroom. Our analysis of teachers' logs also contributed to our regrouping of these findings from this study into two main categories:

- Teachers moving between computer and traditional classrooms changed classroom activities significantly to accommodate the setting, notably decreasing the number and length of whole-class discussions and increasing the number and length of opportunities for writing in the computer classroom, as well as encouraging revision with more in-class activities and peer support in the computer classroom.
- For a variety of reasons, teachers adopted different roles in the traditional and computer classrooms so that in the computer classroom they gave students more control of pacing as well as greater responsibility for initiating dialogue with peers and teachers.

As we discuss in Chapters 5 and 6 of *Transitions* (Palmquist, Kiefer et al., 1998), the computer classrooms we studied became a work site where students consistently engaged in writing that contributed significantly to their final graded papers as well as, and more importantly, to their understanding of the complexity of writing.

Teachers not only adapted class plans and activities as they moved from traditional classroom to computer classroom, but they also adapted their roles in the classroom. In their interviews, teachers suggested that their roles changed in response to the increased number of independent tasks students engaged in while at the computers, the lack of a clear focal point that would allow the teacher to dominate the space of the computer classroom, and greater student engagement with writing as a classroom task – with the latter largely a result of the comparative ease and efficiency of drafting and revising made possible by access to computers.

3. FOLLOW-UP INTERVIEWS WITH TEACHERS IN BOTH CLASSROOM SETTINGS

Without doubt, in the ten years since the initial data collection for the *Transitions* study, teachers have evolved new techniques and adaptations – both to the specific classroom spaces and technologies available and to the shifts necessary for moving from one classroom setting to the other. We recently interviewed Anita, one of the teachers from the original study, asking her to reflect about the key findings from the study noted above. We also interviewed three other teachers who have experience teaching in both traditional and computer classrooms.

Asked to comment on whether large-group discussions are more easily orchestrated in the traditional classroom, Anita responded that she now views large-group discussions in the computer classroom as easier (because of room layout) in the computer classroom than in the traditional classroom:

> I do not think that it is more difficult for me to orchestrate large group discussion in the computer classroom. In fact, I think that it works better for me in the computer classroom because there is an aisle that I can walk around in as we discuss. Because the chairs are placed in a circle, students can see each other; students can't easily hide. Even if the chairs are circled up in the regular classroom, students can fade behind the desk portion of the chairs.

David, who has taught in both classroom settings in our writing program over the past seven years, notes that he no longer sees many differences: "Typically my discussions are comparable, sometimes even better [in the computer classroom] because we can lead in with more effective daily writing on the computer." Comments from Jo, however, who has taught in our program since the late 1980s, emphasize the interplay of elements that contribute to successful large-group discussion:

> It depends on the teacher and the particular class, of course. The computer room is just one of the variables. I always insist on discussion, regardless what room we're in or how crowded conditions may be. I'm also a big fan of Tannen in terms of varying the size/composition of discussion groups. I start with small groups who then share with the class. But students also have to contribute to large-group discussions.... Overall, I do believe that more exciting things happen in traditional class discussions.

Not surprisingly, these teachers evaluate the effectiveness of class activities within a context of personal expectations and preferences, as well as their extensive experiences in the two classroom settings.

Because the amount of time devoted to writing in the classroom itself was so critical in prompting other curricular changes, we asked Anita if this imbalance has continued in her traditional and computer classrooms:

> I definitely ask students to compose more in the computer classroom than I do in the traditional classroom. In the computer classroom, I have them draft and encourage them to work on various sections of their choice. In the traditional classroom, I usually encourage them to draft a particular section such as the introduction or conclusion. A significant difference is that I have students work on their drafts in the computer room for up to or even more than half of the class, whereas, in the traditional classroom, I use whole class discussion and group work more and leave no more than 15 minutes for drafting. I still think that my in-class drafting assignments in the traditional classroom are limited in scope.

Echoing Anita, David also notes that writing in the computer classroom is more efficient for students and thus more effective as a teaching technique. David notes that he tries to assign the same tasks in both settings, but he goes on to say that

> [It's so much] easier to get students to write in computer classrooms. In traditional [classrooms], I have to almost harass at times, but at the very least consistently encourage and nudge. [But] I try to do almost all of the writing activities from the computer sections in the traditional. What I end up doing, though, is taking less time for them and expecting (and typically getting) less from them. I would say that I probably plan for/spend about twice the time writing in computer classrooms.

All the teachers in our follow-up interviews still see the advantages that access to word processing provides for students in the classroom setting – at least so far as producing work – but they also tailor their in-class writing for the traditional class to tasks that they see students can produce comfortably with pen and paper.

Anita's reasons for having students write more often and for longer periods in the computer classroom compared to the traditional classroom continue to reflect the importance of the computer classroom as a workspace:

> I walk around the class reading over shoulders. I am much more apt to walk around the room and read over the shoulders of students in the computer classroom than I am in the traditional classroom. The spacing in the traditional classroom does not allow me free movement so I recognize that I stay at the front of the class more often.

Similarly, Thomas, who has taught writing for more than three decades and has worked in computer classrooms since the mid-1980s, comments that the main advantage of the computer classroom is its ability to serve as an active workspace:

> As I go back and forth, the computer enables them to do actual drafting that becomes part of the project. When I do traditional classes, the writing that I have them do in class is much less actual text production and much more the other kinds of critical reading, awareness of writing process, reflection, looking at rhetorical contexts...I do a lot more writing-to-learn things [in the traditional classroom] on critical reading and rhetorical issues, but in the computer classroom they're doing whatever they need to be doing – writing a draft, looking on the Web for sources, editing their bibliographies, revising. One of the things I love about the computer classroom is that I get to do so many individual tutorial sessions, just 2-3 minutes, sitting down, troubleshooting, looking at writing in progress, what's stumping you, what's working. You can't really do that in a traditional classroom.

Notably, in her follow-up interview, Anita's descriptions of the classroom activities repeatedly emphasize movement and interaction. Anita moves around the room and among the students to stimulate their active participation in class and to increase her availability to answer specific questions. For Anita, hand-in-hand with the notion of a comfortable workspace that promotes writing comes enhanced awareness of student engagement: "When I pace in the computer classroom, as students are working on projects or activities, I am closer to them and they can stop me with questions; I also find myself peering over shoulders which gives me more access to student writing." David also expresses the importance of teacher movement, noting, "I can move much more because there aren't rows to contend with (in a traditional classroom that's too small for a circle)." But as he notes at some length, student attitudes toward computers have changed as along with students' facility in manipulating software applications. He sees new problems emerging with regard to student control in the computer classroom:

> I would say the computer classroom has been getting harder to control over the past few years. My sense is that now students are so comfortable with the technology that they come in and they're right to work, be it on class-related stuff, their email, surfing the Web, or sometimes playing Solitaire. I've also seen a lot more students trying to use email and the net during class. [So] I find less chatting in the negative/disruptive sense in computer classrooms but more individuals who are actively distracting themselves with the computer.

In his interview, Thomas agrees with David's observation, adding that he sees students' computer skills affecting the total context of teaching in the computer classroom:

> I'll see 20 people on task and four doing other things – one's on email, two are playing Solitaire inevitably, or off on Web sites. That's changed what I would do. Fifteen years ago I would have said, "put away that Coloradoan [our local newspaper]; we're on task here." And now I just go over and say, "Wow, that's an interesting game." That's their choice to use their time as they need to. Movement between computer and traditional classrooms has become interesting terrain... The whole landscape of what it means to be a teacher in a classroom has changed. There's so much technology in traditional classroom these days that it seems like a much more seamless transition. Everybody can navigate almost anything. That's a two-year shift – very recent.

Finally, the teachers we interviewed expressed preferences for one setting over the other, but they also recognize, as Anita explains, that teacher preferences affect student reactions:

> I believe that students who have class in the computer classroom feel more inclined to visit me in my office for conferences and feel that I am more approachable. This could be because I prefer to teach in the computer classroom, and it shows. But, I think that the traditional classroom casts preconceptions on the part of the students and further distances student from instructor.

In general, Anita and our other long-time teachers have continued to evolve in their teaching, and a more detailed study of the sort we conducted in 1993-94 would no doubt capture more changes they have made since then in both instructional settings. What the follow-up interviews highlight, however, is the complexity of interactions that affect student and teacher performance in any instructional context.

4. FOLLOW-UP INTERVIEWS ABOUT TEACHER TRAINING

In a parallel effort to influence some of the complex factors teachers must negotiate among as instructional technology is introduced, we have reshaped our teacher-training program for graduate teaching assistants (GTAs). Although we have long promoted computers as key tools for writing instruction, we now also commit significant amounts of time in our training programs to address issues of teaching with nontraditional tools. In particular, we now devote one semester of our GTA training sessions to the ways that various computer resources can supplement instruction in any setting. Because so few of our GTAs will teach in one of our computer classrooms, we concentrate on explanations and examples of using asynchronous postings, email lists, word processing features (especially for peer review), Internet searching in their classes, and Web-based "studios" as part of their teaching repertoire in traditional classrooms. We encourage GTAs to incorporate these computer tools into activities during the training semester so that we can discuss, as a group, the advantages and pitfalls of integrating computer support into traditional classroom courses.

Mindful of specific findings from the study, we began revamping several years ago the syllabus new teachers use when they first teach our introductory college writing course. We now explicitly describe writing activities for class meetings at the beginning of the semester so that teachers can see the advantages of having students write in class – no matter the setting. As the interview comments in the preceding section indicate, however, writing in traditional classrooms still means working against most students' expectations. When Kate first moved from computer classrooms back into a traditional classroom, she analyzed (1999) her experience this way:

> Students don't think of classrooms as places where significant writing and thinking go on. They will take notes and they will write exams, but they don't ordinarily think of classroom time as writing time.... Asking students to write longhand responses now almost guarantees telegraphic writing.

Despite these constraints on in-class writing in traditional classrooms, we explain to new teachers how writing can function in their traditional classrooms, and we encourage them to make in-class writing a key component in their repertoire of classroom activities. As Thomas explains in some detail, however, the differences we stress in our training program are not those between computer and traditional classrooms but those between effective and ineffective uses of in-class writing:

> It's comfortable for the GTAs to have daily writing as a kind of crutch but I have to wean them away from that a little. For me the most effective in-class writing activities are the ones I don't plan but plug in when we're at a point where the discussion is not going the way I want or students haven't had a chance to read critically, and if we're going to have a discussion they need to go back and write something. So I always see these writing tasks as "we need to get focused here." But that's an experienced teacher who can see what's going to happen and adapt the writing to the teaching situation.

As Thomas works with GTAs to discuss these writing situations, his examples, modeling, and class conversations teach GTAs more about using writing as a tool in any classroom setting. GTAs also gain first-hand experience through their teaching and critique of teaching (another key part of our training program) so that they can mimic the decision-making processes of more seasoned teachers.

As other technological resources have become available, we have also worked to integrate them appropriately into our training for new teachers in traditional classrooms. In particular, we encourage "Web publication" of certain final drafts to allow students in each class to see what their peers have accomplished on a given assignment and to promote more authentic audience concerns as students write their academic papers. Regardless of setting, students in our writing classes need to build a sense of the "classroom" community, and "publication" on asynchronous bulletin boards, through email distribution lists, and on specific Web sites promotes a stronger sense of the classroom community than individual writing activities that students rarely share with anyone but their teacher.

In addition, we extend the writing classroom – both the community of writers and the time/space boundaries of the class – by assigning writing on asynchronous discussion forums. As David notes, "This tool is fully integrated into GTAs' orientation program," and Thomas, who teaches a semester-long training course for our new GTAs, makes the discussion forum an integral part of his graduate class.

Thomas also eloquently explains both why our training support needs to keep current with emerging technologies and how our new teachers can accommodate all the technological applications we ask them to consider using:

> The whole landscape of writing has been changed by technology. When you sit back and think about how things are done differently compared to 10 years ago, almost everything has changed. The issue of writing process – I've been reading some stuff in the last week about post-process theory – and it's like all the things that we were deliberately and consciously teaching about process have become second nature. Of course, you start with a draft; it's in the computer. Of course you revise; you get out your computer file. Of course you share things. I think the whole notion of sharing texts – students' texts have become a lot more public because of technology. I always had to spend some time [explaining that] we're a writing community and we share things we write. I always had 30 minutes on that, and now it's totally unnecessary. The whole notion of writing process is integrated in the air we breathe so we don't have to spend time on it now; they get it in grade school and high school. And I see no one who's reluctant to share anything they write with anyone else. Maybe discussion forums have changed that. They've learned a public voice – some more successfully than others, some more ranting than others.

As Thomas notes, however, no matter how important we feel our training for technology support is, "It seems like every year there's a threshold for how much technology GTAs can absorb. We seem to hit that at different points in the semester. But a lot depends on their personal experiences. GTAs have a steep learning curve and then the reaction – 'I'm sorry I can't deal with this.'"

Also, as David notes, GTAs' commitment to learning how to use technological tools is limited by their time and commitment to the short-term teaching program:

> I think back to my own experience and it took me two or three years to get to a point where things like Syllabase[2] or online research or teaching in a computer classroom that I felt comfortable with the basics of those environments and those resources and could then plan off them or do new things or think more about other ways to use them. But it took me a big chunk of time to get there versus GTAs with two years or maybe three years or maybe only one, and I don't think there's any way they can get to that level. It takes a long time to integrate technology effectively into teaching much less use it to directly change how you're teaching or offer new ways to teach. That's hard in terms of a year or two years.

As a result, we continually monitor all the components of our training program to ensure that we're focusing on the technologies that will most benefit the instructional efforts of our graduate teaching assistants. We understand, as well, that not all teachers in our training program will feel equally concerned with mastering tools and techniques. With this in mind, we encourage an ongoing discussion about the technologies that are available to support our classes and the advantages and disadvantages of using them.

Finally, one of our concerns based on the initial study is to break down the simple dichotomy that seems to arise between traditional and computer classrooms. Even experienced professionals, like Anita, react to their personal preferences for the teaching environment and inadvertently privilege one setting over the other. As our profession moves into hybrid (blended face-to-face and online instruction) as well as fully distance or online models of instruction, we increasingly see the importance of extending all classes outside the traditional boundaries of a particular class time and place. Through our integration of classroom-management systems, Web-

---

[2] *Syllabase is an online course management system similar to WebCT or Blackboard. Information on the system can be found at http://www.3gb.com.*

based instructional resources, network communication tools, and Web publishing, we continue to emphasize in our teacher training an approach that integrates technology with writing classes, regardless of where those classes occur – traditional classrooms, networked computer classrooms, or virtual classrooms.

5. CONCLUSIONS WE CAN DRAW FROM BOTH STUDIES

Teachers need to adapt to new instructional contexts, including traditional classrooms, networked computer classrooms, traditional classrooms with extensive out-of-class technological support tools, hybrid classes, and fully online (or virtual) classes. Teachers' ability to adapt will be shaped by myriad concerns – background knowledge, past experience, mental models of teaching, attitudes toward students, and the specific focus of the course in question. Clearly, many of these features are beyond the control of teacher trainers, but we can present new information, model new processes, and help shape attitudes and expectations through training activities.

As the results from the *Transitions* study showed, teachers appropriately adapted their teaching plans and goals to take advantage of specific features of the classroom setting. As our follow-up interviews confirm, the two contexts we have concentrated on (the traditional classroom and the networked computer classroom) present different advantages to teachers. How well they exploit those advantages, we believe, can be enhanced through training. Our program begins with the premise most clearly articulated in Selfe's 1992 argument for technology critics. In this piece, Selfe presents five key suggestions for improving teacher training, but the underpinning of her overall argument is that the most effective teacher training programs teach "educators to think critically about how and when virtual environments can support the educational objectives of teachers in English classrooms" (Selfe 1992: 24). Other researchers agree that educating teachers depends on not just teaching them to use technology but, primarily, to teach with technology when the technology serves students', teachers', and program goals (Francis-Pelton et al., 2000).

In our training program, we build on that initial premise with specific activities that invite new teachers to explore and practice integrating technology into their instructional contexts. We enact a training program that looks much like the one Mewborn and Stanulis (2000) describe, one that emphasizes discussing contexts and technology as an impetus for change, modeling effective teaching, and making the tacit knowledge they have of computer technologies as writers explicit in their teaching of writing. Like Smith (2001), we believe that our GTAs become better teachers when they have direct experience with the computer tools their students use, so we build opportunities for frequent practice into our week-long pre-service training, our semester-long graduate seminar in teaching theory and practice, and our semester-long follow-up sessions in a computer classroom. Although our GTAs may not be as accomplished in reacting quickly to the changing demands of their classrooms as more experienced teachers, we believe the training they receive helps them adjust effectively and appropriately to new teaching contexts. Equally important, we believe that careful introduction to new technologies can help teachers see technology as a possible enhancement to rather than impediment in their teaching.

ASSESSMENT OF ARGUMENTATIVE WRITING

RON OOSTDAM

University of Amsterdam

Abstract. When producing an argumentative text, writers have to solve problems that are specific for that type of text. The nature and severity of these problems, i.e., the specific problem area of argumentation in written discourse, can be characterized with the help of concepts from the pragma-dialectical argumentation theory (Van Eemeren & Grootendorst, 1984). It is assumed that during the writing process language users will have to appeal to knowledge and skills corresponding with these concepts in order to overcome problems. In this chapter the role of specific knowledge and skills in writing argumentative texts is indicated. A summary is given of the different stages of writing discursive texts and the specific problems connected with these stages (section 2). On the basis of the results of an assessment study of argumentation skills, it is illustrated to what extent the marked problems occur in secondary school students' writing (section 3). For some of the problems found, writing advice is formulated (section 4).

Keywords: argumentative texts, argumentation skills, pragma-dialectical argumentation theory, written discourse, assessment study, secondary education, measurement instruments, achievement levels, writing problems, writing advices

1. INTRODUCTION

In general writing is considered as a relatively stable skill that can be influenced by learning and is determined by the knowledge and skills writers rely on during the process of text production. In most cognitive models of writing a distinction is being made between the different components of the writing process, such as generating and selecting content elements, organizing text structure, translating mental representations into linguistic forms and revising text (cf. Bereiter & Scardemalia, 1987; Hayes & Flower, 1980; Kellogg, 1996). Furthermore, it is commonly assumed that writing is a recursive process that involves a constant planning, monitoring and evaluating of writing activities (cf. Van Gelderen & Oostdam, 2003). Speaking about the writing ability of individuals actually refers to a quite heterogeneous underlying cognitive process (cf. De Glopper, 1988). In relation to this process a dis-

---

Oostdam, R. (2004). Assessment of argumentative writing.
In G. Rijlaarsdam (Series Ed.) and Rijlaarsdam, G., Van den Bergh, H. & Couzijn, M. (Vol. Eds.), Studies in writing. Vol. 14, Effective learning and teaching of writing, 2nd Edition, Part 2, Studies in how to teach writing, 427-442.

tinction can be made between general and specific knowledge and skills (cf. Alamargot & Chanquoy, 2001). General knowledge and skills play a rather invariant role during writing irrespective of the type of text (narrative, informative, descriptive, argumentative). Writing a narrative or argumentative text will confront writers for example with the same problems on the level of spelling and punctuation. Also on the level of translation most problems will be invariant of text type: every text requires application of the same criteria for word sequence, the use of text markers and connectives, sentence combining, text coherence, et cetera. However, some texts demand specific knowledge and skills. The review of Hillocks for example (1986) gives an overview of writing studies indicating that syntactical complexity co varies with the differences in writing goals.

In this chapter it is described which specific knowledge and skills are involved in writing an argumentative text (cf. Meuffels, 1982; Oostdam, 1991; Van Eemeren & Grootendorst, 1984). An overview is presented of the different phases in writing an argument and for each phase specific problems that writers have to solve are described. These problems are characterized and defined with concepts from the pragma-dialectical argumentation theory (cf. Van Eemeren & Grootendorst, 1984; Van Eemeren, Grootendorst, Jackson & Jacobs, 1993). Subsequently, based on the results of an assessment study into argumentation skills in the final grades of secondary education, it is illustrated to what extent the marked problems actually occur in students' writing performance.

2. STAGES IN WRITING AN ARGUMENT

The first phase of writing an argument consists in determining the subject, text objective, text type and audience (Van Eemeren & Grootendorst, 1984). The text objective in an argumentative text is fixed: convincing the reader of the acceptability of the standpoint taken. Text type and the audience together determine the functional context of the argument, which is often determined beforehand.

When conceiving an argument a writer has to take up a clear standpoint (also compare Toulmin, 1969). With a standpoint a language user expresses his positive or negative position with respect to an opinion. A language user can explain his position in a standpoint with the help of all kinds of markers ('I think', 'according to me', et cetera). An opinion is formed by the proposition which is expressed in the speech act to which the argument is related (cf. Searle, 1979). The subject of the opinion can among other things relate to facts, actions and attitudes. For a writer it is important to explain with regard to which opinion he has taken a particular standpoint pro or con.

After having explained his standpoint a writer has to generate and select arguments in the second argumentative phase to support his standpoint. In doing so, not only finding arguments pro is involved, but also looking for the rebuttals of possible arguments con. The knowledge of writers about the subject limits the arguments to be generated. Which arguments writers generate will also depend on their knowledge of schemes for finding a subject. A good example of such schemes are stock issues (as used in debating courses), with the help of which it can be checked whether all relevant points come up for discussion in the argument (cf. Braet & Berkenbosch, 1989; Freeley, 1981).

In the third phase the generated arguments will have to be selected. This phase of the writing process consists of drawing up an argumentation structure. The structure of the argumentation brought forward to support the standpoint may be complex (cf. Van Eemeren, Grootendorst & Kruiger, 1987; Freeman, 1992; Oostdam, 1990; Perelman & Olbrechts-Tyteca, 1969; Snoeck Henkemans, 1992; Toulmin, 1969). A distinction has to be made between the main argumentation and the sub-argumentation. The former relates to the main standpoint and the latter to sub-standpoint(s). The relation between standpoint and argument(s) can be explained by markers ('so', 'for', et cetera). With that, a distinction can be made between different types of argumentation structures: single, multiple, coordinate and subordinate (Van Eemeren, Grootendorst, & Kruiger, 1987).

Finally, in the fourth phase the writer will determine the global text structure. In verbal situations the structure of arguments can be characterized in terms of confrontation phase, opening phase, argumentation phase and conclusion phase (Van Eemeren & Grootendorst, 1984). In the confrontation phase it is determined that there is a difference of opinion and the standpoint (or standpoints) is determined univocally. In the opening phase it is indicated that there is a preparedness to solve the difference of opinion by defending the standpoint with the help of argumentation. The subsequent argumentation phase consists of putting forward argumentation to support the standpoint and react to or anticipate possible arguments con. This phase is the most crucial for solving the difference of opinion. Finally, in the conclusion phase it is determined whether the difference of opinion has been solved or not.

It may be assumed that written arguments can also be typified with the help of these phases (cf. Van Eemeren, Grootendorst, Jackson & Jacobs, 1993; Koetsenruijter, 1991; Viskil, 1991). The confrontation phase will then often come about preceding the production of the text. Formulating a standpoint and accompanying arguments will conclude the opening and argumentation phase. The conclusion phase will usually take place outside the text: the success of the attempt to persuade the reader will become evident from the reaction of the reader(s). The sequence of these argumentation phases is less fixed in written arguments than in discussions. It is possible that a writer presents some arguments for rhetorical reasons preceding the standpoint.

The description of the above-mentioned phases seems to presuppose a linear development in the writing process, but determining the text structure may also precede generating the arguments. Neither is it required that these phases of the writing process should be completed consciously. An analytic survey is not made in advance in every case. Arguments can be dreamt up while writing and in the meantime a readjustment of the argument and argumentation structure takes place.

After writing the first version one or more rewriting rounds may follow. While producing and revising the text, a writer has to bear his text objective in mind and in the light of this he constantly has to analyze and evaluate critically the comprehensibility and acceptability of the text. Text analysis and evaluation are inextricably linked to writing (cf. Van Gelderen & Oostdam, 2003).

When analyzing and evaluating the text, the following questions are of importance at the least. Has the standpoint been formulated in a clear way? Is the introduction of the text structure clear? Is the argumentation structure properly ordered and transparent for the reader?

3. DESIGN OF THE ASSESSMENT STUDY

The two main objectives of the study were to investigate (1) the content of educational matter in argumentation in Dutch secondary education and (2) pupils' skill in receptive and productive argumentation towards the end of their education.

To determine pupils' achievement levels a great number of receptive and productive argumentative tests has been presented to the pupils from 136 classes. As a measurement in the final year could not be realized, only pupils of the pre-final school year of the four major tracks in Dutch secondary education were subjected to the tests: junior vocational education (LBO), lower general secondary education (MAVO), higher secondary education (HAVO) and academic secondary education (VWO)[1]. The average ages of pupils of the four tracks differ[2]. Junior vocational education (LBO) and lower general secondary education (MAVO) have four grade levels. The third grade can be compared to the ninth grade of high school. Higher secondary education (HAVO) has five grade levels. Grade level four is comparable to the tenth grade. Academic secondary education (VWO) has six grades, of which the fifth grade is similar to grade eleven of high school[3].

The test battery consisted of a large number of instruments for measuring receptive and productive argumentation skills (cf. Van Eemeren, De Glopper, Grootendorst & Oostdam, 1995; Oostdam, 1990, 1991; Oostdam & De Glopper, 1995, 1999; Oostdam & Eiting, 1991; Oostdam, De Glopper & Eiting, 1994). The tests for the productive skills relate to writing an argumentative text, selecting and ordering arguments, and using argumentative indicators. Within the framework of this chapter I will briefly describe the set-up of the productive tests and discuss some main results on the basis of the test scores of grade nine (LBO: lower tracks, vocational) and grade eleven students (VWO: higher tracks, pre-university). A comparison between these two grades gives some impression about the extent of the differences between tracks (i.e., grade levels) and the specificity of the problems, which occur.

---

[1] *For each track a random sample was made from 129 schools on the basis of the school file of the Ministry of Education for the school year 1988-1989. The average response for all tracks was 28%. The ages of the students range from 15 (3-LBO) to 17 (5-VWO). When we mention differences between tracks in the text, it also concerns differences in age between LBO/MAVO and HAVO/VWO. We label this distinction as lower tracks versus higher tracks.*
[2] *The range of students' ages for each track explains an important part of the variance in achievement levels. Most of the variance, however, is associated with differences in students' aptitudes.*
[3] *For more detailed information about the Dutch school system and education in argumentation skills see Oostdam & Emmelot 1991.*

4. TEST BATTERY

The test battery for the measurement of productive argumentation skills contained a free writing task and three subtests each focused on a particular skill: selecting arguments, arranging arguments and using argumentative indicators.

4.1 Free Writing Task

In the free writing task a discursive text had to be written. The subject of the task was set. The pupils were to either attack or defend the standpoint 'School uniforms have to be introduced on a compulsory basis'. The length of the essay was to be about one page. The pupils were allowed to create their own title. The task emphasized that the standpoint had to be well substantiated, with the purpose of convincing the reader.

The writing task contained no documentation material with arguments pro and con for the standpoint. From try-outs it appeared that a documented writing task provokes the writing out of phrases from the enclosed documentation. In a documented writing task the character of the essays became more contemplative rather than argumentative. Given arguments pro and con in the documentation increase students' apprehension for the standpoint in such a way that they see advantages as well as disadvantages for introducing compulsory school uniforms. As a result of this most students did not clearly attack or defend the standpoint.

Two raters with the help of extensive scoring schemes have evaluated every essay[4]. Among other things it was determined whether texts contained an explicit or implicit main standpoint. It was also determined how many arguments students brought forward to support their standpoint. Five types of arguments were distinguished. 'Arguments pro' support the standpoint taken. In case of a 'negated argument pro' the student contradicts an argument pro, which had been taken up previously. With an 'accepted argument con' the student included an argument against his standpoint without hesitation. If a pupil rejects an argument con without refutation, I speak of a 'non-accepted argument con'. The notion 'refuted contra-argument' refers to an attempt to refute.

Furthermore it has been checked whether an introduction of the subject was presented, at what position the main standpoint was first mentioned and whether or not the essay had an ending.

---

[4] *Nine raters were involved in rating the essays, every essay being rated by two raters (cf. Van den Bergh & Eiting 1989). The consensus between the raters, expressed as the percentage of corresponding scores, is: 87% (presence and nature of main standpoint: Table 1); 83% (nature of the arguments mentioned: Table 2); 85% (introduction subject: Table 6); 70% (position standpoint in text: Table 6); 65% (nature of the ending; Table 6).*

4.2 Selecting Arguments

The skill to select arguments has been measured with a test in which students have to select good arguments to support a given standpoint. The selection of arguments was presented as a preparation for writing an argumentative text. The text consists of two tasks that can be scored univocally. Besides a clear formulation of the standpoint every task contains information about the context and the audience for the text to be written. Four arguments have to be selected out of a list with 16 statements. The remaining statements are distractions: neutral statements or statements which may be interpreted argumentatively, but offer no immediate support for the standpoint. One of the two tasks is given below by way of illustration.

Instruction

When people talk with each other they make all kinds of statements and they often present their standpoints about a certain matter. In order to convince someone of a standpoint valid arguments must be given. For example, supporting the standpoint 'Yvonne is a good treasurer' with the argument 'She always looks very spruce' is not very convincing, for the fact that Yvonne looks very spruce does not mean that she is a good treasurer. It would be much better to support the standpoint 'Yvonne is a good treasurer' with an argument like 'She knows how to handle money'.

In the following task a standpoint is given together with a list of sixteen statements. Choose four statements from that list which can serve as an argument to support the standpoint.

Task

In the Netherlands you are legally required to have your car inspected annually when it is older than three years. From the following list of sixteen statements, choose four that can serve as an argument to support the standpoint: *A legally required yearly car inspection is very important for motorists.* (Statements marked with an asterisk are the ones to be chosen.)

Please note: This standpoint is presented in an information brochure for motorists. It may be clear that in such a brochure only the benefits for motorists are emphasized.

1.* A yearly car inspection warns the motorist on time about serious defects in his car which can endanger the other road users.
2. As a consequence of the yearly car inspection the sale of new cars will increase.
3. Yearly car inspections offer the possibility to check whether the owner is properly insured.
4. A yearly car inspection is a good way to measure the total number of cars on the road.
5.* The yearly car inspection is a cheap way to have major parts of your car checked.
6. A yearly car inspection will increase the number of service garages.
7. Traffic inspections become much easier by the system of yearly car inspection: the test rapport immediately shows whether a car meets the safety requirements.
8. Owners of rejected cars are forced to remove their scrap iron from the road.
9. At the yearly inspection some major parts of the car are checked.
10.* A yearly car inspection increases road safety because cars which constitute a danger for other motorists are removed from the road.
11. A car is condemned when the brakes are in bad shape.

12. Random samples are taken to check whether the yearly car inspection has been done properly.
13. A yearly car inspection is free when an assignment for repairs is given simultaneously.
14.* As a result of the yearly car inspection the risk of buying a car in bad shape is reduced.
15. A yearly car inspection can be done by an independent inspector.
16. The yearly car inspection is only obliged for cars older than three years.

4.3 Arranging Arguments

Pupils' skill in arranging arguments has been measured with a test in which students were asked to sort out 16 arguments for a given standpoint in the shape of a tree diagram. The test consists of two similar tasks, which can be scored univocally. The arguments have been formulated in such a way that their function as main argument or sub-argument can be determined unequivocally. Based on their relation main arguments and sub-arguments form certain intrinsic clusters. In the instruction task, execution is explained explicitly (see below).

Instruction

When people talk with each other they make all kinds of statements and they often present their standpoint about something. In many cases the standpoint is supported by arguments. For example: 'You'd better not buy a television set, because television has a bad influence on children'. In this example the standpoint 'You'd better not buy a television' is supported by the main argument 'Television has a bad influence on children'.

Of course it is also possible to support the main argument by so-called sub-arguments. For example: 'You'd better not buy a television set, because television has a bad influence on children. By television children are confronted with violence daily'. In this case the main argument 'Television has a bad influence on children' is supported by the sub-argument 'Television confronts children with violence daily'.

In the following task a number of main arguments and sub-arguments for a point of view are given but they are not ordered yet. Please order the arguments in such a way that it is clear which are the main arguments and which the sub-arguments.

The following example demonstrates how to fulfil the task.

Standpoint: You'd better not buy a television set

Arguments:

1. Television only offers superficial entertainment.
2. Watching television costs a lot of money.
3. There is a boring quiz on every night.
4. Children are confronted with violence daily.
5. Good newsreels are seldom broadcasted.
6. Television has a bad influence on children.

The standpoint 'You'd better not buy a television set' is supported by the following three main arguments:

1. Television only offers superficial entertainment.
2. Watching television costs a lot of money.
6. Television has a bad influence on children.

The main argument 'Television only offers superficial entertainment' is supported by the following two sub-arguments:
3. Every night there is a dull quiz to be seen.
5. Good newsreels are seldom broadcasted.

The main argument 'Watching television costs a lot of money' is not supported.
The main argument 'Television has a bad influence on children' is supported by the sub-argument:
4. Children are confronted with violence daily.

The above structure of main arguments and sub-arguments can be reproduced in the following schema. The numbers of the main arguments are placed in the left boxes; the numbers of the sub-arguments are placed in the right boxes. You can see that each main argument can be supported by at least four sub-arguments.

Please note: Not all the boxes have to be filled in. However, the number of boxes to be filled in depends on the number of arguments given.

Figure 1. Structural relations between main arguments and sub-arguments

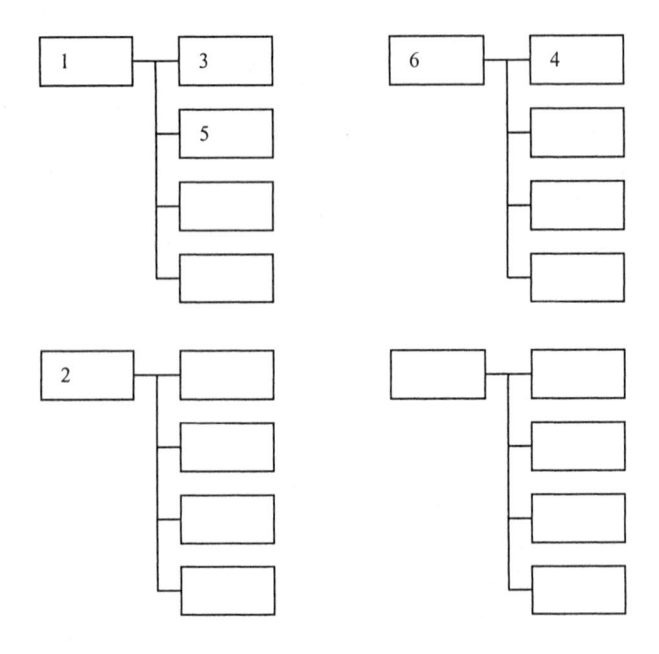

Task

At an air show over the German city of Ramstein three aircrafts of the Italian stunt-flying team Frecce Tricolore (Three coloured arrow) have crashed. As a consequence of this accident forty-nine people were killed including the three pilots and a hundred and sixty people were badly injured. After this accident, stunt flying on air shows became a subject of discussion in the Netherlands. Below, a number of arguments for the standpoint 'Air shows should be forbidden' are presented. Put the numbers of the main arguments in the left-hand boxes and the numbers of the sub-arguments in the right-hand boxes.

1. The aircrafts fly very low.
2. Air shows are a useless pastime.
3. Air shows cost the taxpayer a lot of money.
4. The risk for the pilots increases as a consequence of stunts becoming more sensational.
5. The safety of the public can no longer be guaranteed.
6. Every crashed aircraft costs a couple of millions.
7. People are regularly injured.
8. Attack on the social environment.
9. The cost of maintenance is high.
10. High wages for pilots of the stunt-flying team.
11. Glorification of war material.
12. Air shows are dangerous for the pilots.
13. Many traffic jams for people living in the neighbourhood.
14. Air pollution by exhaust fumes.
15. Fewer possibilities for the pilots to escape in the air.
16. The crowds cause parking problems.

It has been checked what kind of ordering errors students make. Two absolute ordering errors have been distinguished (type 1 and 2): errors within an intrinsic cluster in which a main argument (MA) is labeled sub-argument (SA) or vice versa. There are also two absolute combination errors (type 7 and 8): errors in which statements are mentioned correctly as main arguments or sub-arguments, but in which a sub-argument is placed with a main argument from another intrinsic cluster or in which a sub-argument is lacking. The remaining errors are of a mixed nature. The classification is as follows:
3) SA as MA together with a MA as SA (within the cluster);
4) SA as MA together with a SA as SA (within the cluster);
5) SA as MA together with a MA as SA (outside the cluster);
6) SA as MA together with a SA as SA (outside the cluster);
7) SA as MA without any MA or SA;
8) MA as MA together with MA as SA (outside the cluster);
9) MA as MA together with a SA (outside the cluster);
10) MA as MA and erroneously without SA.

A category of 'other errors' was added to classify arguments mentioned twice or skipped.

4.4 Using Argumentative Indicators

The skill of using argumentative indicators has been measured with a test, which can be scored univocally. In the test an schematically presented argumentation structure (main standpoint with main arguments and sub-arguments) must be transformed into a well-written text. The test consists of two short tasks in which standpoint and arguments are of a neutral nature and have been formulated as simply as possible. The students do not have to order the argumentation anymore. It is clearly indicated to the pupils, which sub-arguments belong to which main arguments. In every task a connection has to be made between 9 ordered statements on 8 sentence borders. For illustration, one of the tasks is given below.

Task

In the following task a number of main arguments and sub-arguments are given for the standpoint 'France is a nice destination for your holiday'. Try to write a well-written text in which all the arguments are used.

- France is a nice destination for your holiday
    - you can go there for any kind of vacation
        - it has fine beaches
        - the cities are worth visiting
    - staying there is affordable
        - hotels are not too expensive
        - you can eat for little money
    - you can spend a lot of time outside
        - most of the time the weather is nice

Please note: only use the arguments given and follow the sequence given. Of course you may change the word sequence and use connectors such as 'because', 'besides', 'moreover', 'so', 'therefore', 'and', et cetera.

Per sentence border it was determined with which linking words or other markers the student has made the connection. The following distinctions were made:
1) structure errors: subordination instead of coordination;
2) structure errors: coordination instead of subordination;
3) direction errors: connector referring forwards instead of referring backwards, adversative connection instead of enumerating;
4) connection errors: wrong use of connectors;
5) enumeration errors: errors in enumeration;
6) frequency errors: the number of sentence borders without a connector or other marking (at 1, 2 and 3 unmarked borders 0 fault, for each additional unmarked border: 1 fault).

A category 'other' was used to classify the number of sentences omitted by the students. The resulting lacking connections between sentences were scored as errors.

5. RESULTS

In discussing some main results I will focus on the following topics: presenting a standpoint, generating arguments, selecting arguments, arranging arguments and using argumentative indicators. As said before I will discuss the results on basis of the test scores of grade nine (LBO: vocational track) and grade eleven students (VWO: pre-university track).

5.1 Presenting a Standpoint

From Table 1 it becomes clear that virtually every pupil adopts an explicit standpoint in his or her essay. It is remarkable that especially many VWO students adopt an implicit standpoint more often. A small number, amounting to 4% at the LBO, does not adopt any standpoint.

Table 1. Presence and Nature of the Main Standpoint (Percentages per Track)

	Vocational (LBO) $n = 195$	Pre-university (VWO) $n = 220$
standpoint explicit	84.6	84.1
standpoint implicit	11.3	14.5
standpoint lacking	4.1	1.4

5.2 Generating Arguments

The average number of arguments brought forward in the argumentative essays differs per track. Between LBO and VWO the difference is considerable: it is almost half a standard deviation of the individual scores. The differences can be traced back to two types of arguments: arguments pro and refuted arguments. The VWO students most often put forward arguments pro and refute most of the arguments con.

Table 2. Nature of Arguments Presented (Average Numbers per Track)

	Vocational (LBO) $n = 195$	Pre-university (VWO) $n = 220$
arguments pro	2.15	2.44
negated arguments pro	0.01	0.00
accepted arguments con	0.24	0.23
non-accepted arguments con	0.07	0.08
refuted arguments	0.09	0.36
total number of arguments:		
M	2.56	3.11
SD	1.17	1.16

5.3 Selecting Arguments

The LBO students select an average of no more than two of the four arguments, whereas the VWO students select an average of about three of the four arguments. This difference is very large: it covers a complete standard deviation.

Table 3. Number of Correctly Selected Arguments, per Track and Task

	Vocational (LBO) task 1 $n = 274$	task 2 $n = 277$	Pre-university (VWO) task 1 $n = 331$	task 2 $n = 328$
M	1.95	1.70	3.27	3.00
SD	0.93	0.88	0.71	0.74

5.4 Arranging Arguments

There are very large differences in the number of ordering errors between the two tracks (see Table 4). Measured by the distribution of the LBO scores, the difference between LBO and VWO amounts to one-and-a-half to two times the standard deviation.

Table 4. Average Number of Arrangement Errors per Type and Total Number of Errors, per Track and Task

type	Vocational (LBO) task 1 $n = 201$	task 2 $n = 191$	Pre-university (VWO) task 1 $n = 320$	task 2 $n = 310$
1	1.17	1.37	0.40	0.53
2	1.03	1.59	0.42	0.44
3	0.79	1.54	0.08	0.32
4	1.01	1.51	0.13	0.14
5	0.35	0.41	0.12	0.45
6	1.27	0.80	0.63	0.68
7	1.52	1.28	0.44	0.66
8	0.14	0.12	0.13	0.05
other	1.91	2.18	0.38	0.52
total number of errors:				
M	9.22	10.81	2.73	3.78
SD	4.80	3.37	2.74	2.85

Error types 5 and 8 do not occur very often. In the LBO the errors are divided over the remaining types rather equally. In VWO not only types 5 and 8 but also types 3 and 4 are relatively infrequent: students still refer to sub-arguments as main arguments (as in types 1 and 2), but in doing so they do not very often make the error of combining statements from different intrinsic clusters.

5.5 Using Argumentative Indicators

The results in Table 5 show considerable differences between tracks with respect to the number of connection errors made. Between LBO and VWO there is a difference of about three quarters up to one standard deviation, measured by the distribution of the LBO. Within the LBO mainly structure errors (type 2) are made: the introduction of a subordinating connection instead of a coordinating one. The other errors are relatively infrequent. Within the VWO all error types are found infrequently, as well as structure errors of type 2.

Table 5. Average Number of Connections Erroneously introduced per Type and Total, per Track and Task

	Vocational (LBO) task 1 $n = 221$	task 2 $n = 221$	Pre-university (VWO) task 1 $n = 307$	Task 2 $n = 307$
structure 1	0.29	0.12	0.08	0.01
structure 2	0.70	0.98	0.17	0.13
direction	0.01	0.03	0.00	0.03
connection	0.00	0.01	0.03	0.08
enumeration	0.27	0.20	0.13	0.10
frequency	0.19	0.23	0.03	0.05
other	1.00	0.92	0.13	0.44
total number of errors				
M	2.46	2.49	0.59	0.85
SD	2.09	2.07	1.12	1.76

5.6 Introducing Argumentation Structure

For every essay it has been checked whether an introduction of the subject is given, at what position the main standpoint is first mentioned and whether or not the essay has an ending (see table 6).

The results show that over a quarter of the LBO students start the essay with an introduction of the subject. In the VWO, half the essays have an introduction. The main standpoint has been placed at the beginning of the text in virtually all cases. The VWO students have a stronger preference for presenting the main standpoint halfway the text. It is remarkable that a relatively large number of the VWO students do not clearly formulate the main standpoint until the end. The percentage of students that repeat the main standpoint in the ending increases from LBO to VWO. Approximately 20% of the texts from all tracks has an ending in which arguments are repeated or summarized. At the LBO half of the essays rated has no ending or an ending, which lacks an intrinsic connection with the main standpoint or arguments mentioned, and at the VWO over a quarter.

Table 6. Parts of the Argumentation Structure, Percentages per Track

	Vocational (LBO)	Pre-university (VWO)
	$n = 195$	$n = 220$
introduction of the subject	26.7	54.1
no introduction of the subject	73.3	55.9
	$n = 170$	$n = 187$
standpoint at beginning of text	68.2	45.5
standpoint halfway the text	21.8	30.5
standpoint at ending of text	9.4	23.5
standpoint exclusively in title	0.6	0.5
	$n = 195$	$n = 220$
ending with repetition standpoint	31.8	51.8
ending with repetition arguments	17.4	19.5
ending: other	50.8	28.6

6. DISCUSSION

Results of the empirical research occasion some writing advice for the educational practice. The following enumeration of writing advice does not pretend to be exhaustive: the advice only relates to problems that have to be ascertained by the assessment study. With writing arguments, other problems may rise. Besides, not all secondary school students will be able to follow the advice without any problem. Between the two groups of students there are substantial differences in the extent to which writing problems arise. These differences suggest that there is a development with regard to the specific aspects of writing arguments. It is not sure that this development can be influenced by education in all cases, but in some cases, there are clear indications in that direction (cf. Janssen & Overmaat, 1990; Overmaat, 1996).

Before presenting writing advices it need to be emphasized that the present situation in the two tracks has changed drastically, because of an educational renewal of the educational system in the Netherlands. As mentioned before the data collection for this assessment took place in the period 1989-1990. However, in the last decade a new national curriculum for secondary education was introduced, partly based upon the concepts of constructivism, to improve students' learning processes. As a result a large number of new methods were brought into circulation. Writing an argumentative text has become a significant part of the final examinations and as a consequence language methods pay much more attention to argumentative skills and both oral and written arguments. A new assessment of students' argumentative writing skills within this new educational context will probably lead to other results as presented in this chapter. In spite of this, it seems plausible that the conclusions of this study are still valid for many other countries with no formal schooling in argumentation on secondary level. Furthermore, the allocated problems still can give direction to the development of effective writing instruction.

Below some concrete writing advices are being formulated. In presenting these advices, the stages in Writing an Argument (section 2) were followed. Each advice is preceded by a summary of the main assessment results concerning the specific problems related to the accompanying writing stage.

A first advice can be formulated as follows: "Adopt an explicit main standpoint, pro or con, and indicate clearly the opinion it relates to". Although most students adopt a clear main standpoint, part of the essays has no main standpoint or only an implicit one. Besides, part of the students takes up a standpoint pro as well as con with respect to the same opinion. This shows clearly that not all students manage to formulate a clear main standpoint.

A second advice concerns generating arguments: "Generate arguments pro as well as con for the main standpoint adopted and provide refutations for the arguments con brought forward". Between 15 and 20% of the students produce less than two arguments. With students from LBO the average number of accepted and non-accepted arguments con exceeds the average number of rebutted arguments con. Therefore, in a relatively large number of essays there will hardly be a successful attempt at persuasion. Schemes for generating relevant arguments pro and con may be helpful. Especially the method of stock issues can be useful: a list with fixed issues may direct the process of generating arguments, because students are looking specifically and systematically for arguments to support the standpoint they have taken up. Such a list is also very helpful in determining whether all relevant items in the argument(ation) are discussed and can also be used during the phase of critical text evaluation.

The third advice is: "Evaluate the relation between the main standpoint and the generated arguments pro and con in the light of the text objective and the audience in order to select arguments". A relatively large number of students is unable to select arguments for a main standpoint. Many students select less than one argument in the test in which 4 correct arguments have to be chosen out of a list of 16 arguments (see Table 3). Education in argumentative writing will have to teach students to select arguments based on an intrinsic evaluation, bearing in mind the text objective and the audience.

With regard to identifying the argumentation structure a fourth advice can be given: "Analyze the intrinsic relation between the selected arguments and determine the main arguments and the sub-arguments which belong to every main argument". Arranging arguments creates a lot of problems for students; a relatively large number of errors are made here. At the LBO it concerns sorting errors as well as ranking order errors. VWO students mainly make ranking order errors: main arguments are called sub-arguments and vice versa. Therefore it seems rather important in writing education to pay attention to sorting arguments by teaching students theoretical knowledge of main and sub-arguments and argumentation structures, and by training them in analyzing intrinsic relations.

A fifth advice is: "Make sure that connections between standpoints and arguments are clear to the reader of the text and that possible markers of connections are correct". Although the introduction of connections does not seem to cause very large problems for most students, a piece of advice may be useful here. As yet, in many of the arguments produced no (implicit or explicit) connection is made. Furthermore, many students erroneously present a coordinating connection as a subordinating connection.

The final advice concerns the global text structure: "Make a text structure in which the different argumentation phases have been clearly arranged for the reader". Many students do not mention the main standpoint until halfway through the text, at the end of the text, or only in the title. Besides a considerable part of the essays has an ending without any intrinsic connection with the argumentation. Knowledge of text schemes seems to be a useful proceeding to teach students how to make a better global text structure (cf. Janssen & Overmaat 1990, Overmaat, 1996).

DIGITAL INFORMATION LITERACY: TEACHING STUDENTS TO USE THE INTERNET IN SOURCE-BASED WRITING

CAROLINE M. STERN

Ferris State University, USA

Abstract. The rich resources of the Internet increasingly call writing faculty to incorporate digital research strategies into source-based writing. Yet, research shows that some students do not have basic competency to use the Internet for academic research. Composition classes can help students to be information literate and know how to effectively find, evaluate, use, communicate and manage both traditional and digital research information that is reliable and valid. Composition teachers can provide guided practice for students who are learning to read and use the Internet in an information literate way. Source-based writing instruction can also alert students to the important difference between the library and the Internet. Lessons in source-based writing can be enhanced by incorporating one of the many widely available, public-domain online-information literacy tutorials that are published by libraries.

Keywords: Internet, literacy, digital literacy, instructional design, source-based writing, composition, libraries, information literacy, online tutorials, Web sites.

1. THE INSTRUCTIONAL DEMANDS OF THE DIGITAL AGE

A recent survey of 1,184 in-coming freshmen at a American public university showed that 87% of the respondents considered themselves to have an intermediate to expert level of skill in using the Internet for school projects (Stern, 2002: 198). The same study alarmingly showed that 35% of those students never or seldom judged the academic reliability of the sources they gleaned from the Internet for school projects. Of even more concern, 92% of those respondents reported that Internet sources are usually, often or always reliable as research sources for school projects (Stern, 2002: 193).

Stern, C. M. (2004). Digital information literacy: Teaching students to use the internet in source-based writing.
In G. Rijlaarsdam (Series Ed.) and Rijlaarsdam, G., Van den Bergh, H. & Couzijn, M. (Vol. Eds.), Studies in writing. Vol. 14, Effective learning and teaching of writing, 2nd Edition, Part 2, Studies in how to teach writing, 443 - 453.

These statistics point to the problem that some students may know how to access the Internet; however, they need formal instruction in using it as a research resource. They are not grasping the concept that the Internet is rife with unregulated and sometimes spurious information.

Educators have long agreed that students benefit from structured bibliographic instruction on how to use academic libraries effectively. Yet, research has yet to be published on the extent to which students at all levels are given systematic and cumulative instruction in how to use the Internet as a research tool and resource. The aforementioned study of Midwestern American in-coming college freshmen showed that only 19% of those surveyed had ever received formal education for using the Internet for academic applications in high school (Stern, 2002: 198). These statistics are a caution to those who would assume that all students come to college prepared to use the Internet for academic research. Just as middle and high school teach students to use libraries, they must systematically and cumulative teaching students to use the Internet as a research tool and resource.

The *Pew Internet and American Life Project* (2002, Sept.15) reports that:

> "One-fifth of today's college students began using computers between the ages of 5 and 8. By the time they were 16 to 18 years old, all of today's current [American] college students had begun using computers.... About half (49%) first began using the Internet in college; half (47%) began using it at home before they arrived at college."

Knowing how to use a computer as an appliance or how to access the Internet does not equate with being an effective researcher any more than being able to walk into a library makes one a scholar or using a pen makes one a writer.

The curricula of all levels of education should carefully consider how to systematically educate students to become digitally information literate – in other words, how students seeking, evaluate, and use digital information for academic purposes. In secondary and higher education and increasingly in elementary schools, students can wrap their hands around lab computer keyboards and click their way across flashing screens to browse, navigate, and cut and paste into and across the cyberspace of the World Wide Web. Yet, educators must ask whether these students know how to judge the reliability of the digital sources they access, whether they can use Boolean search strategies, or whether they know how to read URLs as clues to academic source reliability. Definitive research on students' digital information competencies has yet to be completed in terms of how to design instruction that moves students toward standard digital information literacy competencies.

What is certain is that the Internet changes the way composition faculty teaches source-based writing. As we await the research on exactly how to infuse digital information literacy instruction into the curricula, we can learn some lessons by looking at history.

1.1 History's Lessons about Literacy and Change

Ours is not the first society to blink into the uncertain future posed by dramatic revolutions in learning.

"Plato criticized the use of writing as a medium for carrying thought and values.... [H]e objected to its superficiality... and feared that men would come to rely on writing and would cease to use memory" (Graff, 1991: 24).

Walter Ong (1991), in his study of the writings of Clanchy, concluded that

"[p]eople had to be persuaded that writing improved the old oral methods sufficiently to warrant all the expense and troublesome techniques it involved" (p.96).

History demonstrates that revolutionary methods for transmitting information such as alphabets, pen and paper, the printing press, widespread and affordable mechanical duplication of text, and word processing have reshaped how composition is taught. Likewise, educators must examine how the dramatically new medium of the Internet reshapes source-based writing strategies. Instructional design research provides some clues as to how this can be accomplished.

1.2 Instructional Design for Educational Change

Instructional design researchers acknowledge that educators need to know more about how students use the Internet for academic purposes (Tyner, 1998; Nosich, 2001; Spitzer, Eisenberg, & Lowe, 1998). While the assessment data on students' Internet competencies is being gathered and evaluated by researchers, another segment of the published scholarship is examining the strategies for guiding information literacy instructional design that can be based on traditional literacy instructional design (Askov, 1998; Borgman, 2001; Conrad, 2000).

Student assessment is one of the first steps in the instructional design process for any teaching strategies (Smith and Ragan 1999, Seels and Glasgow 1998, Conrad 2000). Instructional design research is now emerging that assesses what American high school and college students know about using the Internet for research. The data on how students use traditional and digital library sources offer insights into how composition faculty in high school might shape digital information literacy instruction.

The Pew Foundation (2002, Sept. 15) found that

"[n]early three-quarters (73%) of college students say they use the Internet more than the library, while only 9% said that they use the library more than the Internet for information searching."

A survey by this author found that 16% of the in-coming freshmen at a public university had never used their school library in their senior year of high school, 25% used it only one or two times, 28% used it only 3 to 5 times, 15% used it six to ten times, and only 15% had used it more than ten times in the past year (Stern, 2002: 195). This data begs the question of how composition teachers should design instruction in source-based writing when students are reporting that they are not library-users.

Many American high school students know how to get online; however, one must ask whether these same students are digitally information literate? If, as the one survey reported, just 19% of high schools students in the study have ever received formal instruction in using the Internet for school projects and 73% are self taught or learned with a friend, what competencies can these students have for using the Internet as a research tool and resource? Do they know how to construct a keyword search that yields academically reliable sources? Are they able to deconstruct Web pages to determine a site's authority, currency, or biases as a research resource? Even if they are able to evaluate sources, do the students do so?

The survey of incoming college freshmen showed that there was also evidence that a substantial number (36.9%) of the respondents never or seldom judged the reliability of the sources they found on the Internet (Stern, 2002: 193). The survey data demonstrated that a sizable number of students in the sample population did not understand that the Internet is rife with unreliable sources that masquerade as reliable sources.

Additionally, the most significant finding of this survey was that 35% of the students never or seldom critically evaluated the information they found on the Internet and only 36% usually judged the reliability of source. Although students indicated that they are confident in their own ability to effectively use the Internet for academic purposes, the data pointed to a definite need within the target population for basic digital information literacy instruction.

1.3 Teaching Digital Information Literacy

Many educators are considering exactly how the new digital literacies of the information age fit into the already overloaded curriculum. The question also becomes one of who will be responsible for teaching this skills set. A pattern is evolving in high school and higher education in the United States that the composition teacher is taking primary responsibility for teaching Internet research skills. As a result, literacy, long the domain of the composition classroom, has been redefined.

2. INFORMATION LITERACY DEFINED

As early as 1977, B.D. Johnson noted that:

> "literacy...has been stretched beyond the definition of reading and writing letters, not necessarily out of irreverence towards print but as a reaction to technological advancements in communication."

Expanding on traditional literacy skills, information literacy (IL) refers to the ability of students to "recognize when information is needed and have the ability to locate, evaluate, and use effectively the needed information" (ACRL, 2000: 2).

The current literature pertinent to information literacy makes clear that there is a correlation between traditional information literacy (IL) skills and the digital information literacy skills that are demanded of 21st century high school and college students when they use the Internet for academic research (Tyner, 1998; Gilster, 1997; Szczypula, Tschang, & Vikas, 2001; Dolence & Norris, 1999; Lemke, 1998; Head, 1999).

Information literacy is distinct from technological or computer literacy. Computer literacy centers on the ability to manipulate technology and use the computer as an appliance. This is very different from the ability of a student to effectively gather, assess, and use information in both paper-based and digital realms of information. The Association of College and Research Libraries (ACRL), a division of the American Library Association (ALA), acknowledges the unique dependency that information literacy has on computer technology, which it sees as a related, but distinct, competency (ACRL, 2000: 3). Information literacy is a skill set that goes well beyond computer literacy. In many ways, information literacy is tied to critical reading, thinking, and sourced-based writing.

2.1 Composition as the Instructional Base for Information Literacy

Many of the steps in the academic research process remain the same whether the reading and writing are done in paper-based or digital mediums. Balancing the benefits of paper-based and Internet-based research is already addressed in many high school and college composition handbooks that have chapters on research methodology. Handbooks often contain a chapter devoted to guiding students through Internet research methodology and citation format for electronic sources. Because of the relatively nascent state of digital research and writing, the content of these directions often amounts to basic guidance about using the various Internet search engines and some instruction in Boolean search strategies.

While these are important directives, they are incomplete in helping student researchers fully understand all the important differences between the library and the Internet as an academic information sources. Composition faculty who teach source-based writing to middle school through college students can begin any orientation to research skills by helping students understand how libraries are different from the Internet as a research environment.

3. THE LIBRARY AND INTERNET AS INFORMATION SOURCES

3.1 Distinguishing between the Library and Internet as Information Sources

Some faculty resist using the Internet as a research tool and resource for students because they see it as an ungoverned frontier of information compared to the familiar domains of traditional academic libraries. The Internet is a frontier, but it is one that students need to be taught to explore. Because parts of the Internet are not a professionally assembled and organized collection of edited and juried information the way sources in an academic library are, every source must be carefully evaluated for reliability and validity. Faculty and students must be clear in their understanding of how the Internet differs from libraries.

Students benefit from understanding that libraries are one gateway to the Internet; however, libraries are not "domains" of the Internet because library holdings are usually password protected. In other words, full reciprocity does not exist between the Internet and institutional libraries. One may use a library computer to access the Internet; however, by contrast, patrons usually need a password to enter and access the full services of a library using the Internet as their gateway.

Digital libraries do stand at the convergence of paper-based and digital information. No longer simply repositories of paper-text information, many libraries are incorporating into their traditional holdings a diverse collection of digital media in addition to becoming electronic access points to information such as the Internet.

> "Digital libraries are a set of electronic resources and associated technical capabilities for creating, searching, and using information.... The content of digital libraries includes data, metadata that describe various aspects of the data (e.g., representation, creator, owner, reproduction rights), and metadata that consist of links or relationships to other data or metadata, whether internal or external to the digital library" (Borgman, 2001: 210).

In this sense, then, the Internet is a library "holding" because the library is a gateway to the information that the Internet holds.

Some of the key differences between libraries and the Internet are that libraries:
1) Offer information in a patron-centered way unlike the Internet that mediates information for a commercial or sponsor-based interest;
2) Provide a personal and professionally organized and patron-centered system for searching, organizing, and accessing information while the Internet is scanned and studied by search engines that use human and artificial intelligence to index and create directories of information;
3) Select information based on its quality, variety, and relevance and then professionally manage the collection in a prescribed, professional, and consistent way to suit the patron population whereas the Internet is simply a platform for all types of information without regard for quality, publication source, or bias, currency, authorship, or integrity.
4) Build media collections that are organized, accessible, balanced in perspective and scope, archived, and weeded in a way that facilitates patrons while the Internet is simply a publishing platform with few constraints.

In contrast to libraries, the Internet offers few screens to publication. The skill of web authors to create content, the technology of web masters to publish the media, and the ability of the user to access the information are really the primary obstacles to publication of Internet information. Even the conventional legal constraints concerning obscenity, slander, liable, and fraud are not obstacles to publication for renegade Web sites.

Another important difference presented by the Internet is that the quality of presentation of information is not necessarily a clue as to the quality of the content the way it might be with a print publication. The Internet hosts many Web pages that have sophisticated presentation in terms of media applications and graphic design, but these contexts of information are not reliable indicators of the quality of content.

One other service that is missing on the Internet is that of archiving digital information. More than one disappointed researcher has found that some Web sites do not archive information. The Web is dynamic. That is an advantage if one wants the most recent data with no information delay, but it is a significant disadvantage if one needs to retrieve digital information that is no longer posted or archived. Researchers need to be made aware of this dimension to digital information and taught to save digital data to a disc or hard copy for later reference.

The most important contribution of academic libraries is that they have applied professional, scholarly, and objective acquisitions and holdings considerations to the materials in a collection. Internet research can be risky for the novice source-based writer. Composition teachers must, therefore, guide students in learning information literacy skills that will equip learners to use the Internet as an intelligent supplement to library-based research.

4. EQUIPPING STUDENTS TO DO RESEARCH USING THE INTERNET

Because the Internet provides access to a diverse spectrum of current academic and professional resources, it is emerging as a preferred research resource over traditional paper-based sources. In response to this, students from middle school on can benefit from instruction that teaches them to be critically alert and to determine the academic reliability and validity of every Internet source they consult. Students must be equipped to be their own knowledge managers who can:

1) Organize an information search;
2) Use technology that itself requires a competency separate from the subject matter being learned;
3) Design keyword and Boolean search strategies that target the best possible pool of research resources;
4) Employ search skills that consider the various and distinct capabilities of search engines, meta-crawlers, intranets, and browsers;
5) Use critical thinking to evaluate the enormous variance in the quality of information published on the Web;
6) Sort through the large quantity of information available from a wide variety of sources;
7) Separate subject content, media presentation, and information delivery as modes of shaping information quality;
8) Synthesize subject matter information from a variety of sources;
9) Understand that digital information is often dynamic and not "locked" into print the way paper texts are;
10) Apply copyright law and ethics to use information in fair and legal ways;
11) Create communication and information storage that effectively use the appropriate media; and
12) Understand the public nature of information that is published without password protection in full-access media such as the Internet.

These skills represent an expansion, revision, or addition to the traditional information management practices of a paper-based information society. Traditional bibliographic instruction – which has been typically taught by librarians and composition teachers – has always sought to teach student researchers to use critical thinking skills in the gathering, using, and managing of information. But now the onus for bibliographic savvy is placed squarely on individual users more than ever before because so much information exists outside the domain of library collections and traditionally publishing houses.

Recognizing the importance of these skills, the question then becomes how composition teachers might effectively teach these vital research skills in the context of source-based writing.

5. ONLINE RESOURCES FOR TEACHING INFORMATION LITERACY

Learner-centered, online tutorials are emerging as an effective method for delivering digital information literacy instruction. These tutorials can be widely found on the instructional homepages of many libraries. They usually allow learners to start the instruction at a level appropriate to their abilities and knowledge and can be completed without high levels of support from librarians or classroom faculty.

Online tutorials allow information literacy instruction to take place virtually in a systematic, affordable, convenient, and flexible way. For example, the online tutorials may function as lab work attached to an existing class or as independent learning modules that are hosted by the library Web site. Many online tutorials are aimed at minimal exit competency and can be self-paced to lower frustration levels for students. They, therefore, do not involve high stakes testing and employ the principles of guided practice and application-based projects.

The most comprehensive examples of this type of online information literacy instruction can be found on the homepages of research libraries at universities such as the State University of New York at Albany, the University of California at Berkeley, The University of Texas's TILT, Wolfgram Memorial Library at Widener University, Cornell University, and Purdue University.

The instructional design of the newer online tutorials is increasingly interactive and therefore an improvement over the traditional textbook instructions that operate more like a reference source of information than an instructional activity such as the online tutorials employ.

Some of the leaders in online information literacy instruction are:
- Cornell University's guide to effective library research that takes the learners through the research process from identifying a suitable topic, finding supporting materials, and writing the research paper[1]
- Purdue University Library's core education (comprehensive online research education) that covers search strategies, using indexes and catalogs, evaluating sources, and research project planning[2]

The University of Washington information literacy learning web site offers an annotated gateway to fifteen links to other online tutorials that cover topics such as basic to advanced research strategies[3].

The University of California at Berkeley continues its leadership in information literacy instruction with a second-generation tutorial[4]. The online tutorial covers topics such as Boolean searches, search engine capabilities, web basics, electronic database use, and library catalogs and collections. The tutorial unit on evaluating Web pages is a part of a larger review of the research and reading process. The University of California at Berkeley site also demonstrates an understanding of the frustrations that many Web users face by offering trouble-shooting tips and hints for

---

[1] http://www.libaryr.cornell.edu/okuref/research/tutorial.html
[2] http://www.lib.purdue.edu/core/
[3] http://www.lib.washington.edu/uwill/tutorial.html
[4] http://www.lib.berkeley.edu/TeachingLib/Guides/rguides.html

"smart searching." It also does more than simply offer a rubric to evaluate the page and models IL principles with examples taken from Web pages.

The State University of New York (SUNY) Albany's library has its tutorials posted[5] and is another example of a successful second-generation tutorial in information literacy. The site provides an overview of the entire research process with Web page evaluation being only one aspect of that process. The SUNY Albany site focuses on a variety of search strategies for different information sources such as subject guides, search engines, library catalogs, and specific databases. Like the University of California at Berkeley, SUNY Albany's site has a section on the "invisible" or "deep" web, which refers to

> "information stored in searchable databases mounted on the Web. These databases usually search a targeted topic or aspect of a topic. Search engines cannot or will not index this information" (SUNY Albany, 2002).

In the section dedicated to web page evaluation, the SUNY Albany site moves beyond deconstructing web pages to a critical evaluation of material offered in settings such as e mail, list serves, and MOOS/MUDs. It incorporates tutorial units on evaluating audio, visuals, and therefore goes beyond the evaluation of text offered in earlier tutorials. Albany's site truly is cutting edge in terms of the breadth of its content and depth of instruction. It takes the learner screen by screen through the process of evaluating Web pages for a sample research paper in an undergraduate class. Its screens are set up to respond individually to correct and incorrect answers and offer an explanation of why the choice made by the learner was correct or not. It also locks the reader into completing the tutorial by housing sample web sites on its own domain rather than allowing learners to link away from the tutorial. This is an attractive feature because it keeps the learners from being distracted from the learning task by inviting Internet pages.

Probably one of the most attractive instructional aspects of the SUNY Albany page is that it allows learners to e-mail the completion notice for each exercise to an instructor on its campus. This demonstrates the practical understanding that some people are motivated to learn only when they receive recognition for their learning. The tutorial is a splendid demonstration of educational economy since it is automated, convenient, and has applications for a wide variety of disciplines. It is targeted to groups such as students who need an initiation to the whole process of research, so it would be suitable for high school as well as college students.

Another Web site that has also taken the forefront of online information literacy instruction the University of Texas' TILT tutorial[6]. It is a favorite tutorial because of its rich content and easy access. The proof of this is that if one types in the keywords "information literacy tutorial" on Google, TILT is the "I'm Feeling Lucky" pick out of 4,000 plus possible "hits."

The Web site offers an introduction module, three information literacy learning modules, and a follow-up on research methodology. Screen by screen the tutorial guides students through topics such as:

---

[5] *http://library.albany.edu/usered/*
[6] *http://tilt.lib.utsystem.edu/*

- Defining information literacy and understanding the impact of technology on research methodology, including some misconceptions about the Internet;
- Selecting a reliable and valid research source, distinguishing between scholarly and popular sources, using the library and the "library on the web," surfing the Web, using periodical indexes, evaluating all research resources, employ criteria for evaluations and citing print and online information; and
- Effectively searching the library databases and the Web using Boolean strategies. (TILT).

6. TRADITIONAL LITERACY AND INFORMATION LITERACY

The task of moving students to digital information literacy may not be as daunting as it may at first appear. Educators can take comfort in considering that all ages have demanded that scholars be information literate. Just as many of us learned to manage traditional libraries and print-based media, likewise this next generation is learning to much the same in a digital medium. Many of the traditional information literacies have found new contexts in the Internet. For example, all scholars must still consider the authorship, bias, accuracy / verifiability, and currency of any research information they use. This same need is simply translated into the digital realms of the Internet. The Internet sources may not always offer up the clues in the same way as did print materials such as books; however, for those who have come from a tradition of paper-based research there are many correlations between the Internet and books. Some of them include:

- URL's equate with book publishing information and authorship identification,
- Splash pages serve as title pages,
- Hotlinks correspond to foot or endnotes in paper-based text,
- Web search functions are like book indexes,
- Pull down menus are like tables of contents,
- Hypertext approximates reading pages out of sequence, and
- Keywords and HTML tags function as index locators.

There are digital dimensions that do have correlations in paper text such as streaming video, audio, or interactivity. But scholars should be able to scaffold on what they know about communication conventions to understand the implications of these media and options for literacy.

What composition teachers who teach source-based writing can do is to translate their own literacies into the digital domains while holding firm to the basics of research methodologies that have served generations of scholars. What they must also understand is that the Internet is a very different environment for researching information because the onus for evaluating the material rests entirely on the researcher who pulls it from a Web site.

For novice researchers who have yet to hone their critical thinking skills to the point of being adept at Internet research, they would best be served by conducting research – both paper-based and digital – within the domain of a library or under the tutelage of faculty members who can provide the supports, services and technologies necessary. Educators have long understood that modeling and practising a learning principle are important steps in moving learners to become autonomous scholars.

The Internet invites teachers to show students how to use it effectively.

Great strides have been made in developing teaching strategies that use the best tools for information gathering – whether they are the library or the Internet. Equipping life-long learners with critical thinking skills that allow them to navigate all the domains of information is an excellent way to prepare the knowledge mangers of the future for the emerging technologies that we have yet to imagine.

"DOWN THE PLUGHOLE"[1]: THE PITFALLS OF TESTING THE WRITING OF L2 PUPILS

GERI SMYTH

University of Strathclyde, Scotland

Abstract. This chapter considers the difficulties of National Tests in writing for children who are learning to write in an additional language. Samples of writing tests undertaken by such children are considered to analyse where their difficulties might lie. While there has been much written about effective teaching of writing for L2 learners, there has been little research into the testing of L2 writing of such pupils. In an international climate of increased accountability in education and the use of league tables of test results as quality indicators, there is a need to consider the problems of testing writing of children in a language which is not their home language. As the government of the United Kingdom increasingly focus any discourse on literacy on falling standards and lack of literacy skills it becomes increasingly important to consider how the measurement of such skills may disadvantage bilingual pupils. The chapter provides a description of National Tests in writing in Scotland, along with the national criteria for assessing children's writing. In Scotland, children between the ages of 5-14 are tested in Functional, Personal and Imaginative writing in English and are assessed as having attained a prescribed level, A–F.
It is classroom teachers in Scotland who have the responsibility for deciding when a child will be tested and which test papers, from an annual catalogue, will be used. However, there is currently no guidance available to teachers as to how to consider the needs of the growing number of Scottish pupils who are writing in English as an additional language. Previous research by the author (Smyth, 2000) considered the practices of mainstream teachers as they taught bilingual[2] pupils and reported on the dominant cultural models which informed their practice. Gee (1999) defines cultural models as "everyday people's explanations or theories" which are rooted in the practices of socioculturally defined groups of people. An analysis of the ethnographic data resulting from the research found that the master model, which helped to shape and organise the teachers' beliefs and led to a number of related cultural models was that *bilingual pupils need to become monolingual in order to succeed.*

---

[1] *"Down the Plughole" is the title of one of the Imaginative Writing tests to be analysed in the chapter by a consideration of a bilingual child's response to the task. The phrase Down the Plughole is also an English colloquialism meaning 'lost forever'.*

[2] *The term bilingual is used to refer to children who use more than one language in their everyday life (Wiles, 1985).*

Smyth, G. (2004). "Down the Plughole: The pitfalls if testing the writing of L2 pupils.
In G. Rijlaarsdam (Series Ed.) and Rijlaarsdam, G., Van den Bergh, H. & Couzijn, M. (Vol. Eds.), Studies in writing. Vol. 14, Effective learning and teaching of writing, 2nd Edition, Part 2, Studies in how to teach writing, 455 - 467.

I contend that unless teachers are working in a school with a coherent language policy, they do not take account of pupils' bilingualism or biculturalism when choosing or assessing tests. Samples of writing tests completed by children writing in English as an additional language will be discussed in the chapter to evaluate how the errors made in genre and/or the omissions from their writing have resulted from a lack of linguistic and cultural knowledge for which teachers have not accounted, having rather, assumed that the children are working towards monolingualism.

Teaching practice in relation to the tests will be analysed to discuss how adaptations in practice would improve second language writers' ability. The national criteria for assessing the level at which children are writing incorporates aspects of language and style which may not be explicitly taught in the classroom due to teacher assumptions of shared experiences and literacies. The cultural model, derived from the master model defined above, that the bilingual pupil who is not functioning monolingually in English, has learning deficiencies, which require remediation can lead teachers to take a directive approach to support for writing which does little to teach children the purpose of writing or to foster the children's creativity. The teaching of writing can provide valuable opportunities to support and extend bilingual pupils' knowledge about language. Focusing on linguistic and cultural knowledge will enable bilingual pupils to write more successfully and independently rather than stifling children's creativity by taking a very directed approach to the task.

Keywords: bilingual pupils, testing, functional writing, imaginative writing, Scottish education, planning of writing, functions of language, structures of language

1. INTRODUCTION

The discussion in this chapter arises from the writer's concern that the dominant cultural model which informs mainstream teachers' practice with bilingual pupils in Scotland is that bilingual pupils need to become monolingual in order to succeed (Smyth, 2000). This supports the contention of Verhoeven and Durgunoglu that 'Within the majority language context, the first language of a people is considered as a potential source of (un)successful transfer in L2 acquisition, rather than as a language variety in its own right' (Durgunoglu & Verhoeven, 1998: ix). In this context it is perhaps inevitable that the assessment of bilingual pupils' writing in their second language will be erroneous, ignoring the pupils' L1 literacy, which may differ significantly from the literacy of the majority language. Gee (1990) has argued that literacy is ideological, rooted in a particular world view and with a desire for that view of literacy to dominate and to marginalise others. Street (1995, 2001) contends that literacy is not a neutral 'given', but rather that 'The ways in which teachers – and their students interact is already a social practice that affects the nature of the literacy being learned and the ideas about literacy held by the participants, especially the new learners' (Street, 2001: 8). This chapter explores these views of literacy as an ideological, social practice in the context of the writing of bilingual pupils in Scottish schools in test situations and in everyday class work.

2. BACKGROUND

2.1 Education in Scotland

Children in Scotland must start compulsory education between the ages of four and a half and five and a half years old. They attend primary school for six to seven years and secondary school for four to seven years. Education is compulsory between the ages of five and sixteen years old. However nursery education is available for all children from the age of three years old until they start school. The predominant model of teaching in British primary schools is one teacher per age-based class for all curricular areas for one school year.

2.2 Curriculum 5-14

Curriculum guidelines in Scotland for the teaching of English Language[3] include guidance for the teaching of writing, with attainment targets related to three strands of writing: Imaginative, Functional and Personal.

Imaginative writing may include stories, poems or plays in a range of genres. Functional writing involves the use of such forms as letters, reports and instructions. Personal writing draws from personal experience and incorporates discussion of feelings and emotions. As part of the overall assessment arrangements for pupils in schools in Scotland, each pupil aged 5 – 14 years should be tested in Writing whenever evidence from the teacher's continuous assessment indicates that the pupil has attained the targets at a particular level and is ready to move towards the next level. Six levels of achievement, A-F, are provided for within the 5-14 writing curriculum. At levels A-E, the writing test consists of two units, one Imaginative or Personal and one Functional. This chapter will not consider testing at level F, which has only recently been added to the guidelines.

2.3 Multilingual Nature of Scotland

Since the 1950s increasing numbers of children being educated in Scotland have been learning in English while their home language, that is the first language encountered at home, is other than English. Such children will be referred to throughout this chapter as bilingual, that is, 'they use two or more languages in their everyday life (Wiles, 1985)

Until the 1980s the large majority of bilingual pupils in Scottish schools were located in inner city schools, were usually second or third generation and were predominantly from a linguistic background originating from either the Asian subcontinent or Hong-Kong. However new patterns of immigration to the United Kingdom have resulted in pupils from widely disparate linguistic and cultural backgrounds being educated in schools across the country. Many of these schools have little or no history or experience of working with pupils from other than the dominant white, English-speaking background.

A range of factors has contributed to an increase in the number of home languages amongst pupils in Scottish primary schools. Political changes world wide (significantly, the opening of the borders of the former Eastern European Soviet bloc states and war in the former Yugoslavia) along with increased economic mobility (particularly within the member states of the European Union) have resulted in greater numbers of school pupils who have European languages other than English as their first language. Increased inward investment from the Far East and the arrival

---

[3] *English Language 5 - 14.*

of non-European postgraduate students and their families as universities compete to attract overseas students have added to the multilingual make-up of Scottish primary schools. In Glasgow, one of the thirty-two unitary authorities in Scotland and one of the centres for dispersal of asylum seekers, there are now pupils with over sixty home languages. This pattern is replicated across Scotland.

3. EDUCATION FOR BILINGUAL PUPILS IN SCOTLAND

There are a small number of Gaelic-medium schools and classes in Scotland, where children are taught bilingually in Gaelic[4] and English. The majority of children being educated in these classes have English as a first language and their parents have chosen for them to acquire Gaelic in school. Those pupils who are being educated in Gaelic-medium schools or classes, may be tested in either Gaelic or English. Speakers of languages other than English and Gaelic do not have the opportunity to be educated or tested in any language other than English. While pupils being educated in Gaelic medium education are given opportunities to investigate Gaelic literature, other bilingual pupils in Scotland do not have the opportunity in school to read literature in their home language, thus they do not have the ability to draw from the resources of their heritage literature when they write in English. The decreasing resource being allocated to the provision of bilingual teachers in Scottish schools is now only provided to the very early stages of the primary school, with the emphasis being put on using the first language only where it is essential in order to access English.

3.1 Testing the Writing of Bilingual Pupils

The only guidance given to teachers concerning the testing of pupils whose first language is not English is that they should attempt the Writing tests only when their progress suggests that they have attained the targets for Level A and beyond in the normal way, independent of any special support.[5]

Up to level C, all pupils can be given help at the planning stage. This may be done by having a teacher-led class lesson focusing on the completion of the planning page provided with the National Test papers. On one occasion during the research I conducted into mainstream teachers' practices with bilingual pupils, I observed Fiona, an English as an Additional Language (EAL) teacher, working with Asif, a nine-year-old Punjabi speaking boy. Ellen, the class teacher, had given Fiona a copy of the Imaginative Writing National Test which the whole of Asif's language group were going to sit the next day under exam conditions. Ellen wished the EAL teacher to help Asif with the planning of the writing. Fiona is a peripatetic EAL teacher who visits this school twice a week. She had not seen this test before and had difficulty knowing how to support Asif with a decontextualised piece of imaginative writing entitled "Down the plughole":

---

[4] *Gaelic is one of the heritage languages of Scotland.*
[5] *SQA(2001)National Tests in Writing Information for Teachers: 5.*

The Writing Test Papers incorporate a planning page on which children are intended to write notes in response to content questions before writing the complete story. In this case the planning questions were:
1) Where is the plughole?
2) How did the person get into it?
3) What did the person see?
4) How did the person feel?
5) What happened?
6) How does your story end?

The intention is that by noting responses to these questions, the pupils will have a story outline which they will then translate into a full story. The focus of this particular plan is to aid the pupil in the production of a well-sequenced story with a conclusion. Teachers' guidance notes are also provided with the Test to support the teacher in contextualising the story for the class. However Fiona was not given these notes. Due to the pressure on her time as a peripatetic teacher, she started the session with Asif by asking him the first planning question, without any discussion of the purpose of the task or the possible genre of the story.

1	F	Where is the plughole?
	A	Sink, bath.
	F	Where are you – bath or sink?
	A	Bath.
5	F	Write that down.
		Asif wrote 'bath'.
	F	Why are you in the bath?
	A	To do a bath.
	F	Are you dirty or has something happened to get you dirty?
10	A	'Cos I'm dirty.
	F	What have you done to make you dirty?
	A	Fallen in mud.
	F	Write that down. F - A - L - L - E - N.
		Asif wrote 'fallen'.
15	F	What is the sentence you'd write? Make a sentence using these two bits.
	A	I was playing in mud then I fallen then I went in my house then I had a bath.
	F	Write something like that.

The interaction continued in this way with Fiona going through the Planning questions, Asif responding and Fiona helping him to write responses to the Planning questions which it was intended he would use the next day to write the story. This is an Imaginative Writing test, but Fiona at no point took an opportunity to discuss the nature of Imaginative Writing with Asif. Fiona's use of 'you' (lines 3, 7, 9 and 11 above) led Asif to construct the sentence at lines 17-18: 'I was playing in mud then I fallen then I went in my house then I had a bath' which reads as a piece of personal writing rather than imaginative. In this way Asif's creativity was stifled by the directed approach taken to the task. The planning of a piece of writing is a skill in itself, although it is not assessed. If the planning page of the test is not used in the intended way, the child will have difficulty using the plan to support the subsequent writing.

The role, which had been ascribed to the EAL teacher by the school, was to enable the bilingual child to operate in the context of the monolingual assessment procedures. At the end of this session Asif was expected to have planning notes so Fiona helped him to achieve these, thereby missing the opportunity to support his Knowledge about Language which might enable him to write independently more successfully in the future. The cultural model that Asif has learning deficiencies, which require remediation is resulting in a self-fulfilling prophecy.

In addition to issues about the way in which the EAL teacher is being used, there are many issues around the cultural relevance of this text, the teaching and testing of writing and the difficulties of responding imaginatively in a second language.

Children working in an additional language will struggle to express themselves imaginatively, particularly if the required text does not match with the style of storying in their first language. For many children in Scotland whose first language is Punjabi, they and their families will not be literate in Punjabi, as the language is only oral for the Moslem community. Therefore, even if they have been told stories in Punjabi, they will not have read or been read to in their first language and will not have the knowledge of story conventions. Traditional Punjabi tales do not tend to use the same notions of magic as are implied by the planning questions for this National Test. The story is meant to be about *a person* somehow being small enough to go down a plughole and have an adventure. Punjabi, Asif's first language, is not as expressive a language as either English or Urdu and does not use words such as, for example, miniscule or phrases such as *as tiny as an insect*, to describe the type of imaginative situation required. Therefore, for Asif, thinking in Punjabi and translating into English, he is restricted to the very literal answers to Fiona's questions as noted above.

4. THE CONTENT OF THE NATIONAL TESTS

> When I'm choosing which National Tests to use in the school, I have to carefully steer a pathway through the catalogue of options due to the cultural bias of many of the tests and the fact that the concepts which the children are required to write about may be totally out with their knowledge base. (Jane, primary headteacher of a school with a large number of Punjabi speaking children on the role)

A sample of test papers at different levels and requiring different genres will now be discussed to consider what children are expected to know linguistically and culturally in order to succeed in the tests. Some of the criteria for assessing children's writing are indicated by the use of ***bold italics*** in the discussions which follow.

One of the Level D/E Imaginative Writing tests is called "Things that go bump in the Night." The children are required to write an imaginative story about ghosts. While in English, the title might lead monolingual English speaking children to anticipate a ghost story, it is not a title that easily translates into other literacies. The style and typical characters of ghost stories in other literacies may lead the bilingual child to be assessed as not achieving the appropriate level because the writing does not, for example, ***use some of the conventions of storytelling to hold the reader's interest***.

One of the Personal Writing tests at the same Level (D/E), is called "Introducing". This test requires the child to "write an introduction for a friend, – giving a description of his/her appearance as well as his/her character, achievements and qualities you admire. Explain why you like to spend time with this friend."

5. BILINGUAL PUPILS WRITING IN THE NATIONAL TESTS

Tahira, an 11 year old girl, whose first language is Punjabi, filled the three available pages in response to the "Introducing" test. Her description of her friend included the following:

> Sannah has long, curly, bumpy and fat hair that is very soft. She is an average height but is shorter than me. She is older than me –

Tahira does not have some of the English vocabulary she wishes to use to describe her friend's hair. She has been creative in substituting *bumpy* for *wavy* and *fat* for *thick*. Tahira's teachers need to consider the vocabulary she is likely to need in different tasks and ensure that she has a chance to meet and practice this vocabulary. Tahira's piece of writing continues by focusing on the second part of the task, giving descriptions of what she and her friend do together and recounting incidents that have happened to them. She then returns to the description of her friend but uses an unusual language construction:

> Sannah always shares with me to show that she is kind. She reads scary books to show she is a person that loves scary books and films. She always plays inside or outside to show she is adventourous.

A more usual structure to meet the function of describing character and qualities would be

> Sannah is very kind and always shares (her games) with me. She does not frighten easily and loves reading scary books and watching scary films. She is adventurous in the games she plays, both inside and outside.

Although Tahira has a clear context about which to write (her friend, Sannah) she is not used to the English language structures and vocabulary required to describe Sannah and therefore the bulk of her piece of writing focuses on a description of events.

Tahira knows what the task entails and does her best to meet the task demands but has difficulties because she is not sure how to structure her ideas. Although the National Tests have a planning sheet, the focus of these is on vocabulary and sequencing. Perhaps a focus on the appropriate structures to be used to achieve certain functions of language might be more helpful. Certainly, guidance to teachers should incorporate advice on how to use functions and structures of language as a planning tool.[6]

---

[6] *For a discussion of functions and structures of language and guidance on using these as a tool for planning, see Gibbons (1991) and Smyth (2003).*

A piece of class work written by Tahira in the same term focused on the use of imagery to describe a setting for an imaginative piece of writing. Tahira's writing included this description of the setting:

> – the huge blue tree was full of sparkles, like shimmering fairies dancing in the wood. The leaves flapped about like a thousand pixies angry because they are losing their pixie dust. The sun shone brightly amongst the leaves like dazzling diamonds polished perfectly.

From this piece it is clear that Tahira can write descriptively but the test has not enabled her to do so in relation to her friend. Reminders on the test-planning sheet of the style of writing that might be appropriate for this description would have helped Tahira to plan her piece more effectively. Further, the class task focused only on description of the setting, whereas the National Tests in writing demand a complete piece of writing. Recent work on the writing process (Czerniewska, 1992; Graves, 1983; Murray, 1984 and others) has emphasised the need for children as writers to be taught to focus on the process rather than the product, yet the National Tests reverse this practice. The inclusion of a planning page is not an indication that the Scottish Qualifications Authority view writing as a process but rather an acknowledgement that most teaching of writing now involves a planning stage. What is missing from the national tests is the opportunity for conferencing about the writing after the planning stage.

Turning now to the testing at earlier levels, a Level A-C Imaginative Writing test called "A Frightening Experience", requires pupils to write an imagined personal response, about how they felt during a frightening experience. If the frightening experience the child decides to recount, happened outside the school, it is unlikely that the bilingual child thinks about the experience in English, the language of the school. Emotions are more likely to have been expressed in the first language and the child may be assessed as having not achieved the appropriate level because their response *leaves out or repeats details important to the reader's understanding of the writer's feelings or thoughts*.

Asma, an 8-year-old bilingual girl with Punjabi as her first language, wrote this text in response to the 'Frightening Experience' task:

> One night when I was at my auntie's house in my cousin's bedroom these strange noises were coming from the window. I got up and went to look. Suddenly Bang! I got so scard I went into my auntie's room mum said why? are you still awayk? I said mum there is this man how is in Abnah's bedroom and that person is making strange noises. Me and my mum went into the room and my heart was raceing very fast. But when we went in it was my uncle. My uncle was trying to get into the house but the front door was locked so he went and climbed the wall I said to my uncle that I got so scard and that I thought it was someone else. I felt much better that my frightening experience was over.

Asma has included detail to convey her emotions to the reader: *my heart was raceing very fast*. However the story is more of a personal account of an event than an imagined personal response. She has written in detail about her relatives and about the explanation for the frightening experience at the expense of detail about how she felt when she heard the noises or what she thought might be the cause. It seems to have been difficult for Asma to write imaginatively.

The same girl was involved with the rest of her class in writing imaginative stories about having magical powers. This series of lessons was supported by the teacher reading stories to the class and discussing known magical characters. Asma wrote and illustrated a book as a result of this entitled *Winnie the Witch*, extracts from which follow:

> – I got very angry and so I put on my magic gloves and with a whooshing, glittering and amazing shower of sparkling stars shooting out into the air, I turned invisible. – What fun I had that night and the boy never knew where I had gone!
>
> – I waved my magic gloves over the girl and with a shriek she turned into a wicked green slimy frog!
>
> –"It was my magic gloves" I explained as I wondered what other adventures I would have with my wonderful, amazing, fantastic magic gloves! .....

It is clear from these extracts from Asma's book that the story is not based on reality, yet she has most certainly written an exciting imaginative story. In this piece Asma has certainly included details important to the reader's understanding of the writer's feelings or thoughts: *I got very angry; What fun I had that night; I wondered what other adventures I would have –*. She has also used story conventions to hold the reader's interest, including in the closing sentence, *I wondered what other adventures I would have,* giving the reader room to speculate and predict.

> I tend to choose tests that are related to the school or the playground so that the children can write about an event which they have predominantly experienced in English, the language in which they have to write. (Jane, primary head teacher)

This consideration is certainly appropriate for personal writing but may lead to the kind of stilted writing that is apparent in Asma's test piece on a Frightening Experience. If bilingual children are to succeed in writing imaginatively they need the vocabulary, structures and storying conventions to do so and this can only be achieved by spending time in the class reading and discussing stories.

In the tests, both Asma and Tahira have written personal responses about events, rather than the required imaginative genre. Unless they have had experience of reading descriptions of people or frightening stories they are unlikely to be able to improve on these achievements in the context of the tests. Yet for both pupils they are clearly able to write descriptively and imaginatively. Teachers are given the power to decide when a pupil will be tested on the basis that the child is ready. It would seem more appropriate for teachers to be able to record on the basis of such class work as has been done by Asma and Tahira that the girls have achieved a certain level in their writing.

6. REFUGEE PUPILS IN SCOTLAND

In the past two years many of the bilingual pupils in Scottish schools have been the children of asylum seekers and refugees. Often these children have had an education prior to arrival in school in Scotland although this education may have been seriously disrupted. Most of the children are literate in at least one language and many are from educated, professional families. However on arrival in Scotland they may have little or no English. It seems both inappropriate and unjust to test their English writing skills yet it is also unjust not to acknowledge their writing skills in their first language.

> The arrangements for National Testing to have serious flaws when they are applied to refugee pupils. Testing is so closely linked to target setting for schools that the children's needs are not considered. Newly arrived refugee children should not be tested in English, but I have not been able to get support in the school that such pupils should be tested in their home language. (Carol, a teacher of newly arrived refugee pupils in Scotland)

Contrary to the beliefs expressed here by Carol, the children are tested in English as soon as their Basic Interpersonal Communicative Skills (BICS) (Cummins, 1984) suggest to the head teacher that they might pass, thus raising the school target. This takes no account of their Cognitive Academic Language Proficiency (CALP) (Cummins, 1984), their literacy in the first language or the cultural relevance of the tests. For Tamil children, who were taught in English, they could appear fluent on the surface but never have expressed themselves in writing in English. Many Afghan children recently arrived in Scotland may have received a schooling which was illegal, fragmented and focused on the literal rather than the inferential, presenting problems for imaginative writing.

In addition to the cultural difficulties outlined previously in relation to Imaginative and Personal writing, Carol pointed out that the Functional Writing Tests can also prove very difficult. One Level D/E test requires children to write a fictitious letter to their local Member of Parliament, asking for support for a campaign to protect the local environment.

> For a child who has had to flee their country because of the political regime and the knowledge that complaint or dissension can lead to torture and worse, such a piece of writing would be extremely difficult. (Carol)

Further, a practice has developed in Scotland where children are being tested at the first level (A) no matter their age. This can mean that the test being sat, in addition to being culturally irrelevant, is also age-inappropriate.

7. THE WAY FORWARD

So what are the answers? With the increasingly multilingual nature of the country, a national language policy has to be developed that will enable children to be assessed in their own language. School assessment of writing needs to evolve from school based work rather than assuming that all children have the same background of knowledge, experience and literature. Importantly, time needs to be allocated within the curriculum for teachers to share reading and writing with children, exposing classes to a wide range of oral and written genres.

There is an urgent need for teacher education to equip teachers with the skills to recognise the functions and structures of language required by different classroom tasks. Alongside this, schools need to campaign for the Scottish Qualifications Authority not only to be more culturally aware but to give clearer guidance to schools as to arrangements to be made for testing bilingual pupils. This may hopefully avoid the problems that Asif faced when trying to respond to the task "Down the Plughole". The session discussed above continued with Fiona attempting to help Asif with a task for which neither his home background nor his schooling had prepared him.

F		So you're on your own in the bathroom. What's going to happen? Where is the plug?
A		Near the taps.
F		At the end of the bath. That's one of the questions, where is the plughole? Write that down.
		We've got to think of why, how you got down that plughole. What size would you have to be?
A		Two metres.

This final comment of Asif's indicates that he has no idea what the content of the story is about. Asif tried very hard to answer the teacher's questions but the directed approach taken to the task by Fiona did not allow him to overcome the difficulties identified above in relation to the purpose of either planning or imaginative writing. Indeed, the teaching style adopted has led to Asif's writing being metaphorically sent *Down the Plughole*.

He is destined to fail, being unable to write a story which successfully identifies who is involved and tells what happens, includes sufficient detail to make the main sequence of events in the story clear and mostly organises the details of the story logically[7]. This failure will then reinforce the view that he has learning difficulties.

7.1 What Can Be Done? The Personal /Imaginative Writing Distinction

The bilingual learner needs to know the functions and structures of language required for different styles of writing. Use of a planning format such as that given below will help the teacher to identify the specific language demands of the genres. The functions, structures and vocabulary identified here are only a small proportion of those needed for successful personal and imaginative writing. The language required will depend on the task as well as on the age of the learner.

What is important is that the teacher considers in advance what the required language will be and models this for the child. This modeling needs to be done by reading aloud from a range of genres as well as through class writing and focused questions which use the target language, for example, *How would you feel if you were –?* (Personal). *What do you think it might be like ((down the plughole)? What might happen if –?* The use of *might* in these latter two questions will encourage imaginative thought and response, whereas questions such as *Are you dirty or has something happened to get you dirty?* used by Fiona, will encourage a personal response.

---

[7] *Imaginative Writing Level B criteria for Choice and Use of Language and Selection and Organisation of Ideas.*

THE LANGUAGE DEMANDS OF WRITING TASKS

Activities	Functions of language	Structures of language	Specialist vocabulary
Personal writing	Expressing emotion and attitudes, expressing a personal response	Use of first person narrative, I felt –, I know –, I think –, I liked the way –,	Words expressing feelings
Imaginative Writing	Describing characters and setting, narrating	Once upon a time As (cold) as (ice)	Range of adjectives and adverbs, similes

7.2 Bilingual Learners and the Planning of Writing

The importance of planning writing has been well documented (Graves, 1983; Styles, 1989). As discussed, planning is built into the National Tests for writing in the UK. Planning is particularly important for the bilingual child, not only to help them think about the sequence and content of their work but also to enable the teacher to assess if the child may need support with particular functions, structures and vocabulary. The planning of writing however is a skill in itself which needs taught. The purpose and process of the plan need to explained and modeled. The teacher needs to show how he or she approaches the planning of a piece of writing by modeling the planning process to a group or the whole class, using a large sheet of paper and a marker. Depending of the type of writing questions such as *Who is in the story? Where does the story take place? What happens in the story?* will be written on the paper. The teacher should record the characters, setting and plot under these questions, focusing on using the terms characters, setting and plot. Subquestions may then also be recorded on the paper such as *How does the story begin? Describe the main characters / setting; How does the story end?*

On a separate sheet of paper, the teacher should then demonstrate the transition form the plan to the actual story, including the rejection of some of the originally planned ideas and the addition of new ones. This is important so that the child does not believe the plan to be rigid.

For bilingual children particularly, the use of writing partners and/or collaborative planning will be important. The children may work in a group to brainstorm ideas at the planning stage. This will extend the range of ideas and vocabulary used. The children can then individually plan their own work, using some of the group ideas. With a partner the children can question each other about how they will move from one section of the plot to the next, how they will introduce the different characters, how they will use description to build up tension etc.

The 5-14 assessment guidelines for writing, and indeed for all the other curricular areas, have been developed in relation to the linguistic knowledge and experience of the native speaker of English. It is not appropriate to use these same guidelines to assess the development of a bilingual pupil, acquiring English as an additional language. Nor is it appropriate to assess an older bilingual pupil's learning of English by broad descriptions which are normally applied to a six to seven year old native speaker. There is a need for additional, school-based formative assessment of bilingual pupils, to supplement the 5-14 testing arrangements. Further, a national policy for the education and assessment of bilingual pupils needs to be implemented, resourced and monitored to help ensure that bilingual pupils in Scotland are given the opportunity to demonstrate their achievements alongside their monolingual peers.

COMPOSING A SUMMARY

MONICA ALVARADO* & ANA LAURA DE LA GARZA**

*Universidad Autónoma de Querétaro, México & **Escuela Maxei de Querétaro, México

Abstract
Composing a summary is a useful tool for expert readers when they read to learn, but naïve readers have to deal with two main difficulties in expository reading and writing: the text organization and the lack of previous knowledge about a specific topic. We presented a didactic sequence designed to help young children (from 3rd grade of elementary school, nine years old) to compose a summary based on the reading of an expository text. The core of the didactic sequence was to ask the children to cross out or take away everything that wasn't necessary from a given text. The didactic strategy helped the children to find the underlying nodes making them evaluate each part of the text (words, paragraphs, clauses, etc) in relation with the whole text. The identification of endophoric, exophoric references, and the previous information they had about the topic, helped them to manage the text structure successfully.

Keywords: Expository texts, to summarize, reading abilities, main ideas identification, didactical sequence.

1. GENERAL EXPOSITION

One of the goals of elementary school is for students to become efficient readers, able to extract specific information from within a text. This process is multi-tiered. It involves recognizing new information, relating it to previously existing knowledge and finally using it to increase, modify or reject the preexisting information. The greatest part of this reading to learn task is based on texts that provide information on a topic.

Expository texts are characterized by the use of specialized lexicon (related to the topic involved) and by an argumentative structure that requires information ordering that always is related to the topic and the writers' communicative intentions: definition or description of an event, explanation of its origin, description of types or categories involved in a concept, etc. (Boscolo, 1996). This structure is different from the organization of the narrative texts that children are accustomed to. Where

---

Alvarado, M. & De la Garza, A. L. (2004). Composing a Summary.
In G. Rijlaarsdam (Series Ed.) and Rijlaarsdam, G., Van den Bergh, H. & Couzijn, M. (Vol. Eds.), Studies in writing, Volume 14, Effective learning and teaching of writing, 2nd edition, Part 3, Studies in writing-to-learn, 469 - 479.

children's narratives generally follow a progressive time sequence in which a series of episodes are linked by chronology and theme, expository texts may use one of several forms of informational organization. The organization may proceed from general concepts to more specific ones or, to the contrary, from the description of specific cases to a general definition; information may be presented geographically, categorically, or in rank order. Understanding the organization is key to extracting the information needed.

Composing a summary is a useful tool for expert readers when they read to learn. It demands of them identification of the expository organization and the effort of presenting main ideas while maintaining the global coherence of the basic text (Van Dijk, 1983). In this task, as we pointed out before, the readers background in a subject and his intentions in reading have a principal relevance. Composing a summary is in this way a task in between reading and writing (Lerner, 2001).

Naïve readers, have serious problems in identifying main ideas inside an expository text. Some studies (Boscolo, 1996; Englert & Raphael, 1988) have shown that elementary school children have to deal with two main difficulties in expository reading and writing: the first is identification of text organization; the second concerns the effect of the reader's knowledge of the topic that allows him/her to identify the author's position, in other words, the intentions that made him/her follow a specific expository structure.

The didactic procedures commonly used for teaching students how to summarize ignore naïve reader's difficulties with expository texts. They start by asking the children to identify the main ideas of a given text. Later, children have to write these ideas in their own words. Lexical limitation of the students is often recognized, so the didactic procedure includes tasks for identifying unknown words and their meanings. Kaufman & Perelman (1999) and Kaufman & Perelman (in press) have insisted that looking for unknown words has never made comprehension of the text easier. It forces the children focus on isolated items or words losing the global perspective and even more, can lead them to a distorted interpretation of the text.

As opposed to this classical way of teaching, we consider the following premises for our didactic sequence (Kaufman & Perelman, 1999):

1) Not all texts can be summarized: communicative intentions and the text structure restrict this task.
2) The identification of the main ideas of a text is the result of a meticulous analysis of it and not a starting point.
3) Children need an introduction to the topics and subjects studied to facilitate a better global comprehension of the text. This will also help them to make particular inferences to surpass their lexical limitations.
4) For this specific task children must have an explicit goal: to get more information about a topic, to study, to analyze a text, etc.
5) When evaluating a text with summarizing aims, the students should approach the contents in an analytical way. For this reason "studying" occurs in the same passage as reading, evaluating and summarizing the text.
6) Composing a summary is an ability that can begin to be developed at an early age.

In what follows we present a didactic sequence designed to help young children (from third level of elementary school, nine years old) to compose a summary based on the reading of an expository text. We worked with Mexican middle class children. All of them were regular students. The didactic sequence lasted two months with two sessions (one hour each) per week.

2. INTENTIONS

Our intentions were to allow children to:
1) Evaluate overall content of an expositive text.
2) Identify and order its relevant ideas.
3) Locate the nodes of the chosen text.
4) Write a summary with predetermined limitations of space (number and length of lines) using the main ideas they found.

3. ANTECEDENTS

In the process of a scholastic project on the history of the Aztecs, a group of children in the third grade of elementary school (9 years average) began to look for relevant information that would allow them to characterize the culture. As an introduction the teacher of the group initiated different activities such as:
- reading aloud stories and Aztec legends.
- locating the Aztecs geographically and chronologically through known indexes.
- presenting guided readings of expositive texts (encyclopedias, monographs, etc).
- making explanations that complemented information and responded to specific doubts of the children.

4. DESCRIPTION OF THE DIDACTIC SEQUENCE IN TEN STEPS

1) A text was chosen on the Aztec culture that provided well-known and also new information for the children. A state-distributed textbook of the 5th grade of elementary school was chosen with accessible language.
2) The teacher presented the text to the group, reading it aloud. The students remembered previously presented information and they raised some doubts that were discussed in the group.
3) The children were organized by pairs and a copy of the text was given to each pair. With the help of an overhead projector the text was read again with the instruction to "take away everything that is not necessary". The children collectively made suggestions and discussed in order to make decisions about what there was to erase. Once consensus was obtained, the teacher physically crossed out from the transparency whatever the children indicated to her (this was the basic material for all the sequence). The first paragraph of the text was analyzed this way.

4) The instruction was then given to continue in pairs with the task of "taking away everything that is not necessary" in the second paragraph.
5) In a group session the children evaluated (they discussed) the elimination decisions that had been taken. After a consensus was made the text in the transparency was modified.
6) In pairs they continued the task with the remaining text. Whenever they concluded the work on a paragraph the decisions were discussed within the group and the information on the transparency was erased accordingly.
7) The resulting text was read collectively (the transparency was modified in the passage of the didactic procedure) and the children themselves noticed the grammar deficiencies of the text. Within this part of the procedure, unnecessary parts were crossed out again. During this same session they made suggestions to complete the text and to make it legible. The interventions were mainly focused on the verbal agreement, use of nexuses and prepositions. Again the consensual suggestions were written on the transparency.
8) By pairs the children reread the final version and they started the task of writing in one or two lines the main ideas of each paragraph on a 12.5 x 7.5 cm file card.
9) The written results were discussed paying special attention not to alter the chronological sequence of the facts since it was an historical text. A consensus was made about the main ideas of each paragraph.
10) The final version of the summary was written without access to the source text.

5. "LOS AZTECAS" CHARACTERIZATION OF THE TEXT

The chosen text was a chronological description of relevant events in the Aztec culture. It starts talking about the beginning of the tribe (around 1300) when they settled down in Mesoamerica. The text exposes a description of the general conditions of the tribe in different moments of their development until they became the greatest empire that had existed in Mesoamerica (around 1430).

>The Aztecs
>
>When you were in fourth grade you studied the history of the Aztecs or mexicas, as they are also known. You will remember that until the year 1300, they were the last tribe from the arid north to arrive in Mesoamerica. They were a poor and backward people and badly received by the inhabitants of the tolteca culture which were already established in the Valley of Mexico.
>
>The Aztecs wandered for years, without being able to settle down even in the worst lands of the Valley, until the year 1344, when, according to the legend, they found in some abandoned islands the signal that there they should found their city. Once settled, the Aztecs were for several decades under the dominion of the powerful people from Azcapotzalco, whom they served as mercenary soldiers.
>
>By about 1430, the Aztecs had assimilated the culture of the advanced peoples of the Valley and had become an efficient military power. They attacked and defeated Azcapotzalco making themselves one of the strongest dominions in the region. They initiated

then a tremendous military campaign that in only 70 years made them masters of the greatest empire that had ever existed in Mesoamerica.

The aztecs formed an alliance with the dominions of Texcoco and Tacuba, and under the command of great military chiefs such as Moctezuma Ilhuicamina and Ahuitzotl, the aztecs conquered central Mexico, Veracruz, the Guerrero cost, part of Oaxaca and dominated the territory of Soconusco as it border Guatemala. Only very few peoples managed to resist the mexica forces: the purepechas, the tlaxcaltecas and some of the mixtecan dominions.

Los aztecas

Cuando estabas en cuarto grado estudiaste la historia de los aztecas, o mexicas, como también se les conoce. Recordarás que hacia el año 1300, ellos fueron la última tribu del norte árido en arribar a Mesoamérica. Eran un pueblo pobre y atrasado y fueron mal recibidos por los habitantes de los señoríos de origen tolteca ya establecidos en el Valle de México.

Los aztecas vagaron durante años, sin poder establecerse ni en las peores tierras del Valle, hasta que en 1344, según cuenta la leyenda, encontraron en unos islotes abandonados la señal de que ahí deberían fundar su ciudad. Ya asentados, los aztecas estuvieron por varias décadas bajo el dominio del poderoso señorío de Azcapotzalco, al que servían como soldados a sueldo.

Hacia 1430, los aztecas habían asimilado la cultura de los pueblos avanzados del Valle y se habían convertido en un eficiente poder militar. Atacaron y derrotaron entonces a Azcapotzalco y se transformaron en uno de los más fuertes señoríos de la región. Iniciaron así una sorprendente hazaña guerrera, que en sólo 70 años los haría dueños del más grande imperio que había existido en Mesoamérica.

Los aztecas formaron una alianza con los señoríos de Texcoco y Tacuba y bajo el mando de notables jefes militares, como Moctezuma Ilhuicamina y Ahuitzotl, los aztecas conquistaron el centro de México, Veracruz, la costa de Guerrero, parte de Oaxaca y dominaron el territorio de Soconusco, en los límites con Guatemala. Sólo unos cuantos pueblos lograron resistir el empuje mexica: los purépechas, los tlaxcaltecas y algunos señoríos mixtecas.

Según la leyenda, los aztecas partieron de Aztlán, el Lugar de las Garzas o de la Blancura, situado en el norte.

Representación de Chicomóztoc, el Lugar de las Siete Cuevas, sitio de origen de las tribus chichimecas que poblaron el Valle de México.

La fundación de Tenochtitlan, según el Códice Durán.

In terms of Van den Broek & Kremer (2000) when reading is successful, the result is a coherent and usable mental representation of the text, the result of the identification of "nodes" through the management of endophoric and exophoric references related with previous knowledge of the topic. Nodes allow the location of main ideas and the subjacent structure of the text. We considered three nodes inside of the chosen text:
1) Information about when they arrived to Mesoamerica.
2) The difficulties they found to settle down.
3) Information about when they had assimilated other cultures and started being an efficient military power.

6. WHAT DID CHILDREN DO?

To cross out or to clear parts of a given text resulted an overwhelming task for the children who were interpreting it in different ways. Children, at the beginning of the task decided to cross out only minimal parts of the text (prepositions, pronouns and articles) that in general terms altered neither the meaning nor the content of the text. Some children chose to omit comas or periods, showing with this the difficulty of altering a preexisting text. After the intervention of the teacher, the children began to erase greater parts: adjectives, adverbs and verbs that completed the sentences. It was owing to this gradual evaluation of the parts of the text, that the children took the risk of erasing a complete sentence and with this to even reconstruct the global meaning of it. It was in this process that the children started to appreciate the underlying ideas of the text and to hierarchize them, being able to establish the central ideas (nodes).

The following analysis is presented considering modifications that children made to each paragraph of the text. We considered the second and third revision that children did collectively. We try to explain how they came to identify the text structure and the main ideas (nodes) while crossing out different parts of the text.

6.1 First Paragraph

"Cuando estabas en cuarto año estudiaste la historia de"	When you were in fourth grade you studied the history of.	This is an exophoric reference that children crossed it out because they considered it unnecessary information.
"como también se les conoce"	as they are also known	This is an endophoric reference to the Aztecs. As it was known information, children decided to eliminate it.
"ellos"	they	Children eliminated this pronoun because it is included in the verbal ending.
"y atrasado"	and backward people	This is an endophoric reference to the Aztec culture. Children have previous information and they knew the Aztecs were not a backward culture.
"de los señoríos"	of the domains	They consider it as an accessory information.

The first paragraph, after the second revision looked as follows:

> ... la historia de los aztecas o mexicas, hacia el año 1300, fueron la última tribu del norte árido en arribar a Mesoamérica. Eran un pueblo pobre y fueron mal recibidos por los habitantes de origen tolteca ya establecidos en el Valle de México.

After the collective reading and discussion about what was deleted, children decided to eliminate more words on the paragraph, it read as follows:

> Año 1300, última tribu del norte árido en arribar a Mesoamérica. Pueblo pobre, mal recibidos los toltecas ya establecidos en el Valle de México.

This paragraph shows the main ideas that children were able to identify. To get them, they deleted some grammatical elements that made the text difficult to read, but at the same time, this situation let them write the main ideas on a card file that was later used for the summary.

The summary was as follows:

> En el año 1300 los aztecas fueron la última tribu de Aridoamérica en llegar a Mesoamérica. Eran un pueblo pobre y fueron mal recibidos por los habitantes del Valle de México de origen tolteca.

6.2 Second Paragraph

"llegaron a Mesoamérica en 1300, y se establecieron en 1344"	they arrived to Mesoamerica in 1300, and they established there in 1344".	They changed the date (1344) from its place and erased the remaining information, considering it unnecessary.
"unos"	"some"	It is an undetermined plural article, and they considered it accessory information.

The second paragraph, after the second revision looked as follows:

> Los aztecas, sin poder establecerse ni en las peores tierras del Valle, encontraron en 1344 islotes abandonados la señal de que ahí deberían fundar su ciudad. Ya asentados, los aztecas estuvieron por varias décadas bajo el dominio del poderoso señorío Azcapotzalco como soldados a sueldo.

After re-reading this paragraph the children decided there was some more information that could be deleted, arguing that the information was implied in another part of the text or that it was accessory data. The resulting text looked like follows:

> Sin poder establecerse, encontraron en 1344 la señal de que ahí deberían fundar su ciudad. Estuvieron bajo el dominio de Azcapotzalco como soldados a sueldo.

As in the first paragraph, children deleted enough information to get the main ideas out of the text. They followed the same procedure and wrote them on a card file, then afterwards they wrote the summary.

The summary of this part of the text was as follows:

> No podían establecerse porque los toltecas no se los permitían, hasta que encontraron la señal que sus dioses les dieron para fundar su ciudad. Estuvieron varios años dominados por los de Azcapotzalco, tenían que pagarles tributo y servirles como soldados a sueldo.

6.3 Third Paragraph

"hacia"	towards	They substituted this preposition for "en" (in), a shorter one. They change "asimilado" (assimilated) for "copiado" (copied) a more familiar word for them.
"eficiente"	efficient	This is an endophoric reference to military power, they considered it unnecessary information.

The third paragraph, after the second revision it read as follows:

> En 1430 los aztecas habían copiado la cultura de los pueblos avanzados del Valle y se convirtieron en un poder militar.

After the collective reading and discussion about what was deleted, children decided to eliminate more words from the paragraph. It read as follows:

> Copiado la cultura de los pueblos avanzados, se convirtieron en un poder militar.

The summary of this part of the text was as follows:

> Copiaron la cultura de los pueblos avanzados y se convirtieron en un poder militar.

6.4 Fourth Paragraph

"atacaron"	attacked	This is an endophoric reference to the Aztecs. They argued it was implied in "derrotaron" (defeated).
"entonces"	then	They eliminated this nexus for considering it unnecessary information.
		They substituted "transformaron" (transformed) for "conviritieron" (turned into) because they considered it a more familiar word.
"señoríos"	dominions	because it is an endophoric reference to "military power" above in the previous paragraph.
"así"	then	nexus, they argued it was an unnecessary word.
"que"	that	nexus, they argued it was an unnecessary word.
"solo"	only	adverb that is related with the efficient military power. They considered it unnecessary because it was clear for them that "only" 70 years were enough time for the Aztecs to become a great empire.
"haría"	will do	they substituted for "hizo" (did), to maintain the verbal concordance that was used inside the paragraph.

The fourth paragraph, after the second revision looked as follows:

> Derrotaron a Azcapotzalco y se convirtieron en uno de los más fuertes de la región iniciaron una sorprendente hazaña guerrera en 70 años los hizo dueños del más grande imperio que había existido en Mesoamérica.

After the collective reading and discussion about what was deleted, children decided to eliminate more words on the paragraph, it looked like follows:

> Derrotaron a Azcapotzalco y se convirtieron en uno de los más fuertes de la región en 70 años más grande imperio que había existido en Mesoamérica.

The summary of this part of the text was as follows:

> En 70 años lograron el más grande imperio de Mesoamerica.

6.5 Fifth Paragraph

They substituted "formaron una alianza" (they formed and alliance) for "se unieron" (they join together) to use a more familiar expression.

"señoríos"	dominions	endophoric reference implied in previous (Azcapotzalco) and subsequent specific information (Texcoco and Tacuba).
"y"	and	nexus, reiterative term that must be deleted.
"el"	the	unnecessary article to maintain the coherence of the paragraph.
"notables"	notables	endophoric reference to efficient military power. Previous information made them keep only the names of the military chiefs.
"los aztecas"	the Aztecs	reiterative information in the same paragraph.
"dominaron"	dominated	endophoric reference to "conquered".
"los"	the	article. It is an unnecessary term that does not alter the grammar structure of the sentence.
"cuantos"	a few	adverb. It is an unnecessary term that does not alter the grammar structure of the sentence.
"señoríos"	dominions	an endophoric reference to "mixtecas".

The fifth paragraph, after the second revision looked as follows:

> Los aztecas se unieron con los de Texcoco y Tacuba bajo mando de jefes militares, como Moctezuma Ilhuicamina y Ahuitzotl, conquistaron el centro de México, Veracruz, la costa de Guerrero, parte de Oaxaca y el territorio de Soconusco, en límites con Guatemala. Sólo unos pueblos lograron resistir el empuje mexica: los purépechas, los tlaxcaltecas y algunos mixtecas.

After the collective reading and discussion about what was deleted, children decided to eliminate more words from the paragraph, it read as follows:

> Se unieron con los de Texcoco y Tacuba, militares como Moctezuma Ilhuicamina y Ahuitzotl conquistaron cento de México, Veracruz, la costa de Guerrero, parte de Oaxaca y el territorio de Soconusco, resistir el empuje mexica: los purépechas, los tlaxcaltecas y algunos mixtecas.

The summary of this part of the text was as follows:

> Se unieron con los de Texcoco y Tacuba, con jefes militares como Moctezuma y Ahuitzotl conquistaron gran parte del territorio de México. Sólo los purépechas, los tlaxcaltecas y algunos mixtecas pudieron aguantar la fuerza de los mexicas.

It is important to mention that the final version of the summary was not separated into the same number of paragraphs as the original text. Children made decisions about the location of the ideas inside this final text. We transcribe the summary as they wrote it, first in Spanish and then in translation.

Los Aztecas	The Aztecs
En el año 1300 los aztecas fueron la última tribu de Aridoamérica en llegar a Mesoamérica. Eran un pueblo pobre y fueron mal recibidos por los habitantes del Valle de México de origen tolteca. No podían establecerse porque los totecas no se los permitían ç, hasta que encontraron la señal que sus dioses les dieron para fundar su ciudad. Estuvieron varios años dominados por los de Azcapotzalco, tenían que pagarles tibuto y servirles como soldados a sueldo. Copiaron la cultura de los pueblos avanzados y se convirtieron en un poder militar. En 70 años lograron el más grande imperio de Mesoamérica. Se unieron con los de Texcoco y Tacuba, con jefes militares como Moctezuma y Ahuitzotl conquistaron gran parte del territorio de México. Sólo los purépechas, los tlaxcaltecas y algunos mixtecas pudieron aguantar la fuerza de los mexicas.	In 1300 the Aztecs were the last tribe from the arid north to arrive in Mesoamerica. They were poor people and they were badly received by the inhabitants of the Valley of Mexico of Tolteca origin. They weren't able to settle down because the Tolteca culture didn't allow them, until they found the signal that their gods gave them to found their city. They were for several years under the dominion of the people from Azcapotzalco, they had to pay tribute and served them as mercenary soldiers. They copied the culture of the advanced peoples and they become a military power. In 70 years they accomplished the greatest empire of Mesoamerica. They joined with Texcoco and Tacuba people, with military chiefs such as Moctezuma and Ahuitzotl they conquered a large part of the Mexican territory. Only the Purepechas, the Tlaxcaltecas and some Mixtecas managed to resist the Mexica force.

The written summaries helped them to put aside the source text and to express the main content in a personal way. This second activity was fundamental for the children since it provided them with the opportunity to rearrange the content and to choose the best way to write it: concisely and directly. As they eliminated a lot of grammatical elements to obtain the main ideas they had to think and choose new elements to restructure the coherence of the text.

As they analyzed the text in pairs, different decisions about which were the nodes inside each paragraph were expected, but when the collective revision took place it became clear that all the nodes that we identified previously were discovered by the children.

7. CONCLUSIONS

When we started this chapter we assumed that working at a word level, looking for the meaning of each unknown word, is a useless task that often leads the children to misinterpret the global content of a text. Nevertheless, even when children decided to cross out word by word, they never lost the whole meaning of the text. Moreover, the global meaning of the text was reconstructed each time a word was deleted. In terms of the knowledge of difficult words, the children were capable of making inferences supported by the context.

As we have shown the didactic strategy helped the children to find the underlying nodes making them evaluate each part of the text (words, paragraphs, clauses, etc) in relation with the whole text. The identification of endophoric, exophoric references, and the previous information they had about the topic, helped them to manage the text structure successfully. It doesn't mean, of course, they knew all the content of the text. But they could evaluate previous knowledge and modify or increase it in regard to the deep analysis they were making.

In this task children noticed they could eliminate accessory information, even though the text lost its grammatical coherence. The didactic sequence was designed to allow multiple chances to read, elect the unnecessary information and to re evaluate their decisions. In these terms, children could distance themselves from the text and have a more objective position. This meant children could reestablish the grammar coherence when writing the final summaries.

Regarding the way the didactic sequence was directed: we alternated between pairs and collective work. This enriched the development of the task. It allowed children to discuss and contrast their ideas. The final products were summaries with different grammatical elements in which the same nodes could be clearly identified.

Before starting the work with the children, we took the decision to give each pair a file card for writing their summaries in order to limit the physical space, but at the end of the task this was unnecessary because as a result of the analysis of the text they had made, the summaries were brief and concise.

Finally, we tried to show that summarizing is a task that must be initiated at an early age in elementary school to let children face the opportunity of reading expository texts and trying to understand them by identifying the underlying structure and meanings.

ENHANCING THINKING DISPOSITIONS THROUGH INFORMAL WRITING

Experiences in Science Classes

TAMAR LEVIN & TILI WAGNER

Tel Aviv University, Israel

Abstract: This study explores whether, how and why non formal writing in science classroom change students thinking disposition, which are perceived as latent tendencies that motivate and direct abilities toward productive thinking. The study is theory-driven, inspired by a constructivist view of learning, new approaches to science literacy, cognitive and social theories of the writing process, and a theory of thinking disposition. Designed as an action research with a comparative group, the study was conducted in four 8th grade science classrooms for almost two years, and includes 97 students. Measurements of students' thinking dispositions were analyzed prior to the study and at the end, following the implementation of writing experiences that allowed the use of four writing genres. The measurement instruments were developed and validated specifically for the study: thinking disposition questionnaire, reflection questionnaire and 14 writing tasks. Both quantitative and qualitative analysis was performed. The findings provide hard evidence that not only do students who write on science subjects after studying a science topic show progress in all five thinking dispositions measured, but a comparable group of students, who did not receive writing assignments, either failed to make significant progress or made less significant progress than the intervention group. The results also demonstrate that improvement in student thinking dispositions was affected by tasks that, although generically representing different types of rhetorical discourse, nevertheless had similar potential to enhance dispositions.

Keywords: mindfulness; informal writing; scientific literacy; thinking disposition; writing to learn; writing in science; writing genres, action research.

1. INTRODUCTION

This chapter describes a study that relates writing and thinking in the context of science learning. The study explores whether, how and why informal writing experiences in science classes change students thinking dispositions.

Levin, T., & Wagner, T. (2004). Enhancing Thinking Dispositions Through Informal Writing. In G. Rijlaarsdam (Series Ed.) and Rijlaarsdam, G., Van den Bergh, H. & Couzijn, M. (Vol. Eds.), Studies in writing, Volume 14, Effective learning and teaching of writing, 2nd edition, Part 3, Studies in writing-to-learn, 481-497.

For more than two decades the "writing-to-learn" movement has underscored the importance of writing and the value of combining articulate writing with scientific inquiry. "Writing-to-learn" in science is considered a tool for enabling students to develop an understanding of science (Rivard, 1994), a means of improving thinking and communication skills (Keys, 2000), as well as facilitating enculturation into the community of science practitioners (Rowell, 1997). Writing in science, according to Rowell (1997: 46), calls for an ability to "articulate reasons for supporting claims [...] express doubts, ask questions, relate alternative views, and point out what is known". This implies that when writing, both scientists and students deal not only with science contents, but also with the epistemic nature of scientific knowledge (Hofer & Pintrich, 1997).

The underlying assumption of writing to learn in science is that writing is not simply a way of expressing or displaying what one has learned. Writing is itself a fundamental mode of learning (Stehney, 1990). It offers students opportunities to think about what they are learning (Vacca & Linek, 1992), clarifies thought, allows for analytical criticism and reflection, and for ideas to be developed even further. It is also an important discursive tool for organizing and consolidating basic ideas into more coherent and better-structured knowledge (River & Straw, 2000).

It is not surprising therefore, that educators have begun to look more critically at the types of writing that occur in science classrooms, to examine how formal and non formal writing genres in science can contribute to students' growth, and particularly how different types of writing can facilitate student thinking. The unique contribution of this study is its focus on informal writing tasks as a tool for developing thinking dispositions, which Ennis (1996) perceives as latent tendencies exercised reflectively rather than automatically. Thinking dispositions represent therefore characteristics that animate, motivate, and direct abilities toward good and productive thinking and are recognized in the patterns of one's frequently exhibited, voluntary behavior (Ritchhrat, 2001). Based on the idea that thinking dispositions are developed through a process of enculturation, and that thinking dispositions are best enhanced in an environment that reinforces good thinking in a variety of tacit and explicit ways (Tishman, 1994), we would expect that non traditional writing tasks would enhance student thinking dispositions.

This chapter describes a theory-driven study which was inspired and informed by a constructivist view of learning (Vygotsky, 1978; Wertsch, 1991), new approaches to science literacy (Hand, Prain, Lawrence, & Yore, 1999), cognitive and social theories of the writing process (Scardamalia and Bereiter, 1991; Sperling, 1995), and a theory of thinking disposition (Tishman, 1994). It is practically relevant in that it uses writing as learning and thinking tool to generate educational experiences in the science classroom that can help further the aims of literacy and science literacy.

2. SCIENCE LEARNING AND WRITING: A RECIPROCAL PROCESS

Writing can be a powerful tool in helping children to learn science. Hand et al., (1999) argue that among other things, scientific literacy focuses on the student's ability and emotional disposition to understand the meaning of fundamental concepts, major scientific ideas, and scientific processes, and to articulate their understanding clearly both in writing and orally. Famous scientists have addressed this point. Schrodinger (1951), a Nobel laureate, wrote of his own work on quantum mechanics: "...if you cannot in the long run-tell everyone what you have been doing, your doing has been worthless." In the same vein, Heisenberg (1958) wrote, "Even for the physicist, the description in plain language will be a criterion of the degree of understanding that has been reached."

Locke (1992) coined the expression "science as writing" because the artifacts of science are the written traces that scientists leave behind. According to Rymer (1988), scientists are actually tellers of tales, creative writers who make meaning and choose how to do so. Even when preparing written reports of their work for publication, scientists carefully select and use such literary tools as understatement, metaphor, subtle emotional language and other rhetorical devices in order to extend the boundaries of our thinking, and persuade their readers. Thus imagination within writing always informs science (Hildebrand, 1998).

Prominent experts in the field of writing offer a different and complementary perspective advocating the integration of science and writing. Holliday, Yore, and Alverman (1994) perceive a similarity between the generative model of science learning and Bereiter and Scardamalia's (1987) conception of writing as a knowledge-transforming model. Holliday et al. regard both models as interactive, recursive, and constructive. They also recognize a similarity in the reasoning and thinking processes that scientists typically use and the characteristics of discovery writing suggested by Howard and Barton (1986). Both activities – scientific thinking processes and discovery writing – connote exploration, speculation, intuition, imagination, risk taking, and healthy skepticism.

A more concrete view, advanced by Rivard and Straw (2000), argues that inquiry-based science is a particularly powerful instructional and learning context for the integration of science content and language development. By using language in science inquiry, students get to practise and develop complex language forms and functions (Lee & Fradd, 1998), and higher-order thinking skills (Hand et al., 2002). Moreover, language functions such as description, explanation, argumentation and discussion in science research, encourage students to enhance their conceptual understanding (Rosebery et al., 1992; Gaskins et al., 1994). The relationship between science learning and language learning is thus regarded as reciprocal and synergistic (Stoddart et al., 2002).

However, not only language skills are promoted through writing in the science classroom. Integrated writing experiences can serve as an aid in cultivating different genres of science related writing styles such as fiction writing that highlights scientific themes, and expository prose that explores scientific principles (Champagne & Bunce, 1991; Glynn, Yeany, & Britton, 1991). It is therefore likely that writing on the subject of science will help improve student literacy and nurture the ability to utilize diversity of thoughts (Bruner, 1986).

The question we need to ask is why and how is science-related writing so powerful?

3. WRITING AS A MODE OF LEARNING – THEORETICAL MODELS

Authors vary widely in the hypothetical models they suggest to explain the processes underlying learning through writing. Klein (1999, 2000) discusses four important *cognitive* models: (a) point of utterance – i.e., that writers spontaneously generate knowledge as they write; (b) forward search – i.e., that writers externalize their ideas, then reread them in order to develop them further; (c) backward search – this refers to the process whereby writers develop rhetorical goals and sub-goals and then produce new content to meet these goals, and (d) genre hypothesis – which assumes that certain features of text structure cause writers to generate and elaborate information, and that different genres require different cognitive strategies.

The four hypothetical models that Klein suggests represent a cognitive view of writing. This notion of writing, as entailing the mastery of problem solving strategies, has been criticized for representing writing as a controlled, rational and linear process (Galbraith & Torrance, 1999). More specifically, it has been criticized for its focus on the explicit thinking processes and for ignoring the role of social and interactive factors, such as the writer's familiarity with the particular genre in which s/he is writing, or the writer's relationship with the discourse community to which s/he belongs (Tynjala, 2001). This criticism is reflected in Hayes' (1996) revision of the basic Hayes and Flower (1980) model, in which problem solving is reconceptualized as a single component within a more general reflection module and where social and motivational factors and "thinking behind the text" are taken into account.

Since the framework of this study concerns the social approach to writing, including reference to the cognitive dimension of writing, only two out of Klein's four hypothetical models are relevant to us here: these are the backward search hypothesis or knowledge transformation model, and the genre hypothesis. It is hoped that these models will be of assistance in the analysis and interpretation of our data.

Due to its reflective nature, the *Knowledge transformation* model by Bereiter and Scardamalia (1987) is highly compatible with constructivist theories of learning science, which encompasses the evaluation of available hypotheses, claims, and evidence (Holliday et al., 1994). Knowledge transformation is an act of learning involving a dynamic between the subject matter / issues addressed in the writing and the rhetorical requirements of the writing task. This contrasts with knowledge telling, in which writers represent recollections in printed symbols, which essentially remain unaltered. The dynamic of knowledge transformation involves the constant reevaluation and transformation of writer's knowledge. Keys (1999) has suggested that experienced science writers actively deal with both the content and rhetorical requirements in the knowledge transformation process of writing, while novices struggle with the rhetorical aspects of writing. She also argues that the content domain is where problems and beliefs are considered, while problems relating to the expression of content are dealt with in the discourse domain. Keys conceives reflective and mature writing as a dialectical interplay between the two problem domains, in which the output from each domain provides the input for the other, so that questions of language and syntax choice reshape content meaning, while efforts to express content are what drive the composition component.

In terms of this model, this study analyzed a set of qualitative data, which had bearings on the type of thinking dispositions found in student writings with respect to the content and discourse/rhetorical problem domains.

The *genre model* deals with the role of the writer's discourse community, and therefore relates to the social dimension of the writing process. This model suggests that different writing tasks encourage students to invoke different cognitive strategies for processing and encoding information (Langer & Applebee, 1987). Some genres, such as argumentation, comparison and contrast, metaphor, and analogy are thought to require deep processing, including the construction of links between prior knowledge and new knowledge, and between different elements of new knowledge (Wiley & Voss, 1996). Other genres such as listing, defining, or describing require learners to simply focus on one or more concepts in isolation, usually one at a time. On the other hand, analytical tasks such as explaining the real-world applications of scientific concepts call for learners to assemble these in an integrated web of meaning. Asking students to explain scientific phenomenon in writing, enhances their understanding of content (Fellows, 1994; Prain, 1995). Learning logs, and double-entry journals, are also useful strategies for promoting some other aspects of science understanding (Butler, 1991; Willison, 1996).

It is important, however, to note that genres are not viewed as fixed, rigid forms, but as fluid and responsive to the values and goals of the communities of writers who use them (Berkenkotter & Huckin, 1995). This view perceives genres as being socially negotiated within particular rhetorical contexts (Miller, 1984). Accordingly, genres are not only determined by, but determine the knowledge of a community (Bazerman, 1988) and consequently knowledge that is negotiated through genres is not simply content knowledge, but rather complex, disciplinary, epistemological, ideological knowledge. Thus, written genres are tools that students use to learn either about the rhetorical contexts in which they interact, or about the rhetorical representations of the discipline. Within the context of science writing, Prain & Hand (1996) argue that genres help students acquire an appreciation of the particular reasoning skills a task entails, and to understand the goals, rationale and epistemological criteria that guide scientific work in the broader community.

The typical scientific genres including the lab report, experimental article, and the conference paper are considered rhetorical representations of the discipline. Although considered important (Halliday & Martin, 1993), these genres are also viewed as dry and voiceless, and as epitomizing an authoritative, positivistic stance, that dampens interest in science among certain groups in society (Hildebrand, 1996). Consequently, researchers such as Hildebrand (1996) and Prain and Hand (1996), who represent a feminist and postmodern view of science writing tasks, encourage the production of multiple and expressive genres in order to make science more appealing to an assortment of groups in society. For different reasons, Chaopricha (1997) too advocates the use of a variety of genres, arguing that good writers have to cross the boundaries of conventions, discourse, and communities rather than adopt a narrow template for their writing.

Like Keys, (2000) we believe that writing undertaken in science classes should have a pedagogical as well as a disciplinary orientation. In other words, school science writing assignments should contain some characteristics of the writing style that scientists use, but in addition, should also function as pedagogical tools in terms of helping students to construct scientific meaning in any particular genre they use – whether informal or formal. This study therefore offered a choice of different informal writing genres, which allowed students to choose the genre they felt was most appropriate in each learning unit undertaken in the study.

4. WRITING IN SCIENCE - RESEARCH RESULTS

Several studies have suggested that if the goal of learning is the reproduction of facts (knowledge telling), then writing is a less effective method than "studying for a test" (Penrose, 1992). However, when higher-order learning, such as critical thinking, is sought, writing seems to offer an effective learning tool (Tierney et al., 1989). Various research studies have shown that both formal and informal writing tasks/genres enhance student learning because they require students to reflect, consolidate, elaborate, hypothesize, interpret, synthesize and persuade. These processes enhance higher-order thinking, deeper understanding of science concepts, improved use of comprehension strategies, and ability to suggest causal explanations and elaborate predictions. They also encourage conceptual growth, and an appreciation of knowledge as socially and culturally constructed, foster self-awareness of beliefs and conceptions, and develop greater technical writing proficiencies (Connolly, 1989; Schumacher & Nash, 1991; Sutton, 1992; Brown & Campione, 1994; Fellow, 1994; Glynn & Muth, 1994; Rivard, 1994; Keys, 1994; Mason, 1998; Keys, 2000). While most of the results reported in these studies emphasize the contribution of writing to the enhancement of knowledge or thinking that is relevant to science learning, a recent study by Hand et al. (2002) demonstrates that writing experiences with a science class context also contribute to student meta-cognitive understanding of the writing process itself.

Although much has been reported on the effects of informal writing on students' general thinking strategies in a science context, none of the studies have investigated how writing effects student thinking disposition. Studies on the subject of thinking have underscored the importance of dispositions, in the realization that ability alone does not qualify as intelligent behavior. Tishman, Perkins, and Jay (1995) argue that all too often, people know how to think more effectively about something, but are not disposed to do so. For this reason, both Dewey (1930), with his notion of "good habits of mind", and Siegel (1988), with the concept of "critical spirit", have stressed the importance of analyzing thinking from the standpoint of both abilities and disposition. The study discussed here therefore addresses this need in the context of writing-to-learn in science. We believe that since thinking is reciprocally affected by writing, and since thinking dispositions are learned through a process of enculturation, then writing tasks, which reflect a speculative view of science and recognize the multiple interpretations of an experience or data set (Hand et al., 1999) possess the potential to promote disposition.

Basing itself on Tishman's (1994) definition of thinking disposition and Langer's (1993) concept of mindfulness, the study relates to the following five dispositions: (1) viewing phenomena from multiple perspectives, (2) deducing novel categories or distinctions, (3) feeling a need and willingness to think, (4) enjoying the experience of thinking and (5) appreciating meta-cognition.

Therefore, the main question that our study addresses is whether eight-grade students develop thinking dispositions reflecting constructivist habits of mind after working on writing assignments in their regular science classes.

5. METHOD

5.1 Participants and Context

Being part of a larger study that examines the effects of informal writing in science on student thinking dispositions, attitudes toward science and views of writing, this chapter focuses only on the effect of writing on student thinking dispositions. Since the study was interested in hard evidence regarding the effects of writing, we chose to use the scientific approach to action research (Taba & Noel, 1975; Glanz, 1998). This involved employing a research design containing both quantitative and qualitative methodologies, and a "comparative group", which was similar to the intervention group in terms of the students' personal and social characteristics, the science curriculum they studied and also the teachers. More specifically, the study involved a total of four eighth grade classes and 97 students, divided into a total of (48) students in the two intervention classes and (49) students in the two comparative classes. Two teachers took part in the study, each one teaching both the intervention group students and the comparative group students.

The intervention and comparative group studied the following five science topics, in six learning units: Heat and Temperature; Fibers; Reproduction (two units); the Electric Circuit, and Energy. Students in the comparative group were taught the same syllabus and by the same teachers as the students in the intervention group. However, the students in the comparative group were not asked to write anything while actually studying these topics, just at the end of the study, following their learning of the energy unit, for comparative purposes. The study lasted three school semesters (i.e., one and a half years).

5.2 Research Instrument

A thinking disposition questionnaire was developed specifically for this study. The questionnaire comprised 28 items in the form of a 5-point Likert scale ranging from 1 (totally disagree) to 5 (totally agree). To establish the construct validity of the questionnaire, a principal component factor analysis was carried out twice, on two different samples (Wagner, in press). The identical results for the two groups provided 5 factors, which explained a high (78%) percent of the total variance. The five factors are (1) a tendency to view a phenomenon from different angles; (2) an inclination to draw new distinctions; (3) a need and willingness to think; (4) appreciation of meta-cognition and (5) an enjoyment of thinking. Table 1 shows the reliability indices of each factor, and the percentage of variance contributed by each one. It also shows an example of items for each of the factors.

Table 1. Description of Factors and Measures of Reliability

Factor	Example of Items from the questionnaire	Explained Variance (%)	Reliability
Looking at issues from a number of perspectives	Thinking about things in different ways often only leads to more mistakes.	17.19	.95
Drawing new distinctions	It is a good idea to look for differences in things that seem totally similar.	11.91	.93
A need and willingness to think	It is enough for me to simply know the answer to a problem and not necessarily to understand its reasons.	16.83	.94
Appreciation of meta-cognition	Even when I'm carrying out routine tasks, I think a lot about the way I do them.	16.46	.94
Enjoyment of thinking	After I finish something that required a lot of thought, I feel more relief than satisfaction.	15.48	.92

5.2.1 The Informal Writing Tasks

Informal writing tasks are items of writing that are not regularly used in the science class as part of the science discourse (Keys, 1999). Informal writing tasks can also take the form of a genre that is uncharacteristic of the typical science discourse used.

Three informal writing tasks were designed and assigned to 5 of the learning units: the tasks were a fictional story, a debate and a diary. The subject of the task was naturally related to the topic covered by the learning unit. Below are examples of the three writing tasks given for the learning unit on Heat and Temperature:

Examples of Writing Tasks (Unit on Heat and Temperature):

Story: Tell the story of a group of water particles that were heated up from a temperature of 20°C below zero to 150°C above zero.
Diary: An additional sun has appeared in the sky of our planet. The sun radiates continuous heat on the earth. Write a diary of your own or the diary of someone else describing the effect on our world.
Debate: Two children, Dan and David, have an argument:
Dan: In my computer game, the hero shoots a tank using a small rifle and the tank evaporates.
David: That's impossible. The tank is made of iron. Iron is a metal and no heat exists that can cause the tank to evaporate. Continue the argument.

Altogether, 15 tasks were developed for the first five units. Two different tasks: a plan and two related letters were used for the final learning unit (Energy) with both the intervention and the comparative groups. These tasks were constructed so that the data they would be similar, even though the writing genre differs. Changing the type of writing task used for the last learning unit at the end of the study enabled us to compare the difference in writing quality between the intervention and the comparative group after the intervention was completed, while eliminating any possibility that familiarity with a particular genre would affecting the intervention group students' writing.

Writing tasks for the Energy Unit

> The year is 2030. It is after the end of a third World War, caused by international disputes over energy resources. The United Nations decides on a different distribution of energy resources. According to the resolution, no matter where the energy resources are located, they belong to all nations. An international committee is being formed to discuss how to distribute these resources.
> *The Plan*: As a member of the committee, write a proposal for the new energy distribution.
> *Two related letters*: Write two letters to the committee, one from a boy in Saudi Arabia, the other from Israel.

5.3 Design and Procedure

Before, and at the end the study, we measured students' thinking dispositions, both for the intervention group and the comparative group, using the questionnaire. In addition, after completing the first unit (Heat and Temperature), students in both groups were asked to select one of the three writing tasks either the diary, story or discussion, based on their own preference. The reason for allowing the students in the two groups to choose a task representing the different genres is related to the constructivist approach to science learning. According to this approach, this type of procedure will improve the likelihood that each of the students will all find a task that speaks to them personally. It is also concerns the belief that choice is positively related to the student's intrinsic motivation for the task (Cordova & Lepper, 1996).

During the study, students in the intervention group received four writing tasks, at the end of each learning unit, plus a reflection task related to their writing. Students in the comparison group did not receive any additional writing tasks.

Students in the intervention group also received written feedback regarding his/her writing. Finally, on completing the last unit (Energy), both groups of students were asked to select one of the two writing tasks related to the energy unit: a plan and two-related letters.

6. RESULTS

Quantitative Analysis. Table 2 presents the means and standard deviations for each thinking disposition, for the two groups, before, and at the end of the study.

Table 2. Means and Standard Deviations (between brackets) of Thinking Disposition Measures for the Intervention and Comparative Group - Pre- And Post- Test Measures

	Pre-Test Writers N=48	Pre-Test Non-Writers N=49	Post-Test Writers N=48	Post-Test Non-Writers N=49
1. Viewing different perspectives	2.65 (0.95)	2.73 (1.12)	3.97 (0.64)	2.97 (1.14)
2. Drawing new distinctions	2.85 (0.98)	2.59 (1.16)	4.20 (0.54)	2.94 (1.09)
3. A need and willingness to think	3.35 (1.07)	3.14 (1.10)	4.01 (0.74)	3.38 (1.04)
4. Appreciation of meta-cognition	2.89 (0.99)	2.45 (1.04)	3.67 (0.75)	2.79 (1.05)
5. Enjoyment of thinking	3.07 (0.91)	2.66 (0.94)	3.64 (0.70)	2.95 (0.96)

A repeated multivariate analysis on the data (Table 3) demonstrated a significant interaction between the "group and the measurement time", indicating that the growth in thinking dispositions of the intervention group was significantly higher than the growth in thinking dispositions of the comparative group. Similar results were found for all thinking dispositions.

Table 3. Repeated Measures Analysis. Effect of Writing (between Students Effect) and Effect of Time (within students effect): Mean Square and F-values

Dependent Variable	Writing Effect MS	Writing Effect $F(1,95)$	Time Effect MS	Time Effect $F(1,95)$	Interaction Writing*Time $F(1,95)$
Viewing different perspectives	1.73	5.93*	0.20	149.53*	72.85*
Drawing new distinctions	1.68	16.59*	.22	161.63*	53.98**
A Need & willingness to think	1.86	4.57*	0.18	54.86**	13.09**
Appreciation of meta-cognition	1.07	12.43*	0.16	92.83**	14.54**
Enjoyment of thinking	1.39	10.73*	0.18	47.46**	5.17*

Figure 1 and Table 2 present the interaction effect, showing no differences in the thinking disposition, "viewing a phenomenon from different perspectives", between the groups prior to the study, and a significant difference between the pre- and post-measurements for the intervention group (1.66 sd). No significant difference was found for the comparative group (0.21 sd). We also find that the scores for the intervention group at the end of the study were significantly higher than those of the comparative group (1.13 sd).

Figure 1 depicts a somewhat different pattern of interaction for the disposition "drawing new distinction", with significant differences between the measurements before and after the intervention for each of the groups (0.25 sd; 1.56 sd, respectively). However, the growth relating to the intervention group (1.75 sd) was found to be significantly higher than the growth revealed for the comparative group (0.32 sd, respectively). Or, expressed another way, the significant difference between the groups prior to the study (0.24 sd) was smaller than the significant difference between the groups at the end of the study (1.56 sd). The findings also show that at the end of the study, the scores for the intervention group were significantly higher than those of the comparative group.

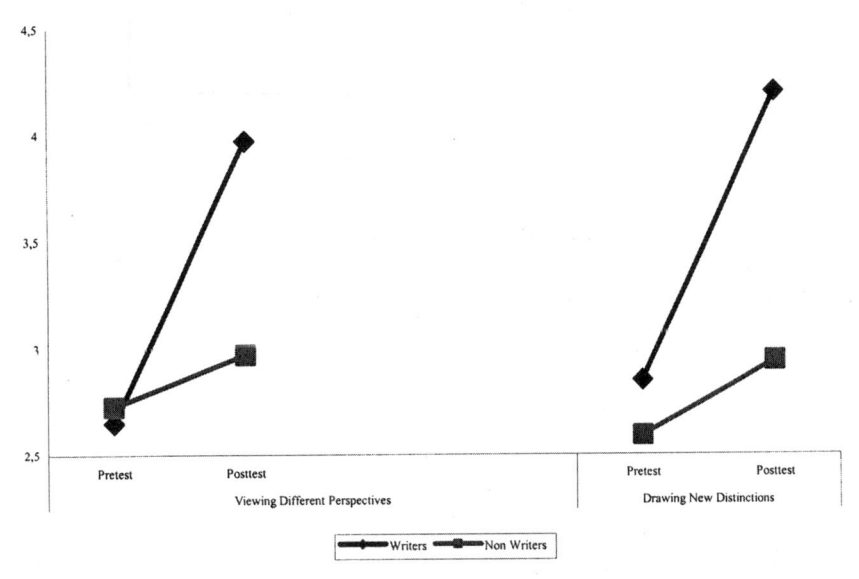

Figure 1. Interaction effect for variables 'Viewing different perspectives' (left hand) and Drawing new distinctions (right hand).

We also found that the intervention group showed significant growth with regard to the "Need and willingness to invest in thinking" disposition, while the comparative group did not. However, the intervention group showed significantly higher growth than the comparative group with regard to "Appreciation of meta-cognition".

No meaningful differences were found for the distribution of tasks selected by the students in the intervention group. Out of 214 students writing tasks, 65, 60 and

89 were stories, diaries and debates respectively. Of the 96 writing tasks students selected at the end of the study, 57 were plans and 39 were two-related letters.

Qualitative analysis. While so far the data has been based on students' self reports, it is also important to explore how student thinking dispositions manifest in their writing. However, due to space limitations we can only provide one illustration relating to the disposition of "Viewing phenomena from different angles / perspectives", showing how students expressed this disposition in two alternative writing tasks at the end of the study: Plan and Letters.

Appendix A shows the categories obtained from the analysis of the written assignments: a plan and letters. The categories, defined for two spheres: content and discourse, reflect the use of either single or multiple views regarding the issues entailed in the tasks. The results of this analysis show that the categories are very similar for the two writing tasks, even though they represent two different types of genres. We can also see from Appendix A and Example 1 that, in terms of content, when a situation is observed from one perspective, the students employ a limited number of unrelated references to science, e.g., one topic, one dimension, one concept or one principle.

Example 1 of a plan using a single viewpoint in the content sphere:

"A Plan: I would distribute oil to each country according to its consumption rate "(61f2)

In this example, only one content dimension is used and the reference to it mentions only consumption. Moreover, the student refers to only one source of energy: oil. In contrast, when a situation is viewed from a multiple, integrated perspective students display an organized network of concepts, ideas, principles and assumptions, and also evaluate their own writing. For example, if a student approaches the question of world energy distribution from a multiple perspective, s/he will discuss the economic, ecological, social, moral and other content factors, besides referring to sub-dimensions for all the dimensions noted. Thus, if a student refers to economical considerations, s/he will also note alternative energy types, and possible ways of saving energy. Viewing an issue from multiple perspectives can also be seen in the attention students pay to the relationship between the content dimensions they used, often organized them in a hierarchical form. It was also found that the hierarchical form was used to suggest priorities for implementing their energy saving plan. The students also tend to conclude their assignment by discussing the strengths and weaknesses of their plan in terms of the content elements they addressed. (see Appendix B).

With regard to the discourse sphere, a situation viewed from a single perspective is expressed in a laconic and fragmented writing style, with non-elaborated text, and only one or a few unreasoned claims or opinions.

Example 2 of a Plan:

"My energy distribution plan is according to the following criteria: economical, ecological, security, political and country size. Thank you" (66f2)

Although in terms of content the student lists several content factors, in terms of discourse, s/he does not elaborate on the content factors listed, nor does s/he explain how the energy distribution plan would address each of those factors. Moreover, the writing contains no assumptions or arguments.

Example 3 of Two Related Letters using a single viewpoint:

> "Letter from a Saudi Citizen: My name is Ahmed and I want to say that in my opinion it is stupid to distribute energy equally. This would not be fair. The energy situation should be kept as it is because that's how it should be.
>
> Letter from an Israeli citizen: My name is Itzik Zohar, and I want to say that the idea of distributing energy equally is a good idea because it should be that way." (78f2)

Both letters make claims and nothing more. In the first letter, the attempt to reason is unrelated to the claim, while in the second letter, it is in fact teleology. In contrast to the single perspective viewpoint above, the multiple, related viewpoint is expressed as a highly elaborated, complete, well-structured, coherent and sometimes creative text, with reasoned arguments and using principles, assumptions etc, and reflection (see Appendix B).

7. DISCUSSION

The study confirms our hypothesis that, when linked to science topics learned in the classroom, informal writing can enhance students thinking dispositions. The study findings provide hard evidence that not only do students who write on science subjects after studying a science topic show progress in all five thinking dispositions measured, but a comparable group of students, who did not receive writing assignments, either failed to make significant progress or made less significant progress than the intervention group. Since we found no other studies of the effects on thinking dispositions of informal, science-related writing, we can only refer to studies that demonstrate improvement in thinking abilities, a dimension of thinking disposition. These studies reveal that informal writing in science can indeed be effective in enhancing higher order thinking skills, performance on higher-order analogy questions (Hand et al., 2002), ability to apply learned knowledge in new situations (Holliday, 1992), reflection on scientific encounter, learning enjoyment and scientific literacy (Keys, 2000).

Nevertheless, we know that merely writing about science does not necessarily ensure that students learn science, learn to write more effectively, or even learn to use writing as a learning or thinking tool (Moore 1993). In other words, not every kind of informal task is likely to have a significant effect on improving thinking dispositions in students. The nature of the tasks (Prain & Hand, 1996; Levin and Geldman, 1997) and the instructional or learning context (Tishman, 1994) have the potential to effectively encourage the learning of science or enhancing thinking, through deliberately and carefully designed writing assignments. Prain & Hand (1996) suggest various considerations that should be taken into account when designing meaningful writing tasks in science. These considerations include attention to writing purpose and type, target readership, transparency of reasoning skills required by the task structure, goals, rationale, and the epistemological criteria underlying scientific work in the relevant community. Other considerations suggested by Britton and Holliday include the importance of searching the interrelationship between the content and discourse aspects of the task, and using tasks that are open-ended, exploratory and personal (Britton, 1970; Holliday et al., 1994).

The three task genres used with the intervention group – debate, story and diary – comply with many of the above criteria. In other words, while these genres may differ in terms of the strategies they encourage students to use, and in their explicit rational and purpose, they are all open-ended, exploratory, involve the personal voice, and most importantly, all three share the potential to enhance students thinking dispositions. For limitations of space, we will only demonstrate this last argument for one disposition, viz., viewing phenomena from single or multiple perspectives. The debate-format writing tasks we developed presented situations where students had to examine different perspectives and either agree with the claims or course of action presented, or take a particular stand and argue for or against the proposition or course of action (Kuhn, 1993). In either case, the dialogical arguments called for students to consider alternative positions. The diary and story tasks also presented situations that required students to approach a situation from a viewpoint not their own and to actually step into another's shoes. For example, they were asked to describe, examine or explain a science related topic from the perspective of someone living in a place very different from earth (*e.g., a planet where the reproductive processes are different from those on earth*), or through the eyes of someone with a very different identity from their own, i.e., not always focused on the human being (e.g., *a water molecule, a sperm or an astronaut*) or through someone or something that lives/exists in a different time, either the past or in the future (e.g., *a ten years old living in England during the Industrial Revolution*), or any combination of these.

The results of the study demonstrate that improvement in student thinking dispositions was affected by tasks that, although generically representing different types of rhetorical discourse, nevertheless had similar potential to enhance dispositions. This implies that not only the form of the task (genre) helps to enhance student thinking dispositions, but also the connection between the genre of the task and its contents. It is the combination where science content, general content and rhetorical discourse intertwine in order to explicitly and quite accurately define the textual context of the writing task and its potential effect. While this may not be totally in line with traditional assumptions and expectations regarding the genre model (Langer & Applebee, 1987), it is nevertheless consistent with the perception of genre as a fluid structure that can meet the needs of the communities of writers who use them (Berkenkotter & Huckin, 1993) and thereby highlights the social nature of writing (Galbraith, 1999).

The study supports and even underscores the importance of viewing both the context in which a text is produced and the context of using it thus demonstrating the social nature of the writing process in the learning of science. It also supports the significance attributed to the dialogical connections between content and discourse when writing is viewed as a process of knowledge transformation (Bereiter & Scardamalia, 1987). Additional proof of the strong relationship between content and discourse is provided by the qualitative data, which show that not only potentially but also practically, in the actual writing, the disposition to view a phenomenon from a single or multiple perspective is expressed through the two spheres of content and discourse, and that the categories indicating how the thinking disposition is reflected in the writings are extremely similar for the two genres – the plan and the two related letters.

Although, for reasons of space constraints, we are unable to report our findings so far for all the thinking dispositions examined in the study, it is worth noting that a similar analysis of the tasks for the remaining dispositions led to similar conclusions. This means that the debate, story and diary that we assigned in the intervention group, could all potentially enriched the thinking dispositions measured by the study. Furthermore, since engaging in the use of different genres of writing brings students to a better appreciation of the personal, tentative and pleasurable side of science (Kyle et al., 1992), we believe that the students' exposure to both selecting their tasks, and to diversity of writing experiences also proved instrumental in enhancing three of the dispositions measured in our study: enjoyment of thinking, need and willingness to think, and appreciation of meta-cognition.

The study findings contribute to an ongoing dispute regarding the most effective types of writing-to-learn tasks for science. While modernists believe that students should learn conventional forms of scientific discourse (Berkenkotter & Huckin, 1995), postmodernists support the use of novel forms of expression that allow students to critique the status quo of the scientific enterprise. Constructivists on the other hand, favor writing forms that facilitate the construction of personal and socially generated meaning (Prain & Hand, 1996). The study reported here supports the use of informal writing tasks, not for their contribution to acquiring science knowledge, but for the thinking dispositions they can encourage. Based on prevailing conceptions of scientific literacy, these dispositions relate to the desired characteristics of scientifically literate individuals and involve abilities and emotional dispositions that reflect the speculative, personal, temporary, and rational attributes of science knowledge and scientific process; skepticism in generating temporal explanations, and plural rather than singular interpretations of world phenomena (Hand, Prain, & Yore, 2001). A willingness and ability to construct explanations of natural phenomena, to test these explanations in many different ways and to convey them to a wide audience is also required (Schwartz & Lederman, 2002).

Our study has therefore demonstrated that the nature and purpose of meaningful informal writing-in-science, along with the contents entailed, suggests various opportunities, responsibilities and hopes with regard to the development of general and scientific literacy alike.

APPENDIX A

	Single perspective	Multiple and Related Perspectives
A. Content Space Plan for Global Energy Distribution	1. Suggests one criterion for energy distribution (economic, social, ecological, etc.) 2. Reference to one aspect of the selected criterion (e.g., just reference to population growth in the context of the economy criterion)	1. Suggests several content criteria for energy distribution, which includes specifying several features of each criterion (See example, Appendix 2) 2. Refers to relationships between different criteria and organizes them based on considerations involving general or science knowledge 3. Applies relevant science knowledge to analyze the text during the reflection process (e.g., refers to benefits and drawbacks of the suggested proposal)
Two Letters addressed to a committee dealing with Global Energy Distribution	1. Uses one criterion to justify a request for energy resources (economic, historical, morale, etc) 2. Uses identical criteria in the two letters. Letters reflect similar interests or similar needs of the letter writers' respective countries	1. Uses several, different prioritized criteria in each letter 2. Uses two different or even opposing criteria in the two letters; offers content based justification for the conflicting needs 3. Uses science knowledge when evaluating the requests in the letters
B. Discourse Space Plan for Global Energy Distribution	1. States limited number of unrelated claims, or assumptions, or principles or conclusions 2. Produces fragmented and laconic, writing structure entailing either an opening, or a main body or an end	1. Presents several claims in the form of assumptions, principles and attitudes, justifies claims and applies criteria with reference to the specific situation presented in the task. 2. presents argumentation to resolve conflicting interests and needs in the proposed plan. (juxtaposition of ideas) 3. writes elaborated and coherent text, which explicitly connects different ideas. Writing structure has a logically related introduction, a main body of text and a conclusion
Two Letters addressed to a committee dealing with Global Energy Distribution	1. Uses a limited number of unrelated and unjustified claims in each letter 2. Produces a fragmented and laconic writing structure entailing either an opening or a main body or an end.	1. Uses several justified claims in the form of assumptions and principles and establishes criteria based on them; applies criteria with reference to the specific situation presented in the task 2. Uses the letters to produce an explicit dialogue with a defined potential reader. Presents justifications and persuasive argumentation regarding the difference of opinion that the two letters express 3. Produces elaborated, coherent text, which explicitly connects different ideas.

APPENDIX B

"Energy: The 3rd World War caused great damages across the entire world. However, perhaps one good thing came out of it: the fact that all of the world's countries have understood the need to stop fighting over energy resources and to try to come to an agreement, that may not be in the best interests of each county, but will definitely not be for the worst, and will certainly ensure greater stability. The following is my proposal for distributing global energy resources:

I propose that energy resources should be distributed according to the following criteria:

1. Different energy resources and their location: one needs to examine in each country: oil, coal, natural gas, uranium deposits for nuclear power (for example, the Arab states are very rich in oil and natural gas, while some European countries have many waterfalls). It is important to ensure that energy could be transferred as directly as possible to avoid losing even more energy.

2. Population: The size of a country's population – the more people there are to consume energy, the greater the resources the country will receive. Thus, for example, China will be allocated relatively large energy resources).

3. Level of development: The more developed countries need more resources: their industries are more highly developed and therefore need more coal and natural gas. Such countries would receive larger quantities of crude oil to meet their transportation fuel requirements). Developing countries would receive enough energy to meet their consumption needs. Each developed country would take a developing country under its patronage and help in its development for a limited number of years. If it failed comply with this condition, the developed country would receive less energy than it deserved.

4. Energy consumption: Sometimes it is not the number of people that determine the level of consumption in a country, and a smaller country might have higher rates of consumption than larger countries. In this type of case, a committee would examine the consumption rate and number of citizens and would need to be persuaded that the higher energy demand was justified.

Regarding consumption, another criterion would be how the energy is used and not how much is used. High consumption countries that waste rather than save energy would receive less than countries that with a proven record of energy saving policies.

The strength of my proposal lies in its effort to distribute energy resources equally, with no political considerations.

The weakness of my proposal is that some countries might not accept it, e.g., countries with small populations and low energy needs with large natural energy resources. Such countries have nothing to gain from this proposal.

Another problem might arise because of conflicting criteria and I didn't set ones and didn't decide which one is preferable.

Perhaps it would help to devise a measure that addresses all the criteria – even a quantitative measure derived by multiplying all the conditions together so that each country receives energy based on its "energy rights" measure.

FOSTERING REFLECTIVE WRITING BY STRUCTURING WRITING-TO-LEARN TASKS

GISSI SARIG

Kibbutzim College of Education, Israel

Abstract. Mature learning and thinking requires a reflective disposition. Due to the relation of writing in general, and reflective writing in particular, to knowledge production – writing may foster reflective learning and thinking in various academic domains. However, while adults may be either inclined or trained towards writing-to-reflect, children need to be educated to engage in it. The aim of the technique presented in this chapter is to offer a strategic framework for structuring & facilitating reflective writing for school children. It comprises nine writing-to-reflect acts: (1) Coordinating expectations from the learning resource at hand; (2) Relating it to prior knowledge; (3) Detecting & diagnosing difficulties in it; (4) Selecting relevant knowledge; (5) Judging the value of the learning source critically; (6) Deliberating its optional interpretations; (7) Transforming its structure conceptually; (8) Re-contextualizing the newly gained knowledge; (9) Linking: Assessing learning outcomes & creating new learning goals. The learners use these nine 'reflection stops' as optional writing opportunities. They select one or several of the 'stops', and start writing about a text they learn from, 'entering' and 're-entering' it by performing the reflective acts each selected stop entails. Wide use of this technique from second to seventh grade has shown that the majority of children & teachers may benefit from using it when it is introduced gradually and exercised flexibly and judiciously.

Keywords: reflective writing; reflective thinking; writing-to-learn; writing instruction; writing techniques

1. THEORETICAL FRAMEWORK

1.1 Introduction

Mature learning and thinking requires a reflective disposition, which Perkins (1995), following Paul (1994), characterizes as high-investment commitment to complex tasks across multiple frames of reference. Due to the relation of writing in general (Bereiter & Scardamalia, 1987; Galbraith, 1999), and reflective writing in particular (Sarig, 1996) to knowledge production – writing may foster a reflective disposition to learning and thinking in various academic domains (Aspinwall & Miller, 1997;

Sarig, G. (2004). *Fostering reflective writing by structuring writing-to-learn tasks.*
In G. Rijlaarsdam (Series Ed.) and Rijlaarsdam, G., Van den Bergh, H. & Couzijn, M. (Vol. Eds.), *Studies in writing, Volume 14, Effective learning and teaching of writing*, 2nd edition, Part 3, *Studies in writing-to-learn*, 499- 517.

Deloney Carey, & Geeman, 1998; Prescott, 2001; Swartzendruber-Putnam, 2000). However, while adults may be either naturally inclined or professionally trained towards writing-to-reflect, children need to be educated and encouraged to engage in it.

In this chapter I will present and demonstrate the *'Reflection Cycle'* (Sarig, 1997), a technique offering a strategic framework for structuring, and thus facilitating, reflective writing for school children. It is a reading-writing-thinking technique, which the young writers use to write/think reflectively about a text they learn. It comprises nine writing-to-reflect acts, entitled writing 'stops', each calling for a different writing task.

1.2 Six Theoretical Underpinnings

The broad Pedagogical and Theoretical Rationale underlying the technique, both as a whole, and in reference to particular tasks within it, rests on several theoretical perspectives: semiotic, communicative, cognitive and political approaches to meaning and knowledge making, and a pedagogy inspired by them. The classical and post-modern notions coming from these approaches clearly represent different schools of thought. However, they all converge into one educational goal underlying the technique: *the design of new knowledge* by learners (Shor & Freire, 1990/1987; Sarig, 1996, 2000), whereby learners re-write texts they read.

The first perspective is Charles Saunders Peirce's view of meaning-making as a semiotic process, which he labeled semiosis (Cornbleth 1985; Dewey 1933; Eco, 1979; Siegel & Carey, 1989; Snyder, 1986). Semiosis combines three inter-related principles. First, it is geared towards a quest for *meaning*, rather than truth. This opens up the road to multiple, subjective, and context-bound interpretations of a single knowledge object. The second principle, a direct implication of the first, is the acceptance of and reliance on the ever-transient, cyclical and interpretive nature of meaning-making. This process is motivated by informed skepticism: given that the meaning of a phenomenon under study is context-bound, and that multiple alternative contexts may underlie it, a meaning product is never to be trusted. Each proposed interpretation is critically examined, and then discarded in favor of another, to be replaced in its own turn by yet another one; hence, the transient nature of the products which semiosis yields. The third principle underlying semiosis is an indirect implication of the first two. In semiosis, one focuses on *processes* of reflection, rather than their products. Its goal is to scrutinize meaning-making decision processes reflectively and critically. Its driving force is a persistent skepticism towards the validity of the mental tools used at any given point in the process. Thus, the de-validation of the transient meaning products is only a by-product of the main process. This allows a view of reflective reasoning as a particular case of semiosis, where the phenomenon under examination is thinking itself.

The second perspective is Bakhtin's (1981) portrayal of the meaning-making phenomenon as a dialogic, inter- and intra-subjective appropriation process. This approach puts an emphasis on the *personalization* process involved in tackling incoming linguistic input. According to this view, we actively transform words, intentions & messages of Others to accommodate our own mental world. Thus, in processing texts of Others, we 'appropriate' them, making them our very own. What we may think and write about them, then, will be infused with our unique view of the world, our own voice. It is interesting to note, that this dialogic process is directed both at ourselves and at Others: we deliberate ideas & messages put to us not only by Others, but also by ourselves. Thus, in processing incoming knowledge dialogically, we 'otherize' ourselves just as we personalize others.

The third perspective underlying the *Reflection Cycle* technique is a political view of epistemic authority, inspired by Michel Foucault's political view of knowledge/power (1981). Foucault offers a post-modern deconstruction of traditional conceptions of authoring knowledge, knowing and manipulating others into knowing – maintaining that it is power which defines knowledge as such. Paulo Freire's pedagogy presents a congruent critical view of knowledge and knowing. He argues that meaningful learning can occur only when learners possess epistemic power, with which 'to wrestle' with ideas and texts and 'write' the world (Shor, & Freire, 1990/1987). Hence, the crucial role of educational empowerment processes in developing critical literacy.

The fourth perspective underlying the technique to be presented here comes from constructivism. To begin with, constructivist educators view complex, cognitively-demanding, 'thoughtful' (Newmann, 1990) and 'mindful' (Langer, 1989; 1993; Salomon, 1983) *understanding performances* (Gardner, 1991; Perkins, 1992) as a mainstay of significant learning. Furthermore, they emphasize the crucial role of keen interest in the object of one's study, as well as his or her reliance on relevant personal prior knowledge on which to construct and create new knowledge. This is considered a pre-condition for significant learning (Fosnot, 1996, in Moursund, 1999). Furthermore, learning is viewed not merely as acquiring new knowledge by constructing something new on the foundations of what is already known. Rather, it is conceptualized as *manipulating* extant 'knowledge objects' (Bereiter & Scardamalia, 1998/1996; following Popper, 1972) and *generating* new ones as well. Thus, within this view, learning is conceived of a high-stake, personalized, individual enterprise.

The fifth theoretical perspective has to do with the specific *psychological dispositions* required for successful coping with complex, high-investment tasks. Perkins and his colleagues (Perkins, Jay, & Tishman, 1993; Langer, 1993; Perkins, 1995) make a strong case for the notion of *reflective intelligence* as a psychological disposition. This notion refers to one's ability to use broad-based strategies in a persistent, imaginative, systematic, self-monitoring and self-managing way – so as to tackle intellectually challenging learning and problem-solving tasks. Faccione (2000) defines this ability as open-mindedness, inquisitiveness, analicity, systematicity, and cognitive maturity.

Finally, the sixth theoretical influence on the *Reflection Cycle* technique to be presented in this chapter, comes from the view of writing as way of getting-to-know (Aspinwall, & Miller 1997; Deloney, Carey, & Geeman, 1998; Prescott, 2001; Sarig, 1996; 1997; Swartzendruber-Putnam, 2000). According to this expressionistic view, the mental state of writing generates a consciousness of knowing. In this state we either discover what we did not realize we knew, and/or we create new objects of knowledge altogether. Thus, one does not necessarily have 'to know' in order to write. It is the other way around: in order to know, one needs to write. Although there is no clear-cut evidence for these claims, (Galbraith, 1999), writers in various domains support it with reports from their authentic writing experiences.

Resting on this diverse rationale, the *Reflection Cycle* technique was developed with the realization that not all learners enjoy or practice a self-initiated disposition for spontaneous, strong-sense reflectivity, or the ambition to put a personal mark on texts written by others. It would rather seem that for other learners, especially children – this cultural habit of mind must be intentionally and explicitly cultivated. The Cycle was thus developed as a set of reflective and critical meaning-making acts, representing what mature learners, who are naturally disposed to critical and reflective learning, do expertly.

2. 'THE REFLECTION CYCLE': A DEMONSTRATION

In this section of the chapter I will describe each stop on the *Reflection Cycle*, and provide examples for its products. The texts, translated from Hebrew[1], were written by fifth and sixth graders from a small suburban elementary school[3].

The first stop on the cycle involves *Coordinating Expectations* from the learning resource at hand (e.g., a printed text of any genre; a play; a movie; a personal experience, etc.). The students working with the *Reflection Cycle* are taught to approach a text with a specific learning-writing goal in mind. In this learning environment all texts brought to class, regardless of genre or complexity level, are subjugated to specific writing goals outside the texts themselves, and are therefore seldom approached solely for their own sake (as they could be when analyzed as wholes for their poetic properties, for instance). The work in this stop helps learners to focus their reading-writing efforts on those aspects of the text, which match their particular learning-writing goals. The purpose of this stop is, then, to approach the text vis-à-vis a specific learning goal in mind. For instance, when writing-to-reflect about Absalom's conspiracy in the second book of Samuel[4], Guy, a sixth grader reminds himself of his learning goal: understanding the role of the three dominant figures in the narrative (text #1):

> In the reflection Cycle on Absalom's mutiny I focused on three dominant figures:
> - Absalom, son of King David
> - King David
> - Joab the son of Zeruiah (chief of David's army)
> since I think they are the 'rounded' figures in this story (whether realistic or popular – I wonder), who put the whole story of the mutiny into motion, sure there are other figures related to the mutiny such as: Ahitophel, Hushai the Archite and more...
> Nevertheless I do not think there are other figures with the same status of the three 'heroes' in Absalom's mutiny. (Guy, sixth grade)

---

[1] *All texts, except in Figures 1 & 2 are translated from Hebrew. In translating the texts, care was taken to maintain the original text segmentation, as well as linguistic, textual and communicative appropriateness level. Similarly, the semantic maps in the chapter (Figures 3 & 4) were formatted as closely as possible to the original source.*

The purpose of the second stop on the Cycle, *Relating to Prior Knowledge*, is to inculcate in learners the intentional habit of mind involved first, in retrieving Prior Knowledge in relation to the text and topic at hand, and second, assessing its quality in terms of relevance, accuracy and completeness. Text #2 (Figure 1) presents a representation of prior knowledge in the form of a semantic map. Having mastered the basic skills involved in semantic mapping, the Anonymous fifth grader who wrote it chose it as a mode of representing his or her extant knowledge on sea & coast pollution – the topic of discourse to be reflected and learned from.

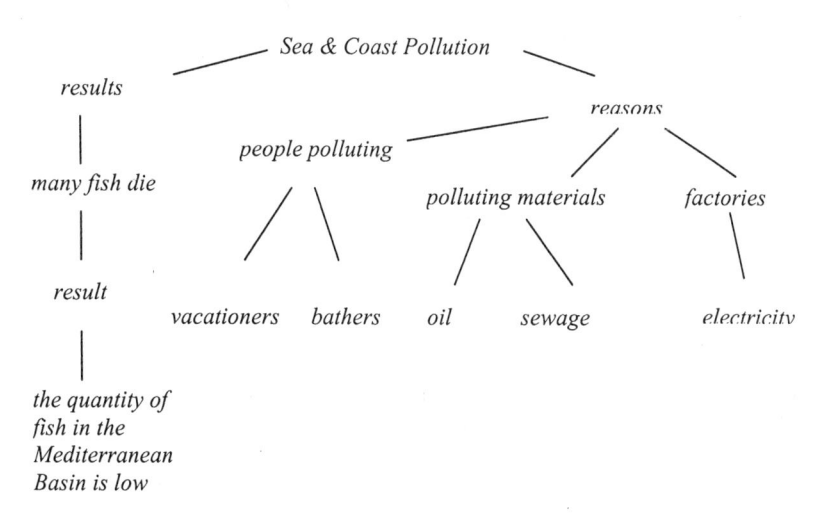

```
                    Sea & Coast Pollution
    results                                    
                                        reasons
       |           people polluting    
   many fish die                       /    \
              /  \         polluting materials   factories
                                /    \              \
    result                                            
              vacationers  bathers  oil  sewage   electricity
       |
   the quantity of
   fish in the
   Mediterranean
   Basin is low
```

Figure 1. Text #2: A semantic map representing prior knowledge by an anonymous fifth grader.

In text #3 (Table 1, left hand side column), Amit, a sixth grader, reflects on a short poem by Shel Silverstein (1981). His or her text offers a more discursive version of the work done with this stop, showing how the young learner, already at home with the technique, works with this stop spontaneously, in interaction with other stops. Parsing the text into stanzas (Gee, 1996; Sarig 2002), and analyzing the thinking moves underlying each, reveals nine reflective acts, five of which implicate relating the text to prior knowledge. These appear on the right hand side column.

Table 1: Text #3: Integrative Use of the Stops on the Reflection Cycle by Amit, Sixth Grade

Text	Stop
(1) In my opinion Shoshi is one of those of our gang who do not try to understand the different (in the case of this story Ariel is the different) and these children sometimes hurt the children severely and sometimes there are cases when they hurt the children less, but they always hurt children, (2) what I really don't understand and I truly do try to understand is how they laugh at the different if all people are different and according to what they decide on the standards of who is different and who is not different. (3) We also always see that the children who got determined as different always try not to be different but for some reason those who are determined as not different will keep on hurting them and probably will never turn them into not different and try to accept those that they decided that they are different so they will turn them too into different. (4) It seems to me that Shoshi could have talked to Ariel if indeed she had wanted to because in the case of the story either there was the teacher or she could have asked his interpreter. (5) Society, which thinks highly of itself, actually does not think of the emotions of others like Shoshi didn't know how Ariel was feeling. (6) I too have a case in which I want to do something, something that up till now only one child in the class has done, and I remember the two or three kids who laughed at him and I am sure hurt him and I am afraid to take the same step, because then they will laugh at me too.	(1) Judging based on re-contextualized prior knowledge (2) Detecting & diagnosing a difficulty (3) Recontextualizing based of prior knowledge (4) Judging based on re-contextualized prior knowledge (5) Judging based on re-contextualized prior knowledge (6) Relating to prior knowledge
(7) According to my opinion Shoshi missed out on a very important message that Ariel tried to communicate to her and she didn't get it (8) and therefore one misses out on beautiful things in life when one doesn't try to understand or when there is no trust between the two.	(7) Judging (8) Transforming & Re-contextualizing
(9) Here in the story it is told about disconnected communication because communication works only when two or more try and make an effort to understand each other…	(9) Transforming

The third stop on the Cycle involves *Detecting & Diagnosing Difficulties* in the text. The first purpose of this stop is to instill in the learners the 'strong-sense' commitment to tackle their difficulties, rather than use them as an excuse to avoid the learning task altogether, as some of them may be inclined to do. It teaches them the habit of analyzing, and thus diagnosing, the sort of difficulty they are facing as a first step toward overcoming it. Working with this stop requires a rich meta-linguistic, meta-strategic database, which, in turn, gets constantly enriched – as the students learn how to analyze, diagnose and label each new difficulty they face for future reference. In spite of the importance of this stop, culturally it is sometimes hard to convince students of all ages that declaring a difficulty in public, let alone document it in writing, is good for you. In some classes students need to undergo an acculturation process, whereby the members of the class reach an agreement on a series of learning values, which they all commit themselves to respect and adopt.

Texts #4 & #5 below present the work of two sixth graders, who have apparently adopted the value of taking pride in one's ability to spot, analyze and diagnose comprehension hurdles. In Text #4 Sharon lists some difficulties she encountered when reading a poem comparing Man to a tree – in the form of discrete questions:

1. What does "nipped" mean?
2. Man is "caught in fire [sic], man gets burnt?
3. "I feel a bitter taste in my mouth", the tree feels a bitter taste?
4. Why is Man "cut off" too, like the tree?
5. Stanza 3, what does it want to say?
6. Why is it written about the tree of the field that "Where was I and where will I be?"
7. Don't we know where we are?
8. Why does Man keep thirsty like the tree of the field?
9. Thirsty for what?
10. Wishing for what?
11. What does the poem want to say?
12. Why the tree of the field particularly?
13. "Buried me", so I am dead? (Sharon, Sixth grade).

In comparison, in text #5 below, Yotam offers a more discursive version of work with this stop. His text allows us to witness the development of his reflective encounter with the biblical affair of the war between the house of Saul and the house of David, in the second book of Samuel:

The chapter has many open questions for which there are no clear answers:
I did not understand for example why Abner crowned the people of Rosheth king. Whereas when Saul was dead, the king returned the rule to David?
In addition, I didn't understand how there could be two kings in the people? Was this acceptable at that period? The people would divide into two groups, and each group would have its own king?
I don't understand what David had been doing for forty years (not taking into consideration the seven years when he ruled the tribe of Judea and Hebron), while Ish-Bosheth ruled over Israel? Was David out of any office?
Another point I didn't understand was why did Abner kill Asahel? Was it out of self-defence? Couldn't he just ignore the provocation and keep on going?... (Yotam, sixth grade).

As these two different instances show, the activity in this stop puts the authority of raising questions and difficulties back in the hands of the learners. It is he or she who wants to know something (the learner) that asks the questions and raises the difficulties – rather than he or she who knows the answers (the teacher). Thus, in adopting the reflective acts involved in this stop, the young learners take active responsibility for their learning difficulties, and by doing so – actually promote comprehension.

In the fourth stop, *Selecting Relevant Knowledge* from the text, learners construct a knowledge base on which to reflect. Text #6, based on 'The Poor Man's Sheep' parable, in the second book of Samuel, offers an example for this in the form of a telegraphic gist.

> There was one poor man and he had only one single sheep, which he loved dearly. There was one rich man and he had lots of sheep and cattle and the rich took the sheep away from the poor man (Anonymous, sixth grade; Presented in handwriting).

In comparison, some learners prefer an idea list format.

In some learning contexts, the work with this stop differs from the traditional 'gist', or 'main ideas' tasks in that – as pointed out earlier – the frame of reference for selecting relevant information is the learning task at hand, rather than the text as a whole. This means that it is not the text as a whole that is under study, but rather the topic of inquiry. In this way, only those idea units from the text that can contribute to furthering the knowledge topic of inquiry will enter the database, on which the reflection will take place.

The fifth stop, *Judging*, engages the learners in direct critical thinking. They may use the stop to relate to moral, ethical or logical aspects of the subject matter with which they take issue; they can reflect on the relevance of the text to their topic of inquiry; its interest level, importance and aesthetic value. Text #7 offers an example for the work in this stop. In this text, Yotam reflects on the dramatic struggle between Saul's and David's followers, in a chapter from the second book of Samuel. He first reflects on the credibility of the story, and its relevance to the realities of life 'here and now'. He then makes a series of moral judgments of the actions taken by its heroes. Finally he judges the level of complexity of the chapter and assesses it as "very complicated for understanding". Nevertheless, finally he re-affirms its value:

> I liked the text because it teaches about games, that finally turn into quarrels – it teaches about one of the reasons because of which civil wars occur. The story is very convincing. Because it is realistic. The text is relevant and timely. Nowadays too civil wars occur. Which include controversies. Slander. Verbal abuse. And even physical violence. Between gangs. Groups of Arabs and Israelis. Secular and conservative people. Jews and Christians. Between parties in the Right and in the Left. And more.
> I think Abner should not have offered Joab at all to get the two armies to play a game. Joab certainly should not have accepted. Both should have been aware of the fact that there could have developed a situation which would lead to war.
> I think that Asahel made a mistake when he provoked Abner. He should not have played it a "hero".
> I think Abner was right when he suggested to stop the war. Joab too was wise when he agreed to stop the war.
> I think that all the bloodshed in this war was uncalled for. After all, the two enemy groups were brother-tribes.
> The chapter is very complicated for understanding, but finally we realize that it is very useful (Yotam, sixth grade).

Work with this stop often merges synergistically with the work on the sixth stop, *Deliberating* issues in the texts, as text #8 below shows. This stop offers the learners a cognitive environment in which to problematize their understanding of the issue at hand. They use it to weigh competing meaning options, explanations and interpretations; to tackle paradoxes, contradictions, text absences & silences and to construct problematic value judgments. Text #8 offers an example for the work done in this stop. In it Guy, a sixth grader, deliberates the complex moral issue of conflicting responsibilities:

> Judging:
>
> Absalom's mutiny starts from Absalom's wish to be king in spite of the sense of guilt over killing Amnon.
> Judging the mutiny is complicated and cumbersome so I will first judge all the dominant figures in the mutiny.
> I will start with Absalom, the creator of the mutiny, in my opinion the beginning of the mutiny could have been on another later date namely, maybe in his heart of hearts David does want Absalom for an heir and if David does not wish so then he can set out on a mutiny.
> King David – David set out on the mutiny after many ploys, such as: Hushai the Archite who offered bad advice to Absalom by means of his weak point – his ego.
> David instructed explicitly not to kill Absalom.
> In my opinion the two stances are correct but still there is only one just stance.
> David is Absalom's father after all (although he had killed Amnon).
> Absalom starts the mutiny with only one thought to kill David so David has to protect himself.
> Joab (David's captain of the guards) Joab disobeyed David, who explicitly said not to kill Absalom Joab killed him with one thought to protect the king. I think Joab was in the right because he murdered just out of respect for David although he did not obey [his] order and that is why he deserves a punishment.
>
> Deliberation:
> In Absalom's mutiny there were many deliberations, and I wrote some of them:
> My first deliberation is, why Absalom did not speak with David about the inheritance of the crown.
>
> Why did David demand not to hurt Absalom although Absalom wants David's death? One important question that is certainly related to the deliberation is: what are David's motives in murdering Absalom?
>
> One motive is known but still [I] know [sic, spelling error in Hebrew] "his silence with David is not clean" namely Joab did many things against David's will and now he does one more thing, The point for thought is did Joab think of the punishment that he will get from David? (Guy, sixth grade)

The seventh stop on the Cycle is *Conceptual Transforming*. In this stop the learners transform pieces of linear information in the text into a coherent, hierarchical whole, on the basis of their personal interpretation of the information relevant to their topic of inquiry. From a dialogic point of view, this stop offers an opportunity for the personalization of the source text, as first, the transformation is based on a personal interpretation of the text, and second, the transformation is based on only those parts of the text, which promote the learners' personal learning goal. From a textual-cognitive point of view, this stop promotes a deeper understanding of the source text, as it involves contemplating the logical relations between its components and their relative rhetorical functions. In doing so, it yields a hierarchically-organized version of the source text. This is why in most cases, the transformed meaning is represented schematically, usually by means of a simple semantic map, to be later developed into a full, discursive text. This sophisticated process thus generates a synergistic interaction between creative acts of mind on the one hand, and structural, systematic thinking, on the other. Text #9 & #10 offer examples for the work done in this stop. Text #9 presents the source text:

> How do unpopular children cope with their situation? The smart ones among them find in the class, or in another class, a faithful friend, whom they can trust. Such a friend helps prevent total isolation and compensates for the frustration caused by the attitude of the majority of children. Such children learn to cope with their share of hurt and insults. These children say that deep inside they cry, and on the outside they play it strong. Anyway, relationship with one child, whose love and support they can count on, is compensation. But there are children who cannot make even one friend, and then they are lonely and hurt (London, 1994:32).

Text #10 (Figure 2 below) presents the map which re-conceptualizes it. In this instance, the Anonymous sixth grader transformed the source text by creating a structure of a comparison between two types of children. This re-conceptualization makes an implicit rhetorical structure, underlying the surface text – explicit. Had the text offered an explicit comparison in the first place, it may have been more reader-friendly. In this way, the transforming stop both promotes a deeper understanding of the source text, and offers learners implicit instruction for writing their own texts in the future.

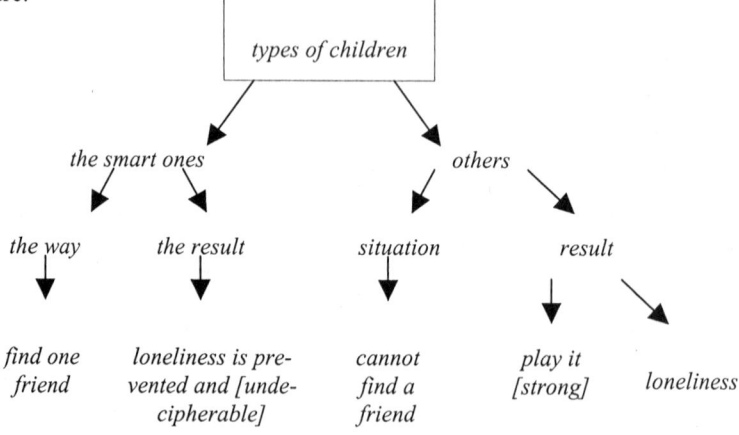

```
                    ┌─────────────────┐
                    │ types of children│
                    └─────────────────┘
                      ↙           ↘
              the smart ones      others
                ↙      ↘          ↙      ↘
           the way  the result  situation  result
              ↓        ↓          ↓       ↓    ↘
           find one  loneliness is pre-  cannot  play it  loneliness
           friend    vented and [unde-   find a  [strong]
                     cipherable]         friend
```

Figure 2. Text #10: The transforming map by an anonymous, sixth grader (presented in handwriting).

The eighth stop on the cycle is *Re-Contextualizing* the newly gained knowledge. In this stop the learners are free to 'take off', as it were, with the new knowledge, and manipulate it in new contexts, breaking away from original learning context and learning goal – as they please. This is, then, actually the only reflective stop where learners are free of the main constraint underlying all the other stops: the specifically defined learning goal controlling the task. This stop provides an outlet for the children's creative drives, and for teachers who may feel the need to break away from the strict constraints of academic writing. Some writers use this stop to let their thoughts wander and hover, as it were, around the topic of discourse, thus enabling them to combine traditional writing with other channels of self-expression. Some learners use the stop for partially-verbal, and even non-verbal reflection. My data include a rich variety of verbal re-contextualizations, such as letters written to authors of the texts and to their relatives; casting the author as a figure in a reportage; T.V. mini-dramas dramatizing the issue at hand; advertisements; poems; interviews and dialogues – as well as non-verbal ones, such as drawings, games, symbols & icons; cartoons and comics. Texts #11 & #12 (Figures 3 & 4) demonstrate the learning products created in this stop. Both are re-contextualizations of the poem "For Man is like The Tree of the Field" by the Israeli poet Nathan Zakh (1988). They present two types of re-contextualizations based on this poem, illustrating two different readings of its message.

In the first (Figure 3), Sharon, a sixth grader, crosses both genre and domain boundaries by recasting the poem as a news item, entitled "A News Flash: A Demonstration for the Sake of Trees". In the item Sharon reports a protest against replacing a green forest near Jerusalem with a shopping Mall. In her reportage, she specifies a place and a date for the imaginary event she creates, as well as the conditions under which a group of contractors intend to build the mall. She describes the scene; quotes the caption on the demonstrators' protest signs and enumerates their arguments. She creates drama by citing bits of fierce dialogue; reporting the tearing down of the contractor's sign designating the forest as a destruction site, and emphasizing the protestor's call to kill themselves along with the trees. Her language choices indicate an attempt to mimic the register of a typical news item. The story is followed by a drawing composed of three icons, re-iterating both the content and rhetorical structure the poem.

Figure 3. An illustration of a poem by Sharon, 6th Grade.

Figure 4 presents an example for an illustrating re-contextualization, more non-verbal in nature, where an Anonymous sixth grader concretizes the message of the same poem by comparing the lower part of a human being to a cut-off tree trunk. He or she then further illustrates the notion by another drawing and two captions, based on the poem: "… Like Man the tree also gets cut off…" and "…Like Man, the tree is also thirsty…"

Figure 4. An illustrating re-contextualization by an anonymous 6th grader.

The last stop on the Cycle, *Linking,* involves assessing learning outcomes and creating future learning goals. In this stop the learners reflect on the contribution of the learning source to their learning goal. This affords them a more educated starting point from which to set new, more focused learning goals, and set out on a search for relevant learning resources. This, in turn, enables them first, to further their knowledge on yet unsettled issues related to their topic of inquiry, and second – to start a new learning cycle by developing new learning goals, now based on an enlarged body of relevant prior knowledge.

Text #13 by Etie, a sixth grader, provides an example for this. Etie uses this stop to produce two sets of questions: "My research questions that this text answers" and "The questions that this text arouses in me":

> This text relates to many of my topics of inquiry, such as the way drug users feel, their lack of communicating to reality and the severity of taking the substance…
>
> My research questions that this text answers are:
> a. What are the causes for drug abuse?
> b. Which organizations deal with drug prevention?
> c. How does the drug abuser feel?
> d. What are the reasons for being dragged to abuse drugs?
> The questions that this text arouses in me:

a. Which types of drugs are there?
b. What is the source of the drugs? Who markets them?
c. Which is the population, that usually abuses drugs?
d. What ways are there for drug withdrawal?
e. How is it possible to stop and prevent the dealers from marketing drugs?
f. How is it possible to stop and prevent youth and adults from abusing drugs? (Etie, sixth grade; Presented in handwriting).

Figure 5 below presents a schematic view of *Reflection Cycle* as a whole.

Coordinating Expectations

Linking: Assessing Learning Outcomes & Creating New Learning Goals

Relating to Prior Knowledge

Re- Contextualizing

Detecting & Diagnosing Difficulties

Conceptual Transforming

Deliberating

Selecting Relevant Knowledge

Judging

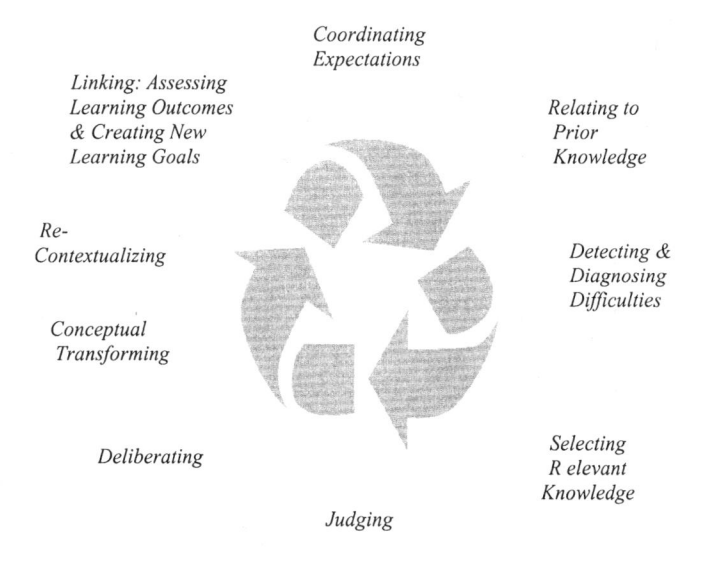

Figure 5. Stops on the reflection cycle: An overview.

3. USES & MISUSES OF THE TECHNIQUE

3.1 Learning Contexts

The *Reflection Cycle* can be used in various learning contexts where reflective thinking is called for. For the most part, it is used in relation to a specific *text* at the heart of the learning event (e.g., in Bible or literature studies) – as in most of the examples above. In this context, reflective writing will be done in dialogic response to a text of any genre used in class (e.g., a textbook chapter; an encyclopedic entry; a web text; a section of a play; a poem; an advertisement; a newspaper article, etc.). For instance, the technique can be applied to a text related to a specifically defined topic, such as 'Coping with Rejection' (as in text #10 above), which the students learn as part of a research project. In another context, the Cycle is used in relation to a certain *topic* – independently of a text, to reflect on extant knowledge related to it. In this learning situation, teachers may use it either as an introduction to a new topic (such as 'Sea & Coast Pollution' – as in text #2 above); as part of a concluding session, or a review. In the last two cases the reflective text that the learners create relates directly to acquired knowledge itself, (as in text #2 above), rather than to a learning source mediating it.

3.2 Recommended Training Procedure & Technique Management

Each stop on the *Reflection Cycle* represents a learning act, which is characteristic of mature learning behavior. Teachers are well advised to conceive of it as a set of *habits of mind*, to be used spontaneously and judiciously – not merely as a linear string of mechanical performances. Thus, once it is exercised and internalized, it can be discarded.

As will be emphasized in section 3.4 below, the training procedure that the *Reflection Cycle* necessitates is highly vulnerable to over-training and misuse. As an attempt to minimize such potential damage, following is a proposal for a recommended training sequence. Clearly, there is more than one 'correct' way to handle the training stage – depending on the multiple constraints that a specific learning situation may entail (e.g., learners' age & cognitive ability level; teaching and learning styles; various school cultures, etc.). Thus, the following proposal should be treated as a general template, which teachers can adapt and then apply to the specific context in which they wish to work with the Cycle.

Four pedagogical principles underlie the proposed sequence:
1) *A gradual shift of control*: As the training progresses, control of the learning process relocates gradually, moving from the teacher to the students. Throughout the training phase it is the teacher who initiates use of the technique; sets the pace & the learning goals; spots and diagnoses misuses in implementing the Cycle, and helps to put slower learners on the right track in case they fail. However, once the Cycle is mastered, it is meant to replace traditional learning tasks, and is to be used by the students independently.
2) *A shift from implicit to explicit instruction*: In the preparatory phases of the training sequence it is recommended that the learners be exposed to various acts on the Cycle implicitly. Thus, explicit metacognitive, metalinguistic & procedural information involved in intelligent use of the cycle will be offered to the learners only at a later stage.
3) *Structured & unstructured use of the stops on the Cycle:* Following the training phase, all the stops on the cycle are to be used recursively, in unpredictable combinations & interactions. This means that there is no telling which of the stops would be selected for use; use of which stop would necessarily entail the use of others, and what the order of the stops selected for use would be. However, it is reasonable to recommend that on the first encounter with a new text to be reflected on, work with the first four stops (*Coordinating expectations; Relating to prior knowledge; Detecting & diagnosing difficulties* and *Selecting relevant knowledge*) precede the work with all others.
4) *Varied learning/teaching formats*: The proposed training process can be applied in various classroom formats – depending on teaching traditions within the

school, teaching and learning styles, and learners' age and ability level. In an ideal situation, intensive group and individual work should follow a short plenary introduction and demonstration of a new stop. Having introduced it, either in the implicit or explicit phase, the teacher can now use smaller-format class configurations to support slow-learners. She or he can supply additional explanation and demonstration of the stops; detect miscomprehension and/or misuse in implementing the stop under study; offer supplementary instruction, etc. To wrap up a session, the class can return to the plenary format, as the whole class shares a selection of students' written products publicly.

Bearing these principles in mind, following is a description of a five-phase training sequence for the *The Reflection Cycle* technique. Phase One involves *inexplicit introduction of the stops*. In this 'practice without preaching' phase, naturally occurring learning contexts can be used as opportunities to practise various stops on the cycle without naming them or explaining what they are all about. For instance, to introduce use of the *Coordinating expectations* stop, each time a new text is approached, the teacher can ask the learners to think/write about the purpose for which they are reading it. Similarly, to introduce the *Relating to prior knowledge* stop, the teacher can make a point to start each new learning unit (e.g., topic, chapter in a book, etc.) by having students write-to-reflect about their prior pieces of knowledge on the topic, and then have them share their products with the whole class. Other stops may be approached indirectly in similar manner.

In parallel, teachers should start creating with the learners *new value systems* in preparation for stops that may generate a cultural clash with competing learning behaviors. For instance, in preparation for the *Detecting & diagnosing difficulties* stop teachers must make a special effort to show their students that they respect their ability to detect, describe, specify and eventually even diagnose their difficulties in comprehending concepts, texts or explanations discussed in and out of class. They must convince their students that contrary to what they may have experienced in other learning environments, in their classes detection of difficulty is respected, praised and rewarded – instead of penalized.

Phase Two of the training initiates *explicit presentation of each stop on the Cycle*. Once the indirect preparation stage is completed, and the students have experienced the stops on the Cycle indirectly and inexplicitly, teachers can launch the explicit and systematic training phase. This should be done as gradually as possible, introducing each stop separately – on different lessons, preferably even on different school days. A recommended way of going about this is to select an intriguing but concise text, and use it repeatedly each time a new stop is added on to the learners repertoire. This can help show the learners how each new stop enriches their thinking about a text they already know.

Phase Three allows temporary *work with the Cycle as a whole*. Once all the stops on the cycle have been explicitly introduced and practiced piecemeal, the students are ready to experience the impact of the full cycle as a whole. To complete this stage, teachers can now select one, or maximum two additional short texts, and have the learners write about each reflectively, using all the stops on the Cycle. At this point it is crucial to avoid over-practice, and restrict the full Cycle practice to a maximum of three texts – preferably dealt on different school days.

Phase Four of the training involves *independent and selective use of the Cycle*. It is now time to introduce the ultimate mode of using of the cycle: spontaneous and judicious selection and implementation of the stops. The students are now expected to use it not only on their teacher's demand – but also on their own initiative. In this unstructured learning environment the children use the 'stops' on the Cycle as optional writing opportunities. They are encouraged to use them cyclically: prior to, during and following the reading of the text to be learnt from, or a topic to process. The students can now be entrusted with the selection of one or multiple stops, from which to write/think about a text or a topic – be it each stop separately, or a few stops interactively. The latter case is demonstrated in text #3 (Table 1 above), which exhibits a series of spontaneous interactions of different stops in various combinations.

The teacher has now turned from initiator to advisor: he or she can now supervise what the students are doing; offer them help, advice, evaluation or extra training – as the case may be. Having completed this phase, the learners are ready to optimize their use of the Cycle and incorporate it into their learning routines in an independent and spontaneous manner.

Phase Five introduces the last stage of the training: *metacognitive & procedural specialization*. By now the learners are ready to be taught how to use the stops on the cycle more knowledgeably, exercising increasing degrees of metacognitive control of the technique. The teachers can now plan special sessions, where they can teach particular theoretical knowledge pertaining to various stops on the Cycle. They can now share with their students metalinguistic terms with which to diagnose comprehension difficulties; procedural knowledge which would help them with semantic mapping; metacognitive strategies with which to monitor the relevance and truth-value of prior knowledge, etc. To introduce these notions and procedures for the first time, teachers can use the plenary format. They can then further develop and elaborate on them in small format exchanges; for instance, they can expand a small group, or an individual feedback session to teach some more advanced metacognitive information. Once teacher and students have established a mutual metalinguistic vocabulary, he or she can use other interactions with the class, both planned and occasional, to further elaborate on any theoretical point called for.

3.3 Benefits for Teachers and Learners

Teachers who use the technique regularly report they find it attractive for several reasons. First, once the training stage is over, the children have full autonomy over the use of the technique in learning from new texts, so the teachers are free of the responsibility for preparing and administering new learning assignments for each learning event. Secondly, they report that children of varying abilities find the Cycle a friendly learning environment – from slow learners with special needs, who are integrated into regular classes, to high-achievers. Third, some teachers admit they find comfort in the structure which the technique brings to what they may perceive as the chaotic freedom of reflective thinking. They can thus use the technique as a learning environment which offers structure within this chaos, without having to give up on a flexible, personalized and open-ended knowledge construction process.

As for the learners, feedback from children and teachers, product analysis, learners' and teachers' documentary logs and classroom observations give rise to several impressions. To begin with, when the Cycle is introduced gradually and exercised flexibly & judiciously, it appears that most children enjoy writing with it and take pride in the texts they create and the knowledge they gain. Secondly, they seem to go through significant learning experiences. In an entry in a documentary log written by a special education fourth grader, he reflected on his learning experience with the *Prior Knowledge* stop, which he used in relation to the topic of 'Peer Pressure'. He commented there with a heightened sense of social and personal awareness, as well as with some wonder and regret, that on that day he and his peers "...found out that unfortunately we knew a lot about the topic." In classrooms where the technique is used as a standard learning procedure, the learners seem to prefer working with it to traditional writing tasks because they experience its learning impact. In a movie documenting work with semantic mapping involved in the *Conceptual transforming* stop (Sarig, 1994), a six grader offered a learned comparison of the technique with traditional learning tasks, such as open-ended questions. He concluded that it is on all counts preferable, as it led to what he characterized s deep, leaning experiences. Finally, the learners seem to pick up writing-to-learn as a natural learning habit, sometimes even initiating it, and suggesting to the teacher to use it when they perceive it is necessary.

3.4 Misuses and Pitfalls

Useful as the Reflection Cycle may be for teachers and students alike, the benefits described above appear to be highly constrained, as the technique is prone to misuse and misapplication. Feedback from learners and teachers, product analysis and classroom observations indicate two major problems. First, for most children, and for that matter, for some teachers, the use of writing as a tool for thinking (and in formal school contexts, for reflective thinking as well) is highly non-habitual. The technique therefore necessitates intensive training. This might, in turn, lead to overuse, or compulsive, rather than free & spontaneous use of the technique. In some cases, over-zealous or anxious teachers tend to 'cram' presentation of the whole Cycle at one time, rather than use occasional opportunities for introducing and exercising it piecemeal – a single relevant 'stop' in a pertinent context, as proposed in section 3.2 above. In extreme cases, teachers might go so far as using the Cycle as the only teaching/learning strategy, and use it repeatedly, without allowing to use it openly and selectively.

Another danger lies in attempts to translate the Cycle, so to speak, into a more familiar, 'normal' task. Teachers and students alike have been observed transforming the Cycle into a list of questions to be answered. There is nothing wrong with operationalizing the stops by using the familiar question form. However, once the children are up against a list of consecutive questions, they may treat the task as such, and produce an efficient list of discrete and consecutive answers. This might lead to flat, non-reflective and contrived products, thus stifling its spirit, missing its point and yielding counter-productive results (Sarig, 2000).

4. CONCLUSION

The technique presented in this chapter offers young learners a structured space in which to acquire reflective habits of mind by means of writing-to-think. When applied openly and judiciously, especially in the acquiring stage, it is rich and flexible enough to suit a variety of disciplinary, inter and multi-disciplinary school topics, and provide individual learners with a space for personalizing new knowledge in a mindful way.

The Cycle offers a practical application for the six theoretical perspectives, which inspired it. It emulates mature semiosis by offering multiple readings of a single text or idea through multiple writing acts and by emphasizing critical deliberation. In so doing, the Cycle creates an empowering learning environment, which encourages and puts to practice abstract dialogic ethics, thus elevating the epistemic status of the learners and enabling them 'to write' the texts of Others – much in the spirit of Bakhtinian philosophy and Freirean pedagogy. The cycle calls for the personalization of incoming knowledge; it capitalizes on learners' extant knowledge and presents them with the opportunity to create new, transformed objects of knowledge. It calls for cognitively demanding understanding performances in an authentic task environment, and thus it may be claimed to practise the basic elements of constructivist approaches to teaching and learning. Finally, the cycle uses writing as an instrument for thinking, thus using the potential of writing to initiate, generate, shape and transform knowledge. In directing the learners to tackle a learning source from reflective and creative perspectives – which for some of them would not come naturally – it cultivates their reflective disposition.

However, as extensive experience with the technique shows, like any teaching heuristic, it, too, can be put to abuse, especially during the training stage. Training learners to use the technique may turn out to be tedious and counter-productive, if it is repeatedly offered to them as a whole. In addition, even at later stages, when it is used mechanically, rather than openly and flexibly, it may lead to stilted, inauthentic writing products.

By now the technique has been used widely enough to merit systematic research. This should focus first on the conditions, under which learners benefit from it: which disciplines, domains, topics and text-types are more suited than others, for optimizing use of the technique? In what ways can its use interact with individual learning styles? A related line of research should focus on the type of gains it may yield, given the right conditions: how can the knowledge gains be characterized and assessed[2]? How does use of the technique interact with the culture of learning in classes where it is used regularly? Another interesting line of research concerns the developmental aspect of using the technique: how long does it take for learners of

---

[2] *Rubrics for assessing reflective writing are offered in Sarig (1996).*

different age groups and cognitive level to master each stop on the cycle? How do they differ in terms of the type of coaching they need until they use the technique spontaneously? The products of such studies may hopefully contribute to further fine-tune this promising, but misuse-prone technique.

AUTHOR'S NOTE

This chapter is an extended version of a paper delivered at the Symposium "Reflection and Metacognition in Primary School Writing", in the bi-annual meeting of SIG Writing (EARLI), Staffordshire University, Staffordshire, July 2002.

ACKNOWLEDGEMENTS

I would like to express my sincere gratitude to Lea Dayan, Dalia Vald and Amalya Sayag of the "Lapid" elementary school in Hod Hasharon and to Zahava Kfir & Yaffa Halabby of the Ministry of Education in the Tel Aviv District, for allowing me to develop and test the 'Reflection Cycle' technique in their schools and classrooms, as well as for sharing with me their students' written products.

I am indebted to Shula Keshet for her expert advice on the meaning of the reflections written by the children on the biblical topics.

I would like to thank Lieve Vanmaele and Roger Beard for their most useful remarks on the various aspects of teaching & using the Reflection Cycle in the classroom.

REFLECTIVE WRITING & REFLECTIVE THINKING

The implications of introducing reflective practice into a professional doctorate programme in Pharmacy

PETE SAYERS

University of Bradford, UK

Abstract. This chapter reports on the use of reflective journals as pieces of assessed work in a recently introduced Doctorate of Pharmacy (DPharm) programme at the University of Bradford, UK. The analysis in this chapter examines the challenges that writing a reflective journal has posed for the students on the DPharm programme. There is a broader context for Pharmacy education as a whole, which this chapter also touches on, as the role of reflection in professional development for pharmacists is a relatively new development. The chapter describes the strategy used by the author to develop reflective writing skills in students whose previous academic writing has been in the style of scientific reports. The author identifies four "interim styles" that students have adopted en route to reflective writing, gives examples of these and offers reasons why these styles emerge. Many of the reasons are in the affective domain. The conclusion is that developing reflective writing requires the development of reflective thinking, and is a personal development issue as much as one of writing development.

Keywords: Reflective writing, reflective journal, reflective thinking, interim styles, tutored practice, personal development, professional development.

1. INTRODUCTION

At the time of publication the Doctorate of Pharmacy (DPharm) has been running for three years. My role is to help students develop their ability to write a reflective journal. This chapter contains some of my own reflection on working with the students on the programme. My approach is that of the practitioner seeking meaning from experience – an approach anchored in Action Research and Ethnomethodology. The chapter contains my reflections on practice from working with three cohorts of students on the DPharm programme. It describes the approach I have taken

Sayers, P. (2004). Reflective writing & reflective thinking. The implications of introducing reflective practice into a professional doctorate programme in Pharmacy.
In G. Rijlaarsdam (Series Ed.) and Rijlaarsdam, G., Van den Bergh, H. & Couzijn, M. (Vol. Eds.), Studies in writing, Volume 14, Effective learning and teaching of writing, 2nd edition, Part 3, Studies in writing-to-learn, 519 - 531.

to help them understand the process of reflective writing. One objective is to reflect on their practice as pharmacists in order to aid their professional development. A second objective is to learn how to write a reflective journal as a piece of academic prose. Developing a reflective style of writing is a challenge for these students. The process of learning this new style of writing has taken the students through a number of interim styles – stages en route to reflective writing. This chapter charts a number of those interim steps towards reflective writing.

To date there have been three students on each year's intake. With such small numbers it is not possible to draw quantitative conclusions. It is, however, possible during the first few years of a programme at this level to identify questions that merit exploration. The interim steps are presented tentatively to stimulate interest and further investigation. All the students have showed these steps to varying extents. What I have attempted in this chapter is to identify these interim steps and to describe them in terms that have offered the students, as individuals and as a group, a way of making sense of them as developmental feedback.

The term "student" may be misleading here – the people involved are experienced hospital pharmacists doing the DPharm programme as part of their professional development. The programme is part-time and work based. Students are allocated a "Clinical Tutor" – a senior colleague in their hospital. The programme is designed to last five years. For each of years 1 to 3 of the programme, students undertake a number of taught modules and produce a portfolio of developments in their clinical practice under the supervision of their clinical tutor. A 2000 word reflective journal is the assessed piece of work that describes the learning from practice – i.e., the professional development derived from the activities recorded in the portfolio. Reflective writing has been introduced as a way of assessing the learning from practice that is implicit in continued professional development to doctoral level. At the end of year 3 students write a further long (10,000 word) reflective journal to provide evidence of their learning and development over the whole of part 1 of the DPharm programme. This is expected to include reflections on academic / research papers as well as clinical practice. During part 2 (the final two years) students do a work-based research project.

My role in the programme is as the university-based tutor for the reflective journal module (culminating in the "long" reflective journal). In effect this has meant helping the students with the 2000 word reflective journals as well. My experience is as an applied linguist who moved from teaching English as a second language into training on cross-cultural communication and implementing equal opportunities policies. I have since become a generic staff developer at the university, responding to requests for assistance from colleagues in a wide variety of disciplines. My previous writing has been on issues in management development and educational development, and how these can be assisted through a personal development approach, i.e., facilitating individual or group learning in a holistic way. It is from this background that I approach the role of helping DPharm students acquire the writing style appropriate for a reflective journal.

There is little history of reflective practice within pharmacy education. Helping students on the DPharm to understand the style and format of a reflective journal has required an equal focus on reflective thinking and action learning, developing the assumption that you can't write reflectively, if you can't make explicit your thinking process. Indeed, to introduce a new style of writing seems to require a new style of thinking. The development of reflective writing has become a wider personal development issue for the students involved.

The idea of the "reflective practitioner" has been developed over a number of years and in a variety of different professions since Schön (1983). There is a wealth of literature on the use of reflection, and reflective journals in Nursing. Burns & Bulman (2000) provide an overview of current issues. Within Pharmacy, developments have come more recently. Purkiss (2002) draws attention to the value of Reflective Practice, and looks forward to progress in coming years.

Within Higher Education (HE) a number of institutions have developed the use of learning logs and reflective writing as assessed work on a variety of courses. Moon (2001) offers guidance on how to write a reflective journal. Brockbank & McGill (1998) give a good overview of techniques available for facilitating reflective learning in HE. Adapting the use of Kolb's (1984) "Learning Cycle", Cowan (1998) describes how iterations of reflection assist student learning when the reflections are made explicit through writing.

In Sayers (2002) I describe how the Reflective Journal was introduced as a piece of assessed work into our Research Supervision Workshop – a staff development course for lecturers at the University. That paper goes on to discuss how requirements for assessment at different levels might be described – how a reflective journal at doctoral "D" level would be expected to differ from a reflective journal at masters "M" level. In this chapter I look at the problems of writing a reflective journal from the perspective of developing student writing – how to help the students develop the style of writing and how to choose appropriate content. I have become increasingly interested in the "interim" styles that students adopt as they develop their ability to write a reflective journal. This chapter explores some of the traps that students can fall into – some examples of the writing styles that students have adopted en route to, or instead of reflective writing – and a way of labelling these, such that the students and their clinical tutors understand how the adopted, interim style differs from the required style.

I named the interim styles:
- Jumping to Conclusions
- The CV (Job application)
- The Campaigning Journalist
- Over Description

Examples are provided from drafts submitted by students for feedback whilst on the DPharm programme.

There are also some wider issues exposed by the introduction of reflective journals into a programme at this level. It raises questions about the education of pharmacists, which encourages students to follow established procedures and expertise. Pharmacy education is traditionally didactic, testing acquisition of knowledge and the safe application of that knowledge. Developments elsewhere in the education of health professionals now put equal emphasis on problem solving, learning in groups and reflecting explicitly on the experience and process of learning. If continued professional development for hospital pharmacists requires them to reflect on their practice, then this has implications for their previous education (at undergraduate and diploma/masters levels) and reveals the need for more research into the sociology of established pharmacy practice.

2. HOW DPHARM STUDENTS DEVELOP THE APPROPRIATE STYLE AND CONTENT

The first point to make here is that there does not seem to be an easy way of explaining in advance, at the beginning of the DPharm programme, what is required to write a good reflective journal. Experience shows that it is very easy to raise anxiety about a new form of assessment and writing. Giving more detail about what is required does not reduce the anxiety. Students have confirmed this later when reviewing their first year on the programme. The students' previous educational experience (rather than an absence of information) was a significant factor increasing the anxiety. Pharmacy students are scientists and as such have been conditioning into writing objective scientific reports. Once they graduate, they do not do a lot of writing. The more detail they were given about the style of a reflective journal the greater the gap appeared to be between their comfort zone (prior conditioning) and what was required. For me there seemed to be two important questions to reflect on: (1) What is the ideal process for acquiring the writing style for a reflective journal, and (2) what approach should I take, as tutor, to facilitate that learning? The second point would also have to include the "unlearning" of previously established styles of writing.

The basis of the approach I adopted was that
1) Writing a reflective journal was a skill development process and
2) There were affective factors inhibiting that development – i.e., previous disposition or experience of writing was increasing rather than decreasing anxiety
3) There may be other personal development issues linked to the writing development and
4) This was a creative process that was going to provide significantly different learning for each individual student.

I gently refused requests from some students and course tutors at the start of the programme for an example of someone else's reflective writing. Firstly, I didn't have any "perfect" examples, and if I had had, they would have probably appeared unattainable, increasing anxiety, rather than offering reassurance. Secondly, creativity would not be achieved by copying. But I have to confess, I was not that confident about this refusal. Perhaps reading other people's reflective journals would help prepare my students. I notice with interest that as, at the time of writing, the third cohort of students start their programme, they are using students in previous cohorts as their main source of information about the process. "It'll become clearer once you get started" was the message.

This suggests that the students are going through a skills development process. Students do understand what a reflective journal is for or about. The problem is the skills they need to develop and produce one. In the Management literature Taylor &

Wright (1988) describe a skills development process for managers learning to appraise staff. Appraisal is an area where there is a similar tension between understanding the concepts and doing it skilfully, and where affective variables play a role in skills development. The link between emotional states and the development of communication skills has also been explored through Neuro-Linguistic Programming (O'Connor & Seymour 1990). The essence of the process described by Taylor & Wright is that skills are learned from feedback gained through "tutored practice".

On that basis I decided that the best way of helping the students on the DPharm to learn how to write a reflective journal was to give them lots of opportunities to practise and to offer encouraging feedback. One of learning points for myself, developed further below, is to identify interim stages in the process of reflective writing, to describe those in a way that was meaningful for the students, and to assist the transition.

Cowan's (1998) model of reflective learning distinguishes three stages of reflection

- Reflection *for* action
- Reflection *in* action, and
- Reflection *on* action.

This provides a useful distinction in the process of producing reflective writing. The required (assessed) reflective journals for the DPharm Practice Units are "reflection **on** action". They provide evidence of learning from, and as a result of the experience recorded in a year's portfolio of clinical practice. The long reflective journal will also be predominantly composed of reflections on action, but this time the data to reflect on may itself be reflection – i.e., previous reflections. Previous reflections may be recorded in a "learning log" containing reflections for action – thoughts about the DPharm before starting the programme – and reflections in action – records of how it felt at the time (during the experience). Although the learning log is private, drafts submitted to me for formative feedback during the programme could contribute to it. It is from these drafts that I take the illustrative examples below.

I asked students to start the process of reflective writing by putting onto paper their thoughts prior to starting the programme: their expectations.

3. JUMPING TO CONCLUSIONS

I established a number of tutorials to give feedback on writing submitted. At the first of these tutorials I noticed something that caused me to reconsider what I was doing. The students were having a conversation between themselves, whilst I was within earshot. They were sounding off about work. Working in a large organisation – in this case the British National Health Service (NHS) – can be very frustrating. The NHS is reputed to be the largest employer in Europe. The British health service is a focus of intense political debate. This has led to a lot of top-down control from government, and a lot of fear of making mistakes. Errors by doctors or pharmacists can bring professionals into critical media focus.

The gist of the students' conversation can be illustrated by one or two phrases that, in one form or another, re-occurred in the conversation.

"Oh well, there's nothing that you can do about that – what else can you expect from the NHS!"

"We all know Dr X (or manager Y) is hopeless!"

Once this kind of judgment has been made (It's hopeless, what else can you expect!), the motivation for reflection will be low. The speaker sees themselves as a victim of the organisation, and unable to engage effectively with it to solve problems. It would be unfair to judge the students on the basis of snippets of conversation, but this was not untypical of what I hear from employees of large organisations, including my own university. Examples of student writing revealed accounting for experience in a similar way. The text seems to jump to conclusions, omitting to make explicit reflection on the experience, which could show how conclusions are reached. §1#1 below is a typical example.

Example 1 – student writing that illustrates the interim style "Jumping to Conclusions"

1#1

I looked back of my previous experiences and concluded that while I would not have missed doing the (postgraduate) diploma, I felt it has almost become something that is expected of a basic grade pharmacist and yet I don't think it fully prepares you for working as a clinical specialist, however, I am hoping the DPharm will allow me to progress further and practice at the highest level.

Despite the advantages of the DPharm, the thought of two years of research fills me with dread. Maybe this is due to a fear of the unknown, or a fear of failure I really don't know. However, my aim is to cross that bridge when I come to it.

1#2

I have done a reasonable amount of continuing education since qualifying, including the postgraduate diploma in clinical pharmacy and continuing education courses. The diploma has certainly influenced my practice although it did not equip me with the skills to continue to develop myself, I have recently thought that it would have been more useful for me to have waited and done the diploma when I had more experience to build it onto.

I feel that the experience I have gained in the last few years working in several different (NHS) Trusts has broadened my mind enough for me to take control of my career direction with the DPharm. Lack of good direction has certainly been a difficulty for me in the past.

It is statements such as " I don't think it fully prepares you for working as a clinical specialist" (§1#1) that attracted my interest. At first glance these provide evidence of reflection. There has clearly been some thinking about the content of the diploma course. At second glance, though, they raise a further raft of questions that are not addressed about what the student learnt on the diploma course, and what it is about being a clinical specialist that could have been better prepared for. There is no evidence in the text submitted, nor was there any suggestion in the initial tutorial meetings that these things had been thought about in any depth. The students were in danger of seeing themselves as victims of an inadequate diploma course.

If the students on the DPharm were to develop as professionals, they would need to take charge of their own development. To be able to record that development in a reflective journal, then the quality of thinking they brought to problem identification, problem definition and problem solving would need to be a focus of our work together. The question shifted from how to develop a writing style, to how to develop a reflective thinking style that can be made explicit and expressed in writing.

One of the objectives of the tutorials became to discuss matters in a reflective style. This means that judgments of people or situations don't stand without investigation. Looking at Kolb's learning cycle, the danger with judgments is they take the learner from "experience" to "theorising" (drawing conclusions) bypassing explicit reflection.

The question I posed to the writer of §1#2 was "How had experience broadened the mind?" rather than to accept the statement unquestioningly. I also wanted to investigate exactly how the student came to conclude that "direction had been a difficulty in the past". The tutorials became conversations that explored issues raised by the students, questioning judgments and refusing to leave stones unturned. "I feel as if I am being psychoanalysed!" said one of the students with feeling during one of these sessions early in the programme. The attention on their inner thoughts was obviously uncomfortable, and something they were unused to. "That's not my intention." I replied, attempting to minimize the discomfort. However, I was using counselling techniques to help the students reflect on the issues raised. After a few sessions the anxiety caused by this attention to inner thoughts diminished, and is now the established way of working for our tutorial meetings.

The students I have worked with have not had difficulty writing in the first person. The shift of writing style from 3rd person + passive voice (the scientific report) to first person + active voice is not difficult. The problem I identified could be summarized as jumping to conclusions, i.e., not exploring the process of reflection that comes between experience and theorising in the Kolb model. Announcing conclusions of thinking in the first person, active voice, but without explicit reflection is the first "interim" style I identified.

Reid (2000) has a diagram of a 6 stage reflective cycle, a revision of Gibbs (1988), which DPharm students have found helpful in making reflection explicit. Her diagram has two stages to reflection, first "feelings", then "evaluation". The first responds to the question "What were you feeling about the experience?" and the second "What was good and bad about the experience?"

4. THE CV

The second interim style derives from the style of active, first person writing that the students have had recent experience of – writing a curriculum vitae (CV). People applying for jobs in professional environments usually have to write a CV which both lists their qualifications and experience, and other experience relevant to the post they are applying for. The letter of application (This may be part of the CV or a separate document) plays up the positive qualities and experience of the applicant and plays down any weaknesses or doubts about suitability. It would never do in a job application to reveal the writer's doubts about any aspect of their work.

A reflective journal, on the other hand, does not read well if all it reveals is what the writer thinks they are good at.

Example 2 – the CV

2#1

I have always regarded the quality of my communication skills to be one of my key strengths. The ability to adjust my approach and language depending on the person to whom I am speaking has helped me to become a well-known and integral part of the pharmacy ward and medical teams. During the last few months, I have become more comfortable dealing with consultants and senior managers from outside the pharmacy department. The chance to spend more than a few weeks as part of the respective teams has added to my confidence and this in turn encourages me to contribute more to clinical decisions.

2#2

Moreover, the responsibility of looking after the changes to the hospital's Intrathecal Chemotherapy Policy not only increased my confidence, but also forced me to become more involved with Risk Management policy and the design of protocols.

2#3

The discussions with Pete Sayers and my D.Pharm peers helped me to focus my ideas on why I had such a negative initial reaction to EBM (Evidence Based Medicine); although my opinion of some protocols and some aspects of EBM remains less favourable than the opinions held by my peers, I am now able to define more accurately why I feel these concepts have their flaws. Moreover, I now recognise the discrete advantages (and disadvantages) that come with the design and application of procedures and protocols. I have learnt from these discussions that it is a very important part of my further development to develop the willingness to set aside previous prejudices.

The writer of these examples intends to provide evidence of learning from practice, but the text – especially §2#1 – reads more like a CV than a reflective journal. That was how it struck me when I first read it – a comment its writer had no difficulty understanding in the feedback I provided. The force of the language is to impress and influence. It justifies the conclusions the student has reached, it doesn't provide reflection on the experience of, for example, being a member of various teams. It expresses conclusions the writer has come to as a result of circumstances. Something (§2#2) "forced me to become more involved with...". The reasons are explored, but the underlying message is of someone overcoming difficulty. The writer here isn't a victim of the organisation – this perspective is that of a survivor.

§2#3 Was written by the same student some time after §s 2#1 and 2#2. It shows a more balanced and reflective style, still trying to impress in its final sentence, but evidence of a change in style. It was the contrast that enabled me to see §s 2#1 and 2#2 as an interim stage. In a later piece of writing, which was more introspective, the same student described a lack of confidence when interacting with others.

My purpose here is not to suggest that the students should play down their achievements, or that the reflective journal is only for confessing doubts and weaknesses. It is easy for feedback about a lack of balance in one direction to be interpreted as a need for the complete opposite. The aim of the reflective journal for the DPharm is to explore issues at the leading edge of current practice, in a balanced way. §2#3 shows the writer has developed a balanced view of Evidence Based Medicine (EBM), but only hints at what the advantages and disadvantages are. There is still room for further reflection.

There are two ways that academic writing typically avoids the problem of writers jumping to conclusions. One is to anchor categorical statements in the established literature of the subject. The other is to reflect on the pros and cons of any question and to draw tentative conclusions based on logic derived from first principles. Both are possible, and to be encouraged within a reflective journal.

5. THE CAMPAIGNING JOURNALIST

The science that pharmacists learn is anchored in chemistry and pharmacology. Most pharmaceutical research is financed by the drug companies and focuses on drug design, and drug testing. There is, as I discovered, relatively little research into the clinical practice of hospital pharmacists. Issues such as patient compliance and evidence-based medicine are complex and when explored by researchers tend to be as much influenced by sociological as scientific factors.

The questions clinical pharmacists pose at the leading edge of their practice are ones where there is less certainty, and hence a greater need for reflection before reaching conclusions.

As a result of the paucity of research into practice, pharmacists seem less aware of fundamental debates in their profession. The politics of their profession seem focused on the government's attempts to control NHS funding, and on the ensuing management of budgets. There does not seem to be a philosophical debate about methods of patient care of anything like the same intensity as the debates about teaching and learning that I am used to within education. This view has been confirmed for me by discussions with a number of senior hospital pharmacists, not just the students on the DPharm.

To say that pharmacists do their job without thinking a great deal about it would be an injustice, but the need to reflect on practice in order to be able to write a reflective journal seems to require more than just the development of a new writing style. The influence of the DPharm is calling into question whether pharmacy education develops people to reflect sufficiently about health care issues. Through doctoral-level qualifications pharmacists hope to be on a par with doctors in the ranks of health professionals. The DPharm programme is causing a number of us to question whether a curriculum weighted in favour of technical knowledge is sufficient to achieve this. Like people in many scientific and technical professions, they are now being asked to develop the sociological and psychological knowledge for what are loosely described as "people skills". This is engendering quite a heated debate within pharmacy education at Bradford.

Strong feelings can be a good trigger for reflection. Where differences in opinions have manifested themselves in the tutorials, the energy for exploring the thinking behind those views has been a good source for reflection. I always invite the students to send me their reflections on the tutorial.

Example 3 is of some writing where students have expressed strong views on issues.

3#1

I feel that some pharmacists reflect unconsciously, however, there needs to be a supportive process to assist them to move to consciously reflecting and at a greater depth. What will be more difficult is encouraging those who are cynical about the value to adopt this approach.

3#2

Some may argue that population data from trials is invalid in the clinical setting because the inclusion criteria are generally tight, and I do see their point. On the other hand, there could never be trials large enough to include a statistically relevant sample size for every subgroup of patient that we might like. There are simply not enough 85 year old ladies with poor renal function, asthma and arthritis willing to trial new medicines for us. Even if they did form an orderly queue, drug companies would not be likely to entertain them with employees and shareholders dependant on the good publicity from initial studies with a new drug. If we can evaluate the limitations of published trials, we can work with them – know your enemy.

This is the interim style I named the "Campaigning Journalist". One of its distinctive features is the phrase: "I feel that.....". Those who have undergone counselling skills training know this as a trap when responding to the question "How do you feel?" "I feel that....." is nearly always followed by a thought, not a feeling. A true feeling doesn't need "that", e.g., I feel sad, I feel frustrated. In a reflective journal "I feel that...." is nearly always followed by a conclusion, e.g., "I feel that something needs doing." The first sentence in §3 #1 does just this. Naming this style the "Campaigning Journalist" enabled the writer to understand exactly why this wasn't the reflective style I was looking for. Reflection requires something a bit more neutral. Reflection comes after strong feelings have been expressed and subsided.

Goleman's (1996) work on Emotional Intelligence suggests that professionals need to be able to work rationally with their emotions. This involves acknowledging the strength of feelings but reflecting rationally on their origins and effects. This is not, I hasten to add, the refusal to acknowledge feelings that is often associated with positivism and scientific method.

Once the campaigning journalist has been triggered it releases a rhetorical style of which Example 3#2 is a good example. This is a different student's work. Again it communicates the force of feeling behind the assertions it makes, but these are more like conclusions than descriptions of reflection. There is an attempt at a balanced view, e.g., "On the one hand....", followed by a contrasting statement in the next sentence. However, the feelings are expressed indirectly and verging on the sarcastic.

Discussions at the tutorials were designed to help the students think through a variety of aspects for every issue raised. The fact that I am not a pharmacist helped. I could ask genuinely naïve questions. I did not have any position to advocate or defend in relation to the topics that generated feelings. The questions I asked enabled the students to articulate both sides of an argument and hence be in a better position to reflect on the argument as a whole – not just their side of it. §3.2 (final sentence) shows some evidence of progress here.

6. OVER DESCRIPTION

The final trap – or interim style – I have identified does not yet have a catchy name. It could best be called "Over Description". It is the problem of describing it (whatever it is) rather than what has been learnt from it. The 2000 word reflective journal requires a succinct account of learning from professional practice, not a description of practice. If description is required it needs to be in the portfolio or an appendix. The thing that needs describing is the learning point, and the reflections that led to that learning.

Example 4

> 4#1
>
> The Drugs & Therapeutics Committee (D&T) has a high profile within the Trust and much of the information concerning its procedures and meeting activity is disseminated to Trust staff via Pharmacy. National standards and guidance for Medicines Information (MI) services highlight the importance of local guidance in medicines management when answering enquiries. The Quality Assurance Programme for Medicines Information Services, produced by the UK Medicines Information Pharmacists Group, indicates that local formularies and guidance should be considered when answering enquiries. In addition, it is acknowledged that continuous intervention is required to ensure compliance to a local formulary.
>
> 4#2
>
> We advertise the MI service as being a source of accurate, timely and current medicines information. However I became concerned that by failing to use information about D&T activity, I was withholding information and therefore not giving our enquirers the comprehensive service we promise. As a MI pharmacist, and therefore potentially the first point of contact for a prescriber, I had not played a full part in disseminating information about D&T procedures and activities. I worried that if a prescriber was not fully informed of the D&T process and available formulary choices, they may write a prescription for a medicine which could not be supplied from Pharmacy. This could cause frustration for the patient and would not present a professional image of the Pharmacy department or the MI service.

§4.1 is typical of a student that needs to ensure the reader understands the context – not an unreasonable wish. However, the style of this example could also be labelled "The Official", as it reads like a formal description, and is impersonal. In §4.2 the explanation of the context, of what's going on around the writer, continues after the pronoun "I" appears. What is missing is the inside story. This is a subtle point, as the final sentence: "This could cause frustration for the patient…" does imply reflection, and the previous sentence "I worried that…" does describe the internal state of the writer. It is not quite clear what the worry is – the personal issue of disappointing a customer, or the task issue of an undeliverable prescription. Hence it is not clear here, what exactly the learning point is. A learning point does emerge later in the text (after the example quoted), but that begs the question of whether such detailed description of the context is needed at the point where the example is taken. Being able to succinctly identify a learning point, and the reflection that led to the learning, is not easy.

This problem of over description occurs in a number of students' writing, and becomes more problematic when reflecting on reading. The temptation is to start writing an essay showing understanding of the content, rather than the reflection on content and the learning points for the reader's practice, which is the goal of the DPharm programme.

7. CONCLUSIONS

My first point in drawing conclusions from writing this chapter is to admit that I have probably demonstrated all the interim styles somewhere here. They are not errors, and may a useful role in a reflective journal. It is a question of balance and purpose. Reflection requires a genuine input from the individual writing the journal. It must be what the writer really wants to write about. On the other hand, as a piece of assessed work for an academic programme, it must also meet its intended or required purpose. The purpose of this chapter is different from the purpose of the reflective journals described in it.

To write a reflective journal, to meet its intended purposes, requires development. My experience of working with the DPharm students suggest that the development required is first and foremost a thinking skill – the ability to make explicit the process of reflection that enables professionals to draw useful, developmental conclusions from experience, to learn explicitly from experience.

Whilst developing the ability to make this thinking explicit in the form of a reflective journal, there is a learning process to go through – learning and unlearning writing skills. The shift from 3rd person to first person writing has taken many of my students through a style of writing, which I have labelled "the CV" and "the Campaigning Journalist". These appear to be useful in developing the presentation of self, and the presentation of reflections triggered by emotion. Being able to identify and describe an interim style has helped students map the gap between a first draft and the desired end product. However, as most of the students whose writing is described in this chapter are still on the programme, the lasting benefits of insights gained thus far are still being identified. The end point – an ideal reflective journal as a piece of academic writing for the DPharm – is still being defined and refined.

There are implications in this for pharmacy education as a whole. The experience of the DPharm programme, and its use of reflective journals as a mode of assessment, is leading to the need for reflective practice to be established earlier in the curriculum – i.e., at undergraduate and postgraduate diploma levels. This has already happened in the curriculum for some other health professionals. Hopefully, graduates of the DPharm programme will be able to demonstrate the value of this approach in the quality of their contribution (written or otherwise) to developments in the analysis of pharmacy practice.

The remaining question to be debated within pharmacy education is how to get the balance right between technical knowledge and personal development in the curriculum. Is the answer to be found in problem-based learning, or some other approach to developing the reflective practitioner?

The introduction of reflective writing into the assessment regime of a professional doctorate has raised a lot of questions for pharmacy education.

WRITING-TO-LEARN: CONDUCTING A PROCESS LOG

RACHEL SEGEV-MILLER

Kibbutzim College of Education, Israel

Abstract: The purpose of the present study, which was conducted within the framework of a more comprehensive one (Segev-Miller, 1997), was to investigate the effect of personal writing on college students' authentic processes of performing a common academic task of writing-from-sources – a literature review – in partial fulfilment of their research requirements. The subjects, 12 elementary education college students, volunteered, at the request of the researcher, to document their performance of the task by means of a process log over an academic year. At the end of the year, the subjects also responded – for the purpose of the present study – to a questionnaire, requiring them to assess the effects of the process log on their writing processes. An analysis of the data obtained from the subjects' responses indicated that conducting the process log facilitated their use of the cognitive intertextual processing and knowledge-transforming strategies of selection, connection and organization of information from the textual sources, which are crucial for the performance of the task. However, the major effect of conducting the process log was to promote the subjects' use of metacognitive strategies, particularly the strategies of self-assessment and self-regulation, which are crucial for significant learning to take place.

Keywords: Cognitive and metacognitive strategies, Knowledge-telling and knowledge-transforming, Personal writing, Process log, Retrospective verbal reporting, Writing-from-sources, Writing-to-learn.

1. INTRODUCTION

Research of academic writing has for over a decade now pointed to the significance of writing to promote learning and critical literacy.[1] Moreover, when combined with reading[2], writing has been found to have more of an effect on learning from texts than either writing or reading separately (Spires, Huntley, & Huffman, 1993; Tier-

---

[1] *For a critique of previous research (i.e., in the 80's) see: Ackerman, 1993; Schumacher & Gradwohl, 1991.*
[2] *Or with other learning activities, e.g., discussion (Dysthe, 1996; Mason, 1998; Probst, 1996).*

Segev-Miller, R. (2004). Writing-to-learn: Conducting a process log.
In G. Rijlaarsdam (Series Ed.) and Rijlaarsdam, G., Van den Bergh, H. & Couzijn, M. (Vol. Eds.), Studies in writing, Volume 14, Effective learning and teaching of writing, 2nd edition, Part 3, Studies in writing-to-learn, 533 - 546.

ney, Soter, O'Flahavan, & McGinley, 1989; Tynjälä, 1998). Indeed, the most common academic writing tasks – so-called "writing-from-sources" – require students to engage in critical processing of textual information and to transform this information rather than to "tell", or reproduce it (Bereiter & Scardamalia, 1987; Flower, Stein, Ackerman, Kantz, McCormick, & Peck, 1990; Greene & Ackerman, 1995; Spivey, 1997).

However, some writing experts (e.g., Britton, Burgess, Martin, McLeod, & Rosen, 1975; Fulwiler, 1986) have deplored the almost total absence from school of personal writing, which is the language closest to thought, or "inner speech" (Vygotsky, 1962), and

> may be at any stage the kind of writing best adapted to exploration and discovery. It is the language that externalizes our first stages in tackling a problem or coming to grips with an experience (Britton et al., 1975:165).

Studies investigating the effects of academic and personal writing have indicated that the latter significantly promoted more higher-order thinking (i.e., analysis) on reading comprehension exams (Blohm, 1991); and that the quality of papers written in personal writing was higher especially in terms of interpretation (Newell, Suszynski, & Weingart, 1989) and elaboration (Beach & Christensen, 1989). However, very few studies investigated the differences between the cognitive processes underlying academic and personal writing. McCrindle and Christensen (1995) found significant differences between two groups of freshmen assigned either an academic (scientific report) or personal (journal) writing task in an introductory biology course. Results elicited from the subjects' responses to a questionnaire (a list of strategies) indicated that personal writing significantly promoted the use of more sophisticated cognitive strategies (elaboration and organization) and metacognitive strategies (assessment and regulation of learning).

With the advent of the Writing-Across-the-Curriculum movement in the mid 70's (Fulwiler & Young, 1990; Hill, 1994), and the Writing-to-Learn movement in the 80's (Newell, 1998; Vacca & Linek, 1992), the personal journal has become a standard component of writing instruction programs at many US colleges. The journal has been used extensively in various other disciplines,[3] with diverse populations,[4] and for different purposes: to report reading, write notes and drafts of papers, assess students' own achievements, report emotional reactions experienced in the learning process, etc. Personal journal writing also provided students with opportunities to examine their development as learners and promoted conceptual change (Ballantyne & Packer, 1995; Gunstone & Northfield, 1992; Jurdak & Zein, 1998) and behavioral change (Dart, Boulton-Lewis, Brownlee, & McCrindle, 1998). Hence there is a variety of terminologies such as: course journal or file, learning journal, personal journal, diary, journal log, learning log, and more recently the process log; and – with the introduction of alternative assessment into the educational system and

---

[3] History (e.g., Downey, 1996; Johns, 1986), literature (e.g., Bowman, 2000; Knickerbocker & Rycik, 2002; Prescott, 2001), math (e.g., Powell, 1997; Silver, 1999), science (Prain & Hand, 1999), etc.

[4] E.g., developmental, see: Olson, Deming, & Valeri-Gold (1994).

the communicative approach into L2 teaching – the portfolio and the dialogue journal, respectively.

Unlike the portfolio (Valencia, Hiebert, & Afflerbach, 1994; Yancey, 1992), which consists of students' best products and serves for the purpose of assessment, and unlike the dialogue journal (Peyton, 1990; Peyton & Reed, 1990), which serves for the purpose of communication between students and teachers, the journal (Anson & Beach, 1990, 1996; Lukinsky, 1991) serves mainly for students to assess themselves and to communicate with themselves.

However, very few writing studies have used the journal as a research instrument. The subjects in these studies were required to document in their journals, or rather process logs, their processes of performing an academic task of writing-from-sources, for the purpose of tapping the strategies they employed (Nelson, 1988; Segev-Miller, 1997; Sternglass, 1988) or to document the time they devoted to performing the task (Greene, 1993). The obvious advantage of the process log over other methods of verbal reporting – interviews or think-aloud protocols – is that it allows researchers to trace the subjects' writing processes over a long period of time (Smith & Stahl, 1993) and to gain insights into these otherwise inaccessible processes. Another advantage of the process log is that because it is retrospective it allows

> writers to explain and reflect on their decisions without interfering directly with their attention to the task, freeing a writer from the "cognitive load" (Afflerbach & Johnston, 1984) that the concurrent verbalization of a think-aloud would require (Greene & Higgins, 1994:118).

In spite of its recent use as an instrument of research into reading and writing processes, the process log seems to be no less reliable than other methods of verbal reporting. Although Afflerbach and Johnston (1984) and Pressley and Afflerbach (1995) hypothesized the existence of significant differences between retrospective and concurrent (think-aloud) data, the studies of Langer (1986), McCarthy (1987), and Segev-Miller (1997, 2000) indicated insignificant or very few differences between the two, which may be accounted for in terms of the inherently different nature of these methods.

The purpose of the present study, which was conducted within the framework of a more comprehensive one (Segev-Miller, 1997), was to investigate the effect of conducting a process log on college students' authentic processes of performing a common academic task of writing-from-sources.

2. METHOD

2.1 Subjects

The subjects, 12 third year elementary education college students, were selected for the comprehensive study on the basis of their scores on Sarig & Folman's (1993) Academic Literacy Test[5], to represent three distinct levels of proficiency, namely,

---

[5] *The Academic Literacy Test (ALT), validated elsewhere (Segev-Miller, 1990), consists of four tasks: a summary, a map, a paraphrase of single texts, and a synthesis of a collection of*

high, medium, and low. At the request of the researcher, the subjects volunteered to conduct a process log,[6] documenting over the academic year their performance of a task of writing-from-sources – a review of the literature from multiple L1 (Hebrew) textual sources – in partial fulfillment of their methodology course requirements.[7]

2.2 Instrument

Once data collection for the comprehensive study was concluded at the end of the academic year, the subjects responded – for the purpose of the present study – to a questionnaire (see: Appendix A, question 1),[8] requiring them to assess the effects of conducting the process log on their performance of the task.

2-3 short texts on the same topic. The ALT was administered to all 150 3rd year elementary education students at the beginning of the academic year. The subjects were then randomly selected from the three distinct proficiency groups which emerged – high (above 80%), medium, and low (below 60%) - four from each group. Other relevant data (i.e., the subjects' scores on the college entrance exams, and on the L1 language and L2 reading exit exams in their 1st year; their GPA in their 1st and 2nd years, etc.) were also collected.
[6] *Unlike the subjects in Nelson's (1988) and Sternglass' (1988) studies, who were required to report only on the planning and revising, and task representation strategies, which they employed, respectively, in the process of performing a task of writing-from-sources, the subjects in the researcher's (1997) comprehensive study were required to provide complete accounts of their processes and of the contexts in which these took place. They were provided with instructions with regard to conducting the process log: E.g., to document on a daily basis thoughts and actions related to the performance of the task from the very beginning of the process (i.e., topic selecting and information seeking), to be candid and elaborate, not to erase anything from the log, etc. The subjects were also required to attach to the process log photocopies of all the textual sources they read and the original copies of all the by-products they wrote (summaries of the textual sources, notes, drafts). Over 3,000 pages (including 769 log pages) were collected. No significant differences between the successful and unsuccessful synthesizers were indicated with regard to the length of their process logs or the degree of elaboration in reporting.*
[7] *Other sources of data for the comprehensive study were weekly individual interviews with the subjects, think-aloud protocols elicited at several stages in the process of performing the task, and analysis of the written by-products and final products. Such a variety of sources would allow for triangulation of the data (see: Van Wijk & Sanders, 1999).*
[8] *The subjects were also required to suggest changes to be introduced into the college academic literacy instruction programs (Appendix A, question 2 & Segev-Miller, 1989, 1991, 1992).*

2.3 Data Analysis[9]

The subjects' responses to question 1 on the questionnaire were parsed into units. The analysis unit in the present study has been defined in terms of a "move" (Deegan, 1995), or the use of a strategy, which could be distinguished from other strategies by the purpose for which it was used. Often such a unit included an elaboration. This is illustrated by the following two units (divided by a double slash) from a subject's response, in which she used the strategies of *selection* and *assessment*, respectively:[10]

> Everything looked important and necessary – I couldn't give anything up. But after a long time during which I tried and retried to put all the important ideas down *[= elaboration = subject accounts for her difficulty in selecting the relevant information from the source text]* I finally did find the most important idea and put it down *[= SELECTION]*. Had it not been for the process log I don't think I would've been able to see it *[= elaboration = accounting for the successful use of the strategy]* // The log also made me see – where I had elaborated on or included too much information, where I had repeated the same mistakes, where I had not emphasized a point enough *[= ASSESSMENT]*.[11]

The analysis of the data yielded 100 units. These were further processed for categories and sub-categories of the strategies used by the subjects.[12]

3. FINDINGS AND DISCUSSION

The analysis of the data indicated two major categories of strategies – cognitive and metacognitive strategies, which the subjects used with a relative frequency of 24% and 76% of the total number of units, respectively. No significant differences were indicated between the successful and unsuccessful subjects[13] with regard to the relative frequencies of their use of cognitive and metacognitive strategics.

This finding is in line with the researcher's (1997) comprehensive study, which indicated no significant differences between the successful and unsuccessful subjects with regard to the total frequencies of all the strategies – both cognitive and metacognitive – they used in the process of performing the task. The study also indicated no significant differences between the two groups with regard to the relative frequencies of their use of metacognitive strategies, although the successful subjects used these strategies with a significantly higher rate of success.

---

[9] *Analysis of the data followed Strauss & Corbin's (1990) grounded theory model, often referred to in the literature as the "constant comparative method of analysis". According to this model, "data are broken down into discrete parts, closely examined, compared for similarities and difference" (p. 62). These units are further conceptualized (i.e., named) and grouped in categories and subcategories which emerge from the data.*
[10] *The quote is from a subject's response, the analysis – in square brackets & Italics.*
[11] *The category of* Assessment *was further divided into sub-categories. The above unit illustrates* Assessment of Product.
[12] *20% of the data were also analyzed by another expert rater to ensure reliability of the analysis; inter-rater agreement was almost 90%.*
[13] *Defined as such on the basis of the scores on their final products in researcher's (1997) study.*

3.1 Cognitive Strategies

The cognitive strategies used by the subjects (see: *Table 1*) were the strategies of selection, connection, and organization of information from the textual sources, with a relative frequency of 41.66%, 33.33%, and 25.00%, respectively, of the total number of units in this category. These strategies are illustrated by quotes from the subjects' responses.[14]

Table 1. Distribution of Cognitive Strategies Used (N = 24)

Strategy	Relative frequency
1.1 selection Everything looked important and necessary – I couldn't give anything up. But (…) I finally did find the most important idea and put it down.	41.66
1.2 connection Putting my thoughts and ideas down on paper helped me (…) and also promoted my thinking – while writing in the log I would think about these things, and then come up with more thoughts and new ideas, especially ideas about how to put these things together, how they are connected.	33.33
1.3 organization Reporting helped me in organizing the information. When I elaborated on my thoughts everything became so much clearer: the organization, what comes before, what comes after.	25.00

Studies of summarizing (for a review see: Kirkland and Saunders, 1991) and writing-from-sources (for a review see: Segev-Miller, 1997) have indicated the difficulties that subjects had selecting, connecting, and organizing information from textual sources, rather than merely copying or quoting it.

The strategies of selection, connection, and organization of information from the textual sources involve intertextual processing and knowledge-transforming, and are, therefore, extremely relevant to the performance of the task of writing-from-sources (Spivey, 1997). Especially relevant is the strategy of connecting, or "inventing" as it is commonly referred to in the literature.[15] When writing from sources, students are required to invent their own macro propositions ("new ideas") from different – sometimes even contradictory – macro propositions of multiple textual sources, and to organize these in a previously non-existent conceptual structure. That is, this strategy requires knowledge-transforming and the production of personal and creative perspectives on the part of students (Chall, 1996; Lohman, 1993).

---

[14] *The quotes have been translated from the subjects' responses in their L1 – Hebrew.*
[15] *For a history of the term see: Crowley (1985).*

These findings, then, indicated that conducting a process log facilitated the subjects' use of the strategies of selection, connection, and organization relevant to the performance of the demanding task of writing-from-sources. The majority of the subjects[16] explicitly attributed their successful use of these strategies to conducting the process log, which served as a tool for thinking and coping with difficulties: "had it not been for the process log", "while writing in the log I would think", "reporting helped me", etc. These findings are in line with Britton et al.'s (1975) conception of personal writing as a means to solving problems.

However, the major effect of conducting a process log on the subjects' performance of the task, according to their own assessments (76% of the total number of analysis units), was to promote their use of metacognitive strategies. This finding is in line with the studies reviewed earlier (see: p. 2), which indicated that personal writing promoted the use of metacognitive strategies.

3.2 Metacognitive Strategies

Current definitions of metacognition include both the learners' declarative and procedural knowledge of cognitive processes (Flavell, 1977/1985) and their ability to assess and plan these processes (Baker & Brown, 1984). They also include, respectively, the learners' self-assessment and self-regulation of cognition (Paris & Winograd, 1990; Paris, 2001).

Table 2. Distribution of Metacognitive Strategies Used (Relative frequency; N = 76)

Strategy	%
2.1 self-assessment	
2.1.1 assessment of product	19.73
...This [reporting] helped me realize how I was writing, that is, if what I was writing was clear to my reader.	
...The log also made me see – where I had elaborated on or included too much information, where I had repeated the same mistakes, where I had not emphasized a point enough.	
2.1.2 assessment of process	
2.1.2.1 assessment of strategy use	32.89
...I suddenly understood I was reading the passage but was unable to do anything significant with it but copy it or quote it.'	
2.1.2.2 assessment of learning progress	7.89
...Sometimes when I wrote things they would seem old to me, and then I knew I had made one more step ahead.	
...There were days when I reported I had done 'nothing'. Is this an important part of writing a paper – the days when you only think, feel tormented, lost?	
2.1.3 assessment of self	

---

[16] 11 of the 12 subjects. Only one subject, in her response to the questionnaire, thought that the think-aloud sessions, which took place at different stages in the process of performing the task, were more helpful than the process log. Unlike the other subjects, she also related in her process log to her think-alouds after each session.

2.1.3.1 as independent learner	10.52
...I think it's easier then to turn to myself for feedback on my writing, during writing, after writing.	
2.1.3.2 as able to transfer	5.26
...This learning process also facilitated my learning in other contexts, in other courses, especially my developing ability to ask myself the right questions.	
...This reporting contributed to my performance of other tasks.	
2.1.3.3 as reader-writer	5.26
...The process of reporting made me understand the connection between my reading and writing – how I write better on account of what I have read, how I go on reading better on account of what I have written or learnt, the knowledge I have gained from my writing.	
...At times, it seemed to me there is hardly any difference between reading and writing in terms of what they require of me.	
2.2 self-regulation	
2.2.1 setting goals	7.89
...The log helped me become more planful, more focused.	
...Reporting made me organize my planning of future moves, of setting my next goals.	
2.2.2 revising procedures	7.89
...Writing in the log helped me very much when I was 'stuck'; and then my conversation with myself helped me find a different way.	
...Reporting made it possible for me to discover a new way to go about writing the paper (...) In the past I used to take a book, sum it up, and only then check whether the information was really relevant. Now I first check by skimming through the table of contents, parts of the book that look promising etc., and then and only then I start summing the book up. I learnt that this way I could also cover more material.	
...As a result of reporting I changed my way of thinking quite often, especially with regard to the organization of the information.	
2.2.3 task representation	2.63
I became more aware of the requirements of the task, that is, having to relate to and synthesize – not just to list – information from multiple sources.	

Studies of reading (e.g., Garner, 1987), writing (e.g., Bereiter & Scardamalia, 1987), and summarizing processes (e.g., Brown, Campione, & Day, 1982) have indicated that the major differences between successful and unsuccessful learners were in the formers' more frequent and more successful use of metacognitive strategies; and that these strategies had a significant effect on their learning and on their ability to transfer it to other learning contexts (Butler & Winne, 1995; Butterfield & Nelson, 1991).

The two categories of metacognitive strategies reported by the subjects in the present study – self-assessment and self-regulation – were further divided into subcategories. These are presented in *Table 2* and illustrated by quotes from the subjects' responses.

The strategies of self-assessment were, then, used with great variety and with higher relative frequency than the strategies of self-regulation – 81.57% and 15.78%, respectively. The subjects assessed their processes with a relatively high frequency (32.89%) in terms of the difficulties they had to "do anything significant", that is to use transforming strategies, especially linguistic transforming strategies; and their products (19.73%) in terms of criteria commonly used to assess product quality (e.g., elaboration, rhetorical purpose, and audience awareness). They also assessed the progress they made (7.89%) and became aware of the effect of incubation on their performance of the task: How doing "nothing (...) is an important part of writing a paper – the days when you only think", as many of them also reported earlier in their process logs. For example:

> And although I didn't write much, it seemed to me I did make progress – this may be a necessary internal step [Log A, p. 45].

> I made a preliminary plan – but I'm still sleeping on it [Log F, p. 58].

This finding is in line with research of the effect of time-on-task on the quality of subjects' writing processes (Rijlaarsdam & Van den Bergh, 1996; Segev-Miller, 1997), and with Sternglass' (1988: 122) argument that

> just as time is crucial in the planning process, so is it central to the notion of incubation (...) Incubation is often described as an insight or illumination of a creative idea as the result of a period of unconscious work following preliminary work in becoming familiar with a problem.

Indeed, the subjects reported that conducting the process log was also a process of "sudden" or "unexpected" insights: "I suddenly understood", "and then I knew", "after I started reporting I found out", "the log made me see", "the log made it possible for me to discover", etc. These findings are in line with the conception of writing as a process of discovery (Galbraith, 1992, 1996), and with the processes of successful synthesizers (McGinley, 1992; Segev-Miller, 1997; Sternglass, 1988), which were determined to a large extent by discovery, rather than by planning, while writing.

The subjects also reported that conducting the process log helped them to assess themselves as learners. First, the findings – with regard to the subjects' assessment of themselves as independent learners capable of providing their own feedback (10.52%) and of transferring the knowledge they acquired in the process of performing the task, without any explicit instruction, to other learning contexts (5.26%) – indicated the subjects' evolving confidence in their abilities, or their self-efficacy, epitomized in the following quote:

> I felt I had to report to myself, not to anyone else but ME.

These findings are in line with studies (Guthrie & Wigfield, 1997; Landis, 2002; Raedts, 2002; Zimmerman & Bandura, 1994), indicating the effect of students' self-efficacy on their successful performance of reading and writing tasks.

Second, the findings – with regard to the subjects' assessment of themselves as readers-writers (5.26%) and the connections they found between their reading and writing processes "in terms of what they require" – are in line with the conception of these processes as parallel processes of meaning construction, drawing on a common repertoire of cognitive, communicative and linguistic strategies (Tierney & Shanahan, 1996). Finally, the findings – with regard to the connections the subjects found between their reading and writing processes in terms of "how I write better on account of what I have read", etc., – are in line with the conception of reading and writing as reciprocal, or mutually informative, processes serving as input and output for each other (Tierney & Shanahan, 1996).

In addition to the strategies of self-assessment, the subjects used strategies of self-regulation, albeit with a relatively lower frequency. Self-regulation has been defined as the ability to successfully use and monitor strategies, such as setting goals (Zeidner, Boekaerts, & Pintrich, 2000; Zimmerman, 2000). The subjects in the present study reported that conducting the process log "helped" them and "made it possible" for them to regulate themselves: both in planning and setting goals (7.89%), and in revising their procedures and substituting the strategies they used to solve problems (e.g., writing block) with more successful ones (7.89%). These findings are in line with studies which have indicated that students' self-regulation had a significant effect on their learning (Schraw, 1998; Schunk & Zimmerman, 1994). Some of their self-regulation (2.63%) had to do with the subjects' representation of the task that they had been assigned. Task representation has been defined as:

> an interpretive process which translates the rhetorical situation – as a writer reads it – into the act of composing. As such it is the major bridge which links the public context of writing with the private process of an individual writer (...). The task as students represent it to themselves is, by definition, the one they perform, but that representation is *subject to many influences and may evolve in surprising ways during writing* (Flower, 1987:1-2).[17]

Indeed, the subjects in the present study reported that their initial knowledge-telling representation of the task – "just to list" – which studies of writing in academic institutions (e.g., Bridgeman & Carlson, 1984) indicated was quite common, had, with the help of the process log, evolved into the more complex and cognitively demanding representation of knowledge-transforming – "to relate to and synthesize (...) information from multiple sources".[18,19]

4. CONCLUSION

The findings of the present study indicated that, according to the subjects' own assessments, conducting a process log had a significant effect on their performance of an authentic task of writing-from-sources in terms of the strategies they used:
1) The cognitive strategies of intertextual processing and knowledge-transforming – selection, connection, and organization – relevant to the performance of the task of writing-from-sources;
2) The metacognitive strategies of self-assessment (of product, process, and self) and of self-regulation, which are crucial for successful reading and writing, or for learning in general.

These strategies were often absent from students' processes in previous studies of writing-from-sources. Although Flower (1989:26) argued for "writing's epistemic potential to transform knowledge rather than to report knowledge," studies of writing-from-sources have indicated that writing as a process of knowledge-

---

[17] *Italics added.*
[18] *However, in the 1997 study they reported having difficulties in implementing their new task representation, and were not all successful at it. No significant differences between the successful and unsuccessful synthesizers with regard to this strategy were indicated there.*
[19] *For a similar change as a result of explicit instruction see: Segev-Miller (2002a, 2002b).*

transforming does not come easily to most subjects. Penrose (1992:491) has already warned that "students can engage in writing without much thought, without the active involvement or critical reflection we associate with participating or generating knowledge in the discipline" (see also: Ackerman, 1993). Indeed, most unsuccessful synthesizers (and one successful synthesizer) in the researcher's (1997) comprehensive study conceived of academic writing as a "technical" aspect of the performance of the task, an act of putting information or crystallized thoughts down on paper:[20]

> I write what I want to say (...) I think before I write [Log H, p. 2].

The successful synthesizers, on the other hand, conceived of writing as a process of inquiry and "thinking on paper", and used the process log too for this very purpose, as one of the subjects wrote in her response to the questionnaire:

> While reporting I was forced to think 'on paper' about what I was thinking or doing (...). I found out I was actually talking to myself, saying things like 'well, I think...' or 'If I write like this, then...' or 'Maybe it would be better if...', etc.

Another subject wrote in her final process log entry:

> And THANK YOU [i.e., the researcher] so much for this opportunity (...). It was so becoming for me to accompany these unbelievable processes I've been experiencing with my 'thinking log'. I finished going over the log. I feel this is saying good bye to it before I submit it to you for the last time [Log E, p. 90].

The "active involvement and critical reflection" which, according to Penrose, are often absent from students' academic writing, may be promoted by engaging students in personal writing. In contrast with the dichotomous approach, which argued that students must be "weaned" from personal writing in order to acquire academic writing (Flower, 1979; Stotsky, 1986), many agree today that high-quality academic writing is the outcome of personal engagement (Di Pardo, 1990; Fulwiler, 1989; Lantolf & DiCamilla, 1994; Mlynarczyk, 1991; Vanett & Jurich, 1990).[21] The process log, in which students are required to document by means of personal writing their performance of an academic writing task is, in light of the findings of the present study, a suitable instrument for students to exercise this kind of writing, i.e., writing to learn.

In the common academic context, students are not only required to perform cognitively demanding tasks of writing-from-sources with very little explicit instruction, but are also assessed on the basis of their written products. A more valid assessment in line with current learning theories (for a review see: Tynjälä, 2001) and current trends of alternative assessment, which is anchored in an authentic learning context, should take into account process measures as well (Birenbaum & Dochy, 1996). The process log can be used for this purpose.[22] To quote Lambert (in Fulwiler, 1986:192):

---

[20] This was evident also in the significantly fewer drafts they wrote.
[21] Kieft & Rijlaarsdam (2002) have in this spirit suggested a symbiosis of the literature curriculum (i.e., writing to learn) with the skills curriculum (i.e., learning to write).
[22] The assessment criteria will, of course, depend on the purpose and nature of the process log (Segev-Miller, in progress).

> The journal is the place to fail. That is, a place to try, experiment, test one's wings. For the moment judgment, criticism, evaluation are suspended: What matters is the attempt, not the success of the attempt.

This approach is illustrated by one of the subjects' entries already in the first week of conducting her process log:

> And I noticed that I skip a lot of letters, or write other letters. Maybe I have to go again over what I have written, but this is associative writing, very unorganized logically, also the punctuation and the tone are not always in place, 'but this is a log, not a paper', I tell myself to relax [Log B, p. 11].

Indeed, another subject made a similar distinction between the log and the paper in her response to the questionnaire:

> Writing in the process log has been for me a kind of learning which, now that I think of it, seems to me to be more important than the paper itself; that is, the knowledge I acquired to write the paper is something I found in books, but this writing [i.e., in the log] is something inside me that I have never known about.

This quote is reminiscent of Fulwiler's (1989:171) argument that "Journals are more useful than formal papers, because writers remain free to respond to their educational world as they see fit." It is also in line with the findings of studies, which compared academic and personal writing (e.g., McCrindle & Christensen, 1995) and indicated the advantages of the latter to learning.

The process log can, however, be used for instructional purposes as well. The process log may help the instructor trace her students' learning processes and gain cognitive, affective and contextual insights into her students' otherwise inaccessible "black box", and to revise or modify her instruction accordingly.

It is, therefore, crucial that the instructor read her students' logs, in spite of their personal nature, to make sure that they are making good use of the log. In addition, it is most desirable that the instructor also conduct a process log, even write in class while her students are writing, and read out to them from hers. Beyond the personal benefit the instructor may gain from conducting a process log, this may contribute to an atmosphere of mutual trust, and to the validity of the students' writing. For the same purpose, it is suggested that students share parts of their logs with their classmates, read out to them and discuss their individual differences.

The following are suggestions for using the process log either inside or outside the classroom:[23]

Documenting the performance of academic reading-writing tasks: The students may be required, as were the subjects in the researcher's (1997) comprehensive

---

[23] *These have been tried out by the researcher in different courses. The most recent use of the process log is in her (in progress) follow-up study of the long-term effects of explicit strategy instruction on her 2002b subjects' writing from sources. These are currently enrolled in the researcher's seminar course and have been documenting their performance of writing the literature review for their research papers. For further suggestions, especially with regard to more structured logs, see: Cantrell et al. (2000); Commander & Smith (1996); McIntosh & Draper (2001).*

study, to document their processes of performing a writing task from the very beginning: selecting a topic, searching for information, processing the sources of information (selecting, etc.), coping with problems encountered, etc. The students will be required to submit their logs on a regular basis or to relate to them at their student-instructor conferences, or to submit the log with the final paper.

Documenting learning processes: The students may be required to summarize their classnotes after every lesson, or their reading assignments before every lesson, and to gradually and systematically synthesize the knowledge they are acquiring during the course. They may also be required at the end of the course to review their logs, highlight what they consider to be their more significant experiences, and relate to them as the final entry in their logs. Thus the process log will represent the students' authentic learning processes, and be submitted at the end of the course instead of a paper or test.

Documenting learning outcomes, such as conceptual change and strategic development:
- *Conceptual change*: At the beginning of a course, or at the beginning of every new chapter in the course, the students may be required to write definitions of their own to key terms introduced by the lecturer. At the end of the lesson or course the students will be required to redefine these terms, in order to find out how their initial conceptions have changed or evolved, and also to relate to these changes. This requirement may be combined with the technique of concept mapping, which serves to reveal students' knowledge structures, by means of graphic representation. The underlying assumption of this technique (Mahler, Hoz, & Fischl, 1991) is that it is possible to improve students' ability to learn by promoting their ability to organize concepts for the purpose of storing them or expanding the students' repertoire of connections among these concepts.
- *Strategic development:* In a course offering explicit instruction of learning strategies, the students may be required to analyze their own process logs at different stages in their learning, to investigate their development as strategic learners, as it is reflected in the findings obtained from the analysis. Thus the process log will serve both as a source and as a means for the students to learn about themselves and to further develop their metacognitive awareness.

Documenting the performance of L2 reading-L1 writing tasks: EFL college students[24] may be required, when performing a reading-writing task (e.g., asking or answering questions, summarizing), to simultaneously conduct a "double entry" log (see: Barell, 1991) in their mother tongue.[25] In the log they will relate to difficulties encountered in the process of performing the task, the strategies used to cope with these, etc. The rationale underlying the use of L1 in the double-entry log is twofold: First, English for these students is the language of reference rather than the language of thought (Cohen, 1995a, 1995b; Kern, 1994). If students are required to think about what they are reading or how they are thinking, they should be allowed to

---

[24] *I.e., students majoring in disciplines other than English, and taking a course in EFL academic reading in partial fulfillment of their academic requirements.*
[25] *Cf. Williams Mlynarczyk's (1998) ESL students, who conducted their journals in English as L2 in her writing course.*

think in the language they are used to thinking in, namely, their L1 (Hebrew in the case of most of the students' at the researcher's college). Second, for learning to be significant, it should be as authentic as possible and prepare them for their professional careers as elementary and middle school teachers: At college as well as in the future they will have to read in English, but they will almost always write in Hebrew. They should, therefore, be required to perform L2 reading-L1 writing tasks and document these in L1.[26]

Drafting an academic paper: Although the process log focuses on the process, it may also serve as a source for the writing of an academic paper. Thus, students may be required to enclose their practice assignments, or drafts, to their logs as in the case of the portfolio. The students will be required later to select one draft and revise it into a finished product.

AUTHOR'S NOTE

Two earlier versions of the present study were presented at the 30th International Conference of IATEFL (The University of Keele, Stoke-on-Trent, UK, April 9-12, 1996) and the 31st Annual TESOL Convention (Orlando, FL, USA, March 11-15, 1997).

APPENDIX A. QUESTIONNAIRE

Dear Student,

Please, respond to the following questions in detail. Your response is very important for the purpose of concluding the study you have been taking part in. In the study you were required to document your performance of the task of writing a review of the literature for your 3rd year methodology project paper by means of a process log.

The questions are:
1) Has the process log facilitated your performance of the task? How?
2) In light of your experience with the process log, do you have any suggestions to make with regard to the college curriculum? With regard to further research of the issue of writing a project paper?

Thank you for your cooperation.

---

[26] *For the theoretical and pragmatic rationale of the EFL reading curriculum at the researcher's college see: Segev-Miller (1992, 1994); and for the model of EFL reading assessment using L1 - Segev-Miller (1995).*

LEARNING BY WRITING HYPERTEXT: A RESEARCH BASED DESIGN OF UNIVERSITY COURSES IN WRITING HYPERTEXT

ELMAR STAHL & RAINER BROMME

University of Muenster, Germany

Abstract. In this chapter the design of university courses about writing hypertext is presented. The aim of these courses is to teach students how to write hypertext in a way that supports their knowledge acquisition in the subject matter to be processed. To achieve this objective, reflection on the design of hypertext is used to foster comprehension of the contents. The courses encompass five teaching units to present how to work with the features of hypertext appropriately. The instructional program of the courses was developed by taking theoretical ideas and empirical research about reading and writing traditional texts and hypertexts into account. Each of the units covers one of the aspects, which have to be dealt with during the process of writing hypertext: a) developing a basic understanding for hypertext, b) designing nodes, c) organizing an overall structure, d) considering multiple audience perspectives and e) setting links. The main elements of the instructional program are described in detail. An overview of the theoretical background and some concrete examples from the courses are given for each unit. The discussion shall embed this approach within the field of computer-based teaching.

Keywords: audience, discourse knowledge, hypermedia, hypertext, knowledge transforming, learning by design, teaching methods, writing, writing hypertext.

1. INTRODUCTION

In this chapter we report about university courses in writing hypertext. The rationale for the courses is the rapid spread of hypertexts in form of Internet pages during the last years. Via World Wide Web hypertexts have become the most common format of digital texts. Recent software developments have made it easy for everybody to write their own hypertexts. Accordingly, writing hypertext in form of Internet pages has become very popular during the last years. There are a growing number of courses in writing hypertext being offered in schools and universities. These courses

---

Stahl, E., & Bromme, R. (2004). Learning by writing hypertext: A research based design of university courses in writing hypertext.
In G. Rijlaarsdam (Series Ed.) and Rijlaarsdam, G., Van den Bergh, H. & Couzijn, M. (Vol. Eds.), Studies in writing, Volume 14, Effective learning and teaching of writing, 2nd edition, Part 3, Studies in writing-to-learn, 547 - 559.

are based on the assumption that writing hypertext may foster an active, cooperative and constructive learning process about the subject matter to be processed (e.g., Bromme & Stahl, 2002).

Research on writing traditional texts has shown that writing can activate thinking processes and contribute towards deepening one's own knowledge (e.g., Rijlaarsdam, Couzijn & Van den Bergh, 1996). Similar learning effects can be considered for writing hypertext.

Another advantage of hypertext lies in its features (nodes, links, and multi-linear structure) that place particular constraints on the design of the documents. These features are necessary to present information in a way that is compatible with the reading-process on computer screens. For example, information must be fragmented to separate nodes to keep readers from scrolling through long texts. Therefore it is necessary to order the text fragments through links to form a comprehensible structure. Thus writing hypertext consists of writing comprehensible text fragments, deciding about the number and location of links, designing an overall structure of the document and anticipating different ways of navigating through the hypertext (see Bromme & Stahl, 2002, 1999; Stahl, 2001). Dillon (2002) pointed out that authoring hypertext "is text production with the need to reconsider how we convey and exploit structure beyond the cues that authors (and readers) have relied upon for centuries (p. 65)".

We assume that the features of hypertext support a writing process that can be compared with "knowledge transforming" described by Bereiter and Scardamalia (1987). Knowledge transforming means that writing can only contribute to knowledge acquisition, if a text is formulated within a continuous interaction between the content-related knowledge (on the topic addressed in the text) and the discourse knowledge (this includes knowledge about genre, text structure, and how to adapt a text towards a specific audience). This problem-oriented procedure (see e.g., Hayes, 1996, Kellogg, 1994) requires authors to reflect on and extend their own knowledge.

These theoretical ideas about learning by writing traditional texts provide a helpful heuristic to examine conditions and processes of learning by writing hypertext. If the features of hypertext are considered consciously, a learning process comparable with knowledge transforming might be initiated. Thus writing hypertext might support knowledge acquisition in the following way (Bromme & Stahl, 2002, Stahl, 2001):

1) Writing nodes requires an author to discriminate between semantic concepts so that they can be presented as text units, each one being comprehensible by itself. As a result, writing nodes can contribute to the comprehension of concepts and conceptual differences within a subject matter.
2) Thinking about necessary links requires the processing of semantic relations between the concepts explained in different nodes. A thoughtful application of links can thereby contribute to the comprehension of semantic relations.
3) When planning the overall structure an author has to comprehend the content structure of the subject matter. Because of their multi-linearity hypertexts can be read in different ways. Thus authors have to anticipate possible audience perspectives to create flexible ways of reading their hypertext. This might contribute to a deeper comprehension of semantic structures within the subject matter

and to a more flexible use of this new knowledge (e.g., Jacobson & Spiro, 1995).

These knowledge-transforming processes described above represent an ideal case. We do not expect learners to profit "intuitively" in this way from writing hypertext. For example, it is not easy to keep the balance between thinking about the subject matter and the surface features of the hypertext (Dillon, 2002). Courses in schools and universities in writing hypertext often pay too much attention to the design of hypertext. The consequence is that students' comprehension of the subject matter, presented by their hypertexts, is a superficial one (Bereiter, 2002). Therefore it is necessary to find instructions that support learners in using the features of hypertext in a way that fosters possible knowledge-transforming processes.

We developed instructional units to teach university students how to use the features of hypertext consciously. This instructional program is mainly based on results from research on writing hypertext in secondary schools and several experimental studies about knowledge acquisition by writing hypertext (Bromme & Stahl, 1999, 2001, 2002, Stahl, 2001).

The main elements of the courses will be described in detail. For each unit a short overview of the theoretical and empirical background is given. Over the last years these courses have been taught several times. This enables us to report about practical experiences with them.

The university courses of writing hypertext are a part of the psychology masters program (diploma). They are offered as seminars on instructional media, which take two semesters i.e., one year. During the first semester students are introduced to theories about different kinds of media like texts, pictures, and multimedia. During the second semester, students have to write a hypertext about a predefined topic. They work in collaboration with each other and design the hypertext for an anticipated audience. These courses have two purposes: on the one hand, students should gain practical knowledge in writing hypertext. This should contribute to their literacy of designing learning environments. On the other hand, they should learn how to use writing hypertexts as a method to foster their own knowledge acquisition.

For the last four years we have also experimented with the implementation of writing hypertext in other seminars. In these seminars students learn about basics of educational psychology. Usually each student presents a paper about one topic followed by a short discussion. This means that students have an active role during their own presentations but a passive one during the presentations by others. This results in deeper knowledge about the topic that they present themselves but only superficial knowledge about the other topics. To avoid this, the role of the student in the new seminar is constantly an active one. All students write a hypertext of the seminar's topics in collaboration with each other.

As described above, a fundamental challenge of writing hypertext is to match the design of the document and the contents that is presented: the semantic structure of the contents should determine the structure of the hypertext; and the features of hypertexts determine how the contents should be presented. The students are gradually taught how to deal with this interaction of content and discourse knowledge.

Reflection on this interaction is supported by five instructional units, which are presented below. Each unit covers one of the aspects, which have to be dealt with during writing hypertext:

> Unit 1. Developing a basic understanding for hypertext in comparison to other genres of text.
> Unit 2. Developing design of nodes.
> Unit 3. Organizing an overall structure of the hypertext.
> Unit 4. Considering multiple audience perspectives.
> Unit 5. Setting and evaluating concrete links.

In the following section each unit is described. We explain the importance of the unit and present concrete examples from our courses to show how the students dealt with these requirements.

2. INSTRUCTIONAL PROGRAM OF WRITING HYPERTEXT

2.1 Unit 1. Developing a Basic Understanding for Hypertext Compared to Other Genres

During the first unit, students have to develop a metaphor that is appropriate to represent the contents of the hypertext. Stable patterns of presentations for traditional text formats have emerged over the centuries and serve as guides for authors as well as recipients (e.g., Landow, 1994). Newspapers, books, articles, etc. follow conventions of style and layout (Dillon, 2002). This knowledge about texts is important for text comprehension (e.g., Hayes, 1996; Kintch & Yarbrough, 1982) and text production (e.g., Bereiter & Scardamalia, 1987; Kellogg, 1994; Torrance, 1996). For digital genres like hypertext such regularities have just begun to emerge (Dillon & Gushrowski, 2000; Foltz, 1996; Rouet & Levonen, 1996). Therefore the first unit in our courses deals with the development of a collective idea of hypertext in a way that might initiate knowledge transforming.

This requires two levels: on the first level, students have to understand the fundamental features of hypertext and the differences compared to traditional text formats in general. If they are asked to write hypertexts, students will need a shared concept of hypertext to plan and communicate about it in a way that fosters their comprehension of the contents. On the second level, students have to develop an idea of the *concrete* structure of their hypertext. They should use this idea to plan the design of their hypertext in a way that helps anticipated readers to navigate through their hypertext.

In the area of designing computer software such general ideas are often communicated by metaphors. One example for this is the desktop metaphor, which is widely used to communicate graphically oriented user interfaces. Metaphors assist in linking new information to existing knowledge (Indurkhya, 1993). They structure perception and handling of the environment they refer to (Kim & Hirtle, 1995).

The use of metaphors to explain hypertext is also widespread (Gall & Hannafin, 1994; Hammond, 1993; Nielsen, 1993). The most common ones are book metaphors and space metaphors (McKnight, Dillon, & Richardson, 1991).

A *book metaphor* compares hypertexts with traditional books. Its advantage is the comparison of hypertexts (as a new text format) with the prototype of text formats (a book), which is familiar to every user. On the other hand, users may associate a book metaphor too closely with the idea of increasing linearity and reducing complexity, which can be seen as a disadvantage (Stahl, 2001; Tergan, 1997). This can be concluded from studies on navigation in hypertexts. Gray (1990, 1995), for example, showed that inexperienced users often apply linear mental models to hypertexts, and this leads to problems of navigation and information processing because they trigger wrong expectations. Leventhal, Teasley, Instone, Rohlman, and Farhat (1993) offered different functions for navigation and information search to their participants. They reported that users particularly select those functions corresponding to the use of a book, although others would be more useful. Tergan (1997) reported that inexperienced users often work with hypertext in the same way they do with linear texts, for example by "paging" through the nodes.

A *space metaphor* compares hypertexts with virtual information nets in which users can move around and seek for information (Gall & Hannafin, 1994; Kim & Hirtle, 1995). Concepts like "navigation" are typical for spatial associations. By using a space metaphor it should be possible to link new information with fundamental sensory experiences gained by everyone in their environment (in the sense of Lakoff, 1990; Lakoff & Johnson, 1980). Cunningham, Duffy, and Knuth (1993) as well as Turner and Dipinto (1992) reported that students who work on hypertexts for any period of time develop spatial metaphors to talk about their hypertexts. Levin, Stuve, and Jacobson (1999) did a study on mental representations of Internet users with different degrees of expertise. They found that increasing expertise leads to multiple representations of the Internet. Most of these representations can be conceived as spatial metaphors.

Bromme and Stahl (1999, 2001; Stahl, 2001) examined the influences of a book and a space metaphor on writing hypertext. They observed six classes in secondary schools, which wrote hypertexts about regular subject matters. The effects of both metaphors were also tested in an experiment. Their results confirmed that a book metaphor evokes an idea about hypertext that focuses on reducing complexity and sequencing information. In contrast, a space metaphor generates an idea of network-like connected information.

Therefore we conclude that a space metaphor is more suitable for emphasizing the potential complexity of hypertext in a way that facilitates comprehension of the complexity of its contents. We ask our students in the first unit of our courses to find a certain (spatial) metaphor that they can use to structure the subject matter in an appropriate way.

Figure 1a gives an example of a visualization of such a space metaphor. In this course students were asked to write a hypertext about the different forms of psychological therapy. The anticipated audience of this hypertext was laypersons in psychology, which wanted to get comprehensible introductions about the different forms of therapy. To facilitate navigation the students chose a metaphor of a therapy center. The first node of their hypertext presents a drawing of a reception with four doors leading to different forms of therapy (psychoanalysis, behavior therapy, client-centered therapy, and systemic therapy).

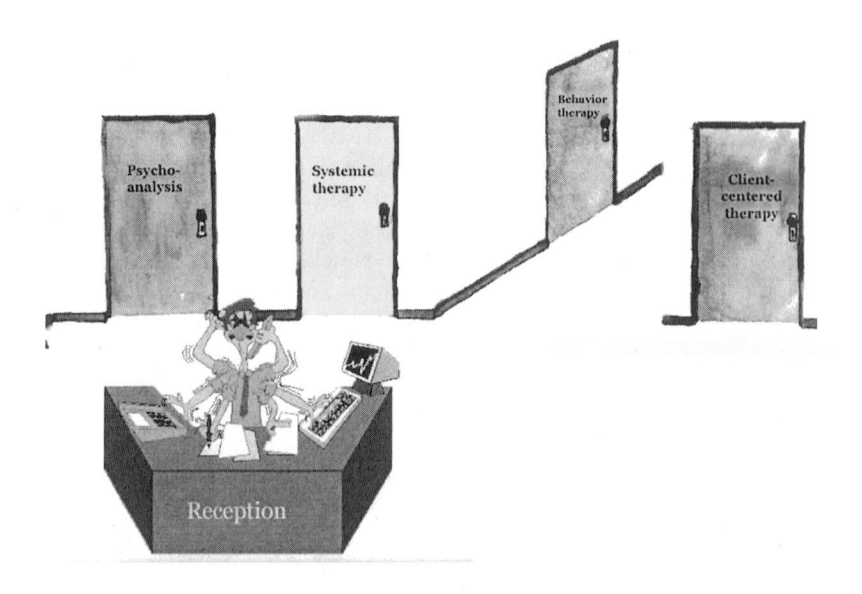

Figure 1. Reception of the therapy center, a hypertext about forms of psychological therapy.

The reader is able to enter the corresponding therapy room by point-and-click on one of the doors. For example, when a reader decides to "go" into the room for psychoanalysis, she enters a "typical" scenario within this therapy presented as a cartoon (figure 2).

All four rooms are presented as such cartoons of typical scenarios during the therapies. In each cartoon similar icons are integrated. The icons represent the various themes that are explained in the hypertext. For example, the light bulb is linked to nodes explaining the main idea of the therapy. A mouse click on the picture on the wall leads to nodes presenting information about the therapy founders (figure 3), and the filing cabinet links to descriptions of therapeutic case studies.

Apart from being motivating, the metaphor of a therapy center serves the two purposes described above. Firstly, it determines the design of the hypertexts and enhances their usability by giving a navigational aid to the readers. Secondly – and more importantly – it sets constraints on the design of the hypertexts which help the students to plan the structure of their hypertext, and by doing so, to elaborate and (re-) structure their own knowledge about the forms of therapy.

Figure 2. Psychoanalysis room within the therapy center.

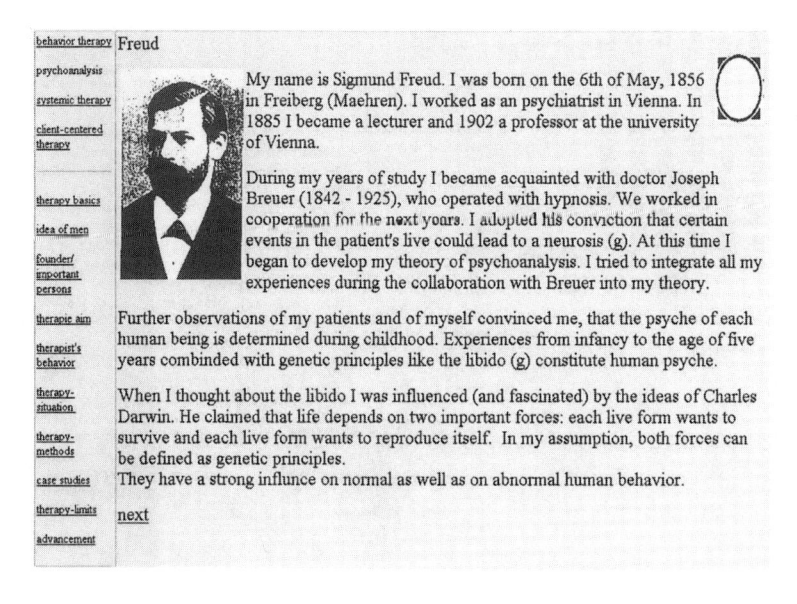

behavior therapy	**Freud**
psychoanalysis	My name is Sigmund Freud. I was born on the 6th of May, 1856 in Freiberg (Maehren). I worked as an psychiatrist in Vienna. In 1885 I became a lecturer and 1902 a professor at the university of Vienna.
systemic therapy	
client-centered therapy	
therapy basics	During my years of study I became acquainted with doctor Joseph Breuer (1842 - 1925), who operated with hypnosis. We worked in cooperation for the next years. I adopted his conviction that certain events in the patient's live could lead to a neurosis (g). At this time I began to develop my theory of psychoanalysis. I tried to integrate all my experiences during the collaboration with Breuer into my theory.
idea of men	
founder/ important persons	
therapie aim	Further observations of my patients and of myself convinced me, that the psyche of each human being is determined during childhood. Experiences from infancy to the age of five years combinded with genetic principles like the libido (g) constitute human psyche.
therapist's behavior	
therapy-situation	When I thought about the libido I was influenced (and fascinated) by the ideas of Charles Darwin. He claimed that life depends on two important forces: each live form wants to survive and each live form wants to reproduce itself. In my assumption, both forces can be defined as genetic principles.
therapy-methods	
case studies	They have a strong influnce on normal as well as on abnormal human behavior.
therapy-limits	next
advancement	

Figure 3. A node about Sigmund Freud, the founder of psychoanalysis.

2.2 Unit 2. Developing the Design of Nodes

During the second unit, students have to decide which concepts of the subject matter they want to include. They also have to write nodes explaining each one of these concepts.

Nodes present information in a fragmented form (Whalley, 1993). Up to now there are no clear guidelines about how to design an "ideal" node. It is reasonable to claim that the design of the nodes depends on the aim of the hypertext. If an author assumes that her audience only wants to read printouts, such a fragmentation in short text units should be avoided. But if the aim is to foster knowledge-transforming processes, it seems necessary to enhance the students' awareness of concepts and conceptual delimitations. A widespread recommendation is to design nodes following a "just enough" principle (Gerdes, 1997). Each node should only contain the necessary amount of information. Details or examples should be presented in separate nodes, which can be read whenever required. Each node should also be written in a way that can be called "cohesive closeness" (Gerdes, 1997). It means that the main information in each node must be comprehensible without reading further nodes. Stahl (2001) reported about five school classes that wrote hypertexts. He concluded that those classes had learned the most about the contents, which had taken these two principles into account.

Figure 4. Example of a node.

Correspondingly, our students are asked to explain only one main concept per node. Figure 4 shows an example of such a node. In this course students had to write a hypertext about the role of media for learning. The example presents a node taken from the subtopic "text comprehension". The text outlines the differences between textbase and situation model within the CI-model of Kintsch (1998). The picture on the left hand side presents a visualization of this content: how a surface structure of a text is transformed into a situation model.

It is important to note that nodes can be seen as drafts during this stage of the writing process. This means that during the following three units described below, it is often necessary to rewrite the nodes. The typical cycles of planning, translation, and revision during writing (see Hayes 1996) are also part of our courses. Planning phases in each of the five units require revision phases of the material developed so far.

2.3 Unit 3. Organizing an Overall Structure of the Hypertext

During the third unit, students are asked to discuss the macrostructure (in sense of Kintsch, 1998) of the contents and how to transfer it into the structure of the hypertext.

Thus the aim of this unit is to foster students' comprehension of the semantic structure. This unit also offers the possibility to check, whether every important concept is presented within the nodes, or if something crucial is missing. A promising way is the construction of an overview structure of the nodes.

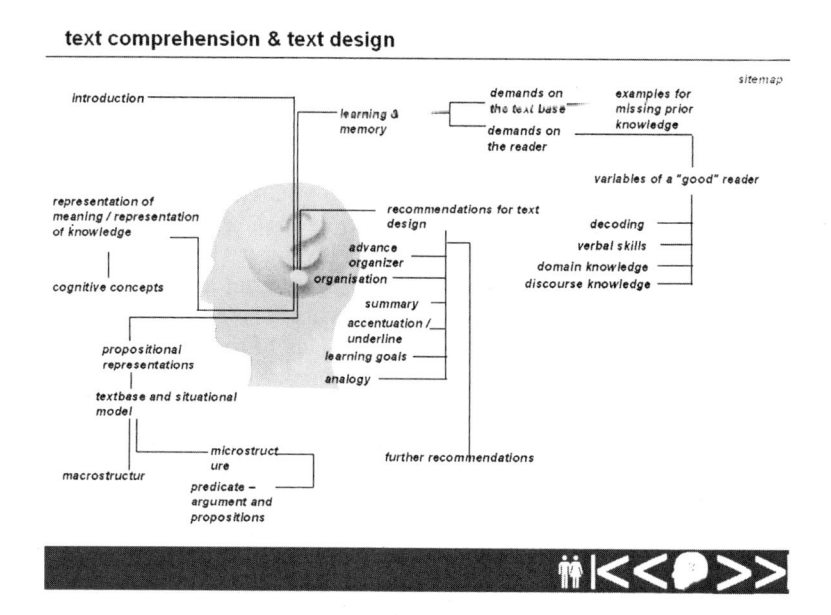

Figure 5. Structural overview of the contents of a hypertext.

Bromme and Stahl (1999) reported about secondary school classes, which made printouts of their nodes, attached them to the blackboard, structured and connected them with the help of woolen yarn. In our university courses we use a procedure consisting of concept mapping techniques to expatiate the semantic structure. Students are asked to develop a graphical overview of the contents of their hypertexts, which are designed for an anticipated audience. The audience should be able to use this overview to orient themselves within the contents. It should facilitate their navigation through the hypertext.

Figure 5 presents an example of a structural overview of a hypertext concerning the role of media for learning. A mouse click on one of the concepts opens the corresponding node.

If the students have developed a metaphor as presented in unit one, it is possible to include this graphical overview in the metaphor. For example, a metaphor like the "therapy center" can include such an overview at the reception. Every visitor can "ask" for the overview plan by clicking on the reception.

2.4 Unit 4. Considering Multiple Audience Perspectives

During the fourth unit, the students are asked to structure their contents considering different audience perspectives and to present multiple ways of navigation. In most cases semantically complex subject matters can be organized in different ways. Due to the multi-linear structure of hypertext, an author should offer the user a variety of ways to read through the nodes.

Since content coherence is a fundamental prerequisite for understanding texts (Kintsch, 1998), the author has to find a balance between flexible ways of reading the hypertext and a possible loss of coherence (Foltz, 1996). Ideally, the author should think about possible audience perspectives and should try to imagine, which contents and structure might be desired by an audience with a particular reading aim. If authors are asked to take different audience perspectives into account, knowledge could be acquired in a way that supports its flexible application.

This expectation is based on the Cognitive Flexibility Theory (CFT, e.g., Jacobson & Spiro, 1995). CFT discusses how knowledge about an ill-structured domain can be acquired in a way that ensures its flexible use. The goal is to stimulate learning transfer. According to CFT one reason for a lack of transfer is an inappropriate instruction method that usually oversimplifies complex contents. Therefore Jacobson and Spiro (1995) suggested instruction methods that emphasize complexity – through, for example, multiple representations of the domain. They consider hypertext as an appropriate tool, because their structural features facilitate presentations of the same contents from different perspectives. Bromme and Stahl transferred this assumption to the writing of hypertext. They examined the effects of taking different audience perspectives during the writing of hypertext into account (Bromme & Stahl, 2001, Stahl, 2001). Their results showed that adopting different perspectives encourages reflection on the structure of the hypertexts and the content structures.

This lead to higher transfer knowledge compared to a group that wrote hypertexts without reflecting about different audiences.

Correspondingly, we ask our students to anticipate audiences with differing perspectives / reading goals, to create multiple reading paths though the hypertext. A possibility to achieve this are guided tours. Guided tours present a common navigational tool in hypertexts. They suggest which nodes should be read in which kind of order by readers with different aims, and can be realized through special links and visualizations. Thus students have to take different audience perspectives into account and plan appropriate guided tours for each one of these perspectives. Another possibility is to create different structural overviews for audiences with different perspectives.

To develop such navigational tools students have to reflect on the contents from different perspectives in a way that their own understanding for the macrostructure of the contents is enhanced.

2.5 Unit 5. Setting and Evaluating Concrete Links

During the fifth unit, students are asked to discuss concrete links that they are placing in their hypertexts.

The availability of links is a fundamental aspect of hypertext environments. They have two important and closely related functions: firstly, they enable the user to navigate within the hypertext. In case that hypertexts do not have any additional functions like search functions, links are the only way to move around within a hypertext. A user has to rely on links if she wants to get to the desired text passage (Dillon, 1996). Therefore the selection of offered links has a great influence on the recipient's navigation: Wright (1993) presented research findings showing that in a course of reading a hypertext, the recipient's willingness to look up certain concepts in a glossary can be influenced significantly by the localization and design of the links. In line with this viewpoint Welsh, Murphy, Duffy and Goodrum (1993) reported that changes in the number of links per node and their localization within the nodes altered the user's navigation behavior significantly.

Secondly, links represent the semantic relations between the node contents. The recipients have to interpret the links on this semantic level. Therefore problems of comprehension could arise, if recipients do not know where a link leads to or if they have inappropriate expectations about its purpose. A main reason of disorientation in hypertexts and for superficial comprehension is a misinterpretation of links (Gray, 1995).

According to the two functions of links, the thoughtful placing of links is an important demand on the authors of hypertexts (Landow, 1994). To foster knowledge transformation it is important that students understand the semantic relations between the concepts. They should also use the task of setting links to discuss concrete semantic relations between the contents of the nodes.

Bromme and Stahl examined how far the comprehension of the semantic relationships, expressed by means of links, could be improved by asking participants to classify each link they set (Stahl, 2001). Their results showed that classifying links according to semantic type encouraged a deeper elaboration of the relations between the node contents.

In our courses we try to enhance the awareness and comprehension of semantic relations by asking our students to justify each link that they want to set. A student has to explain to the others, which kind of semantic relation she wants to express by a link, and why this relation might be important in the context of this particular node.

Discussing links between nodes might also result in modifications of the nodes. For example, it might be necessary to rewrite some parts of a node to integrate a reference to another node. This unit can also lead to a deeper understanding of the macrostructure of the topic and therefore it might result in a revision of structural overviews as well.

These five units enable us to teach the students gradually how to deal with the features of hypertexts in a way, that the reflection about the structure of the hypertexts and its contents is fostered.

As described above, each unit might result in revisions of the material developed so far. Therefore the process of writing hypertext can be seen as a circular process, even if the units are arranged in an instructional sequence.

It is also important to note that the technical transformation of the material into hypertexts should be the last step of the sequence. The students shouldn't construct their hypertext before the drafts of the nodes, the links, the overall structure, the guided tours, and the metaphors are finished. If the five units have been accomplished thoroughly, this technical transformation is an easy and fast process.

We assume that our instructional program supports a process comparable to the one of knowledge transforming that results in deeper knowledge about the subject matter and leads to a hypertext of higher quality.

3. DISCUSSION

In this chapter we present the design of our computer-based university courses. Most university courses that integrate computer-based teaching use computers for retrieving information, learning with the help of interactive environments, or fostering net-based cooperation.

These aspects can be integrated in our courses as well, but they do not represent the main idea. Our students use computers to search for information, but only insofar, that they can refer to this information within their own hypertexts. They are also able to integrate other representations like pictures, films, and audio documents into their nodes, to support comprehension of the contents, which they are presenting. Constructing this kind of hypermedia demands solving some further problems, like finding coherent combinations of text, pictures, and animations. But the main principles for constructing hypermedia and writing hypertext are the same. It is also possible to integrate computer-mediated cooperation in our courses. Students from different universities are able to write hypertexts in net-based cooperation. Furthermore, our students can cooperate virtually with each other, either complementary to or instead of face-to-face communication. These elements of computer-based teaching are possibilities but no necessities to represent our main ideas.

Our instructional program represents the "old" didactical method of learning by writing. We combine this method with the possibilities and demands of hypertext. The courses build on the original idea of hypertext, intended by its "founders", Bush, Nelson, and Engelbart (see Landow, 1994). Alongside the potential of fast access to large amounts of information, they stressed the opportunity for users to change hypertexts themselves and to construct their own text documents: "[...] in hypertext the function of reader merges with that of author and the division between the two is blurred. [...] Technology transforms readers into reader-authors or "wreaders" [...]" (Landow, 1994: 14).

During the courses that we have run so far, we had to deal with different problems. Firstly, it is necessary that the students have some prior knowledge about the contents that they want to present, *before* they plan their hypertexts. The process of writing hypertexts can then support further elaborating, expansion, and transformation of this knowledge. We recommend that the first third of a course should be used to read and discuss the respective topic. After that, students are prepared to start with unit one.

Secondly, the technical aspect should be considered closely. A computer room and some experience with the required software are necessary. We are using software like FrontPage, Netscape composer or PowerPoint, which is easy to handle. Most students have prior experience with this software and it is sufficient to create nice designs. The mastery of more complex software is too time consuming. The targeted balance between content and design would be annulled, if the technical implementations were too extensive.

We consider the process of designing a hypertext to be a process of writing because of the following reasons: firstly, most information in hypertexts is presented in text-form, and thus the main activity of a hypertext author is to write. We agree with Dillon (2002) that the differences between writing traditional texts and hypertexts are based on the multi-linear structure of hypertexts. Therefore it is interesting to examine how far theories of writing can be transferred to writing hypertext. We assume that the similarities between writing in these different text formats are much larger than their differences. The process of writing hypertext is mainly a process of planning, translation, and revision of text, even if some units in our courses are mainly focusing on aspects like setting links and metaphorical explanations.

Secondly – as Hayes (1996) pointed out – models of writing should try to include effects of a wide range of components, like visual and spatial features of texts, combinations of texts with other representations like pictures and graphs, the medium, different genres, social contexts, motivational aspects of writing, and so on. Our courses and studies about writing hypertext are designed to contribute to such an aim.

THE EFFECT OF STUDENT PRIOR EXPERIENCE, AT-TITUDES, AND APPROACHES ON PERFORMANCE IN AN UNDERGRADUATE SCIENCE WRITING PROGRAM

CHARLOTTE E. TAYLOR & HELEN DRURY

University of Sydney, Australia

Abstract. Designing a program to teach writing within the science curriculum may not be effective if we do not understand what factors influence success in the writing process. We therefore collected data to create a profile of the characteristics of our incoming undergraduate science students with reference to their prior experiences, attitudes and approaches to writing. Significant correlations were found between the extent of prior experience, positive attitudes and type of approach to writing. Comprehensive prior experience and a positive attitude correlated strongly with subsequent success in the first semester writing program in biology. Students without these characteristics may therefore be entering our program with a clear disadvantage. The data were used to propose changes to the writing program particularly in the areas of preparation, practice and feedback phases of the cycle of learning. These curriculum changes are designed to create a more positive student perception of the teaching and learning context so that students can adapt a more effective approach to writing in the sciences and hence improve the quality of their learning outcomes.

Keywords: prior writing experiences, approaches to writing, attitudes to writing, science writing curriculum.

1. INTRODUCTION

1.1 The Values of Writing in the Degree Program

It is essential that students in science learn to communicate effectively within their discipline using the appropriate scientific writing genres (Keys, 1999), since this is one of the most important skills for a successful career in science (Moore, 1994). The value of possessing or developing good writing skills, and having a facility with

---

Taylor, C. E., & Drury, H. (2004). The effect of student prior experience, attitudes, and approaches on performance in an undergraduate Science Writing Program.
In G. Rijlaarsdam (Series Ed.) and Rijlaarsdam, G., Van den Bergh, H. & Couzijn, M. (Vol. Eds.), Studies in writing, Volume 14, Effective learning and teaching of writing, 2nd edition, Part 3, Studies in writing-to-learn, 561-573.

the language of the discipline is thus an integral and explicit part of the academic environment. The extent to which undergraduates embrace this concept will determine their initial, and possibly only, degree of success in academic writing activities. However, there are a number of obstacles to providing an appropriate training and assessment for all undergraduates (Clanchy & Ballard, 1995).

In this context it is essential to know which learning activities best help students (Lea & Street, 1998), since interventions designed to help develop writing skills may have little effect if students are lacking in confidence or motivation, have a poor approach to learning, or see writing as unimportant. The level of independence exhibited by students during the writing process may also be linked to their previous experience and success in writing. Students entering undergraduate science programs thus bring with them experiences and attitudes, which will influence their approach to writing tasks, and may affect their subsequent performance in such tasks.

1.2 Student Experience of and Attitudes to Writing

Students arriving in new academic environments carry with them very varied experiences of learning both in terms of quantity and quality (Prosser and Trigwell, 1999). The way in which these prior experiences mirror the new situation and prepare students for new learning activities may play a major role in their subsequent success both in terms of changing or retaining a learning approach and in terms of the student's attitude to the activities. Incoming students' prior experiences have been acknowledged to some extent in developing teaching strategies for integration with curriculum material (Sander, Stevenson, King, & Coates, 2000).

The attitudes of incoming science students in biology, and their effect on performance in writing programs, have been documented by Moore (1993). He found that students were initially often hostile to writing activities, perceiving them to be outside the discipline. They did not like writing, did not want to do any in their courses, had poor skills in writing, and little motivation or understanding of improving. Moore demonstrated that designing a positive approach and learning experience encouraged students to want to do more writing and drew them into a cycle of learning to write.

1.3 Student Approaches to Writing

Biggs (1987a) defined a number of different approaches that student adopt when given learning tasks. These can be characterized in terms of deep surface and strategic approaches and were originally perceived as being relatively stable in a number of learning activities. Surface approaches are characterized by reproduction of knowledge, whereas deep approaches are at the 'transformational end of learning' (Brockbank & McGill, 1998) where the learner goes beyond reproduction to the abstraction of meaning. A strategic approach to learning may focus predominantly on addressing the demands of assessment (Entwistle, 1998), such that aims involve strategies and learning behaviors, which will maximize marks such as organizing material and having a calculated, well-managed approach to study.

However these approaches now tend to be seen as being contextualized by students and therefore may change if tasks encourage this (Prosser & Trigwell, 1999). In the present study, questions from the Study Process Questionnaire devised by Biggs (1987a & b) and the Approaches to Study Inventory of Entwistle (1998) were adapted to a context specific activity, namely academic writing in science. Such an approach had previously been used successfully to work with students' perceptions of different types of assessment tasks (Scouller, 1998).

1.4 The Scientific Writing Program

The writing program in first year biology at The University of Sydney is characterized by a series of phases, which form a cycle of learning experiences (Settlage, 2000) (Table 1). Inherent in the process is the necessity for communication of expectations between teachers and students, so that key areas of the writing process can be developed through a good working and learning relationship. This is accompanied by a sequential presentation of concepts and activities (Lea, 1998), plus a presentation of tasks, which allows students to demonstrate their competence to teachers, and to themselves (Nightingale, 1988). Integration with the discipline material is seen as an essential component of this building process. In this way writing is not just for communicating, but also helps to develop analytical abilities, knowledge construction and retention. The cycle also acknowledges that most learning probably occurs outside the teacher's sphere of influence (Biggs 1987a): the role of teacher becomes one of facilitating the environment in which the learning occurs.

Table 1. Stages and Key Elements of the Writing Program within the Biology Curriculum

Stages	Sequencing
Preparing	Make explicit: …course expectations (i.e.: information about assignments, number, timing, % of marks etc.); …by guidelines, modeling etc. assignment types i.e.: genre expectations; …assessment criteria.
Practising	Create space for practice of writing different genres or parts of genres after giving guidelines on these and before assessing them. Set writing tasks progressively so that they build on previous tasks in terms of the demands of content and genre.
Feedback	Give feedback: ….on practice writing. Direct feedback so that it can be used in the assessed assignment; …on assessed writing as soon as possible after submission.
Reflection	Allow students to reflect on their writing practice and performance after each assignment is returned to students with their own individual feedback. Reflect on how they write, what they learn from writing, etc. Direct reflections towards action for the next assignment.

In the preparation phase of the cycle the emphasis is on making explicit the course goals and expectations, including assessment criteria, in terms of writing and exemplifying and modeling the genres students will be writing. The writing phase of the cycle concentrates on providing opportunities for practice and discussion of the scientific genres in a student centered, non-threatening environment (Nicol *et al.*, 1994). In the feedback phase, students submit a draft report for diagnostic, formative feedback from their teachers before final submission for assessment purposes. Giving formative feedback involves students in reflection on what they have written and what changes they are going to make. This use of feedback provides a model for the final reflection stage when individual and generalized feedback on the present task needs to be applied to the next task.

2. AIMS OF THIS STUDY

This chapter reports on a survey of students' prior writing experience, attitudes and approaches (Biggs, 1987a and b) to scientific writing in their first year of a science degree program. These data are compared with a profile of the student writer in terms of their report writing performance and literacy assessment (The MASUS Procedure: Bonanno and Jones, 1997) as well as their overall success in the final course examination. In this way, we can determine the extent to which experiences and attitudes are related to students' approaches to writing and writing outcomes, as well as overall performance, during the early stages of their degree program. The research outcomes on students' attitudes, experiences and approaches can then be used to develop teaching and learning strategies to improve the effectiveness of the scientific writing program, especially for low achieving students or students with poor attitudes and approaches and negative past experiences.

3. METHODS AND DATA ANALYSIS

175 volunteers from the first year biology cohort (N = 1180) at The University of Sydney were surveyed, on entry to the university in semester 1, with a pre-writing questionnaire. At the end of the semester the same students were asked to complete a post-writing questionnaire, and results of this survey will be reported in a separate paper. Questions were designed to provide information specifically about three areas of the student experience of writing. These areas are
1) quantitative and qualitative measures of prior experience of writing,
2) attitudes to the experiences of writing,
3) approaches to writing.
Data was also recorded for a fourth area
4) performance indicators prior to, and after, participation in the writing program.
Prior experience questions gave information about the range and number of writing tasks. The number of science assignments and the number of other written assignments completed in the previous year were surveyed, and the breadth of science writing tasks was ascertained as a composite score of types of scientific writing at-

tempted – lab experiments, scientific literature report, science essay discussing ones views on a topic, group assignments and other tasks being the options available.

Attitudes to writing were assessed using questions about the degree of success in written assignments, ability to cope with written tasks, and perceived ability to write in good English. A specific 'attitude' component was also constructed from information about perceptions of
- Entry qualifications,
- Assignment writing skills,
- Ability to plan and organize writing.

Students were asked to rate themselves in these areas in comparison to other students in the cohort.

Students' approach to writing was determined using a modified series of questions from the Study Process Questionnaire of Biggs (1987a), with further input from questionnaires of Scouller (1998), and Entwistle (1998).

Writing performance was investigated using data from the University Admissions Index (UAI), plus assessment marks from the first year biology course. The latter comprised the mark for the laboratory report and the final course mark. In addition a literacy assessment was carried out on a subset of 80 students for their laboratory report. Literacy was ranked in four areas, which represent a spectrum of perspectives on the students' writing, from a macro level to a micro level. These areas are:
- Transfer and integration of relevant reference material,
- Use of an appropriate genre structure,
- Academic style and cohesion,
- Correct grammar.

Student responses were analyzed by a Pearson Correlation Analysis and a cluster analysis. The correlation analysis determined the relationship between pairs of variables, and indicated how the components of the writing experience relate to each other. The cluster analysis detected characteristics of sub groupings of students, thus providing information about how individual students experience the components of the writing experience. The validity of the 'surface', 'deep' and 'strategic' items for approaches to writing, was determined using a Cronbach α analysis.

4. RESULTS

4.1 Characteristics of the Student Cohort

The students sampled had a mean entry grade (UAI) of 87.9 on a scale of 1-100, compared with a mean of 86.5 for the whole cohort. The volunteers were thus a representative subset of the group. The majority of the respondents were recent school leavers (84% finished during the previous year) and 75% designated English as their home language. Since most students were recent school leavers their writing experiences at school were those mainly reported. The mean final mark for the course was 60.97% and for the laboratory report was 70.25%.

4.2 Reliability Analysis and Correlation Analysis

There was strong correlation between the attitude items on the questionnaire, and it was thought that they were measuring the same underlying factor. A reliability analysis gave an alpha value of .73, so these three variables were combined to give an "attitude to assignment writing" factor.

An analysis of the approaches to writing data showed that the deep approach to writing factor consisted of 10 items with a reliability alpha of .69. The surface approach to learning consisted of 10 items with a reliability alpha of .62, and the strategic approach to learning consisted of 10 items with a reliability alpha of .71. Although the reliability value for the surface approach is marginal, the results mirror those from similar studies (Trigwell, Prosser & Waterhouse, 1999). Revision of some of the surface items may be applicable in future studies. Pearson correlation coefficients for all variables are shown in Appendix A and discussed below.

4.3 Prior Experiences of Writing

The breadth of types of prior writing experiences was positively and significantly correlated with the numbers of writing tasks completed ($r = .43$ and $r = .41, p = .01$). It was also positively and significantly correlated with deep and strategic approaches to writing and with an attitude of coping well with previous writing experiences ($r = .46, r = .45, r = -.38, p = .01$). Breadth of experience correlated negatively and significantly with a surface approach to writing ($r = -.39, p = .01$)

4.4 Attitude to Writing

Student attitudes to writing showed significant correlations with a number of variables. There was a negative correlation with surface approach to writing ($r = -.45, p = .01$), and positive correlations with both deep ($r = .40, p = .001$) and strategic ($r = .39, p = .01$) approaches to writing. Attitude was also positively correlated with a perception of coping well with writing ($r = .56, p = .01$) and receiving good grades for writing ($r = .55, p = .01$). There was a significant negative correlation between attitude and a perception that English was not a problem when writing ($r = -.39, p = .01$). It should be noted that this was the only measure of students' experience of writing that correlated with performance in the course as indicated by the final grade ($r = .27, p = .05$).

4.5 Approaches to Writing

Deep approaches to writing correlated positively and significantly with strategic approaches ($r = .74, p = .01$), with a positive attitude to writing ($r = .40, p = .01$), and with perceptions of coping well with writing tasks ($r = .49, p = .01$).

Strategic approaches to writing showed a similar pattern of correlations. Surface approaches to writing showed no significant positive correlations, but correlated negatively and significantly with deep approaches to writing ($r = -.40, p = .01$), breadth of writing experience ($r = .39, p = .01$), receiving good grades for previous writing tasks ($r = -.37, p = .01$), and having a positive attitude to writing ($r = -.45, p = .01$).

4.6 Performance in Writing

Indicators of overall performance such as UAI and final mark generally showed fewer significant correlations with other variables. However UAI ($r = .45, p = .01$) showed a positive significant correlation with attitude to writing ($r = .50, p = .01$), as well as with receiving good grades ($r = 0.51, p = .01$) and coping well with prior writing tasks ($r = .28, p = .05$) In addition all performance indicators (UAI, final grade and lab report grade) correlated with each other at the $p = .01$ level of significance. Similarly, report literacy showed few significant correlations other than with performance indicators (UAI, $r = .48, p = .01$; Lab report grade, $r = 0.73, p = 0.01$; Final grade, $r = .61, p = .01$). It also correlated significantly coping successfully with previous writing assignments ($r = .43, p = .01$). Literacy correlations were based on a smaller sample of the original ($n = 41$), as complete data could not be obtained for every variable in this area.

4.7 Cluster Analysis

Results of a cluster analysis using Ward's minimum variance method indicated a three-cluster solution (based on the magnitude of the increasing value of the Squared Euclidean Distance between clusters) as shown in Table 2.

Cluster 1 is characterized by a group of students who have low scores for questions relating to surface approaches to writing, and high scores for questions relating to deep approaches to writing. They have a positive attitude to writing, cope well with writing tasks and have previously received good grades for written tasks.

The second cluster comprises a group of students who have low scores for questions relating to surface approaches to writing, and low scores for questions relating to deep approaches to writing. They have a poor attitude to writing and feel that they cope poorly with writing tasks.

The third cluster is characterized by students who have poor grades for the current writing tasks and the course in general, but feel that they can cope well with writing tasks and have a positive attitude. They have average scores for questions relating to deep, surface and strategic approaches to writing and therefore seem to be disengaged from the activity.

Since the sample size was smaller for items relating to performance (UAI) and literacy (Lab report literacy), they were not included in the original cluster analysis. However, means and standard deviations for these items for each cluster were calculated, as shown in Table 3, and these show similar trends to the other performance indicators in clusters 1 and 3, and a negative trend for cluster 2 suggesting that students in this cluster perform poorly in these areas.

Table 2. Summary Statistics for Prior Experience, Attitudes and Approaches to Writing using Cluster Analysis

Variable	Cluster 1 (n = 38) M	SD	Cluster 2 (n = 50) M	SD	Cluster 3 (n = 12) M	SD
Prior experiences						
Number of previous writing tasks	0.34	1.18	-0.39	0.66	0.27	1.14
Number of other writing tasks	0.08	0.94	0.02	0.99	0.05	1.18
Breadth of previous writing tasks	0.28	0.89	-0.25	1.01	0.27	1.09
Previously received good grades for writing	0.52	0.99	-0.35	0.95	0.11	0.66
English grammar not a problem	0.48	0.67	-0.49	1.04	0.54	0.89
Attitudes to writing						
Coped well with previous writing tasks	0.60	0.68	-0.59	0.85	0.69	1.19
Attitude to writing	0.59	0.87	-0.57	0.92	0.40	0.92
Approaches to writing						
Surface approach to writing	-0.65	0.96	0.47	0.70	-0.16	1.40
Deep approach to writing	0.62	0.55	-0.68	0.91	0.13	0.99
Strategic approach to writing	0.64	0.56	-0.52	0.95	-0.06	1.15
Performance outcomes						
Lab report grade	0.40	0.58	0.19	0.59	-1.97	1.10
Final course grade	0.39	0.81	0.03	0.79	-1.43	1.20

Statistically significant at p<0.01 for all items except Number of other assignments (p = .965) and Breadth of previous writing tasks (p = .028).

Table 3. Summary Statistics for UAI, and Report Literacy using Cluster Analysis

Variable	Cluster 1 n	M	SD	Cluster 2 N	M	SD	Cluster 3 N	M	SD
Performance indicators									
UAI	22	0.51	0.67	30	-0.09	1.03	10	-0.63	0.98
Report literacy	28	0.27	0.99	38	-0.08	1.00	3	-0.13	0.71

Statistically significant at p<0.5 for report literacy and at p<0.01 level for UAI.

5. DISCUSSION

The results focus on the relationships between variables, which comprise the learning of writing for undergraduate students, as well as identifying clusters of students as a function of their experiences of the writing process. These data are discussed in terms of creating a profile of individual students as they begin the first year writing program. They are also used to suggest changes to the writing curriculum to better help students learn academic writing.

5.1 Creating a Student Profile

The data above describe a number of key characteristics of our students with respect to writing. The profile of an incoming student focuses on their attitude to writing, which has been moulded by their previous experiences and approaches. Thus students with extensive and positive experiences in writing arrive with a positive attitude and adopt successful writing approaches and cope well with our undergraduate writing program. This broadly describes the 38% of students in cluster 1. However, the majority of students (50%), as described by cluster 2, tend to identify more with surface approaches to writing and this, combined with little prior writing experience and a largely negative approach tends to result in average to poor performance. Finally a small minority of students (12% in cluster 3) are failing as measured by performance indicators, have not adopted a consistent approach to writing and have largely limited and negative prior experiences.

The fact that a positive attitude to writing related more significantly to the extent of previous experience, and perceptions of success in writing experience rather than to UAI shows that incoming students who can identify with these characteristics can be expected to succeed in their writing. We can therefore further support the development of positive attitudes to writing – by enhancing the status of the writing experiences we provide, emphasizing the importance of practice and approach as well as raising confidence through positive, formative feedback. The significant association of poor attitude with negative prior writing experiences in terms of coping, practice and grades, combined with a surface approach to writing points to the possibility of identifying a cohort of low-achieving student writers who will need more help and direction to learn within the existing writing program. Armed with this information we can thus make changes to the writing curriculum to account for our different student profiles emphasizing the development of a positive attitude to writing through building confidence.

5.2 Changes to the Scientific Writing Program Based on Research Outcomes

Our research outcomes emphasize the importance of taking into account what students bring with them – their attitudes, experiences and approaches – to the new teaching/learning context of writing in the sciences at university. Therefore, the initial phase of the writing program, the preparation phase, is a critical site for student reflection on where they are in terms of writing and where they need to be if they are to succeed in writing in the sciences at university.

In this preparation phase, the questionnaire, which allowed us to create a student profile, can be used as an instrument for reflection for students and a diagnostic tool for both students and teachers. For students, this self diagnostic tool can introduce an opportunity for reflection on their own individual experiences, attitudes and approaches to writing and make them aware of the factors involved in writing development as they move from a school to a university context. This increased awareness can provide a context for change in attitude and in approach, which may not have been previously considered, as many students would have unconsciously applied their existing attitudes and approaches to the new context. For teachers, the profile allows us to know our students better and where they are along the continuum of experience, attitudes and approaches. It can be used to identify students who may be disadvantaged or at risk of failing in writing as well as students who are low achievers or who are just coping or passing in terms of their writing performance. These students can be monitored and given more support during the subsequent phases of the program, especially those parts which are designed to improve students' confidence and develop a positive attitude to writing in science.

Many students – more than 50% in our sample – reported some degree of anxiety about the kinds of writing they would be expected to do in first-year biology, recognizing that this is a new and unfamiliar context. However, having a positive and confident attitude to writing, as the research data shows, is linked to success in assignment writing. Therefore, the preparation phase of the program needs to reduce these anxiety levels, which are associated with entering a new learning context. Many of the activities in the preparation phase already aim to make the new context explicit in terms of course requirements, genre expectations and examples etc. However, although genres are modeled in a progressive way, students' prior experiences and understandings of, for example, the genre of the laboratory report are not taken into account or built on. Our research data suggests that it is important to make the connection between what students already understand and know about the product and process of report writing (and some students will have had very little, if any, experience of writing this genre) and the requirements of the new context. In the same way, although teachers' expectations of student writing are made explicit through discussion of assessment criteria, students need to relate these criteria to their prior understanding of what good writing is. For example, we have now introduced an activity that exemplifies the criteria for success in university science writing. This involves students examining two short example texts on the biology topic they are currently studying, one of which presents a number of problems in terms of content, structure and language. Based on comparisons of these texts, students work out their own assessment criteria before comparing these to criteria used by teachers in marking written work. In this way, largely abstract evaluation criteria are made concrete through exemplification.

The writing phase of the program, which focuses on practice, can also be used as a site to explore the approaches students adopt towards writing and in this way move students towards best practice approaches. Deep or strategic approaches to writing tasks need to be re-inforced and re-interpreted in the new university context. Clearly, it is of critical importance for those students identified as adopting a surface approach to have an opportunity to learn about and successfully practise a new approach. Since the writing phase already involves students in preparing draft practice reports for discussion and feedback from teachers and peers, best practice approaches can be made explicit in this context. For example, strategic approaches such as planning within a time frame, working out the requirements of the task, outlining an answer, drafting and re-drafting and proof reading; and deep approaches such as, understanding the point of the assignment, showing the relationships between ideas, and critically reflecting on both content and form while writing can be discussed and exemplified. The research data shows strong correlations among these approaches and previous success in assignment writing.

The feedback phase is a critical site for promoting positive attitudes in weaker, less confident students. It can provide a positive learning experience rather than simply summative evaluation of their writing, which may be perceived as having a negative bias. Students are presented with diagnostic feedback, which they need to apply to the writing of their final draft if they are to get good marks. In this way, there is a strong incentive for acting on the feedback and this of necessity involves students in reflection on what they have written and what changes they are going to make, thus fostering a deep approach to writing. Weaker students, if they learn from their feedback, almost certainly gain good or improved marks and this can be a significant event for students who are used to performing poorly in writing. This success can be a catalyst for creating a more positive attitude to writing.

In the final reflection stage, individual and generalized feedback on the present task needs to be applied to the next task. Such an application poses a challenge for students who are used to seeing curriculum topics and assignments in a compartmentalized way. The survey data did not directly collect information in this area but the fact that most students saw little connection between their writing in biology and their future writing in a professional context suggests that students are not used to linking their experiences across courses and disciplines, let alone to the real world. Our research suggests that as students move onward and upward through the science undergraduate curriculum, they will need to reassess their writing experiences, attitudes and approaches. This means that writing development needs to be integrated progressively within and between courses in the undergraduate science curriculum so there is a continuum from first to third year and onward into the honors year. Creating such a curriculum certainly poses a challenge for us.

6. CONCLUSION

The scientific writing program provides an environment for helping students to improve and develop writing skills within a supportive discipline-based community of peers and teachers. As much as possible, it aims to take into account the attitudes, experiences and approaches that students bring with them, as it is these that will influence learning outcomes in the new context (Lea & Street, 1998). It allows for space and time in the curriculum for students to reflect on their current writing knowledge and practices and compare these with the requirements of the new disciplinary culture of the university. As this new culture and its writing practices are gradually made explicit to students, spaces for reflection on and re-thinking of writing products and practices are necessary so that students can adapt, change and practise writing new texts in new ways with feedback and guidance from peers and teachers. By providing feedback on draft reports, with incentives for participation as students engage in the process, we aim to encourage a deeper approach to writing, with associated advantages for continuing engagement and improvement.

ACKNOWLEDGMENTS

Thanks to Associate Professor Michael Prosser and Dr. Paul Ginns for their help and advice with the statistical analyses.

Appendix A. Pearson Correlation Coefficients for performance, student experiences, attitudes and approaches to writing (listwise n = 62). Correlation value appears first, followed by the probability that this is due to chance. ** Correlation is significant at the 0.01 level (2-tailed); * significant at the 0.05 level (2-tailed)

		2	3	4	5	6	7	8	9	10	11	12	13
1.	Number of previous science tasks	.363** .004	.409** .001	.170 .185	-.012 .928	.307* .015	.198 .123	-.134 .297	.216 .092	.293* .021	.109 .397	-.090 .487	-.139 .282
2.	Number of other writing tasks	1	.427** .001	.333** .008	.012 .925	.222 .083	.113 .381	-.194 .132	.223 .082	.210 .101	.039 .762	-.024 .854	.006 .966
3.	Breadth of previous writing tasks		1	.223 .081	-.118 .361	.378** .002	.264* .038	-.394** .002	.463** .000	.447** .000	.024 .854	-.106 .414	-.111 .390
4.	Previously received good grades for writing			1	-.235 .066	.341** .007	.549** .000	-.368** .003	.182 .157	.250 .050	.508** .000	.209 .104	.156 .225
5.	English grammar not a problem				1	-.233 .068	-.389** .002	.256* .045	-.166 .196	-.239 .061	-.324* .010	-.054 .678	.069 .592
6.	Coping well with previous writing tasks					1	.564** .000	-.306* .015	.493** .000	.400** .001	.280* .028	.041 .754	.007 .959
7.	Attitude to writing						1	-.448** .000	.400** .001	.392** .002	.498** .000	.273* .032	.050 .699
8.	Surface approach to writing							1	-.400** .001	-.280* .028	-.195 .129	-.117 .365	.022 .865
9.	Deep approach to writing								1	.738** .000	.036 .784	-.033 .802	.023 .862
10.	Strategic approach to writing									1	.057 .662	.003 .985	.026 .844
11.	University Admission Index (UAI)										1	.683** .000	.452** .000
12.	Final grade											1	.710** .000
13.	Lab report grade												1

CHILDREN'S WRITING STRATEGIES: PROFILES OF WRITERS

ANAT SHAPIRA* & RACHEL HERTZ-LAZAROWITZ**

*Gordon College of Education, Haifa, **Haifa University, Israel*

Abstract. The goal of the study was to investigate via Writing Strategies Interviews (WSI) and Writing Think Aloud Procedure (WTAP), the use of writing strategies defined as actions and behaviors used by the writer to solve problems in the writing process. A writer's profile was defined as the average score for each of the four theory-based clusters used: Meta-cognitive strategies, cognitive strategies, social strategies and affective strategies. After the participants (352 sixth grade students from Arab and Jewish schools) completed a self-report Likert-type Writing Strategies Questionnaire (WSQ), 31 randomly selected participants were further engaged in an interview (WSI), and in a think aloud procedure (WTAP), regarding writing, and their composition was scored.

The findings indicated that the children could be classified through the WSQ, according to one of three profiles of strategy use; a *General* profile, an *Affective* profile, and a *Social* profile. The interviews and the think aloud procedure further validated the profiles and gave in-depth descriptions of the children's' use of writing strategies.

The chapter discusses the contribution of qualitative methods to a theoretical understanding of writing as a process, and its implications for education.

Keywords: writing strategies, writers' profiles, elementary school.

1. INTRODUCTION

1.1 Writing as a Component of Literacy

Writing is a process of language production and of active meaning construction (Hatch, 1992; Wixon & Stone, 1977) and a problem-solving activity (Flower & Hayes, 1979; Peregoy & Boyle, 1993). The development of writing skills sets special challenges for the writer, since it requires capacity for language production and articulation. The writer has to coordinate many components, and a long-term effort

---

Shapira, A., & Hertz-Lazarowitz, R. (2004). Children's writing strategies: Profiles of writers. In G. Rijlaarsdam (Series Ed.) and Rijlaarsdam, G., Van den Bergh, H. & Couzijn, M. (Vol. Eds.), Studies in writing, Volume 14, Effective learning and teaching of writing, 2nd edition, Part 3, Studies in writing-to-learn, 574-586.

is required for the achievement of a high level of performance (Zimmerman & Bandura, 1994).

According to the principles of constructivist structuralism (Piaget 1970a, 1970b;Vygotsky 1962; 1978) literacy is acquired in a social context and develops through social interactions, where students learn its foundations through partnership, exploring, and building (Hoskisson, 1979; Teale, 1984). The most important factor in this process is the development of a self-monitoring mechanism, which ensures that the student is an active participant in her own course of development, not just a passive receiver of knowledge passed on to them by others (Montgomery, 1992). Students who direct and manage their own learning, are more likely to achieve academic success than those who do not. They set higher goals for themselves, and constantly engage in new tasks, even in the face of difficulties (Zimmerman & Bandura, 1994).

1.2 Strategies as a Helping Tool in the Writing Process

Researches recommend helping students by providing them with suitable strategies for solving problems that are a part of the writing process (Applebee & Langer, 1983; O'Malley & Chamot, 1990; Oxford, 1990). These strategies act as scaffolds, which can help students identify thinking skills and basic cognitive processes. Skilled writers use a rich repertoire of strategies, and are able to employ strategies compatible with the assignment at hand. One problem that hinders students is their difficulties in using their existing knowledge with regard to learning strategies, and in adjusting their thinking processes (Flavell, Miller & Miller, 1993). This stems from their tendency not to combine their meta-cognitive knowledge and their skills within a unified conceptual framework. As a result, many skills remain inactive, and writers find it difficult to implement them outside the context in which they were learned (Kuhn, Schauble & Garcia-Mila, 1992).

Strategies are a means utilized by the writer to solve problems that arise in the writing process. These are actions and behaviors that reflect cognitive, social, and affective processes, occurring before, during and after the writing process. Many researchers (Neiman, 1978; Oxford, 1989; Zimmerman & Martinez-Pons, 1986), who focused on the development of vocabulary, grammar, listening, speaking, reading and writing, classified strategies into various categories, according to the type of information-processing required from the learner.

By its nature, strategy use in the process of language production is very broad and involves many aspects. To explore it systematically, we examined a strategy-use classification method borrowed from the teaching of a second language. This method suits a wide variety of subjects, from reading in one's first language to acquiring new languages. According to this classification, strategies used in the process of language production can be divided into four clusters: meta-cognitive, cognitive, social, and affective (O'Malley & Chamot, 1990).

1.3 Meta-cognitive Strategies

These include global skills and are aimed at the development of self-awareness regarding the level of understanding, motivation, and approach to all skills. They embrace planning, goal setting, preparing for action, focusing, using schemata, activity monitoring, evaluation of its success, and the search for practice opportunities (Oxford, 1990).

1.3.1 Cognitive Strategies

These are personal strategies, which are appropriate for the individual learner on the one hand, and for the task at hand on the other hand. Cognitive strategies involve a manipulation of the task through the use of language. This is carried out through: physical activities (such as: using a dictionary, summarizing, organizing, reading out loud); through mental functions (such as: imagery, applying a schema – attributing new knowledge to existing knowledge, guessing, analyzing, and reasoning), and compensation strategies which include overcoming obstacles and writing limitations by various means, such as self-initiated breaks, listening to music, etc. (Oxford, 1990).

1.3.2 Social Strategies

These consist of interaction among writers and with teachers, and include asking for help, asking questions, asking for correction, and developing an awareness of the thoughts and feelings of others. Studies show that peer and teacher feedback improves written outcomes (Beach, 1979; Kerlitz-Nissim, 1998; Samway, 1993; Williams & Colomb, 1993; Yagelski, 1995).

1.4 Affective Strategies

These strategies can be of a positive or negative nature. The use of negative affective strategies such as avoidance, passiveness, difficulty in concentrating, and showing lack of concern, can eventually lead to dropping out of the task (Oxford, 1990). The goal of strategy use training is to uproot the use of negative strategies and to strengthen the use of positive ones such as self-relaxation techniques, self-rewarding and self-talk regarding one's ability to successfully complete the assignment (Anderson, 1988).

The four clusters of the strategies are not isolated. According to the social cognitive theory of self-regulation (Zimmerman & Martinez-Pons, 1986; Zimmerman & Bandura, 1994, Zimmerman, 2000), affective and cognitive states are interrelated, and they are further related to the meta-cognitive state of the learner which regulates planning, monitoring, and evaluation. Self-regulation acts through a system of psychological sub-functions, which includes action-monitoring, personal standards for evaluating and directing one's performance, and consistent self-regulation even in the face of difficulties or competing distractions. This ability for self-regulation develops both with age, and with training.

In the initial phase of the present study Marom & Hertz-Lazarowitz (2002), studied children's' profiles of using writing strategies. 352 children (Arabs and Jews) answered a 41 items Likert type Writing Strategies Questionnaire (WSQ), (Alpha 80.) which related to four clusters of strategies meta-cognitive, cognitive, social and affective (see Appendix A). The Ward's method of cluster analysis which allows the classification of variables into groups without defining them beforehand was used. The analysis creates empirically distinct groups with similar attributes (Aldenderfer & Blashfield, 1984; Marom, 1997). The profile of a writer was defined as a participant's mean score on each of the four strategy clusters; the analysis identified three profiles of writers:

- Profile 1 – The General profile consisting of participants who scored a higher than average score on all four clusters the meta- cognitive, cognitive, social and affective clusters (46.9% of the participants).
- Profile 2 – The Affective profile, consisting of participants who scored high on the affective cluster and lower than average of all other clusters (35.4%).
- Profile 3 – The Social profile – consisting of participants who won average or higher scores on the social cluster (17.7%).

Most prominent in this analysis was the abundant use of affective strategies in profiles 1 and 2. Overall, 80 % of the participants scored the highest (3.54) on the affective cluster as measured by the WSQ (on a range of 1-5). The scant use of social strategies in profile 2 was also prominent (2.51) as compared with the relatively high use of social strategies (3.00) in profile 3. We were puzzled by the absence of a distinct Cognitive profile (Marom & Hertz-Lazarowitz, in press).

2. THE STUDY DESIGN

2.1 The Aims of the Present Study

The focus in this study is on in depth understanding of the writing process by employing qualitative methods of inquiry. We used a Writing Strategies Interview (WSI) and a Writing Think-Aloud Procedure (WTAP) to obtain information about the various abilities of writers, who differed in level of motivation and learning style (Abbott & Wingard, 1981; Oxford, 1990).

We assumed that at the age of 12, in sixth grade, the participants were in a developmental stage where they had already acquired some knowledge regarding their thinking processes, and had enough writing experience and language abilities to allow them to clearly to express their thoughts regarding the use of strategies.

2.2 Participants

Thirty-one children (10% of the larger sample of 352) were randomly selected for a Writing Strategies Interview (WSI) and a Writing Think-Aloud Procedure (WTAP).

2.3 Procedure

After completing the Writing Strategies Questionnaire (WSQ) the participants (31) were invited to a quiet room in the school for an individual session where they were interviewed about their use of strategies and asked to write a composition on a topic of their choice. While writing they were asked to think aloud. The interview and the think aloud lasted about an hour and were recorded and transcribed (Marom, 1997).

In view of the problematic nature of the reliability of children's reporting in think-aloud procedures, and in order to assure their cooperation, participants were prepared before the think-aloud procedure (Johnston, 1992; Meichenbaum, 1977). The think-aloud procedure was demonstrated to the participants, before they were asked to engage in thinking about their own writing. We also conducted a dialogue which included questions regarding the processes participants underwent while they were writing specific words or sentences. Emphasis was placed on questions of the 'what' and 'which' type instead of the 'why' and 'how' type, since it was found that the second type of questions could interfere with a child's attempts to verbalize her thoughts (Blank, 1973). The researcher wrote observational notes while the child was in the WTAP. In the interview, participants were asked open questions. Next, the participants wrote free compositions for 20 minutes on a subject of their own choice. Some of the topics students suggested were- relationships with friends and family members, dreams about peace and their hobbies. The compositions were scored (range 1-100).

2.4 Measurements and Scoring

The Writing Think Aloud Procedure. The main goal of the WTAP and the Writing Strategies Interview (WSI) was to give the participants a room to voice unique strategies, and enrich and broaden the closed Likert-type statements of the Writing Strategies Questionnaire (WSQ). However, the two qualitative measures (the think aloud and the interview) and the quantitative measure of the WSQ were conceptually linked.

In the think aloud procedure each of the participants was asked to voice out loud his or her thoughts regarding the writing process as he or she went through the process before, during and after writing. The writers were observed as they composed the text. The coding of the WTAP is presented in Appendix B.

Writing Strategies Interview (WSI). A structured interview about writing was conducted with the same 31 participants. It consisted of 40 open and general questions that matched the themes of the Likert-type WSQ and were related to the Meta- cognitive, Cognitive, Social and Affective clusters. The WSI was mainly conducted in Hebrew, but in the interviews with the Arab children an Arabic-speaking translator was available to help when needed (Marom, 1997).

An example of the general questions in the interview is: "What do you do in order to overcome difficulties?" In the WSQ parallel items were: "When I encounter difficulties I tell myself positive things". "When I encounter difficulties I stop writing". Participants' responses in the interview were grouped by strategy clusters and ranked on a scale from 1 (never) to 5 (always).

The following are several key statements taken from the interview, which demonstrate this:

> "I love to write in my room [or] in my library booth. I find it comfortable because it's a little dark and quiet." (Meta-cognitive strategy- planning)

> "We learned about the sacrifice of Isaac in the Torah. I connected this with places I see daily. The sacrifice of Isaac was done on a high place so [while I was writing – A.M.], I imagined a high block of apartments like the one we used to live in, in the north." (Cognitive strategy)

> "When I can't write I drink water, go out to play a little, and come back later, and then it succeeds." (Affective strategy)

> "I prefer to write with a partner, like if I don't understand something I ask my partner." (Social strategy).

Based on the transcriptions of the interviews and the think-aloud procedures the strategies that the participants devised were classified into the four strategy clusters and were coded on a five-point scale (1-low to 5-high) according to a pre-planned scale similar to the one used in the WSQ. For example, a participant's response in the interview was:

> "I think about the subject before writing", "I think about the structure of the composition and I think about the content" (indicates planning). "I revise the composition while writing it" (indicates monitoring) and "I edit my composition after writing" (indicates evaluation).

Such a transcript was scored as high (5) if a participant indicated that he or she did so *always* and low if he or she indicated they did it *rarely*. These statements were classified as belonging to the meta-cognitive cluster as they corresponded to several items in this cluster in the WSQ An example is: "I plan my composition before I start writing"; "When writing I stop in the middle and review what I had written" and "I try to evaluate my composition".

3. RESULTS

3.1 Correlation of Measurements

The use of qualitative and quantitative measures provided a rich empirical and phenomenological understanding of writing in this age group. We followed the same theoretical conceptualization of four clusters of strategies and so we could correlate the different measures. We found moderate to high correlation between the two quantitative measures the WSI and the WTAP ranging from .34 to .41 (significant at .005 level) on three clusters (the exception being the social cluster). We found high and significant correlations between the qualitative WSQ and the quantitative WSI ranging from .43 to .53 on all four clusters (all significant at .005 level). Finally correlations between the WSQ and the WTAP were significant and high only on the affective cluster (.35) (Marom & Hertz-Lazarowitz, 2002). Thus we conclude that investigating children's' use of strategies for writing requires a combination of methods as the process is extremely rich and complex. Each methodology makes contribution to the educational and theoretical implication of writing development. From the interviews and the think aloud procedure we learned that children devote a great deal of thinking to their writing and develop an awareness of the strategies they use. We learned that there are distinct profiles of writers with idiosyncratic characteristics.

3.2 Profiles of Writers: Two Cases

3.2.1 Jasmine

Jasmine is an affective profile student. Her scores were; 4.00 on the Affective strategies cluster, 2.33 on the Social strategies cluster, 2.17 on the Cognitive strategies cluster and 2.92 on the Meta-Cognitive strategies cluster, her composition score was 93. Each account relates to her use of strategies.

The affective domain. Jasmine feels happy whenever the word "writing" is mentioned. The reason for this is her joy in expressing things. Writing is easy for her and she initiates writing on her own at home. She especially likes to write about peace, because for her if there is no peace there is no life. She was frustrated when she wrote a composition about the autumn, because it was short and dull. The composition of which she felt most proud was titled: "If I were a clock". In this composition she wrote that if she were a clock she would prolong the beautiful hours in which people feel good and shorten those in which people feel bad, as in times of war. When she faces difficulties in her writing process, she "does some thinking" and then carries on. She recommends "thinking for a long time". Only when she is in a bad mood, or if the weather is too hot or cold, does Jasmine abstain from writing.

The social domain. Jasmine prefers to write alone "because I like to think by myself and do not like to get help from anybody". She is willing to discuss her writing but only after she has finished it, "so I won't take any ideas from anyone else. I like to think for myself". After she is done she likes to get feedback, "but not bad feedback, because then I'll think that I was wrong, and it's an unpleasant situation".

The cognitive domain. Jasmine writes a draft for each composition but does not plan her writing ahead. While she writes she asks herself questions, such as whether her ideas or the examples she wants to give are appropriate.

The meta-cognitive domain. Jasmine makes sure that her compositions have a beginning and an end, characters, location of events, and a main idea. She examines what she has written, "at the end of each sentence, to see if it's correct and appropriate". She usually does not plan the way her composition will end, but waits for a point where she feels that she can end it.

In the open part of her Writing Strategies Questionnaire where students freely added comments about their writing behavior, Jasmine wrote that she liked writing stories and sometimes even her thoughts. She corresponded with her friends and kept a diary. She usually wrote at home, and preferred to write in her room. "I prefer to be alone, not in the classroom, so that I can think for myself, without anybody's help and without any noise."

Jasmine's composition was titled: Forcing myself.

> "If I were peace I would force myself upon all the nations in the world, because peace is the most beautiful thing in the world, and without it there is no happiness. There is another wish and that is to be a clock that rules time so that I can make the seconds and hours in which people are happy longer, and shorten the seconds of the miserable war that man does not like."

3.3 Tzachi

Tzachi is also an affective profile student. His score on the affective strategy cluster was relatively lower than the mean score received by participants in this profile (Affective 2.92; Social 2.75; Cognitive 3.00; Meta-cognitive 3.17). His written output scored 60. Each of the following accounts relates to his use of strategies:

The affective domain. Tzachi is "okay" with writing. "It is not that I hate it, it's not a big deal but..." it opens your feelings...like, if I have a secret that bugs me, this (writing) would be a good friend of mine." Writing is not difficult "when you want to". At the same time he finds it difficult, "for example, sometimes I am in a bad mood, I don't feel like doing it and no ideas come to me". If he is told to write and the subject does not interest him, he will try to avoid it – "I'm on strike." But "if I must do it, then I must...I write something but it's not what I really want...but if I can choose, I'm sure not going to write." His most satisfying writing experience was an ongoing story that he wrote on his own initiative about his dog. The most frustrating experience for him is dictation. During the think-aloud procedure, he said that if he had to show what he wrote he "would tear it pieces, and look for all kind of stupid things like spelling mistakes".

The social domain. When experiencing difficulties, Tzachi prefers to write with a partner, but prefers to write alone if things are going well. "I either overcome them (the difficulties) or ask somebody". He wishes to get feedback on his writing only when he thinks that it is good; "if it looks stupid to me then – no". If the feedback is not entirely positive he does not want to hear it. "When they tell me bad things – I don't want to hear it." Even positive feedback causes him discomfort, "good things I also don't want to hear, and it embarrasses me a little".

The cognitive domain. Tzachi uses cognitive strategies. If he has enough time, he writes a draft for his compositions, "not in the classroom because I need the time to write the composition". Sometimes he starts writing over from the beginning in the middle of the composition; he examines what he has written while in the process. "Let's say I write a passage, and I haven't finished it, I read it over again to check it." Tzachi sees images in his thoughts: " even while I'm writing and also when I am not writing. When I walk, I think about something. I want to explain it to somebody – so I explain how it looks. In my writing I also imagine what the picture looks like".

The Meta-cognitive domain. When he thinks about writing, Tzachi assumes that good writing is "deep, meaningful writing, and looks good". He usually thinks before starting to write. He doesn't plan the structure of his composition. He reads his composition again both in the course of the process and at its end, "all the time so I make sure I haven't made mistakes or have spelling mistakes." He does not write differently for different audiences. Only when his writing is personal is it different in character.

Tzachi's composition (no title was given):

> "We got our dog in April 29.4.96; With some three more puppies (female); One dog we gave to one family who are friends of ours, and another one to another family; that gave the puppies to someone outside of Ayalon. Yesterday I went to my friend's and saw that his dog had grown up much. His bitch is called Harry and our bitch we called Mocha."

3.4 Conclusion

Jasmine and Tzachi both belong to profile 2, but they differ mainly in the manner in which they use affective strategies. While Jasmine uses positive affective strategies, Tzachi uses negative ones. Jasmine is willing to invest time and mental resources to think when she faces difficulties. Writing comes very easy to her, and this is reflected in the high score for her composition. From what Tzachi said we might conclude that he does not like to write at all, that writing generates feelings of difficulty and frustration in him. Tzachi does not manage easily with difficulties in the writing process; he prefers to "go on strike" and at best, to write only because he is forced to do so. Interestingly, frustration arises mainly with assignments such as dictation, (which is not writing in our sense) but this student hates it and associates it with writing. In spite of his negative affective attitude to writing Tzachi may initiate his own writing when he is interested in the topic.

4. DISCUSSION

Our study showed that children in sixth grade could be identified as having different profiles as writers; this was based on their self-report about use of different strategies, in three measures. The students could further describe their inner world of writing in quantitative and qualitative forms and so the measures we developed have reliability and validity, and can contribute to future research on writing development. The most common profile in this age group was the Affective profile and the least common one was the Meta-cognitive. The Affective profile writers produced the compositions that scored the highest.

What did we learn about children's writing strategies? We began our conceptualization on children writing strategies based on the literature (O'Malley & Chamot, 1990; Oxford, 1990) and accordingly we made a distinction between cognitive and meta-cognitive strategies. Our data furnished support for the four clusters conception, but not for the existence of a distinct cognitive profile. It seems that at this age students find it difficult to distinguish meta-cognitive from cognitive strategies, because what is defined as meta-cognitive can also function as cognitive. At other times, strategies from these two clusters were used simultaneously. We have many examples from the interview and the think aloud procedure to illustrate this. One example of this overlap is from the think-aloud protocol: The interviewee started to relate how she lost her way home in first person; as she was telling her story she decided to change the text and use the persona of a boy to describe this experience. She reported these shifts, and it seems that she was involved in a meta-cognitive analysis of her meta-cognitive and cognitive strategies, which in this case overlapped. The often-sketchy boundaries between the different strategy clusters have already been described in the literature (Neiman et al., 1978; O'Malley & Chamot, 1990). The think-aloud procedure provided by its qualitative description an additional confirmation regarding the profiles conceptualization, and demonstrated the central role of the affective strategies for the children.

The literature would lead us to expect that the higher the strategy-use profile, the better the written output, since skilled writers use a rich variety of strategies, matching their use to the assignments at hand (Brown et. al, 1983; Chamot & Kupper, 1989). Our data showed that children who scored high on all clusters (profile 1), and children using affective (profile 2), scored higher than the children who used social strategies (profile 3), with profile 2 children producing the best writing compositions. In this age group, children we did not identify children who used mainly cognitive and meta-cognitive strategies so we conclude that in this age group we didn't identify in the specific task of free writing – the affective strategies are very central to its development and production. The general profile writers perhaps did not achieve the highest score for their written outputs because of the gap between their meta-cognitive and cognitive knowledge of strategies and their ability to implement it at their age level.

In future research the nature and structure of the writing task should be further studied. Will children report in their interview or WTAP on using similar or different strategies when they face a factual writing task? Does the finding that profile 2 children scored the highest reflect the match between their profile and the writing task? Maybe the free writing assignment led participants to an affective inclined expression, making the assignment more appropriate for those scoring high on the affective strategy cluster, which is why they had greater success in it.

5. IMPLICATIONS FOR EDUCATION

A literature review shows that many teachers have little awareness of the issue of strategies, and little knowledge regarding the processes through which students can be taught strategies that fit specific skills. Teachers often tend to suggest the use of strategies, that match their own learning style (O'Malley & Chamot, 1990; Oxford, 1989). Understanding a student's profile of strategy usage allows the teacher access into his or her internal world where specific components of the process can be observed. These observations can make the teachers' awareness of the writer's thoughts and actions performed in his or her writing process; This may help the teachers to direct young writers to use their knowledge of strategies to improve their writing and to develop writing skills, which will thereby originate from internal motivation.

Findings of the qualitative analysis indicate that participants who like to write are best characterized as using mostly positive affective strategies in the writing process. Those who find writing difficult must be trained to eliminate negative affective strategies and use positive affective ones in order to overcome difficulties in the writing process. In addition, they should be encouraged to use social strategies. The findings in the present study indicate that participants, who find writing difficult, need to use social strategies (like asking for help) in order to complete their assignment.

The results of many studies, (Applebee & Langer, (1983); Samway, (1993), on the relationship between the use of social strategies and the improvement in the quality of writing, suggest that their use is recommended. Also appeals for help which are mastery-oriented should be encouraged, meaning that the helper should focus on such processes that will lead the help-seeker to achieve his or her goal independently (Nelson-Le-Gall, 1992). Teachers and peers, can encourage the use of such social strategies (Kerlitz-Nissim, 1997).

APPENDIX A – QUESTIONNAIRE STRUCTURE

Meta-Cognitive Strategies

I plan before I start writing.
I try to evaluate what I have written
I think of the way I organize my writing.
After writing I tend to check what I have written.
I plan my writing to the end before I start writing.
I ask myself: Have I progressed with my writing?
I compare my writing to the writing of others
When writing I stop in the middle and review what I have written.
When I write I imagine things related to the topic of my composition.
I don't plan my writing ahead.
I prefer to write by myself.
A lot of reading improves my writing.

Cognitive Strategies

I make side notes while I write.
I ask myself questions related to the subject of my composition while I write.
I prepare a draft.
I use books or other written materials when writing.
I usually write chapter headings when I write.
I look for spelling mistakes while I write.
While writing I try to imagine the things I'm writing about.

Social Strategies

I would like to plan my compositions with a friend.
I like to write down my thoughts without discussing them with others.

I like it when somebody helps me with my writing.
I would like to know what people think about what I have written.
When I write I ask the teacher questions.
I don't like to discuss my writing with others.
I would like to write with a friend.
When I write I ask my friends for help.
When I write, I like to discuss my ideas with another person.

Affective Strategies

I love to write.
I deal with difficulties I have while I write.
When I'm being encouraged, my writing improves.
I talk to myself to encourage myself while I write.
I think that writing is boring.
I write from my own free will in my spare time.
I like to write about topics that I choose.
I think writing is interesting.
When I find it hard to write I tell myself positive things.
I convince myself that I can finish the writing assignment.
I write even if no one asks me to.
When I have difficulties I stop writing.

APPENDIX B – THINK ALOUD CODING

Meta-cognitive Strategies

Components: planning, monitoring and evaluation	
Use of planning, monitoring and evaluation	5
Partial use of a strategy (at least two out of three components)	4
Use of one of the components	3
Use of one of the components without completion*	2
No evidence of use of any of the strategy components	1

For example, monitoring part of the composition

Cognitive Strategies

Components: imagery, asking questions, paragraphing, punctuation, organization, correction, writing a draft	
Use of the above mentioned components (at least five components)	5
Partial use of strategies (at least two of the components)	4
Use of one of the strategy components	3
Use of one of the strategy components without completion*	2
No use of any of the strategy components	1

*For example, partial organization of the composition.

Social Strategies

Components: asking for help, asking questions for clarification, asking for feedback (by addressing friends, the teacher or resources)

Use of the above mentioned strategies	5
Partial use of strategies (at least two of the components)	4
Use of one of the strategy component	3
Use of one of the strategy components-dependency oriented appeal for help*	2
No evidence of use of any of the strategy components	1

(Le-Gall, 1992); For example, addressing the teacher using the phrase: I don't know

Affective Strategies

Components: Self talk – self-encouragement, positive statements as for the ability to end the task successfully. Relaxation – taking a break, drinking water, addressing another issue. Self-rewarding as soon as progress related to the task at hand has been made.

Use of all the above mentioned components	5
Partial use of the strategies(at least two of the components)	4
Use of one of the strategy components	3
No use of any of the strategy components	2
Use of negative affective strategies*	1

For example, avoidance, passiveness, difficulty in concentrating, showing lack of concern, dropping out.

WRITING-TO-LEARN AND GRAPH-DRAWING AS AIDS OF THE INTEGRATION OF TEXT AND GRAPHS

GISELLA PAOLETTI

University of Trieste, Italy

Abstract. Comprehending instructional texts often requires the integration of verbal and visual information. Visual information (especially diagrams) can be helpful for relating and integrating pieces of information and can therefore contribute to mental model building. However, they often fail in achieving any contribution to the instructional process, because of a number of factors.
In fact, readers often neglect illustrations and rely too much on textual information. Even when they pay attention to pictorial information, learners often obtain the overall meaning of pictures the easiest and fastest way possible, through low-level processing that gives the learner the illusion of having understood. Moreover, graphs used in textbooks may be difficult to understand, because they often assume an *information-telling* perspective that does not help readers understand a text's most important data and numerical trend. A further problem is that texts and graphs are often placed far apart from each other and therefore require the learner to scan the page in search of a diagram corresponding to a printed sentence.
The aim of this investigation is to verify whether the use of two well-known study strategies (writing-to-learn and drawing visual organizers, i.e., graph drawing) can stimulate the integration of a text's propositions with visual information. Forty-two University students were asked to read a newspaper article (containing one written text and six diagrams) and either to prepare a written reformulation of the text or to draw a visual organizer summarizing the textual information.
An analysis of the participants' written notes (i.e., an external and controllable product of task instructions) and of their results in a delayed test provided us with information on the usefulness of the two strategies for information integration and for the monitoring of text comprehension.
An analysis of overall group main effects revealed significant differences among instructional conditions for total scores and for scores on diagram and integration questions, but not for text questions. The group of students who drew graphs outperformed the others (the writing-to-learn and reading-only groups) on all measures requiring the integration of textual and graphic information.

Keywords: Writing-to-learn, graph-drawing, comprehension monitoring, text-graph integration

Paoletti, G. (2004). *Writing-to-learn and graph-drawing as aids if the integration of text and graphs*.
In G. Rijlaarsdam (Series Ed.) and Rijlaarsdam, G., Van den Bergh, H. & Couzijn, M. (Vol. Eds.), *Studies in writing, Volume 14, Effective learning and teaching of writing, 2nd edition, Part 3, Studies in writing-to-learn,* 587-597.

1. INTRODUCTION

The purpose of the following experiment was to gather evidence on if and how *graph drawing* and *writing-to-learn* can contribute to the comprehension and learning of a *text-with-pictures*, i.e., whether or not these strategies can improve text-picture integration, inconsistency detection, and as the ranking of important information.

Many texts, hypertexts, and multimedia presentations require the learner to analyze verbal, as well as iconic, information. Indeed, it is believed that illustrations, diagrams, and animations have a positive effect on text comprehension and learning (Levin, Anglin e Carney, 1987; Mayer, 2001), because they can induce cognitive processes, such as visual chunking, mental imagery, and parallel processing (Winn, 1987). Since pictorial information represents concepts spatially in networks and thereby informs us on how such concepts are related (Winn, 1987), it may serve to help reorganize textual information (Hegarty, Just & Carpenter, 1991), by contributing to mental model building (Gyselinck & Tardieu, 1994, 1999; Schnotz, Picard & Henninger, 1994) and to dual encoding (Paivio, 1971, 1986).

Given all the promising characteristics of pictorial information, one might ask why it is necessary to increase picture effectiveness by writing-to-learn or graph-drawing. The main reason concerns the need to encourage effortful processing of the information contained in texts and illustrations. Indeed, researchers have become more and more aware of its potential, but also of the fact that in educational practice little of that potential is being realized (Peeck, 1994).

When people read a text, they construct the referential representation incrementally (Kintsch & van Dijk, 1978), when a diagram accompanies the text, readers must integrate information presented in two different media, by alternating between reading the text and inspecting the diagram (Hegarty, Just & Carpenter, 1991). Learners are required to split their attention and cognitive resources between, and to mentally integrate, two or more related sources of information. Furthermore, eye fixation studies have demonstrated the text's central role in controlling the reader's attention. Indeed, the process of constructing a representation from text and diagrams is directed by the text. These studies also show that readers first try to build representations from the text alone and tend to neglect accompanying illustrations, relying too much on textual information, or carrying out low-level processing of pictorial information.

The situation becomes more problematic when graphs assume an *information-telling* perspective that does not inform readers of a text's most important data and numerical trends (Shah, Mayer & Hegarty, 1999) and when text and corresponding pictures are placed far apart (Sweller, 1988; Mayer, 2001).

1.1 The Comprehension of a Text Accompanied by Diagrams

Problems in text-graph integration can arise because of a learner's individual characteristics (e.g., her/his prior knowledge, processing methods, etc.), or due to the text itself (distance between a text and accompanying diagram, knowledge-telling perspective, etc.).

On a basic level, learners may not benefit from graphs, because they lack sufficient knowledge for making sense and interpreting the convention used (Hegarty, Just & Carpenter, 1991). However, even when learners are able to decode graphs' signs, they may experience comprehension failures, because they lack the appropriate strategies for integrating texts and visual organizer information (Moore, 1993). Students may not look at illustrations in texts, because they believe they can get all the information they need from what they read (Winn, 1987; Peck, 1987). They therefore try to get the overall meaning of the picture easily and rapidly through low-level processing, which gives the learner the illusion of having understood (Weidenmann, 1994). However, even if short exposure to graphic information is adequate for abstracting the main topic, further fixations are needed to obtain more detailed information (Hegarty, Just & Carpenter, 1991). One of the consequences of shallow processing is that inconsistencies between text and pictures are often not detected (Peek, 1987).

Concerning a text's characteristics, a graph may be not effective because a *split-attention effect* can arise, because in order to render instructional material intelligible, diverse sources of available information must be mentally integrated (Chandler & Sweller, 1992). We know that the amount of attention given to a diagram is influenced by its proximity to the part of the text referring to it. We also know that readers pay more attention to diagrams presented after referring sentences, as long as the text directs the processing of diagrams by referring to them (Hegarty, Just & Carpenter, 1991; Whalley & Fleming, 1975). Text and corresponding pictures are often situated far apart from each other and therefore require the learner to scan one or more pages in search of a diagram corresponding to a printed sentence (Sweller, 1988; Mayer, 2001). The additional cognitive load associated with integrating text and pictures may indeed exceed available attentional resources (Moreno & Mayer, 1999). Moreover, graphs used in textbooks may be difficult to understand because they are not designed to effectively communicate the main point of a text. They often assume an *information-telling* (*knowledge-telling*) perspective that does not inform readers of the text's most important data and numerical trends (Shah, Mayer & Hegarty, 1999). In this case, instead of selecting or highlighting the most important information, the author represents all information in the graph, thereby forcing the reader to process and select the relevant data.

1.2 The Effect of Graph Drawing and Writing-To-Learn

There are many assumptions concerning the contributions to comprehension and learning of graph drawing and writing-to learn. To illustrate the present work's hypothesis regarding their contribution to text-graph integration, some of these assumptions and some evidence against them are described here below.

First, it should be mentioned that some researchers believe that not simply the presence of a graph improves comprehension, but the *act of constructing a graph* (Dean & Kulhavy, 1981). Visual organizers, such as time lines, Venn diagrams, concept maps, causal chains, and graphs, create a visual statement that can support and organize thought and give students and teachers the opportunity to consider alternative structures, to elaborate on what is already known, and to correct misconceptions (Clarke, 1992, Dansereau, 1985). Graph-drawing helps students scan, sort, and organize information and can be helpful for relating and integrating pieces of information (Winn, 1994). It encourages students to select and rank text ideas and to connect them, in order to produce an integrated representation (Vidal-Abarca, Gilabert & Garcia Madruga, 1994).

On the other hand, it is not clear if students always profit from graph-drawing. Problems may arise because students can have difficulty interpreting quantitative information, because they do rather poorly in connecting related but distinct conceptual domains (Novack, 1985), and because they are often unable to isolate important variables (de Jong & van Joolingen, 1998). Students, who rarely receive training in graph-drawing, may not be able to restructure material in a new form (Aureli & Ottaviani, 1992) and can have a hard time comparing different graphs (Linn, Layman & Nachmias, 1987). In other words, graph-drawing has many potentialities, the realization of which, however, depend on a learner's individual ability and knowledge. The same may be said about writing-to-learn.

Writing-to-learn can help students think critically and construct new knowledge; it can stimulate the integration of textual information, as well as the connection between textual information and prior knowledge (Langer, 1986; Marshall, 1987; Spivey 1997, Hand et al., 2001; Nelson, 2001; Tynjälä, 1998a, b, 1999). Moreover, it is associated with more effective and long-lasting recall than that resulting from other learning strategies (Kirby & Woodhouse, 1993; Hand, Prain & Yore, 1999; Paoletti, 1996; Tynjälä, 1998, 1999). In fact, it is believed that writing-to-learn activates deeper text processing, and, by giving material different form and organization, that it contributes to the formation of macrostructures, which can be recalled more easily than the text's original sequence of propositions.

On the other hand, results on writing-to learn continue to be mixed (Ackerman, 1993; Klein, 1999). Students often show a tendency to elaborate and summarize a text in small segments (consistent with the *piecemeal processing explanation,* Garner, 1981), without integrating pieces of information appearing in non-adjacent sentences, and to repair internal inconsistencies by using external knowledge sources, i.e., by relying on uncontrolled elaborative inferences (Paoletti, in press).

1.3 Aim of the Study

The experiment reported here was designed to establish if and when graph-drawing and writing-to-learn positively influence learners' comprehension processes – in particular, information integration and the selection and ranking of important information - and their recall.

Forty-two University students were asked to elaborate assigned material by reading a newspaper article. The two experimental groups received further instructions to either preparing a written reformulation of the text or to drawing a graph summarizing the textual information. The material was one page long and contained one written text and six diagrams (line graphs), which introduced a set of factors related to good performance in secondary school. The assigned material had been selected in such a way that, to fully comprehend it, text and diagrams had to be matched, connected, compared, and integrated.

The hypotheses can be stated as follows:
1) Graph drawing and writing-to-learn are both strategies which help learners restructure material in a new form and organization.
2) The product of *writing-to-learn* should maintain a sequential form, but information may be ranked and linked in an original way: writing-to-learn should stimulate participants' integration of textual information and the detection, selection, and reorganization of important information (at least when participants are overtly requested to do so).
3) Conversely, writing to learn may focus the learner's attention on the text (and only on the text). Therefore, it may not enhance either text-graph inconsistency detection, or information ranking (for the pieces of information mentioned only in the graphs).
4) Graph drawing should force the processing of quantitative details, and of relationships among variables. Therefore, learners should be better able to construct a representation of the relevant quantitative information (which allows precise information ranking) in the graph-drawing conditions. Conversely, text analysis may not be so precise as in the writing-to-learn condition.

2. METHOD

2.1 Participants

Sixty University students were asked to participate in this experiment for course credit. All participants had completed, at minimum, all of their second year courses.

Participants were randomly allocated to three groups of 20 learners each (writing-to-learn, graph-drawing, and reading only). Some participants from each group dropped out after the first stage, so that there was a total of 42 learners who completed all stages of the experiment: reading only (N = 18), writing-to-learn (N = 16), and graph-drawing (N = 8).

2.2 Procedure

During the study sessions, all participants received a written copy of the text to be read. Written instructions were provided on a separate sheet of paper.

Participants were given learning instructions that directed their attention towards the problematic aspects of the article and asked the experimental groups to either prepare a written summary of the text or to draw a graph highlighting the most important information in the article. Control group subjects were instructed to read the article carefully.

The following day, all the students were asked to answer questions assessing memory for information explicitly presented in the text and in the graph, as well as questions requiring text-graph integration.

2.3 Material

The material consisted of a newspaper article, which described the results of a study conducted by the Italian Ministry of Education. The article described the profile of a model Secondary school student and illustrated six factors associated with good scholastic results. The text was accompanied by a set of six line-graphs. The text listed all six factors and gave quantitative data for the top two factors (parents' level of scholastic achievement, and number of books read). The graphs gave extensive quantitative data for each factor.

The text did not direct the processing of graphs by referring to them. Learners had to decide if and when to process the graphs, and had to select the appropriate graph. Text and graphs assumed an *information-telling perspective*: they did not highlight the article's most important data and numerical trends (the reader had to construe them). The text and graphs presented data in a way that required a great deal of mental effort. Only a precise analysis of the graphs (which used different ranges and, at a superficial glance, gave the idea that all illustrated factors were equally important) allowed readers to rank the factors' relative influence on success.

The article did not keep internal coherence of information under control and indeed, contained a series of inconsistencies between textual information and graphic information. For example, let us compare information in the text (Fig. 1) and in the graph (Fig. 2) regarding the influence of a mother's level of scholastic achievement on success.

From the data we can confirm that parents' cultural level is of fundamental importance. A mother with a high school or University degree has children with the best scholastic results. They obtain 70 in an evaluation scale ranging from 40 to 80. Students with mothers without degrees, i.e., with only an elementary school certificate, all obtain scores under 50...

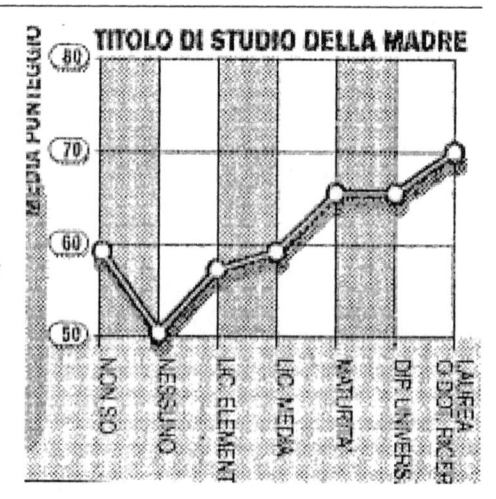

Figure 1. Text.   Figure 2. Graph[1].

---

[1] Translation of the Italian Terms: Titolo di studio della madre = Mother's study degree; Media punteggio = average score; Laurea o dot. Ricer. = Laurea degree or PhD; Dip.Univers. = Bachelor Diploma; Maturita' = High School Diploma; Lic. Media = Junior

The comparison between text and graph reveals that:
- The text refers to a scale between 40 and 80, though the graph shows values between 50 and 80;
- The text says that the son of a mother with an elementary school certificate doesn't exceed 50, while in the graph his score reaches almost 60.

The "natural" characteristics of the article, i.e., demanding information ranking, and internal inconsistencies, were exploited in order to produce a measure of text-graph integration, as described in the following paragraph.

2.4 Measures

Data consisted of: a) students' written notes, i.e., outputs of the study session and b) their answers on a post-test. The following day, participants responded to a set of multiple-choice questions, some of which could be answered by considering either textual or graphic information only and some of which could be answered only after integrating text and graphs. Integration questions examined: a) if the students ranked information by analyzing text and graphs and b) if they detected text-graph inconsistencies. Inconsistency detection provided a measure of the degree to which readers monitored for congruency among ideas expressed in the article. Indeed, an essential prerequisite to evaluating texts for internal consistency is the integration of separate propositions, and inconsistency detection indicates that information was integrated (Baker, 1985).

The purpose of this measure was to answer the following questions:
1) Were the students who used writing-to-learn or graph-drawing better able to remember textual and graphic information?
2) Were they stimulated to integrate textual and graphic information?
3) Did they detect internal inconsistencies?
4) Did they retain a representation that ranked the most important factors?

3. RESULTS

Let us first examine quantitative results from the post-test. Means and standard deviations are displayed in Table 1.

The graph-drawing group obtained, on average, better results for line graph questions, for integration questions, and consequently, for total scores. Their results on the text questions were not worse than those of the other groups. It should be noted that for text questions, the writing-to-learn group produced, on average, no better results than the graph-drawing group or the control group. The writing group performed more poorly than the reading-only group on line-graph questions.

High School License; Lic. Elementare = Primary School License; Nessuno = Nessuno; Non So = Not Known.

Table 1. Means and Standard Deviations of the Three Experimental Groups

	Writing-to-learn Mean	SD	Graph-drawing Mean	SD	Reading only Mean	SD
Text questions	1.6	0.6	1.7	0.5	1.6	0.5
Line graph questions	2.0	0.8	3.7	0.9	2.6	0.7
Integration questions	1.2	1.0	3.4	1.5	1.3	1.1
Total score	4.8	1.3	8.8	1.3	5.5	1.1

A series of analyses of variance were conducted to verify the significance of the descriptive data. Even if sample sizes were dissimilar, a test for homogeneity of variance showed that group variance was not unequal. The dependent variable was test scores on the multiple-choice items.

The analysis of overall group main effects revealed significant differences among instructional conditions for total scores, $F(2, 39) = 17.523$, $MS = 26.157$, $p = <.0001$, for graph question scores, $F(2, 39) = 11.846$, $MS = 7.042$, $p = <.0001$, and for integration scores $F(2, 39) = 9.960$, $MS = 14.026$, $p = .0003$, but not for text questions $F(2, 39) = .207$, $MS = 0.56$, $p = .8142$.

Post hoc analyses (Fisher PLSD) showed significant differences for graph question scores between the graph-drawing group's scores and the other groups (Table 2), as well as for questions requiring text-graph integration (Table 3), and consequently, on overall scores.

Table 2. Questions on Graphs: Post Hoc Differences between Groups

Comparison	Mean Diff.	Crit. Diff.	p-value
Writing, drawing	-1.625	.675	<.0001
Writing, control	-.549	.536	.0450
Drawing, control	1.076	.663	.0022

Table 3. Integration Questions: Post Hoc Differences between Groups

Comparison	Mean Diff.	Crit. Diff.	p-value
Writing, drawing	-2.062	1.039	.0003
Writing, control	035	.825	ns
Drawing, control	2.097	1.020	

No significant differences were found between groups for text information questions. A re-examination of Table 2 shows a difference between the writing group and the control group. The control group did better than the writing group on graph questions, when the questions did not require text-graph integration, but only for memory of factual information. It appears that the text-writing assignment did absorb all the students' attention and left no room for graph analysis. However, text analysis did not result in better recall on textual information questions for the writing condition group.

An analysis of study outputs may contribute to understand some of the findings. Besides inducing effortful processing of the textual and graphic information, the outputs served as an external and controllable product of task instructions.

The writing-to-learn group produced linear texts, which maintained the original text structure (listing, but not ranking, relevant factors). Some of the important pieces of information were selected but not ranked, and no quantitative details were included, not even for factors for which the article provided quantitative information. Inconsistency detection was not evident.

In the graph-drawing group two alternative solution patterns were evident: line graph and bar chart production, both of which demonstrated that pieces of information from the article had been compared and that important information had been selected and ranked. Students' graphs were far from complete and accurate, however, and inconsistency detection was not evident.

In conclusion, which of our expectations were verified? As expected, the product of writing-to-learn maintained a sequential form, since the order of information in students' notes corresponded to that of the original material with no apparent attempt at reorganization. Results on the post-test showed that memory for graphs was not good, and text-graph inconsistency detection was almost null.

Graph-drawing seems to have forced the processing of graphic as well as textual information. The learners in this group[2] selected and ranked information and were able to detect text-graph inconsistencies.

4. CONCLUDING REMARKS

Writing-to-learn and drawing-graphs are generally held to be strategies that activate deep levels of processing. Both can stimulate information integration and reorganization, by restructuring the information in a new form more suitable for memory storage.

From the results of this study, it is possible to conclude that when the material consists of text-and-pictures and the pictures are to be fully analyzed (i.e., when they are not merely descriptive or representational), a writing-to-learn strategy may be not adequate to insure the integration of textual with pictorial information.

---

[2] *In this respect, we wish to mention that the loss of subjects in the graph-drawing group might imply some sort of bias in the findings. A replicate experiment with a larger number of subjects would be desirable.*

Eye movement studies have demonstrated that the text is often the preferred point of entry to (and often the only source of) information (Lewensteing, 2000; Hegarty, Just, & Carpenter, 1991). A strategy that focuses attention on the text, such as writing a summary, can induce the kind of selective operations (see, Nelson, 2001) that lead to omitting and ignoring of visual information.

Graph drawing not only allows easier comparison among rich data sets, but it can stimulate more detailed processing, and especially, the construction of connections among pieces of information and between texts and pictures.

In the present study, students who wrote summaries – even if they were well acquainted with this strategy – did not integrate text and pictures. On the other hand, students who drew graphs did integrate textual and pictorial information, probably because they had to process the text, as well as understand the graphs.

Various theoretical explanations can account for the superior performance of the graph-drawing group:

- The Generation Effect (Slamecka & Graf, 1978),
- Level/Type of processing (Craik & Lockhart, 1972; Hyde & Jenkins, 1969),
- Transfer-Appropriate Processing (Nelson, Walling, McEnvoy, 1979; Tulving & Bower, 1974),
- Material Appropriate Processing (McDaniel & Einstein, 1989).

The *generation effect* (Slamecka & Graf, 1978) refers to the idea, not at all new in education, that there is an advantage to learning by doing. An active involvement of the learner is more beneficial than the merely passive reception of the same information. Given the computing difficulties of our task, one may think that an externally-provided diagram might be easier to remember than the encoding a learner might generate on his or her own (Bellezza, 1996; Shah, Mayer & Hegarty, 1999). Our data, however, seems to confute this idea. Students who generated graphs remembered more information than students who were merely exposed to the graphs (the control group). Moreover, the writing-to-learn group generated texts, but in many cases these participants reproduced the list-like form of the original text. Writing was apparently interpreted as a skimming activity with no evidence of integration (Brown, Day & Jones, 1983).

According to the *levels-of-processing* view (Craik & Lokhart, 1972; Hyde & Jenkins, 1969), memory for events is determined by the type of processing that is performed on the to-be-encoded material. Items that receive only superficial analyses are assumed more poorly retained than inputs subjected to deeper semantic analyses. Writing-to-learn is assumed a strategy that stimulates *deep processing* of the text. Giving the material a different form and organization should, in theory, contribute to form macrostructures, which can be recalled more easily than the text's original sequence of propositions. However, in our study, the students who produced written texts, i.e., summaries of the article, limited their involvement to the elaboration of the written part, and did not focus on the graphs and their integration with the text. On the other hand, graph drawing forced students to select and rank text ideas and to connect the text and graphs, in order to produce a comprehensible representation of the article. Therefore, the graph-drawing group was more able to monitor the article for its internal coherence.

The *transfer appropriate processing framework* (Nelson, Walling, McEnvoy, 1979; Tulving & Bower, 1974) concerns how the goodness of a particular acquisition activity is defined, relative to a particular learning goal. Consider the demands of our post-test: besides memory for facts, it required establishing the position of various factors in a hierarchy and detecting text-graph inconsistencies. It is possible that graph drawing allowed participants to acquire more information on these items, though the writing group may have had the potential for being equally accurate on other kinds of information, which was not tested.

The *material-appropriate processing* framework (McDaniel & Einstein, 1989) assumes that two types of elaboration (individual item and relational processing) are important for learning and that adjuncts (learning strategies) and texts induce a particular type of processing: the greater the degree to which the adjunct and text facilitate complementary types of processing, the greater the influence on learning.

"A picture is worth a thousand words" is a widely used proverb. A prerequisite for a picture to have an effect on a mental representation is that readers recognize the utility of the picture and spend sufficient time processing it. Illustrations and graphs are supposed to help students understand study material. However, we should start asking how systematically students have been trained to process and understand graphs, not to mention how they have been trained to monitor text (and text-graph) coherence.

REFERENCES

Abbott, G. & Wingard, P. (1981). *The teaching of English as an international language*. Glasgow and London: Collins.
Abbott, V., & Black, J. B. (1986). Goal-related inferences in text comprehension. In J. A. Galambos, R. P. Abelson, & J. B. Black (Eds.), *Knowledge structures*. Hillsdale: Lawrence Erlbaum.
Ackerman, J. M. (1993). The promise of writing-to-learn. *Written Communication, 10*, 334-370.
Adam, J. M. (1992). *Les textes: types et prototypes. Récit, description, argumentation, explication, dialogue* [Texts: types and prototypes. Narration, description, explanation, dialogue]. Paris: Nathan.
Adam, J-M. (1995). Hacia una definición de la secuencia argumentativa. *Comunicación, Lenguaje & Educación, 25*, 9-22.
Adams, M. J. (1990). *Beginning to read: Thinking and learning about print. A summary*. Champaign, IL: Center for the Study of Reading, The Reading Research and Education Center and University of Illinois at Urbana-Champaign.
Afflerbach, P., & Johnston, P. (1984). On the use of verbal reports in reading research. *Journal of Reading Behavior, 16*, 307-322.
Akiguet, S. (1997). Amorce de la compétence argumentative écrite chez des enfants de neuf, dix et onze ans. *Archives de Psychologie, 65*, 29-48.
Akiguet, S., & Piolat, A. (1996). Insertion of connectives by 9- to 11-year old children in an argumentative text. *Argumentation, 10*, 253-270.
Alamargot, D. (2000, September). *Third Workshop on Argumentative Text Processing, Earli Sig-Writing*, Verona, September 6th. Paper discussant of symposium.
Alamargot, D., & Chanquoy, L. (2001). *Studies in writing: Vol. 9. Through the models of writing*. Dordrecht: Kluwer Academic Publishers.
Albertini, J. (1993). Critical literacy, whole language and teaching of writing to deaf students: who should dictate to whom? *Tesol Quarterly, 27*(1), 59-73.
Aldenderfer, M., & Blashfield, R. (1984). *Cluster analysis*. California: Sage.
Alexander, P. A., Schallert, D. L., & Hare, V. C. (1991). Coming to terms: How researchers in learning and literacy talk about knowledge. *Review of Educational Research, 61*, 315-343.
Alexander, R. J. (1992). *Policy and practice in primary education*. London: Routledge.
Algulin, I. (1977). *Den orfiska reträtten. Studier i svensk 40-talslyrik och dess litterära bakgrund* [The Orphic retreat: Studies in Swedish poetry of the 1940's]. Unplished doctoral dissertation. Stockholm: Stockholm Studies of Literature.
Allal, L. (1985). Processus de régulation interactive dans le cadre d'un jeu de mathématique à l'école primaire. *Revue internationale de psychologie appliquée, 34*, 83-104.
Allal, L. (1988). Vers un élargissement de la pédagogie de maîtrise: Processus de régulation interactive, rétroactive et proactive. In M. Huberman (Ed.), *Assurer la réussite des apprentissages scolaires* (pp. 86-126). Neuchâtel: Delachaux, & Niestlé.
Allal, L. (1993). *Self-regulation in classroom writing activities*. Paper presented at the 5th meeting of the European Association for Research on Learning and Instruction, Aix-en Provence.
Allal, L. (2000). Metacognitive regulation of writing in the classroom. In G. Rijlaarsdam & E. Espéret (Series Eds.), & A. Camps & M. Milian (Vol. Eds.), *Studies in writing: Vol. 6. Metalinguistic activity in learning to write* (pp. 145-166). Amsterdam: Amsterdam University Press.
Allal, L. (2001). Situated cognition and learning: From conceptual frameworks to classroom investigations. *Revue Suisse des Sciences de l' Education, 23*, 407-422.
Allal, L., & Saada-Robert, M. (1992). La métacognition: Cadre conceptuel pour l'étude des régulations en situation scolaire. *Archives de Psychologie, 60*, 265-296.
Allal, L., Rouiller, Y., & Saada-Robert, M. (1995). Autorégulation en production textuelle: Observation de quatre élèves de 12 ans. *Cahier d' Acquisition et de Pathologie du Langage, 13*, 17-35.

Althusser, L. (1971). *Ideology and ideological state apparatuses. In Lenin and philosophy*. Trans. Ben Brewster. New York and London: Monthly Review Press.

Ambroise, C., Auriac-Peyronnet, E., Jandot, C., & Rage, F. (submitted). The Links between philosophical discussion and Conceptualization *vs* linearization processes in argumentation field with young writers. *L1-Educational Studies in Language and Literature*.

Anderson, G. L., Herr, K., & Nihlen, A. S. (1994). *Studying your own school: An educator's guide to qualitative practitioner research*. Thousand Oaks, CA: Corwin Press, Inc.

Anderson, J. (1988). *Cognitive skills and their acquisition*. Hillside, NJ: Lawrence Erlbaum.

Anderson, J. R. (1987). Skill acquisition: Compilation of weak-method problem solutions. *Psychological Review, 94,* 192-210.

Anderson, J. R. (1990). *Cognitive psychology and its implications* (3rd ed.). New York: Freeman.

Anderson, R. C. (1978). Schema-directed processes in language comprehension. In J. W. Pellegrino, & A. M . Lesgold (Eds.), *Cognitive psychology and instruction* (pp. 67-82). New York: Plenum Press.

Angèlil-Carter, S. (2000). *Stolen language?: Plagiarism in writing*. Harlow, England: Pearson Education.

Anson, C., & Beach, R. (1990, March). *Research on writing to learn: The interesting case of academic journals*. Paper presented at the Annual Meeting of the Conference on College Composition and Communication (Chicago, IL, March 22-24).

Anson, C., & Beach, R. (1996). *Journals in the classroom: Writing to learn*. Norwood, MA: Christopher Gordon.

Antos, G. (1982). *Grundlagen einer Theorie des Formulierens* [Foundations to a theory of discourse formulation]. Tübingen: Niemeyer.

Anula, J. J. (in preparation). *Multifuncionalidad y reformulación en la construcción de discursos sobre la inmigración* [Multifuncionality and reformulation in the discourse construction about immigration]. PhD Thesis in preparation. Universidad Nacional de Educación a Distancia (O.U.), Madrid, Spain.

Applebee, A. (1984). Writing and reasoning. *Review of Educational Research, 54*(4), 577-596.

Applebee, A., & Langer, J. (1983). Instructional scaffolding: Reading and writing as natural language activities. *Language Arts, 60*(2), 168-175.

Ashwell, T. (2000). Patterns of teacher response to student writing in a multiple-draft composition classroom: Is content feedback followed by form feedback the best method? *Journal of Second Language Writing, 9*(3), 227-257.

Askov, E. N., & Bixlet, B. (1998). Transforming adult literacy instruction through computer-assisted instruction. In D. Reinking, M. McKenna, L. D. Labbo, & R. D. Kieffer (Eds.), *Handbook of literacy and technology: Transformation in a post-typographical world* (pp.167-184). Mahwah, New Jersey: Lawrence Erlbaum.

Aspinwall, L., & Miller, L. D. (1997). Students' reliance on writing as a process to learn first semester calculus. *Journal of Instructional Psychology, 24* (4), 253-61.

Association of College and Research Libraries (ACRL) (2000). *Information literacy competency standard for higher education*. Chicago: American Library Association.

Association of College, & Research Libraries (ACRL) (2000*). Standards for university libraries: Evaluation of performance*. Retrieved April 3, 2003, from http://www.ala.org/acrl/ilcomstan.html.

Atkinson, R. Levin, J., Kiewra, K., Meyers, T., Kim, S., Atkinson, L., Renandya, W., & Hwang, Y. (1999). Matrix and mnemonic text-processing adjuncts: Comparing and combining their components. *Journal of Educational Psychology, 2,* 342-357.

Atwell, N. (1987). *In the middle: Writing, reading, and learning with adolescents*. Portsmouth, NH: Heinemann.

Aureli, E., & Ottaviani, M. G. (1992). Insegnanti e testi: due aree di condizionamento per l'insegnamento della statistica nelle scuole secondary. *Induzioni, 4,* 33-36.

Auriac-Peyronnet E., Martinet, P., & Peyronnet, A (in preparation). The impact of philosophical discussion about the "petit frère tombé du ciel" on the argumentative abilities in special class c.l.i.s.

Auriac-Peyronnet, E. (1998, June-July). *Effects of oral practice and cooperative discussion on argumentative text writting by 10-12 year old children. Paper presentend at the 2nd international workshop on argumentative text processing*. June 30-July 1, Poitiers University.

Auriac-Peyronnet, E. (1999, June). Argumenter en CM1 et CM2: le croisement de l'oral et de l'écrit (Argue in CM1 and CM2 elementary classroom: the cross between oral and written aspects), *Troisième congrès International d'Actualité de la Recherche en Education et Formation*. Bordeaux University, 28-30 Juin 1999.

Auriac-Peyronnet, E. (2001). The impact of oral training on argumentative texts produced by 10- and 11-year-old children: Exploring the relation between narration and argumentation. *European Journal of Psychology of Education, 16*, 299-317.
Auriac-Peyronnet, E. (Ed.). (2003). *Je parle... Tu parles... Nous apprenons. Coopération et argumentation au service des apprentissages. (I speak... You speak... We are learning. The links between Co-operation and Argumentation to learn)*. Bruxelles: De Boeck Université, coll. Pédagogie.
Auriac-Peyronnet, E. (*submitted, accepted, in revision*). The role of moral values as a factor influencing the quality of production of argumentative texts in 11-year-old pupils, *Written communication*.
Auriac-Peyronnet, E., & Daniel, M. F. (2002). The specifics of philosophical dialogue: A case study of pupils aged 11 and 12 years. *Thinking, 16*(1), 23-31.
Auriac-Peyronnet, E., & Gombert, A. (2000, September). Effects of collective moral values on argumentative text produced by 11-13 year old children. *Third workshop on argumentative text processing, Earli Sig-Writing*. Verona, September 6th 2000.
Auriac-Peyronnet, Martinet, P., Peyronnet, A. Torregrosa, E., & Tressol, J. F. (2002, July). Faire aussi des Sciences en CLIS1 – Classe d'intégration scolaire – [Study sciences in special integrated classroom too]. *6ème Biennale de l'éducation et de la formation* (p.16). Paris: July 3-6 2002.
Austin, J. L. (1962). *How to do things with words*? London: Oxford University Press.
Austin, J. L. (1976). *How to Do Things with Words* (2nd edition, edited by J. O. Urmson, & M. Sbisà. London, etc.: Oxford University Press.
Ausubel, D. P. (1962). A subsumption theory of meaningful verbal learning and retention. *Journal of General Psychology, 66*, 213-224.
Ausubel, D. P. (1963). *The psychology of meaningful verbal learning*. New York: Grune & Stratton.
Baker, L. (1985). How do we know when we don't understand? Standards for evaluating text comprehension. In D. L. Forrest-Pressley, G. E. Mackinnon, & T. Gary Waller, *Metacognition, cognition and human performance*, (pp. 155-205). Orlando: Academic Press.
Baker, L., & Brown, A. L. (1984). Metacognitive skills in reading. In P. D. Pearson (Ed.), *Handbook of reading research* (pp. 353-394). New York: Longman.
Bakhtin, M. (1981). *The dialogic imagination*. Austin, Texas: University of Texas Press.
Bakhtin, M. (1986). The problem of speech genres. *Speech genres and other late essays*. Austin, Texas: University of Texas Press.
Bakhtin, M. M. (1978). *Esthétique et théorie du roman* [Aesthetic and theory of the novel]. Paris: Gallimard.
Bakhtin, M. M. (1985). *Estética de la creación verbal* [Aesthetic of verbal creation]. México: Siglo Veintiuno Editores.
Bakhtin, M. (1981). Discourse in the novel. In M. Holquist (Ed.), C. Emerson, & M. Holquist (Trans.), *The dialogic imagination: Four essays by M. M. Bakhtin* (pp. 259-422). Austin: University of Texas Press (Original work published in 1934-1935).
Bal, M. (1977). *Narratologie: Essais sur la signification narrative dans quatre romans modernes* [Narratology: Essays about narrative meaning in four modern novels]. Paris: Klinscksieck.
Ballantyne, R., & Packer, J. (1995). Making connections: Using student journals as a teaching/learning aid. Monograph (Gold Guide No. 2). Canberra, Australian Capital Territory: Higher Education Research and Development Society of Australia.
Balslev, K., & Saada-Robert, M. (2002). Expliquer l'apprentissage situé de la litéracie: Une démarche inductive/déductive [Explaining situated learning of literacy: An inductive/deductive approach]. In F. Leutenegger, & M. Saada-Robert (Eds.), *Expliquer et comprendre en sciences de l'éducation* (pp. 111-129). Bruxelles: De Boeck.
Bamberg, M. (1997). *Narrative development, Six approaches*. Mahwah, NJ: Lawrence Erlbaum.
Bandura, A. (1977). *Social learning theory*. Englewood Cliffs: Prentice Hall.
Bandura, A. (1986). *Social foundations of thought and action: A social-cognitive theory*. Englewood Cliffs: Prentice Hall.
Bang, M. G. (1986). The grey lady and the strawberry snatcher. New York: Four Winds Press.
Barell, J. (1991). *Teaching for thoughtfulness: Classroom strategies to enhance intellectual development*. New York: Longman.
Barnes, D.(1976). From communication to curriculum. Harmondsworth: Penguin.
Barthes, R. (1966). *Critique et verité* [Critic and truth]. Paris: Seuil.
Barthes, R. (1970). *S/Z*. Paris: Seuil.
Barthes, R. (1973). *Le plaisir du texte* [The pleasure of the text]. Paris: Seuil.

Bartlett, E. J. (1982). Learning to revise: Some component processes. In M. Nystrand (Ed.), *What writers know: The language, process, and the structure of written discourse* (pp. 345-363). New York: Academic Press.

Barton, S., & Sanford, A. (1993). A case study of anomaly detection: Shallow semantic processing and cohesion establishment. *Memory, & Cognition, 4*, 477-487.

Baudrillard, J. (1994). *The illusion of the End.* Cambridge: Polity Press.

Bazerman, C. (1988). *Shaping written knowledge: The genre and activity of the experimental article in science.* Madison: University of Wisconsin Press.

Beach, R. (1979). The effects of between draft teacher evaluation versus student self-evaluation on high school students' revising of rough drafts. *Research in the Teaching of English, 13*, 111-119.

Beach, R., & Christensen, M. (1989, March). *Discourse conventions in academic response journals.* Paper presented at the Annual Meeting of the Conference on College Composition and Communication (Seattle, WA, March 16-18).

Beard, R. (1984). *Children's writing in the primary school.* Sevenoaks: Hodder & Stoughton.

Beard, R. (1999). *The National Literacy Strategy: Review of research and other related evidence.* London: Department for Education and Employment.

Beard, R. (2000a). *Developing writing 3-13.* London: Hodder & Stoughton.

Beard, R. (2000b). Research and the National Literacy Strategy. *Oxford Review of Education, 26*(3&4), 421-436.

Beaugrande, R. de (1984). *Text production: Toward a science of composition.* Norwood, New Jersey: Ablex Publishing Corp.

Beausoleil, J.-R., & Daniel, M. F. (1991). L'identification des dimensions philosophiques dans les dialogues des élèves [The identification of philosophical factors in pupils discussions], *Arrimages, 7&8,* 17-23.

Béguelin, M. J. (2002). Unidades de lengua y unidades de escritura. Evolución y modalidades de la segmentación gráfica [Units of language and units of writing. Evolution and modalities of griten segmentation]. In E. Ferreiro (Ed.), *Relaciones de (in)dependencia entre oralidad y escritura* (pp. 31-52). Barcelona: Gedisa.

Belcher, D., & Hirvela, A. (Eds.). (2001). *Linking literacies: Perspectives on reading-writing connections.* Ann Arbor: University of Michigan Press.

Bellezza, F. S. (1996). Mnemonic methods to enhance storage and retrieval. In E. L. Bjork, & R. A. Bjork (Eds.), *Memory* (pp. 345-380). New York: Academic Press.

Bennett, T. (1984). Texts in history: The determination of readings and their texts. *Australian Journal of Communication, 5&6*, pp.3-11.

Bentolila, A. (1994). La relation entre la pratique de l'oral et la lecture [The relationship between oral practice and reading]. *Lettre d'Information de l'Association Langage Lecture Orthographe, 17,* 2-3.

Bereiter, C. (2002). Emergent versus presentational hypertext. In R. Bromme, & E. Stahl (Eds.), *Writing hypertext and learning. Conceptual and empirical approaches. Advances in learning and instruction series* (pp. 73-78). Amsterdam: Pergamon.

Bereiter, C., & Scardamalia, M. (1982). From conversation to composition. In R. Glaser (Ed.), *Advances in instructional Psychology* (Vol. 2, pp. 1-64). Hillsdale, NJ: Lawrence Erlbaum.

Bereiter, C., & Scardamalia, M. (1987). Knowledge telling and knowledge transforming. In: *The Psychology of written composition* (pp. 10-13, 349-358). Hillsdale, NJ: Lawrence Erlbaum.

Bereiter, C., & Scardamalia, M. (1987). *The psychology of written composition.* Hillsdale, NJ: Lawrence Erlbaum.

Bereiter, C., & Scardamalia, M. (1993). Composing and Writing. In R. Beard (Ed.), *Teaching literacy: balancing perspectives.* London: Hodder & Stoughton.

Bereiter, C., & Scardamalia, M. (1998/1996). Rethinking learning. In: D. R. Olson, & N. Torrance, *The handbook of education and human development* (pp. 485-513). Oxford: Blackwell Publishers.

Berge, K. L. (1988). *Skolestilen som genre. Med påtvungen penn* [School style as a genre. With an inflicted pen]. Lillehammer.

Bergsten, S. (1994). *Lyrikläsarens handbok* [The handbok of the poetry reader]. Lund: Studentlitteratur.

Berkenkotter, C., & Huckin, T. N. (1995). *Genre knowledge in disciplinary communication: Cognition/culture/power.* Hillsdale, NJ: Lawrence Erlbaum.

Berliner, D. C., & Calfee, R. C. (Eds.). (1996). *Handbook of educational psychology.* New York: Macmillan.

REFERENCES

Bernárdez, E. (1995). Teoría y epistemología del texto [Theory and epistemology of text]. Madrid: Cátedra.

Bétrix Koehler, D. (1991). *Dis-moi comment tu orthographies, je te dirai qui tu es: Analyse des performances orthographiques des élèves de 5e et 6e.* (Report No 91.02). Lausanne: Centre Vaudois de recherches pédagogiques.

Bialystok, E. (1991). *Language processing in bilingual children.* Cambridge, UK: Cambridge University Press.

Biggs, J. B. (1987a). *Student approaches to learning and studying.* Melbourne: Australian Council for Educational Research.

Biggs, J. B. (1987b). *Study process questionnaire manual.* Melbourne: Australian Council for Educational Research.

Birenbaum, M., & Dochy, F. (1996). (Eds.), *Alternatives in assessment of achievements, learning, processes, and prior knowledge.* Boston: Kluwer Academic Publishers.

Bizzell, P. (1982). Cognition, context and certainty: What we need to know about writing. *Pre/text, 3,* 213-214 (Reproduced in V. Vitanza, (Ed.). (1993): The First Decade (pp 65-92). Pittsburgh, Pa: University of Pittsburgh Press.).

Black, K. (1989). Audience analysis and persuasive writing at the college level. *Research in the Teaching of English, 3,* 231-253.

Blank, M. (1973). Eliciting verbalization from young children in experimental tasks: A methodological note. *Child Development, 46,* 254-257.

Blohm, P. J. (1991, April). Effect of journal writing tactic and implementation on levels of comprehending world history text. Paper presented at the American Educational Research Association Conference (Chicago, IL., April 3-7).

Bochner, J. H., Albertini, J. A., Samar, V. J., & Metz, D. A. (1992). External and diagnostic validity of the NTID writing test: An investigation using direct magnitude estimation and principal component analysis. *Research in the Teaching of English, 26*(3), 299-314.

Boëthius, U. (1990). Högt och lågt inom kulturen. Moderniseringsprocessen och de kulturella hierarkierna. In J. Fornäs & U. Boëthius (Eds.), *Ungdom och kulturell modernisering.* FUS-rapport nr 2, pp 59-93. Stockholm: Stehag.

Bonanno, H., & Jones, J. (1997). *The MASUS procedure: Measuring the academic skills of university students.* Sydney: Learning Centre, The University of Sydney.

Borel, M. J. (1981). L'explication dans l'argumentation: approche sémiologique [Explanation within argumentation: a semiotic approach]. *Langue Française, 50,* 20-38.

Borgman, C. L. (2001). Digital libraries and virtual universities. In F. T. Tschang, & T. Della Senta, (Eds.). *Access to knowledge. New information technologies and the emergence of the virtual university* (pp. 207-240). New York: United Nations University/ Institute of Advanced Studies.

Boscolo, P. (1996). The use of information in expository text writing. In C. Pontecorvo, M. Orsolini, B. Burge, & L. Resnick. (Eds.), *Children's early text construction* (pp. 219-230). New Jersey: Lawrence Erlbaum.

Boscolo, P., & Mason, L. (1997, August). *Writing and conceptual change. What changes? Paper presented at the Writing-to-learn in classroom context,* Paper presented at the 7th EARLI Conference, Athens.

Boscolo, P., & Mason, L. (2001). Writing to learn, writing to transfer. In G. Rijlaarsdam (Series Ed.) & P. Tynjälä, L. Mason, & K. Lonka (Vol. Eds.). *Studies in writing: Vol. 7. Writing as a learning tool.* Dordrecht: Kluwer Academic Publishers.

Bottomley, D. M., Henk, W. A., & Melnick, S. A. (1997/1998). Assessing children's views about themselves as writers using the Writer Self-Perception Scale. *The Reading Teacher, 51*(4), 286-295.

Bouchard, R. (1988). Lire pour réécrire (des discours mathématiques en classe). Reformulation et énonciation [Reading to rewrite (mathematical discourses in the classroom). Reformulation and uttering]. *Études de Linguistique Appliquée, 71,* 34-50.

Bouchard, R. (1993). Interaction comme moyen d'étude didactique. Interaction et processus de production écrite. Une étude de pragmatique impliquée [Interaction as a means for a didactic study. Interaction and written composition process. A study in implied pragmatics]. In J.-F. Halté (Ed.), *Inter-Actions. L'interaction, actualités de la recherche et enjeux didactiques* (pp. 137-199). Metz: Université de Metz.

Bouchard, R. (1996). Dialogue, co-action et construction des contextes en situation de travail: L'écriture (collective) comme artisanat [Dialog, co-action and context construction within the task: (collective) writing as a craft]. In S. Cmerjrkova, A. Hoffmanova, et al. (Eds.), *Dialoganalyse Vi, referate de 6. Arbeitstagung.* Prag/Tübingen: Niemeyer.

Bouffard-Bouchard T., Parent S., & Larivée S. (1991a). Compétences cognitives, capacités d'apprentissage et métacognition.(cognitive skills, learning capacity and metacognition). *Journal International de Psychologie, 26,* 723-744.

Bouffard-Bouchard T., Parent S., & Larivée S. (1991b). Influence of self-efficacy on self-regulationand performance among junior and senior high school age students. *International Journal of Behavioral Development, 14*(2), 56-79.

Bower, G. H., & E. R. Hilgard (1981). *Theories of learning* (5th ed.). Englewood Cliffs: Prentice-Hall.

Bowman, C. A. (2000). Creating connection: Challenging the text and student writers. *English Journal, 89*(4), 78-84.

Braaksma, M. A. H., Rijlaarsdam, G., & Van den Bergh, H. (2002). Observational Learning and the Effects of Model-Observer Similarity. *Journal of Educational Psychology, 94,* 405-415.

Braaksma, M. A. H., Rijlaarsdam, G., Van den Bergh, H., & Van Hout-Wolters, B. (in press). Observational learning and effects on orchestration of writing processes. *Cognition and Instruction, 22*(1).

Braaksma, M. A. H., Van den Bergh, H., Rijlaarsdam, G., & Couzijn, M. (2001). Effective learning activities in observation tasks when learning to write and read argumentative texts. *European Journal of Psychology of Education, 1,* 33-48.

Braaksma, M., Rijlaarsdam, G. van den Bergh, H., & van Hout-Wolters, B. (2002, July). *Observational learning and its effects on the orchestration of writing processes.* Paper presented at SIG Writing Conference, Stafford, UK.

Braet, A. , Moret, L., Schoonen, R., & Sjoer, E. (1993). Zo haal je een hoog cijfer voor je examenopstel: adviezen van en voor leerlingen [This is the way to a high grade for your exam essay. Advice to and from students]. *Tijdschrift voor Taalbeheersing, 15, 173-192.*

Braet, A., & Berkenbosch, R. (1989). *Debatteren over beleid* [Debating about policy]. Groningen: Wolters-Noordhoff.

Brakel Olson, V. L. (1990). The revising process of sixth-grade writers with and without peer feedback. *Journal of Educational Research, 84* (1), 22-29.

Brandt, D. (1986). Toward an understanding of context in composition. *Written Communication, 3,* 139-157.

Brandt, D. (1992). The cognitive as the social: An ethnomethodogical approach to writing process research. *Written Communication, 9,* 315-355.

Brassart, D. G. (1990). Explicatif, argumentatif, descriptif, narratif, et quelques autres. Notes de travail [Explanatory text, argumentative text, descriptive text, narrative text and other types of text. Working notes]. *Recherches, 13,* 21-60.

Brassart, D. G. (1995). Elementos para una didáctica de la argumentación en la escuela primaria. *Comunicación, Lenguaje y Educación, 25,* 41-50.

Brassart, D. G., & Veevaert, A. (1992). *Enseigner, apprendre le texte argumentative.* Lille: CRDP.

Brassart, D.-G. (1985). Les Enfants comprennent-ils des énoncés argumentatifs? [Did children understand argumentative utterances?]. *Repères, 65,* 15-21.

Brassart, D.-G. (1987). *Le développement des capacités discursives chez l'enfant de 8 à 12 ans: le discours argumentatif – étude didactique –* [The development of discourses competencies by children of 8 to 12 years – a didactical study –]. Unpublished doctoral dissertation. Strasbourg.

Brassart, D.-G. (1988). La gestion des contre-arguments dans le texte argumentatif écrit chez les élèves de 8 à 12 ans et les adultes compétents [The cognitive management of counter-arguments in argumentative written text in 8-12 years olds children and Adults]. *European Journal of Psychology of Education, 4*(1), 51-69.

Bräten I., & Olaussen B. S. (1997). The relationship between motivational beliefs and learning strategy use among Norvwegian college students. *Contemporary Educational Psychology, 23,* 182-194.

Breetvelt, I., Van den Bergh, H., & Rijlaarsdam, G. (1994). Relations between writing processes and text quality: When and how? *Cognition and Instruction, 12*(2), 103-123.

Bridgeman, B., & Carlson, S. B. (1984). A survey of academic writing tasks. *Written Communication, 1,* 247-280.

Britton, J. (1971). *Language and learning.* Harmondsworth: Penguin.

Britton, J., Burgess, T., Martin, N., McLeod, A., & Rosen, H. (1975). *The development of writing abilities.* London: MacMillan Education.

REFERENCES

Brockbank, A., & McGill, I (1998). *Facilitating reflective learning in higher education,* SRHE / Open University, Buckingham.
Bromme, R., & Stahl, E. (1999). Spatial metaphors and writing hypertexts: Study within schools. *European Journal of Psychology of Education, 14*, 267-281.
Bromme, R., & Stahl, E. (2001). The idea of 'hypertext' and its implications on the process of hypertext writing. In W. Frindte, T. Köhler, P. Marquet, & E. Nissen (Eds.), *IN-TELE 99 – Interned-based teaching and learning 99, Vol.3 Internet Communication* (pp. 302-308). Frankfurt am Main: Peter Lang.
Bromme, R., & Stahl, E. (Eds.). (2002). *Writing hypertext and learning. Conceptual and empirical approaches.* London: Pergamon.
Bronckart, J. P. et al. (1997). *Activité langagière, textes et discours: pour un interactionisme sociodiscursif* [Discursive activity, texts and discourses: Towards a sociodiscursive interactionism]. Neuchâtel: Delachaux & Niestlé.
Bronckart, J.-P., Bain, D., Schneuwly, B., Davaud, C., & Pasquier, A. (1985). *Le fonctionnement des discours* [The function of discourse. A psychological model and a method of analysis]. Neuchâtel: Delachaux & Niestlé.
Brossard, M., & Fijalkow, J. (1998). *Apprendre à l'école: Perspectives Piagétiennes et Vygotskiennes* [Learning at school: Piagetian's and Vygotskian's perspectives]. Bordeaux: Presses Universitaires de Bordeaux.
Brossell, G. (1983). Rhetorical specification in essay examination topics. *College English, 45*(2), 165-173.
Brown, A. L. (1992). Design experiments: Theoretical and methodological challenges in creating complex interventions in classroom settings. *Journal of the Learning Sciences, 2*, 141-178.
Brown, A. L., & Campione, J. C. (1994). Guided discovery in a community of learners. In K. McGilly (Ed.), *Classroom lessons: Integrating cognitive theory and classroom practice* (pp. 229-270). Cambridge, MA: MIT Press/Bradford Books.
Brown, A. L., & Palinscar, M. S. (1982). Inducing strategic learning from texts by means of informed, self-control training. *Topics in Learning, & Learning Disabilities, 2*, 1-17.
Brown, A. L., Campione, J. C., & Day, J. D. (1982). Learning to learn: On training students to learn from texts. *Educational Researcher, 10*, 14-21.
Brown, A., Bransford, J., Ferrara, R., & Campione, J. (1983). Learning, Remembering, and Understanding. In P. H. Mussen (Ed.), *Carmichael's manual of child psychology, Vol 3,* pp. 77-166. New Jersy: John Wiley Publishers.
Brown, A., Day, J., & Jones, R. (1983). The development of plans for summarizing texts. *Child Development, 54*, 968-979.
Brown, H. D. (2001). *Teaching by principles: An interactive approach to language pedagogy* (2nd ed.). White Plains, N. Y.: Addison Wesley Longman.
Brown, J. S., Collins, A., & Duguid, P. (1989). Situated cognition and the culture of learning. *Educational Researcher, 18*(1), 32-42.
Bruffee, K. (1985). *A short course in writing* (3rd ed.). Boston: Little, Brown.
Bruner J. (1983). *Le développement de l'enfant. Savoir faire, savoir dire* [The child development. Knowing to do, knowing to say]. Paris: PUF.
Bruner, J. (1984). *Acción, pensamiento y lenguaje* [Action, thinking and language]. Comp. J. J. Linaza. Madrid: Alianza.
Bruner, J. (1986). *Actual minds, possible worlds.* Cambridge, MA: Cambridge University Press.
Bruner, J. (1996). *La cultura de la educación* [The culture of education]. Madrid: Visor.
Bruner, J. S., Olver, R. R., & Greenfield P. M. (1966). *Studies in cognitive growth.* New York: John Wiley and Sons.
Bucheton, D., & Chabanne, J. C. (Mars 2002). L'évaluation des écrits intermédiaires à l'école et au college [Evaluation of intermediate writing in school and college]. *Colloque L'écriture et son apprentissage. Question pour la didactique, apports de la didactique.* Paris: 21-23 Mars.
Buckingham, D., & Sefton-Green, J. (1994). *Cultural studies goes to school: Reading and teaching popular media.* London: Taylor, & Francis.
Bühler, K. (1934). *Sprachtheorie* [Theory of language]. Stuttgart/New York: Gustav Fischer (Reprinted in 1982).
Burns, & Bulman (Eds.). (2000). *Reflective practice in nursing* (2nd Edition). Oxford: Blackwell.

Burtis, P. J., Bereiter, C., Scardamalia, M., & Tetroe, J. (1983). The development of planning in writing. In B. M. Kroll, & G. Wells (Eds.), *Explorations in the development of writing* (pp. 153-174). John Wiley & Sons.

Butler, D. L., & Winne, P. H. (1995). Feedback and self-regulated learning: A theoretical synthesis. *Review of Educational Research, 65*(3), 245-282.

Butler, J. (1991). Science and thinking: The write connection. *Journal of Science Teacher Education, 2*(4), 106-110.

Butterfield, E. C., & Nelson, G. D. (1991). Promoting positive transfer of different kinds. *Cognition and Instruction, 8*(1), 69-102.

Cagliari, L. C. (2001). Como alfabetizar: 20 anos em busca de soluções [How to teach/learn to read and write: 20 years in search of solution]. *Letras de Hoje, 36*(3), 47-66.

Caillier, J. (1999). *Interactions entre pairs et didactique de l'oral.* Mémoire de DEA de Sciences du Langage. Montpellier: Université Paul-Valéry.

Caillier, J. (2001). Le courant "maîtrise de la llengue" [The field of linguistics hablities]. In Tozzi (Ed.), *L'éveil de la pensée réflexive à l'école primaire* (pp.61-68). Paris, Montpellier: Hachette & CNDP.

Calkins, L. M. (1986). *The art of teaching writing.* Portsmouth, NH: Heinemann.

Calkins, L. M. (1994). *The art of teaching writing* (New edition). Portsmouth, NH: Heinemann.

Callaghan, M., & Rothery, J. (1988). *Teaching factual writing: A genre-based approach.* Sydney: Metropolitan East disadvantaged schools programme.

Camps, A. & Milian, M. (Eds.). (2000). *El papel de la actividad metalingüística en el aprendizaje de la escritura* [Metalinguistic activity in learning to write]. Rosario, Argentina: Homo Sapiens.

Camps, A. (1994a). L'ensenyament de la composició escrita [Teaching written composition]. Barcelona: Barcanova.

Camps, A. (1994b). Projectes de llengua entre la teoria i la pràctica [Language projects between theory and practice]. *Articles de Didàctica de la Llengua i la Literatura, 2,* 7-20 (Spanish translation, 1996: Proyectos de Lengua entre la teoría y la práctica, Cultura y Educación, 2, pp. 43-57).

Camps, A. (1995). Aprender a escribir textos argumentativos: Características dialógicas de la argumentación escrita. *Comunicación, Lenguaje y Educación, 25,* 51-63.

Camps, A., & Dolz, J. (1995). Introducción: Enseñar a argumentar: un desafío para la escuela actual. *Comunicación, Lenguaje y Educación, 25,* 5-8.

Camps, A., Guasch, O., Milian, M., & Ribas, T. (1997). Activitat metalingüística durant el procés de producció d'un text argumentatiu [Metalinguistic activity along the process of writing an argumentative text]. *Articles, 11,* 13-28.

Cantrell, R. J., Fusaro, J. A., & Dougherty, E. A. (2000). Exploring the effectiveness of journal writing on learning social studies: A comparative study. *Reading Psychology, 21*(1), 1-11.

Caramazza, A., & Hillis, A. E. (1991). Lexical organization of nouns and verbs in the brain. *Nature, 349,* 788-790.

Carruthers, M. J. (1992). *The book of memory: A study of memory in medieval culture.* Cambridge: Cambridge University Press.

Carugati, F. (1988). Interactions, déstabilisations, conflits. In A.-N. Perret-Clermont, & M. Nicolet (Eds.), *Interagir et connaître: Enjeux et régulations sociales dans le développement cognitif* (pp. 93-100). Fribourg: Delval.

Caspi, M. (1985). *Approach to creative Self-remaking.* Jerusalem: Hebrew University of Jerusalem.

Catach, N. (1980). *L'orthographe française: Traité théorique et pratique avec des travaux d'application et leurs corrigés.* Paris: Nathan.

Catach, N. (1980). La punctuation [Punctuation]. *Langue Francaise, 45,* 55-68

Cauzinille-Marmèche E. (1991). Apprendre à utiliser sa connaissance pour la résolution de problèmes: analogie et transfert [Learning to use one's cognition for problem solving. Comparisons and transfer]. *Bulletin de Psychologie, Tome XLIV, 399,* 156-164.

Cazden, C. (1986). Classroom discourse. In M. Wittrock (Ed.), *Handbook of research on teaching* (3rd ed., pp. 432-463). New York: Macmillan.

Cazden, C. (1988). *Classroom discourse. The language of teaching and learning.* Heinemann: Educational Books, Inc.

Cederlund, J., & Severinson Eklundh, K. (n.d). *JEdit: The logging text editor for Macintosh.* Stockholm, Sweden: IPLab, Department of Numerical Analysis and Computing Science, Royal Institute of Technology (KTH).

Central Advisory Council for Education (1967). *Children and their primary schools* (The Plowden Report). London: Her Majesty's Stationery Office.

Chaib, C. (1996). Ungdomsteater och personlig utveckling. En pedagogisk analys av ungdomars teaterskapande [Youth theatre and personal development. A pedagogical analysis of young people's theatre production]. Göteborg: Pedagogiska institutionen, University of Lund.

Chall, J. S. (1996). *Stages of reading development* (2nd ed.). Fort Worth, TX: Hartcourt Brace.

Chamot, A., & Kupper, L. (1989). Learning strategies in foreign language instruction. *Foreign Language Annals, 1*, 12-24.

Champagne, A. B., & Bunce, D. M. (1991). Learning-theory-based science teaching. In S. M. Glynn, R. H. Yeany, & B. K. Britton (Eds.), *The psychology of learning science* (pp. 21-41). Hillsdale, NJ: Lawrence Erlbaum.

Chandler, P., & Sweller, J. (1992). The split-attention effect as a factor in the design of instruction. *British Journal of Educational Psychology, 62*, 233-246.

Chanquoy, L. (2001). How to make it easier for children to revise their writing: A study of text revision from 3rd to 5th grades. *British Journal of Educational Psychology, 71*, 15-41.

Chaopricha, S. (1997). Coauthoring as learning and enculturation: A study of writing in biochemistry. Unpublished doctoral dissertation, University of Wisconsin, Madison, WI.

Cheung, M. (1996). *Implementing process writing in Hong Kong secondary schools: A case study of the effect of an innovation-related in-service programme on the process and outcomes of teachers' opinion*. Unpublished doctoral dissertation. Hong Kong: City University of Hong Kong.

Glynn, S. M., Yeany, R. H., & Britton, B. K. (1991). *The psychology of learning science*. Hillsdale, NJ: Lawrence Erlbaum.

Clanchy, J., & Ballard, S. (1995). Generic skills in the context of higher education. *Higher Education Research and Development, 14*(2), 155-166.

Clark, H. H. (1977). Bridging. In P. N. Johnson-Laird, & P. C. Wason (Eds.), *Thinking. Readings in cognitive science* (pp.411-420). Cambridge: Cambridge University Press.

Clarke, J. H. (1992). Using visual organizers to focus on thinking. *Journal of Reading, 3*, 526-534.

Clifford, J. (1981). Composing in stages: The effects of a collaborative pedagogy. *Research in the Teaching of English, 15*(1), 37-58.

Clyne, M. (1999). Writing, testing and culture. In B. Doecke (Ed.), Responding to students' writing: continuing conversations (pp.165-176). Norwood: AATE.

Cohen, A.D. (1991). Strategies in Second Language Learning: Insights form Research. R. Phillipson et al. (Eds.), *Foreign/Second Language Pedagogy Research* (pp. 107-119). Clevedon (UK): Multilingual Matters Ltd.

Cohen, A. D. (1995a). In which language do/should multilinguals think? *Language, Culture, and Curriculum, 8*(2), 99-113.

Cohen, A. D. (1995b). The role of language of thought in foreign language learning. *Working Papers in Educational Linguistics, 11*(2), 1-11.

Cohen, L. & Maion, L. (1994). *Research methods in education*. London: Routledge.

Cohen, J. (1968). Weighted kappa: Nominal scale agreement with provision for scaled disagreement or partial credit. *Psychological Bulletin, 70* (4), 213-220.

Coirier, P. & Golder, C. (1993). Production of supporting structure: Developmental study. *European Journal of Psychology of Education, 2*, 1-13.

Coirier, P., Andriessen, J., & Chanquoy L. (1999). From planning to translating: The specificity of argumentative writing. In G. Rijlaarsdam & E. Espéret (Series Eds.) & J. Andriessen & P. Coirier (Vol. Eds.), *Studies in weiring: Vol 5. Foundations of argumentative text processing* (pp. 1-28). Amsterdam: Amsterdam University Press.

Coirier, P., Favart, M., & Chanquoy, L. (2002). Ordering and structuring ideas in text: From conceptual organization to linguistic formulation. *European Journal of Psychology of Education, 17*, 157-175.

Collins, A., Brown, J. S, & Newman, S. E. (1989). Cognitive apprenticeship: Teaching the craft of reading, writing and mathematics. In L. B. Resnick (Ed.), *Knowing, learning and instruction* (pp. 453-494). Hillsdale, NJ: Lawrence Erlbaum.

Coltier, D. & Gentilhomme, F. (1989). Repérage des genres de l'explicatif et production d'explications [Looking for explanatory genres and giving explanations]. *Repères, 77*, 53-75.

Coltier, D. (1986). Approches du texte explicatif [Approaches to the explanatory text]. Pratiques, 51, pp. 3-21.

Combettes, B., & Tomassone, R. (1988). Le texte informatif [The informative text]. Bruxelles: De Boeck.

Commander, N. E., & Smith, B. D. (1996). Learning logs: A tool for cognitive monitoring. *Journal of Adolescent and Adult Literacy, 39*(6), 446-453.

Conche, M. (2000). Il faut avant tout former la capacité de juger [We have to teach the judgement competencies]. *JDI, 7,* 19-19.

Connell, R. W., Ashenden, D. J., Kessler, S., & Dowsett, G. W. (1982). *Making the difference: Schools, families and social division.* North Sydney: Allen and Unwin.

Conolly, P. (1989). Writing and the ecology of learning. In P. Conolly, & T. Vilardi (Eds.), *Writing to learn in mathematics and science* (pp. 1-14). New York: Teacher College Press.

Conrad, K., & Training Links (2000). *Instructional design for web-based training.* Amherst: HRD Press.

Cook, V. (2001). Using the first language in the classroom. *The Canadian Modern Language Review/ La Review Canadienne des Langues Vivantes, 57*(3), 402-423.

Cook-Gumperz, J. (1986). *The social construction of literacy.* Cambridge: Cambridge University Press.

Cope, B., & Kalantzis, M. (Eds.). (1993). *The powers of literacy. A genre approach to teaching writing.* London: Falmer Press.

Cordova, D., & Lepper, M., (1996). Intrinsic motivation and the process of learning: Beneficial effects of contextualization, personalization, and choice. *Journal of Educational Psycholocy, 88,* 715-738.

Cornbleth, C. T. (1985). Critical thinking & cognitive processes. In W. B. Stanley et al. (Eds.), *Review of Research in Social Studies in Education* (1976-1983) (pp. 64-11). Washington, D.C. National Council for the Social Studies.

Cornell University Library. Online library tutorial (1998). Retrieved April 3, 2003 from, http://campusgw.library.cornell.edu/ cgi-in/manntom2.cgi/ section=help&URL=newhelp/newhelp.html

Cotteron, (1995). ¿Secuencias didácticas para enseñar a argumentar en la escuela primaria? *Comunicación, Lenguaje y Educación, 25,* 79-94.

Couzijn, M. (1999). Learning to write by observation of writing and reading processes: Effects on learning and transfer. *Learning and Instruction, 9,* 109-142.

Couzijn, M., & Rijlaarsdam, G. (1996). Learning to read and write argumentative text by observation. In G. Rijlaarsdam, H. van den Berg, & M. Couzijn (Eds.), *Studies in writing: Vol. 2. Effective teaching and learning of writing: Current trends in tesearch* (pp. 253-273). Amsterdam: Amsterdam University Press.

Couzijn, M., & Rijlaarsdam, G. (1996). Learning to write by reader observation and written feedback. In G. Rijlaarsdam, H. Van den Bergh, & M. Couzijn (Eds.), *Studies in writing: Vol. 2. Effective teaching and learning of writing: Current trends in research* (pp 224-253). Amsterdam: Amsterdam University Press.

Cowan J, (1998). *On becoming an innovative university teacher.* Open University Press.

Crahay, M. (1981). Contrôler et réguler une approche interactive. *Education et Recherche, 3*(2), 151-183.

Craik, F., & Lockhart, R. (1972). Levels of processing: A framework for memory research. *Journal of Verbal Learning and Verbal Behavior, 18,* 257-273.

Crawford, K., Gordon, S., Nicholas, J., & Prosser, M. (1998). Qualitatively different experiences of learning mathematics at university. *Learning and Instruction, 8*(5), 455-468.

Creemers, B. P. M. (1994). *The Effective Classroom.* London: Cassell.

Crowhurst, M. (1987, April). *The effect of reading instruction and writing instruction on reading and writing persuasion.* Paper presented at the Annual Meeting of the American Educational Research Association, Washington, D.C. (Ed 281148).

Crowley, S. (1985). Invention in nineteenth century rhetoric. *College Composition and Communication, 36*(*1*), 51-60.

Crystal, D. (2001). *Language and the internet.* Cambridge: Cambridge University Press.

Cuenca, M. J. (1995). Mecanismos lingüísticos y discursivos de la argumentación. *Comunicación, Lenguaje y Educación, 25,* 23-40.

Culioli, A. (1990). *Pour une linguistique de l'énonciation* [Towards a linguistic of uttering]. 2 vols. Paris: Ophrys.

Cullen J. L. (1985). Children's ability to cope with failure: Implication of a metacognitive approach for classroom. In D. L. Forrest-Presley, G E. Mac Kinnon, & T. G. Walker (Eds.), *Metacognition, cognition and Human performance* (vol. 2, pp. 267-300). INC, Orlando, FL: Academic Press.

Culler, J. (1982). *On deconstruction. Theory and criticism after structuralism.* Ithaca: Cornell University Press.

Cumming, A. (1989). Writing expertise and second language proficiency. *Language Learning, 39,* 81-135.

REFERENCES

Cummins, J. (1984). *Bilingualism and special education: Issues in assessment and pedagogy*. Clevedon: Multilingual Matters.

Cunningham, D. J., Duffy, T. M., & Knuth, R. A. (1993). The textbook of the future. In C. McKnight, A. Dillon, & J. Richardson (Eds.), *Hypertext: A psychological perspective* (pp. 19-49). New York: Ellis Horwood.

Curriculum Development Council (1983). *Syllabuses for secondary schools: English*. Hong Kong: Curriculum Development Council.

Curriculum Development Council (1999). *Syllabuses for secondary schools: English language*. Hong Kong: Curriculum Development Council.

Curriculum Development Council (2001). *Learning to learn*. Hong Kong: Curriculum Development Council.

Czerniewska, P. (1992). *Learning about writing*. Oxford: Blackwell

Dahl, R. *James and the giant peach*. New York: Puffin, 1961 [Spanish version 1996. *James y el melocotón gigante*. Madrid: Santillana.]

Daniel, M.-F. (1992/1997). *La philosophie et les enfants. Les modèles de Lipman et de Dewey* [The Philosophy and the children. Lipman's and Dewey's models]. Montréal: Ed. Logiques. Bruxelles: DeBoeck & Belin.

Daniel, M.-F., & Pallascio, R. (1997). Community of inquiry and community of philosophical inquiry: conceptual analysis and application to the children's classroom. *Inquiry The Journal of Critical Thinking, 17*(1), 51-67.

Dansereau, D. (1985). Learning strategy research. In J. Segal, S. Chipman, & R. Glaser (Eds.). *Thinking and learning skills: Vol. 1* (pp. 209-240). Hillsdale, NJ: Lawrence Erlbaum.

Darling-Hammond, L. (Ed.). *Review of Research in Education* (Volume 20). Washington, DC: AERA.

Darras, F. & Delcambre, I. (1989). Ce qu'ils font et ce qu'ils en disent: analyse des procédures rédactionnelles d'élèves de 2ème [What they do and what they say they do. Analysis of the composition processes of second-form pupils]. *Recherches, 11*, 13-52.

Dart, B. C., Boulton-Lewis, G. M., Brownlee, J. M., & McCrindle, A. R. (1998), Changes in knowledge of learning and teaching through journal writing. *Research Papers in Education, 13*(3), 291-318.

David, J. & Jaffré, J. P. (1997). Le rôle de l'autre dans les procédures métagraphiques [The role of the other in the metagraphic processes]. *Recherches, 26*, 155-168.

Day J. D., French L. A., & Hall L. K. (1985). Social influence on cognitive development. In D. L. Forrest-Presley, G. E. Mac Kinnon, & T. G. Walker (Eds.), *Metacognition, cognition and Human performance* (vol. 2, pp. 33-54). INC, Orlando, FL. Academic Press

De Corte, E. (1990). Acquiring and teaching cognitive skills; A state-of-the-art of theory and research. In P. J. Drenth, J. A. Sergeant, & R. J. Takens (Eds.), *European perspectives in psychology* (Vol. 1, pp. 237-263). London: John Wiley.

De Corte, E. (1996). Instructional psychology: Overview. In E. De Corte, & F. E. Weinert (Eds.), *International encyclopedia of developmental and instructional psychology* (pp. 33-43). Oxford, UK: Pergamon.

De Corte, E. (2000). Marrying theory building and the improvement of school practice: A permanent challenge for instructional psychology. *Learning and Instruction, 10*, 249-266.

De Gaulmyn, M. M. (1994). La rédaction conversationnelle: Parler pour écrire [The conversational composing: Speaking to write]. *Le français aujourd'hui, 108*, 73-81.

De Glopper, K. (1986). *Onderzoeksdossier project internationale vergelijking van het stelvaardigheidsonderwijs. Instrumenten en procedures uit het onderzoek naar de stelvaardigheid van leerlingen in het derde leerjaar LTO, MAVO, HAVO en VWO* [Research dossier. Project international comparison of education in written composition. Instruments and procedures used for the study of writing performance of 9th graders]. Amsterdam: SCO.

De Glopper, K. (1988). *Schrijven beschreven: inhoud, opbrengsten en achtergronden van het schrijfonderwijs in de eerste vier leerjaren van het voortgezet onderwijs* [Writing described: Subject matter, results and background of writing education in the first four grades of secondary education]. Den Haag: SVO.

De Glopper, K. (1988). The results of the international scoring sessions. In: T. P. Gorman, A. C. Purves, & R. E. Degenhart (Eds.), *The IEA study of written composition I: The international writing tasks and scoring scales*. Oxford: Pergamon Press.

De Jong, F. P. C. M, & B. H. A. M Van Hout-Wolters (1993). Knowledge construction, self-regulation and process-oriented instruction. In: B. Van Hout-Wolters, & F. De Jong (Eds.), *Process-oriented instruction and learning from text.*
De Jong, T., & Van Joolingen, W. (1998). Scientific discovery with computer simulations of conceptual domains. *Review of Educational Research, 2,* 179-201.
De Jonge, H., & Wielenga, G. (1973). *Statistische methoden voor psychologen en sociologen* [Statistical methods for psychologists and sociologists]. Groningen: Tjeenk Willink.
De Lemos, C. T. G. (1998). Sobre a aquisição da escrita: Algumas questões [On the acquisition of writing: Some questions]. In R. Rojo (Org.), *Alfabetização e letramento. Perspectivas lingüísticas* (pp. 13-31). Campinas, SP: Mercado de Letras.
De Man, P. (1971). *Blindness and insight. Essays in the rhetoric of contemporary criticism.* New York: Oxford University Press.
Dean, R. S., & Kulhavy, R. W. (1981). Influence of spatial organization on prose learning. *Journal of Educational Psychology, 73,* 57-64.
Dearing, R. (1994). *The National Curriculum and its Assessment: Final Report.* London: School Curriculum and Assessment Authority.
Deegan, D. H. (1995). Exploring individual differences among novices reading in a specific domain: The case of law. *Reading Research Quarterly, 30* (2), 154-170.
Deloney, L. A., Carey, M. J., & Geeman, H. G. (1998). Using electronic journal writing to foster reflection and provide feedback in an introduction to clinical medicine. *Academic Medicine, 73*(5), 574-75.
Denzin, N. K. (1989). *The research act* (3rd ed.). Englewood Cliff, NJ: Prentice Hall.
Department for Education and Employment (1998a). *The National Literacy Strategy: Framework for teaching.* London: Author.
Department for Education and Employment (1998b). *The National Literacy Strategy: Literacy training pack.* London: Author.
Department for Education and Employment (1999). *The National Curriculum: Handbook for primary teachers in England, Key Stages 1 and 2.* London: Author, & Qualifications and Curriculum Authority.
Department for Education and Employment (2000). *Grammar for Writing.* London: Author.
Department for Education and Employment (2001). *Developing Early Writing.* London Author.
Department of Education and Science (1975). *A Language for Life* (The Bullock Report). London: Her Majesty's Stationery Office.
Department of Education and Science (1978). *Primary Education in England.* London: Her Majesty's Stationery Office
Dewey, J. (1916). *Democracy and education: An introduction to the philosophy of education.* New York: The Macmillan Company.
Dewey, J. (1930). Human nature and conduct. New York: The Modern Biblioteca.
Dewey, John. (1933). *How we think.* Boston: D. C. Heath.
Di Pardo, A. (1990). Narrative knowers, expository knowledge. *Written Communication, 7,* 59-95.
Díez, C. (2002). *La interacción social y la construcción del conocimiento en el inicio lectoescritor. Un estudio longitudinal* [The social interaction and the knowledge construction in the early literacy: a longitudinal study]. Unpublished doctoral dissertation. Universidad Nacional de Educación a Distancia (O.U.). Madrid, Spain.
Díez, C., Pardo, P., Lara, F., Anula, J. J. & Gónzalez, L. (1999). *La interacción en el inicio de la lectoescritura* [The interaction at the beginning of literacy]. Madrid: Ministerio de Educación & Cultura.
Dillon, A. (1996). Myths, misconceptions, and an alternative perspective on information usage and the electronic medium. In J.-F. Rouet, J. J. Levonen, A. Dillon, & R. J. Spiro (Eds.), *Hypertext and Cognition* (pp. 25-42). Mahwah: Lawrence Erlbaum.
Dillon, A. (2002). Writing as design: Hypermedia and the shape of information space. In R. Bromme, & E. Stahl (Eds.), *Writing hypertext and learning. Conceptual and empirical approaches. Advances in learning and instruction series* (pp. 63-72). Amsterdam: Pergamon.
Dillon, A., & Gushrowski, B. (2000). Genres and the web – is the home page the first digital genre? *Journal of the American Society for Information Science, 51*(2), 202-205.
DiPardo, A., & Freedman, S. W. (1988). Peer response groups in the writing classroom: Theoretic foundations and new directions. *Review of Educational Research, 58,* 119-149.
Dixon, J. (1967). *Growth through English.* Oxford: Oxford University Press.

Doecke, B. (2002). The Little Company: Australian English teachers and the challenge of education reform. *English Teaching: Practice and Critique, 1.1*, 54-65, www.t.mc.waikato.ac.nz/english/ETPC.
Doecke, B., & McClenaghan, D. (1998). Reconceptualising Experience: Growth Pedagogy and Youth Culture. In W. Sawyer, K. Watson, & E. Gold (Eds.), *Reviewing English* (pp.46-56). Sydney: St Clair Press.
Doecke, B., & McKnight, L. (2003). Handling irony: Forming a professional identity as an English teacher. In B. Doecke, D. Homer, & H. Nixon (Eds.), *English teachers at work: Narratives, counter narratives and arguments* (pp.97-108). Adelaide: Wakefield Press.
Doecke, B., Homer, D., & Nixon, H. (Eds.). (2003). *English teachers at work: Narratives, counternarratives and arguments*. Kent Town: Wakefield Press.
Doise, W., Mugny, G., & Perret-Clermont, A. N. (1975). Social interaction and the development of cognitive operations. *European Journal of Social Psychology, 5*, 367-383.
Dolence, M., & Norris, D. M. (1999). *Transforming higher education: A vision for learning in the 21st century*. New York: Society for College and University Planning.
Doly A-M. (1996a). Motivation et métacognition [Motivation and metacognition]. *Cahiers Pédagogiques, «La motivation»*, 59-63.
Doly A-M. (1996b). Réussir pour motiver [Succeeding to motivate]. *Cahiers Pédagogiques, «La motivation»*, 70-74.
Doly A-M. (1999). Métacognition et médiation à l'école [Metacognition and Motivation at school]. In M. Grangeat (Ed.), *La métacognition, une aide au travail des élèves* (pp. 17-61). ESF, Paris.
Doly A-M. (2000). La métacognition pour apprendre à l'école [Metacognition for learning at school] *Cahiers Pédagogiques, 381*, 35-40.
Doly A-M.(1998). Métacognition et pédagogie: Enjeux et propositions pour l'introduction de la métacognition à l'école [Metacognition and pedagogy: Aims and propositions for introduction of metacognition at school]. Unplished doctoral dissertation, Lyon 2 University, France.
Dolz, J. (1995). Escribir textos argumentativos para mejorar su comprensión. *Comunicación, Lenguaje y Educación, 25*, 65-77.
Dolz, J. (Mars 2002). *L'écriture d'une explication en chimie à l'école primaire. Apprentissage de l'écriture et rapport au savoir* [Writing an explication in chemist at elementary school. The learning of writing and the access to the knowledge]. Colloque L'écriture et son apprentissage. Question pour la didactique, apports de la didactique, Paris, 21-23 Mars 2002.
Dolz, J., & Pasquier, A. (1994). Enseignement de l'Argumentation et Retour sur le Texte (1) [The teaching of Argumentation and the feedback to the writing text]. *Repères, 10*, 163-181.
Dornyei, Z., & Csizer, K. (1998). Ten commandments for motivating language learners: Results of an empirical study. *Language Teaching Research, 2*, 203-229.
Douglas, J. Y. (1994). Technology, pedagogy, and context: A tale of two classrooms. *Computers and Composition, 11*(3), 275-282.
Dourish, P. & Bellotti, V. (1992). Awareness and coordination in shared workspaces. *Conference proceedings on Computer-supported cooperative work* (pp. 107-114).
Downey, M. T. (1996). *Writing to learn history in the intermediate grades*. Final report. (Technical Report Project No. 2). The Center for the Study of Writing and Literacy, Berkeley, CA, & Pittsburgh, PA.
Dreyfus, H., & Dreyfus, S. (1986). *Mind over machine: The power of human intuition and expertise in the era of the computer*. New York: Free Press.
Driscoll, M. P. (1994). *Psychology of learning for instruction*. Boston: Allyn, & Bacon.
Duncker, K. (1935). *Zur Psychologie des produktiven Denkens* [Concerning Psychology of Productive Thinking]. (Reprinted in 1963). Berlin: Springer.
Durgunoglu, A. Y., & Verhoeven, L. (1998). *Literacy Development in a Multilingual Context: crosscultural perspectives*. Mahwah, NJ: Lawrence Erlbaum.
Dysthe, O. (1996). The multivoiced classroom. *Written Communication, 13*(3), 385-425.
Eco, U. (1979). The role of the reader's place in American thought. *Semiotica, 1*(2), 21-37.
Ehri, L. (1990). Movement into words reading and spelling. How spelling contributes to reading. In J. M. Mason (Ed.), *Reading and writing connections*. Boston: Allyn, & Bacon.
Ehri, L. (1997). Learning to read and learning to spell are one and the same, almost. In C. A. Perfetti, L. Rieben, & M. Fayol (Eds.), *Learning to spell* (pp. 237-269). Mahwah, NJ: Lawrence Erlbaum.
Elbow, P. (1973). *Writing without teachers*. London: Oxford University Press.

Elbow, P. (1981). *Writing with power: Techniques for mastering the writing process.* New York: Oxford University Press.
Elshout, J. J., & M. V. J. Veenman (1992). Relation between intellectual ability and working method as predictors of learning. *Journal of Educational Research, 85,* 134-143.
Emig, J. (1971). *The composing processes of twelfth graders* (Research Report No. 3). Urbana, IL: National Council of Teachers in English.
Englert, C. S., & Raphael, T. E. (1988). Constructing well-formed prose: Process, structure and metacognitive knowledge. *Exceptional Children, 54,* 513-520.
Ennis, R. H. (1996). Critical thinking dispositions: Their nature and assessability. *Informal Logic, 18*(2&3), 129-147.
Entwistle, N. (1998). Improving teaching through research on student learning. in J. J. F. Forest (Ed.), *University teaching: International perspectives* (pp. 458). New York: Garland Publishing Inc.
Epstein-Jannai, M. (1996). The reader who imagine his role. *Helkat Lashon, 23,* 244-258. (Hebrew)
Epstein-Jannai, M. (1999). The reader, the detective and the reading frame. *Machshavot Ktuvot, 16,* 14-27. (Hebrew).
Epstein-Jannai, M. (2000). Some remarks about the reader and the reader process in Borges' short story "The theme of the traitor and the hero". *Alei Siah, 43,* 149-160. (Hebrew).
Epstein-Jannai, M. (2001). Writing as a testimony for reading: An approach to the concept of genre as a frame for meaning construction. *Script, 2,* 103-132. (Hebrew).
Erixon, P.-O. (2003). *Drömmen om den rena kommunikationen. Om lyriksskrivning i gymnasieskolan* [The Dream of the undisguised communication. About poem writing at upper secondary school]. Lund: Studentlitteratur.
Espéret, E. (1984). Processus de production: Genèse et rôle du schéma narratif dans la conduite de récit. In M. Moscato, & G. P.-L. Bonniec (Eds.), *Le langage, construction et actualisation* (pp. 179-197). Rouen: Université de Rouen.
Espéret, E. (1989). De l'acquisition du langage à la construction des conduites langagières (From language acquisition to construction of language behaviours). In G. Netchine-Grynberg, *Développement et fonctionnement cognitifs chez l'enfant* (pp. 121-135). Paris: Presses Universitaires de France.
Espéret, E. (1989). Training in narrative structure: Effects on children's story writing at different structural levels. In P. Boscolo (Ed.), *Writing: Trends in European research* (pp. 33-41). Padova: UPSEL Editore.
Esperet, E. (1999). Commentary. Teaching and learning to write: Cognitive and social processes at work. *Learning and Instruction, 9,* 229-233.
Fabre, C. (1987). La réécriture dans l'écriture. Le cas des ajouts dans les écrits scolaires [Rewriting while writing. The case of added elements in pupils' texts]. *Études de Linguistique Appliqueé, 68,* 15-39.
Fabre, C. (1990). *Les brouillons d'écoliers ou l'entrée dans l'écriture* [Pupils' drafts or entering the written world]. Grenoble: Creditel/L'Atelier du texte.
Faccione, P. (2000). Reasoned judgment and revelation: The relation of critical thinking and Bible study. *Critical thinking and the study of Bible in the age of new media.* A consultation sponsored by the American Bible Society, Research Center for Scripture and Media, NY, NY.
Faigley, L., & Witte, S. (1981). Analysing revision. *College Composition and Communication, 32,* 400-414.
Faigley, L., Cherry, R. D., Joliffe, D. A., & Skinner, A. M.(1989). *Assessing Writer's Knowledge and Processes of Composing.* Norwood, NJ: Ablex.
Fairclough, N. (1992). *Discourse and social change.* Cambridge, England: Polity Press.
Fayol M. (1985). *Le récit et sa construction, une approche de psychologie cognitive* [The narration and its building up. An approach of cognitive psychology]. Neuchatel, & Paris: Delachaux & Niestlé.
Fayol M., & Monteil J-M. (1994). Stratégies d'apprentissage/apprentissage de stratégies [Strategies of learning/learning of strategies]. *Revue Française de Pédagogie, 106,* 91-110.
Fayol, M. (1983). L'acquisition du récit: Un bilan des recherches. *Revue française de pédagogie,* No 62, 65-82.
Fayol, M. (1997). *Des idées au texte: Psychologie cognitive de la production verbale, orale et écrite.* Paris: PUF.
Fayol, M., & Schneuwly, B. (1987). La mise en texte et ses problèmes. In J.-L. Chiss, J.-P. Laurent, J.-C. Meyer, H. Romian, & B. Schneuwly (Eds.), *Apprendre/enseigner à produire des textes écrits* (pp. 223-240). Bruxelles: De Boeck.

Feilke, H. (1993). Schreibentwicklungsforschung: Ein kurzer Überblick unter besonderer Berücksichtigung prozessorientierter Schreibfähigkeiten. [Research on the development of writing. A review stressing process-oriented writing skills]. *Diskussion Deutsch, 24*(129), 17-34.

Feilke, H. (1996). From syntactical to textual strategies of argumentation. Syntactical development in writen argumentation texts by students aged 10 to 22. *Argumentation, 10*(2), 197-212.

Fellows, N. J. (1994). A window into thinking: Using student writing to understand conceptual change in science learning. *Journal of Research in Science Teaching, 31*, 985-1002.

Fenoglio, I., & Boucheron-Pétillon (Eds. 2003 *sous presse*). Processus d'écriture et traces linguistiques [Writing processes and linguistics marks]. *Langages, 149*.

Ferreiro, E. (1988). L'écriture avant la lettre [Writing before the Knowledge of Letters]. In H. Sinclair (Ed.), *La production de notations chez le jeune enfant* (pp. 17-70). Paris: PUF.

Ferreiro, E. (1991). Desarrollo de la alfabetización. Psicogénesis [Development of literacy]. In Y. M. Goodman (Ed.), *Los niños construyen su lectoescritura*. Aique, Argentina.

Ferreiro, E., & Teberosky, A. (1979). *Los sistemas de escritura en el desarrollo del niño* [The systems of writing in the children development]. Siglo XXI, México.

Ferreiro, E., & Zucchermaglio, C. (1996). Children's use of punctuation marks: The case of reported speech. In C. Pontecorvo, M. Orsolini, B. Burge, & L. B. Resnick (Eds.), *Children's early text construction*. Mahwah, NJ: Lawrence Erlbaum.

Ferreiro, E., (1999). Oral and written words. Are they the same units? In T. Nunes (Ed.), *Learning to read: An integrated view from research and practice*. Dordrecht, The Netherlands: Kluwer Academic Publishers.

Ferris, D., & Hedgcock, J. S. (1998). *Teaching ESL composition: Purpose, process and practice*. Mahwah, NJ: Lawrence Erlbaum.

Ferris, D., & Roberts, B. (2001). Error feedback in L2 writing classes: How explicit does it need to be? *Journal of Second Language Writing, 10*(3), 161-184.

Fitz-Gibbon, C. T. (1998). OFSTED: Time to Go? *Managing Schools Today, 7*(6), 22-25.

Fitz-Gibbon, C. T., & Stephenson-Forster, N. J. (1999). Is OFSTED helpful? An evaluation using social science criteria. In C. T. Cullingford (Ed*.), An inspector calls: Ofsted and its effect on school standards* (pp. 97-118). London: Kogan Page.

Flack, V. F., Afifi, A. A., Lachenbruch, P. A., & Schouten, A. J. A. (1988). Sample size determinations for the two rater kappa statistic. *Psychometrika, 53*(3), 321-325.

Flanders, N. A. (1970). *Analysing teaching behaviour*. Addison-Wesley, Reading, Massachusetts

Flavell J. H. (1985). Developpement métacognitif [Metacognitive development]. In Bideaud J. & Richelle M. (Eds.), *Psychologie développementale, problèmes et réalités* [Developmental psychology, problems and realities] (pp.30-41). Liège: Mardaga.

Flavell, J. H. (1976). Metacognitive aspects of problem solving. In L. B. Resnick (Ed.), *The nature of intelligence* (pp. 231-235). Hillsdale, NJ: Lawrence Erlbaum.

Flavell, J. H. (1977/1985). *Cognitive development* (2nd ed.). Englewood Cliffs, NJ: Prentice-Hall.

Flavell, J., Miller, P., & Miller, S. (1993). *Cognitive development*. Englewood Cliffs, NJ: Prentice-Hall.

Florio, S. & Clark, C. M. (1982). The functions of writing in an elementary classroom. *Research in the Teaching of English, 16*(2), 115-130.

Flower, L. (1979). Writer-based prose. A cognitive basis for problems in writing. *College of English, 41*, 19-37.

Flower, L. (1987). *The role of task representation in reading-to-write* (Reading-to-Write Report No. 2). The Center for the Study of Writing, Pittsburgh, PA, & Berkeley, CA.

Flower, L. (1989). Cognition, context and theory building. *College Composition and Communication, 40*, 282-311.

Flower, L. (1989). *Negotiating academic discourse*. (Reading-to-Write Report No. 29). The Center for the Study of Writing, Pittsburgh, PA, & Berkeley, CA.

Flower, L. (1994). *The construction of negotiated meaning: A social cognitive theory of writing*. Detroit: Wayne State University Press.

Flower, L. S, & Hayes, J. R. (1980). The dynamics of composing: Making plans and juggling constraints. In C. H. Frederiksen, & J. P. Dominic (Eds.), *Writing: The nature, development and teaching of written communication* (pp. 39-58). Hillsdale, NJ: Lawrence Erlbaum.

Flower, L. S., Hayes, J. R., Carey, L., Schriver, K., & Stratman, J. (1986). Detection, diagnosis and the strategies of revision. *College Composition and Communication, 37*(1), 16-55.

Flower, L., & Hayes, J. R. (1981). A cognitive process theory of writing. *College Composition and Communication, 32*, 365-387.

Flower, L., Stein, V., Ackerman, J., Kantz, M., McCormick, K., & Peck, W. (1990). *Reading-to-write: Exploring a cognitive and social process.* New York: Oxford University Press.

Foltz, P. W. (1996). Comprehension, coherence, and strategies in hypertext and linear text. In J.-F. Rouet, J. J. Levonen, A. Dillon, & R. J. Spiro (Eds.), *Hypertext and Cognition* (pp. 109-136). Mahwah, NJ: Lawrence Erlbaum.

Fosnot, C. T. (1996). *Constructivism: Theory, perspectives, and practice.* New York: Teachers College Press.

Foucault, M. (1969). *L'archeologie du savoir* [Archeology of knowledge]. Paris: Gallimard.

Foucault, M. (1981). *Power/Knowledge: Selected interviews and other writings.* Random House, Inc.

Francis-Pelton, L., Farragher, P., & Riecken, T. (2000). Content based technology: Learning by modeling. *Journal of Technology and Teacher Education, 8*(3), 177-86.

François, F. (1981). *Syntaxe et mise en mots, analyse différentielle des comportements linguistiques des enfants.* Paris: Ed. du CNRS.

François, F., Hudelot, C., & Sabeau-Jouannet E. (1984). *Conduites linguistiques chez le jeune enfant (Linguistics behaviours of young children).* Paris: Presses Universitaires de France.

Fraser, J. (2001). A comparison of the writing in English of British deaf students and non-native hearing students. Unpublished Master thesis. King's College, London, UK.

Freedman, A. (1996, October). ReActivating Genre: ReGENERating discourse theory, research and pedagogy. European writing conferences. Barcelona: October 1996.

Freedman, S. W. & Sperling, M. (1985). Teacher-student interacion in the writing conference: Response and Teaching. In S. W. Freedman (Ed.), *The Acquisition of written language: Response and revision.* Norwood, NJ: Ablex.

Freedman, S. W. (1987). *Peer response in two ninth-grade classrooms.* Berkeley, CA: Center for the Study of writing.

Freedman, S. W. (1987). The acquisition of written composition: Response and revision. Norwood, NJ: Ablex.

Freedman, S. W., Flower, L., Hull, G., & Hayes, J. R. (1995). *Ten years of research: Achievements of the National Center for the Study of Writing and Literacy.* Technical Report 1-C. Berkeley, Ca, & Carnegie Mellon, Pa: NCSWL.

Freeley, A. J. (1981). *Argumentation and debate. Reasoned decision making* (5th ed.). Belmont, CA: Wadsworth.

Freeman, J. B. (1992). *Dialectics and the macrostructure of arguments. A theory of argument structure.* Berlin/New York: Foris/De Gruyter.

Freire, P., & Shor, I. (1987). *A pedagogy for Liberation.* USA: Bergin and Garvey.

Freud, A. (1942). *The ego and the mechanisms of defence.* London: The Hogarth Press.

Frijda, N. H., & Elshout, J. J. (1976). Probleemoplossen en denken [Problem solving and thinking]. In J. A. Michon, E. G. J. Eyckman, & L. F. W. de Klerk (Eds.), *Handboek der psychonomie* (pp. 413-446). Deventer: Van Loghum Slaterus.

Frith, U. (1985). Beneath the surface of developmental dyslexia. In K. E. Patterson, J. C. Marshall, & M. Coltheart (Eds.), *Surface dyslexia neuropsychological and cognitive studies or phonological reading* (pp. 301-330). Hillsdale, NJ: Lawrence Erlbaum.

Frow, J. (1995). *Cultural Studies and Cultural Value.* Oxford: Clarendon Press.

Fulwiler, T. (1986). Journals across the disciplines. In T. Newkirk (Ed.), *To compose: Teaching writing in the high school* (pp. 186-197). Portsmouth, NH: Heinemann.

Fulwiler, T. (1989). Responding to student journals. In C. M. Anson (Ed.), *Writing and response: Theory, practice, and research* (pp. 149-173). Urbana, IL: National Council of Teachers of English.

Fulwiler, T., & Young, A. (1990). (Eds.), *Programs and methods for writing across the curriculum.* Upper Montclair, NJ: Boynton/Cook.

Galbraith, D. (1992). Conditions for discovery through writing. *Instructional Science, 21,* 45-72.

Galbraith, D. (1996). Self-monitoring, discovery through writing and individual differences in drafting strategy. In G. Rijlaarsdam, H. Van den Bergh, & M. Couzijn. (Eds.), *Studies in writing: Vol. 1. Theories, models and methodology in writing research* (pp. 121-144). Amsterdam: Amsterdam University Press.

Galbraith, D. (1999a). Conceptual processes in writing: From problem solving to text production. In G. Rijlaarsdam & E. Espéret (Series Eds.) & M. Torrance & D. Galbraith (Vol. Eds.), *Studies in writing:*

Vol.4. Knowing what to write: Conceptual processes in text production (pp.1-13). Amsterdam: Amsterdam University Press: Amsterdam.

Galbraith, D. (1999b). Writing as a knowledge-constituting process. In M. Torrance, & D. Galbraith (Eds.), *Studies in writing: Vol. 4. Knowing what to write: Conceptual processes in text production* (pp. 139-160). Amsterdam: Amsterdam University Press.

Galbraith, D., & Rijlaarsdam, G. (1999). Effective strategies for the teaching and learning of writing. *Learning and Instruction, 9*, 93-108.

Galbraith, D., & Torrance, M. (1999). Conceptual processes in writing: from problem solving to text production. In: G. Rijlaarsdam, & E. Esperet (Series Eds.), & M. Torrance, & D. Galbraith (vol. Eds.), *Studies in Writing. Vol 4. Knowing what to write: conceptual processes in text production* (pp. 1-12). Amsterdam: Amsterdam University Press.

Gall, J. E., & Hannafin, M., J. (1994). A framework for the study of hypertext. *Instructional Science, 22*, 207-232.

Gárate, M., & Melero, M. A. (2000, September). Paper presented at the EARLI SIG Writing conference 2000. Verona, September 7-9, 2000.

Garcia-Debanc C. (1986). Intérêt des modèles du processus rédactionnel pour une pédagogie de l'écriture [Advantage of models for redactionnels procedures for writing training]. *Pratiques, 49*, 23-65.

Garcia-Debanc, C. & Roger, Ch. (1986). Apprendre à rédiger des textes explicatifs [Learning to compose explanatory texts]. *Pratiques, 51*, 55-76.

Gardner, H. (1991). *The Unschooled mind: How children think and how schools should teach.* New York: Basic Books.

Garner, R. (1981). Monitoring of passage inconsistency among poor comprehenders: a preliminary test of the piecemeal processing explanation. *Journal of Educational Psychology, 74*, 159-162.

Garner, R. (1987). *Metacognition and reading comprehension.* Norwood, NJ: Ablex.

Gaskins, I. W., Guthrie, J. T., Satlow, E., Ostertag, L. S., Byrne, J., & Connor, B. (1994). Integrating instruction of science, reading, and writing: goals, teacher development, and assessment. *Journal of Research in Science Teaching, 31*, 1039-1056. (Special issue: The reading-science learning-writing connection)

Gass, S., & Mackey, A. (2002). *Stimulated recall methodology in second language research.* Mahwah, NJ: Lawrence Erlbaum.

Gavelek J. R., & Raphael, E. (1985). Metacognition and the role of questioning activities. In D. L. Forrest-Presley, G. E. Mac Kinnon, & T. G. Walker (Eds.), *Metacognition, cognition and Human performance* (Vol. 2, pp. 103-136). INC, Orlando, FL. Academic Press.

Gee, J. P. (1990). *Social Linguistics and Literacies: Ideologies In Discourses* London: Falmer Press

Gee, J. P. (1991). What is Literacy? In C. Mitchell, & K. Weiler (Eds.), *Re-writing literacy: Culture and the discourse of the other* (pp. 3-11). New York: Bergin and Garvey.

Gee, J. P. (1996). Discourse analysis: Status, solidarity and social identity. In: *Social linguistics and literacies: Ideology in discourses* (pp. 90-121). PA: Taylor, & Francis.

Gee, J. P. (1999). *An introduction to discourse analysis theory and method.* London: Routledge.

Geist, U. (1989). Givne former, faste mønstre [Given forms, well known patterns]. In Gunnarsson, B.-L., Liberg, C., & Wahlén, S. (Eds.), *Skrivande, Rapport från ASLA:s nordiska symposium.* Uppsala: ASLA.

Genette, G. (1972). *Figures III.* Paris: Seuil.

Gerdes, H. (1997). *Lernen mit Text und Hypertext* [Learning with text and hypertext]. Berlin, Germany: Pabst.

Gere, A. R. & Stevens, R. (1985). The language of writing groups: How oral response shapes revision. In S. W. Freedman (Ed.), *The acquisition of written language: Response and revision* (pp. 85-105). Norwood, NJ: Ablex.

Gérouit, C., Roussey, J.-Y., & Piolat, A. (july 2002). *Effects of notetaking on writing argumentation by 10-12 year-old children.* Paper presented at the EARLI SIG-Writing 02 Conference, Stafford University, 10-13 July, 2002.

Gibbons, P. (1991). *Learning to learn in a second language.* New South Wales: PETA.

Gibbs, G. (1998). *Learning by doing. A guide to teaching & learning methods.* Further Education Unit, Oxford Brookes University.

Gilly, M. (1988). Interaction entre pairs et constructions cognitives: Modèles explicatifs. In A.-N. Perret-Clermont, & M. Nicolet (Eds.), *Interagir et connaître: Enjeux et régulations sociales dans le développement cognitif* (pp. 19-28). Fribourg: Delval.

Gilster, P. (1997). *Digital literacy*. New York: Wiley.
Girolami, A. (2001). *Contrôle des optitudes à la lecture et à l'ecriture. CALE* [Assessing reading and writing skills]. Montreuil: Editions du Papyrus.
Girolami-Boulinier, A. (1984). *Les niveaux actuels dans la pratique du langage oral et écrit* [Current levels in the practice of oral and written language]. Paris: Masson.
Girolami-Boulinier, A. (1987). Language: pour une pédagogie de l'immédiateté [Language: For an immediate pedagogy]. *Bulletin de la Société Alfred Binet et Théodore Simon, 610* (I), 30-47.
Girolami-Boulinier, A. (1988). *Les premiers pas scolaires. Acquisitions indispensables pour prévenir l'échec scolaire* [First steps in schooling. Crucial acquisitions to prevent academic failure]. Issy-les-Moulineaux: EAP.
Girolami-Boulinier, A. (1989). *La grammaire langage en 20 leçons* [The grammar language in 20 lessons]. Issy-les-Moulineaux: EAP
Girolami-Boulinier, A. (1993). *L'apprentissage de l'oral et de l'écrit* [Education in speaking and writing skills]. (Collection "Que sais-je?", nr. 2717). Paris: PUF.
Girolami-Boulinier, A. (2000). Mise en place de la grammaire française [The use of French grammar]. In A. Girolami-Boulinier et al. (Eds.), *Le français au troisième millénaire. Comment faire vivre la langue?* (pp. 71-83). Montreuil: Editions du Papyrus
Girolami-Boulinier, A., & Cohen-Rak, N. (1985). S.O.S au C.E.S. [S.O.S. in the C.E.S.]. *Bulletin de la Société Alfred Binet et Théodore Simon, 604* (III), 6-14.
Girolami-Boulinier, A., & Pinto, M. da G. (1996). English, French and Portuguese spelling in the 4th school year. In S. Contento (Ed.), *Psycholinguistics as a multidisciplinarily connected science. Proceedings of the 4th ISAPL International Congress (June 23-27, 1994)* (vol. II, pp. 35-40). Cesena: Società Editrice Il Ponte Vecchio.
Glanz, J. (1998). *Action research: An educational leader's guide to school improvement*. Norwood, MA: Christopher-Gordon.
Glynn, S. M., & Muth, D. (1994). Reading and writing to learn science: Achieving scientific literacy. *Journal of Research in Science Teaching, 31*, 1057-1073. (Special issue: The reading-science learning-writing connection).
Golder, C. (1996). *Le développement des discours argumentatifs* [The development of argumentative discourses]. Lausanne, Paris: Delachaux, & Niestlé.
Goleman, D. (1996). *Emotional intelligence, why it can matter*. London: Bloomsbury.
Gombert J. E. (1991). Le rôle des capacités métalinguistiques dans l'acquisition de la langue écrite *(The rôle of metalinguistic capacities in written language acquisition)*. *Pratiques, 3*, 114-126.
Gombert, J. E. (1998). L'étayage de deux points de vue contraries. Etude chez de jeunes rédacteurs de 10 à 13 ans. In R. Vion (Ed.), *Les sujets et leurs discours. Enonciation et interaction* (pp. 23-45). Aix-en Provence: Presses de l'Université de Provence.
Gombert, J.-E., Bryant, P., & Warrick, N. (1997). Children's use of analogy in learning to read and to spell. In C. A. Perfetti, L. Rieben, & M. Fayol (Eds.), *Learning to spell* (pp. 221-235). Mahwah, NJ: Lawrence Erlbaum.
Goodman, Y. (1991). Las raíces de la alfabetización [Roots of literacy. *En Más allá de la alfabetización, Infancia y Aprendizaje, número extraordinario (pp. 29-42)*.
Goodwin, Ch. (1979). The interactive construction of a sentence in natural conversation. In G. Psathas (Ed.), *Everyday language: Studies in ethnomethodology* (pp. 97-121). New York: Irvington Publishers.
Goody J. (1979). *La raison graphique:* Minuit, Paris.
Gordon, C. J., & Braun, C. (1985). Metacognitive processes: Reading and writing narrative discourse. In B. L. Forrest-Pressley, G. E. Mackinnon, & T. G. Walter (Eds.), *Metacognition, cognition and human Performance* (pp. 1-75). New-York: Academic Press.
Gorman, T. P., Purves, A. C., & Degenhart, R. E. (1988). *The IEA study of written composition. Writing tasks and scoring scales*. Oxford: Pergamon Press-IEA.
Grabe, W., & Kaplan, R. B. (1996). *Theory and practice of writing*. London and New York: Addison Wesley Longman.
Graff, H. J. (1991). *The legacies of literacy: Continuities and contradictions in western culture and society*. Bloomington: Indiana University Press.
Graham, S., & Harris, K. R. (2000). The role of self-regulation and transcription skills in writing and writing development. *Educational Psychologist, 35*(1), 3-12.

Graham, S., Berninger, V. W., Abbott, R. D., Abbott, S. P., & Whitaker, D. (1997). The role of mechanics in composing of elementary school students: A new methodological approach. *Journal of Educational Psychology, 89*, 170-182.

Grainger, T. (1997). *Traditional storytelling in the primary classroom.* Leamington Spa: Scholastic.

Graves, D. (1984). A researcher learns to write: Selected articles and monographs. Portsmouth, NH: Heinemann.

Graves, D. H. (1983). *Writing: Teachers and children at work.* Portsmouth, NH: Heinemann.

Gray, S. H. (1990). Using protocol analyses and drawings to study mental model construction. *International Journal of Human Computer Interaction, 2*(4), 359-378.

Gray, S. H. (1995). Linear coherence and relevance: Logic in computer-human 'conversations'. *Journal of Pragmatics, 23*, 627-647.

Green, B., & Bigum, C. (1993). Aliens in the classroom. *Australian Journal of Education, 37*(1), 119-141.

Greene, S. (1993). The role of task in the development of academic thinking through reading and writing in a college history course. *Research in the Teaching of English, 27*(1), 46-75.

Greene, S., & Ackerman, J. M. (1995). Expanding the constructivist metaphor: A rhetorical perspective on literacy research and practice. *Review of Educational Research, 65*(4), 383-420.

Greene, S., & Higgins, L. (1994). Once upon a time: The use of retrospective accounts in building theory in composition. In P. Smagorinsky (Ed.), *Speaking about writing: Reflections on research methodology* (pp. 115-140). Sage Series In Written Communication, Vol. 8. Thousand Oaks, CA: Sage.

Gregory, S. (1996). Bilingualism and the education of deaf children. Paper presented at the Bilingualism and the education of Deaf children: Advances in Practice. University of Leeds, UK.

Grésillon, A. (1994). *Eléments de critique génétique. Lire les manuscrits modernes* [Elements of genesis criticism. Reading modern manuscripts]. Paris: Presses Universitaires de France.

Grize, J. B. (1990). *Logique et langage* [Logic and language]. Paris: Ophrys.

Gruber, S. (1995). Re: Ways we contribute: Students, instructors, and pedagogies in the computer-mediated writing classroom. *Computers and Composition, 12*(1), 61-78.

Grugeon, E., Hubbard, L., Smith, C., & Dawes, L. (1998). *Teaching listening and speaking in the primary school.* London: David Fulton Publishers.

Gubern, M. M. (1999). Commentary: Strategies for effective research on the teaching and learning of writing. *Learning and Instruction, 9*, 223-228.

Gülich, E. (1986). L'organisation conversationelle des énoncés inachevés et de leur achèvement [The conversational arrangement of unfinished utterances and their completion]. *DRLAV*, 34-35, 161-182.

Gülich, E. (1993). *Procédés de formulation et travail conversationnel: éléments d'une théorie des processus de la production discursive* [Formulation procedures and conversational work: elements to a theory of discursive production]. XXe. Congrès International de Linguistique et Philologie Romanes. Tome II. Section II. Analyse de la conversation. Université de Zürich, 1992. Tübingen: Francke Verlag.

Gunstone, R., & Northfield, J. (1992, April). *Conceptual change in teacher education: The centrality of metacognition.* Paper presented at the Annual Meeting of the American Educational Research Association (San Francisco, CA, April 20-24).

Guthrie, J. T., & Wigfield, A. (1997). *Reading engagement: Motivating readers through integrated instruction.* Newark, DL: IRA.

Gyselinck, V., & Tardieu, H. (1994). Illustrations, mental models and comprehension of instructional text. In W. Schnotz, & W. Kulhavy (Eds.), *Comprehension of Graphics* (pp.139-152). Amsterdam: North-Holland.

Haas, C. (1989). Does the medium make a difference? Two studies of word processing on planning. *Research in the Teaching of English, 23*(2), 181-207.

Haas, C. (1996). *Writing technology: studies on the materiality of literacy.* Hillsdale, NJ: Lawrence Erlbaum.

Habermas, J. (1996). *Kommunikativt handlande. Texter om språk, rationalitet och samhälle* [Communicative acting. Texts and language, rationality and society]. Göteborg: Daidalos.

Habermas, J. (1998). *Borgerlig offentlighet. Kategorierna "privat" och "offentligt" i det moderna samhället* [The Bourgeois public sphere. The categories "private" and "public" in modern society]. Lund: Arkiv moderna klassiker.

Hadot, P. (1997). *Philosophy as a way of life.* Oxford: Blackwell.

Hakuta, K. (1986). *Mirror of language: The debate on bilingualism.* New York: Basic Books.

Hall, N. (1989). *Writing with Reason*. London: Hodder, & Stoughton.
Halliday, M. A. K. (1978). *Language as social semiotic*. London: Edward Arnold.
Halliday, M. A. K. (1990). *Spoken and written language*. Cambridge, England: Cambridge University Press.
Halliday, M. A. K., & Hasan R. (1989). *Language, context and text: Aspects of language in a social-semiotic perspective* (Part A, pp. 3-49). Victoria, Australia: Deakin University Press.
Halliday, M. A. K., & Martin, J. R. (1993). *Writing science: Literacy and discursive power*. Pittsburgh, PA: University of Pittsburgh Press.
Halté, J.-F. (1989). Discours explicatif: état et perspectives de la recherche [Explanatory discourse: state of the art and research perspectives]. *Repères, 77*, 95-109.
Hammond, N. (1993). Learning with hypertext: Problems, principles and prospects. In C. McKnight, A. Dillon, & J. Richardson (Eds.), *Hypertext: A psychological perspective* (pp. 51-69). New York: Ellis Horwood.
Hand, B., Prain, V., & Wallace, C. (2002). Influences of writing tasks on students' answers to recall and higher-level test questions. *Research in Science Education, 32*, 19–34.
Hand, B., Prain, V., & Yore, L. (2001). Sequential writing tasks' influence on science learning. In G. Rijlaarsdam (Series Ed.) & P. Tynjälä, L. Mason, & K. Lonka (Vol. Eds.), *Studies in writing: Vol. 7. Writing as a Learning Tool: Integrating Theory and Practice* (pp. 105-129). Dordrecht: Kluwer Academic Publishers.
Hand, B., Prain, V., Lawrence, C., & Yore, L. D. (1999). A writing in science framework designed to enhance science literacy. *International Journal of Science Education, 21*, 1021-1035.
Harpin, W (1976). *The second 'R': Writing development in the junior school*. London: Allen, & Unwin.
Harris, L. D., & Wambean, C. A. (1996). The Internet-based composition classroom: A study in pedagogy. *Computers and Composition, 13*(3), 353-371.
Hatch, G. (1992). Reviving the rodential model for composition: Robert Zoellner's alternative to Flower and Hayes. *Rhetoric Review, 10*(2), 244-248.
Hativa, N. (2000). Teacher thinking, beliefs, and knowledge in higher education: An introduction. *Instructional Science, 28*(5&6), 331-34.
Hativa, N., Barak, R., & Simhi, E. (1999, April). *Expert university teachers: Thinking, knowledge and practice regarding effective teaching behaviors*. Annual meeting of the American Educational Research Association (Montreal, Quebec, April 19-23, 1999).
Hayes, J. R. (1996). A new framework for understanding cognition and affect in writing. In C. M. Levy, & S. Ransdell (Eds.), *The science of writing: Theories, methods, individual differences and applications* (pp. 1-27). Mahwah, NJ: Lawrence Erbaum Associates.
Hayes, J. R., & Flower, L. (1980). Identifying the organization of writing processes. In L. W. Gregg, & E. R. Steinberg (Eds.), *Cognitive processes in writing: An interdisciplinary approach* (pp. 3–30). Hillsdale, NJ: Lawrence Erlbaum.
Hayes, J. R., & Flower, L. S. (1980b). Writing as problem solving. *Visible Language, 14* (4), 388-399.
Hayes, J. R., & L. S. Flower (1980b). Writing research and the writer. *American Psychologist, 41*, 1106-1113.
Hayes, J. R., Flower, L. S, Schriver, K. A., Stratman, J. F., & Carey, L. (1987). Cognitive processes in revision. In S. H. Rosenberg (Ed.), *Advances in applied psycholiguistics: Vol. 2. Reading, writing and language learning* (pp. 176-240). Cambridge: Cambridge University Press.
Head, A. (1999). *Design wise: A guide for evaluating the interface design of information resources*. Medford, N.J.: Information Today, Inc.
Healy, M. (1982). Using student writing response groups in the classroom. In Camp, G. (Ed.), *Teaching Writing: Essays from the Bay Area Writing Project*. Portsmouth, New Hampshire: Boynton/Cook Publishers.
Heath, S. B. (1983). *Ways with words: Language, life and work in communities and classrooms*. Cambridge, England: CUP.
Hegarty, M. Carpenter, & P. Just, M. (1991). Diagrams in the comprehension of scientific texts. In R. Barr, M. Kamil, P. Mosenthal, & P. Pearson (Eds). *Handbook of reading research* (pp. 641-668). Mahwah, NJ: Lawrence Erlbaum.
Heisenberg, W. (1958). *Physics and philosophy: The revolution in modern science*. New York: Harper, & Row.
Her Majesty's Inspectorate (1991). *English Key Stage 1: A Report by HM Inspectorate on the first year, 1989-90*. London: Her Majesty's Stationery Office.

Her Majesty's Inspectorate (1992*). English Key Stages 1, 2 and 3: A report by HM Inspectorate on the second year 1990-91*. London: Her Majesty's Stationery Office.
Her Majesty's Inspectorate (1999). *The National Literacy Strategy: An evaluation of the first year*. London: Office for Standards in Education.
Her Majesty's Inspectorate (2000). *The Teaching of Writing in Primary Schools: Could do better*. London: Office for Standards in Education.
Her Majesty's Inspectorate (2002). *The National Literacy Strategy: The first four years 1998-2002*. London: Office for Standards in Education.
Herman, R., Holmes, S., & Woll, B. (1999). *Assessing British Sign Language development: Receptive skills test*. Coleford, England: Forest Bookshop.
Higgins, L., Flower, L., & Petraglia, J. (1992). Planning text together: The role of critical reflection in student collaboration. *Written Communication, 9*, 48-84.
Hildebrand, G. M. (1996, April). *Writing in/forms science learning*. Paper presented at the NARST Annual Meeting, St. Louis, April. ERIC: ED 393 694
Hildebrand, G. M. (1998). Disrupting hegemonic writing practices in school science. *Journal of Research in Science Teaching, 35*, (4), 345-362.
Hill, C. A. (1994, March). *Writing-to-learn as a rationale for writing across the curriculum*. Paper presented at the Annual Meeting of the 45th Conference on College Composition and Communication (Nashville, TN, USA, March 16-19).
Hillocks, G. (1984). What works in teaching composition: A meta-analysis of experimental treatment studies. *American Journal of Education, 93*, 133-170.
Hillocks, G. (1986). *Research in written composition: New directions for teaching*. Urbana, IL: ERIC Clearinghouse on Reading and Communication Skills and National Conference on Research in English.
Hillocks, G. (1986). The writer's knowledge: Theory, research and implications for practice. In D. Bartholomae & A. R. Petrowsky (Eds.), *The teaching of writing* (pp. 71-94). Chicago, IL.
Hillocks, G. (1995). *Teaching writing as reflective practice*. New York: Teachers College Press.
Hofer, B, & Pintrich, P. R. (1997). The development of epistemological theories: Beliefs about knowledge and knowing and their relation to learning. *Review of Educational Research, 67*(1), 88-140.
Holliday, W. G. (1976). Teaching verbal chains using flow diagrams and texts. *AV Communication Review, 24*, 63-78.
Holliday, W. G. (1992). Helping college science students read and write: Practical research based suggestions. *Journal of College Science Teaching, 21*, 58-61.
Holliday, W. G., Yore, L. D., & Alvermann, D. E. (1994). The reading-science learning-writing connection: Breakthroughs, barriers, and promises. *Journal of Research in Science Teaching, 31*, 877-896. (Special issue: The reading-science learning-writing connection)
Holt-Reynolds, D. (1992). Personal history-based beliefs as relevant prior knowledge in course work. *American Educational Research Journal, 29*(2), 325-49.
Holt-Reynolds, D. (1994). When agreeing wit the professor is bad news for preservice teacher educators: Jeanneane, her personal history, and coursework. *Teacher Education Quarterly, 21*(1), 13-35.
Hoskisson, K.(1979). Learning to read naturally. *Language Arts, 56*, 489-496.
Howard, V. A., & Barton, J. H. (1986*). Thinking on paper*. New York: Quill.
Howe, A., & Johnson, J. (1992). *Common bonds: Storytelling in the classroom*. London: Hodder and Stoughton.
Huang, S. (2000). The nature of an EFL teacher's audiotaped and written feedback on student writing: A case study. *ERIC Document 438728*.
Hunter, I. (1988). *Culture and government: The emergence of literary education*. London: Macmillan Press.
Huot, B. (1990). The literature of direct writing assessment: Major concerns and prevailing trends. *Review of Educational Research, 60*(2), 237-263.
Hyde, T. S, & Jenkins, J. J. (1969). The differential effects of incidental tasks on the organization of recall of a list of highly associated words. *Journal of Experimental Psychology, 82*, 472-481.
Hyland, F., & Hyland, K. (2001). Sugaring the pill: Praise and criticism in written feedback. *Journal of Second Language Writing, 10*(3), 185-212.
Indurkhya, B. (1992). *Metaphor and cognition* (Vol. 13). Dordrecht: Kluwer Academic Publishers.
IRDP (n.d.). *Enquête PISA 2000. Compétences des élèves romands de 9e année: Oremiers résultats* [PISA 2000 survey. Skills among Swiss Romand 9th year school children: first results]. Conférence

Intercantonale de l'Instruction Publique de la Suisse Romande et du Tessin. IRDP (Institut de Recherche et de Documentation Pédagogique). Available at http://www.irdp.ch/ocde-pisa/pisa2000.htm, visited on the 08.03.2002

Irigaray, L. (1985). *Parler n'est jamais neuter* [Speak is never neutral]. Paris: Eds. Minuits.

Iser, W. (1974). *The act of reading: A theory of aesthetic response.* Baltimore: Johns Hopkins University.

Jacobson, M. J., & Spiro, R. J. (1995). Hypertext learning environments, cognitive flexibility, and the transfer of complex knowledge: An empirical investigation. *Journal of Educational Computing Research, 12*(4), 301-333.

Jacques, F. (1988). Trois stratégies interactionnelles conversation, négociation, dialogue [Three strategy of interaction: conversation, negotiation, dialogue]. In Gelas, Cosnier, Kerbrat-Orecchioni, *Echanges sur la conversation* (pp.45-67). Lyon: Presses Universitaires.

Jaffré, J. P. (1995). Invention et acquisition de l'écriture: Éléments d'une linguistique génétique [Invention and acquisition of writing: elements of genetic linguistics]. *Linx, 31*, 49-64.

Jaffré, J. P. (1997). From writing to orthography: The functions and limits of the notion of system. In. C. A. Perfetti, L. Rieben, & M. Fayol (Eds.), *Learning to spell* (pp. 3-21). Mahwah, NJ: Lawrence Erlbaum.

Jakobson, R. (1960). Linguistics and poetics. In T. A. Sebeok (Ed.), *Style in language* (pp. 350-377). Cambridge, MA: M.I.T. Press.

Jakobson, R. (1963). *Essais de linguistique générale* [General linguistic essays]. Paris: Editions de Minuit (Collection Points, n.° 17).

James, C. (1998). *Errors in language learning and use. Exploring error analysis.* Harlow: Longman.

Janssen, T., & M. Overmaat (1990). *Tekstopbouw en stelvaardigheid: Een onderzoek naar de effecten van twee experimentele methoden voor tekstopbouw* [Effects of instruction of organizational techniques on aspects of written composition]. Lisse: Swets & Zeitlinger.

Johns, A. M. (1986). Journalogs: Tools for acquainting students with history and the task demands of an advanced history class. *The History and Social Science Teacher, 21*(3), 180-183.

Johnson, B. D. (1977). Visual literacy, media literacy, and mass communication for English instruction. *Dissertation Abstract International, 38,* 6581A (University Microfilms No. 78-5287)

Johnson, H., & Seifert, C. (1999). Modifying mental representations: comprehending corrections. In H. van Oostendorp & S. Goldman (Eds.), *The construction of mental representations during reading*, (pp. 303-317). Mahwah, NJ: Lawrence Erlbaum.

Johnston, P. (1992). Telling thinking: evaluation through thinking out loud. *Constructive evaluation of literate activity.* New York & London: Longman.

Jordan, C. E. (1986). The comprehending and composing process of good writers who are good readers and poor writers who are good readers. (Doctoral dissertation, Temple University, 1986). *Dissertation Abstracts International, 47* (8), DA86274678.

Juranville, A (1994). L'ecriture [Writing]. *Revue philosophique de la France et de l'etranger, 2*, 167-180.

Jurdak, M., & Zein, R. A. (1998). The effect of journal writing on achievement in and attitude toward mathematics. *School Science and Mathematics, 98*(4), 421-419.

Kaufman, A., & Perelman, F. (1999). El resumen en el ámbito escolar. *Revista Latinoamericana de Lectura, 20,* 4.

Kaufman, A., & Perelman, F. (in press). *Resúmenes escritos: Contradicciones de su enseñanza entre 4o y 7o año de EGB.* Anuario de investigaciones No 9. Facultad de Psicología, Universidad de Buenos Aires.

Kavanagh, J. F. (1991). Preface. In J. F. Kavanagh (Ed.), *The language continuum. From infancy to literacy* (pp. vii-ix). Parkton, Maryland: York Press.

Kellogg, R. T. (1994). *The psychology of writing.* New York: Oxford University Press.

Kellogg, R. T. (1996). A model of working memory in writing. In C. M. Levy, & S. Ransdell (Eds.), *The science of writing: Theories, methods, individual differences and applications* (pp. 57-71). Mahwah, NJ: Lawrence Erbaum.

Kemmis, S., & McTaggart, R. (Eds.). (1988). *The action research planner.* Victoria: Deakin University Press.

Kent-Drury, R. (1998). Finding a place to stand: Negotiating the spatial configuration of the networked computer classroom. *Computers and Composition, 15*(3), 387-408.

Kerlitz-Nissim, T. (1997). *The development of writing following peer feedback in classes Implementing new methods of literacy.* Unpublished MA thesis, Faculty of Education, Haifa University.

Kern, R. G. (1994). The role of mental translation in second language reading. *Studies in Second Language Acquisition, 16* (4), 441-461.
Keys, C. (1999). Revitalizing Instruction in Scientific Genres: Connecting knowledge production with writing to learn in science. *Science Education, 83*, 115-130.
Keys, C. W. (1994). The development of scientific reasoning skills in conjunction with collaborative writing assignments: An interpretative study of six ninth-grade students. *Journal of Research in Science Teaching, 31*, 1003-1022.
Keys, C. W. (2000). Investigating the thinking processes of eighth grade writers during the composition of a scientific laboratory report. *Journal of Research in Science Teaching, 37*(7), 676-690.
Kiefer, K. (1991). Computers and Teacher Education in the 1990s and Beyond. In G. Hawisher, & C. Selfe (Eds.), *Evolving perspectives on computers and composition studies: Questions for the 1990s* (pp. 117-131). Urbana, IL: NCTE, 1991.
Kiefer, K. (1999, May). *Readjusting to an old space: Back to the Blackboard*. Computers and Writing Conference, May 1999.
Kieft, M., & Rijlaarsdam, G. (2002, July). *Writing about literature in modern textbooks: An analysis*. Paper presented at the 8th International conference of the European Association for Research on Learning and Instruction, Writing SIG (Staffordshire University, Stafford, UK, July 10-13).
Kim, H., & Hirtle, S. C. (1995). Spatial metaphors and disorientation in hypertext browsing. *Behaviour, & Information Technology, 14*(4), 239-250.
Kintsch, W. (1998). *Comprehension: A paradigm for cognition*. New York: Cambridge University Press.
Kintsch, W., & van Dijk, T. A. (1978). Toward a model of text comprehension and production, *Psychological Review, 85*, 363-394.
Kintsch, W., & Yarbrough, J. C. (1982). Role of rhetorical structure in text comprehension. *Journal of Educational Psychology, 74*(6), 828-834.
Kirby, J., & Woodhouse, R. (1993, August). *Depth of processing in learning from text*. Paper presented at the 5th EARLI Conference, Aix-en-Provence.
Kirkland, M. R., & Saunders, M. A. P. (1991). Maximizing student performance in summary writing: Managing the cognitive load. *TESOL Quarterly, 25*(1), 105-122.
Kleiman, A. B. (1998). Ação e mudança na sala de aula: uma pesquisa sobre letramento e interação [Action and change in the classroom: A study of literacy and interaction]. In R. Rojo (Org.), *Alfabetização e letramento. Perspectivas lingüísticas* (pp. 173-203). Campinas, SP: Mercado de Letras.
Klein, P. D. (1999). Reopening inquiry into cognitive processes in writing-to-learn, *Educational Psychology Review, 3*, 203-270.
Klein, P. D. (1999). Learning science through writing: The role of rhetorical structures. *The Alberta Journal of Educational Research, 45*, 132–153.
Klein, P. D. (2000). Elementary students' strategies for writing-to-learn in science. *Cognition and Instruction, 18*(3), 317–348
Klem, E, & Moran, C. (1992). Teachers in a strange LANd: Learning to teach in a networked writing classroom. *Computers and Composition, 9*(3), 5-22.
Kluwe, R. H. (1987). Executive decisions and regulation of problem solving behavior. In F. E. Weinert, & R. H. Kluwe (Eds.), *Metacognition, motivation and understanding* (pp. 31-64). Hillsdale, N.J.: Lawrence Erlbaum.
Knickerbocker, J. L., & Rycik, J. (2002). Growing into literature: Adolescents' literary interpretation and appreciation. *Journal of Adolescent and Adult Literacy, 46*(3), 196-208.
Kobayashi, H., & Rinnert, C. (1992). Effects of first language on second language writing: translation versus direct composition. *Language Learning, 42*(2), 183-215.
Koetsenruijter, W. (1991). A strategy for the dialectical reconstruction of the confrontation stage. In F. H. van Eemeren, R. Grootendorst, J. A. Blair, & Ch. A. Willard (Eds.), *Proceedings of the second international conference on argumentation* (pp. 441-447). Amsterdam: Sic Sat.
Kolb, D., (1984). *Experiential learning*. Prentice Hall, New York.
Kollberg, P. (1998). *S-notation – a computer based method for studying and representing text composition*. Unplished doctoral dissertation. Stockholm, Sweden: Department of Numerical Analysis and Computing Science, Royal Institute of Technology (KTH).
Kotschi, Th. (1986). Procédés d'évaluation et de commentaires metadiscursifs comme stratégies interactives [Evaluation procedures and metadiscursive comments as interactive strategies]. *Cahiers de linguistique française, 7*, 207-230.

Koutsoubou, M. (in preparation). Deaf ways of writing narratives: a bilingual approach from Greek deaf students. Unpublished Ph.D Thesis, City University, London, UK.
Krafft, U. & Dausendschön-Gay, U. (1993). La coordination des activités conversationnelles: types de contract [Coordinating conversational activities: types of contract]. *XXe. Congrès International de Linguistique et Philologie Romanes. Tome II. Section II. Analyse de la conversation* (pp. 95-108). Université de Zürich, 1992. Tübingen: Francke Verlag.
Krashen, S. (1982). *Principles and practices in second language acquisition.* Oxford: Pergamon.
Krashen, S. (2001). Bilingual education works. Retrieved 10 April, 2003, from www.rethinkingschools.org/Archives/15_02/Bi152.htm
Krashen, S., & Terrell, T. (1983). *The natural approach: Language acquisition in the classroom.* Oxford: Pergamon.
Kress, G. & van Leeuwen, T. (2001). *Multimodal discourse: The modes and media of contemporary communication.* London: Arnold.
Kress, G. (1997). *Before writing: Rethinking the paths to literacy.* London and New York: Routledge.
Kress, G. (2000). A curriculum for the future. *Cambridge Journal of Education, 35*(1), 133-145.
Kress, G. (2003). *Literacy and the new media age.* London and New York: Routledge.
Kress, G., Jewitt, C., Ogborn, J. and Tsatsaelis, C. (2001). *Multimodal teaching and learning: The rhetorics of the science classroom.* London and New York: Continuum.
Kristeva, J. (1971). *Le texte du roman* [The text of the novel]. Paris: Seuil.
Kristeva, J. (1984). *Revolution in poetic language.* New York: Colombia University Press.
Kuhl, J., & Kraska, K. (1989). Self-regulation and metamotivation: Conceptual mechanisms, development, and assessment. In R. Kanjer, P. L. Ackerman, & R. Cudeck (Eds.), *Abilities, motivation, and methodology.* Hillsdale, N.J.: Lawrence Erlbaum.
Kuhn, D. (1993). Science as argument: Implications for teaching and learning scientific thinking. *Science Education, 77*(3), 319-337.
Kuhn, D., Schauble, L., & Garcia-Mila, M. (1992). Cross domain development of scientific reasoning. *Cognitive Instruction, 9*, 285-327.
Kyle, W. C., Abell, S. K., Roth, W.-M., & Gallagher, J. J. (1992). Toward a mature discipline of science education. *Journal of Research in Science Teaching, 29*, 1015-1018.
Labov, W. (1997). *Some further steps in narrative analysis.* Retrieved 14 July, 2003, from http://www.ling.upenn.edu/~wlabov/sfs.html.
Lahire B. (1993). *Culture écrite et inégalités scolaires. Sociologie de l'échec à l'ecole* [Writing culture and inequalities at school. Sociology of failure at school]. Lyon: PU Lyon.
Lakoff, G. (1990). *Women, fire, and dangerous things.* Chicago: University of Chicago Press.
Lakoff, G., & Johnson, M. (1981). *Metaphors we live by.* Chicago: The University of Chicago Press.
Landis, D. (2002). Reading engaged readers: A cross-cultural perspective. *Journal of Adolescent and Adult Literacy, 45*(6), 472-487.
Landis, J. R., & Koch, G. G. (1977). The measurement of observer agreement for categorial data. *Biometrics, 33*, 159-174.
Landow, G. P. (1994). What's a critic to do? Critical theory in the age of hypertext. In G. P. Landow (Ed.), *Hyper/Text/Theory* (pp. 1-48). London: Johns Hopkins.
Langdon, M. (1961). *Let the children write: an explanation of intensive writing.* London: Longman.
Langer, E. (1989). *Mindfulness.* Reading: MA: Addison-Wesley.
Langer, E. (1993). A mindful education. *Educational Psychology, 28*(1), 43-50.
Langer, J. (1986). *Children reading and writing.* Norwood, NJ: Ablex.
Langer, J. (1986). Learning through writing: Study skills in the content areas. *Journal of Reading, 2,* 400-410.
Langer, J. A., & Applebee, A. (1987). *How writing shapes thinking: A study of teaching and learning* (NCTE Research Report No. 22). Urbana, IL: National Council of Teachers of English.
Lantolf, J. P., & DiCamilla, F. (1994). The linguistic analysis of private writing. *Language Sciences, 16*(3-4), 347-369.
Lausberg, H. (1998). *Handbook of Literary Rhetoric.* Leiden: E. J. Brill.
Lea, J., & Levy, M. (1999). Working memory as a resource in the writing process. In G. Rijlaarsdam & E. Espéret (Series Eds.) & M. Torrance, & G. Jeffery (Vol. Eds.). *Studies in Writing: Vol. 3. The cognitive demands of writing. Processing capacity and working memory effects in text production* (pp 63-83). Amsterdam: Amsterdam University Press.

References

Lea, M. R. (1998). Academic Literacies and learning in higher education: Constructing knowledge through texts and experience. *Studies in Education of Adults, 30*(2), 156-171.

Lea, M. R., & Street, B. (1998). Student writing in Higher education: an academic literacies approach. *Studies in Higher Education, 23,* 157-172.

LeCourt, D. (1998). Critical pedagogy in the computer classroom: Politicizing the writing space. *Computers and Composition, 15*(3), 275-296.

Lee, I. (1997). ESL learners' performance in error correction in writing: Some implications for teaching. *System 25*(4), 465-477.

Lee, I. (2002). Teaching coherence to ESL students: A classroom inquiry. *Journal of Second Language Writing, 11*(2), 135-159.

Lee, O., & Fradd, S. H. (1998). Science for all, including students from non-English-language backgrounds. *Educational Researcher, 27,* 12-21.

Leech, G. N., & Short, M. H. (1981). *Style in fiction: A linguistic introduction to english fictional prose.* London: Longman.

Lemke, J. L. (1998). Metamedia literacy: Transforming meanings and media. In D. Reinking, M. McKenna, L. D. Labbo, & R. D. Kieffer (Eds.), *Handbook of Literacy and Technology: Transformation in a post-typographical world* (pp.283-302). Mahwah, NJ: Lawrence Erlbaum.

Lerner, D. (2001). *Leer y escribir en la escuela.* México: Fondo de Cultura Económica, Mexico City.

Levelt, W. J. M. (1989). *Speaking. From intention to articulation.* Second printing, 1991. A Bradford Book. Cambridge, Massachusetts/London, England: The MIT Press.

Leventhal, L. M., Teasley, B. M., Instone, K., Rohlman, D. S., & Farhat, J. (1993). Sleuthing in Hyper-Holmes: An evaluation of using hypertext vs. a book to answer questions. *Behaviour & Information Technology, 12,* 149-164.

Levin, J. A., Stuve, M. J., & Jacobson, M. J. (1999). Teachers' conceptions of the Internet and the world wide web: A representational toolkit as a model of expertise. *Journal of Educational Computing Research, 21,* 1-23.

Levin, J., Anglin, G. Carney, R. (1987). On empirically validating functions of pictures in prose. In D. Willows, H. Houghton (Eds.), *The psychology of illustration.* (vol. 1., Basic Research, pp. 51-86). New York: Springer-Verlag.

Levine, M. (2001). *Educational care: A system for understanding and helping children with learning differences at home and in school.* Cambridge, MA: Educators Publishing Services.

Levine, T., & Geldman Caspar, Z. (1997). What can be learned from informal student writings in a science context? *School Science and Mathematics; Bowling Green, 97,* 359-367.

Lewensteing, M. (2000). *Eyetracking: a closer look.* www.poynter.org/centerpiece/ 071200.htm.

Lewis, M., & Wray, D. (1995*). Developing children's non-fiction writing: working with writing frames.* Leamington Spa: Scholastic.

Lieberman, J. N. (1977). *Playfulness. Its relationship to imagination and creativity.* London: Academic Press.

Lightbown, P., & Spada, N. (1993). *How languages are learned.* Oxford: Oxford University Press.

Lindgren, E., & Sullivan, K. P. H. (2003). Stimulated recall as a trigger for increasing noticing and language awareness in the L2 writing classroom: A case study of two young female writers. *Language Awareness.*

Lindgren, E., & Sullivan, K. P. H. (April, 2002). *Analysing and presenting on-line revision.* Paper presented at The first key-stroke logging symposium, Umeå, Sweden.

Linn, M. , Layman, J., & Nachmias, R. (1987). Cognitive consequences of micro-computer-based laboratories: Graphing skills development. *Journal of Contemporary Educational Psychology, 12,* 244-253.

Lipman, M. (1991). *Thinking in education.* [translated by Decostre, N. (1995). *À l'école de la pensée*]. Bruxelles: De Boeck Université.

Littlewood, W. (1981). *Communicative language teaching: An introduction.* Cambridge: Cambridge University Press.

Lo, A. (1992). Language experience stories. In M. Lau, & M. Murphy (Eds.), *Developing writing: Purposes and practices* (pp. 32-59). Hong Kong: Institute of Language in Education, Education Department.

Locke, D. (1992). *Science as writing.* New Haven: Yale University Press.

Lohman, D. F. (1993). Teaching and testing to develop fluid abilities. *Educational Researcher, 22*(7), 12-21.

London, Y. (1994). *Yaron London Speaks with Children About Friendship.* Edited by Y. Schiff with Z. Galillee, J. Chagrin, & A. Gelman (p. 32). Avivim (In Hebrew).

Lotman, J. (1974). *Den poetiska texten* [The poetic text]. Stockholm: Pan/Norstedts.

Lowyck, J., & Vanmaele, L. (1992a). How to put language in a child's mind: The development of 'Scriptor' as a computer tool for writing. In P. Kommers, D. H. Jonassen, & J. T. Mayes (Eds.), *Cognitive tools for learning* (pp. 215-226). Berlin/Heidelberg/New York: Springer.

Lowyck, J., & Vanmaele, L. (1992b). Schrijven door jonge leerlingen. Een verkenning [Youngsters writing. An exploration]. *Tijdschrift voor Taalbeheersing, 14*(3), 206-220.

Luke. A. (2001). The Queensland 'New Basics': An Interview with Allan Luke. *English in Australia,* 129-130, pp. 132-140.

Lukinsky, J. (1991). Reflective withdrawal through journal writing. In J. Mezirow (Ed.), *Fostering critical reflection in adulthood* (pp. 213-234). San Francisco, CA: Jossey-Bass.

Lumbelli, L. (1985). *Psicologia dell'Educacazione. Comunicare a scuola* [Psychology of education. Communicating at school]. Bologna: Il Mulino.

Lumbelli, L. (1988). *Incoraggiare a leggere* [Encouraging to read]. Firenze: La nuova Italia.

Lumbelli, L.(1986). Focusing on text comprehension as a problem-solving task. A fostering project for culturally deprived children. In C. Cornoldi, & J. Oakhill (Eds.). *Reading comprehension difficulties: processes and intervention,* (pp. 301-330). Hillsdale, NJ: Lawrence Erlbaum.

Lumbelli, L., & Camagni, C. (1993). Can comprehensibility in writing be improved by revising oral language? In G. Eigler, & T. Jechle (Eds.), *Writing. Current trends in European Research* (pp. 197-213). Freiburg: Hochschule Verlag.

Lumbelli, L., Paoletti G., & Frausin, T. (1999). Improving the ability to detect comprehension problems: From revising to writing. *Learning and Instruction, 9,* 143-166.

Lumbelli, L., Paoletti, G., Camagni, C., & Frausin, T. (1996). Can the ability to monitor local coherence in text comprehension be transferred to writing? In G. Rijlaarsdam, H. Van den Bergh, & M. Couzijn (Eds.), *Studies in writing: Vol. 2. Effective teaching and learning of writing. Current trends in research* (pp 207-223). Amsterdam: Amsterdam University Press.

MacLachlan, G., & Reid, R. (1994). *Framing and Interpretation.* Melbourne: Melbourne University Press.

Maehr, M. L., & Meyer, H. A. (1997). Understanding motivation and schooling: Where we've been, where we are, and where we need to go. *Educational Psychology Review, 9,* 371-409.

Mager, W., Bos, A., & Van der Auwera, L. (1991/1993). *WAPSO-batterij.* Brasschaat: C.A.P. (Coördinatieteam Antwerpen Psycho-diagnostiek V.Z.W.). [WAPSO-intelligence test, Brasschaat: C.A.P.: Coordination Team Psycho-diagnostics of Antwerp].

Mahler, S., Hoz, R., & Fischl, D. (1991). Didactic uses of concept mapping in higher education: Applications in medical education. *Instructional Science, 20,* 25-47.

Maingueneau, D. (1990). Éléments de linguistique pour le texte littéraire [Linguistic elements to an analysis of literary text]. Paris: Bordas.

Malinowsky, B. (1923). The problem of meaning in primitive languages. In C. K. Ogden, & I. A. Richards (Eds.), *The meaning of meaning* (pp. 296-336). New York: Harcout, Brace and World, Inc.

Mannoni, O. (1979). *La otra escena. Claves de lo imaginario* [The other stage. Keys of the Imaginary]. Buenos Aires: Hachette.

Marcuschi, L. A. (1998). A língua falada e o ensino de português [Spoken language and the teaching of Portuguese]. In N. B. Bastos (Org.), *Língua Portuguesa. História, perspectivas, ensino* (pp. 101-119). São Paulo: IP-PUC/SP-EDUC.

Marcuschi, L. A. (2001). *Da fala para a escrita. Atividades de retextualização* [From the spoken to the written. Retextualisation activities] (2nd Ed.). São Paulo: Cortez Editora.

Marom, A& Hertz-Lazarowiz, R. (2002). Use of strategies in the writing process. *Script, 5-6,* 101-127 (Hebrew).

Marom, A. (1997). *The use of strategies in the writing process.* Research work submitted at the Faculty of Education at the Haifa university (Hebrew).

Marshall, C. (1997). Annotation: from paper books to the digital library. *Proceedings of the 2nd ACM international conference on Digital libraries* (pp 131-140).

Marshall, J. (1987). The effects of writing on students' understanding of literary texts. *Research in the Teaching of English, 1,* 30-63.

Martin, J. R. (1989). *Factual writing: Exploring and challenging social reality.* London: Oxford University Press.

Mason, L. (1998). Sharing cognition to construct scientific knowledge in school context: The role of oral and written discourse. *Instructional Science, 26*(5), 359-389.
Matsuhashi, A. (1987). Revising the plan and altering the text. In A. Matsuhashi (Ed.), *Writing in real time: Modelling production processes* (pp.197-223). Norwood, NJ: Ablex Publishing Company.
Maturana, H. R., & Varela, F. J. (1987). *The Tree of Knowledge: The Biological Roots of Human Understanding.* Boston and London: New Science Library.
Maybury, B. (1967). *Creative writing for juniors.* London: Batsford.
Mayer, C., & Akamatsu, C. T. (1999). Bilingual-Bicultural models of literacy education for deaf students: considering the claims. *Journal of Deaf Studies and Deaf Education, 4*(1), 1-8.
Mayer, R. (2001). *Multimedia Learning.* Cambridge: Cambridge University Press.
Mayer, R. E. (1983). *Thinking, problem solving, cognition.* New York: Freeman
McCarthy, L. P. (1987). A stranger in strange lands: A college student writing across the curriculum. *Research in the Teaching of English, 21,* 233-265.
McClenaghan, D. (2001). Norman Bates, Abba and Annoying Neighbours. *English in Australia, 129-130,* 78-88.
McCrindle, A. R., & Christensen, C. A. (1995). The impact of learning journals on metacognitive and cognitive processes and learning performance. *Learning and Instruction, 5,* 167-185.
McCutchen, D. (1986). Domain knowledge and linguistic knowledge in the development of writing ability. *Journal of Memory and Language, 25,* 431-444.
McCutchen, D. (1996). A capacity theory of writing: Working memory in composition. *Educational Psychology Review, 8*(3), 299-325.
McCutchen, D. (2000). Knowledge, processing, and working memory: Implications for a theory of writing. *Educational Psychologist, 35*(1), 13-23.
McDaniel, M. A. & Einstein, G. O. (1989). Material-appropriate processing: A contextualist approach to reading and studying strategies. *Educational Psychology Review, 1,* 113-145.
McGhie-Richmond, D. R., Jordan, A., & Underwood, K. (2002, April). *Discovering the general in the particular: A case study of an exemplary teacher's beliefs.* Annual Meeting of the American Educational Research Association (New Orleans, LA, April 1-5, 2002).
McGinley, W. J. (1992). The role of reading and writing while composing from sources. *Reading Research Quarterly, 27*(3), 226-249.
McIntosh, M. E., & Draper, R. J. (2001). Using learning logs in mathematics: Writing to learn. *Mathematics Teacher, 94*(7), 554-557.
McKnight, C., Dillon, A., & Richardson, J. (1991). *Hypertext in context.* Cambridge: Cambridge University Press.
Meichenbaum, D. (1977). *Cognitive behaviour modification.* New York and London: Plenum Press.
Mélot A-M. (1991). Contrôle des conduites de mémorisation et métacognition *(control of the memorisation behaviour and metacognition). Bulletin de Psychologie,* Tome XLIV, 399, 138-146.
Mélot A-M., & Corroyer D. (1992). Organization of Metacognive Knowledge: a Condition for Strategies Use in Memorization. *European Journal of Education, 7,* 23-37.
Menez, M. (1984). Stratégies de guidage et processus cognitifs sollicités. *Bulletin de psychologie, 37,* 167-172.
Mercer, M. (1969). *Frog, where are you?* New York: Puffin Books.
Mercer, N. (1995). *The guided construction of knowledge: Talk amongst teachers and learners.* Clevedon: Multilingual Matters.
Meuffels, B. (1982). *Studies over taalvaardigheid* [Studies into language skills]. Unpublished doctoral dissertation. University of Amsterdam.
Mewborn, D. S., & Stanulis, R. N. (2000). Making the tacit explicit: Teacher educators' values and practices in a co-reform teacher education program. *Teacher Education Quarterly, 27*(3), 5-22.
Miller, C. R (1984). Genre as social action. *Quarterly Journal of Speech, 70,* 151-167.
Mlynarczyk, R. (1991). Is there a difference between personal and academic writing? *TESOL Journal, 1*(1), 17-20.
Montgomery, D. E. (1992). Young children's theory of knowing: The development of a folk epistemology. *Developmental Review, 12,* 410-430
Moon, J (2001). *Reflections in learning and professional development.* London: Kogan Page.
Moore, P. J. (1993). Metacognitive processing of diagrams, maps and graphs, *Learning and Instruction, 3,* 215-226.

Moore, R. (1993). Does writing about science improve learning about science? *Journal of College Science Teaching, 22*(4), 212-217.
Moore, R. (1994). Writing as a tool for learning biology. *Bioscience, 44*(9), 613-617.
Moran, C. (1998). From a high-tech to a low-tech writing classroom: You can't go home again. *Computers and Composition, 15*(1), 1-10.
Moreno, R., & Mayer, R. (1999). Cognitive principles of multimedia learning: The role of modality and contiguity. *Journal of Educational Psychology, 2,* 358-368.
Morino, H. (1998). *Writing and reading: Exploring their similarities in teaching: Suggestions for high school English teachers in Japan.* ERIC Document 423697.
Morris, D. (1977). *Manwatching.* London: Jonathan Cape Ltd.
Mortimore, P., Sammons, P., Stoll, L., Lewis, D., & Ecob, R. (1988). *School Matters: The junior years.* Wells: Open Books.
Mosconi, G. (1978). *Il pensiero discorsivo* [Thinking and Discourse]. Bologna: Il Mulino.
Mounty, J. L. (1993). *Signed language development checklist.* Princeton, N.J.: Educational Testing Service.
Moursund, D. G. (1999). The case for PBL. In: *Project-Based learning using information technology,* (Chapter 4). Eugene, OR: International Society for technology in Education. Retrieved September 10, 2003, from http://www.uoregon.edu/~moursund/PBL%20Book%201999/
Murray, D. (1984). *Write to learn.* New York: Holt, Rinehart and Winston
Murray, D. M. (1987). *Write to learn.* New York: Holt, Rinehart, and Winston.
Mussen, P. H., (Ed.). Flavell, J. H., & Markman, M. (Eds.). (1983). *Carmichael's manual for child psychology, 3,* 77-166. New York: John Wiley Publishers.
Neiman, N., Frohlich, M., Stern, H., & Todesco, A. (1978). *The good language learner.* Toronto: Ontario Institute for Studies in Education.
Nelson Le-Gall, Sh. (1992). Children's instrumental help-seeking: Its role in the social acquisition and construction of knowledge. In R. Hertz-Lazarowitz, & N. Miller (Eds.), *Interaction in cooperative groups – The theoretical anatomy of group learning* (pp. 49-68). Cambridge: Cambridge University Press.
Nelson, D., Walling, J., & McEnvoy, C. (1979). Doubts about depth. *Journal of Experimental Psychology: Human Learning and Memory, 1,* 24-44.
Nelson, J. (1988). Examining the practices that shape student writing: Two studies of college freshmen writing across the disciplines. Unpublished doctoral dissertation. Carnegie Mellon University, Pittsburgh, PA.
Nelson, N. (2001). Writing to learn. One theory, two rationales. In G. Rijlaarsdam (SeriesEd.) & P. Tynjälä, L. Mason, & K. Lonka (Vol. Eds.), *Studies in writing: Vol.7. Writing as a learning tool: Integrating theory and practice* (pp. 23-36). Dordrecht: Kluwer Academic Publishers.
Neuwirth, C., Kaufer, D., Chandhok, R., Morris, J. (1990). Issues in the design of computer support for co-authoring and commenting cscw applications. *Proceedings of acm cscw'90 conference on computer-supported cooperative work* (pp.183-195).
New London Group. (1996). A pedagogy of multiliteracies: Designing social futures. *Harvard. Educational Review, 66,* 60-92.
Newell, A. (1980). Reasoning, problem solving and decision processes: The problem space as a fundamental category. In R. S. Nickerson (Ed.), *Attention and performance* (pp. 693-719). Hillsdale, NJ: Lawrence Erlbaum.
Newell, A., & Simon, H. A. (1972). *Human problem solving.* Englewood Cliffs, NJ: Prentice-Hall.
Newell, G. (1998). How much are we the wiser?: Continuity and change in writing and learning in the content areas. *97th Yearbook of the National Society for the Study of Education* (pp. 178-202). Chicago, IL: University of Chicago Press.
Newell, G., Suszynski, K., & Weingart, R. (1989). The effects of writing in reader-based and writer-based mode on students' understanding of two short stories. *Journal of Reading Behaviour, 21*(1), 37-57.
Newman, D., Griffin, P., & Cole. M. (1989). *The construction zone: Working for cognitive change in school.* Cambridge: Cambridge University Press.
Newmann, F. M.(1990). Qualities of thoughtful social studies classes: An empirical profile. *Curriculum Studies, 22-23,* 253-275 .
Ng, E., & Bereiter, C. (1992). Three levels of goal-orientation in learning. *The Journal of Learning Sciences, 1,* 243-73.

Nicol, D. J., Kane, K., & Wainwright, C. (1994). Improving laboratory learning through group work and structured reflection and discussion. *Education, Training and Technology International, 31*(4), 302-318.
Nielsen, J. (1993). *Hypertext and hypermedia*. London: Academic Press Professional.
Nightingale, P. (1988). Understanding processes and problems in student writing. *Studies in Higher Education, 13*(3), 263-283.
Noonan, K. (2000). Why we were wrong about bilingual education. Retrieved 5 April, 2003, from http://education.guardian.co.uk/old/tefl/story/0,10044,395171,00.html
Norman, D. A., & Rumelhart, D. E. (1975). *Explorations in cognition. Memory and knowledge*. San Francisco: Freeman.
Nosich, G. (2001). *Learning to think things through: A guide to critical thinking in the curriculum*. Upper Saddle River: Prentice Hall.
Novack, J. (1985). Metalearning and metaknowledge strategies to help students learn how to learn. In L. West, & A. Pines, (Eds.), *Cognitive structure and conceptual change* (pp. 189-209). New York: Academic Press.
Nunan, D. (1990). Action research in the language classroom. In J. C. Richards, & D. Nunan (Eds.), *Second language teacher education* (pp. 62-81). New York: Cambridge University Press.
Nunberg, G. (1990). *The linguistics of punctuation*. Stanford, CA: Center for the Study of Language and Information.
Nystrand, M. (1986). Learning to write by talking about writing: A summary of research on intensive peer review. In M. Nystrand (Ed.), *The structure of written communication: Studies in reciprocity between writers and readers* (pp. 179-211). Orlando, FL: Academic Press.
Nystrand, M. (1989). A social-interactive model of writing. *Written Communication, 6*, 66-85.
Nystrand, M. (1990). Sharing Words. The Effects of Readers on Developing Writers. *Written Communication, 7*(1), 3-24.
Nystrand, M., Greene, S., & Wiemelt, J. (1993). Where did composition studies come from? An intellectual history. *Written Communication, 10*(3), 267-333.
Nyström, C. (2000). *Gymnasisters skrivande. En studie i genre, textstruktur och sammanhang* [Writing in upper secondary school: genre, text structure and cohesion]. Uppsala: Skrifter utgivna av Institutionen för nordiska språk vid Uppsala universitet.
O'Connor, J., & Seymour, J. (1990). *Introducing neuro-linguistic programming*. New York: Crucible Books.
O'Hara, K., & Sellen, A. (1997). A comparison of reading paper and on-line documents. *Proceedings of ACM CHI 97 Conference on human factors in computing systems, vol. 1*, 335-342
O'Hare, F. (1973). *Sentence-combining: Improving student writing without formal grammar instruction*. Illinois: National Council of Teachers of English.
O'Malley, M., & Chamot, A.(1990). *Learning strategies in second language acquisition*. Cambridge: Cambridge University Press.
OECD (2000). *Measuring Student Knowledge and Skills: The PISA 2000 Assessment of Reading, Mathematical and Scientific Literacy*. Available at http://www.pisa.oecd.org/docs/assess.htm, visited on the 19.03.2002
OECD (2001). *Knowledge and skills for life. First results from the OECD Programme for International Student Assessment (PISA)2000. Education and skills*. OECD, Organisation for Economic Co-operation and Development. Paris: OECD Publications.
Office for Standards in Education (1995). *English: A review of inspection findings 1993/94*. London: Her Majesty's Stationery Office.
Office for Standards in Education (1998). *The Annual Report of Her Majesty's Chief Inspector of Schools: Standards and quality in Education 1996/97*. London: The Stationery Office.
Olson, D. (1994). *The world on paper*. Cambridge, MA: Cambridge University Press.
Olson, D. R., & Kamawar, D. (2002). Writing as a form of quotation. In J. Brockmeier, M. Wang and D. R. Olson (Eds.), *Literacy, narrative and culture*. Richmond, Surrey: Curzon.
Olson, J. R., Deming, M. P., & Valerie-Gold, M. (1994). Dialogue journals: Barometers for assessing growth in developmental learners. *Journal of Developmental Education, 18*, 26-30.
Olson, V. B. (1990). The revising processes of sixth-grade writers with and without peer feedback. *Journal of Educational Research, 84*, 22-29.
Ong, W. (1991). *Orality and literacy*. New York: Metheum.

Oostdam, R. J. (1990). Empirical research on the identification of singular, multiple and subordinate argumentation. *Argumentation, 4*, 2, 223-234.
Oostdam, R. J. (1991). *Argumentatie in de peiling. Een aanbod- en prestatiepeiling van argumentatievaardigheden in het voortgezet onderwijs* [Assessment study to argumentation skills in Dutch secondary education]. Amsterdam: SCO-Kohnstamm Institute.
Oostdam, R. J., & de Glopper, K. (1999). Students' skill in judging argument validity. In Frans H. van Eemeren, Rob Grootendorst, J. Anthony Blair, & A. Willard (Eds.), *Proceedings of the Fourth International Conference of the International Society for the Study of Argumentation* (pp. 621-625). Amsterdam: Sic Sat.
Oostdam, R. J., & M. H. Eiting (1991). The measurement of receptive argumentation skills: The identification of points of view in single and multiple disputes. In F. H. van Eemeren, R. Grootendorst, J. A. Blair, & Ch. A. Willard (Eds.), *Proceedings of the Second International Conference on Argumentation* (pp. 636-671). Amsterdam: Sic Sat.
Oostdam, R. J., & Y. W. Emmelot (1991)/ Education in argumentation skills at Dutch secondary schools. In F. H. van Eemeren, R. Grootendorst, J. A. Blair, & Ch. A. Willard (Eds.), *Proceedings of the Second International Conference on Argumentation* (pp. 1121-1126). Amsterdam: Sic Sat.
Oostdam, R. J., de Glopper, K., & M. H. Eiting (1994). Argumentation in written discourse: secondary school students' writing problems. In Frans H. Van Eemeren, & Rob Gootendorst (Eds.), *Studies in Pragma-Dialectics* (pp. 130-141). Amsterdam: Sic Sat.
Oostdam, R., & de Glopper, K. (1995). Argument form and cognitive components. In F. H. van Eemeren, R. Grootendorst, J. Anthony Blair, & A. Willard (Eds.), *Reconstruction and application. Proceedings of the third ISSA conference on argumentation: Vol. 3* (pp. 327-336). Dordrecht: Sic Sat.
Ormerod, F. and Ivani, R. (2001). Materiality in children's meaning-making practices. *Visual Communication, 1*, 65-9.
Ormerod, F., & Ivani, R. (2000). Texts in practices: Interpreting the physical characteristics of children's project work. In Barton, D., Hamilton, M., & Ivani, R. (Eds.). *Situated literacies: Reading and writing in context*. London and New York: Routledge.
Ormrod, J. E. (2003). *Educational psychology: Developing learners* (4th ed). Upper Saddle River, N. J.: Pearson Education.
Orsolini, M., & Pontecorvo, C. (1986). Disputare e construire. Processi di conoscenza nell'interazione verbale tra bambini [Debating and constructing. Process of knowledge in verbal interaction between children]. *Età evolutiva, 30*, 63-76
Orsolini, M., Pontecorvo, C., & Amoni, M. (1989). Discutere a scuola: interazione sociale e attività cognitiva [Discussing at school: social interaction and cognitive action]. *Giornale Italiano di Psicologia, 16*(3).
Overmaat, M. (1996). *Schrijven en lezen met tekstschema's: effectief onderwijs in de bovenbouw van het voortgezet onderwijs* [Effects of structural schema training on writing and reading in secondary education, with English summary]. Unpublished doctoral dissertation. Amsterdam: SCO.
Ovsiannikov I. A,. Arbib M., & McNeill T. (1999). Annotation Technology. *International Journal of Human-Computer Studies, 50*(4), 329-36.
Oxford R. (1990). *Language learning strategies*. Boston: Heinle and Heinle.
Oxford, R. (1989). The best and the worst. *Foreign Language Annals, 22*(1), 23-39.
Paivio, A. (1971). *Imagery and verbal processes*. New York: Holt, Rinehart, & Winston.
Paivio, A. (1986). *Mental representation. A dual coding approach*. New York: Oxford University Press.
Pallascio, R., & Lafortune, L. (Eds.). (2000). *Pour une pensée réflexive en education* [In favour to adopt a reflexive thinking in education]. Québec: Presses Universitaires du Québec, coll. Éducation Recherche.
Palmquist, M., Kiefer, K. Hartvigsen, J., & Godlew, B. (1998). *Transitions: Teaching writing in computer-supported and traditional classrooms*. Norwood: Ablex Publishing Corp.
Pålson, E. (1998). *Revision strategies in young foreign language writing*. Stockholm: Technical report TRITA-NA-P9802, IPLab-143, Department of Computing Science, Royal Institute of Technology.
Pander Maat, H. (1994). *Tekstanalyse: een pragmatische benadering* [Text analysis. A pragmatic approach]. Groningen: Martinus Nijhoff.
Paoletti, G. (1996). Apprendere scrivendo: l'effetto della riformulazione del testo [Learning by writing: the effect of text reformulation]. In B. Vertecchi (Ed.), *Per una nuova qualita' della scuola* (pp. 253-267). Napoli: Tecnodid.

Paoletti, G. (2004). Writing-to-learn and the analysis of text coherence. *Proceedings of the EARLI writing conference 2000,* Verona, Italy.
Paris S. G., & Winograd G. W. (1990). How metacognition can promote academic learning and instruction. In B. J. Jones, & L. Idol, *Dimensions of thinking and cognitive instruction* (pp.15-33). Hillsdale, NJ: Lawrence Erlbaum.
Paris, S. G. (2001). Classroom applications of research on self-regulated learning. *Educational Psychologist, 36*(2), 89-101.
Pasquier, A., & Dolz, J. (1990). Pratiques de textes informatifs. *Education et Recherche, 12*(2), 148-165.
Patterson, A. (2000). Australia: Questions of Pedagogy. In R. Peel, A. Patterson, and J. Gerlach (Eds.), *Questions of english: Ethics, aesthetics, rhetoric and the formation of the subject in England, Australia and the United States* (pp.233-300). London and New York: Routledge.
Paul, P. V. (2001). *Language and deafness*. San Diego: Singular Thompson Learning.
Paul, R. (1994). Teaching critical thinking in the strong sense. In K. S. Walters (Ed.), *Re-thinking reason: New perspectives on critical thinking* (pp. 181-198). Albany: SUNY Press.
Peeck, J. (1987). The role of illustrations in processing and remembering illustrated texts. In D. Willows, & H. Houghton (Eds.), *The Psychology of illustration* (pp. 115-150). New York: Springer-Verlag.
Peeck, J. (1994). Enhancing graphic-effects in instructional texts: Influencing learning activities. In W. Schnotz, & W. Kulhavy (Eds.), *Comprehension of graphics* (pp. 291-302). Amsterdam: North-Holland.
Peled, N. (1996). Characteristics of school literacy development. *Ba'Mihlala, 8,* 115-175.
Pennycook, A. (1996). Borrowing other's words: Text, ownership, memory, and plagiarism. *TESOL Quarterly, 30*, 201-30.
Penrose, A. M. (1992). To write or not to write: Effects of task and task interpretation on learning through writing. *Written Communication, 9,* 465-500.
Peregoy, S. F., & Boyle, O. F. (2001). *Reading, writing, and learning in ESL: A resource book for K-12 teachers* (3rd ed.). New York: Longman.
Peregoy, S., & Boyle, O. (1993). *Reading, writing and learning in ESL*. New York and London: Longman.
Perelman, C., & Olbrechts-Tyteca, L. (1958). *Traité de l'argumentation. La nouvelle rhétorique* [The new rhetoric. A treatise on argumentation]. Paris: Presses Universitaires de France.
Perelman, Ch., & Olbrechts-Tyteca, L. (1969). *The new rhetoric: A treatise on argumentation*. Notre Dame, Indiana: University of Notre Dame Press.
Perfetti, C. A. (1997). The psycholinguistics of Spelling and Reading. In C. A. Perfetti, L. Rieben, & M. Fayol (Eds.), *Learning to spell* (pp. 20-38). Mahwah, NJ: Erlbaum.
Perkins, D. (1995). *Outsmarting IQ: The science of learnable intelligence*. New York: The Free Press.
Perkins, D. N. (1992). *Smart schools: From training memories to educating minds*. New York: The Free Press.
Perkins, D. N. (1995). L'individu-plus. Une vision distribuée de la pensée et de l'apprentissage [Person-plus. A distributed vision concerning thought and learning]. *Revue Française de Pédagogie, 111,* 57-71.
Perkins, D. N., & Salomon, G. (1989). Are cognitive skills context-bound? *Educational Researcher, 18*(1), 16-25.
Perkins, D. N., Jay, E., & Tishman, Sh. (1993). New conceptions of thinking: From ontology to education. *Educational Psychologist, 28*(1), 67-85.
Perkins, D., Jay, I., & Tishman, S. (1993). Beyond abilities: A dispositional theory of thinking. *Merril Palmer Quarterly, 39*(1), 1-21.
Peters, M. (1985). *Spelling: Caught or taught? A new look*. London: Routledge.
Peters, R. S. (Ed.). (1969). *Perspectives on Plowden*. London: Routledge, & Kegan Paul.
Pew Internet and American Life Project (2002, September 15). *The Internet goes to college: How students are living in the future with today's technology*. Retrieved April 15, 2003 from http://www.pewintern.org.
Peyton, J. (1990). *Students and teachers writing together: Perspectives on journal writing*. Alexandria, VA: TESOL.
Peyton, J., & Reed, L. (1990). *Dialogue journal writing with non-native English speakers: A handbook for teachers*. Alexandria, VA: TESOL.
Piaget J. (1974). *La prise de conscience* [The Sudden awarness]. Paris: PUF.
Piaget, J. (1926). *The language and the thought of the child*. New York: Harcourt, Brace, & World.

Piaget, J. (1962). *Play, Dreams and Imitation in Childhood*. London: Routledge.
Piaget, J. (1970a). *Main trends in inter-disciplinary research*. NY: Harper.
Piaget, J. (1970b). *Main trends in psychology*. NY: Harper.
Pienemann, M. (1998). *Language processing and second language development: Processability theory*. Amsterdam: John Benjamin's Publishing Company.
Pinto, M. da G. (1999). Spelling and writing in Portuguese primary school children. To what extent do these processes/skills depend on a mastering of orality and on adequate reading methods. In M. da G. Pinto, J. Veloso, & B. Maia (Eds.), *Psycholinguistics on the threshold of the year 2000. Proceedings of the 5th International Congress of the International Society of Applied Psycholinguistics* (pp. 503-511). Porto: Faculdade de Letras da Universidade do Porto.
Pinto, M. da G. (2001, July). *The importance of indirect, semi-direct and silent direct reading techniques/methods in improving oral language, reading, and spelling*. Paper presented at the 3rd IAIMTE Conference, University of Amsterdam, The Netherlands, 11-13 July 2001.
Pinto, M. da G. L. C. (1994). *Desenvolvimento e distúrbios da linguagem* [Language development and disorders]. Porto: Porto Editora (Colecção Linguística Porto Editora, n° 3).
Pinto, M. da G. L. C. (1997). A ortografia e a escrita em crianças portuguesas nos primeiros anos de escolaridade. Até que ponto dependem estas habilidades de um bom domínio do oral e de métodos adequados de leitura? [Spelling and writing in Portuguese children in early schooling. How far do these skills depend on a good oral mastery of the language and suitable reading methods?]. *Revista da Faculdade de Letras do Porto – Línguas e Literaturas, 14*, 7-58.
Pinto, M. da G. L. C. (1998). *Saber viver a linguagem. Um desafio aos problemas de literacia* [Knowing how to experience language. A challenge to the problems of literacy]. Porto: Porto Editora (Colecção Linguística Porto Editora, n° 11).
Piolat, A. (1990). *Vers l'amélioration de la rédaction de texte*. Dossier d'habilitation à diriger des recherches. Not published. Université de Provence, Aix-en-Provence.
Piolat, A., & Roussey, J-Y., & Gombert, A. (1999). The development of argumentative schema in writing. In G. Rijlaarsdam & E. Espéret (Series Eds.) & J. Andriessen & P. Coirier (Vol. Eds.), *Studies in Writing: Vol. 5. Foundations of argumentative text processing* (pp. 117-135). Amsterdam, Amsterdam University Press.
Pontecorvo, C. (1987). Discussing for reasoning: the role of argument in knowledge construction. In E. De Corte, J. G. L. C. Lodewijks, R. Parmentier, & P. Span (Eds.), *Learning and Instruction. Publication of the European Association for Research on learning and Instruction* (pp. 1-82). Oxford/Leuven: Leuven University Press.
Pontecorvo, C., Castiglia, D. and Zucchermaglio, C. (1989). Discorso e ragionamento scientifico nelle discussioni in classse [Discourse and scientific reasoning in the classroom discussion]. *Scuola e Città, 10*, 447-461.
Poon, A. Y. K. (2001). Don't learn English in the Chinese way, Ming Pao, 15 June. (In Chinese)
Pope, R. (1995). *Textual intervention*. London/New York: Routledge.
Popper, K. R. (1972). *Objective knowledge: An evolutionary approach*. Oxford: Clarendon Press.
Porter, R. P. (1998). The case against bilingual education. *The Atlantic Monthly, 281*(5), 28-39.
Pouit, D., & Golder C. (1996). Peut-on faciliter l'argumentation écrite ? Effets d'un schéma de texte, d'une liste d'idées et d'un thème familier [Can we support argumentative writing? The impact of a text's schema, a listing of ideas and a familiar thematic]. *Archives de Psychologie, 64*, 179-199.
Pouit, D., & Golder, C. (1997). Il ne suffit pas d'avoir des idées pour défendre un point de vue. La récupération des idées peut-elle faciliter la production écrite d'une argumentation chez les enfants de 11 à 17 ans [It's not enough to dispose of some ideas to argue to position. Can the recovery of ideas help 11-17 years olds children to write?]. *Revue de Psychologie de l'Education, 3*, 33-52.
Powell, A. B. (1997). Capturing, examining, and responding to mathematical thinking through writing. *Clearing House, 71*(1), 21-25.
Prain, V. (1995). Helping students identify how writers signal purpose in autobiographical writing. *Journal of Reading, 38*, 476-481.
Prain, V., & Hand, B. (1996). Writing for learning in secondary science: Rethinking practices. *Teaching and Teacher Education, 12*, 609–626.
Prain, V., & Hand, B. (1999). Students' perceptions of writing for learning in secondary school science. *Science Education, 83*(2), 151-162.
Prescott, H. M. (2001). Helping students say how they know what they know. *The Clearing House, 74*(6), 327-331.

Pressley, M., & Afflerbach, P. (1995). *Verbal protocols of reading: The nature of constructively responsive reading.* Hillsdale, NJ: Lawrence Erlbaum.
Price, M. (2002). Beyond 'Gotcha!': situating plagiarism in policy and practice. *College Composition and Communication, 54*, 88-115.
Prior, P. (1998). *Writing/Disciplinarity. A sociohistoric account of literate activity in the academy.* Mahwah, NJ: Lawrence Erlbaum.
Pritchard, R. J. (1993). Developing writing prompts for reading response and analysis. *English Journal, 82*(3), 24-32.
Pritchard, R. J., & Marshall, J. C. (1994). Evaluation of a tiered model for staff development in writing. *Research in the Teaching of English, 28* (3), 259-285.
Pritchard, R. J., & Marshall, J. C. (2002a). Professional development in healthy vs. unhealthy districts: Top ten characteristics based on research. *School Leadership and Management, 22*(1), 113-141.
Pritchard, R. J., & Marshall, J. C. (2002b). Do NWP teachers make a difference: Findings from research on district-level staff development. *The NWP Quarterly, 24*(3), 32-38.
Probst, R. (1996). Reader-response theory in the middle school. In K. Beers, & B. G. Samuels (Eds.), *Into focus: Understanding and creating middle school readers* (pp. 125-138). Norwood, MA: Christopher Gordon.
Prosser, M., & Trigwell, K. (1999). *Understanding learning and teaching: The experience in higher education.* London: Society for Research into Higher Education, Ltd.
Purdue University Library. Comprehensive online research education (CORE). Retrieved April 3, 2003, from http://core.lib.purdue.edu/
Purkiss, R. (2002). Reflective practice. *Pharmacy Management, 18*(1), 8-10.
Qualifications, & Curriculum Authority (1998). *The grammar papers.* London: Author.
Qualifications, & Curriculum Authority (1999). *Not whether but how.* London: Author.
Quintilian (1961). *Institutio Oratoria* (with an English Translation by H. E. Butler), Cambridge, MA: Harvard University Press.
Rabinowitz, P. (1987). *Before reading. Narrative conventions and the politics of interpretation.* Ithaca and London: Cornell University Press.
Raedts, M. (2002, July). *The role of self-efficacy beliefs and task knowledge in writing.* Paper presented at the 8th International Conference of the European Association for Research on learning and Instruction Writing SIG (Staffordshire University, Stafford, UK, 10-13 July).
Rametti, F. (1993). *Punto per punto: Evoluzione dell'uso della punteggiatura nei bambini de scueola elementare* [Point to point: Evolution in the use of punctuation in primary school children]. Unpublished doctoral dissertation. Università degli Studi La Sapienza, Faculty of Psychology, Rome.
Ramonet, I. (1995, January). El pensamiento único. *Le Monde Diplomatique, January 1995* (Spanish edition).
Reid, B. (2000). The role of the mentor to aid reflective practice. Burns, & Bulman (Eds.), *Reflective Practice in Nursing* (2nd Edition). Blackwell, Oxford.
Reid, I. (2002). Wordsworth Institutionalized: The Shaping of an Educational Ideology. *History of Education, 31*, 15-37.
Reid, I. (2003). The Persistent Pedagogy of 'Growth'. In B. Doecke, D. Homer, & H. Nixon (Eds.). *English teachers at work: Narratives, counter narratives and arguments* (pp.97-108). Adelaide: Wakefield Press.
Reigeluth, C. M. (Ed.). (1999). *Instructional-design theories and models. Vol. II: A new paradigm of instructional theory* (pp. 633-651). Mahwah, N.J: Lawrence Erlbaum.
Remond M., & Quet F. (1999). Apprendre à comprendre l'écrit. Psycholinguistique et métacognition: l'exemple du CM2 [Learning to understand writing. Psycholinguistic and metacognition: example in classroom of 10-11 years old pupils]. *Repères, 19,* 203-225.
Renshaw, P. (1998). Sociocultural pedagogy for new times: Reframing key concepts. *Australian Educational Researcher, 25*(3), 83-99.
Richards, C. (Ed.). (1982). *New directions in primary education.* Lewes: Falmer Press.
Richards, J. C., & Lockhart, C. (1996). *Reflecting teaching in second language classroom.* Cambridge: Cambridge University Press.
Richards, J. C., & Rodgers, T. S. (2001). *Approaches and methods in language teaching* (2nd ed.). Cambridge: Cambridge University Press.

Rieben, L., & Saada-Robert, M. (1997). Relations between word-search strategies and word-copying strategies in children aged 5 to 6 years old. In. C. A. Perfetti, L. Rieben, & M. Fayol (Eds.), *Learning to spell* (pp. 295-319). Mahwah, NJ: Erlbaum.

Rijlaarsdam (1993, April). *Learning, whose learning? Autonomous learning in language education.* Paper 5th Int. Convention on Language and Education. March 22-26 1993 Norwich: University of East Anglia.

Rijlaarsdam, G. (1986). *Effecten van leerlingenrespons op aspecten van stelvaardigheid.* [Effects of peer response on aspects of writing skills]. PhD thesis. Amsterdam: SCO.

Rijlaarsdam, G. (1987, March). *Effects of peer evaluation on writing performance, writing processes, and psychological variables.* Paper presented at the 38th Annual Meeting of the Conference on College Composition and Communication, Atlanta, USA. ED 284 288.

Rijlaarsdam, G. (Series Ed.), & L. Björk, G. Bräuer, L. Rienecker, & P. Stray Jörgensen (Vol. Eds.) (2003). *Studies in Writing: Vol 12. Teaching Academic Writing in European Higher Education.* Dordrecht: Kluwer Academic Publishers.

Rijlaarsdam, G. and team (2003, August). Studying processes in writing and reading literary fiction: outcomes for researchers, & learners. Keynote at 10th European conference for Research on Learning, & Instruction. In L. Mason, S. Andreuzza, B. Arfè, & L. Del Favero (Eds.), *Abstracts.* 10th European conference for Research on Learning, & Instruction (p. 188). Padua: CLEUP.

Rijlaarsdam, G., & Couzijn, M. (2000). Stimulating awareness of writing in the writing curriculum. In G. Rijlaarsdam & E. Espéret (Series Eds.), & A. Camps & M. Milian (Vol. Eds.), *Studies in writing: Vol 6. Metalinguistic activity in learning to write* (pp. 167-202). Amsterdam: Amsterdam University Press.

Rijlaarsdam, G., & Van den Bergh, H. (1996). The dynamics of composing: An agenda for research into an interactive compensatory model of writing: Many questions, some answers. In C. M. Levy, & Ransdell, S. (Eds.), *The science of writing: Theories, methods, individual differences, and application* (pp. 107-125). Mahwah, NJ: Erlbaum.

Rijlaarsdam, G., van den Bergh, H., & Breetvelt, I. (1993, August). *Metacognitive activities related to text quality in written composition processes.* Paper presented at the Fifth European conference for Research on Learning and Instruction, Aix-en-Provence, France.

Rijlaarsdam, G., van den Bergh, H., & Couzijn, M. (Eds.). (1996). *Studies in Writing. Volume 2: Effective teaching and learning of writing. Current Trends in research.* Amsterdam: Amsterdam University Press.

Rimmon-Kenan, S. (1983). *Narrative Fiction – Contemporary Poetics.* London: Methuen.

Ritchhart, R. (2001). From IQ to IC: A dispositional view of intelligence. *Roeper Review, 23*(3), 143-150.

Rivard, L. P. (1994). A review of writing to learn in science: Implications for practice and research. *Journal of Research in Science Teaching, 31*, 969–983.

Rivard, L. P., & Straw, S. B. (2000). The effect of talk and writing on learning science: an exploratory study. *Science Education, 84,* 566–593.

Rochex J-Y. (1995). *Le sens de l'expérience scolaire.* Paris: PUF.

Rodda, M., & Eleweke, C. J. (2000). Theories of literacy development in limited English proficiency deaf people: a review. *Deafness and Education International, 2*(2), 101-113.

Rodrigues, D, & Rodrigues, R. (1989). How word processing is changing our teaching: New technologies, new approaches, new challenges. *Computers and Composition, 7*(1), 13-25.

Rodriguez, H. (1999). The domain help system. Technical report TRITA-NA-P9912, CID-56, NADA.

Rogers, C. (1969). *Freedom to learn.* Columbus, OH: Merrill Publishing Company.

Rogers, C. R. (1951). *Client-centered therapy.* Chicago, Ill: Houghton Mifflin.

Rojo, R. (2001). Letramento escolar, oralidade e escrita em sala de aula: Diferentes modalidades ou gêneros do discurso? [Literacy in school, speaking and writing in the classroom: Different modalities or types of discourse]. In I. Signorini (Org.), *Investigando a relação oral/escrito e as teorias do letramento* (pp. 51-74). Campinas, SP: Mercado de Letras.

Romano, T. (2000). *Blending genre, altering style: Writing multi-genre papers.* Portsmouth, New Hampshire: Boynton/Cook.

Rosat M., Dolz J., & Schneuwly B. (1991). Et pourtant... ils révisent. Effets de deux séquence didactiques sur la réécriture de textes [And yet..., they review. Result of two didactic lessons about rewriting]. *Repères, 4,* 22-45.

Rosebery, A. S., Warren, B., & Conant, F. R. (1992). Appropriating scientific discourse: Findings from language minority classrooms. *Journal of Research in Science Teaching, 33,* 569–600.

Rouet, J.-F., & Levonen, J. J. (1996). Studying and learning with hypertext: Empirical studies and their implications. In J.-F. Rouet, J. J. Levonen, A. Dillon, & R. J. Spiro (Eds.), *Hypertext and cognition* (pp. 9-23). Mahwah, NJ: Lawrence Erlbaum.
Roulet, E. (1987). Complétude interactive et connecteurs reformulatifs [Interactive completion and reformulation connectors]. *Cahiers de linguistique française, 8,* 111-140.
Roulet, E., & et al. (1987). *L'articulation du discours en français contemporain* [The discourse articulation of modern French]. Peter Lang: Bern.
Roussey J-Y, & Piolat A. (1991). Stratégies experts de contrôle rédactionnel et définition du but [Expert control writing strategies and goal definition]. *Repère, 4,* 15-32.
Roussey, J.-Y., & Gombert, A. (1992). Ecriture en dyade d'un texte argumentatif par des enfants de huit ans. *Archives de psychologie, 60,* 297-315.
Roussey, J.-Y., Piolat, A., & Guercin, F. (1990). Revising strategies for different text types. *Language and Education, 4*(1), 51-65.
Rowell, P. A. (1997). Learning in school science: The promises and practices of writing. *Studies in Science Education, 30,* 19–56.
Rubin, D. L. (1988). Introduction: Four dimensions of social construction in written communication. In B. A. Rafoth, & D. L. Rubin (Eds.), *The social construction of written communication* (pp. 1-36). Norwood, NJ: Ablex.
Rumelhart, D. E. (1980). Schemata: The building blocks of cognition. In R. J Spiro, B. C. Bruce, & W. F. Brewer (Eds.), *Theoretical issues in reading comprehension* (pp. 33-58). Hillsdale, NJ: Lawrence Erlbaum.
Rumelhart, D. E., & Ortony, A. (1977). The representation of knowledge in memory. In R. C. Anderson, J. Rand, & W. E. Montague (Eds.), *Schooling and the acquisition of knowledge* (pp. 99-136). Hillsdale, NJ: Lawrence Erlbaum.
Russel, C. (1985). *Peer conferencing and writing revision: A study of relationships* (Service Bulletin No 48). Wisconsin: Council of Teachers of English.
Rymer, J. (1988). Scientific composing processes: How eminent scientists write journal articles. In D. A. Jolliffe (Ed.), *Advances in Writing Research: Volume 2.* Norwood: Ablex.
Saada-Robert, M., & Balslev, K. (2001). Emergent literacy in the classroom. In R. Nata (Ed.), *Progress in Education, vol. 4* (pp. 139-167). Huntington, N.Y.: Nova Science Publishers.
Saada-Robert, M., & Balslev, K. (sous presse). Au-delà d'une évidence pluridisciplinaire: Étude de la litéracie émergente en situation scolaire [Going beyond a generally aknowledged pluridisciplinar approach: Study of emergent literacy in school context]. In G. Chatelanat, C. Moro, & M. Saada-Robert (Eds.), *Science ou sciences de l'éducation. Sondages au cœur de la recherche.* Berne: Peter Lang.
Saada-Robert, M., & Favrel, J. (2000). Litéracie émergente en situation scolaire: Étude exploratoire de la logographie [Emergent literacy in school context: Exploratory study of logography]. In M. Almgrem, A. Barrena, M.-J. Ezeizabarrena, I. Idiazabal, & B. MacWhinney, *Research on child language acquisition* (pp. 232-249). Somerville, Mass.: Cascadilla Press.
Saada-Robert, M., & Hoefflin, G. (2000). Image et texte: Leur utilisation à l'école par des enfants de 4 ans [Picture and text: How are they used by 4 year-old children in school?]. *Archives de Psychologie, 68,* 83-98.
Salomon, G. (1983). The differential investment of mental effort in learning from different sources, *Educational Psychologist, 18,* 42-50.
Salomon, G., & D. N. Perkins (1989). Rocky roads to transfer: Rethinking mechanims of a neglected phenomenon. *Educational Psychologist, 24*(2), 113-142.
Salomon, G., Globerson, T., & Guterman, E. (1989). The computer as a zone of proximal development: Internalizing reading-related metacognitions from a reading partner. *Journal of Educational Psychology, 81*(4), 620-627.
Salomon, G., Perkins, D. N., & Globerson, T. (1991). Partners in cognition: Extending human intelligence with intelligent technologies. *Educational Researcher, 20*(3), 2-9.
Samway, K. (1993). This is hard, isn't it? Children evaluating writing. *TESOL Quarterly, 27*(2), 233-257.
Sander, P., Stevenson, K., King, M., & Coates, D. (2000). University students' expectations of teaching. *Studies in Higher Education, 25(3),* 309-323.
Sarig, G. (1994). From world structure to text structure. An educational-documentary film, Kibbutzim College of Education (In Hebrew).

Sarig, G. (1996). Academic literacy as ways of getting-to-know: What can be assessed. In M. Birenbaum, & F. J. R. C. Dochy (Eds.), *Alternatives in assessment of achievements, learning processes and prior knowledge* (pp.161-201). Boston/Dordrecht/London: Kluwer Academic Publishers.

Sarig, G. (1997). Going round the Reflection Cycle: Reflective Writing. In G. Sarig, *To write a thing: Writing-to-think* (pp. 97-139). Hed Artzi Publishing House (In Hebrew).

Sarig, G. (2000). *The spirit of things: Emergent academic literacy*. Yesod Publishing House, the Academic Library (In Hebrew).

Sarig, G. (2002, March). *Analyzing stream-of-consciousness style writing products to promote self-understanding*. Paper delivered at the WDHE annual Meeting. University of Leicester, March, 2002.

Sarig, G., & Folman, S. (1993). An integrative test of academic literacy: Theoretical and pragmatic rationale. *Education and its context: Kibbutzim College Annals, 15*, 125-144. (In Hebrew).

Sayers, P. (2002). Reflective Journals: Issues of Assessment, Relevance and Style. In Graal, M. (Ed.), *Changing contexts for teaching, & learning. Proceedings of the 8th Annual Writing Development In Higher Education Conference*, University of Leicester.

Scardamalia, M., & Bereiter, C. (1987). Knowledge telling and knowledge transforming in written composition. In S. Rosenberg (Ed.), *Advances in applied linguistics: Vol. 2. Reading, writing and language learning* (pp. 142-175). Cambridge, MA: Cambridge University Press.

Scardamalia, M., & Bereiter, C. (1991). Literate expertise. In K. A. Ericsson, & J. Smith (Eds.), *Toward a general theory of expertise* (pp. 172-194). Cambridge, MA: Cambridge University Press.

Scardamalia, M., Bereiter, C., & Fillion, B. (1981). *Writing for results: A source book of consequential composing activities*. Ontario: Ontario Institute for Studies in Education Press.

Scardamalia, M., Bereiter, C., & Goelman, H. (1982). The role of production factors in writing ability. In M. Nystrand (Ed.), *What writers know* (pp. 173-210). New York: Academic Press.

Schank, R. (1990/1998). *Tell me a story. Narrative and intelligence*. Evanston, Illinois: Northwestern University Press.

Scharnhorst, U. & Büchel, F. P. (1990). Cognitive and metacognitive components of learning: Search for the locus of retarded performance. *European Journal of Psychology of Education, 5*(2), 207-230.

Scheerens, J. (1992). *Effective Schooling: Research, theory and practice*. London: Cassell.

Schegloff, E. A. (1982). Discourse as an interacional achievement: some uses of uh huh and other things that come between sentences. In D. Tannen (Ed.): Analyzing discourse: Text and talk. Georgetown University Roundtable on Languages and Linguistics, 1981. Washington: Georgetown University Press, pp. 71-93.

Schneuwly, B. (1988). *Le langage écrit chez l'enfant: La production des textes informatifs et argumentatifs*. Neuchâtel: Delachaux et Niestlé.

Schneuwly, B., Rosat, M. C., & Dolz, J. (1989). Les organisateurs textuels dans quatre types de textes écrits. Etude chez des eleves de 10, 12 et 14 ans. *Langue Française, 81*, 52-69.

Schnotz, W., Picard, E. Henninger, M. (1994). The use of graphics and texts in contructing mental models. In W. Schnotz, & W. Kulhavy (Eds.). *Comprehension of Graphics* (pp. 185-206). Amsterdam: North-Holland.

Schoenfeld, A. H. (1998). Toward a Theory of Teaching-in-Context. http://www-gse.berkeley.edu/ Faculty/ aschoenfeld/TechInContext/teaching-in-context.html.

Schön, D. (1983). *The reflective practitioner*. New York: Basic Books.

Schoonen, R., van Gelderen, A., de Glopper, K., Hulstijn, J., Snellings, P., Simis, A., & Stevenson, M. (2002). Linguistic knowledge, metacognitive knowledge and retrieval speed in L1, L2 and EFL writing. In G. Rijlaarsdam (Series Ed.) & S. Ransdell, & M. L. Barbier (Vol. Eds.), *Studies in Writing: Vol. 11. New directions for research in L2 writing* (pp. 101-122). Dordrecht: Kluwer Academic Publishers.

Schraw, G. (1998). Promoting general metacognitive awareness. *Instructional Science, 26*, 113-125.

Schriver, K. A. (1989). Evaluating text quality: the continuum from text-focused to reader-focused methods. *IEEE Transactions on professional communication, 32*, 238-55.

Schriver, K. A. (1991). Plain language through protocol-aided revision. In E. R. Steinberg (Ed.). *Plain language: Principles and Practice*. Detroit, Michigan: Wayne State University Press.

Schriver, K. A. (1992). Teaching writers to anticipate readers' needs: A classroom-evaluated pedagogy. *Written Communication, 9*, 179–208.

Schriver, K. A. (1992). Teaching writers to anticipate readers' needs: A classroom-evaluated pedagogy. *Written Communication, 9*, 179-208.

Schrodinger, E. (1951). *Science and humanism: Physics in our time.* Cambridge, England: Cambridge University Press.
Schubauer-Leoni, M. L. (1986). Le contrat didactique: Un cadre interprétatif pour comprendre les savoirs manifestés par les élèves en mathématique. *European Journal of Psychology of Education, 1,* 139-153.
Schumacher, G., & Gradwohl, J. M. (1991). Conceptualizing and measuring knowledge change due to writing. *Research in the Teaching of English, 25,* 67-96.
Schunk, D. H. (1991). *Learning theories. An educational perspective.* New York: Merril-Macmillan.
Schunk, D. H., & Zimmerman, B. J. (Eds.). (1994). *Self-regulation of learning and performance: Issues and educational applications.* Hillsdale, NJ: Lawrence Erlbaum.
Schwartz, R. S., & Lederman, N. (2002). It's the nature of the beast: The influence of knowledge and Intentions on learning and teaching nature of Science. *Journal of Research in Science Teaching,* 29(4), 331-59.
Scollon, R. (1995). Plagiarism and ideology: Identity in intercultural discourse. *Language in Society, 24.*
Scouller, K. M. (1998). The influence of assessment methods on students' learning approaches: multiple choice question exam versus assignment essay. *Higher Education, 35,* 453-472.
Searle, J. R. (1969). *Speech Act. An essay in the philosophy of language.* London: Cambridge University Press.
Searle, J. R. (1979). *Expression and meaning. Studies in the theory of speech acts.* Cambridge: Cambridge University Press.
Seels, B., & Glasgow, Z. (1998). *Making instructional design decisions* (2nd ed.). Columbus: Prentice Hall.
Sefton-Green, J. (2000). Beyond school: Futures for English and media education. *English in Austra-lia (127-128), 14-23.*
Sefton-Green, J., & Nixon, H. (2003). Can "English" cope? The challenges of popular culture, digital technologies and curriculum change. In B. Doecke, D. Homer, & H. Nixon (Eds.), *English teachers at work: Narratives, counter narratives and arguments* (pp.242-254). Adelaide: Wakefield Press.
Segev-Miller, R. (1989). *Linguistic processing in EFL study-summarizing.* Seminar Paper. The School of Education, The Hebrew University of Jerusalem, Jerusalem.
Segev-Miller, R. (1990). *Survey of ALT (Academic Literacy Test) assessment of college seniors.* Kibbutzim College of Education: Tel Aviv.
Segev-Miller, R. (1991). *A proposal for a 3-year Hebrew (L1) writing instruction program.* The Committee for the Improvement of Academic Literacy. Kibbutzim College of Education: Tel Aviv.
Segev-Miller, R. (1992). *A proposal for an EFL (L2) reading instruction program.* The Committee for the Improvement of Academic Literacy. Kibbutzim College of Education, Tel Aviv.
Segev-Miller, R. (1994). Replanning the EFL reading course: A theoretical rationale. *ISRATESOL Newsletter, 10,* 3-6.
Segev-Miller, R. (1995). A model of EFL academic reading assessment. *ISRATESOL Newsletter, 12,* 15.
Segev-Miller, R. (1997). *Cognitive processes in discourse synthesis.* Unpublished doctoral dissertation. The Hebrew University of Jerusalem, Jerusalem.
Segev-Miller, R. (2000, February). *Retrospective and on-line verbal reporting as instruments of research into reading and writing processes.* The Annual Conference of UTELI: The organization of University Teachers of the English Language in Israel (University of Haifa, Haifa, Israel, February 1).
Segev-Miller, R. (2002a, July). *Writing from sources: The effect of explicit instruction on college students' processes and products.* Paper presented at the 8th International conference of the European Association for Research on Learning and Instruction, Writing SIG (Staffordshire University, Stafford, UK, July 10-13).
Segev-Miller, R. (2002b, October). *The effect of explicit instruction on college English majors' writing from sources: Processes and products.* Paper presented at the Annual Conference of The Israeli Educational Research Association (Bar-Ilan University, Ramat Gan, Israel, October 2-3).
Segev-Miller, R. (in progress). *The long-term effects of explicit instruction of intertextual processing strategies: A follow up.*
Selfe, C. (1992). Preparing English teachers for the virtual age: The case for technology critics. In G. E. Hawisher, & P. LeBlanc (Eds.), *Re-imagining computers and composition: Teaching and research in the virtual age* (pp. 24-42). Portsmouth, NH: Boynton-Cook.

Selman, R. L. (1980). *The growth of interpersonal understanding: Developmental and clinical analyses.* New York: Academic Press.

Settlage, J. (2000). Understanding the learning cycle: Influence on abilities to embrace the approach by preservice elementary school teachers. *Science Education, 84,* 43-50.

Severinson Eklundh, K. (1992). Problems in achieving a global perspective on the text in computer based writing. *Instructional Science, 21,* 73-84.

Severinson Eklundh, K., & Kollberg, P. (1995). Computer tools for tracing the writing process: from keystroke records to S-notation. In G. Rijlaarsdam, H. van den Bergh & M. Couzijn (Eds.), *Studies in writing: Vol. 1. Theories, models and methodology in writing research* (pp. 526-541). Amsterdam University Press, Amsterdam.

Severinson Eklundh, K., & Kollberg, P. (1996). A computer tool and framework for analysing on-line revisions. In C. M. Levy, & S. Randsdell (Eds.), *The Science of writing* (pp. 163–188). Mahwah, NJ: Lawrence Erlbaum.

Seymour, P. H. (1997). Foundations of orthographic development. In. C. A. Perfetti, L. Rieben, & M. Fayol (Eds.), *Learning to spell* (pp. 319-339). Mahwah, NJ: Lawrence Erlbaum.

Shah, P., Mayer, R., & Hegarty, M. (1999). Graphs as aids to knowledge construction: signaling techniques for guiding the process of graph comprehension. *Journal of Educational Psychology, 4,* 690-702.

Shanahan, T., & R. G. Lomax (1986). An analysis and comparison of theoretical models of the reading-writing relationship. *Journal of Educational Psychology, 178,* 116-123.

Sharples, M. (1999). *How we write: Writing as creative design.* London and New York: Routledge.

Sheerin, Y., & Barnes, D. (1991). School writing. Buckingham: Open University Press.

Sheridan, J. (1995). An overview and some observations. In J. Sheridan (Ed.). *Writing-across-the-curriculum and the academic library. A guide for librarians, instructors, and writing program directors* (pp. 3-22). Westport, CT: Greenwood Press.

Sherman, J. (1992). Your own thoughts in your own words. *ELT Journal, 46,* 190-198.

Shimron, Y. (1993). Promoting literacy – the contribution of Dina Feitelson. *Maagaley Kriyah, 2*(2), 5-9 (in Hebrew).

Shimron, Y. (1996). Personal Communication.

Shor, I., & Freire P. (1990/1987). *A Pedagogy for Liberation.* Tel Aviv: Mifras. (Translated into Hebrew by N. Goober).

Siegel, H. (1988). *Educating reason: Rationality, critical thinking, and education.* NY: Routledge.

Siegel, M., & Carey, R. F. (1989). *Critical thinking: A semiotic perspective.* Monographs on Teaching Critical Thinking No. 1. ERIC: ED 30 3802.

Siegel, S., & Castellan, N. J. (1989). *Nonparametric statistics for the behavioral sciences.* New York: McGraw-Hill.

Silliman, E. R., Jimerson, T. L., & Wilkinson, L. C. (2000). A dynamic systems approach to writing assessment in students with language learning problems. *Topics in Language Disorders, 20*(4), 45-64.

Silver, J. W. (1999). A survey on the use of writing-to-learn in mathematics classes. *The Mathematics Teacher, 92*(5), 388-389.

Silverstein, S. (1981). Deaf Donald. In: *A light in the attic* (p. 143). NY: Harper, & Row Publishers, Inc. Hebrew Translation (1993) by B. & S. Hendel. Sifrey Aliyat Gag: Yedi'ot Aharonot, & Sifrey Hemed.

Simone, R. (1996). Reflections on the comma. In C. Pontecorvo, M. Orsolini, B. Burge & L. B. Resnick (Eds.), *Children's early text construction.* Mahwah, NJ: Lawrence Erlbaum.

Sinclair-de Zwart, H. (1972). A possible theory of language acquisition within the general framework of Piaget's developmental theory. In P. Adams (Ed.), *Language in thinking. Selected readings* (pp. 364-373). Middlesex: Penguin Education. Reprinted, 1973.

Skon, L., Johnson, D. W., & Johnson, R. T. (1981). Cooperative peer interaction versus individual competition and individualistic efforts: Effects on the acquisition of cognitive reasoning strategies. *Journal of Educational Psychology, 73*(1), 83-92.

Slamecka, N., & Graf, P. (1978). The generation effect: delineation of a phenomenon. *Journal of Experimental Psychology: Human, Learning and Memory, 6,* 592-604.

Sloate, P. L., & Voyat, G. (1983). Language and imitation in development. *Journal of Psycholinguistic Research, 12*(2), 199-222.

Slobin, D. (1996). From thought and language to thinking for speaking. In J. J. Gumperez, & S. C. Levinson (Eds.), *Rethinking linguistic relativity*. Cambridge: Cambridge University Press.

Smith, J. (2001). Modeling the social construction of knowledge in ELT teacher education. *ELT Journal, 55*(3), 221-27.

Smith, M. C., & Stahl, N. A. (1993). The use of the reading diary for obtaining reading behavior data among adults. In J. L. Johns (Ed.), *Literacy: Celebration and challenge*. Illinois Reading Council. Silver Anniversay Monographs (#ED 362844).

Smith, P. L., & Ragan, T. J. (1999). *Instructional design* (2nded.). New York: Wiley.

Smyth, G. (2000). *'I feel this challenge but I don't have the background'*: Teacher's responses to their bilingual pupils in 6 Scottish primary schools: An ethnographic study. Unpublished doctoral dissertation, Open University.

Smyth, G. (2003). *Helping bilingual pupils to access the curriculum*. London, David Fulton

Snoeck Henkemans, A. F. (1992). *Analysing complex argumentation: The reconstruction of multiple and coordinatively compound argumentation in a critical discussion*. Amsterdam: Sic Sat.

Snowman, J. (1986). Learning tactics and strategies. In G. D. Phye, & T. Andre (Eds.), *Cognitive classroom learning: Understanding, thinking and problem solving* (pp. 243-275). Orlando, FL: Academic Press.

Snyder, S. (1986). The literacy-logic debate: Towards a clarification from a peircean perspective on logic. Unpublished Doctoral thesis. Indiana University.

Soares, M. (1998). *Letramento. Um tema em três gêneros* [Literacy. One theme, three genres]. Belo Horizonte: Autêntica Editora. 2.ª edição, 4.ª reimpressão, 2001.

Sonnenschein, S., & Whitehurst, G. J. (1983). Training referential communication skills: The limits of success. *Journal of Experimental Child Psychology, 35*, 426-36.

Sonnenschein, S., & Whitehurst, G. J. (1984). Developing referential communication: A hierarchy of skills. *Child Development, 55*, 1936-1945.

Sperber, D., & Wilson, D. (1986). *Relevance: Communication and cognition*. Oxford: Blackwell.

Sperling, M. (1996). Revising the writing-speaking connection: Challenges for research on writing and writing instruction. *Review of Educational Research, 66* (1), pp. 53-86.

Spires, H. A., Huntley, L. E., & Huffman, L. E. (1993). Developing a critical stance toward text through reading and writing. *Journal of Reading, 37*, 114-122.

Spitzer, K. L., Eisenberg, M. B., & Lowe, C. A. (1998). *Information literacy: Essential skills for the information age*. Syracuse, New York: ERIC Clearinghouse.

Spivey, N. N. (1997). *The constructivist metaphor: Reading, writing, and the making of meaning*. San Diego, CA: Academic Press.

Sprenger-Charolles, L., & Casalis, S. (1996). *Lecture et Ecriture: Acquisition et troubles du développement* [Reading and Writing: Acquisition and developmental disturbances]. Paris: Presses Universitaire de France.

Sprenger-Charolles, L., Siegel, L., & Béchennec, D. (1997). L'acquisition de la lecture et de l'écriture en français: Étude longitudinale [Acquisition of Reading and Writing in French: A longitudinal study]. In. C. A. Perfetti, L. Rieben, & M. Fayol (Eds.), *Learning to spell* (pp. 339-360). Mahwah, NJ: Lawrence Erlbaum.

Stahl, E. (2001). *Hyper-Text-Schreiben: Die Auswirkungen verschiedener Instruktionen auf Lernprozesse beim Schreiben von Hypertext* [Hyper–Text-Writing: Effects of different instructions on learning processes during the writing of hypertext]. Münster: Waxmann.

State University of New York at Albany (SUNY) (2002). *User education homepage*. Retrieved April 3, 2003, from http://library.albany.edu/usered/.

Statistix (1989). *Version 3.1. NH Analytical Software*. P0 Box, 13204, St. Paul, MN 55113.

Stehney, A. K. (1990). A writing program and its lessons for mathematicians. In A. Sterrett (Ed.), *Using writing to teach mathematics* (pp. 26–29). Washington, DC: Mathematical Association of America.

Stein, N., & Bernas, R. (1999). The early emergence of argumentative knowledge and skill. In G. Rijlaarsdam & E. Espéret (Series Eds.), & J. Andriessen & P. Coirier (Vol. Eds.), *Studies in Writing: Vol. 5. Foundations of argumentative text processing* (pp. 97-116). Amsterdam: Amsterdam University Press.

Stern, C. M. (2002). Assessing entry-level digital information literacy of in-coming college freshmen. *Dissertation Abstracts International, 63*, no. 05A (2002): p. 1746.

Sternglass, M. (1988). *The presence of thought: Introspective accounts of reading and writing*. Advances in Discourse Processes (Vol. 34). Norwood, NJ: Ablex.

Stevenson. M., & Schoonen, R. (July, 2002). *Writing processes in a third language*. Paper presented at Writing 02, Stafford, UK.
Stoddart, T., Pinal, A., Latzke, M. & Canaday, D. (2002). Integrating Inquiry Science and Language Development for English Language Learners. *Journal of Research in Science Teaching, 39*(8), 664–687.
Stodolsky, S. (1984). Frameworks for studying instructional processes in peer work-groups. In P. Peterson, L. Wilkinson, & M. Hallinan (Eds.), *The social context of instruction: Group organization and group processes* (pp. 107-124). Orlando: Academic press.
Stotsky, S. (1986). On learning to write about ideas. *College Composition and Communication, 37*(3), 276-293.
Strauss, A. T., & Corbin, J. (1990). *Basics of qualitative research: Grounded theory procedures and techniques*. Newbury Park, CA: Sage.
Street, B. (1995). *Social literacies: Critical approaches to literacy in development, ethnography and education*. London: Longman.
Street, B. (Ed.). (2001). *Literacy and development: Ethnographic perspectives*. London: Routledge.
Styles, M. (1989). *Collaboration and writing*. Milton Keynes: Open University Press.
Sullivan, K. P. H., & Lindgren, E. (2002). Self-assessment in autonomous computer aided L2 writing. *ELT Journal, 56(3)*, 258-266.
Sullivan, K. P. H., Kollberg, P., & Pålson, E. (1998). Trace-it – a computer tool with application to the second language classroom. *BABEL: Journal of the Australian Federation of Modern Language Teachers Associations Inc, 33*(1), 22-28.
Sutton, C. (1992). *Words, science and learning*. Buckingham, UK: Open University Press.
Sutton, C. (1995). Quelques questions sur l'écriture et la science: une vue personnelle d'outre-manche [Some issues on writing and science: a personal view from beyond the Manche]. *Repères, 12*, 37-52.
Swartzendruber-Putnam, D. (2000). Written reflection: Creating better thinkers, better writers. *English Journal, 90*, 88-93.
Sweller, J. (1988). Cognitive load during problem solving: effects of learning. *Cognitive Science, 12*, 257-285.
Sylva, T., & Kapper, J. L. (2001a). Bibliography of recent scholarship in second language writing. *Journal of Second Language Writing, 10* (3), 213-223.
Sylva, T., & Kapper, J. L. (2001b). Selected bibliography of recent scholarship in second language writing. *Journal of Second Language Writing, 10* (4), 305-313.
Sylva, T., & Kapper, J. L. (2002). Selected bibliography of recent scholarship in second language writing. *Journal of Second Language Writing, 11* (2), 161-171.
Szcypula, J., Tschang, F. T., & Vikas, O. (2001). Reforming the educational knowledge base: Course content and skills in the Internet age. In F. T. Tschange, & T. Della Senta (Eds.), *Access to knowledge: New information technologies and the emergence of the virtual university* (pp. 93-128). New York: United Nations University/ Institute of Advanced Studies.
Taba, H. (1966). *Teaching strategies and cognitive functioning in elementary school children*. San Francisco, CA: San Francisco State University.
Taba, H., & Noel, E. (1957). *Action research: A case study*. Washington, DC: Association for Supervision and Curriculum Development.
Taylor, C. E., & Drury, H. (1996). Teaching writing skills in the science curriculum. *Research and Development in Higher Education, 19,* 160-164.
Taylor, D. S., & Wright, P. L. (1988). *Developing interpersonal skills through tutored practice*. Prentice Hall, London.
Teale, W. (1984). Toward a theory of how children learn to read and write naturally. *Language Arts, 59*, 555-570.
Teese, R. (2000). *Academic success and social power: Examinations and inequality*. Melbourne: Melbourne University Press.
Tergan, S.-O. (1997). Misleading theoretical assumptions in hypertext/hypermedia research. *Journal of Educational Multimedia and Hypermedia, 6*, 257-283.
Thacker, P. R. (1990). Effects of text organization on reading in ninth-grade good and poor readers and writers. (Doctoral dissertation, Harvard University, 1990). *Dissertation Abstracts International, 51* (6), DA9032467.

Thacker, P. R. (1991). *Text organization in reading: What ninth grade good and poor readers and writers know.* Washington, D.C.: Office of Educational Research and Improvement. (ERIC Document Reproduction Service No. ED 347 501).

The Ministry of Education and Science (1994). *Läroplan för gymnasieskolan* [The Swedish National Curriculum]. Stockholm: Utbildningsdepartementet.

Thomson, J. (1987). *Understanding teenagers reading: Reading processes and the teaching of literature.* North Ryde: Methuen Australia.

Thorndike, E. L., & Woodworth, R. S. (1901). The influence of improvement in one mental function upon the efficiency of other functions. *Psychological Review, 8,* 247-261.

Thorndyke, P. W., & Hayes-Roth, B. (1979). The use of schemata in the acquisition of knowledge. *Cognitive Psychology, 11,* 82-106.

Tierney, R. J., & Shanahan, T. (1996). Research on the reading-writing relationship: interactions, transactions, and outcomes. In R. Barr, M. L. Kamil, P. Mosenthal, & P. D. Pearson (Eds.), *Handbook of reading research, Vol. 2* (2nd ed., pp. 246-309). New York: Longman.

Tierney, R. J., Soter, A., O'Flahavan, J. F., & McGinley, W. (1989). The effects of reading and writing upon thinking critically. *Reading Research Quarterly, 24,* 134-173.

Tishman, S. (1994). What makes a good thinker: A look at thinking dispositions. *Harvard Graduate School of Education Alumni Bulletin, 39*(1), 7-9.

Tishman, S., Perkins, D. N., & Jay, E. (1995). *The thinking classroom: Learning and teaching in a culture of thinking.* Needham Heights: Allyn and Bacon.

Tjukovskij, K. (1976). *Från två till fem år. Om barns språk, dikt och fantasi* [From two to five. About children's language, poetry and fantasy]. Stockholm: Gidlund.

Tolchinsky, L., & Simó, R. (2001). *Escribir y leer a través del curriculum.* Barcelona. ICE Universitat de Barcelona/Horsori.

Tomlinson, D. (1994). Errors in the research into the effectiveness of grammar teaching. *English in Education, 28*(1), 20-26.

Torrance, M. (1996). Is writing expertise like other kinds of expertise?. In G. Rijlaarsdam, H. Van den Bergh,, & M. Couzijn (Eds.), *Studies in writing: Vol. 1. Theories, models and methodology in writing research* (pp. 3-9). Amsterdam: Amsterdam University Press.

Torrance, N., & Olson, D. R. (1985). Oral and literate competencies in the early school years. In D. R. Olson, N. Torrance and A. Hildyard (Eds.), *Literacy, language and learning: The nature and consequences of reading and writing.* Cambridge, UK: Cambridge University Press.

Toulmin, S. E. (1958). *The uses of argument.* Cambridge: Cambridge University Press.

Toulmin, S. E. (1969). *The uses of argument.* 2nd ed. Cambridge: Cambridge University Press.

Trigwell, K., Prosser, M., & Waterhouse, F. (1999). Relations between teachers' approach to teaching and students' approaches to learning. *Higher Education, 37,* 57-70.

Truscott, J. (1998). Noticing in second language acquisition: a critical review. *Second Language Research, 14*(2), 103-135.

Tsang, W. K., Wong, M., & Yuen, H. K. (2000). Feedback to writing: Focusing on grammar, or content, or both. In C. S. Li, A. Lin, & W. K. Tsang (Eds.), *Language and education in postcolonial Hong Kong* (pp. 317-332). Hong Kong: Linguistic Society of Hong Kong.

Tulving, E., & Bower, G. (1974). The logic of memory representations. In G. Bower (Eds.), *The psychology of learning and motivation* (pp. 265-301). New York: Academic Press.

Turner, A. V., & Dipinto, V. M. (1992). Students as hypermedia authors: Themes emerging from a qualitative study. *Journal of Research on Computing in Education, 25,* 187-198.

Turner, V. (2000). Deaf children and literacy: Identifying appropriate tools and learning environment. *Deaf Worlds, 16*(1), 17-25.

Turner-Bisset, R. (1999). The knowledge bases of the expert teacher. *British Educational Research Journal, 25*(1), 39-55.

Tyner, K. (1998). *Literacy in a digital world: Teaching and learning in the age of information.* Mahwah, NJ: Lawrence Erlbaum.

Tynjälä, P. (1998a.). Writing as a tool for constructive learning: Students' learning experiences during an experiment. *Higher Education, 36,* 209-230.

Tynjälä, P. (1998b). Traditional studying for examination versus constructivist learning tasks: do learning outcomes differ? *Studies in Higher Education, 23,* 173-189.

Tynjälä, P. (1999). Towards expert knowledge? A comparison between a constructivist and a traditional learning environment in the university. *International Journal of Educational Research, 31,* 355-442.

Tynjälä, P. (2001). Writing, learning, and the development of expertise in higher education. In G. Rijlaarsdam (Series Ed.) & P. Tynjälä, L. Mason, & K. Lonka (Vol. Eds.), *Studies in writing: Vol. 7. Writing as a learning tool* (pp. 37-56). Dordrecht: Kluwer Academic Publishers.

Tynjälä, P. (2001, April). *Writing as a learning tool*. Paper presented at the Annual Meeting of the American Educational Research Association (Seattle, WA, April 10-14).

University of California at Berkeley. (2001, December). *Instruction and tutorials*. Retrieved April 3, 2003, from http://www.lib.berkeley.edu/TeachingLib/Guides/rguides.html

University of Washington (2003). *Information Literacy Learning*. Retrieved April 15, 2003 from http://www.lib.washington.edu/uwill/tutorial.html.

Urbano, H. (1999). Variedades de planejamento no texto falado e no escrito [Types of planning in spoken and written texts]. In D. Preti (Org.), *Estudos de língua falada. Variações e confrontos* (pp. 131-151). São Paulo: Humanitas Publicações-FFLCH/USP (Projetos Paralelos-NURC/SP (Núcleo USP), 3). 2.ª edição.

Vacca, R. T., & Linek, W. M. (1992). Writing to learn. In J. W. Irwin, & M. A. Doyle (Eds.), *Reading/Writing connections: Learning from research* (pp. 145-159). Newark, DL: IRA.

Valencia, S. W., Hiebert, E. H., & Afflerbach, P. P. (1994). (Eds.). *Authentic reading assessment: Practices and possibilities*. Newark, DL: IRA.

Van den Akker, J., Branch, R., Gustafson, K., Nieveen, N., & Plomp, Tj. (Eds.) (1999). *Design approaches and tools in education and training* (pp. 125-136). Dordrecht: Kluwer Academic Publishers.

Van den Bergh, H. (1988). Onderzoek naar functionele doelstellingen voor het moedertaalonderwijs [Research on functional goals for education in mother tongue. Educational Studies]. *Pedagogische Studiën, 65*(4), 139-148.

Van den Bergh, H., & M. H. Eiting (1989). A method of estimating rater reliability, *Journal of Educational Measurement, 26*(1), 29-40.

Van den Broek, P., & Kremer, K (2000). The mind in action: What it jeans to comprehend during reading. In D. Taylor, D. Graves, & P. Van den Broek (Eds.), *Reading for meaning*. Columbia: Teachers College Press.

Van der Aalsvoort, M., & Van der Leeuw, B. (1982). *Leerlingentaal en school. De rol van taal in elke onderwijsleersituatie* [Pupil's language and school. The function of language in school education]. Enschede: VALO-Moedertaal.

Van der Geest, A. J. M. (1990). Schrijven beschreven? Psychometrie versus inhoudelijke analyse [Research on functional goals for education in mother tongue. Educational Studies]. *Tijdschrift voor Taalbeheersing, 12*(2), 120-131.

Van der Pool, E., & van Wijk, C. (1995). Proces en strategie in een psycho-linguïstisch model van schrijven en lezen [Process and strategy in a psycho-linguistic model of writing and reading]. *Tijdschrift voor Onderwijsresearch, 20*, 200-214.

Van Dijk, T. (1983). *La ciencia del texto*. Buenos Aires: Paidós

Van Eemeren, F. H., & Grootendorst, R. (1992). *Argumentation, communication, and fallacies. A pragma-dialectical perspective*. Hillsdale, NJ: Lawrence Erlbaum.

Van Eemeren, F. H., & R. Grootendorst (1984). *Speech acts in argumentative discussions. A theoretical model for the analysis of discussions directed towards solving conflicts of opinion*. Dordrecht: Foris Publications.

Van Eemeren, F. H., de Glopper, K., Grootendorst, R., & Oostdam, R. (1995). Identification of unexpressed premises and argumentation schemes by students in secondary school. *Argumentation and Advocacy, 31*(3), 151-162.

Van Eemeren, F. H., de Glopper, K., Grootendorst, R., & Oostdam, R. J. (1994). Student performance in identifying unexpressed premisses and argumentation schemes. In F. H. van Eemeren, & R. Grootendorst (Eds.), *Studies in Pragma-Dialectics* (pp. 89-103). Amsterdam: Sic Sat.

Van Eemeren, F. H., Grootendorst, & Kruiger, T., (1987). *Handbook of argumentation theory. A critical survey of classical backgrounds and modern studies*. Berlin/New York: Foris/De Gruyter.

Van Eemeren, F. H., Grootendorst, R., Jackson, S., & Jacobs, S. (1993). *Reconstructing argumentative discourse*. Tuscaloosa/London: the University of Alabama Press.

Van Eemeren., F. H., & Grootendorst, R. (1999a). Developments in argumentation theory. In G. Rijlaarsdam & E. Espéret (Series Eds.) & J. Andriessen & P. Coirier (Vol. Eds.), *Studies in Writing: Vol. 5. Foundations of Argumentative Text Processing* (pp. 43-57). Amsterdam: Amsterdam University Press.

References

Van Eemeren., F. H., & Grootendorst, R. (1999b). From analysis to presentation: A Pragma-dialectical Approach to Writing Argumentative Texts. In G. Rijlaarsdam & E. Espéret (Series Eds.) & J. Andriessen & P. Coirier (Vol. Eds.), *Studies in Writing: Vol. 5. Foundations of Argumentative Text Processing* (pp. 59-73). Amsterdam: Amsterdam University Press.

Van Gelderen, A., & Oostdam, R. (2004). Revision of form and meaning in learning to write comprehensible text. In G. Rijlaarsdam (Series Ed.) & L. Allal, L. Chanquoy, & P. Largy (Vol. Eds.), *Studies in Writing: Vol. 13. Revision: Cognitive and instructional processes*. Amsterdam: Kluwer Academic Press.

Van Hout-Wolters (1992). *Cognitieve strategieën als onderwijsdoel* [Cognitive strategies as a goal of education]. Inaugural address, University of Amsterdam. Groningen: Wolters-Noordhoff.

Van Kraayenoord C. E, & Schneider W. E. (1999). Reading achievement: Metacognition, reading self-concept and interest: a study of German students en grades 3 and 4. *European Journal of Psychology of Education, 14*, 305-324.

Van Waes, L. (1992). The influence of the computer on writing profiles. In H. Pander Maat, & M. Steehouder (Eds.), *Studies of functional text quality. Utrecht Studies in Language and Communication 1* (pp.173-186). Amsterdam: Rodopi Publishers.

Van Wijk, C. (1999). Conceptual process in argumentation: A developmental perspective. In G. Rijlaarsdam & E. Espéret (Series Eds.) & M. Torrance & D. Galbraith (Vol. Eds.). *Studies in writing: Vol 4. Knowing what to write. Conceptual proceses in text production*. Ámsterdam: Amsterdam University Press.

Van Wijk, C., & Sanders, T. (1999). Identifying writing strategies through text analysis. *Written Communication, 16*(1), 51-75.

Vanett, L., & Jurich, D. (1990). The missing link: Connecting journal writing to academic writing. In J. Peyton (Ed.), *Students and teachers writing together: Perspectives on journal writing* (pp. 23-33). Alexandria, VA: TESOL.

Vanmaele, L. (2002). *Leren schrijven van informatieve teksten. Een ontwerponderzoek bij beginners secundair onderwijs.* [Learning to write informative texts. A design experiment with novices secondary education]. Leuven: Universitaire Pers.

Vasudevan V., & Palmer M. (1999). *On Web annotations: Promises and pitfalls of current Web infrastructures*. Paper at the 32nd Hawaii international conference on system sciences.

Vérin, A. (1995). Mettre par écrit ses idées pour les faire évoluer en sciences [Putting one's own ideas in written words to let them make a step forward in sciences]. *Repères, 12*, 21-36.

Vermunt, J. (1995). Process-oriented instruction in learning and thinking strategies. *European Journal of Psychology of Education, 10*, 325-349.

Vermunt, J. D. H. M. (1992). *Leerstijlen en leerstrategieën in het Hoger Onderwijs*. [Doctoral dissertation]. Lisse: Swets & Zeitlinger.

Vermunt, J., & Lowyck, J. (2000). Leeractiviteiten en procesgericht onderwijs [Learning activities and process-oriented instruction]. In G. T. M. ten Dam, J. F. M. J. van Hout, C. Terlouw, & J. Willems (Eds.), *Onderwijskunde hoger onderwijs: handboek voor docenten* (pp. 30-55). Assen: Van Gorcum.

Vidal-Abarca, E., Gilabert, R., & Garcia Madruga, J. (1994). Idea-mapping techniques: Effects on recall, comprehension and learning. In F. de Jong, & B. van Hout-Wolters (Eds.), *Process-oriented instruction and learning from text* (pp. 51-65). *Amsterdam:* VU University Press.

Viskil, E. (1991). Argumentation and composition: Modelling argumentative writing. In F. H. van Eemeren, R. Grootendorst, J. A. Blair, & Ch. A. Willard (Eds.), *Proceedings of the second international conference on argumentation* (pp. 1135-1143). Amsterdam: Sic Sat.

Voss, J. F., Greene, T. R., Post, T. A., & Penner, P. C. (1983). Problem solving skill in the social sciences. In G. H. Bower (Ed.), *The psychology of learning and motivation: Advances in research theory, 17* (pp. 165-213). New York: Academic Press.

Voss, J. F., Wiley, J., & Sandak, R. (1999). Reasoning in the construction of argumentative texts. In G. Rijlaarsdam & E. Espéret (Series Eds.) & J. Andriessen & P. Coirier (Vol. Eds.), *Studies in Writing: Vol. 5. Foundations of argumentative text processing* (pp. 1-28). Amsterdam, Amsterdam University Press.

Vygotski L. (1985). *Pensée et langage* [Thought and language]. Paris: PUF.

Vygotsky L. S. (1978). *Mind in society: The development of higher psychological processes* (E. Hanfmann, & G. Vakar, Trans.). Cambridge, MA: Massachusetts Institute of Technology Press.

Vygotsky, L. (1962). *Thought and language* (E. Hanfmann, & G. Vakar, Trans.). Cambridge, MA: MIT Press.

Vygotsky, L. S. (1978). *Mind in society. The development of higher psychological processes* (Translated into English by M. Cole, V. John-Steiner, S. Scribner, & E. Souberman). Cambridge, MA: Harvard University Press.

Walshe, R. D. (1981). *Every child can write*! Rozelle: Primary English Teaching Association.

Wang, W., & Wen, Q. (2002). L1 use in the L2 composing process: An exploratory study of 16 Chinese EFL writers. *Journal of Second Language Writing, 11*, 235-246.

Wason, P. C. (1980). Specific thoughts on the writing process. In L. W. Gregg, & E. R. Steinberg (Eds.), *Cognitive processes in writing* (pp. 129-137). Hillsdale, NJ: Lawrence Erlbaum.

Weidenmann, B. (1994). Codes of instructional pictures. In W. Schnotz, & W. Kulhavy (Eds.), *Comprehension of graphics* (pp. 29-42). Amsterdam: North-Holland.

Wells, G. (1999). *Dialogic inquiry: Towards sociological practice and theory of education.* Cambridge: Cambridge University Press.

Welsh, T. M., Murphy, K. P., Duffy, T. M., & Goodrum, D. A. (1993). Accessing elaborations on core information in a hypermedia environment. *Educational Technology Research and Development, 41*(2), 19-34.

Wertheimer, M. (1945). *Productive Thinking.* New York: Harper.

Wertsch, J. V. (1991). *Voices of the mind: A sociocultural approach to mediated action.* Cambridge, Mass.: Harvard University Press.

Whalley, P. (1993). An alternative rhetoric for hypertext. In C. McKnight, A. Dillon, & J. Richardson (Eds.), *Hypertext: A psychological perspective* (pp. 7-17). New York: Ellis Horwood.

Whalley, P. C., & Fleming, R. W. (1975). An experiment with a simple recorder of reading behaviour. *Programmed Learning and Educational Technology, 12*, 120-123.

Widdowson, H. G. (1978). *Teaching language as communication.* Oxford: Oxford University Press.

Widener Library. (2001, July). *Checklist for an informational web page.* Retrieved April 3, 2003, from http://www.muse.widener.edu/Wolfgram-Memorial-Library/webevaluation/inform.htm

Wiles, S. (1985). Language and Learning in Multiethnic classrooms: strategies for supporting bilingual students. In Wells, G., & Nicholls, J. (Eds.), *Language and learning an interactional perspective*, (pp 83-93). Bristol: Falmer Press.

Wiley J., & Voss, J. F. (1996). The effects of playing historians on learning in history. *Applied Cognitive Psychology, 10*, 563-572.

Wilhelm, J. D. (1997). *'You Gotta BE the Book': Teaching engaged and reflective reading with adolescents.* New York: Teachers College Press.

Wilkinson, A. (1971). *The foundations of language.* Oxford: Oxford University Press.

Wilkinson, A., Barnsley, G., Hanna, P., & Swan, M. (1980). *Assessing language development.* Oxford: Oxford University Press.

Williams Mlynarszyk, R. (1998). *Conversations of the mind: The uses of journal writing for second language writers.* Mahwah, NJ: Lawrence Erlbaum.

Williams, J., & Colomb, J. (1993). The case for explicit teaching: Why what you don't know, won't help you. *Research in the Teaching of English, 27*, 252-264.

Willingham, D. B., Nissen, M. J., & Bullemer, P. (1989). On the development of procedural knowledge. *Journal of Experimental Psychology: Learning, Memory and Cognition, 15*, 1047-1060.

Willison, J. (1996). How R U integrating handson, writing, and reading for understanding in your students' science learning? *Australian Science Teachers Journal, 42*(4), 8-14.

Winn, B. (1987). Charts, graphs, and diagrams in educational materials. In D. Willows, & H. Houghton (Eds.), *The Psychology of illustration* (pp. 152-198). New York: Springer-Verlag.

Winn, W. (1994). Contributions of perceptual and cognitive processes to the comprehension of graphics. In W. Schnotz, & W. Kulhavy (Eds.), *Comprehension of graphics* (pp. 3-28). Amsterdam: North-Holland.

Witte, S. (1992). Context, text, intertext: Toward a constructionist semiotic of writing. *Written Communication, 9*, 237-308.

Witte, S. P. (1985). Revising, composing theory, and research design. In S. W. Freedman (Ed.), *The acquisition of written language: Response and revision* (pp. 250-284). Norwood, NJ: Ablex.

Witte, S. P. (1987). Pre-text and composing. *College Composition and Communication, 38*, 347-425.

Wixon, V., & Stone, P. (1977). Getting it out getting it down. *English Journal, 66*, 70-72.

Wolfe, J., (2002). Annotation technologies: A software and research review, *Computers and Composition, 19*(4), 471-497.

Wong B. Y. L. (1985). Metacognition and learning disabilities. In D. L. Forrest-Presley, G. E. Mac Kinnon, & T. G. Walker (Eds.), *Metacognition, cognition and human performance* (vol. 2, pp. 137-175). *INC, Orlando, FL. Academic Press.*

Wordsworth, W. (1950) Ode: Intimations of Immortality from Recollections of Early Childhood. In William Wordsworth: *Selected Poetry.* Ed. M. Van Doren. New York: The Modern Library.

Wray, D. & Lewis, M. (1993). Primary children's use of information books. *Reading, 26,* 19-24.

Wray, D. & Lewis, M. (1997). *Extending literacy: Children's reading and writing non-fiction.* London and New York: Routledge.

Wray, D. (1985). *Teaching information skills through project work.* Sevenoaks, Kent, UK: Hodder and Stoughton.

Wray, D., Medwell, J., Fox, R., & Poulson, L. (2000). The teaching practices of effective teachers of literacy. *Educational Review, 52*(1), 75-84.

Wright, P. (1993). To jump or not to jump: Strategy selection while reading electronic texts. In C. McKnight, A. Dillon, & J. Richardson (Eds.), *Hypertext: A psychological perspective* (pp. 137-152). New York: Ellis Horwood..

Wyse, D. (2001). Grammar for Writing? A critical review of empirical evidence. *British Journal of Educational Studies, 49*(4), 411-427.

Yagelski, R. P. (1995). The role of classroom context in the revision strategies of student writers. *Research in the Teaching of English, 29*(2), 216-238.

Yancey, K. B. (1992). *Portfolios in the classroom: An introduction.* Urbana, IL: NCTE.

Yando, R., Seitz, V., and Zigler, E. (1978). *Imitation: A developmental perspective.* Hillsdale, NJ: Lawrence Erlbaum.

Yoshinaga-Itano, C., & Downey, D. M. (1998). The effect of hearing loss on the development of metacognitive strategies in written language. *The Volta Review, 98*(1), 97-143.

Yussen S. R. (1985). The role of metacognition in contemporary theories of cognitive development. In D. L. Forrest-Presley, G. E. Mac Kinnon, & T. G. Walker (Eds.), *Metacognition, cognition and human performance.* (Vol.1, pp. 253-284. INC, Orlando, FL: Academic Press.

Zakh, Nathan. (1988). For Man is like The Tree of the Field. In: *For man is like the tree of the field: Poems, & songs* (p. 16). Tamuz Publishing House. (In Hebrew)

Zeidner, M., Boekaerts, M., & Pintrich, P. (2000). Self-regulation: Directions and challenges for future research. In M. Boekaerts, P. Pintrich, & M. Zeidner (Eds.), *Handbook of self-regulation* (pp. 750-768). San Diego, CA: Academic Press.

Zesiger, P., & de Partz, M.-P. (1994). Perturbations du langage écrit: Les dyslexies et les dysgraphies [Disturbances of written language: Dyslexia and dysgraphia]. In X. Seron, & M. Jeannerod (Eds.), *Neuropsychologie humaine* (pp. 419-423). Liège: Mardaga.

Zhu, W. (2001). Interaction and feedback in mixed peer response groups. *Journal of Second Language Writing, 10*(4), 251-276.

Ziehe, T. (1989). *Närhet och distans? i Kulturanalyser – ungdom, utbildning, modernitet* [Culture analysis – youth, education and modernity]. Stockholm/Stehag: Symposion.

Zimmerman, B. J. (2000). Attaining self-regulated learning: A socialcognitive perspective. In M. Boekaerts, P. Pintrich, & M. Zeidner (Eds.), *Handbook of self-regulation* (pp. 13-39). San Diego, CA: Academic Press.

Zimmerman, B. J., & Bandura, A. (1994). Impact of self-regulatory influences on writing course attainment. *American Educational Research Journal, 31*(4), 845-862.

Zimmerman, B. J., & Schunk, D. H. (1989). *Self-regulated learning and academic achievement: Theory, research and practice.* New York: Springer Verlag.

Zimmerman, B., & Bandura, A. (1994). Impact of self-regulatory influences on writing course attainment. *American Educational Research Journal, 31*(4), 845-862.

Zimmerman, B., & Martinez Pons, M. (1986). Development of a structured interview for assessing student use of self-regulated learning strategies. *American Educational Research Journal, 23*(4), 614-628.

AUTHOR INDEX

Abbott, G., 577
Abbott, V., 199
Ackerman, P. L., 533
Ackerman, J., 533, 534
Ackerman, J. M., 533, 534, 543, 590
Adam, J. M., 64, 326, 335
Adam, J-M., 325, 326
Adams, M. J., 48
Afflerbach, P., 535
Akamatsu, C. T., 152, 153
Akiguet, S., 326
Alamargot, D., 272, 303, 336, 428
Albertini, J., 151
Aldenderfer, M., 577
Alexander, P. A., 394
Alexander, R. J., 277, 280, 394
Algulin, I., 134
Allal, L., 77, 79, 80, 83, 89
Althusser, L., 129
Ambroise, C., 302
Amoni, M., 92
Anderson, G. L., 146
Anderson, J., 576
Anderson, J. R., 215, 225, 250, 258
Anderson, R. C., 395
Andriessen, J., 182, 324
Angèlil-Carter, S., 369
Anglin, G., 588
Anson, C., 535
Anula, J. J., 15, 91, 95
Applebee, A., 485, 494, 575, 584
Arbib, M., 107
Ashwell, T., 306
Askov, E. N., 445
Aspinwall, L., 499, 501
Atwell, N., 143
Aureli, E., 590
Auriac-Peyronnet, E., 8, 292, 295, 302, 363
Austin, J. L., 182, 210, 395
Ausubel, D. P., 412

Baker, L., 200, 539, 593
Bakhtin, M., 351, 352, 370, 371, 500
Ballantyne, R., 534
Ballard, S., 562
Balslev, K, ., 10, 17, 18, 20

Bamberg, M., 155
Bandura, A., 200, 245, 257, 541, 575, 576
Bang, M. G., 155, 462
Barell, J., 545
Barnes, D., 126, 130
Barthes, R., 351
Bartlett, E. J., 200, 212
Barton, D., 200, 483
Barton, J. H., 200, 483
Barton, S., 200, 483
Baudrillard, J., 356
Bazerman, C., 485
Beach, R., 534, 535, 576
Beausoleil, J.-R., 292, 295
Béchennec, D., 24
Béguelin, M. J., 48
Belcher, D, ., 306
Bellezza, F. S., 596
Bellotti, V., 108
Bennett, T., 124
Bentolila, A., 32
Bereiter, C., 63, 79, 80, 200, 242, 260, 284, 286, 303, 325, 331, 394, 396, 400, 427, 482, 483, 484, 494, 499, 501, 534, 540, 548, 549, 550
Berge, K. L., 135
Bergsten, S., 134
Berkenbosch, R., 429
Berkenkotter, C., 485, 494, 495
Berliner, D. C., 417
Bernas, R., 326
Bialystok, E., 152
Biggs, J. B., 562, 563, 564, 565
Bigum, C., 122, 130
Birenbaum, M., 543
Bizzell, P., 60
Björk, L., 11
Black, J. B., 199, 200
Black, K., 199, 200
Blank, M., 578
Blashfield, R., 577
Blohm, P. J., 534
Bochner, J. H., 395, 409
Boekaerts, M., 542
Boëthius, U., 134
Bonanno, H, ., 564
Borel, M. J., 64

Borgman, C. L., 445, 448
Bos, A., 398
Boscolo, P., 323, 469, 470
Bottomley, D. M., 145
Bouchard, R., 71, 72, 74
Bouffard-Bouchard, T., 383, 384
Boulton-Lewis, G. M., 534
Bower, G., 241, 242, 596, 597
Bower, G. H., 241, 242, 596, 597
Bowman, C. A., 534
Boyle, O., 306, 574
Boyle, O. F., 306, 574
Braaksma, M. A. H., 4, 185, 200, 243, 259, 260, 261
Braet, A., 215, 429
Brakel Olson, V. L., 400
Branch, R., 14
Brandt, D., 60
Brassart, D.-G., 64, 295, 325, 326, 334
Bräuer, G., 11
Braun, C., 80
Breetvelt, I., 80, 395
Bridgeman, B,., 542
Britton, B. K., 483
Britton, J., 6, 7, 130, 277, 395, 494, 534, 539
Brockbank, A., 521, 562
Bromme, R., 13, 547, 548, 549, 551, 556, 557
Bronckart, J.-P., 60, 81
Brossard, M., 293, 298
Brossell, G., 395
Brown, A., 314, 583, 596
Brown, A. L., 79, 397, 486, 539, 540
Brown, H. D., 306, 314, 316
Brown, J. S., 88, 396
Brownlee, J. M., 534
Bruffee, K., 81
Bruner, J., 92, 97, 171, 355, 385, 388, 483
Bryant, P., 19
Bucheton, D., 304
Buckingham, D., 124
Bühler, K., 395
Bunce, D. M., 483
Burgess, T., 534
Burtis, P. J., 79
Butler, D. L., 540
Butler, J., 485
Butterfield, E. C., 540

Cagliari, L. C., 33
Caillier, J., 294
Calfee, R. C., 417
Calkins, L. M., 143, 285
Callaghan, M., 276, 278, 287
Camagni, C., 181, 184, 187, 201
Campione, J., 486, 540
Campione, J. C., 486
Cantrell, R. J., 544

Caramazza, A., 19
Carey, L., 80
Carey, M. J., 500, 501
Carey, R. F., 500
Carlson, S. B., 542
Carney, R., 588
Carpenter, P., 588, 589, 596
Carruthers, M. J., 172
Casalis, S., 24
Caspi, M., 351, 353
Castellan, N. J., 402
Castiglia, D., 99, 100
Catach, N., 47, 83
Cauzinille-Marmèche, E., 383, 385
Cazden, C., 80, 99, 331
Cederlund, J., 262
Chaib, C., 132
Chall, J. S., 538
Chamot, A., 575, 582, 583
Champagne, A. B., 483
Chandler, P., 589
Chanquoy, L., 182, 259, 260, 272, 273, 303, 324, 336, 428
Chaopricha, S., 485
Cheung, M., 306
Christensen, C. A., 534, 544
Christensen, M., 534, 544
Clanchy, J., 445, 562
Clark, C. M., 63, 198
Clarke, J. H., 590
Clifford, J., 400
Clyne, M., 121
Coates, D., 562
Cohen, A. D., 11, 81, 545
Cohen, J., 81, 402, 405
Cohen, L., 306
Cohen-Rak, N., 31, 33, 40, 41, 43
Coirier, P., 182, 303, 324, 326
Collins, A., 88, 396
Colomb, J., 576
Coltier, D., 64
Combettes, B., 64
Commander, N. E., 544
Conche, M., 303
Connell, R. W., 129
Connor, B., 523
Conrad, K., 445
Cook, V., 152
Cook-Gumperz, J., 61
Cope, B., 287, 351, 352
Corbin, J., 537
Cordova, D., 489
Cornbleth, C. T., 500
Couzijn, M., 1, 6, 7, 10, 13, 16, 50, 185, 188, 209, 243, 259, 260, 261, 323, 396, 397, 400, 548
Cowan, J., 521, 523

Crahay, M., 80
Craik, F., 596
Creemers, B. P. M., 280
Crowhurst, M., 405
Crowley, S., 538
Crystal, D., 39, 45
Csizer, K., 316
Cuenca, M. J., 325
Culioli, A., 69
Culler, J., 350
Cumming, A., 153
Cummins, J., 464
Cunningham, D. J., 551
Czerniewska, P., 462

Dahl, R., 51, 389
Daniel, M.-F., 8, 292, 293, 295, 303
Dansereau, D., 590
Darling-Hammond, L., 417
Darras, F., 72
Dart, B. C., 534
David, J., 12, 72, 102, 128, 195, 196, 287, 372, 421, 422, 423, 424, 425, 488, 502, 505, 506, 507
Day, J., 385, 596
Day, J. D., 385, 540, 596
De Corte, E., 394, 397, 398
De Gaulmyn, M. M., 72
De Glopper, K., 215, 242, 398, 427, 430
De Jong, F. P. C. M., 258
De Jonge, H., 402
De Lemos, C. T. G., 33, 34
De Man, P., 362
de Partz, M.-P., 19
Dean, R. S., 589
Dearing, R., 278
Deegan, D. H., 537
Degenhart, R. E., 188
Delcambre, I., 72
Deloney, L. A., 500, 501
Deming, M. P., 534
Denzin, N. K., 146
Dewey, J., 7, 171, 178, 486, 500
Di Pardo, A., 543
DiCamilla, F., 543
Díez, C., 15, 91, 95, 103
Dillon, A., 548, 549, 550, 557, 559
DiPardo, A., 81
Dipinto, V. M., 551
Dixon, J., 130
Dochy, F. J. R. C., 543
Doecke, B., 9, 13, 14, 124, 129, 130
Doise, W., 80
Dolence, M., 446
Dolz, J., 81, 303, 304, 324, 325, 334, 382
Dornyei, Z., 316
Douglas, J. Y., 122, 125, 126, 128, 130, 418

Dourish, P., 108
Downey, D. M., 155, 534
Draper, R. J., 544
Dreyfus, H., 172
Dreyfus, S., 172
Drury, H., 13, 15
Duffy, T. M., 551, 557
Duguid, P., 88
Duncker, K., 183, 396
Durgunoglu, A. Y., 456
Dysthe, O., 533

Eco, U., 500
Ehri, L., 18, 19, 21, 24
Einstein, G. O., 596, 597
Eisenberg, M. B., 445
Eiting, M. H., 430, 431
Elbow, P., 81, 396
Eleweke, C. J., 152
Elshout, J. J., 242, 396
Emmelot, Y. W., 430
Englert, C. S., 470
Ennis, R. H., 482
Entwistle, N., 562, 563, 565
Epstein-Jannai, M., 349, 350, 352, 353, 356
Erixon, P.-O., 9, 131, 132
Espéret, E., 79, 80, 292

Fabre, C., 72
Faccione, P., 501
Faigley, L., 213, 266
Fairclough, N., 370
Farhat, J., 551
Favrel, J., 21
Fayol, M., 18, 79, 80, 82, 303, 382, 384
Feilke, H., 326, 394, 400
Fellows, N. J., 485
Ferreiro, E., 19, 21, 22, 25, 47, 48, 49, 56, 91
Ferris, D., 305, 306
Fijalkow, J., 293, 298
Fischl, D., 545
Fitz-Gibbon, C. T., 280
Flack, V. F., 405
Flanders, N. A., 99
Flavell, J. H., 77, 382, 539, 575
Fleming, R. W., 589
Florio, S., 63
Flower, L. S., 60, 63, 78, 79, 80, 105, 165, 200, 243, 259, 303, 382, 396, 427, 484, 534, 542, 543, 574
Folman, S., 535
Foltz, P. W., 550, 556
Fosnot, C. T., 501
Foucault, M., 351, 501
Fradd, S. H., 483
Francis-Pelton, L., 426
François, F., 303

Fraser, J., 155
Frausin, T., 185, 201, 204
Freedman, A., 61
Freedman, S. W., 63, 81
Freeley, A. J., 429
Freeman, J. B., 429
Freud, A., 171, 553
Frijda, N. H., 396
Frith, U., 18, 19, 20, 21, 24, 29
Frow, J., 124
Fulwiler, T., 534, 543, 544

Galbraith, D., 8, 200, 261, 274, 284, 396, 484, 494, 499, 502, 541
Gall, J. E., 550, 551, 584, 586
Gárate, M., 7, 8, 9, 10, 328
Garcia Madruga, J., 590
Garcia-Debanc, C., 64, 382
Garcia-Mila, M., 575
Gardner, H., 501
Garner, R., 540, 590
Gaskins, I. W., 483
Gass, S., 262
Gee, J. P., 124, 455, 456, 503
Geeman, H. G., 500, 501
Geist, U., 7, 9, 15, 120, 169
Genette, G., 360, 362
Gentilhomme, F., 64
Gerdes, H., 554
Gere, A. R., 63
Gérouit, C., 298
Gibbons, P., 461
Gibbs, G., 525
Gilabert, R., 590
Gilly, M., 78
Gilster, P., 446
Girolami, A., 35
Girolami-Boulinier, A., 31, 33, 34, 35, 36, 37, 40, 41, 42, 43, 44, 45
Glanz, J., 487
Glasgow, Z., 445, 458
Globerson, T., 77, 80
Glynn, S. M., 483, 486
Gold, E., 534
Golder, C., 292, 293, 296, 302, 326
Goleman, D., 528
Gombert, A., 19, 81, 295, 326, 334
Gombert, J. E., 19, 335, 382
Goodman, Y. M., 91
Goodrum, D. A., 557
Goodwin, Ch., 72
Gordon, C. J., 80
Gorman, T. P., 188
Grabe, W., 305, 306, 316, 317
Gradwohl, J. M., 533
Graf, P., 596
Graff, H. J., 445

Graham, S., 260, 272
Grainger, T., 310
Graves, D., 63, 126, 130
Graves, D. H., 143, 285, 462, 466
Gray, S. H., 551, 557
Green, B., 122, 130
Greene, S., 534, 535
Gregory, S., 152
Grésillon, A., 303
Griffin, P., 331
Grize, J. B., 64
Grootendorst, R., 182, 183, 248, 427, 428, 429, 430
Gruber, S., 418
Grugeon, E., 310
Gubern, M. M., 59, 198
Gülich, E., 72
Gunstone, R., 534
Gushrowski, B., 550
Gustafson, K., 14
Guterman, E., 77
Guthrie, J. T., 541
Gyselinck, V., 588

Haas, C., 264
Habermas, J., 131, 135
Hadot, P., 350
Hakuta, K., 152
Hall, N., 277
Halliday, M. A. K., 61, 395, 485
Halté, J.-F., 64
Hammond, N., 550
Hand, B., 288, 482, 483, 485, 486, 493, 495, 534, 590
Hannafin, M. J., 550, 551
Hare, V. C., 289, 394
Harpin, W., 277
Harris, K. R., 260, 272
Harris, L. D., 418
Hatch, G., 574
Hativa, N., 417
Hayes, J. R., 60, 63, 78, 79, 80, 105, 212, 243, 259, 303, 382, 396, 427, 484, 548, 550, 555, 559, 574
Hayes-Roth, B., 395
Head, A., 446
Healy, M., 171
Heath, S. B., 61, 62
Hedgcock, J. S., 305, 306
Hegarty, M., 588, 589, 596
Heisenberg, W., 483
Henk, W. A., 145
Henningsen, M., 588
Herman, R., 154
Herr, K., 146
Hertz-Lazarowitz, R., 13, 574, 577, 580
Hiebert, E. H., 535

Author Index

Higgins, L., 79, 535
Hildebrand, G. M., 483, 485
Hilgard, E. R., 241, 242
Hill, C. A., 534
Hillis, A. E., 19
Hillocks, G., 8, 210, 213, 214, 242, 284, 285, 394, 428
Hirtle, S. C., 550, 551
Hirvela, A., 306
Hoefflin, G., 21
Hofer, B., 482
Holliday, W. G., 483, 484, 493, 494
Holmes, S., 154
Holt-Reynolds, D., 417
Hoskisson, K., 575
Howard, V. A., 483
Howe, A., 310
Hoz, R., 545
Huang, S., 306
Huckin, T. N., 485, 494, 495
Huffman, L. E., 533
Hull, G., 63
Hunter, I., 129
Huntley, L. E., 533
Huot, B., 395
Hyde, T. S., 596
Hyland, F., 306
Hyland, K., 306

Indurkhya, B., 550
Instone, K., 551
Iser, W., 351
Ivani, R., 368, 372, 379

Jackson, S., 428, 429
Jacobs, S., 428, 429
Jacobson, M. J., 549, 551, 556
Jacques, F., 292
Jaffré, J. P., 19, 72
Jakobson, R., 45, 395
James, C., 51, 125, 126, 127, 128, 153, 155, 167, 276
Jandot, C., 302
Janssen, T., 440, 442
Jay, E., 486, 501
Jenkins, J. J., 596
Jimerson, T. L., 153
Johns, A. M., 534
Johns, J. L., 534
Johnson, B. D., 360, 446
Johnson, D. W., 80, 360
Johnson, H., 200, 360
Johnson, J., 310, 360
Johnson, M., 360, 551
Johnson, R. T., 80, 360
Johnston, P., 535, 578
Jones, J., 564

Jones, R., 596
Jordan, C. E., 144
Juranville, A., 350
Jurdak, M., 534
Jurich, D., 543
Just, M., 172, 235, 359, 373, 444, 452, 588, 589, 596

Kalantzis, M., 287, 351, 352
Kamawar, D., 47, 49
Kantz, M., 534
Kaplan, R. B., 305, 306, 316, 317, 372
Kapper, J. L., 306
Kaufman, A., 470
Kavanagh, J. F., 32
Kellogg, R. T., 243, 427, 548, 550
Kemmis, S., 309, 315
Kent-Drury, R., 418
Kern, R. G., 545
Keys, C. W., 482, 484, 485, 486, 488, 493, 561
Kiefer, K., 15, 418, 420
Kieft, M., 543
Kim, H., 550, 551
King, M., 342, 502, 507, 562
Kintsch, W., 555, 556, 588
Kirby, J., 590
Kirkland, M. R., 538
Kleiman, A. B., 32
Klein, P. D., 200, 484, 590
Klem, E., 418
Kluwe, R. H., 79
Knickerbocker, J. L., 534
Knuth, R. A., 551
Kobayashi, H., 153
Koch, G. G., 405
Koetsenruijter, W., 429
Köhler, T., 83
Kolb, D., 521, 525
Kollberg, P., 261, 262, 264, 266
Kotschi, Th., 71
Koutsoubou, M., 14, 16, 151, 154
Krashen, S., 152, 306, 307
Kraska, K., 242
Kremer, K., 473
Kress, G., 123, 368, 369, 370, 378, 379
Kristeva, J., 351, 370
Kruiger, T., 429
Kuhl, J., 242
Kuhn, D., 494, 575
Kulhavy, R. W., 589
Kupper, L., 583
Kyle, W. C., 495

Labov, W., 155
Lafortune, L., 303
Lakoff, G., 360, 551
Landis, D., 405, 541

Landis, J. R., 405, 541
Landow, G. P., 550, 557, 559
Langdon, M., 126
Langer, E., 486, 501, 584
Langer, J. A., 155, 485, 494, 535, 575, 590
Lantolf, J. P., 543
Lara, F., 15, 91
Larivée, S., 383
Lawrence, C., 482
Layman, J., 590
Lea, J., 336, 517, 563
Lea, M. R., 517, 562, 563, 571
LeCourt, D., 418
Lederman, N., 495
Lee, I., 306, 483
Lee, O., 306, 483
Leech, G. N., 169, 177
Lemke, J. L., 446
Lepper, M., 489
Lerner, D., 470
Levelt, W. J. M., 43
Leventhal, L. M., 551
Levin, J., 12, 14, 15, 481, 493, 551, 588
Levin, J. A., 12, 14, 15, 481, 493, 551, 588
Levonen, J. J., 550
Levy, C. M., 336
Lewensteing, M., 596
Lewis, D., 287
Lewis, M., 368, 369
Li, C. S., 102, 332
Lieberman, J. N., 355
Lightbown, P., 151, 152, 153
Lindgren, E., 6, 13, 259, 261, 262, 266
Linek, W. M., 482, 534
Linn, M., 590
Lipman, M., 291, 292, 303
Littlewood, W., 306, 315
Lo, A., 315, 538
Locke, D., 483
Lockhart, C., 309
Lockhart, R., 596
Lohman, D. F., 538
Lomax, R. G., 245
London, Y., 60, 61, 151, 277, 280, 367, 370, 508
Lowe, C. A., 445
Lowyck, J., 14, 16, 393, 394, 406
Lukinsky, J., 535
Lumbelli, L., 7, 8, 10, 50, 97, 181, 184, 185, 187, 197, 201, 203, 204

Mackey, A., 262
MacLachlan, G., 126
Maehr, M. L., 316
Mager, W., 398
Mahler, S., 545
Maingueneau, D., 69

Manion, L., 306
Mannoni, O., 350
Marcuschi, L. A., 32, 45
Marom, A., 13, 574, 577, 578, 580
Marshall, C., 106
Marshall, J., 590
Marshall, J. C., 142
Martin, J. R., 351, 352, 356, 485
Martin, N., 285, 534
Martinet, P, ., 295
Mason, J. M., 533
Mason, L., 323, 486, 533
Matsuhashi, A., 267
Maturana, H. R., 171
Maybury, B., 277
Mayer, C., 152, 153
Mayer, R., 588, 589, 596
Mayer, R. E., 250
McCarthy, L. P., 535
McClenaghan, D., 9, 13, 14, 15, 122, 124, 125, 128, 129, 130
McCormick, K., 534
McCrindle, A. R., 534, 544
McCutchen, D., 260, 261, 272, 394
McDaniel, M. A., 596, 597
McEnvoy, C., 596, 597
McGhie-Richmond, D. R., 417
McGill, I ., 521, 562
McGinley, W., 541
McGinley, W. J., 534
McIntosh, M. E., 544
McKnight, C., 550
McKnight, L., 129
McLeod, A., 534
McNeill, T., 107
McTaggart, R., 309, 315
Meichenbaum, D., 578
Melero, M. A., 7, 8, 9, 10, 328
Melnick, S. A., 145
Menez, M., 80
Mercer, M., 155
Mercer, N., 127
Meuffels, B., 213, 428
Mewborn, D. S., 426
Meyer, H. A., 316
Meyer, J.-C., 316
Milian, M., 6, 10, 14, 59, 72
Miller, C. R ., 485
Miller, L. D., 499, 501
Miller, P., 575
Miller, S., 575
Mlynarczyk, R., 543, 545
Montgomery, D. E., 575
Moon, J ., 521
Moore, P. J., 589
Moore, R., 493, 561, 562
Moran, C., 418

Moreno, R., 589
Moret, L., 215
Morino, H., 306
Morris, D., 171
Morris, J., 171
Mortimore, P., 277, 280
Mosconi, G., 183, 184
Mounty, J. L., 154
Moursund, D. G., 501
Mugny, G., 80
Murphy, K. P., 557
Murray, D., 462
Murray, D. M., 143
Muth, D., 486

Nachmias, R., 590
Nash, J. G., 486
Neiman, N., 575, 583
Nelson, D., 536, 596, 597
Nelson, G. D., 536, 540
Nelson, J., 535, 536
Nelson, N., 536, 590, 596
Neuwirth, C., 106, 107
Newell, A., 396
Newell, G., 534
Newman, D., 331
Newman, S. E., 396
Newmann, F. M., 501
Ng, E., 242
Nicol, D. J., 564
Nielsen, J., 550
Nieveen, N., 14
Nightingale, P., 563
Nihlen, A. S., 146
Nixon, H., 121
Noel, E., 487
Noonan, K., 152
Norman, D. A., 395
Norris, D. M., 446
Northfield, J., 534
Nosich, G., 445
Novack, J., 590
Nunan, D., 309
Nunberg, G., 48, 51
Nystrand, M., 60, 81
Nyström, C., 131, 132

Olaussen, B. S., 383, 384
Olbrechts-Tyteca, L., 182, 195, 429
Olson, D., 534
Olson, D. R., 47, 49, 51, 534
Olson, J. R., 51, 92, 534
Olson, V. B., 81, 534
Ong, W., 445
Oostdam, R. J., 11, 15, 254, 427, 428, 429, 430
Ormerod, F., 368, 372, 379
Ormrod, J. E., 316

Orsolini, M., 92
Ortony, A., 395
Ottaviani, M. G., 590
Overmaat, M., 405, 440, 442
Oxford, R., 276, 575, 576, 577, 582, 583

Packer, J., 534
Paivio, A., 588
Palinscar, M. S., 79
Pallascio, R., 293, 303
Palmer, M., 107, 144, 147
Palmquist, M., 15, 420
Pålson, E., 261
Pander Maat, H., 395, 409
Paoletti, G., 7, 10, 12, 15, 185, 197, 201, 204, 587, 590
Parent, S., 383
Paris, S. G., 383, 384, 539
Pasquier, A., 81, 303
Patterson, A., 129
Paul, P. V., 152, 163
Paul, R., 152, 163, 499
Pearson, P., 267
Pearson, P. D., 267
Peck, W., 534, 589
Peeck, J., 588
Peled, N., 355
Pennycook, A., 369
Penrose, A. M., 486, 543
Peregoy, S., 574
Peregoy, S. F., 306
Perelman, C., 181, 182, 183, 195
Perelman, Ch., 429
Perelman, F., 470
Perfetti, C. A., 18, 19
Perkins, D., 73, 80, 88, 258, 486, 499, 501
Perkins, D. N., 73, 80, 88, 258, 486, 499, 501
Perret-Clermont, A. N., 80
Peters, M., 277
Peters, R. S., 276
Peyronnet, A., 295, 302, 303
Peyton, J., 535
Piaget, J., 18, 169, 172, 177, 183, 385, 575
Picard, E., 588
Pienemann, M., 261
Pinto, M. da G. L. C., 10, 38, 44, 45
Pintrich, P. R., 482, 542
Piolat, A., 298, 326, 334, 382
Plomp, Tj., 14
Pontecorvo, C., 47, 56, 92, 99, 100
Poon, A. Y. K., 2, 8, 13, 14, 15, 305, 317
Pope, R., 178
Popper, K. R., 501
Porter, R. P., 152, 380
Post, T. A., ., 192, 203, 207, 246, 319, 332, 490, 594
Pouit, D., 296

Powell, A. B., 534
Prain, V., 482, 485, 493, 495, 534, 590
Prescott, H. M., 500, 501, 534
Pressley, M., 535
Price, M., 369
Prior, P., 147, 264, 334, 369, 503, 515, 564, 566, 568
Pritchard, R. J., 14, 142, 143
Probst, R., 533
Prosser, M., 562, 563, 566, 572
Purkiss, R., 521
Purves, A. C., 188

Rabinowitz, P., 350
Raedts, M., 541
Ragan, T. J., 445
Rage, F., 302
Ramonet, I., 324
Raphael, E., 383
Raphael, T. E., 470
Reed, L., 535
Reid, B., 525
Reid, I., 129, 130
Reid, R., 126
Reigeluth, C. M., 14
Renshaw, P., 127
Richards, C., 277
Richards, J. C., 309, 314
Richardson, J., 550
Rieben, L., 17, 18, 19, 21, 25, 29
Rienecker, L., 11
Rijlaarsdam, G., 1, 4, 6, 7, 8, 10, 11, 13, 16, 80, 185, 188, 200, 209, 211, 214, 241, 243, 260, 261, 274, 284, 323, 395, 396, 397, 400, 409, 541, 543, 548
Rimmon-Kenan, S., 362
Rinnert, C., 153
Rivard, L. P., 482, 483, 486
Roberts, B., 306
Rochex, J.-Y., 382, 384, 391
Rodda, M., 152
Rodgers, T. S., 314
Rodrigues, D., 417, 418
Rodrigues, R., 417, 418
Rodriguez, H., 13, 109
Roger, Ch., 2, 64, 517
Rogers, C., 143
Rogers, C. R., 187, 203
Rohlman, D. S., 551
Rojo, R., 32
Romano, T., 368
Rosat, M., 382
Rosebery, A. S., 483
Rosen, H., 534
Rothery, J., 287
Rouet, J.-F., 550
Rouiller, Y., 6, 10, 77, 83

Rouiller, Y., 672
Roulet, E., 72, 293
Roussey, J-Y., 80, 81, 298, 326, 334, 382
Rowell, P. A., 482
Rubin, D. L., 61, 62
Rumelhart, D. E., 395
Russel, C., 81
Rycik, J., 534
Rymer, J., 483

Saada-Robert, M., 10, 17, 18, 19, 20, 21, 25, 29, 77, 79, 83
Salomon, G., 77, 80, 88, 258, 501
Samway, K., 576, 584
Sandak, R., 325
Sander, P., 562
Sanders, T., 536
Sanford, A., 200
Sarig, G., 12, 499, 500, 501, 503, 515, 516, 535
Saunders, M. A. P., 500, 538
Sayers, P., 5, 12, 521, 526
Scardamalia, M., 63, 72, 79, 80, 81, 200, 260, 284, 285, 286, 303, 325, 331, 394, 396, 400, 482, 483, 484, 494, 499, 501, 548, 550
Schallert, D. L, ., 394
Schank, R., 355
Schauble, L., 575
Scheerens, J., 280
Schegloff, E. A., 72
Schneuwly, B., 79, 82, 83, 326, 382
Schnotz, W., 588
Schoenfeld, A. H., 419
Schön, D., 521
Schoonen, R., 215, 265, 267
Schraw, G., 542
Schriver, K. A., 80, 188, 200, 201, 213, 214, 215, 235, 236
Schrodinger, E., 483
Schumacher, G., 486, 533
Schumacher, G. M., 533
Schunk, D. H., 200, 242, 245, 257, 258, 542
Schwartz, R. S., 495
Scollon, R., 369
Scouller, K. M., 563, 565
Searle, J. R., 182, 210, 227, 395, 428
Seels, B., 445
Sefton-Green, J., 121, 124, 126
Segev-Miller, R., 12, 533, 535, 536, 538, 541, 542, 543, 546
Seifert, C., 200
Selfe, C., 426
Sellen, A., 106
Selman, R. L., 336
Settlage, J., 563
Severinson Eklundh, K., 120, 261, 262, 264, 266

Author Index

Seymour, J., 523
Seymour, P. H., 19, 21, 24
Shah, P., 588, 589, 596
Shanahan, T., 245, 541
Sharples, M., 370
Sheerin, Y., 126
Sheridan, J., 324
Sherman, J., 369
Shor, I., 500, 501
Short, M. H., 169, 177
Siegel, H., 486
Siegel, L., 24, 402
Siegel, M., 500
Silliman, E. R., 153, 155
Silver, J. W., 534
Silverstein, S., 503
Simó, R., 324
Simon, H. A., 396
Simone, R., 47, 48
Sinclair-de-Zwart, H., 34
Sjoer, E., 215
Skon, L., 80
Slamecka, N., 596
Sloate, P. L., 171
Slobin, D., 151
Smith, B. D., 544
Smith, C., 544
Smith, J., 426, 544
Smith, M. C., 535, 544
Smith, P. L., 445, 544
Smyth, G., 14, 455, 456, 461
Snoeck Henkemans, A. F., 429
Snowman, J., 394
Snyder, S., 500
Soares, M., 32
Sonnenschein, S., 215, 226, 245, 255, 257
Soter, A., 534
Spada, N., 151, 152, 153
Sperber, D,., 178, 179
Sperling, M., 63, 482
Spires, H. A., 533
Spiro, R. J., 549, 556
Spitzer, K. L., 445
Spivey, N. N., 534, 538, 590
Sprenger-Charolles, L., 24
Stahl, E., 13, 547, 548, 549, 551, 554, 556, 557
Stahl, N. A., 535
Stanulis, R. N., 426
Stehney, A. K., 482
Stein, N., 326
Stein, V., 326, 534
Stephenson-Forster, N. J., 280
Stern, C. M., 13, 443, 444, 445, 446
Sternglass, M., 535, 536, 541
Stevens, R., 63
Stevenson, K., 562
Stevenson, M., 267

Stoddart, T., 483
Stodolsky, S., 80
Stotsky, S., 543
Stratman, J., 80
Strauss, A. T., 537
Straw, S. B., 226, 238, 482, 483
Stray Jörgensen, P., 11
Street, B., 456, 562, 571
Stuve, M. J., 551
Styles, M., 466
Sullivan, K. P. H., 261, 262, 265, 266, 274
Suszynski, K., 534
Sutton, C., 64, 486
Swartzendruber-Putnam, D., 500, 501
Sweller, J., 588, 589

Taba, H., 406, 412, 487
Tardieu, H., 588
Taylor, C. E., 13, 15
Teale, W., 575
Teasley, B. M., 551
Teberosky, A., 91, 92
Teese, R., 121, 126
Tergan, S.-O., 551
Terrell, T., 306
Tetroe, J., 79
Thacker, P. R., 144
Thomson, J., 125
Thorndike, E. L., 214
Thorndyke, P. W., 395
Tierney, R. J., 486, 534, 541
Tishman, S., 482, 486, 493
Tishman, Sh., 501
Tjukovskij, K., 134
Tolchinsky, L., 92, 324
Tomassone, R., 64
Tomlinson, D., 287
Torrance, M., 484, 550
Torrance, N., 51
Torregrosa, E. ., 295
Toulmin, S. E., 182, 326, 334, 428, 429
Tressol, J. F., 295
Trigwell, K., 562, 563, 566
Truscott, J., 261
Tsang, W. K., 306
Tschang, F. T., 446
Tulving, E., 596, 597
Turner, A. V., 551
Turner, V., 151, 152
Turner-Bisset, R., 417
Tyner, K., 445, 446
Tynjälä, P., 274, 534, 543, 590

Urbano, H., 39

Vacca, R. T., 482, 534
Valencia, S. W., 535

Van den Akker, J., 14
Van den Bergh, H., 1, 4, 13, 80, 185, 213, 243, 323, 395, 409, 431, 541, 548
Van den Broek, P., 473
Van der Aalsvoort, M., 394, 395
Van der Geest, A. J. M., 395, 409
Van der Leeuw, B., 394, 395
Van der Pool, E., 394
Van Dijk, T., 470
Van Dijk, T. A., 470
Van Eemeren, F. H., 182, 183, 248, 427, 428, 429, 430
Van Gelderen, A., 427, 429
Van Hout, J. F. M. J., 258
Van Kraayenoord, C. E., 383
Van Wijk, C., 331, 394, 536
Vanett, L., 543
Vanmaele, L., 14, 16, 393, 394, 396, 517
Varela, F. J., 171
Veenman, M. V. J., 242
Veevaert, A., 334
Veloso, J., 46
Verhoeven, L., 456
Vérin, A., 64
Vermunt, J. D. H. M., 211, 242, 406
Vidal-Abarca, E., 590
Vikas, O., 446
Viskil, E., 429
Voss, J. F., 325, 396, 485
Voyat, G., 171

Walling, J., 596, 597
Walshe, R. D., 127
Wambean, C. A., 418
Wang, W., 152
Warrick, N., 19
Wason, P. C., 396
Waterhouse, F., 566
Weidenmann, B., 589
Weingart, R., 534
Wells, G., 126
Welsh, T. M., 557
Wen, Q., 152
Wertheimer, M., 183
Wertsch, J. V., 369, 375, 482
Whalley, P., 554
Whalley, P. C., 589

Whitehurst, G. J., 215, 226, 245, 255, 257
Widdowson, H. G., 306, 315
Wielenga, G., 402
Wigfield, A., 541
Wiles, S., 455, 457
Wiley, J., 325, 485
Wilhelm, J. D., 125
Wilkinson, A., 277, 287
Wilkinson, L. C., 153
Williams, J., 545, 576
Willison, J., 485
Wilson, D., 178, 179
Winn, B., 588, 589
Winn, W., 590
Winne, P. H., 540
Witte, S. P., 60, 200, 266, 267
Wixon, 574
Wolfe, J., 108
Woll, B., 154
Wong, M., 306, 383
Woodhouse, R., 590
Woodworth, R. S., 214
Wordsworth, W., 130
Wray, D., 287, 368, 369, 417
Wright, P., 557
Wright, P. L., 523
Wyse, D., 289

Yagelski, R. P., 576
Yancey, K. B., 535
Yando, R., 171
Yarbrough, J. C., 550
Yeany, R. H., 483
Yore, L. D., 482, 483, 495, 590
Yoshinaga-Itano, C., 155
Young, A., 337, 534
Yuen, H. K., 306

Zakh, N., 509
Zeidner, M., 542
Zein, R. A., 534
Zesiger, P., 19
Zhu, W., 306
Ziehe, T., 131, 135
Zimmerman, B. J., 200, 242, 245, 258, 541, 542, 575, 576
Zucchermaglio, C., 92, 99, 100

SUBJECT INDEX

academic text, 5
academic writing, 12, 109, 369, 508, 519, 527, 530, 533, 534, 543, 562, 563, 569
achievement levels, 427, 430
action research, 14, 305, 306, 308, 309, 315, 318, 481, 487
adverbs, 39, 174, 466, 474
agreement
    general, 36, 39, 43, 66, 81, 84, 101, 102, 133, 182, 314, 325, 335, 358, 360, 402, 405, 472, 497, 505, 537
    rule, 43
    subject-verb, 314
alphabetic language, 51
alphabetic writing, 23
ambiguities, 217
analogy, 147, 485, 493
annotation, 105, 106, 107, 108, 109, 110, 111, 112, 113, 115, 116, 117, 118, 119, 120, 378
annotation interface, 105, 107, 116, 120
approaches
    strategic approaches, 562, 566, 567, 570, 571
approaches to writing, 561, 562, 564, 565, 566, 567, 568, 569, 570, 573
argument
    argument and counterargument, 323
    argumentation, 4, 7, 16, 181, 182, 183, 184, 185, 186, 187, 188, 189, 190, 193, 194, 195, 247, 248, 254, 291, 292, 293, 297, 302, 303, 324, 325, 326, 329, 334, 335, 341, 342, 346, 427, 428, 429, 430, 431, 436, 439, 440, 441, 442, 483, 485, 496
    counterargument, 181, 182, 183, 184, 185, 186, 187, 188, 189, 192, 193, 195, 214, 248, 331
    phase, 429, 442
    philosophical, 295
    process, 182
    skills, 297, 427, 428, 430, 431
    structure, 4, 254, 429, 430, 436, 439, 440, 441
        complex, 249, 254, 256
        compound, 248
        subordinate, 248, 254, 256
    written, 182, 295, 324, 325

argumentative writing, 7, 181, 324, 335, 427, 440, 441
assessment
    arrangement, 275, 276, 283, 457
    cards, 387
    collective assessment, 391
    criteria, 543, 563, 564, 570
    formative, 467
    self-assessment, 141, 533, 539, 540, 542
    task, 125, 563
    writing assessment, 233, 306
assessment study, 427, 428, 430, 440
associations, 353, 354, 551
attitudes to writing, 561, 562, 566, 569
audience
    adaptation, 260, 266, 272
    addressed, 200
    anticipated audience, 549, 551, 556
    audience perspective, 547, 548, 550, 556, 557
    authentic, 424
    awareness, 148, 209, 540
    intended, 200
    orientation, 273, 274
    public, 144
    real, 82, 126
authentic text
    real-life text, 176
automatization, 272
awareness
    audience, 148, 209, 540
    awareness of revision, 263, 267
    awareness raising, 5, 7, 10
    critical, 281
    genre, 10
    language awareness, 31, 35, 39
    linguistic, 40
    linguistic awareness, 40
    metacognitive, 82, 149, 259, 260, 261, 274, 545
    meta-critical, 126
    morphological awareness, 38, 39
    phonemic, 21, 26
    phonological, 17, 20, 21, 29
    reader, 6, 10
    self-awareness, 75, 486, 576
    the alphabetic principle, 21

the alphabetic system, 20

bilingual, 14, 15, 151, 152, 153, 154, 155, 156, 159, 161, 163, 164, 371, 455, 456, 457, 458, 460, 462, 463, 465, 466, 467
bilingual pupils, 455, 456, 457, 458, 463, 465, 467
bilingualism, 14, 16, 151, 152, 153, 163, 456
blank spaces, 22, 53

capital letter, 47, 48, 49, 52, 53, 54, 55, 56, 87, 98, 101, 279, 388
centralisation, 275, 276, 280
child language, 374
Chinese, 56, 311, 313, 314, 317
chunks, 369, 373, 377, 378
classroom setting, 80, 82, 324, 399, 417, 419, 420, 421, 422, 424, 426
clinical tutor, 520, 521
cognitive
  cost, 382
  functioning, 382
  resources, 259, 260, 267, 272, 588
  strategy, 12, 185, 395, 484, 485, 534, 538, 542, 574, 576, 579, 581, 582, 583
cognitive and metacognitive strategies, 537
collaboration
  collective performance, 102
collaboration, 77, 80, 81, 85, 88, 91, 93, 101, 105, 261, 400, 549
collaborative
  composition, 59, 65, 73, 74
  learning, 59
  writing, 59, 63, 72, 78, 87, 214
comment
  critical, 214
  digital, 105
  evaluative, 214
  indirect post-reading, 232
  on-line, 223
  post-reading, 213, 235
  self-generated, 213, 217, 227, 232
  written, 209, 210, 214, 217, 218, 219, 224, 225, 227, 231, 232, 233, 234, 235
commentary tasks, 215
competence
  language competence, 398, 402, 403, 404, 407
  strategic competence, 11
complexity, 4, 9, 15, 21, 38, 45, 63, 79, 82, 124, 125, 155, 286, 291, 326, 331, 345, 407, 420, 423, 428, 502, 506, 551, 556
composition
  collaborative composition, 59, 65, 73, 74
  process, 59, 63, 65, 66, 74, 75
  reader oriented, 2
  sentence oriented, 2

strategies, 59
supported composition, 286, 287
task, 63
composition lesson, 2, 307
compositional arrangement, 377
comprehension
  monitoring, 197, 587
computer classrooms, 15, 417, 418, 419, 420, 421, 422, 423, 424, 425, 426
conceptual change, 534, 545
conceptualisation, 9, 291, 299, 302, 304, 326, 329
constraints, 183, 303, 349, 352, 357, 362, 370, 424, 448, 495, 508, 512, 548, 552
constructing
  knowledge, 61, 63, 92, 127, 233
constructing knowledge, 362
constructivism, 2, 440
constructivist, 23, 24, 25, 91, 92, 93, 96, 103, 481, 482, 484, 487, 489, 501, 516, 575
content
  element, 427, 492
  structure, 408, 548, 556
context interaction, 59, 61, 74
control
  control activities, 304
  control process, 383
  internal control, 382, 385
  local planning, 206
  locus of control, 381
  metacognitive control, 80, 382, 385, 514
  process, 395
  self-control, 381
  strategic control, 243
  strategic control, 243
correcting, 81, 84, 105, 109, 113, 119, 170, 235, 285, 332, 333, 335, 576, 585
course tutor, 522
curriculum development, 122, 287
cycle of learning, 561, 562, 563

deaf student, 14, 151, 152, 153, 154, 161, 163, 164
derivation, 86
descriptions, 165, 174, 226, 228, 229, 233, 237, 238, 239, 278, 377, 388, 422, 461, 463, 467, 528, 552, 574
determiners, 35, 37, 38, 39
development
  communicative strategies, 103
  creativity, 349
  cultural development, 385
  intentional cognition, 8
  of writing, 306, 574
  professional development, 281, 287, 519, 520, 522
  staff development, 144, 521

strategic development, 545
developmental
   model, 17, 18
   stages, 19
didactic sequence, 4, 9, 14, 21, 47, 49, 50, 52, 56, 57, 75, 393, 469, 470, 471, 479
differentiating, 99
direct writing, 8, 151
disagreements, 95
discourse analysis, 91
discourse knowledge, 547, 548, 549
discourse strategies, 95
drafting
   rough drafting, 143, 231, 287, 420, 421, 422, 571
drawing, 19, 21, 24, 27, 126, 198, 202, 239, 288, 312, 314, 315, 316, 364, 368, 370, 372, 374, 375, 378, 379, 429, 491, 509, 510, 525, 530, 541, 551, 587, 588, 589, 590, 591, 594, 595, 596, 597
Dutch, 247, 430

editing, 105, 109, 115, 143, 149, 153, 281, 287, 377, 378, 396, 422
educational level
   elementary education, 47, 52, 88, 291, 292, 303, 350, 355, 381, 444, 469, 470, 471, 479, 502, 517, 574, 592, 593
   higher education, 11, 409, 444, 446
   Kindergarten, 17, 18, 20, 21, 25, 26, 350, 355
   primary education, 2, 8, 9, 64, 276, 277, 305
   secondary
      upper secondary, 131, 132, 136, 139, 339
educational strategy, 184
elaboration, 60, 61, 64, 68, 71, 74, 105, 234, 267, 360, 400, 406, 534, 536, 537, 540, 558, 596, 597
emergent writing, 17, 18, 19, 20, 21, 22, 24, 26, 29
English, 2, 3, 9, 37, 46, 51, 52, 54, 70, 73, 109, 110, 118, 119, 121, 122, 124, 126, 127, 128, 129, 130, 262, 263, 275, 276, 277, 278, 279, 280, 281, 282, 283, 284, 285, 286, 287, 288, 289, 305, 306, 307, 308, 309, 310, 311, 312, 313, 314, 315, 316, 317, 318, 319, 340, 342, 344, 345, 371, 391, 426, 455, 456, 457, 458, 460, 461, 462, 463, 464, 466, 467, 520, 545, 546, 565, 566, 568, 573
English language, 122, 311, 316, 317, 318, 461
environments, 9, 13, 32, 364, 380, 425, 426, 525, 557, 558, 562
error
   correction, 306
   detection, 242

evaluation
   content, 398, 404, 412
   criteria, 235, 381, 384, 386, 387, 389, 570
   formative, 75
   procedure, 188
   process, 185
   summative, 571
expertise, 7, 61, 63, 64, 75, 81, 144, 172, 177, 185, 188, 206, 229, 241, 242, 260, 326, 343, 356, 388, 396, 397, 443, 448, 452, 469, 470, 517, 521, 537, 551

feedback
   by authentic reader, 212
   by reader, 50, 211
   indirect reader feedback, 235
   peer feedback, 143
French, 48, 70, 81, 88, 303, 350
function words, 161, 163
functional writing, 456
functions of language, 456, 461

generalization, 11, 217, 218, 302, 342, 346
generating
   content, 4, 8, 10
genre
   awareness, 10
   creative genre, 131
   digital genre, 550
   discourse genre, 61
   expectation, 563, 570
   expressive genre, 485
   factual genre, 287
   feature, 2, 283, 284
   imaginative genre, 463
   internal schools genre, 131
   model, 485, 494
   non-narrative, 371
   research genre, 367, 369
   scientific genre, 485, 564
   social genre, 379
   structure, 565
   text genre, 260
   theory, 275, 287
genre, 2, 9, 10, 122, 123, 132, 134, 135, 170, 199, 248, 261, 275, 283, 284, 287, 317, 342, 346, 349, 350, 351, 352, 353, 355, 357, 362, 363, 364, 367, 368, 374, 375, 377, 378, 456, 459, 484, 485, 486, 488, 489, 494, 502, 509, 511, 548, 563, 565, 570
genre hypothesis, 484
grammatical reference, 275, 288
graph-drawing, 587, 588, 590, 591, 593, 594, 595, 596
grapheme, 28, 44, 86
guided writing, 275

handwriting, 278, 506, 508, 511
Hebrew, 353, 355, 502, 507, 536, 538, 546, 578
homophone, 86
hypermedia, 547, 558
hypertext, 4, 13, 107, 110, 547, 548, 549, 550, 551, 552, 554, 555, 556, 557, 558, 559

imaginative writing, 456, 458, 464, 465
imitation, 7, 22, 23, 25, 169, 170, 171, 172, 173, 175, 176, 177, 178, 179, 245, 370
immediate grasping of the meaning of verbal productions, 31
in-class writing, 417, 422, 424
indirect
    indirect approach, 184
indirect object, 36, 39
individual differences, 28, 544
individual utterance, 370
induction, 146, 169
inductively, 95, 251
inference, 197, 198, 199, 201, 202, 204, 205, 208, 238, 332, 334
inflection, 342, 346
inner speech, 534
input at the right level, 259
instruction
    direct teaching, 11
    explicit teaching, 396, 408
instructional design, 397, 443, 445, 450
integrative method in teaching writing, 305
interact, 6, 65, 79, 101, 178, 192, 315, 368, 369, 370, 419, 456, 485, 516
interference, 43, 152, 154, 161, 164
Internet, 111, 264, 423, 443, 444, 445, 446, 447, 448, 449, 451, 452, 453, 547, 551
inter-textuality, 351, 367
intonation, 48, 50
invented spelling, 19, 20
Italian, 49, 191, 435, 592

keystroke logging, 259
knowledge
    content knowledge, 380, 393, 394, 397, 398, 405, 409, 485
    discursive knowledge, 394, 405, 408
    genre knowledge, 10
    knowledge building, 59
    language, 456
    strategic knowledge, 394, 396, 397, 407
    writing system, 5, 49
    written language, 91
knowledge production, 499
knowledge transforming, 63, 74, 260, 394, 396, 547, 548, 550, 558

language
    activity, 60
    additional language (L2 or L3), 455, 456, 460, 467
    creativity, 45
    education, 245
    emotional language, 483
    exercise, 35, 36, 37
    first language (L1), 6, 17, 34, 152, 153, 191, 259, 260, 262, 264, 265, 267, 269, 270, 271, 272, 273, 274, 306, 456, 536, 538, 545, 546
    first language (L1), 152, 259, 260, 456, 457, 458, 460, 461, 462, 464, 575
    function, 92
    home language, 455, 457, 458, 464, 565
    majority language, 456
    manipulation, 38, 39
    method, 31, 33, 34, 36, 39, 40, 44, 440
    native language, 340
    of the discipline, 562
    performance, 81
    play, 40, 289
    policy, 456, 464
    production, 574, 575
    rule, 4
    second language (L2), 151, 152, 153, 305, 306, 310, 455, 456, 535, 536, 545, 546
    second language (L2), 61, 151, 152, 260, 261, 315, 316, 318, 456, 460, 520, 575
    structure of language, 45
    study, 278
    style, 105
    target language, 152, 153, 308, 310, 314, 315, 465
    task, 4
    use, 4, 6, 7, 10, 11, 154, 163, 169, 210, 307, 312, 357, 396, 400, 401, 407, 427, 428
    user, 4, 6, 7, 210, 427, 428
language awareness, 31, 35, 39
language development, 32, 36, 39, 483
language learning, 307, 314, 369, 483
language method, 31, 33, 34, 36, 39, 40, 44, 440
language of thought, 545
language production, 574, 575
language structuration, 31
learner characteristics
    deafness, 14, 151, 152, 153, 154, 161, 163, 164
    learning deficiency, 456, 460
    learning difficulty, 465, 505
    learning disability, 141
    learning expert, 383
    learning habit, 515

learning strategies, 14, 18, 60, 92, 410, 545, 575, 590, 597
learning strategy, 515
learning style, 15, 516, 577, 583
learner type, 15
learning
  assignment, 514
  content, 2
  goal, 11, 59, 244, 258, 368, 397, 499, 502, 507, 508, 510, 512, 597
  language learning process, 369
  objective, 75, 249, 254
  outcomes, 11, 130, 242, 243, 418, 499, 510, 545, 561, 571
  result, 11
  situation, 92, 211, 244, 261, 511, 512
  task, 4, 5, 11, 15, 207, 244, 451, 504, 506, 512, 515, 562
  test, 247
  theory, 13, 257, 543
  unit, 12, 486, 487, 488, 489, 513
  unlearning, 522, 530
learning act, 4, 5, 6, 7, 11, 15, 214, 243, 244, 245, 257, 367, 397, 399, 400, 407, 412, 413, 512, 533, 562
learning activity, 4, 5, 6, 7, 11, 15, 214, 243, 244, 245, 257, 367, 397, 399, 400, 407, 412, 413, 533, 562
learning aim
  concept learning, 250
  literacy learning, 281, 368
  second language learning, 261
learning and teaching processes, 349
learning context, 12, 75, 483, 493, 506, 508, 511, 513, 540, 541, 543, 569, 570
learning environments, 513, 549
learning experience, 367, 515, 562, 571
learning goal
  learning agenda, 211
  learning objective, 75, 249, 254
learning method, 274
learning mode
  action learning, 520
  active learning, 169, 285
  by observation, 209, 242, 245, 247, 255, 257, 258
  by reader observation, 211
  enquiry learning, 368
  experiential learning, 211, 212
  experimental learning, 169
  higher-order learning, 486
  independent learning, 450
  learning by design, 547
  learning by doing, 241, 242, 244, 245, 247, 251, 255, 257, 258, 596
  learning mode
    observational learning, 14, 169, 181, 185, 188, 194, 196, 197, 200, 241, 245, 258, 259, 260
    metacognitive learning, 381
    observational, 14, 169, 181, 185, 188, 194, 196, 197, 200, 241, 245, 258, 259, 260
    participative learning, 323, 328, 329
    problem, 531
    self-regulated learning, 185
    situated learning, 2
learning object
  learning of science, 493, 494
  learning to read, 17, 18, 20, 246, 257, 443
  learning to write, 3, 5, 9, 14, 17, 20, 63, 89, 95, 153, 173, 209, 215, 217, 241, 246, 257, 259, 260, 369, 382, 387, 455, 543
learning practice, 350
learning process, 20, 91, 92, 93, 96, 103, 171, 211, 212, 213, 233, 242, 244, 257, 261, 345, 354, 440, 512, 530, 534, 540, 544, 545, 548
  learning curve, 382, 425
  learning enjoyment, 493
  process of learning, 11, 29, 75, 105, 520, 521
  quality of learning, 14, 232
learning tool, 12, 242, 346, 486
  learning cycle, 510, 525
  learning dialogue, 276
  learning journal, 534
  learning log, 521, 523, 534
learning transfer, 556
learning-to-write, 4, 5, 11, 13, 209, 211, 215, 233, 244
lexical items, 40, 43
lexical nature and function identification, 31
libraries, 377, 443, 444, 447, 448, 450, 452
linearity, 295, 548, 551
linguistic knowledge, 466
linguistic system, 153, 163
literacy
  digital literacy, 443
  information literacy, 443, 444, 445, 446, 447, 449, 450, 451, 452
literacy acquisition, 21
  assessment, 564, 565
  progress, 91
  skills, 151, 152, 153, 446, 455
  stages of literacy, 100
literacy agency, 32
literacy group, 95
literacy learning, 281, 368
literacy practice, 9, 121, 122, 124, 127, 130
literacy requirement, 34
literacy teaching, 275
  literacy curriculum, 3
  literacy education, 367
  literacy event, 14, 32, 60

literacy hour, 2, 281, 283, 286
literacy lesson, 2, 275, 283
literacy scaffolding, 317
literacy standard, 287
local coherence, 184, 197, 198, 199, 201, 207, 208
locus of control, 381

main ideas identification, 469
meaning-making, 124, 500, 502
measurement instruments, 427, 481
memory
  working memory, 42, 74, 259, 260, 261, 272
memory, 22, 34, 40, 41, 42, 43, 185, 186, 198, 201, 212, 216, 229, 232, 331, 336, 350, 351, 384, 445, 591, 595, 596, 597
metacognition, 12, 77, 79, 197, 383, 384, 385, 386, 394, 539
metacognitive awareness, 82, 149, 259, 260, 261, 274, 545
metaphor, 169, 178, 374, 375, 483, 485, 550, 551, 552, 556
methodology
  dual or triple task, 4
mindfulness, 481, 486
model
  of writing, 277, 396
monitoring
  comprehension, 197, 587
monitoring, 11, 59, 75, 78, 79, 80, 89, 118, 147, 153, 197, 198, 199, 200, 201, 207, 208, 211, 215, 242, 243, 244, 257, 279, 381, 383, 384, 427, 501, 575, 576, 579, 585, 587
motivation, 135, 169, 185, 316, 369, 381, 382, 383, 384, 386, 387, 391, 392, 489, 524, 562, 576, 577, 583
multi-modality, 367

narrative, 42, 47, 49, 57, 77, 78, 80, 82, 122, 123, 124, 125, 141, 142, 143, 147, 148, 155, 166, 191, 203, 305, 306, 310, 313, 314, 315, 316, 317, 319, 325, 346, 350, 355, 357, 361, 362, 374, 378, 381, 385, 387, 388, 391, 428, 466, 469, 502
narrative method in teaching writing, 305, 317
National Literacy Strategy, 275, 279, 280, 281, 282, 284, 286, 289
National Policy, 275
non formal writing, 481, 482
noticing, 184, 200, 259, 260, 261
noun/pronoun expansions, 31

online tutorials, 443, 450
oral discourse, 181, 184, 187
oral language, 7, 31, 32, 33, 35, 37, 40, 42, 45, 46, 50, 206, 325, 382

orthography, 31, 34, 40, 44, 410
outlining, 400, 408, 412, 571
overgeneralisation, 153

passive voice, 174, 525
PBI (Peer-Based Instruction), 259, 260, 262, 263, 265, 266, 267, 268, 269, 270, 271, 272, 273, 274
peer interaction, 77, 78, 80, 81, 88, 89
peer response, 214
performance
  language performance, 81
  mechanical performance, 512
  problem-solving performance, 198
  reading performance, 46
  teacher performance, 15, 423
  test performance, 281
  writing performance, 243, 544
  writing performance, 144, 149, 153, 212, 285, 288, 393, 401, 402, 428, 564, 570
performance indicator, 564, 567, 569
personal development, 5, 519, 520, 521, 522, 531
personal writing, 459, 463, 533, 534, 539, 543, 544
philosophical dialogue, 291, 292, 293, 294, 295, 303
phonographic, 21, 22, 23, 24, 25, 26, 28, 29
phonological, 17, 20, 22, 28, 29, 35, 40
phonological component, 22
plain language, 483
planner, 309
planning
  content, 393, 396, 400, 407, 408, 411
planning of writing, 198, 204, 456, 466
plural, 39, 475, 495
poetry, 6, 9, 125, 131, 132, 133, 134, 135, 138, 139, 277, 281, 353
popular culture, 121, 122, 126, 129, 361
Portuguese, 35, 37, 38, 39, 43, 44
pragma-dialectical argumentation theory, 427, 428
pre-established, 369
pre-school, 37, 91
primary school, 2, 12, 32, 37, 39, 43, 127, 275, 276, 277, 278, 279, 280, 281, 283, 287, 289, 291, 292, 305, 306, 307, 308, 310, 311, 315, 317, 318, 323, 367, 456, 457, 458
prior writing experiences, 561, 566, 569
private, 9, 107, 131, 132, 135, 136, 137, 138, 139, 140, 255, 312, 352, 370, 523, 542
problem solving, 11, 19, 170, 181, 184, 185, 383, 395, 396, 400, 407, 484, 521, 525
procedural criteria, 381
procedural facilitation, 8
process log, 533, 534, 535, 536, 537, 539, 541, 542, 543, 544, 545, 546

SUBJECT INDEX

process of composition, 60, 63, 65
process-product, 91
production rule, 250
production space, 61
professional development, 281, 287, 519, 520, 522
pronunciation, 33, 42, 43
pseudo letters, 93
public, 9, 18, 64, 81, 107, 127, 128, 131, 135, 136, 140, 144, 190, 191, 425, 435, 443, 445, 449, 505, 542
punctuation, 5, 31, 40, 42, 43, 47, 48, 49, 50, 51, 52, 53, 54, 55, 56, 57, 58, 260, 266, 284, 288, 342, 345, 346, 388, 428, 544, 585
punctuation marks, 47, 48, 49, 50, 52, 53, 54, 56, 284
punctuation system, 48

question mark, 53, 56, 57, 118, 279, 288
question paper, 340
question type
 comprehension question, 312
 guiding, 2, 307
 higher-order question, 280
 planning question, 459, 460
 reflection question, 481
 supportive question, 6
quotation, 50, 51, 52, 55, 56, 359, 370

reader
 reader feedback, 50, 211
reading
 direct reading, 33, 34, 45
 indirect reading technique, 33, 40, 41, 44
 semi-direct and silent direct reading, 31, 40
 semi-direct reading, 33, 43
 silent reading, 33, 34, 43, 44
reading abilities, 469
reading and writing processes, 11, 257, 349, 363, 535, 541
reference material, 565
referential communication, 226
reflective
 journal, 5, 519, 520, 521, 522, 523, 525, 526, 527, 528, 529, 530
 style, 520, 525, 526, 528
 thinking, 12, 499, 511, 514, 515, 519, 520, 525
 writing, 5, 12, 499, 500, 511, 516, 519, 520, 521, 522, 523, 531
regulation
 metacognitive, 77, 78, 79, 89
regulation of learning, 242, 244, 534
reliability, 190, 226, 229, 231, 443, 444, 446, 447, 449, 487, 537, 566, 578, 582
research tool

questionnaire, 65, 133, 264, 328, 332, 390, 487, 488, 489, 533, 534, 536, 537, 539, 543, 544, 564, 566, 570
 Study Process Questionnaire, 563, 565
reviewer, 105, 106, 107, 109, 111, 113, 115, 116, 117, 118, 119, 414
reviewing, 78, 79, 105, 130, 286, 522
revising, 4, 68, 81, 89, 143, 149, 197, 200, 201, 204, 205, 206, 207, 208, 218, 224, 225, 229, 281, 333, 396, 400, 407, 412, 420, 422, 427, 429, 536, 540, 542
 transformation unit, 83
revision
 on-line, 266
 strategy, 396, 413
revision ability, 204
revision lesson, 81
revision process
 awareness of revision, 263, 267
 frequency of revision, 259, 260
 monitoring of revision, 208
 on-line revision, 266
 revision activit, 80, 88, 210, 224, 232
 revision during writing, 555
 revision episode, 68
 revision operation, 68
 revision strategy, 396, 413
revision process, 80, 114, 120, 204, 208, 260, 273, 396
revision quality, 209
revision task, 197
revision type
 balance revision, 269
 discourse juncture revision, 267
 pre-text revision, 267
 revision of speech planning, 184
 revision of text, 559
 self-revision, 232
 spelling revision, 86
 surface revision, 272
 text revision, 80, 198, 213
 text-based revision, 259, 260
 typographical revision, 267
rhythm, 149

scaffolding, 2, 8, 9, 10, 91, 97, 125, 283, 316, 396, 401
scheme
 argumentative, 9, 195, 323, 325, 326, 332, 334
science writing curriculum, 561
scientific literacy, 481, 482, 493, 495
Scottish, 455, 456, 457, 458, 462, 463, 464
scribbles, 21, 22, 23, 25, 29
secondary education, 11, 409, 427, 428, 430, 440

segmentation, 20, 21, 22, 23, 25, 28, 29, 66, 83, 84, 86, 166, 502
self-efficacy, 381, 384, 386, 391, 541
self-reflection, 143, 146, 149, 242
self-regulation, 77, 78, 89, 141, 142, 147, 149, 188, 211, 242, 260, 381, 383, 386, 395, 396, 533, 539, 540, 542, 576
semantic level, 557
semiotic resource, 121, 123
semiotics, 95, 367
sentence construction, 31, 401, 410, 413
shared writing, 2, 275, 283, 286, 287, 288, 289
sign language, 151, 152, 153, 154, 161, 163, 164
silent, 31, 33, 34, 43, 44, 45, 93, 223, 234
situated
   learning, 2
   point of view, 18
   research, 17, 18, 20
   writing, 25
situation
   classroom situation, 14, 121, 122, 303, 386
   communicative situation, 11, 18, 72, 75, 92
   conflict, 418
   discursive situation, 59, 75
   ecological, 326
   natural, 95
   polemic, 324
   problem, 203
   problem-solving, 181
   realistic, 210
   rhetorical, 542
   situation of working, 75
   task situation, 28, 215
   test, 456
   work, 99, 100
   writing situation, 60, 62, 64, 75, 234, 424
situatuated
   cognition, 88
social
   context, 20, 59, 60, 65, 126, 171, 198, 248, 277, 418, 559, 575
   environment, 352, 435
   interaction, 57, 61, 79, 89, 259, 261, 575
   mediation, 33, 34, 63, 75, 276, 289, 381, 384, 385
   relationship, 9, 121, 124, 130
source-based writing, 369, 443, 444, 445, 447, 449, 452
Spanish, 48, 49, 51, 52, 70, 91, 93, 100, 327, 350, 477
specification, 127, 346
specificity, 50, 292, 295, 430
speech
   act, 4, 5, 16, 182, 227, 228, 229, 247, 395, 428
   chain, 34, 35, 38

direct speech, 47, 50, 51, 52, 53, 54, 55, 56, 57, 176
indirect speech, 47, 50, 54, 55, 57, 176
intellectual speech, 95
oral speech, 10
quoted speech, 47, 49, 51, 54, 56, 57
reported speech, 49, 52, 55, 56, 57
song, 33, 42
turn, 66
speech act theory, 182, 395
speech therapy, 350, 355
spelling, 4, 17, 18, 19, 20, 21, 27, 28, 29, 33, 42, 43, 54, 86, 87, 88, 119, 120, 239, 260, 266, 272, 277, 278, 279, 281, 314, 317, 342, 346, 391, 401, 410, 413, 428, 507, 581, 582, 584
spoken word, 22, 23, 24, 28
starting point, 92, 96, 131, 132, 135, 357, 361, 470, 510
status, 194, 242, 280, 403, 495, 502, 516, 569
strategic
   act, 140, 217
   control, 243
   learner, 545
strategy
   affective strategy, 581, 583
   cognitive strategy, 579
   communicative strategy, 379
   detour strategy, 184
   domino strategy, 406
   knowledge-constituting strategy, 395, 396, 407
   metacognitive strategy, 381
   stealing strategy, 171
strategy use, 519, 539, 574, 575, 576
structure of speech, 293
structures of language, 456, 461, 464, 465
style
   interim style, 5, 12, 519, 520, 521, 524, 525, 528, 529, 530
   narrative style, 42
   oral style, 45
   rhetorical style, 528
   rules, 172
   written style, 43
Sweden, 105, 109, 118, 131, 132, 139, 259, 262, 264
Swedish, 119, 120, 131, 132, 134, 136, 259, 260, 262, 263, 264, 266, 274
syllable, 19, 22, 25, 38, 39, 92
synchronous discussion forums, 417
synthesis writing
   source text, 373, 378, 379, 472, 478, 507, 508, 537

task representation, 59, 536, 540, 542
teacher

SUBJECT INDEX

composition teacher, 445, 446, 449, 452
teacher training, 311, 417, 426
teacher-student interaction, 181, 420
teaching
    and learning, 14, 18, 20, 59, 60, 65, 75, 169, 170, 171, 177, 291, 309, 310, 353, 512, 513, 516, 527, 561, 564
    educational style, 96
    methods, 276, 278, 288, 309, 315, 316, 398, 547
    poetry, 131
    teaching style, 91, 92, 93, 96, 99, 103, 191, 465
    writing and reading, 131
teaching writing, 17, 131, 140, 277, 305, 306, 307, 308, 309, 310, 314, 316, 318, 339, 340, 383, 408, 418
    instructional unit, 549, 550
    model text, 174
    scales of text, 8
    teaching unit, 547
technology critics, 417, 426
testing, 2, 14, 246, 247, 274, 278, 380, 398, 403, 404, 450, 455, 456, 457, 458, 460, 462, 465, 467, 521, 527
text
    organization, 8, 359, 395, 469, 470
    quality, 209, 213, 216, 217, 218, 226, 227, 228, 232, 259, 263, 267, 269, 270, 272, 273, 274, 399, 403
text analysis, 204, 206, 345, 356, 402, 591, 595
text based activity
    analysis, 204, 206, 345, 356, 402, 591, 595
    constructing, 257, 354
    elaboration, 204
    production, 6, 8, 72, 78, 80, 81, 82, 85, 87, 88, 89, 178, 210, 243, 244, 261, 323, 333, 369, 422, 427, 548, 550
    revising, 81, 396, 427
    text-based changes, 266, 267, 273
text comprehension, 197, 198, 199, 334, 550, 555, 587, 588
text feature
    coherence, 198, 428
    general, 8, 10, 250
    length, 208
    overall quality, 209, 213, 216, 217, 218, 226, 227, 228, 232, 259, 263, 267, 269, 270, 272, 273, 274, 399, 403
    quality criteria, 399
    structure, 248, 249, 254, 256, 273, 393, 394, 396, 399, 400, 404, 405, 406, 408, 409, 410, 412, 413, 414, 415, 427, 429, 430, 442, 469, 470, 474, 479, 484, 548, 595
    textual gaps, 204
text genre
    academic text, 5
    annotated text, 107, 108, 114, 115, 119, 120
    argumentative, 7, 8, 10, 173, 174, 175, 181, 182, 183, 184, 185, 188, 191, 192, 193, 241, 247, 248, 249, 250, 251, 252, 253, 254, 257, 258, 259, 265, 274, 295, 323, 324, 325, 326, 327, 328, 329, 330, 332, 333, 334, 336, 427, 428, 430, 432, 440
    cultural text, 9, 123
    descriptive, 262, 263, 269
    digital text, 13, 547
    discursive, 427, 431, 507
    explanatory, 59, 63, 75
    expository, 469, 470, 471, 479
    expository, 469, 470, 471, 479
    factual text, 132
    hypertext, 4, 13, 107, 110, 547, 548, 549, 550, 551, 552, 554, 555, 556, 557, 558, 559
    instruction, 3, 5, 14, 29, 59, 77, 89, 142, 143, 145, 150, 152, 170, 171, 187, 188, 222, 223, 224, 226, 233, 244, 245, 247, 258, 265, 308, 311, 323, 328, 401, 418, 423, 425, 433, 444, 445, 446, 447, 449, 450, 451, 471, 472, 508, 512, 513, 536, 541, 542, 543, 544, 545, 556
    instructive, 209, 213, 216, 217, 218, 225, 229, 232, 233, 587
    literary text, 69, 170, 355
    manual, 209, 210, 213, 214, 215, 217, 218, 224, 225, 226, 228, 229, 233, 234
    media text, 9, 123, 127
    narrative, 47, 77, 78, 82, 141, 143, 147, 191, 203, 381, 385, 387, 391, 469
    poetic text, 135
text genre, 260
text production
    attempted text, 59, 65, 72, 74
    context of production, 61, 62, 63, 69, 74, 75
    dyadic text production, 77
    individual text production, 77, 87
    intended text, 80, 212, 408
    joint text, 77, 78, 82
    narrative text, 77, 78, 82, 142
    oral text, 80, 187, 294
    process, 6, 78, 79, 261
text production, 6, 8, 72, 78, 80, 81, 82, 85, 87, 88, 89, 178, 210, 243, 244, 261, 323, 333, 369, 422, 427, 548, 550
text structure
    hierarchical, 114, 410
    linear, 551, 595
    textual level, 11
text type, 4, 132, 211, 213, 239, 247, 250, 251, 351, 352, 399, 428
text-graph integration, 587, 588, 589, 591, 593, 594, 595
textual experience, 38

textual genre, 45
theme, 4, 10, 11, 13, 113, 141, 147, 149, 276, 302, 340, 470
thinking aloud, 197, 210, 214, 219, 227, 231, 329
thinking disposition, 12, 481, 482, 485, 486, 487, 489, 490, 492, 493, 494, 495
transfer, 4, 6, 10, 11, 75, 77, 78, 82, 83, 88, 143, 153, 163, 184, 210, 213, 214, 215, 225, 241, 245, 246, 247, 255, 256, 257, 267, 269, 274, 275, 287, 291, 300, 301, 302, 304, 325, 378, 383, 384, 385, 386, 393, 401, 402, 403, 408, 456, 540, 555, 556, 557, 597
transformations, 79, 82, 83, 84, 85, 86, 87, 88, 89, 183, 367, 368, 375, 378, 379
translating, 4, 34, 40, 78, 79, 89, 105, 427, 460, 502, 578
translation, 35, 51, 54, 60, 151, 154, 163, 164, 263, 393, 428, 477, 555, 559
tutored practice, 519, 523
tutoring
  expert tutor, 388
  online tutor, 443, 450
  peer tutor, 80
  private tutor, 312
  tutored practice, 519, 523
  tutorial, 422, 450, 451, 524, 525, 528
  tutorial unit, 450, 451
  tutoring, 381, 385, 386, 387, 388, 389, 390
type of text, 61, 80, 82, 208, 211, 215, 217, 232, 267, 323, 325, 427, 428

unit
  discrete unit, 35, 38, 40, 44
  idea unit, 33, 41, 506
  linguistic unit, 36, 38, 45
  text unit, 548, 554
  thematic unit, 360
  unit of analysis, 48, 95, 198
  word unit, 22
unlearning, 522, 530
utterances, 59, 65, 69, 93, 98, 102, 181, 186, 188, 195, 237, 351

validity
  ecological, 197, 206
variety, 1, 19, 22, 24, 25, 49, 92, 155, 158, 159, 229, 244, 277, 280, 351, 353, 361, 420, 448, 449, 451, 456, 482, 485, 509, 516, 520, 521, 528, 534, 536, 540, 556, 575, 583
vocabulary enlargement, 31
voice, 69, 144, 148, 292, 341, 362, 369, 375, 379, 425, 494, 501, 525, 578
Vygotskian perspective, 7, 326

web sites, 451
whole-language, 91

word
  chaining, 406
  head word, 31, 36, 37, 38, 39, 45
  sequence, 428, 436
word class, 289
word processing, 264, 422, 423, 445
word processor, 106, 107
word type
  function words, 161, 163
working memory, 42, 74, 259, 260, 261, 272
writing advices, 427, 440, 441
writing conventions, 353
writing development, 275, 519, 522, 570, 571, 580, 582
writing from sources, 538, 544
writing genres, 287, 481, 486, 561
writing hypertext, 13, 547, 548, 549, 550, 551, 558, 559
writing in science, 481, 487, 493, 570
writing in the classroom, 18, 421
writing instruction, 14, 60, 78, 209, 212, 417, 423, 441, 443, 499, 534
writing pedagogy, 169, 170, 171, 177, 213, 306
writing problems, 92, 264, 407, 427, 440
writing process, 5, 6, 8, 9, 13, 24, 57, 59, 66, 68, 78, 79, 82, 105, 142, 143, 146, 147, 151, 154, 169, 171, 178, 210, 211, 212, 213, 214, 230, 239, 240, 244, 253, 257, 259, 260, 261, 262, 263, 264, 272, 274, 284, 286, 293, 303, 327, 349, 351, 353, 354, 361, 374, 396, 397, 400, 401, 402, 405, 406, 422, 425, 427, 429, 462, 481, 482, 485, 486, 494, 533, 535, 541, 548, 555, 561, 562, 563, 569, 574, 575, 577, 578, 580, 582, 583, 584
writing production, 21
writing strategy
  knowledge telling, 74, 260, 484, 486
  knowledge transforming, 63, 74, 260, 394, 396, 547, 548, 550, 558
writing teaching, 323
writing techniques, 499
writing to summarize, 12, 470, 479, 538, 540, 545, 576, 587, 590
writing workshop, 127, 141, 143, 150, 349, 350, 352, 355, 364
writing-from-sources, 12, 533, 534, 535, 536, 538, 539, 542, 543
writing-to-learn, 3, 11, 13, 14, 15, 319, 422, 481, 482, 486, 495, 499, 515, 543, 587, 588, 589, 590, 591, 593, 595, 596
written discourse, 62, 427
written language, 27, 31, 32, 33, 37, 40, 45, 46, 59, 60, 61, 62, 72, 74, 83, 93, 144, 151, 153, 155, 289, 325, 394
written production, 20, 27, 28, 49, 50, 57, 61, 204, 382

written productions, 49, 57, 382

zone of proximal development, 259, 261, 331, 398

LIST OF CONTRIBUTORS

Mónica Alvarado, Professor of Language Education, Facultad de Psicología, Universidad Autónoma de Querétaro, México. monicalvardo@yahoo.com

José Jerónimo Anula Alameda, Tutor Lecturer of the UNED, Associated Centre of Santa Cruz de Tenerife, Spain. joseanula@terra.es

Emmanuèle Auriac-Peyronnet, Professor of Psychology, Laboratory of Psychology of Interaction, University of Nancy II, & Universitary Institute of Formation of Teachers of Clermont Fd, France. epeyronnet@auvergne.iufm.fr

Kristine Balslev, Doctoral Assistant, Faculty of Psychology and Educational Sciences, University of Geneva, Switzerland, kristine.balslev@pse.unige.ch

Roger Beard, Reader in Literacy Education, School of Education, University of Leeds, UK. R.F.Beard@education.leeds.ac.uk

Rainer Bromme, Professor for Educational Psychology, Psychological Institute III, University of Muenster, Germany. bromme@uni-muenster.de

Sandra Brunsberg, Lecturer in English, Unit for Language and Communication, Royal Institute of Technology (KTH), Stockholm, Sweden. sandra@lib.kth.se

Michel Couzijn, Senior lecturer in Language Education, Graduate School of Teaching and Learning, University of Amsterdam, The Netherlands. M.J.Couzijn@uva.nl

Sergio Crasnich, Lecturer of Experimental Education, Dept. of Psychology, University of Triest, Italy. sergio.crasnich@tin it

Marie-France Daniel, Professor of Philosophy, Interdisciplinary Center of Research on Learning and Development, University of Montreal, Canada. Marie-france.daniel@umontreal.ca

Cristina Díez Vegas, Pre-school teacher. Doctor in Psychology. Freelance research in collaboration with the Universidad Nacional de Educación a Distancia (UNED –OU-) and the Burgos University. cdiez@terra.es

Brenton Doecke, Associate Professor, Faculty of Education, Monash University Clayton, Australia 3800. Brenton.Doecke@Education.monash.edu.au

Anne-Marie Doly, Maître de Conférence in Education Sciences, University Institute of teachers training (IUFM) of Auvergne, France. amdoly@auvergne.iufm.fr

Milly Epstein-Jannai - Head of the Textual Studies Program, The School for Multidisciplinary Studies, Beit Berl College, Israel. millyeps@zahav.net.il

Per-Olof Erixon, Associate professor, Department of Creative Studies in Teacher Education, Umeå University, Sweden. per-olof.erixon@educ.umu.se

Milagros Gárate, Professor of Developmental and Educational Psychology, Department of Education of University of Cantabria, Spain. garatem@unican.es

Ana Laura de la Garza, Elementary School Teacher, Escuela Maxei, Querétaro, México.maxei@unimedia.com.mx

Uwe Geist, Senior lecturer (retired) in Danish Language, Department of Language and Culture, Roskilde University, Danmark. uwe@ruc.dk

Rachel Hertz-Lazarowitz, Professor of Psychology and Education, Haifa University, Faculty of Education, Israel 31905. rachelhl@construct.haifa.ac.il

Ron L. Honeycutt, Visiting Assistant Professor, Department of Curriculum and Instruction, North Carolina State University, Reading/Writing Specialist for Wake County Public Schools, Raleigh, NC USA. stay_the_course@msn.com

Kate Kiefer, Professor of English and University Distinguished Teaching Scholar, Department of English, Colorado State University, United States of America, Kate.Kiefer@ColoState.edu

Maria Koutsoubou, Ph.D researcher, Department of Language and Communication Sciences, City University, UK. m.koutsoubou@city.ac.uk

Fernando Lara Ortega, Professor of the Evolutional and Education Psychology. Science Department at Burgos University, Spain. flara@ubu.es

Tamar Levin, Professor of Education; Tel Aviv University, School of Education, Israel; tamil@post.tau.ac.il

Eva Lindgren, PhD candidate, Secondary school teacher, Department of Modern Languages, Umeå University, Sweden. eva.lindgren@engelska.umu.se.

Joost Lowyck, professor of educational technology, Centre for Instructional Psychology and Technology, Catholic University of Leuven, Belgium. Joost Lowyck@ped.kuleuven.ac.be.

Lucia Lumbelli, Professor of Experimental Education, Dept. of Psychology, University of Triest, Italy. lumbelli@units.it

Katia Mazurczak, Assistant, Faculty of Psychology and Educational Sciences, University of Geneva, Switzerland, katia.mazurczak@pse.unige.ch

Douglas McClenaghan, Masters Research student, Faculty of Education, Monash University, & Secondary school teacher (English), Viewbank Secondary College, Viewbank Melbourne Victoria. mcclenaghan.douglas.j@edumail.vic.gov.au

Ángeles Melero, Lecturer of Developmental and Educational Psychology, Department of Education of University of Cantabria, Spain. meleroma@unican.es

Marta Milian, Senior lecturer in Language Education (Didàctica de la llengua) in the Faculty of Education, Universitat Autònoma de Barcelona, Spain, Department de Didàctica de la Llengua i la Literatura. Faculty of Education. Universitat Autònoma de Barcelona, Spain. marta.milian@uab.es

Susanne Munch, senior master, secondary scool teacher, Frederiksværk Gymnasium, Denmark. susanne.munch@email.dk

Rob Oliver, PhD Candidate, Institute of Education, University of London, robolivers@yahoo.co.uk

Ron Oostdam, Senior researcher, SCO-Kohnstamm Institute, Centre for the Study of Language Learning, University of Amsterdam, The Netherlands. ron@educ.uva.nl

Gisela Paoletti, Researcher, Department of Psychology, University of Triest, Italy. paolet@units.it

Mike Palmquist, Professor of English and University Distinguished Teaching Scholar, Department of English, Colorado State University, United States of America, Mike.Palmquist@ColoState.edu.

Pilar Pardo de León, Associate Professor of the Department of Evolutional and Education Psychology Department, UNED. ppardo@psi.uned.es

Maria da Graça Pinto, Professor in Linguistics, Faculty of Arts, University of Porto, Portugal, mgraca@letras.up.pt

Anita Y.K. Poon, Assistant Professor in language education, Department of Education Studies, Hong Kong Baptist University, Hong Kong.

Ruie J. Pritchard, Professor, Department of Curriculum and Instructor, Interim Associate Dean for Academic Affairs, College of Education, North Carolina State University, USA. Ruie_pritchard@ncsu.edu

Henrry Rodriguez, Research engineer. Interaction and Presentation, Laboratory NADA, Royal Institute of Technology (KTH), Stockholm, Sweden. henrry@nada.kth.se

Yviane Rouiller, Professor, School for Teacher Education, Lausanne, Switzerland. yviane.rouiller@eduvd.ch

Gert Rijlaarsdam, Professor of Innovative Language Education, Graduate School of Teaching and Learning, University of Amsterdam, The Netherlands. G.C.W.Rijlaarsdam@uva.nl

Madelon Saada-Robert, Professor of Situated Learning, Faculty of Psychology and Educational Sciences, University of Geneva, Switzerland, madelon.saada@pse.unige.ch

Gissi Sarig, Senior lecturer of Language Education & Academic Director of Professional Development Resource Complex, Kibbutzim College of Education, Israel. sarig@macam.ac.il

Pete Sayers, Staff Development Adviser University of Bradford, UK. p.l.sayers@bradford.ac.uk

Rachel Segev-Miller, Lecturer, The English Department & The Center of Academic Literacy, Kibbutzim College of Education; The English Department & The Graduate Program in Language Education, Levinsky College of Education, Tel Aviv, Israel. aki@macam.ac.il

Anat Shapira, Ph.d candidate, Haifa University, and Lecturer of EFL and Philosophy of Education, Gordon College of Education, Haifa, Israel, 35705. a_shapira@walla.co.il

Geri Smyth, Senior lecturer, Primary Education Department, University of Strathclyde, Scotland. g.smyth@strath.ac.uk

Elmar Stahl, Assistent Professor for Educational Psychology, Psychological Institute III, University of Muenster, Germany, stahlel@psy.uni-muenster.de

Caroline M. Stern, PhD, Associate Professor Department of Languages and Literature, 3040 Arts & Sciences Commons, 820 Campus Drive Ferris State University, United States of America.

Huub Van den Bergh, associate professor in Language Behavior, University of Utrecht, The Netherlands. Huub.H.vandenbergh@let.uu.nl

Lieve Vanmaele, senior researcher, Centre for Instructional Psychology and Technology, Catholic University of Leuven, Belgium. Lieve.Vanmaele@ped.kuleuven.ac.be

Sofía A. Vernon, Professor of Educational Psychology, Facultad de Psicología, Universidad Autónoma de Querétaro, México.sofiavernon@prodigy.net.mx, sofiavernon@yahoo.com.mx

Tili Wagner, Ph.D candidate at Tel Aviv University and a Teacher at Beit Berl College, Israel, tiliw@zahav.net.il

Paula Zermeño, Elementary school teacher, Escuela Maxei, Querétaro, México. pzeross@yahoo.com.mx

Studies in Writing

7. P. Tynjälä et al. (eds.): *Writing as a Learning Tool.* 2001
   ISBN HB 0-7923-6877-0; PB 0-7923-6914-9
8. L. Tolchinsky (ed.): *Developmental Aspects in Learning to Write.* 2001
   ISBN HB 0-7923-6979-3; PB 0-7923-7063-5
9. D. Alamargot and L. Chanquoy: *Through the Models of Writing.* 2001
   ISBN HB 0-7923-6980-7; PB 0-7923-7159-3
10. T. Olive and C.M. Levy (eds.): *Contemporary Tools and Techniques for Studying Writing.* 2001   ISBN HB 1-4020-0035-9; PB 1-4020-0106-1
11. S. Ransdell and M-L. Barbier (eds.): *New Direction for Research in L2 Writing.* 2002   ISBN HB 1-4020-0538-5; PB 1-4020-0539-3
12. L. Björk, G. Bräuer, L. Rienecker and P. Stray Jörgensen (eds.): *Teaching Academic Writing in European Higher Education.* 2003
    ISBN HB 1-4020-1208-X; PB 1-4020-1209-8
13. L. Allal, L. Chanquoy and P. Largy (eds.): *Revision: Cognitive and Instructional Processes.* 2004   ISBN HB 1-4020-7729-7
14. G. Rijlaarsdam, H. van den Bergh, M. Couzijn (eds.) *Effective Learning and Teaching of Writing: A Handbook of Writing in Education.* 2004
    ISBN HB 1-4020-2724-9; PB 1-4020-2725-7

For Volumes 1-6 please contact Amsterdam University Press, at www.aup.nl